# A
# HISTORY OF THE SIKHS

FROM
THE ORIGIN OF THE NATION

TO
THE BATTLES OF THE SUTLEJ

BY
JOSEPH DAVEY CUNNINGHAM
LIEUTENANT OF ENGINEERS, AND CAPTAIN IN THE ARMY OF INDIA

EDITED BY
H.L.O. GARRETT, M.A., I.E.S.
PROFESSOR OF HISTORY GOVERNMENT COLLEGE, LAHORE

# LOW PRICE PUBLICATIONS
## DELHI - 110052

*Sales Office :*
**D.K. Publishers Distributors (P) Ltd.**
1, Ansari Road, Darya Ganj
New Delhi - 110002
Phones : 3261465, 3278368
Fax : 091-011-3264368


First Published      1849
Revised              1915
Reprinted            1990, 1996, 1997


CUNNINGHUM, JOSEPH DAVEY (1812-1851)


*Published By :*
**LOW PRICE PUBLICATIONS**
B-2, Vardhaman Palace,
Nimri Commercial Centre,
Ashok Vihar, Phase - IV, Delhi - 110 052
Tel.: 7401672, Fax : 091-011-7138265


*Printed At :*
**D.K. Fine Art Press (P) Ltd.**
Delhi - 110052


**PRINTED IN INDIA**

## EDITOR'S NOTE

THE author's original spelling of Indian names is archaic and almost intolerable to the modern reader. I have therefore adopted the modern accepted spelling, and for the arduous work of transliteration I am indebted to L. Tej Ram, M.A., Professor of Mathematics at the Randhir College, Kapurthala.

The author's text and notes have remained unaltered, but where necessary I have added additional notes, which will be found in brackets.

By permission of the Government of the Punjab, I am enabled to reproduce some of the results obtained by the recent examination of the manuscript records of the Sikh days, which have long been lying in the archives of the Civil Secretariat. In this connexion I have been greatly assisted by L. Sita Ram Kohli. M.A., the research student in charge of the work. Apart from this, he has been of great help in preparing the entire volume and, in particular, in the drawing up of the Bibliography. Finally, I tender my very grateful thanks to the Hon. Mr. J. P. Thompson, I.C.S., Chief Secretary to the Government of the Punjab, who has kindly looked through the manuscript and to whom I am indebted for many valuable hints and suggestions.

H. L. O. GARRETT.

LAHORE,
*November* 1915.

# INTRODUCTORY

THE original edition of Capt. Cunningham's book appeared in 1849. A second edition was finished in 1851, but, as is explained in the second preface by his brother, this edition did not make its appearance till 1853, after the death of the author. The second edition did not differ materially from the first beyond certain re-arrangements and certain additions to the notes, with the exception of Chapter IX. This chapter, which deals with the events leading up to, and the progress and result of, the first Sikh War, was considerably modified in the second edition. Even in this form the chapter contains many statements of an injudicious nature. Indeed, as the result of certain strictures upon the policy of the Government of India in dealing with Gulab Singh of Jammu, the author was dismissed from his employment in the Political Department by the Honourable East India Company and sent back to regimental duty. These strictures, together with a note upon the subsequent punishment meted out to the author, will be found in their proper place in Chapter IX.

To turn to the volume as a whole. The author, as he tells us in his own prefatory note, spent eight years of his service (from 1838 to 1846) in close contact with the Sikhs, and that too during a very important period of their history. His experiences began with the interview between Lord Auckland and Ranjit Singh in 1838 and lasted down to the close of the first Sikh War, when he became resident in Bhopal. The result of his eight years' residence was to give him a great insight into the history of the Sikhs and to inspire in him a partiality which is only too clearly visible in his handling of the events leading up to the outbreak of hostilities with the British. The whole book bears evidence of most meticulous care, and the voluminous footnotes show the breadth and variety of the author's study.

Chapter I deals with the country and its people. There is a detailed description of the industries of the Punjab and its dependencies, much of which has been rendered archaic by the natural march of events. The ethnological part of this chapter has been carefully done, though this again is in need of supplementation in the light of modern research. It seems hardly necessary to guide the modern reader in this direction when so many excellent gazetteers are now available, but for a very lucid summary of He Hill States of the Punjab and their peoples, a subject in which the author is a little difficult to follow, reference may well be made to an article (in vol. iii of *The Journal of the Punjab Historical Society*) by Messrs. Hutchison and Vogel, which is admirably explicit and is supplemented by a short bibliography on the subject.

Chapter II is concerned with the old religions of India. Here again knowledge has moved forward and much of the author's information is archaic. His conception of the lingam and its significance, for example, is not in consonance with modern theory. Unfortunately, too, he lived before the days when the labours of the Archaeological Department had thrown a flood of light upon the teaching of Buddha and the prevalence of his religion in India. Indeed, his only reference to the British in this connexion is an accusation of iconoclasm which reads strangely to a modern generation. His account of 'modern reforms' naturally stops at an early point, and he seems to have been led into the somewhat erroneous conclusion that the whole Indian world—Hindu and Muhammadan—at the time that he wrote, was moving in the direction of a new revelation. As I have pointed out in a supplementary note, the tendency is rather, in the case of both creeds, towards a reversion to ancient purity and the removal of accretions and corruptions. The chapter concludes with an account of Guru Nanak and his teaching.

Chapter III is concerned with the lives and teaching of the Gurus. The gradual spread of the Sikh religion in the Punjab led to the establishment of a sort of *imperium in imperio*. This development caused Mughal emperors to follow a line of policy much like that adopted by the Roman emperors when confronted by the rising organization of the Christian Church. This policy—one of repression and persecution—caused a profound modification of the whole Sikh system. The simple altruism of the early days was laid aside and, under Gobind Singh, the tenth and last Guru, the Sikhs became a definite fighting force. At first the armies of the Khalsa met with little success, and the death of Gobind Singh in 1708, followed by that of Banda, his successor in the command of the armies, in 1716, seemed to sound the knell of Sikh hopes and ambitions. But

# INTRODUCTORY

the fervour of their belief rose triumphant over persecution, and the Sikhs found their opportunity in the years of disorder which followed the death of the Emperor Bahadur Shah in 1712.

Chapter IV relates the gradual establishment of Sikh independence down to 1764. Northern India was a wild welter of confusion. The Mughal Empire was falling rapidly to pieces under the repeated blows of invaders from north and south. First Nadir Shah and his Persian hosts, and then the Afghan Ahmad Shah Durrani, swept down upon the imperial capital. Like Rome of old, Delhi felt again and again the hand of the spoiler, and its glories became a thing of the past. The advent of the Marathas upon the scene seemed at first the prelude to the establishment of Hindu supremacy in the north of India. But the battle of Panipat (1761) proved fatal to their ambitions and left the stage open for the development of a new power in the Punjab.

Amid all this confusion the Sikhs gradually achieved their independence. At first they were mere bands of plunderers, but gradually these bands became united into a formidable fighting force. In 1748 the army of the Khalsa became a recognized organization under Jassa Singh, and though it frequently suffered defeat, it never lost its definite character after that date. The Sikhs sustained their greatest disaster at the hands of the Afghans at Ludhiana in 1762, but the waves of Afghan invasion had spent their strength. In 1763, at Sirhind, the Sikhs avenged their defeat of the previous year and permanently occupied the province of Sirhind. In the following year, which witnessed the last Afghan invasion, they became masters of Lahore. and in the same year, at a meeting at Amritsar, organized themselves into a ruling political system, described by the author as a 'theocratic confederate feudalism'. The condition of the Punjab during these years of bloodshed and disorder was miserable in the extreme. To find any parallel in European history one would have to go back to the days of King Stephen in England or to some of the worst episodes of the Thirty Years' War. Waris Shah, the author of the story of *Hir and Ranjha*, who flourished during this period, gives, in the epilogue of this poem, a vivid account of the state of the country :

Fools and sinners give counsel to the world,
The words of the wise are set at naught.

No man tells the truth or cares for justice,
Telling what is untrue has become the practice in the world.

With violence men commit flagrant iniquity,
In the hands of tyrants there is a sharp sword.
There is no Governor, Ruler, or Emperor.
The country and all the people in it have been made desolate.

Great confusion has fallen on the country,
There is a sword in every man's hand.
The purdah of shame and modesty has been lifted
And all the world goes naked in the open bazaar.

Thieves have become leaders of men.
Harlots have become mistresses of the household.
The company of devils has multiplied exceedingly,
The state of the noble is pitiable.
Men of menial birth flourish and the peasants are in
great prosperity.

The Jats have become masters of our country,
Everywhere there is a new Government.[1]

The Sikhs had become a nation and, in theory, a united
nation, but in actual fact such was far from being the
case. The new State was composed of a number—
twelve is the usually recognized total—of leagues or
'Misals'. Instead of uniting and forming a solid State,
these 'Misals' were almost constantly engaged in civil
war, grouping and regrouping in the struggle for pre-
eminence. It needed a strong hand to check these in-
ternecine disputes, and, fortunately for the Punjab,
Ranjit Singh appeared on the scene. The career of the
one-eyed Lion of the Punjab is fully described in the
text and needs but little reference at this point. The
Maharaja's real career commences with his acquisition
of Lahore in 1799. From that date he steadily extended his sway over the whole Punjab. Many books have
been written on the career of this remarkable man
and upon the system of comparatively orderly government which he introduced. There exist in the Secretariat at Lahore a number of manuscript records
(accounts, muster rolls, pay sheets, &c.) of his government. These are now under examination, and it is
hoped that a great deal of additional light will be
thrown upon his system of government as a result. The

[1] [I am indebted to Mr. C. F. Usborne, C.S., for the above
translation.]

papers that have been examined up to the present time
(1915) show how actively Ranjit Singh interested himself in the details of his administration. As regards his
character, he was not altogether without faults. Temperance and chastity were not his conspicuous virtues.
But with all his shortcomings, he was a strong and
able ruler admirably suited to the conditions of the
time. The Maharaja's territorial expansion brought
him into contact with the Cis-Sutlej States, which
were under English protection, and so into contact
with the English. The result of this was the Treaty
of 1809, which Ranjit Singh loyally observed down to
his death in 1839, although at times he showed symp-
toms of irritation at the rising power of the English.

The death of Ranjit Singh in 1839 was the signal
for the outbreak of a series of palace revolutions, in
which the army of the Khalsa played a part hardly
dissimilar from that of the Praetorian Guards at their
very worst. This period of the story is fully dealt with
by the author in Chapter VIII. The disorder culmi-
nated in the crossing of the Sutlej by the Sikh forces
and the consequent outbreak of the first Sikh War.
From this point of the story the partiality of the author
causes many of his statements to be viewed with suspicion. In his eyes the war represents a national tide
of self-preservation rising against the ever-encroaching
power of England. Such was far from being the case,
and very different motives actuated the corrupt administration of Lahore. Terrified of the power of the
army, that administration flung its legions across the
Sutlej in the hope that they would be either annihilated or so seriously crippled as to cease to be a danger
in the future. At the same time the outbreak of hostilities would divert attention from the shortcomings
of the central government—a political manoeuvre
strongly reminiscent of some of the actions of Napoleon
III. The author gives a somewhat turgid description
of the battles of the war—indeed, the language in the
account of the battle of Sobraon reminds one of the
story of the battle in the poems of Mr. Robert Montgomery—and he concludes his narrative by some
general remarks upon English policy in India. From
the latter I have removed some passages which are not
only injudicious but which have been stultified by the
march of events.

Beyond a bare reference the author does not touch
on the second Sikh War and the resultant annexation
at all; but, as he was transferred to Bhopal at the con-

clusion of the first war, he probably lost touch with Punjab politics.

It is not possible in a short introduction of this nature to follow the history of the Sikhs in detail since the Punjab came under British control. That the Sikhs settled down peacefully and loyally under the new regime is sufficiently borne out by the records of the Mutiny, when the newly raised Sikh regiments—many of them composed of the disbanded regiments of the Khalsa army—did excellent service. The Sikhs have displayed their warlike aptitude in other fields since 1857 and are to be found to-day taking their share in the great European War.

In 1911 the Sikh population of the Punjab numbered a little over two millions out of a total population of some twenty-three and a half millions. As regards modern conversions to Sikhism and the relation of that religion to Hinduism, Mr. Candler has the following interesting remarks in an article which appeared in *Blackwood's Magazine* in September 1909 : The truth is that the Sikhs have only partially rid themselves of caste. They were able to suppress the instinct so long as it endangered their existence, but when they became paramount in the Punjab and the Khalsa was sufficient for its own needs, the old exclusive Brahmanical spirit returned. The influence of Ranjit Singh's Court increased this retrogressive tendency, and in spite of the Guru's teaching it is not always easy for a low-caste Hindu to become a Sikh to-day. Still, it is not always impossible. The acceptance or rejection of a convert is likely to depend on whether the majority in the district Singh Sabha or Sikh Council is conservative or progressive. The so-called Conservative Party is naturally exclusive, while the so-called Progressive Party are really purists who would revert to the injunctions of Nanak and Gobind. They are ready to receive all converts whom they believe to be genuine, of whatever caste. The Sikhs now number a little over two millions, and in the last ten years the numbers have only risen in proportion to the general increase in the Punjab. The lack of converts is due as much to apathy as to obstacles placed in the way by the priests.'

**H. L. O. GARRETT**

# BIOGRAPHICAL NOTE

## ON THE CUNNINGHAM FAMILY

ALLAN CUNNINGHAM, the father of the author of this volume, was born in the parish of Keir, Dumfriesshire, in 1784. Although apprenticed to his elder brother, then a stonemason, he soon showed a literary bent. At the age of eighteen he made the acquaintance of Hogg, the Ettrick shepherd, and the acquaintance ripened into a warm friendship. Early in the nineteenth century he commenced his career as an author, and his poems began to appear in various periodicals. When R. H. Cromek, the engraver, was travelling in Scotland in 1809, collecting Scottish songs, he met Cunningham, who showed him some of his work. Upon Cromek's advice Cunningham then went up to London to try his fortune at literature. For some years he worked both as a mason and as a literary man, producing a number of poems in the *Day* and the *Literary Gazette*. In 1814, Chantrey, the sculptor, to whom he had been introduced by Cromek, engaged him as his superintendent of works, and this connexion lasted down to Chantrey's death, in 1841. During this period he produced a quantity of literary work of a varied nature. He had become acquainted with Sir Walter Scott, when the latter was sitting for Chantrey, and in 1820 submitted to him a drama, *Sir Marmaduke Maxwell*. It was considered unsuitable to the stage, but Scott was favourably impressed with the style. In 1825 appeared *The Songs of Scotland, Ancient and Modern,* which contained the well-known sea song, 'A Wet Sheet and a Flowing Sea.' His connexion with Chantrey gave him an intimate knowledge of the artistic world, which he turned to account in his *Lives of the Most Eminent British Painters, Sculptors, and Architects,* which he published from 1829-33. His last important work was an edition of Burns, which appeared in 1834. Late in life he made the acquaintance of Caryle, who had a warm regard for him. Cunningham died in 1842, leaving five sons and a daughter.

Joseph Davey Cunningham, the eldest son and the

author of the present volume, was born in 1812. At an early age he showed such aptitude for mathematics that his father was advised to send him to Cambridge. But as he was keenly desirous of becoming a soldier a cadetship in the East India Company's service was procured for him, through the good offices of Sir Walter Scott. After a brilliant career at Addiscombe he sailed for India in 1834, and was at first employed on the staff of the chief engineer of the Bengal Presidency. In 1837 he was appointed assistant to Colonel (afterwards Sir Claude) Wade, the political agent on the Sikh frontier. For the next eight years he held various appointments under Colonel Wade and his successors, and at the time of the outbreak of the first Sikh War was political agent in the State of Bahawalpur. Upon the commencement of hostilities he was attached first to the staff of Sir Charles Napier and then to that of Sir Hugh Gough. He was present, as political officer, with the division of Sir Harry Smith at the battles of Buddawal and Aliwal. At Sobraon he served as an additional aide-de-camp to the Governor-General, Sir Henry Hardinge. His services earned him a brevet and the appointment of political agent to the State of Bhopal. In 1849 appeared his *History of the Sikhs*. As has been noted elsewhere in this edition, the views taken by the author were anything but pleasing to his superiors. As a punishment, he was removed from his political appointment and sent back to regimental duty. The disgrace undoubtedly hastened his death, and soon after his appointment to the Meerut Division of Public Works he died suddenly at Ambala, in 1851.

Like Joseph Davey Cunningham, his younger brothers inherited their father's literary abilities. Alexander, the second brother, had a distinguished career in India. He, too, obtained his cadetship through the influence of Sir Walter Scott, and arrived in India in 1833. Lord Auckland appointed him one of his aides-de-camp, and while on the Governor-General's staff he visited Kashmir, then almost an unknown country. He served with distinction in the Gwalior campaign of 1843 and acted as executive engineer of Gwalior until the outbreak of the first Sikh War. In this war and also in the second Sikh War he did good service and then returned to Gwalior. In 1856 he was appointed chief engineer in Burma (after a brief period of service in Multan, where he designed the Vans Agnew and Anderson monument), and remained there till 1858. He was transferred to the North-Western

Provinces in 1858, and remained there till his retirement in 1861 with the rank of major-general.

It was at this stage that he commenced his archaeological career. The Government of India decided to appoint an archaeological surveyor, and Cunningham, who during his whole career in India had displayed the greatest activity in this direction, was appointed to the post. This he held (with an interval from 1865 to 1870) down to his final retirement in 1885. His work in this capacity is too well known to need detailed treatment in a note of this nature. He continued his interest in Indian archaeology after his retirement, and the collection of coins in the British Museum bears testimony to his generosity. He died in 1893 as Sir Alexander Cunningham, having been created a K.C.I.E. in 1887.

Peter Cunningham, the third brother, under whose editorship the second edition of this book appeared in 1853, was a well-known antiquary. He held an appointment in the Audit Office, which he obtained through Sir Robert Peel in 1834. His chief work was the *Handbook of London,* which first appeared in 1849 and is still regarded as a standard authority. He also edited a large number of books—the collected letters of Horace Walpole (1857) and the works of Oliver Goldsmith (1854) being well-known examples of his work. He retired from the public service in 1860 and died in 1869.

Francis Cunningham, the youngest brother, also served in India. He joined the Madras army in 1838 and won distinction at the siege of Jalalabad. He retired from the army in 1861, and after his retirement devoted himself to literature, for which he displayed the family aptitude. He published editions of Marlowe (1870), Massinger (1871), and Ben Jonson (1871). His death took place in 1875.

# BIBLIOGRAPHY

## SECTION A. PRINTED BOOKS

### (1) ENGLISH

Archer, J. H. Laurence. *Commentaries on the Punjab Campaign* (1848-9). London, 1878.

Baird, J. G. A. *Private Letters of the Marquess of Dalhousie.* Blackwood, 1910.

Banerjee. *Evolution of Khalsa.*

Broadfoot, Major. *Career of Major George Broadfoot, C.B., in Afghanistan and the Punjab.* London, 1888.

Burnes, Sir A. *Travels into Bokhara.* London, 1834.

Burton, Lt.-Col. R. G. *The First and Second Sikh Wars.* Simla, 1911.

Chopra, G. L. *The Punjab as a Sovereign State.* 1928.

Coley, J. *Journal of the Sutlej Campaign* (1845-6). London, 1856.

Cotton, J. J. *Life of General Avitabile.* Calcutta, 1906.

*Despatches of Lords Hardinge and Gough and General Sir Harry Smith, &c., relative to the Engagements of Moodkee, Ferozeshah, &c.* (2nd edition.) London, 1846. (Olivier, Pall Mall.)

Dunlop, J. *Multan, during and after the Siege.* London, 1849.

Edwardes, Sir H. B. (vol. i), and H. Merivale (vol. ii). *Life of Sir H. Laurence.* London, 1872.

Fane, H. E. *Five Years in India,* 1835-39. (Author was aide-de-camp to Lord Auckland.) London, 1842.

Foster, G. *A Journey from Bengal to England through North India, Kashmir, Afghanistan, and Persia, into Russia* (1783-4). London, 1798.

Ganda Singh and Teja Singh. *History of the Sikhs.*

Gardner, A. *Memoirs of Col. A. Gardner.* London (re-edited), 1898.

*Gazetteer of the Punjab.* Provincial Series of the *Imperial Gazetteer of India.* Oxford, 1908.

Gough, Sir C., and A. D. Innes. *The Sikhs and the Sikh Wars.* London, 1897.

Gough, Lord. *Despatches of Lord Gough* (Parliamentary Papers, 1846).

Griffin, L. H. *Ranjit Singh* ('Rulers of India' Series). Oxford, 1892.

Gupta, H. R. *History of the Sikhs* in 3 vols.

Hardinge, Lord. *Despatches of Lord Hardinge* (Parliamentary Papers, 1846).

Honigberger, J. M. *Thirty-Five Years in the East.* (The author was court physician at Lahore for some time.) London, 1852.

Huegel, C. von. *Travels in Kashmir and the Country of the Sikhs.* Written in German, translated by T. B. Jervis. London, 1845.

Humbly, W. W. W. *Journal of a Cavalry Offic* · (*Sikh Campaign,* 1845-6). London, 1854.

Irvine, W. *The Later Moguls. Journal of the Asiatic Society of Bengal,* vols. lxiii (1894), lxv (1896), lxvii (1898).

Jacquemont, V. *Letters from India* (translated). London, 1835.

Kaye, Sir J. W. *Life and Correspondence of Lord Metcalfe.* London, 1854.

Khazan Singh. *History and Philosophy of the Sikh Religion.* Lahore, 1914.

Latif, M. *A History of the Punjab.* Calcutta, 1891.

Laurence. J. *The Sikhs and their Country. Journal of the Asiatic Society of Bengal,* vol. iii.

Laurence, Major W. M. *Some Passages of the Life of an Adventurer in the Punjab.* Delhi, 1842.

Macauliffe, M. A. *The Sikh Religion, its Gurus, Sacred Writings, and Authors.* 6 vols. Oxford, 1909.

Macgregor, W. L. *The History of the Sikhs.* London, 1846.

Malcolm, J. *A Sketch of the Sikhs.* London and Bombay, 1812.

Marshman, J. C. *Memoirs of Sir H. Havelock.* London, 1860.

Masson, C. *Narrative of Various Journeys in Balochistan, Afghanistan, and the Punjab* (1826-38). 3 vols. London, 1842.

Massy, C. F., and Griffin, L. H. *The Chiefs and Families of Note in the Punjab,* 1909. Revised ed., 1907.

Mohana Lala. *Travels in the Punjab, Afghanistan, Turkistan.* London, 1846.

Moorcroft and Trebeck. *Travels in the Himalayan Provinces* (1819-25), edited by H. H. Wilson. London, 1841.

Narang, G. C. *Transformation of Sikhism.*

Osborne, W. G. *Court and Camp of Runjeet Singh.* (Author was military secretary to Lord Auckland.) London, 1840.

Prinsep, H. T. *The Origin of the Sikh Power in the Punjab.* Calcutta, 1834.

Rait, R. S. *Life of Hugh, Viscount Gough.* Constable, London, 1903.

Sethi, R. R. *Lahore Darbar.* New Delhi, 1950.

Sinha, N. K. *Ranjit Singh,* 1933.

Smyth, G. *History of the Reigning Family of Lahore.* Calcutta, 1847.

Steinbach Lt.-Col. H. *The Punjab.* (Author was employed in

Ranjit Singh's army for about eight years.) London, 1845.

Thackwell, E. J. *Narrative of the Second Sikh War.* London, 1851.

Thorburn, S. S. *The Punjab in Peace and War.* Blackwood. London, 1904.

Wade, C. *Our Relations with the Punjab.* London, 1823.

### (2) PERSIAN

Amar Nath, Diwan. *Zafar Nama-i-Ranjit Singh.* A very important source of information concerning the reign of Ranjit Singh. The author was for some time a paymaster of the Irregular Cavalry forces of the Lahore Darbar. The book was edited with notes and introduction by Sita Ram Kohli in 1928.

Buti Shah. *Tarikh Punjab.* The author Ghulam Muhiy-ud-Din *alias* Buti Shah, was in the service of the British at Ludhiana. He wrote his book in 1848 at the suggestion of Col. Ochterlony.

Kanhya Lal. *Ranjit Nama.* Lahore, 1876.

Khafi Khan. *Muntakhab ul lubab.* (Translation in *History of India as told by its own Historians.* Elliot and Dowson. Vol. vii. 1877.)

Mohsin Fani. *Dabistan.* (Translation by D. Shea and A. Troyer. London, 1843.) (Author was a contemporary of Gurus Har Gobind and Har Rai, VIth and VIIth Gurus.)

Sohan Lal. *Diary of Ranjit Singh or Umdat-ul-Tawarikh.* 1885. The MS. copy of this book in Bankipur Oriental Public Library closes at 1831. The published copy goes down to 1849. (Sohan Lal was Ranjit Singh's Court vakil and historian. A very faithful narrative of Ranjit Singh's life.)

## SECTION B.   DOCUMENTS, UNPUBLISHED MSS.

1. Sarup Lal. *Tarikh-Sikhan.* (MSS. undated.)
2. *State Records.* MSS. Civil Secretariat, Punjab, 1812-49.
     Official documents of Ranjit Singh's government. Papers of various descriptions. Civil and military departments. Written in the Persian language.
3. *Records of Ludhiana, Ambala, and Delhi agencies.* MSS. Civil Secretariat, Punjab, 1804-49.
     Dispatches and communications between the Sikh Government and the East India Company and their Agents. Written in English.
4. *In the Library of the India Office.*
     M. Ali ud din. *Ibrat Nama.* M. Khya Bux. *Sher Singh Nama. Tarikh Mulki-i-Hazara.*

# ADVERTISEMENT TO THE
## SECOND EDITION, 1853

THE sheets of this Edition were seen and corrected by their Author, and were ready for publication several months previous to his death, in February, 1851. The reasons—of a painful, though temporary character—for the delay in the appearance of the work will be found in a Memoir already written and to be published hereafter, when regard for the living will no longer interfere with the truth of History.

The author fell a victim to the truth related in this book. He wrote History in advance of his time, and suffered for it; but posterity will, I feel assured, do justice to his memory.

My brother's anxiety to be correct was evinced in the unceasing labour he took to obtain the most minute information. Wherever he has been proved to be wrong—and this has been in very few instances—he has, with ready frankness, admitted and corrected his error. In matters of opinion he made no change—not from obstinacy, but from a firm conviction that he was right.

The new notes to this Edition contain some information of moment, contributed by Lord Gough, Sir Charles Napier, and others, and all received my brother's sanction.

The printed materials for the recent History of India are not of that character on which historians can rely. State Papers, presented to the people by 'both Houses of Parliament', have been altered to suit the temporary views of political warfare, or abridged out of mistaken regard to the tender feelings of survivors.[1] In matters of private life, some tenderness may be shown to individual sensitiveness, but History, to be

---

[1] The character and career of Alexander Burnes have both been misrepresented in those collections of State Papers which are supposed to furnish the best materials of history, but which are often only one-sided compilations of garbled documents, —counterfeits, which the ministerial stamp forces into currency, defrauding a present generation, and handing down to posterity a chain of dangerous lies.—KAYE, *Affghanistan*, ii. 13.

of any value, should be written by one superior to the influences of private or personal feelings. What Gibbon calls 'truth, naked, unblushing truth, the first virtue of more serious history', should alone direct the pen of the historian; and truth alone influenced the mind and guided the pen of the Author of this book.

PETER CUNNINGHAM.

KENSINGTON,
   18th January, 1853.

# AUTHOR'S PREFACE TO THE
## SECOND EDITION

IN this Second Edition the author has made some alterations in the text of the last chapter, where it seemed that his readers had inferred more than was meant, but the sense and spirit of what was originally written have been carefully preserved, notwithstanding the modifications of expression now introduced. Throughout the grammatical imperfections detected on reperusal have been removed; but no other changes have been made in the text of the first eight chapters. Some notes, however, altogether new, have been added, while others have been extended; and such as by their length crowded a series of pages, and from their subject admitted of separate treatment, have been formed into Appendices.

The author's principal object in writing this history has not always been understood, and he therefore thinks it right to say that his main endeavour was to give Sikhism its place in the general history of humanity, by showing its connexion with the different creeds of India, by exhibiting it as a natural and important result of the Muhammadan Conquest, and by impressing upon the people of England the great necessity of attending to the mental changes now in progress amongst their subject millions in the East, who are erroneously thought to be sunk in superstitious apathy, or to be held spell-bound in ignorance by a dark and designing priesthood. A secondary object of the author's was to give some account of the connexion of the English with the Sikhs, and in part with the Afghans, from the time they began to take a direct interest in the affairs of these races, and to involve them in the web of their policy for opening the navigation of the Indus, and for bringing Turkestan and Khorasan within their commercial influence.

It has also been remarked by some public critics and private friends, that the author leans unduly towards the Sikhs, and that an officer in the Indian army should appear to say he sees aught unwise or objectionable in the acts of the East India Company and its delegates is at the least strange. The author has, indeed,

constantly endeavoured to keep his readers alive to
that undercurrent of feeling or principle which moves
the Sikh people collectively, and which will usually
rise superior to the crimes or follies of individuals. It
was the history of *Sikhs,* a new and peculiar nation,
which he wished to make known to strangers; and he
saw no reason for continually recurring to the duty
or destiny of the English in India, because he was
addressing himself to his own countrymen who know
the merits and motives of their supremacy in the East,
and who can themselves commonly decide whether the
particular acts of a viceroy are in accordance with the
general policy of his government.  The Sikhs, moreover, are so inferior to the English in resources and
knowledge that there is no equality of comparison
between them.

The glory to England is indeed great of her Eastern
Dominion, and she may justly feel proud of the increasing excellence of her sway over subject nations;
but this general expression of the sense and desire of
the English people does not show that every proceeding of her delegates is necessarily fitting and far-seeing.
The wisdom of England is not to be measured by the
views and acts of any one of her sons, but is rather to
be deduced from the characters of many.  In India it
is to be gathered in part from the high, but not always
scrupulous, qualities which distinguished Clive, Hastings, and Wellesley, who acquired and secured the
Empire; in part from the generous, but not always
discerning, sympathies of Burke, Cornwallis, and Bentinck, who gave to English rule the stamp of moderation and humanity; and also in part from the ignorant
well-meaning of the people at large, who justly depre-
cating ambition in the abstract vainly strive to check
the progress of conquest before its necessary limits
have been attained, and before the aspiring energies of
the conquerors themselves have become exhausted. By
conquest, I would be understood to imply the extension
of supremacy, and not the extinction of dynasties, for
such imperial form of domination should be the aim
and scope of English sway in the East.  England should
reign over kings rather than rule over subjects.

The Sikhs and the English are each irresistibly
urged forward in their different ways and degrees towards remote and perhaps diverse ends : the Sikhs, as
the leaders of a congenial mental change; the English,
as the promoters of rational law and material wealth;
and individual chiefs and rulers can merely play their

parts in the great social movements with more or less of effect and intelligence. Of the deeds and opinions of these conspicuous men, the Author has not hesitated to speak plainly but soberly, whether in praise or dispraise, and he trusts he may do both, without either idly flattering or malignantly traducing his country, and also without compromising his own character as a faithful and obedient servant of the State; for the soldiers of India are no longer mere sentinels over bales of goods, nor is the East India Company any longer a private association of traffickers which can with reason object to its mercantile transactions being subjected to open comment by one of its confidential factors. The merits of the administration of the East India Company are many and undoubted; but its constitution is political, its authority is derivative, and every Englishman has a direct interest in the proceedings of his Government; while it is likewise his country's boast that her children can at fitting times express in calm and considerate language their views of her career, and it is *her* duty to see that those to whom she entrusts power rightly understand both their own position and *her* functions.

25th October, 1849.

# PREFACE TO THE FIRST EDITION [1]

ONE who possesses no claims to systematic scholar-ship, and who nevertheless asks the public to approve of his labours in a field of some difficulty, is bound to show to his readers that he has at least had fair means of obtaining accurate information and of coming to just conclusions.

Towards the end of the year 1837, the author re-ceived, through the unsolicited favour of Lord Auck-land, the appointment of assistant to Colonel Wade, the political agent at Ludhiana, and the officer in charge of the British relations with the Punjab and the chiefs of Afghanistan. He was at the same time required as an engineer officer, to render Ferozepore a defensible post, that little place having been declared a feudal escheat, and its position being regarded as one of military im-portance. His plans for effecting the object in view met the approval of Sir Henry Fane, the Commander-in-Chief; but it was not eventually thought proper to do more than cover the town with a slight parapet, and the scheme for reseating Shah Shuja on his throne seemed at the time to make the English and Sikh Gov-ernments so wholly one, that the matter dropped, and Ferozepore was allowed to become a cantonment with scarcely the means at hand of saving its ammunition from a few predatory horse.

The author was also present at the interview which took place in 1838, between Ranjit Singh and Lord Auckland. In 1839 he accompanied Shahzada Taimur and Colonel Wade to Peshawar, and he was with them when they forced the Pass of Khaibar, and laid open the road to Kabul. In 1840 he was placed in adminis-trative charge of the district of Ludhiana; and towards the end of the same year, he was deputed by the new frontier agent, Mr. Clerk, to accompany Colonel Shel-ton and his relieving brigade to Peshawar, whence he returned with the troops escorting Dost Muhammad Khan under Colonel Wheeler. During part of 1841 he was in magisterial charge of the Ferozepore district, and towards the close of that year, he was appointed

[1] Published in 1 vol. 8vo. 19th March, 1849.

—on the recommendation again of Mr. Clerk—to proceed to Tibet to see that the ambitious Rajas of Jammu surrendered certain territories which they had seized from the Chinese of Lassa, and that the British trade with Ladakh, &c., was restored to its old footing. He returned at the end of a year, and was present at the interviews between Lord Ellenborough and Dost Muhammad at Ludhiana, and between his lordship and the Sikh chiefs at Ferozepore in December 1842. During part of 1843 he was in civil charge of Ambala; but from the middle of that year till towards the close of 1844, he held the post of personal assistant to Colonel Richmond, the successor of Mr. Clerk. After Major Broadfoot's nomination to the same office, and during the greater part of 1845, the author was employed in the Bahawalpur territory in connexion with refugee Sindhians, and with boundary disputes between the Daudputras and the Rajputs of Bikaner and Jaisalmer. When war with the Sikhs broke out, the author was required by Sir Charles Napier to join his army of co-operation; but after the battle of Ferozeshah, he was summoned to Lord Gough's head-quarters. He was subsequently directed to accompany Sir Harry Smith, when a diversion was made towards Ludhiana, and he was thus present at the skirmish of Badowal and at the battle of Aliwal. He had likewise the fortune to be a participator in the victory of Sobraon, and the further advantage of acting on that important day as an aide-de-camp to the Governor-General. He was then attached to the head-quarters of the Commander-in-Chief, until the army broke up at Lahore, when he accompanied Lord Hardinge's camp to the Simla Hills, preparatory to setting out for Bhopal, the political agency in which state and its surrounding districts, his lordship had unexpectedly been pleased to bestow upon him.

The author was thus living among the Sikh people for a period of eight years, and during a very important portion of their history. He had intercourse, under every variety of circumstances, with all classes of men, and he had at the same time free access to all the public records bearing on the affairs of the frontier. It was after being required in 1844, to draw up reports on the British connexion generally with the states on the Sutlej, and especially on the military resources of the Punjab, that he conceived the idea, and felt he had the means, of writing the history whcih he now offers to the public.

The author's residence in Malwa has been bene-

ficial to him in many ways personally; and it has also
been of advantage in the composition of this work, as
he has had the opportunity of becoming acquainted
with the ideas and modes of life of the military colonies
of Sikhs scattered through Central India.

SEHORE, BHOPAL,
   *December* 9, 1848.

# NOTE

In the references, and also in the text, from Chap. V to the end of the volume, the names of military officers and civil functionaries are quoted without any nice regard to the rank they may have held at the particular time, or to the titles by which they may have been subsequently distinguished. But as there is one person only of each name to be referred to, no doubt or inconvenience can arise from this laxity. Thus the youthful, but discreet Mr. Metcalfe of the treaty with Ranjit Singh, and the Sir Charles Metcalfe so honourably connected with the history of India, is the Lord Metcalfe of riper years and approved services in another hemisphere. Lieutenant-Colonel, or more briefly Colonel, Pottinger, is now a Major-General and a Grand Cross of the Bath; while Mr. Clerk has been made a knight of the same Order, and Lieutenant-Colonel Lawrence has been raised to an equal title. Captain, or Lieutenant-Colonel, or Sir Claude Wade, mean one and the same person : and similarly the late Sir Alexander Burnes sometimes appears as a simple lieutenant, or as a captain, or as a lieutenant-colonel. On the other hand, Sir David Ochterlony is referred to solely under that title, although, when he marched to the Sutlej in 1809, he held the rank of lieutenant-colonel only.

# CONTENTS

## CHAPTER I

### THE COUNTRY AND PEOPLE

## CHAPTER II

### OLD INDIAN CREEDS, MODERN REFORMS, AND THE TEACHING OF NANAK

#### UP TO A. D. 1539

# CONTENTS

## CHAPTER III

### THE SIKH GURUS OR TEACHERS, AND THE MODIFICATION OF SIKHISM UNDER GOBIND

#### A. D. 1539-1716

## CHAPTER IV

## THE ESTABLISHMENT OF SIKH INDEPENDENCE
### A. D. 1716-64

# CONTENTS

## CHAPTER V

## FROM THE INDEPENDENCE OF THE SIKHS TO THE ASCENDANCY OF RANJIT SINGH AND THE ALLIANCE WITH THE ENGLISH

### 1765—1808-9

## CHAPTER VI

## FROM THE SUPREMACY OF RANJIT SINGH TO THE REDUCTION OF MULTAN, KASHMIR, AND PESHAWAR

### 1809—1823-4

## CHAPTER VII

### FROM THE ACQUISITION OF MULTAN, KASHMIR, AND PESHAWAR TO THE DEATH OF RANJIT SINGH

#### 1824-39

# CONTENTS XLIII

## CHAPTER VIII

### FROM THE DEATH OF MAHARAJA RANJIT SINGH TO THE DEATH OF WAZIR JAWAHIR SINGH

#### 1839-45

# CONTENTS

## CHAPTER IX

### THE WAR WITH THE ENGLISH

### 1845-6

# APPENDIXES

# CONTENTS

# CONTENTS

# A HISTORY OF THE SIKHS

## CHAPTER I

## THE COUNTRY AND PEOPLE

Geographical Limits of Sikh Occupation or Influence—Climate,
Productions, &c. of the Sikh Dominions—Inhabitants, Races,
Tribes—Religions of the People—Characteristics and
Effects of Race and Religion—Partial Migrations of Tribes—
Religious Proselytism.

DURING the sixteenth and seventeenth centuries of Geographical limits.
the Christian era, Nanak and Gobind, of the Kshattriya
race, obtained a few converts to their doctrines of religious reform and social emancipation among the Jat
peasants of Lahore and the southern banks of the Sutlej.
The 'Sikhs', or 'Disciples', have now become a nation;
and they occupy, or have extended their influence, from
Delhi to Peshawar, and from the plains of Sind to the
Karakoram mountains. The dominions acquired by the
Sikhs are thus included between the 28th and 36th
parallels of north latitude, and between the 71st and
77th meridians of east longitude; and if a base of four
hundred and fifty miles be drawn from Panipat to the
Khaibar Pass, two triangles, almost equilateral, may
be described upon it, which shall include the conquests
of Ranjit Singh and the fixed colonies of the Sikh
people.

The country of the Sikhs, being thus situated in a Climate, produc-
medium degree of latitude, corresponding nearly with tions, &c.
that of northern Africa and the American States, and
consisting either of broad plains not much above the
sea level, or of mountain ranges which rise two and
three miles into the air, possesses every variety of climate and every description of natural produce. The
winter of Ladakh is long and rigorous, snow covers the
ground for half the year, the loneliness of its vast soli-
tudes appals the heart, and naught living meets the eye;
yet the shawl-wool goat gives a value to the rocky Grain, and
wastes of that elevated region, and its scanty acres yield shawl wool
unequalled crops of wheat and barley, where the stars of Ladakh.
can be discerned at midday and the thin air scarcely
bears the sound of thunder to the ear.[1] The heat and

[1] Shawl wool is produced most abundantly, and of the

Silks, in-
digo, and
cotton of
Multan.

the dust storms of Multan are perhaps more oppressive
than the cold and the drifting snows of Tibet; but the
favourable position of the city, and the several over-
flowing streams in its neighbourhood, give an importance, the one to its manufactures of silks and carpets,
and the other to the wheat, the indigo, and the cotton
of its fields.[1] The southern slopes of the Himalayas are

finest quality, in the steppes between the Shayuk and the main
branch of the Indus.   About 100,000 rupees, or £10,000 worth
may be carried down the valley of the Sutlej to Ludhiana and
Delhi. (Journal Asiatic Society of Bengal, 1844, p. 210.)   The
importation into Kashmir alone is estimated by Moorcroft
(Travels, ii. 165) at about £75,000, and thus the Sutlej trade
may represent less than a tenth of the whole.

Moorcroft speaks highly of the cultivation of wheat and
barley in Tibet, and he once saw a field of the latter grain in
that country such as he had never before beheld, and which, he
says, an English farmer would have ridden many miles to have
looked at.   (Travels, i. 269, 280.)

The gravel of the northern steppes of Tibet yields gold in
grains, but the value of the crude borax of the lakes surpasses,
as an article of trade, that of the precious metal.

In Yarkand an intoxicating drug named churrus, much used
in India, is grown of a superior quality, and while opium could
be taken across the Himalayas, the Hindus and Chinese carried
on a brisk traffic of exchange in the two deleterious com-
modities.

The trade in tea through Tibet to Kashmir and Kabul is of
local importance.   The blocks weigh about eight pounds, and
sell for 12s. and 16s. up to 36s. and 48s. each, according to the
quality. (Cf. Moorcroft, Travels, i. 350, 351.)

[1] The wheat of Multan is beardless, and its grain is long
and heavy.   It is exported in large quantities to Rajputana, and
also, since the British occupation, to Sind to an increased extent.
The value of the carpets manufactured in Multan does not
perhaps exceed 50,000 rupees annually. The silk manufacture
may be worth five times that sum, or, including that of Bahawalpur, 400,000 rupees in all; but the demand for such fabrics
has markedly declined since the expulsion of a native dynasty
from Sind.   The raw silk of Bokhara is used in preference to
that of Bengal, as being stronger and more glossy.

English piece-goods, or (more largely) cotton twists to be
woven into cloth, have been introduced everywhere in India;
but those well-to-do in the world can alone buy foreign articles,
and thus while about eighteen tons of cotton twist are used by
the weavers of Bahawalpur, about 300 tons of (cleaned) cotton
are grown in the district, and wrought up by the villagers or
exported to Rajputana.

The Lower Punjab and Bahawalpur yield respectively
about 750 and 150 tons of indigo. It is worth on the spot from
9d. to 1s. 6d. the pound.   The principal market is Khorasan; but
the trade has declined of late, perhaps owing to the quantities
which may be introduced into that country by way of the Persian Gulf from India. The fondness of the Sikhs, and of the
poorer Muhammadans of the Indus, for blue clothing, will
always maintain a fair trade in indigo. [It seems hardly necessary to state that the prosperity of the Western Punjab to-day

periodically deluged with rain, which is almost unknown beyond the snow, and is but little felt in Multan or along the Indus. The central Punjab is mostly a bushy jungle or a pastoral waste; its rivers alone have rescued it from the desert, but its dryness keeps it free from savage beasts, and its herds of cattle are of staple value to the country; while the plains which immediately bound the hills, or are influenced by the Indus and its tributaries, are not surpassed in fertility by any in India. The many populous towns of these tracts are filled with busy weavers of cotton and silk and wool, and with skilful workers in leather and wood and iron. Water is found near the surface, and the Persian wheel is in general use for purposes of irrigation. Sugar is produced in abundance, and the markets of Sind and Kabul are in part supplied with that valuable article by the traders of Amritsar, the commercial emporium of Northern India.[1] The artisans of Kashmir, the varied productions of that famous valley, its harvests of saffron, and its important manufacture of shawls, are well known and need only be alluded to.[2] The plains of Attock and Peshawar no longer shelter the rhinoceros which Babar delighted to hunt, but are covered with rich crops of rice, of wheat, and of barley. The moun-

*Black cattle of the central Punjab.*

*The Persian wheel used for irrigation.*

*Sugar of the upper plains.*

*The saffron and the shawls of Kashmir.*

*Rice and wheat of Peshawar.*

depends principally upon its grain, and that cultivation has received a great stimulus from the canal system.

As regards the second paragraph of the note the statement about the consumption of foreign cotton, &c., reads strangely to a modern generation.—Ed.]

[1] In 1844 the customs and excise duties of the Punjab amounted to £240,000 or £250,000 or to one-thirteenth of the whole revenue of Ranjit Singh, estimated at £3,250,000. ['Under the present system of decentralization in finance, the Imperial Government delegates to the Punjab Government the control of expenditure on the ordinary administrative services, together with the whole or a certain proportion of certain heads of revenue sufficient to meet those charges. Of the various heads of revenue, post-office, telegraphs, railways, opium, and salt are entirely Imperial. Land revenue, stamps, excise, income tax, and major irrigation works are divided between the Imperial and Provincial Governments in the proportion of one-half to each. Minor irrigation works and some minor heads are divided in varying proportions, while the revenue from forests, registration, courts of law, jails, police, and education are wholly provincial, as well as the income of district boards and municipalities. The Budget for 1914-15 shows a total revenue (including opening balance) of Rs. 6,44,50,000 and a total expenditure of Rs. 5,00,29,000, leaving a closing balance of Rs. 1,44,21,000.'— *Indian Year Book*, 1915.]

[2] Mr. Moorcroft (*Travels*, ii. 194) estimates the annual value of the Kashmir manufacture of shawls at £300,000, but this seems a small estimate if the raw material be worth £75,000 alone (*Travels*, ii. 165, &c.), that is, 1,000 horse loads of 300 pounds, each pound being worth 5s.

tains themselves produce drugs and dyes and fruits;
their precipitous sides support forests of gigantic pines,
and veins of copper, or extensive deposits of rock salt
**Drugs, dyes,** and of iron ore are contained within their vast outline.
**and metals** The many fertile vales lying between the Indus and
**of the hills.** Kashmir are perhaps unsurpassed in the East for salu-
brity and loveliness; the seasons are European, and the
violent 'monsoon' of India is replaced by the genial
spring rains of temperate climates.

**Inhabi-** The people comprised within the limits of the Sikh
**tants.** rule or influence, are various in their origin, their language, and their faith. The plains of Upper India, in
which the Brahmans and Kshattriya had developed a
peculiar civilization, have been overrun by Persian or
Scythic tribes, from the age of Darius and Alexander to
that of Babar and Nadir Shah. Particular traces of the
successive conquerors may yet perhaps be found, but
**Immigration** the main features are: (1) the introduction of the Muh-
**of the Jats,** ammadan creed; and (2) the long antecedent emigration
**and introdu-** of hordes of Jats from the plains of Upper Asia. It is not
**ction of** necessary to enter into the antiquities of Grecian 'Getae'
**Muhamma-** and Chinese 'Yuechi', to discuss the asserted identity
**danism.** of a peasant Jat and a moon-descended Yadu, or to try
to trace the blood of Kadphises in the veins of Ranjit
Singh. It is sufficient to observe that the vigorous Hindu
civilization of the first ages of Christianity soon
absorbed its barbarous invaders, and that in the lapse
of centuries the Jats became essentially Brahmanical
in language and belief. Along the southern Indus they
soon yielded their conscience to the guidance of Islam;
those of the north longer retained their idolatrous faith,
but they have lately had a new life breathed into them;
they now preach the unity of God and the equality of
man, and, after obeying Hindu and Muhammadan
rulers, they have themselves once more succeeded to
sovereign power. [1] The Musalman occupation forms
the next grand epoch in general Indian history after
the extinction of the Buddhist religion; the common
speech of the people has been partially changed, and
the tenets of Muhammad are gradually revolutionizing
the whole fabric of Indian society; but the difference of
race, or the savage manners of the conquerors, struck
the vanquished even more forcibly than their creed,
and to this day Jats and others talk of 'Turks' as synonymous with oppressors, and the proud Rajputs not
only bowed before the Musalmans, but have perpetua-
ted the remembrance of their servitude by adopting

[1] See Appendix I.

'Turkhana', or Turk money, into their language as the equivalent of tribute.

In the valley of the Upper Indus, that is, in Ladakh and Little Tibet, the prevailing caste is the Bhoti subdivision of the great Tartar variety of the human race. Lower down that classical stream, or in Gilgit and Chulass, the remains of the old and secluded races of Dardus and Dungars are still to be found, but both in Iskardo and in Gilgit itself, there is some mixture of Turkoman tribes from the wilds of Pamer and Kashkar. The people of Kashmir have from time to time been mixed with races from the north, the south, and the west; and while their language is Hindu and their faith Muhammadan, the manners of the primitive Kash or Katch tribes, have been influenced by their proximity to the Tartars. The hills westward from Kashmir to the Indus are inhabited by Kukas and Bambas, of whom little is known, but towards the river itself the Yusufzaïs and other Afghan tribes prevail; while there are many secluded valleys peopled by the widely spread Gujars, whose history has yet to be ascertained, and who are the vassals of Arabian 'saiyids', or of Afghan and Turkoman lords.

The Tartars of Tibet.

The ancient Dardus.

Turkomans of Gilgit.

The Kashmiris

and their western neighbours,

Kukas Bambas, Gujars, &c.

In the hills south of Kashmir, and west of the Jhelum to Attock and Kalabagh on the Indus, are found Gakhars, Gujars, Khattars, Awans, Janjuas, and others, all of whom may be considered to have from time to time merged into the Hindu stock in language and feelings. Of these, some, as the Janjuas and especially the Gakhars, have a local reputation. Peshawar and the hills which surround it, are peopled by various races of Afghans, as Yusufzais and Mohmands in the north and west, Khalils and others in the centre, and Afridis, Khattaks, and others in the south and east. The hills south of Kohat, and the districts of Tank and Bannu, are likewise peopled by genuine Afghans, as the pastoral Waziris and others, or by agricultural tribes claiming such a descent; and, indeed, throughout the mountains on either side of the Indus, every valley has its separate tribe or family, always opposed in interest, and sometimes differing in speech and manners. Generally it may be observed, that on the north, the Afghans on one side, and the Turkomans on the other, are gradually pressing upon the old but less energetic Dardus, who have been already mentioned.

The Gakhars and the Janjuas.

The Yusufzais, Afridis, &c.

Waziris, and other Afghans.

In the districts on either side of the Indus south of Kalabagh, and likewise around Multan, the population is partly Baluch and partly Jat, intermixed, however,

Baluchis, Jats, and Rains, of

with other tribes, as Aroras and Rains, and towards the
mountains of Suleiman some Afghan tribes are likewise
to be found located.    In the waste tracts between the

Indus and Sutlej are found Juns, Bhutis, Sials, Kurruls,
Kathis, and other tribes, who are both pastoral and
predatory, and who, with the Chibs and Buhows south
of Kashmir, between the Jhelum and Chenab, may be

the first inhabitants of the country, but little reclaimed
in manners by Hindu or Muhammadan conquerors; or
one or more of them, as the Bhutis, who boast of their
lunar descent, may represent a tribe of ancient invaders
or colonizers who have yielded to others more powerful
than themselves. Indeed, there seems little doubt of the
former supremacy of the Bhuti or Bhati race in North-
Western India: the tribe is extensively diffused, but the
only sovereignty which remains to it is over the sands
of Jaisalmer. [1]    The tracts along the Sutlej, about Pakpattan, are occupied by Wattus and Johiya Rajputs, [2]
while lower down are found some of the Langah tribe,
who were once the masters of Uch and Multan.

The hills between Kashmir and the Sutlej are possessed by Rajput families, and the Muhammadan invasion seems to have thrust the more warlike Indians,
on one side into the sands of Rajputana and the hills of
Bundelkhand, and on the other into the recesses of the
Himalayas.    But the mass of the population is a mixed

The Dog-
ras and
Kanets of
the Hima-
layas.

The Kohlis
of the Hi-
malayas.

race called Dogras about Jammu, and Kanets to the
eastward, even as far as the Jumna and Ganges, and
which boasts of some Rajput blood. There are, however,
some other tribes intermixed, as the Gaddis, who claim
to be Kshattriya, and as the Kohlis, who may be the
aborigines, and who resemble in manners and habits,
and perhaps in language, the forest tribes of Central
India.    Towards the snowy limits there is some mixture
of Bhutis, and towards Kashmir and in the towns there
is a similar mixture of the people of that valley.

[1] The little chiefship of Karauli, between Jaipur and Gwalior, may also be added. The Raja is admitted by the genealo-
gists to be of the Yadu or Lunar race, but people sometimes say
that his being an *Ahir* or *Cowherd* forms his only relationship
to Krishna, the pastoral Apollo of the Indians.

[2] Tod (*Rajasthan*, i. 118) regards the Johiyas as extinct;
but they still flourish as peasants on either bank of the Sutlej,
between Kasur and Bahawalpur: they are now Muhammadans.
The Dahia of Tod (i. 118) are likewise to be found as cultivators and as Muhammadans on the Lower Sutlej, under the
name of Deheh, or Dahur and Duhur; and they and many other
tribes seem to have yielded on one side to Rahtor Rajputs, and
on the other to Baluchis.

The central tract in the plains stretching from the *The Jats of* Jhelum to Hansi, Hissar, and Panipat, and lying to the *the central* north of Khushab and the ancient Dipalpur, is inhabited *plains* chiefly by Jats; and the particular country of the Sikh people may be said to lie around Lahore, Amritsar, and even Gujrat to the north of the Sutlej, and around Bhatinda and Sunam to the south of that river. The one tract is pre-eminently called Manjha or the middle land, and the other is known as Malwa, from, it is said, some fancied resemblance in greenness and fertility to the Central Indian province of that name.  Many other *mixed with* people are, however, intermixed, as Bhutis and Dogras, *Gujars,* mostly to the south and west, and Rains, Rurs, and *Rajputs.* others, mostly in the east.  Gujars are everywhere *Pathans,* numerous, as are also other Rajputs besides Bhutis, *and others.* while Pathans are found in scattered villages and towns.  Among the Pathans those of Kasur have long been numerous and powerful, and the Rajputs of Rahon have a local reputation. Of the gross agricultural popu- *Relative* lation of this central tract, perhaps somewhat more *proportions* than four-tenths may be Jat, and somewhat more than *of some* one-tenth Gujar, while nearly two-tenths may be Raj- *principal* puts more or less pure, and less than a tenth claim to *races.* be Muhammadans of foreign origin, although it is highly probable that about a third of the whole people profess the Musalman faith.[1]

In every town and city there are, moreover, tribes of religionists, or soldiers, or traders, or handicrafts- men, and thus whole divisions of a provincial capital may be peopled by holy Brahmans[2] or as holy Saiyids, by Afghan or Bundela soldiers, by Kshattriyas, Aroras, *Kshattri-* and Banias engaged in trade, by Kashmiri weavers, and *yas and* by mechanics and dealers of the many degraded or in- *Aroras of* ferior races of Hindustan. None of these are, however, *the cities.* so powerful, so united, or so numerous as to affect the surrounding rural population, although, after the Jats, the Kshattriyas are perhaps the most influential and enterprising race in the country.[3]

[1] See Appendix II.

[2] In the Punjab, and along the Ganges, Brahmans have usually the appellation of Missar or Mitter (i.e. Mithra) given to them, if not distinguished as Pandits (i.e. as doctors or men of learning). The title seems, according to tradition, or to the surmise of well-informed native Indians, to have been intro- duced by the first Muhammadan invaders, and it may perhaps show that the Brahmans were held to be worshippers of the sun by the Unitarian iconoclasts.

[3] See Appendix III.

The wandering Changars.

Of the wandering houseless races, the Changars are the most numerous and the best known, and they seem to deserve notice as being probably the same as the Chinganehs of Turkey, the Russian Tzigans, the German Zigueners, the Italian Zingaros, the Spanish Gitanos, and the English Gypsies. About Delhi the race is called Kanjar, a word which, in the Punjab, properly implies a courtezan dancing girl.[1]

The religions of the Sikh country.

The Lamaic Buddhists of Ladakh.

The Shiah Muhammadans of Bultee.

The Sunni Muhammadans of Kashmir, Peshawar, and Multan.

The Brahmanist hill tribes.

The Sikhs of the central plains mixed with Brahmanists and Muhammadans.

The limits of Race and Religion are not the same, otherwise the two subjects might have been considered together with advantage. In Ladakh the people and the dependent rulers profess Lamaic Buddhism, which is so widely diffused throughout Central Asia, but the Tibetans of Iskardo, the Dardus of Gilgit, and the Kukas and Bambas of the rugged mountains, are Muhammadans of the Shiah persuasion. The people of Kashmir, of Kishtwar, of Bhimbar, of Pakhli, and of the hills south and west to the salt range and the Indus, are mostly Sunni Muhammadans,[2] as are likewise the tribes of Peshawar and of the valley of the Indus southward, and also the inhabitants of Multan, and of the plains northward as far as Pind-Dadan-Khan, Chiniot, and Dipalpur. The people of the Himalayas, eastward of Kishtwar and Bhimbar, are Hindus of the Brahmanical faith, with some Buddhist colonies to the north, and some Muhammadan families to the south-west. The Jats of 'Manjha' and 'Malwa' are mostly Sikhs, but perhaps not one-third of the whole population between the Jhelum and Jumna has yet embraced the tenets of Nanak and Gobind, the other two-thirds being still equally divided between Islam and Brahmanism.

Hindu shopkeepers of Muhammadan cities.

In every town, excepting perhaps Leh, and in most of the villages of the Muhammadan districts of Peshawar and Kashmir, and of the Sikh districts of Manjha and Malwa, there are always to be found Hindu traders and shopkeepers. The Kshattriya prevail in the northern towns, and the Aroras are numerous in the province of Multan. The Kashmiri Brahmans emulate in intelligence and usefulness the Maratha Pandits and the Babus of Bengal; they are a good deal employed in

[1 For the whole question of Indian gipsies the reader is referred to an article on 'The Indian Origin of the Gipsies in 'Europe', by Mr. A. C. Woolner, which appears in vol. ii of the *Journal of the Punjab Historical Society*.]

2 The author learns from his brother, Major A Cunningham who has twice visited Kashmir, that the Muhammadans of that valley are nearly all Shiah, instead of Sunni, as stated in the text.—J.D.C.

official business, although the Kshattriya and the Aroras are the ordinary accountants and farmers of revenue. In 'Malwa' alone, that is, about Bhatinda and Sunam, can the Sikh population be found unmixed, and there it has passed into a saying, that the priest, the soldier, the mechanic, the shopkeeper, and the ploughman are all equally Sikh.

There are, moreover, in the Punjab, as throughout India, several poor and contemned races, to whom Brahmans will not administer the consolations of religion, and who have not been sought as converts by the Muhammadans. These worship village or forest gods, or family progenitors, or they invoke a stone as typical of the great mother of mankind; or some have become acquainted with the writings of the later Hindu reformers, and regard themselves as inferior members of the Sikh community. In the remote Himalayas, again, where neither Mulla, nor Lama, nor Brahman, has yet cared to establish himself, the people are equally without instructed priests and a determinate faith; they worship the Spirit of each lofty peak, they erect temples to the limitary god of each snow-clad summit, and believe that from time to time the attendant servitor is inspired to utter the divine will in oracular sentences, or that when the image of the Daitya or Titan is borne in solemn procession on their shoulders, a pressure to the right or left denotes good or evil fortune.[1]

The characteristics of race and religion are everywhere of greater importance than the accidents of position or the achievements of contemporary genius; but the influences of descent and manners, of origin and worship, need not be dwelt upon in all their ramifications. The systems of Buddha, of Brahma, and of Muhammad are extensively diffused in the Eastern world, and they intimately affect the daily conduct of millions of men. But, for the most part, these creeds no longer inspire their votaries with enthusiasm; the

---

[1] In the Lower Himalayas of the Punjab there are many shrines to Guga or Goga, and the poorer classes of the plains likewise reverence the memory of the ancient hero. His birth or appearance is variously related. One account makes him the chief of Ghazni, and causes him to war with his brothers Arjun and Surjan. He was slain by them, but behold ! a rock opened and Guga again sprang forth armed and mounted. Another account makes him the lord of Durd-Durehra, in the wastes of Rajwara, and this corresponds in some degree with what Tod (Rajasthan, ii. 447) says of the same champion, who died fighting against the armies of Mahmud.

faith of the people is no longer a living principle, but
a social custom,—a rooted, an almost instinctive deference to what has been the practice of centuries. The
Tibetan, who unhesitatingly believes the Deity to dwell
incarnate in the world, and who grossly thinks he
perpetuates a prayer by the motion of a wheel, and the
Hindu, who piously considers his partial gods to delight
in forms of stone or clay, would indeed still resist the
uncongenial innovations of strangers; but the spirit
which erected temples to Sakya the Seer from the
torrid to the frigid zone, or which raised the Brahmans
high above all other Indian races, and which led them
to triumph in poetry and philosophy, is no longer to be
found in its ancient simplicity and vigour. The Buddhist and the reverer of the Vedas, is indeed each satisfied
with his own chance of a happy immortality, but he is
indifferent about the general reception of truth, and,
while he will not himself be despotically interfered
with, he cares not what may be the fate of others, or
what becomes of those who differ from him. Even the
Muhammadan, whose imagination must not be assisted
by any visible similitude, is prone to invest the dead
with the powers of intercessors, and to make pilgrimages to the graves of departed mortals;[1] and we should
now look in vain for any general expression of that
feeling which animated the simple Arabian disciple,
or the hardy Turkoman convert, to plant thrones across
the fairest portion of the ancient hemisphere. It is true
that, in the Muhammadan world, there are still many
zealous individuals, and many mountain and pastoral
tribes, who will take up arms, as well as become passive
martyrs, for their faith, and few will deny that Turk,
and Persian, and Pathan would more readily unite for
conscience's sake under the banner of Muhammad, than
Russian, and Swede, and Spaniard are ever likely to
march under one common 'Labarum'. The Musalman
feels proudly secure of his path to salvation; he will
resent the exhortations of those whom he pities or con-

Brahman-
ism and
Buddhism
rather
forms than
feelings;

yet strong
to resist
innovation.

Muhamma-
danism,
although
corrupted,
has more of
vitality.

All are
satisfied
with their
own faith.

[1 Such a phenomenon is not confined to Islam alone. It
would seem to be a characteristic development in many religions. When once what one may call the 'human touch' weak-
ens, and when the gulf separating the worshipper and the
founder of his creed seems sharply defined, there is a tendency
to interpose some form of mediation to bridge such an imaginary gulf. To such a feeling Catholic Europe owes the introduction of the worship of the Blessed Virgin and the invocation of
countless saints. To such a feeling, also, Buddhism owes the
introduction of the Bodhisattva or Pusas—the mediators for lost
souls. And it will further be found that in course of time such
mediating forces tend to lose their general character and to
become localized tutelary powers.—ED.]

temns as wanderers, and, unlike the Hindu and the
Buddhist, he is still actively desirous of acquiring merit
by adding to the number of true believers. But Buddhist, and Brahmanist, and Muhammadan have each an
instructed body of ministers, and each confides in an
authoritative ritual, or in a revealed law. Their reason
and their hopes are both satisfied, and hence the
difficulty of converting them to the Christian faith by
the methods of the civilized moderns. Our missionaries,
earnest and devoted men, must be content with the
cold arguments of science and criticism; they must not
rouse the feelings, or appeal to the imagination; they
cannot promise aught which their hearers were not
sure of before; they cannot go into the desert to fast,
nor retire to the mountain-tops to pray; they cannot
declare the fulfilment of any fondly cherished hope of
the people, nor, in announcing a great principle, can
they point to the success of the sword and the visible
favour of the Divinity. No austerity of sanctitude con-
vinces the multitude, and the Pandit and the Mulla can
each oppose dialectics to dialectics, morality to morality, and revelation to revelation. Our zealous preachers
may create sects among ourselves, half Quietist and half
Epicurean, they may persevere in their laudable resolution of bringing up the orphans of heathen parents,
and they may gain some converts among intelligent
inquirers as well as among the ignorant and the indi-
gent, but it seems hopeless that they should ever
Christianize the Indian and Muhammadan worlds.[1]

*and can-
not be rea-
soned into
Chris-
tianity.*

The observers of the ancient creeds quietly pursue
the even tenor of their way, self satisfied and almost
indifferent about others; but the Sikhs are converts to
a new religion, the seal of the double dispensation of
Brahma and Muhammad: *their* enthusiasm is still
fresh, and *their* faith is still an active and a living
principle. *They* are persuaded that God himself is

*Sikhism an
active and
pervading
principle.*

[1] The masses can only be convinced by means repudiated
by reason and the instructed intellect of man, and the futility
of endeavouring to convince the learned by argument is exemplified in Martyn's Persian Controversies, translated by Dr.
Lee, in the discussion carried on between the Christian missionaries at Allahabad and the Muhammadan Mullas at
Lucknow, in Ram Mohan Roy's work on Deism and the Vedas,
and in the published correspondence of the T'atubodhni Subha of
Calcutta. For an instance of the satisfaction of the Hindus with
*their* creed, see Moorcroft, *Travels,* i. 118, where some Udasis
commend *him* for believing, like them, in a God ! [Col. Kennedy
(*Res. Hind. Mythol.,* p. 141) states that the Brahmans think
little of the Christian missionaries (as propagandists), although
the English have held authority in India for several generations.—J.D.C.]

present with them, that He supports them in all their endeavours, and that sooner or later He will confound *their* enemies for His own glory. This feeling of the Sikh people deserves the attention of the English, both as a civilized nation and as a paramount government. Those who have heard a follower of Guru Gobind declaim on the destinies of his race, his eye wild with enthusiasm and every muscle quivering with excitement, can understand *that* spirit which impelled the naked Arab against the mail-clad troops of Rome and Persia, and which led our own chivalrous and believing forefathers through Europe to battle for the cross on the shores of Asia. The Sikhs do not form a numerous sect, yet their strength is not to be estimated by tens of thousands, but by the unity and energy of religious fervour and warlike temperament. They will dare much, and they will endure much, for the mystic 'Khalsa' or commonwealth; they are not discouraged by defeat, and they ardently look forward to the day when Indians and Arabs and Persians and Turks shall all acknowledge the double mission of Nanak and Gobind Singh.

The characteristics of race are perhaps more deep-seated and enduring than those of religion; but, in considering any people, the results of birth and breeding, of descent and instruction, must be held jointly in view. The Jats are known in the north and west of India as industrious and successful tillers of the soil, and as hardy yeomen equally ready to take up arms and to follow the plough. They form, perhaps, the finest rural population in India. On the Jumna their general superiority is apparent, and Bhartpur bears witness to their merits, while on the Sutlej religious reformation and political ascendancy have each served to give spirit to their industry, and activity and purpose to their courage.[1] The Rains, the Malis, and some

*The Jats industrious and high-spirited.*

---

[1] Under the English system of selling the proprietary right in villages when the old freeholder or former purchaser may be unable to pay the land tax, the Jats of Upper India are gradually becoming the possessors of the greater portion of the soil, a fact which the author first heard on the high authority of Mr. Thomason, the Lieutenant-Governor of the North-Western Provinces. It is a common saying that if a Jat has fifty rupees, he will rather dig a well or buy a pair of bullocks with the money than spend it on the idle rejoicings of a marriage. ['Socially the landed classes stand high, and of these the Jats, numbering nearly five millions, are the most important. Roughly speaking, one-half of the Jats are Mahomedan, one-third Sikh, and one-sixth Hindu. In distribution they are ubiquitous and are equally divided over the five divisions of the province.'—*Indian Year Book,* 1915.]

others, are not inferior to the Jats in laboriousness and sobriety, although they are so in enterprise and resolution. The Rajputs are always brave men, and they form, too, a desirable peasantry. The Gujars everywhere prefer pasturage to the plough, whether of the Hindu or Muhammadan faith. The Baluchis do not become careful cultivators even when long settled in the plains, and the tribes adjoining the hills are of a disposition turbulent and predatory. They mostly devote themselves to the rearing of camels, and they traverse Upper India in charge of herds of that useful animal. The Afghans are good husbandmen when they have been accustomed to peace in the plains of India or when they feel secure in their own valleys, but they are even of a more turbulent character than the Baluchis, and they are everywhere to be met with as mercenary soldiers. Both races are, in truth, in their own country little better than freebooters, and the Muhammadan faith has mainly helped them to justify their excesses against unbelievers, and to keep them together under a common banner for purposes of defence or aggression. The Kshattriya and Aroras of the cities and towns are enterprising as merchants and frugal as tradesmen. They are the principal financiers and accountants of the country; but the ancient military spirit frequently reappears amongst the once royal 'Kshattriya', and they become able governors of provinces and skilful leaders of armies.[1] The industry and mechanical skill of the stout-limbed prolific Kashmiris are as well known as their poverty; their tameness of spirit, and their loose morality. The people

*The Rains and some others scarcely inferior as tillers of the ground.*

*The peasant Rajputs. The Gujars a pastoral people.*

*The Baluchis pastoral and predatory.*

*The Afghans industrious, but turbulent.*

*The Kshattriyas and Aroras enterprising but frugal.*

*The Kashmiris skilful, but tame and spiritless.*

[1] Hari Singh, a Sikh, and the most enterprising of Ranjit Singh's generals, was a Kshattriya; and the best of his governors, Mohkam Chand and Sawan Mal, were of the same race. The learning of Bolu Mal, a Khanna Kshattriya, and a follower of the Sikh chief of Ahluwalia, excites some little jealousy among the Brahmans of Lahore and of the Jullundur Doab; and Chandu Lal, who so long managed the affairs of the Nizam of Hyderabad, was a Khattri of Northern India, and greatly encouraged the Sikh mercenaries in that principality, in opposition to the Arabs and Afghans. The declension of the Kshattriya from soldiers and sovereigns into traders and shopkeepers, has a parallel in the history of the Jews. Men of active minds will always find employment for themselves, and thus we know what Greeks became under the victorious Romans, and what they are under the ruling Turks. We likewise know that the vanquished Moors were the most industrious of the subjects of mediaeval Spain; that the Mughals of British India are gradually applying themselves to the business of exchange, and it is plain that the traffickers as well as the priests of Saxon England, Frankish Gaul, and Gothic Italy must have been chiefly of Roman descent.

of the hills south and east of Kashmir are not marked by any peculiar and well-determined character, excepting that the few unmixed Rajputs possess the personal courage and the pride of race which distinguish them elsewhere, and that the Gakhars still cherish the remembrance of the times when they resisted Babar and aided Humayun. The Tibetans, while they are careful cultivators of their diminutive fields rising tier upon tier, are utterly debased in spirit, and at present they seem incapable of independence and even of resistance to gross oppression. The system of polyandry obtains among them, not as a perverse law, but as a necessary institution. Every spot of ground within the hills which can be cultivated has been under the plough for ages; the number of mouths must remain adapted to the number of acres, and the proportion is preserved by limiting each proprietary family to one giver of children. The introduction of Muhammadanism in the west, by enlarging the views of the people and promoting emigration, has tended to modify this rule, and even among the Lamaic Tibetans any casual influx of wealth as from trade or other sources, immediately leads to the formation of separate establishments by the several members of a house.[1] The wild tribes of Chibs and Buhows in the hills, the Juns and Kathis, and the Dogras and Bhutis of the plains, need not be particularly described; the idle and predatory habits of some, and the quiet pastoral occupations of others, are equally the result of position as of character. The Juns and Kathis, tall, comely, and long-lived races, feed vast herds of camels and black cattle, which furnish the towns with the prepared butter of the east, and provide the people themselves with their loved libations of milk.[2]

*The unmixed Rajputs.*

*The Tibetans plodding and debased.*

*The custom of polyandry one of necessity.*

*The Juns and Kathis pastoral and peaceful.*

[1] Regarding the polyandry of Ladakh, Moorcroft (*Travels*, ii. 321, 322) may be referred to, and also the *Journal of the Asiatic Society of Bengal* for 1844, p. 202, &c. The effects of the system on bastardy seem marked, and thus out of 760 people in the little district of Hungrung, around the junction of the Sutlej and Pittee (or Spiti) rivers, there were found to be twenty-six bastards, which gives a proportion of about one in twenty-nine; and as few grown-up people admitted themselves to be illegitimate, the number may even be greater. In 1835 the population of England and Wales was about 14,750,000 and the number of bastards affiliated (before the new poor law came into operation) was 65,475, or 1 in about 226 (Wade's *British History*, pp. 1041-55); and even should the number so born double those affiliated, the proportion would still speak against polyandry as it affects female purity.

[2] On milk sustained, and blest with length of days,
　　The Hippomolgi, peaceful, just, and wise.
　　　　　　*Iliad*, xiii. COWPER'S TRANSLATION.

The limits of creeds and races which have been described must not be regarded as permanent. Throughout India there are constant petty migrations of the agricultural population taking place. Political oppression, or droughts, or floods cause the inhabitants of a village, or of a district, to seek more favoured tracts, and there are always chiefs and rulers who are ready to welcome industrious emigrants and to assign them lands on easy terms. This causes some fluctuation in the distribution of races, and as in India the tendency is to a distinction or separation of families, the number of clans or tribes has become almost infinite. Within the Sikh dominions the migrations of the Baluchis up the Indus are not of remote occurrence, while the occupation by the Sindhian Daudputras of the Lower Sutlej took place within the last hundred years. The migration of the Dogras from Delhi to Ferozepore, and of the Johiyas from Marwar to Pakpattan, also on the Sutlej, are historical rather than traditional, while the hard-working Hindu Mehtums are still moving, family by family and village by village, eastward, away from the Ravi and Chenab, and are insinuating themselves among less industrious but more warlike tribes.

*Partial migrations of tribes and proselytism in religion. Causes of migrations.*

*Recent migration of the Baluchis up the Indus, and of the Daudputras up the Sutlej. Migrations of the Dogras, Johiyas, and Mehtums.*

Although religious wars scarcely take place among the Buddhists, Brahmanists, and Muhammadans of the present day, and although religious fervour has almost disappeared from among the professors at least of the two former faiths, proselytism is not unknown to any of the three creeds, and Muhammadanism, as possessing still a strong vitality within it, will long continue to find converts among the ignorant and the barbarous. Islamism is extending up the Indus from Iskardo towards Leh, and is thus encroaching upon the more worn-out Buddhism; while the limits of the idolatrous 'Kafirs', almost bordering on Peshawar, are daily becoming narrower. To the south and eastward of Kashmir, Muhammadanism has also had recent triumphs, and in every large city and in every Musalman principality in India there is reason to believe that the religion of the Arabian prophet is gradually gaining ground. In the Himalayas to the eastward of Kishtwar, the Rajput conquerors have not carried Brahmanism beyond the lower valleys; and into the wilder glens, occupied by the ignorant worshippers of local divinities, the Buddhists have recently begun to advance, and Lamas of the red or yellow sects are now found where none had set foot a generation ago. Among the forest tribes of India the influence of the Brahmans continues

*Islamism extending in Tibet; and generally perhaps in towns and cities. Lamaic Buddhism progressive in some parts of the Himalayas.*

Brahman-
ism like-
wise
extending
in the
wilder
parts of
the plains.

But the
peasantry
and me-
chanics
generally
are becom-
ing seced-
ers from
Brahma-
nism.

to increase, and every Bhil, or Gond, or Kohli who acquires power or money, desires to be thought a Hindu rather than a 'Mlechha';[1] but, on the other hand, the Indian laity has, during the last few hundred years, largely assumed to itself the functions of the priest-hood, and although Hinduism may lose no votaries, Gusains and secular Sadhs usurp the authority of Brahmans in the direction of the conscience.[2] The Sikhs continue to make converts, but chiefly within the limits of their dependent sway, for the colossal power of the English has arrested the progress of their arms to the eastward, and has left the Jats of the Jumna and Ganges to their old idolatry.

[1] Half of the principality of Bhopal, in Central India, was founded on usurpations from the Gonds, who appear to have migrated in force towards the west about the middle of the seventeenth century, and to have made themselves supreme in the valley of the Narbada about Hoshangabad, in spite of the exertions of Aurangzeb, until an Afghan adventurer attacked them on the decline of the empire, and completely subdued them. The Afghan converted some of the vanquished to his own faith, partly by force and partly by conferring Jagirs, partly to acquire merit and partly to soothe his conscience, and there are now several families of Muhammadan Gonds in the possession of little fiefs on either side of the Narbada. These men have more fully got over the gross superstition of their race, than the Gonds who have adopted Hinduism.

[2 The recent spread of the 'Marwari' traders over the cen-tre, and to the south and east of India, may also be noticed, for the greater number of them are Jains. These traffickers of Rajputana seem to have received a strong mercantile impulse about a hundred years ago, and their spirit of enterprise gives them at the same time a social and a religious influence, so that many families of Vaishnava or Brahmanical traders either incline to Jainism or openly embrace that faith. Jainism is thus extending in India, and conversion is rendered the more easy by the similarity of origin and occupation of these various traders, and by the Quietism and other characteristics common to the Jains and Vaishnavas.—J.D.C.]

# CHAPTER II

## OLD INDIAN CREEDS, MODERN REFORMS, AND THE TEACHING OF NANAK, UP TO 1539 A.D.

The Buddhists—The Brahmans and Kshattriyas—Reaction of Buddhism on victorious Brahmanism—Latitude of orthodoxy—Shankar Acharj and Saivism—Monastic orders—Ramanuj and Vaishnavism—The Doctrine of 'Maya'—The Muhammadan conquest—The reciprocal action of Brahmanism and Muhammadanism—The successive innovations of Ramanand, Gorakhnath, Kabir, Chaitan, and Vallabh —The reformation of Nanak.

THE condition of India from remote ages to the present time, is an episode in the history of the world inferior only to the fall of Rome and the establishment of Christianity. At an early period the Asiatic peninsula, from the southern 'Ghats' to Himalayan mountains, would seem to have been colonized by a warlike sub-division of the Caucasian race, which spoke a language similar to the ancient Medic and Persian, and which here and there, near the greater rivers and the shores of the ocean, formed orderly communities professing a religion resembling the worship of Babylon and Egypt —a creed which, under varying types, is still the solace of a large portion' of mankind. 'Aryavarta', the land of good men or believers, comprised Delhi and Lahore, Gujrat and Bengal; but it was on the. banks of the Upper Ganges that the latent energies of the people first received an impulse, which produced the peculiar civilization of the Brahmans, and made a few heroic families supreme from Arachosia to the Golden Chersonese. India illustrates the power of Darius and the greatness of Alexander, the philosophy of Greece and the religion of China; and while Rome was contending with Germans and Cimbri, and yielding to Goths and Huns, the Hindus absorbed, almost without an effort, swarms of Scythic barbarians : they dispersed Sacae,[1]

*India and its successive masters.*

*The Buddhists.*

*The Brahmans and Kshattriyas.*

[1] Vikramajit derived his title of Sakari from his exploits against the Sacae (Sakae). The race is still perhaps preserved pure in the wilds of Tartary, between Yarkand and the Mansarawar Lake, where the *Sokpos* called Kelmaks (Calmucs) by the Muhammadans, continue to be dreaded by the people

The
Muham-
madans.

The Chris-
tians.

Brahman-
ism strug-
gling with
Buddhism
becomes
elaborated.

they enrolled Getae among their most famous tribes,[1] and they made others serve as their valiant defenders.[2] India afterwards checked the victorious career of Islam, but she could not wholly resist the fierce enthusiasm of the Turkoman hordes; she became one of the most splendid of Muhammadan empires, and the character of the Hindu mind has been permanently altered by the genius of the Arabian prophet. The well-being of India's industrious millions is now linked with the fate of the foremost nation of the West, and the representatives of Judaean faith and Roman polity will long wage a war of principles with the speculative Brahman, the authoritative Mulla, and the hardy believing Sikh.

The Brahmans and their valiant Kshattriyas had a long and arduous contest with that ancient faith of India, which, as successively modified, became famous as Buddhism.[3] When Manu wrote, perhaps nine cen-

of Tibet. [A dread effectually removed by the systematic conquest of Eastern Turkestan by the Chinese during the nineteenth century.—ED.]

[1] The Getae are referred to as the same with the ancient Chinese Yuechi and the modern Jats, but their identity is as yet, perhaps, rather a reasonable conclusion than a logical or critical deduction.

[2] The four Agnikula tribes of Kshattriyas or Rajputs are here alluded to, viz. the Chohans, Solunkees, Powars (or Prumárs), and the Purihars. The unnamed progenitors of these races seem clearly to have been invaders who sided with the Brahmans in their warfare, partly with the old Kshattriyas, partly with increasing schismatics, and partly with invading Graeco-Bactrians, and whose warlike merit, as well as timely aid and subsequent conformity, got them enrolled as 'fireborn', in contradistinction to the solar and lunar families. The Agnikulas are now mainly found in the tract of country extending from Ujjain to Rewah near Benares, and Mount Abu is asserted to be the place of their miraculous birth or appearance. Vikramajit, the champion of Brahmanism, was a Powar according to the common accounts.

[3] The relative priority of Brahmanism and Buddhism continues to be argued and disputed among the learned. The wide diffusion at one period of Buddhism in India is as certain as the later predominance of Brahmanism, but the truth seems to be that they are of independent origin, and that they existed for a long time contemporaneously; the former chiefly in the south-west, and the latter about Oudh and Tirhut. It is not, however, necessary to suppose, with M. Burnouf, that Buddhism is purely and originally Indian (*Introduction à l' Histoire du Buddhisme Indien*, Avertissement i), notwithstanding the probable derivation of the name from the Sanskrit 'Buddhi', intelligence; or from the 'bo' or 'bodee', i.e. the *ficus religiosa* or peepul tree. The Brahmanical genius gradually received a development which rendered the Hindus proper supreme

Its achievements and characteristics.

turies before Christ, when Alexander conquered, and even seven hundred years afterwards, when the obscure Fahian travelled and studied, there were kingdoms ruled by others than 'Aryas'; and ceremonial Buddhism, with its indistinct apprehensions of a divinity, had more votaries than the monotheism of the Vedas, which admitted no similitude more gross than fire, or air, or

throughout the land; but their superior learning became of help to their antagonists, and Gautama, himself a Brahman or a Kshattriya, would appear to have taken advantage of the knowledge of the hierarchy to give a purer and more scientific form to Buddhism, and thus to become its great apostle in succeeding times. [The whole subject, however, is complicated in the extreme; and it is rendered the more so by the probability that the same Gautama is the author of the popular 'Nyaya' system of Philosophy, and that Buddha himself is one form of the favourite divinity Vishnu; although the orthodox explain *that* circumstance by saying the Preserving Power assumed an heretical character to delude Deodas, king of Benares, who by his virtues and authority endangered the supremacy of the Gods. (Cf. Kennedy, *Res. Hind. Mythol.*, p. 248, &c)—J.D.C.] Of the modern faiths, Saivism perhaps most correctly represents the original Vedic worship. (Cf. Wilson, *As. Res.*, xvii. 171, &c., and *Vishnu Puran*, preface, lxiv.) *Jainism* and *Vaishnavism* are the resultants of the two beliefs in a Buddhist and Brahmanical dress respectively, while *Saktism* still vividly illustrates the old superstition of the masses of the people, whose ignorant minds quailed before the dread goddess of famine, pestilence, and death. The most important monument of Buddhism now remaining is perhaps the 'tope' or hemisphere, near Bhilsa in Central India, which it is a disgrace to the English that they partially destroyed a generation ago in search of imaginary chambers or vessels containing relics, and are only now about to have delineated, and so made available to the learned. The numerous *bas-reliefs* of its singular stone enclosure still vividly represent the manners as well as the belief of the India of Asoka, and show that the Tree, the Sun, and the Stupa (or 'tope') itself —apparently the type of Meru or the Central Mount of the World—were, along with the impersonated Buddha, the principal objects of adoration at that period, and that the country was then partly peopled by a race of men wearing high caps and short tunics, so different from the ordinary dress of Hindus. [It is now usually accepted that by about 600 B.C. Brahmanism was generally the chief religion of India, and the probable date of the birth of Gautama (567 B.C.) makes Buddhism the younger of the two religions. It seems hardly necessary to add that, since the author wrote the above note, our knowledge of Buddhism in India has been enormously· increased by the careful researches of the Archaeological Department. These have resulted in the discovery of a very large number of Buddhist remains which—in great contrast to the iconoclastic vandalism mentioned by the author—have been carefully preserved. Collections of such remains may be seen in many museums in India—there is one typical collection in the Central Museum in Lahore—and to such collections and the various descriptive works on the subject the reader is referred.—ED.]

the burning sun.[1] During this period the genius of
Hinduism became fully developed, and the Brahmans
rivalled the Greeks in the greatness and the variety
of their triumphs. Epic poems show high imaginative
and descriptive powers, and the Ramayana and Mahabharata[2] still move the feelings and affect the character
of the people. Mathematical science was so perfect,
and astronomical observation so complete, that the
paths of the sun and moon were accurately measured.[3]
The philosophy of the learned few was, perhaps, for the
first time, firmly allied with the theology of the believing many, and Brahmanism laid down as articles of
faith, the unity of God, the creation of the world, the
immortality of the soul, and the responsibility of man.
The remote dwellers upon the Ganges distinctly made

[1] 'There seem to have been no images and no visible types
of the objects of worship,' says Mr. Elphinstone, in his most
useful and judicious *History* (i. 73), quoting Professor Wilson,
*Oxford Lectures,* and the *Vishnu Puran;* while, with regard to
fire, it is to be remembered that in the Old Testament, and
even in the New, it is the principal symbol of the Holy Spirit.
(Strauss, *Life of Jesus,* 361.) The Vedas, however, allude to
personified energies and attributes, but the monotheism of
the system is not more affected by the introduction of the
creating Brahma, the destroying Siva, and other minor powers,
than the omnipotence of Jehovah is interfered with by the
hierarchies of the Jewish heaven. Yet, much has to
be learnt with regard to the Vedas and Vedantism, notwithstanding the invaluable labours of Colebrooke and others, and
the useful commentary or interpretation of Ram Mohan Roy.
(*Asiatic Researches,* viii; *Transactions Royal Asiatic Society,*
i and ii; and Ram Mohan Roy on the Vedas.) The translation
of the *Vedant Sar* in Ward's *Hindoos* (ii. 175), and the improved version of Dr. Roer (*Journal Asiatic Society of Bengal,*
February 1845, No. 108), may be consulted with advantage.
If translators would repeat the Sanskrit terms with expanded
meanings in English, instead of using terms of the scholastic
or modern systems which seem to them to be equivalent, they
would materially help students to understand the real doctrine
of the original speculators.

[2] These epics are rarely read *in extenso* by a modern
generation, owing to a lack of knowledge of Sanskrit and also
to their enormous length and the numerous later interpolations.
A literal translation in English of the Mahabharata was made
by Mr. P. C. Roy in 1894. But it is intolerably lengthy and,
for a simple summary of this Indian epic, the reader is
referred to *The Great War of India,* by Thakur Rajendra Singh,
published in Allahabad in 1915.—Ed.]

[3] The so-called solar year in common use in India takes
no account of the precession of the equinoxes, but, as a sidereal year, it is almost exact. The revolution of the points of
intersection of the ecliptic and equator nevertheless appears
to have been long known to the Hindus, and some of their
epochs were obviously based on the calculated period of the
phenomenon. (Cf. Mr. Davis's paper in the *As. Res.,* vol. ii,
and Bentley's *Astronomy of the Hindoos,* pp. 2-6, 88.)

known that future life about which Moses is silent or
obscure,[1] and that unity and omnipotence of the Creator
which were unknown to the polytheism of the Greek
and Roman multitude,[2] and to the dualism of the Mith-
raic legislators; while Vyasa perhaps surpassed Plato
in keeping the people tremblingly alive to the punishment which awaited evil deeds.[3] The immortality of the

[1] One is almost more willing to admit that, in effect, the
Jews generally held Jehovah to be *their* God only, or a limitary
divinity, than that the wise and instructed Moses (whom
Strabo held to be an Egyptian priest and a Pantheist, as quoted
in *Volney's Ruins,* chap. xxii, § 9 note) could believe in the
perishable nature of the soul; but the critical Sadducees nevertheless so interpreted their prophet, although the Egyptians
his masters were held by Herodotus (*Euterpe,* cxxiii) to be the
first who *defended* the undying nature of the spirit of man.
Socrates and Plato, with all their longings, could only feel
assured that the soul had more of immortality than aught
else. (*Phaedo,* Sydenham and Taylor's translation, iv. 324.)

[2] The unknown God of the Athenians, Fate, the avenging
Nemesis, and other powers independent of Zeus or Jupiter,
show the dissatisfaction of the ancient mind with the ordinary
mythology [yet the unity of the Godhead was the doctrine of
the obscure Orpheus, of Plato the transcendentalist, and of
such practical men as Cicero and Socrates.—J.D.C.]; and unless
modern criticism has detected interpolations, perhaps both
Bishop Thirlwall (*History of Greece,* i. 192, &c.) and Mr.
Grote (*History of Greece* i. 3 and chap. xvi, part i generally)
have too much disregarded the sense which the pious and
admiring Cowper gave to Homer's occasional mode of using
'theos'. (*Odyssey,* xiv with Cowper's note, p. 48, vol. ii, edition
of 1802.) [Cf. also the care of the Greek or the Roman in
addressing a deity, and in particular Zeus or Jupiter, in his
particular 'capacity' most suited to the occasion.—ED.]

[3] Ritter (*Ancient Philosophy,* ii. 387) labours to excuse
Plato for his '*inattention*' to the subject of duty or obligation,
on the plea that the Socratic system did not admit of necessity or of a compulsory principle. [Nevertheless, Socrates, *as
represented by Xenophon,* may be considered to have held
Worship of the Gods to be a *Duty* of Man. (See the *Memorabilia,* b. iv, c. iii, iv, vi, and vii.)—J.D.C.] Bacon lies open
in an inferior degree to the same objection as Plato, of under-
rating the importance of moral philosophy (cf. Hallam's
*Literature of Europe,* iii. 191, and Macaulay, *Edinburgh Review,* July 1837, p. 84); and yet a strong sense of duty towards
God is essential to the well-being of society, if not to systems
of transcendental or material philosophy. In the East, however, philosophy has always been more closely allied to theology than in civilized Greece or modern Europe. Plato, indeed,
arraigns the dead and torments the souls of the wicked (see
for instance *Gorgias,* Sydenham and Taylor's translation, iv,
451), and practically among men the doctrine may be effective
or sufficient; but with the Greek piety is simply justice towards the gods, and a matter of choice or pleasure on the part
of the imperishable human spirit. (Cf. Schleiermacher's *In-
troductions to Plato's Dialogues,* p. 181, &c., and Ritter's *Ancient
Philosophy,* ii. 374.) Nor can it be distinctly said that Vyasa
taught the principle of grateful righteousness as now under-

soul was indeed encumbered with the doctrine of trans-migration,[1] the active virtues were perhaps deemed less meritorious than bodily austerities and mental abstrac-tion, and the Brahman polity was soon fatally clogged with the dogma of inequality among men, and with the institution of a body of hereditary guardians of religion.[2]

Brahman-ism vic-torious over Buddhism.

The Brahmans succeeded in expelling the Buddh-ist faith from the Indian peninsula, and when Shankar Acharj journeyed and disputed nine hundred years after Christ, a few learned men, and the inoffensive half-conforming Jains,[3] alone remained to represent the

stood to be binding on men, and to constitute their duty and obligation; and probably the Indian may merely have the advantage of being a theological teacher instead of an onto-logical speculator.

[1] The more zealous Christian writers on Hindu theology seize upon the doctrine of transmigration as limiting the free-dom of the will and the degree of isolation of the soul, when thus successively manifested in the world clouded with the imperfection of previous appearances. A man, it is said, thus becomes subject to the Fate of the Greeks and Romans. (Cf. Ward on *The Hindoos*, ii; Introductory Remarks, xxviii, &c.) But the soul so weighed down with the sins of a former existence does not seem to differ in an ethical point of view, and as regards our conduct in the present life, from the soul encumbered with the sin of Adam. Philosophically, the no-tions seem equally but modes of accounting for the existence of evil, or for its sway over men. [See also note 7, p. 39. J.D.C.] [Socrates, who inculcated every *active* virtue, never-theless admitted, 'that he who wanted least was nearest to the Divinity; for to need nothing was the attribute of God.' (*Memorabilia*, b.1,c.vi,s.10.) J.D.C.]

[2] See Appendix IV, on 'Caste'.

[3] The modern Jains frankly admit the connexion of their faith with that of the Buddhists, and the Jaini traders of Eastern Malwa claim the ancient 'tope' near Bhilsa, as virtually a temple of their own creed. The date of the general recogni-tion of the Jains as a sect is doubtful, but it is curious that the 'Kosh', or vocabulary of Amar Singh, does not contain the word Jain, although the word 'Jin' is enumerated among the names of Mayadevi, the regent goddess of the material universe, and the mother of Gautama, the Buddhist patriarch or prophet. In the Bhagavad, again, Baudh is represented as the son of Jin, and as about to appear in Kikat Des, or Bihar. (See Colonel Kennedy, *Res. Hind. Mythol.*, pp. 243-50.) Amar Singh, the author of the Sanskrit 'Kosa', or vocabulary, was himself a Buddhist; and he is differently stated to have flouri-shed in the first century before, or in the fifth after, Christ (Colonel Kennedy, as above, pp. 127, 128), but in Malwa he is traditionally said to have been confuted in argument by Shankar Acharj, which would place him in the eighth or ninth century of our era.—J.D.C.] ['Jainism is professed by a com-paratively small sect, and it tends to shade off into ordinary Hinduism. Many Jains employ Brahmans in their domestic worship, venerate the cow, and often worship in Hindu tem-

'Mlechhas', the barbarians or 'gentiles' of Hinduism.
The Kshattriyas had acquired kingdoms, heathen
princes had been subdued or converted, and the Brahmans, who ever denounced as prophets rather than
preached as missionaries, were powerless in foreign
countries if no royal inquirer welcomed them,
or if no ambitious warrior followed them. Hinduism had
attained its limits, and the victory brought with it the
seeds of decay. The mixture with strangers led to a
partial adoption of their usages, and man's desire for
sympathy ever prompted him to seek an object of worship more nearly allied to himself in nature than the
invisible and passionless divinity.[1] The concession of a
simple black stone as a mark of direction to the senses,[2]
no longer satisfied the hearts or understandings of the

Loses its<br>unity and<br>vigour.

ples. Jainism and Buddhism have much in common, and up
to recent years Jainism was believed to be an offshoot of
Buddhism. It is now known that it originated independently
of, though at the same time as, Buddhism; that is, in the sixth
century before Christ.'—Holderness, *Peoples and Problems of
India*. (See Stevenson, *The Heart of Jainism*. Oxford University Press, 1915.)—ED.]

[1] Mr. Elphinstone (*History of India*, i. 189) observes that
Rama and Krishna, with their human feelings and congenial
acts, attracted more votaries than the gloomy Siva; and I have
somewhere noticed, I think in the *Edinburgh Review*, the truth
well enlarged upon, viz. that the sufferings of Jesus materially
aided the growth of Christianity by enlisting the sympathies
of the multitude in favour of a crucified God. The bitter remark of Xenophanes, that if oxen became religious their gods
would be bovine in form, is indeed most true as expressive of
a general desire among men to make their divinities anthropomorphous. (Grote, *History of Greece*, iv. 523, and Thirlwall,
*History*, ii. 136.)

[2] Hindu Saivism, or the worship of the Lingam, seems
to represent the compromise which the learned Brahmans
made when they endeavoured to exalt and purify the superstition of the multitude, who throughout India continue to this
day to see the mark of the near presence of the Divinity in
everything. The Brahmans may thus have taught the mere
fetichist, that when regarding a simple black stone, they
should think of the invisible ruler of the universe; and they
may have wished to leave the Buddhist image worshippers
some point of direction for the senses. That the Lingam is
typical of reproductive energy seems wholly a notion of later
times, and to be confined to the few who ingeniously or perversely see recondite meanings in ordinary similitudes. (Cf.
Wilson, *Vishnu Puran*, preface, lxiv [and Colonel Kennedy
(*Res. Hind. Mythol.*, pp. 284, 308), who distinctly says the
Lingam and Yoni are not held to be typical of the destructive
and reproductive powers; and that there is nothing in the
Purans to sanction such an opinion.—J.D.C.].) [The latter
part of the author's note, which begs the whole question of
phallic worship, is hardly in agreement with modern theory.
—ED.]

people, and Shankar Acharj, who could silence the Buddha materialist, and confute the infidel Charvak,[1] was compelled to admit the worship of Virtues and Powers, and to allow images, as well as formless types, to be enshrined in temples. The 'self-existent' needed no longer to be addressed direct, and the orthodox could pay his devotions to the Preserving Vishnu, to the Destroying Siva, to the Regent of the Sun, to Ganesh, the helper of men, or to the reproductive energy of nature personified as woman, with every assurance that his prayers would be heard, and his offerings accepted, by the Supreme Being.[2]

Shankar Acharj methodizes polytheism, A. D. 800-1000

The old Brahman worship had been domestic or solitary, and that of the Buddhists public or congregational; the Brahman ascetic separated himself from his fellows, but the Buddhist hermit became a coenobite, the member of a community of devotees; the Brahman reared a family before he became an anchorite, but the Buddhist vowed celibacy and renounced most of the pleasures of sense. These customs of the vanquished had their effect upon the conquerors, and Shankar Acharj, in his endeavour to strengthen orthodoxy, enacted the double part of St. Basil and Pope Honorius.[3] He established a monastery of Brahman

Reaction of Buddhism on Brahmanism.

Shankar Acharj establishes ascetic orders, and gives pre-eminence to Saivism.

---

[1] Professor Wilson (*Asiatic Researches*, xvi. 18) derives the title of the Charvak school from a Muni or seer of that name; but the Brahmans, at least of Malwa, derive the distinctive name, both of the teacher and of the system, from *Charu*, persuasive, excellent, and *Vak*, speech—thus making the school simply the logical or dialectic, or perhaps sophistical, as it has become in fact. The Charvakites are wholly materialist, and in deriving consciousness from a particular aggregation or condition of the elements of the body, they seem to have anticipated the physiologist, Dr. Lawrence, who makes the brain to secrete thought as the liver secretes bile. The system is also styled the Varhusputya, and the name of Vrihaspati, the orthodox Regent of the planet Jupiter, became connected with Atheism, say the Hindus, owing to the jealousy with which the secondary or delegated powers of Heaven saw the degree of virtue to which man was attaining by upright living and a contemplation of the Divinity; wherefore Vrihaspati descended to confound the human understanding by diffusing error. (Cf. Wilson, *As. Res.*, xvii. 308, and Troyer's *Dabistan*, ii. 198, note.)

[2] The five sects enumerated are still held to represent the most orthodox varieties of Hinduism, [and of the eighteen Purans, five only give supremacy to one form of Divinity over others. (Colonel Kennedy, *Res. Hind. Mythol.*, pp. 203, 204.) —J. D. C.]

[3] All scholars and inquirers are deeply indebted to Professor Wilson for the account he has given of the Hindu sects in the sixteenth and seventeenth volumes of the *Asiatic Researches*. The works, indeed, which are abstracted, are in the hands

ascetics; he converted the solitary 'Dandi', with his staff and waterpot, into one of an order, a monk or friar, at once coenobitic and mendicant, who lived upon alms and who practised chastity.[1] The *order* was rendered still further distinct by the choice of Siva as the truest type of God, an example which was soon followed; and, during the eleventh century, Ramanuj established a fraternity of Brahmans, named after himself; who adopted some refined rules of conduct, who saw the Deity in Vishnu, and who degraded the Supreme Being by attributing to him form and qualities.[2] A conse-

*[margin: Ramanuj establishes other orders with Vishnu as a tutelary god, A. D. 1000-1200.]*

of many people in India, particularly the Bhagat Mala (or History of the Saints) and its epitomes; but the advantage is great of being able to study the subject with the aid of the notes of a deep scholar personally acquainted with the country. It is only to be regretted that Professor Wilson has not attempted to trace the progress of opinion or reform among sectaries; but neither does such a project appear to have occurred to Mr. Ward, in his elaborate and valuable but piecemeal volumes on the Hindus. Muhsin Fani, who wrote the *Dabistan*, has even less of sequence or of argument, but the observations and views of an intelligent, although garrulous and somewhat credulous, Muhammadan, who flourished nearly two centuries ago, have nevertheless a peculiar value; and Capt. Troyer's careful translation has now rendered the book accessible to the English public. [Colonel Kennedy, in his valuable *Researches*, takes no notice of the modern reformers : and he even says that the Hindu religion has remained unchanged for three thousand years (p. 192, &c.); meaning, however, it would seem, that the Unity of the Godhead is still the doctrine of Philosophy, and that Brahma, Vishnu, and Siva are still the principal divinities of Polytheism.—J.D.C.]

[1] Shankar Acharj was a Brahman of the south of India, and according to Professor Wilson (*As. Res.*, xvii. 180), he flourished during the eighth or ninth century : but his date is doubtful, and if, as is commonly said, Ramanuj was his disciple and sister's son, he perhaps lived a century or a century and a half later. He is believed to have established four muths, or monasteries, or denominations, headed by the four out of his ten instructed disciples, who faithfully adhered to his views. The adherents of these four are specially regarded as 'Dandis', or, including the representatives of the six heretical schools, the whole are called 'Dasnames'. (Cf. Wilson, *As. Res.*, xvii. 169, &c.)

[2] Ramanuj is variously stated to have lived some time between the beginning of the eleventh and the end of the twelfth century. (Wilson, *As. Res.*, xvi. 28, note.) In Central India he is understood to have told his uncle that the path which he, Shankar Acharj, had chosen, was not the right one; and the nephew accordingly seceded and established the first four 'sumprdaees', or congregations, in opposition to the four muths or orders of his teacher, and at the same time chose Vishnu as the most suitable type of God. Ramanuj styled his congregation that of Sri, or Lakshmi. The other three were successively founded by, first, Madhav; secondly, by Vishnu Swami and his better-known follower Vallabh; and thirdly, by Nimbharak or Nimbhaditya. These, although all Vaishnavis, called their

quence of the institution of an order or fraternity is the necessity of attention to its rules, or to the injunctions of the spiritual superior. The person of a Brahman had always been held sacred. It was believed that a pious Buddhist could disengage his soul or attain to divinity even in this world; and when Shankar Acharj rejected some of his chosen disciples for nonconformity or disobedience, he contributed to centre the growing feelings of reverence for the teacher solely upon a mortal man;

Spiritual teachers or heads of orders arrogate infallibility.

and, in a short time, it was considered that all things were to be abandoned for the sake of the 'Guru', and that to him were to be surrendered 'Tan, Man, Dhan', or body, mind, and worldly wealth.[1] Absolute submission to the spiritual master readily becomes a lively impression of the divinity of his mission; the inward evidences of grace are too subtle for the understanding of the barbaric convert; fixed observances take the place of sentiment, and he justifies his change of opinion by some material act of devotion.[2] But faith is the usual test of sincerity and pledge of favour among the sectarians of peaceful and instructed communities, and the reformers of India soon began to require such a declaration of mystic belief and reliance from the seekers of salvation.

Scepticism and heresy increase.

Philosophic speculation had kept pace in diversity with religious usage: learning and wealth, and an extended intercourse with men, produced the ordinary tendency towards' scepticism, and six orthodox schools opposed six heretical systems, and made devious attempts to acquire a knowledge of God by logical deductions from the phenomena of nature or of the human mind.[3] They disputed about the reality and the eternity of matter; about consciousness and understanding; and about life and the soul, as separate from, or as identical with one another and with God. The results

---

assemblies or schools respectively after Brahma, and Siva, and Sannakadik, a son of Brahma. (Cf. Wilson, *As. Res.,* xvi. 27, &c.)

[1] Cf. Wilsón, *As. Res.,* xvi. 90.

[2] The reader will remember the fervent exclamation of Clovis when, listening after a victory to the story of the passing and death of Christ, he became a convert to the faith of his wife, and a disciple of the ancient pastor of Rheims: 'Had I been present at the head of my valiant Franks, I would have revenged his injuries.' (Gibbon, *Decline and Fall of the Roman Empire,* vi. 302.) The Muhammadans tell precisely the same story of Taimur and Husain the son of Ali: 'I would have hurried', said the conquering Tartar, 'from remotest India, to have prevented or avenged the death of the martyred Imam.'

[3] See Appendix V.

were, the atheism of some, the belief of others in a limitary deity, and the more general reception of the doctrine of 'Maya' or illusion, which allows sensation to be a true guide on this side of the grave, but sees nothing certain or enduring in the constitution of the material world; a doctrine eagerly adopted by the subsequent reformers, who gave it a moral or religious application.[1] *The dogma of 'Maya' receives a moral application.*

Such was the state of the Hindu faith or polity a thousand years after Christ. The fitness of the original system for general adoption had been materially impaired by the gradual recognition of a distinction of race ; the Brahmans had isolated themselves from the soldiers and the peasants and they destroyed their own unanimity by admitting a virtual plurality of gods, and by giving assemblies of ascetics a pre-eminence over communities of pious householders. In a short time the gods were regarded as rivals, and their worshippers as antagonists. The rude Kshattriya warrior became a politic chief, with objects of his own, and ready to prefer one hierarchy or one divinity to another; while the very latitude of the orthodox worship led the multitude to doubt the sincerity and the merits of a body of ministers who no longer harmonized among themselves. *General decline of Brahmanism.*

A new people now entered the country, and a new element hastened the decline of corrupted Hinduism. India had but little felt the earlier incursions of the Arabs during the first and second centuries of the 'Hijri'; and when the Abbasides became caliphs, they were more anxious to consolidate their vast empire, already weaknened by the separation of Spain, than to waste their means on distant conquests which rebellion might soon dismember. The Arab, moreover, was no longer a single-minded enthusiastic soldier, but a selfish and turbulent viceroy; the original impulse given by the prophet to his countrymen had achieved its limit of conquest, and Muhammadanism required a new infusion of faith and hardihood to enable it to triumph over the heathens of Delhi and the Christians of Constantinople. This awakening spirit was acquired partly from the mountain Kurds, but chiefly from the pastorai Turkomans, who, from causes imperfectly understood, were once more impelled upon the fertile and wealthy south. During the ninth century, these warlike shepherds began to establish themselves from the Indus to the Black Sea, and they oppressed and protected the empire of Muhammad, as Goths and Vandals and their *Early Arab incursions into India but little felt.* *Muhammadanism receives a fresh impulse on the conversion of the Turkomans.*

[1] See Appendix VI.

own progenitors had before entered and defended and absorbed the dominions of Augustus and Trajan. Tughril Beg and Saladin are the counterparts of Stilicho and Theodoric, and the Mullas and Saiyids of Bagdad were as anxious for the conversion of unbelievers as the bishops and deacons of the Greek and Latin Churches. The migratory barbarians who fell upon Europe became Christians, and those who plundered Asia adopted, with perhaps greater ease and ardour, the more congenial creed of Islam. Their vague unstable notions yielded to the authority of learning and civilization, and to the majesty of one omnipotent God, and thus armed with religion as a motive, and empire as an object, the Turks precipitated themselves upon India and upon the diminished provinces of the Byzantine Caesars.

Muhammad invades India, A.D. 1001.

Muhammad crossed the Indus in the year 1001, not long after Shankar Acharj had vainly endeavoured to arrest the progress of heresy, and to give limits to the diversity of faith which perplexed his countrymen. The Punjab was permanently occupied, and before the sultan's death, Kanauj and Gujrat had been overrun. The Ghaznivides were expelled by the Ghoris about 1183. Bengal was conquered by these usurpers, and when the Ibak Turks supplanted them in 1206, Hindustan became a separate portion of the Muhammadan world. During the next hundred and fifty years the whole of India was subdued; a continued influx of Mughals in the thirteenth, and of Afghans in the fifteenth century, added to their successive authority as rulers, gradually changed the language and the thoughts of the vanquished. The Khiljis and Tughlaks and Lodis were too rude to be inquisitorial bigots; they had a lawful option in tribute, and taxation was more profitable, if less meritorious, than conversion. They adopted as their own the country which they had conquered. Numerous mosques attest their piety and munificence, and the introduction of the solar instead of the intractable lunar year, proves their attention to ordinary business and the wants of agriculture.[1]    The

Hindustan becomes a separate portion of the Muhammadan world under the Ibaks. A.D. 1206.

---

[1] The solar, i.e. really sidereal year, called the 'Shabur San', or vulgarly the 'Sur San', that is, the year of (Arabic) months, was apparently introduced into the Deccan by Tughlak Shah towards the middle of the fourteenth century of Christ, or between 1341 and 1344, and it is still used by the Marathas in all their more important documents, the dates being inserted in Arabic words written in Hindi (Marathi) characters. (Cf. Prinsep's *Useful Tables*, ii. 30, who refers to a Report by Lieut.-Colonel Jervis, on Weights and Measures.) The other 'Fasli'. or 'harvest' years of other parts of India, were not introduced until the reigns of Akbar and Shah Jahan, and they mostly

Muhammadans became Indianized; and in the sixteenth century the great Akbar conceived the design
of establishing a national government or monarchy
which should unite the elements of the two systems:
but political obedience does not always denote social
amalgamation, and the reaction upon the Muslim mind
perhaps increased that intolerance of Aurangzeb which
hastened the ruin of the dynasty.

*And the conquerors become Indianized.*

The influence of a new people, who equalled or
surpassed Kshattriyas in valour, who despised the
sanctity of Brahmans, and who authoritatively proclaimed the unity of God and his abhorrence of images,
began gradually to operate on the minds of the multitudes of India, and recalled even the learned to the
simple tenets of the Vedas, which Shankar Acharj had
disregarded.  The operation was necessarily slow, for
the imposing system of powers and emanations had
been adapted with much industry to the local or peculiar divinities of tribes and races, and in the lapse of
ages the legislation of Manu had become closely inter-
woven with the thoughts and habits of the people. Nor
did the proud distinctions of caste and the reverence
shown to Brahmans fail to attract the notice and the
admiration of the barbarous victors.  Shaikhs and
Saiyids had an innate holiness assigned to them, and
Mughals and Pathans copied the exclusiveness of
Rajputs.  New superstition also emulated old credulity.
'Pirs' and 'Shahids', saints and martyrs, equalled
Krishna and Bhairon in the number of their miracles,
and the Muhammadans almost forgot the unity of God
in the multitude of intercessors whose aid they
implored.  Thus custom jarred with custom, and
opinion with opinion, and while the few always fell
back with confidence upon their revelations, the Koran
and Vedas, the public mind became agitated, and found
no sure resting-place with Brahmans or Mullas, with
Mahadev or Muhammad.[1]

*Action and reaction of Muhamma-danism and Brah-manism.*

*The popu-lar belief unsettled.*

continue to this day to be used, even by the English, in revenue
accounts. The commencement of each might, without much
violence, be adapted to the 1st of July of any year of the Christian era, and the Muhammadans and Hindus could at the same
time retain, the former the Hijri, and the latter the Shak
(Saka) and Sambat names of the months respectively. No
greater degree of uniformity or simplicity is required, and the
general predominance of the English would render a measure
so obviously advantageous of easy introduction.

[1] Gibbon has shown (*History*, ii. 356) how the scepticism
of learned Greeks and Romans proved favourable to the growth
of Christianity, and a writer in the *Quarterly Review* (for June
1846, p. 116) makes some just observations on the same subject.
The cause of the scepticism is not perhaps sufficiently attributed

Ramanand
establishes
a compre-
hensive
sect at Be-
nares,
about
A.D. 1400;

The first result of the conflict was the institution, about the end of the fourteenth century, of a comprehensive sect by Ramanand of Benares, a follower of the tenets of Ramanuj. Unity of faith or of worship had already been destroyed, and the conquest of the country by foreigners diminished unity of action among the ministers of religion. Learning had likewise declined, and poetic fancy and family tradition were allowed to modify the ancient legends of the 'Purans' or chronicles, and to usurp the authority of the Vedas.[1]

to the mixture of the Eastern and Western superstitions, which took place after the conquests of Alexander, and during the supremacy of Rome.

Similarly, the influence of Muhammadan learning and civilization in moulding the European mind seems to be underrated in the present day, although Hallam (*Literature of Europe*, i. 90, 91, 149, 150, 157, 158, 189, 190) admits our obligations in physical and even in mental *science;* and a representative of Oxford, the critical yet fanciful William Gray (*Sketch of English Prose Literature*, pp. 22, 37), not only admires the *fictions* of the East, but confesses their beneficial effect on the Gothic genius. The Arabs, indeed, were the preservers and diffusers of that science or knowledge which was brought forth in Egypt or India, which was reduced to order in Greece and Rome, and which has been so greatly extended in particular directions by the moderns of the West. The pre-eminence of the Muhammadan over the Christian mind was long conspicuous in the metaphysics of the schoolmen, and it is still apparent in the administrative system of Spain, in the common terms of astronomical and medicinal science, and in the popular songs of feudal Europe, which ever refer to the Arabian prophet and to Turks and Saracens, or expatiate on the actions of the Cid, a Christian hero with a Musalman title.

Whewell (*History of Inductive Science*, i. 22, 276), in demonstrating that the Arabs did very little, if aught, to *advance* exact science, physical or metaphysical, and in likening them to the servant who had the talent but put it not to use, might yet have excused them on the plea that the genius of the people was directed to the propagation of religious truth—to subjecting the Evil Principle to the Good in Persia, to restoring Monotheism in India, and to the subversion of gross idolatry in regions of Africa still untrodden by Europeans. With this view of the English Professor may be contrasted the opinion of Humboldt, who emphatically says that the Arabs are to be regarded as the proper founders of the *physical sciences*, in the sense which we are now accustomed to attach to the term. (*Kosmos*, Sabine's trans., ii. 212.)

[1] Modern criticism is not disposed to allow an ancient date to the Purans, and doubtless the interpolations are both numerous and recent, just as the ordinary copies of the rhapsodies of the Rajput Bhat, or Bard, Chand, contain allusions to dynasties and events subsequent to Pirthi Raj and Mahmud. The difficulty lies in separating the old from the new, and perhaps also objectors have too much lost sight of the circumstance that the criticized and less corrupted Ramayana and Mahabharata are only the chief of the Purans. They seem needlessly inclined to reject entirely the authority or authenticity of the conventional

The heroic Rama was made the object of devotion to
this new sect of the Middle Ganges, and as the doctrine
of the innate superiority of Brahmanas and Kshattriyas
had been rudely shaken by the Muhammadan ascendancy, Ramanand seized upon the idea of man's
equality before God. He instituted no nice distinctive
observances, he admitted all classes of people as his
disciples, and he declared that the true votary was
raised above mere social forms, and became free or
liberated.[1] During the same century the learned
enthusiast Gorakhnath gave popularity, especially in
the Punjab, to the doctrine of the 'Yog', which belonged
more properly as a theory or practice to the Buddhist
faith, but which was equally adopted as a philosophic
dogma by the followers of Vyasa and of Sakya. It
was, however, held that in this 'Kalyug', or iron age,
fallen man was unequal to so great a penance, or to the

*and intro-
duces hero-
worship;
but main-
tains the
equality of
true be-
lievers be-
fore God.*

*Gorakh-
nath estab-
lishes a
sect in the
Punjab,*

*and main-
tains the*

Eighteen Chronicles, merely because eulogiums on modern
families have been introduced by successive flatterers. Nevertheless, the Purans must rather be held to illustrate modes of
thought, than to describe historical events with accuracy. [Colo-
nel Kennedy (*Res. Hind, Mythol.* pp. 130, 153, &c.) regards
them as complementary to the Vedas, explaining religious and
moral doctrines, and containing disquisitions concerning the
illusive nature of the universe, and not as in any way intended
to be historical.—J.D.C.]

[1] Cf. *Dabistan,* ii. 179, and Wilson, *As. Res.,* xvi. 36, &c.
Professor Wilson remarks (ibid., p. 44, and also xvii. 183), that
the sects of Shankar Acharj and Ramanuj included Brahmans
only, and indeed chiefly men of learning of that race. The
followers of Ramanand, or the Vaishnavas, were long violently
opposed to the Saivic denominations; so much so, according to
tradition, that they would not, on any account, cross the Narbada river, which is held to be peculiarly sacred to Mahadev
or Mahesh, but would rather, in performing a journey, go round
by its sources.

Among the people of Central India there is a general persuasion that the Narbada will one day take the place of the
Ganges as the most holy of streams; but the origin of the feeling is not clear, as neither is the fact of the consecration of the
river to Siva. At Maheshwar, indeed, there is a whirlpool,
which, by rounding and polishing fallen stones, rudely shapes
them into resemblances of a Lingam, and which are as fertile
a source of profit to the resident priests as are the Vaishnava
fossil ammonites of a particular part of the Himalayas. The
labours of the whirlpool likewise diffuse a sanctitude over all
the stones of the rocky channel, as expressed in the vernacular
sentence, 'Rehwa ke kunkur sub sunkur suman,' i.e. each stone
of the Narbada (Rehwa) is divine, or equal to Siva.

Maheshwar was the seat of Sahsar Babu, or of the hundred-
handed Kshattriya king, who was slain by Paras Ram, of the
not very far distant town of Nimawar, opposite Hindia; a probable occurrence, which was soon made the type, or the cause, of
the destruction of the ancient warrior race by the Brahmans.
The same is declared by the Siva Puran. (Colonel Kennedy, *Res.
Hind. Mythol.,* p. 309, note.)— J.D.C.]

equalizing
effect of
religious
penance;

but causes
further
diversity
by adopting
Siva as the
type of God.

The Vedas
and Koran
assailed
by Kabir,
a disciple
of Rama-
nand, about
A.D. 1450:

and the
mother
tongue of
the people

attainment of complete beatitude; but Gorakh taught that intense mental abstraction would etherialize the body of the most lowly, and gradually unite his spirit with the all-pervading soul of the world. He chose Siva as the deity who would thus bless the austere perseverance of his votaries of whatever caste; and, not content with the ordinary frontal marks of sects and persuasions, he distinguished his disciples by boring their ears, whence they are familiarly known as the 'Kanphata', or ear-torn Jogis.[1]

A step was thus made, and faith and abandonment of the pleasures of life were held to abrogate the distinctions of race which had taken so firm a hold on the pride and vanity of the rich and powerful. In the next generation, or about the year 1450, the mysterious weaver Kabir, a disciple of Ramanand, assailed at once the worship of idols, the authority of the Koran and Shastras, and the exclusive use of a learned language. He addressed Muhammadans as well as Hindus, he urged them to call upon him, the invisible Kabir, and to strive continually after inward purity. He personified creation or the world as 'Maya', or as woman,

---

[1] Cf. Wilson (As. Res., xvii. 183, &c.) and the Dabistan (Troyer's translation, i. 123, &c.). In the latter, Muhsin Fani shows some points of conformity between the Jogis and the Muhammadans. With regard to Yog, in a scientific point of view, it may be observed that it corresponds with the state of abstraction or self-consciousness which raised the soul above mortality or chance, and enabled it to apprehend the 'true' and to grasp Plato's 'idea', or archical form of the world, and that neither Indians nor Greeks considered man capable, in his present imperfect condition, of attaining to such a degree of 'union with God' or 'knowledge of the true'. (Cf. Ritter, Ancient Philosophy, Morrison's translation, ii. 207, 334-6, and Wilson, As. Res., xvii. 185.) Were it necessary to pursue the correspondence further, it would be found that Plato's whole system is almost identical, in its rudimental characteristics, with the schemes of Kapil and Patanjal jointly : thus, God and matter are in both eternal: Mahat, or intelligence, or the informing spirit of the world, is the same with nous or logos, and so on. With both God, that is 'Poorsh' in the one and the Supreme God in the other, would seem to be separate from the world as appreciable by man. It may further be observed that the Sankhya system is divided into two schools independent of that of Patanjal, the first of which regards 'Poorsh' simply as life, depending for activity upon 'adrisht', chance or fate, while the second holds the term to denote an active and provident ruler and gives to vitality a distinct existence. The school of Patanjal differs from this latter, principally in its terminology and in the mode (Yog) laid down for attaining bliss—one of the four subdivisions of which mode, viz. that of stopping the breath, is allowed to be the doctrine of Gorakh, but is declared to have been followed of old by Markand, in a manner more agreeable to the Vedas, than the practice of the recent Reformer.

prolific of deceit and illusion, and thus denounced used as an
man's weakness or his proneness to evil. Practically instrument.
Kabir admitted outward conformity, and leant towards But asce-
Rama or Vishnu as the most perfect type of God. Like ticism still<br>upheld.
his predecessors, he erringly gave shape and attributes
to the divinity, and he further limited the application
of his doctrines of reform, by 'declaring retirement from
the world to be desirable, and the 'Sadh', or pure or
perfect man, the passive or inoffensive votary, to be
the living resemblance of the Almighty. The views,
however, of Kabir are not very distinctly laid down
or clearly understood; but the latitude of usage which
he sanctioned, and his employment of a spoken dialect,
have rendered his writings extensively popular among
the lower orders of India.[1]

In the beginning of the sixteenth century the Chaitan
reforms of Ramanand were introduced into Bengal by preaches
Chaitan, a Brahman of Nadia. He converted some religious
Muhammadans, and admitted all classes as members of reform in<br>Bengal,
his sect. He insisted upon 'Bhakti', or faith, as chast- A.D. 1500.
ening the most impure; he allowed marriage and Insists
secular occupations; but his followers abused the usual upon the
injunction of reverence for the teacher, and some of efficacy of
them held that the Guru was to be invoked before faith, and<br>admits of
God.[2] About the same period Vallabh Swami, a Brah- secular oc-
man of Telingana, gave a further impulse to the cupations.

[1] Cf. the *Dabistan*, ii. 184, &c., Wilson, *As. Res.*, xvi. 53, and
Ward's *Hindoos*, iii. 406. Kabir is an Arabic word, meaning the
greatest, and Professor Wilson doubts whether any such person
ever existed and considers the Kabir of Muhsin Fani to be the
personification of an idea, or that the title was assumed by a
Hindu free-thinker as a disguise. The name, however, although
significant, is now at least not uncommon, and perhaps the ordinary story that Kabir was a fondling, reared by a weaver, and
subsequently admitted as a disciple by Ramanand, is sufficiently
probable to justify his identity. His body is stated to have been
claimed both by the Hindus and Muhammadans, and Muhsin
Fani observes that many Muhammadans became Bairagis, i.e.
ascetics of the modern Vaishnava sect, of which the followers
of Ramanand and Kabir form the principal subdivisions. (*Dabistan*, ii. 193.) As a further instance of the fusion of feeling then,
and now, going forward, the reply of the Hindu deist, Akam-
nath, to the keepers of the Kaba at Mecca may be quoted. He
first scandalized them by asking where was the master of the
house; and he then inquired why the idols had been thrown out.
He was told that the works of men were not to be worshipped;
whereupon he inquired whether the temple itself was not reared with hands, and therefore undeserving of respect (*Dabistan,*
ii. 117)

[2] For an account of Chaitan and his followers, cf. Wilson,
*Asiatic Researches*, xvi. 109, &c., and Ward, on *The Hindoos*, iii.

Vallabh
extends the
reforma-
tion to the
south,

and fur-
ther dis-
counten-
ances celi-
bacy, abou'
A.D. 1550.

reformation in progress, and he taught that married teachers were not only admissible as directors of the conscience, but that the householder was to be preferred, and that the world was to be enjoyed by both master and disciple. This principle was readily adopted by the peaceful mercantile classes, and 'Gusains', as the conductors of family worship, have acquired a commanding influence over the industrious Quietists of the country; but they have at the same time added to the diversity of the prevailing idolatry by giving pre-eminence to Bala Gopal, the *infant* Krishna, as the very God of the Universe.[1]

Recapitu-
lation.

Thus, in the beginning of the sixteenth century, the Hindu mind was no longer stagnant or retrogressive; it had been leavened with Muhammadanism, and changed and quickened for a new development. Ramanand and Gorakh had preached religious equality, and Chaitan had repeated that faith levelled caste. Kabir had denounced images, and appealed to the people in their own tongue, and Vallabh had taught that effectual devotion was compatible with the ordinary duties of the world. But these good and able men appear to have been so impressed with the nothingness of this life, that they deemed the amelioration of man's social condition to be unworthy of a thought. They aimed chiefly at emancipation from priestcraft, or from the grossness of idolatry and polytheism. They formed pious associations of contented Quietists, or they gave themselves up to the contemplation of futurity in the hope of approaching bliss, rather than called upon their fellow creatures to throw aside every social as well as religious trammel, and to arise a new people freed from the debasing corruption of ages. Tey perfected forms of dissent rather than planted the germs of nations, and their *sects* remain to this day as they left them. It was reserved for *Nanak* to perceive the true principles of reform, and to lay those broad foundations which enabled his successor *Gobind* to fire the minds of his countrymen with a new nationality, and to give practical effect to the doctrine that the lowest is equal with the highest, in race as in creed, in political rights as in religious hopes.

The re-
forms par-
tial, and
leading to
sectarian-
ism only.

Nanak's
views more
compre-
hensive
and pro-
found.

467, &c.; and for some apposite remarks on Bhakti or faith, see Wilson, *As. Res.*, xvii. 312.

[1] See Wilson, *Asiatic Researches*, xvi. 85, &c.; and for an account of the corresponding Vaishnava sect of Madhav, which has, however, a leaning to Saivism, see also Wilson, *As. Res.*, xvi. 100. (See also Appendix VII for some remarks on the Metaphysics of Indian Reformers.)

Nanak was born in the year 1469, in the neighbour- 1469-1539.
hood of Lahore.[1]  His father, Kalu, was a Hindu of Nanak's
the Bedi subdivision of the once warlike Kshattriyas, birth and
and he was, perhaps, like most of his race, a petty early life.
trader in his native village.[2]  Nanak appears to have A.D. 1469.
been naturally of a pious disposition and of a reflecting
mind, and there is reason to believe that in his youth
he made himself familiar with the popular creeds both
of the Muhammadans and Hindus, and that he gained
a general knowledge of the Koran and of the Brahmanical Shastras.[3]  His good sense and fervid temper

[1] Nanak is generally said to have been born in Talwandi,
a village on the Ravi above Lahore, which was held by one
Rai Bhua of the Bhutti tribe. (Cf. Malcolm, *Sketch of the Sikhs*,
p. 78, and Forster, *Travels*, i. 292-3.) But one manuscript account states that, although the father of Nanak was of Talwandi, the teacher himself was born in Kanakatch, about fifteen
miles southerly from Lahore, in the house of his mother's parents. It is indeed not uncommon in the Punjab for women to
choose their own parents' home as the place of their confinement, especially of their first child, and the children thus born
are frequently called Nanak (or Nanki, in the feminine), from
*Nanke*, one's mother's parents. Nanak is thus a name of usual
occurrence, both among Hindus and Muhammadans, of the poor
or industrious classes. The accounts agree as to the *year* of
Nanak's birth, but differ, while they affect precision, with
regard to the *day of the month* on which he was born. Thus one
narrative gives the 13th, and another the 18th, of the month
Kartik, of the year 1526 of Vikramajit, which corresponds with
the latter end of 1469 of Christ.

[2] In the *Siar ul Mutakharin* (Brigg's translation, i. 110) it
is stated that Nanak's father was a grain merchant, and in the
*Dabistan* (ii. 247) that Nanak himself was a grain factor. The
Síkh accounts are mostly silent about the occupation of the
father, but they represent the sister of Nanak to have been married to a corn factor, and state that he was himself placed with
his brother-in-law to learn, or to give aid, in carrying on the
business.

[3] A manuscript compilation in Persian mentions that
Nanak's first teacher was a Muhammadan. The *Siar ul Mutakharin* (i. 110) states that Nanak was carefully educated by one
Saiyid Hasan, a neighbour of his father's, who conceived a
regard for him, and who was wealthy but childless. Nanak is
further said, in the same book, to have studied the most approved writings of the Muhammadans. According to Malcolm
(*Sketch*, p. 14), Nanak is reported, by the Muhammadans, to
have learnt all earthly sciences from Khizar, i.e. the prophet
Elias. The ordinary Muhammadan accounts also represent
Nanak, when a child, to have astonished his teacher by asking
him the hidden import of the first letter of the alphabet, which
is almost a straight stroke in Persian and Arabic, and which is
held even vulgarly to denote the unity of God. The reader will
remember that the apocryphal gospels state how Christ, before
he was twelve years old, perplexed his instructors, and explained to them the mystical significance of the alphabetical characters. (Strauss, *Life of Jesus*, i. 272.)

left him displeased with the corruptions of the vulgar faith, and dissatisfied with the indifference of the learned, or with the refuge which they sought in the specious abstractions of philosophy; nor is it improbable that the homilies of Kabir and Gorakh had fallen upon his susceptible mind with a powerful and enduring effect.[1]    In a moment of enthusiasm the ardent inquirer abandoned his home, and strove to attain wisdom by penitent mediation, by study, and by an enlarged intercourse with mankind.[2]    He travelled, perhaps, beyond the limits of India, he prayed in solitude, he reflected on the Vedas and on the mission of Muhammad, and he questioned with equal anxiety the learned priest and the simple devotee about the will of God and the path to happiness.[3]    Plato and

**The mental struggles of Nanak.**

[1] Extracts or selections from the writings of Kabir appear in the *Adi-Granth*, and Kabir is often, and Gorakh sometimes, quoted or referred to.

[2] A chance meeting with some Fakirs (Malcolm, *Sketch*, pp. 8, 13) and the more methodical instructions of a Dervish (*Dabistan*, ii. 247) are each referred to as having subdued the mind of Nanak, or as having given him the impulse which determined the future course of his life. In Malcolm may be seen those stories which please the multitude, to the effect that although Nanak, when the spirit of God was upon him, bestowed all the grain in his brother-in-law's stores by charity, they were nevertheless always found replenished; or that Daulat Khan Lodi, the employer of Nanak's brother-in-law, although aware that much had really been given away, nevertheless found everything correct on balancing the accounts of receipts and expenditure.

The Sikh accounts represent Nanak to have met the Emperor Babar, and to have greatly edified the adventurous sovereign by his demeanour and conversation, while he perplexed him by saying that both were kings and were about to found dynasties of ten. I have traced but two allusions to Babar by name, and one by obvious inference, in the *Adi-Granth*, viz. in the Asa Rag and Tailang portions, and these bear reference simply to the destruction of a village, and to his incursions as a conqueror. Muhsin Fani (*Dabistan*, ii. 249) preserves an idle report that Nanak, being dissatisfied with the Afghans, called the Mughals into India.

[3] Nanak is generally said to have travelled over the whole of India, to have gone through Persia, and to have visited Mecca (cf. Malcolm, *Sketch*, p. 16, and Forster, *Travels*, i. 295-6), but the number of years he employed in wandering, and the date of his final return to his native province, are alike uncertain. He had several companions, among whom Mardana, the rababi or harper (or rather a chanter, and player upon a stringed instrument like a guitar), Lahna, who was his successor, Bala, a Sindhu Jat, and Ram Das, styled Buddha or the Ancient, are the most frequently referred to. In pictorial representations Mardana always accompanies Nanak. When at Mecca, a story is related that Nanak was found sleeping with his feet towards the temple, that he was angrily asked how he dared to dishonour the house of the Lord, and that he replied.

Bacon, Des Cartes and Alghazali, examined the current philosophic systems of the world, without finding a sure basis of truth for the operations of the intellect; and, similarly, the heart of the pious Nanak sought hopelessly for a resting-place amid the conflicting creeds and practices of men. All was error, he said; he had read Korans and Purans, but God he had nowhere found.[1] He returned to his native land, he threw aside the habit of an ascetic, he became again the father of his family, and he passed the remainder of his long life in calling upon men to worship the One Invisible God, to live virtuously, and to be tolerant of the failings of others. The mild demeanour, the earnest piety, and persuasive eloquence of Nanak, are ever the themes of praise, and he died at the age of seventy, leaving behind him many zealous and admiring disciples.[2]

Could he turn his feet where the house of God was not?' (Malcolm, *Sketch of the Sikhs*, p. 159.) Nanak adopted, sometimes at least, the garb of a Muhammadan Dervish, and at Multan he visited an assembly of Musalman devotees, saying he was but as the stream of the Ganges entering the ocean of holiness. (Cf. Malcolm, *Sketch*, p. 21. and the *Siar ul Mutakharin*, i. 311.)

[1] There is current a verse imputed to Nanak, to the effect that—

'Several scriptures and books had he read,
But one (God) he had not found:
Several Korans and Purans had he read,
But faith he could not put in any.'

The *Adi-Granth* abounds with passages of a similar tenor, and in the supplemental portion, called the Ratan Mala, Nanak says, 'Man may read Vedas and Korans, and reach to a temporary bliss, but without God salvation is unattainable.'

[2] The accounts mostly agree as to the date of Nanak's death, and they place it in 1596 of Vikramajit, or 1539 of Christ. A Gurmukhi abstract states precisely that he was a teacher for seven years, five months, and seven days, and that he died on the 10th of the Hindu month Asauj. Forster (*Travels*, i. 295) represents that he travelled for fifteen years. Nanak died at Kartarpur, on the Ravi, about forty miles above Lahore, where there is a place of worship sacred to him. He left two sons, Sri Chand, an ascetic, whose name lives as the founder of the Hindu sect of Udasis, and Lachmi Das, who devoted himself to pleasure, and of whom nothing particular is known. The Nanak-putras, or descendants of Nanak, called also Sahibzadas, or sons of the master, are everywhere reverenced among Sikhs, and if traders, some privileges are conceded to them by the chiefs of their country. Muhsin Fani observes (*Dabistan*. ii. 253) that the representatives of Nanak were known as Kartaris, meaning, perhaps, rather that they were held to be holy or devoted to the service of God, than that they were simply residents of Kartarpur.

1469-1539.

The excel-
lences of
Nanak's
doctrine.

The god-
head.

Muham-
madans
and Hindus
equally
called on to
worship
God in
truth.

Nanak combined the excellences of preceding reformers, and he avoided the more grave errors into
which they had fallen. Instead of the circumscribed
divinity, the anthropomorphous God of Ramanand and
Kabir, he loftily invokes the Lord as the one, the sole,
the timeless being; the creator, the self-existent, the
incomprehensible, and the everlasting. He likens the
Deity to Truth, which was before the world began,
which is, and which shall endure for ever, as the ultimate idea or cause of all we know or behold.[1]  He
addresses equally the Mulla and the Pandit, the
Dervish and the Sannyasi, and tells them to remember
*that* Lord o.' Lords who has seen come and go number-
less Muhammads, and Vishnus, and Sivas.[2]  He tells
them that virtues and charities, heroic acts and
gathered wisdom, are nought of themselves, that the
only knowledge which availeth is the knowledge of
God;[3] and then, as if to rebuke those vain men who
saw eternal life in their own act of faith, he declares
that they only can find the Lord on whom the Lord

[1] See the *Adi-Granth* in, for instance, the portion called
*Gowree Rag*, and the prefatory *Jup*, or prayer of admonition
and remembrance. Cf. also Wilkins, *Asiatic Researches*, i. 289.
&c.

'Akalpurik', or the Timeless Being, is the ordinary Sikh
appellation of God, corresponding idiomatically with the Almighty', in English. Yet Gobind, in the second *Granth* (Hazara
Shabd portion), apostrophizes Time itself as the only true God,
for God was the first and the last, the being without end, &c.

Milton assigns to time a casual or limited use only, and
Shakespeare makes it finite:

'For time, though in eternity applied
To motion, measures all things durable
By present, past, and future.'

*Paradise Lost*, v.

'But thought's the slave of life, and life, time's fool;
And time, that takes survey of all the world,
Must have a stop.'

*I Henry IV*, v. iv.

Three of the modern philosophizing schools of India,
viz. a division of the Sankhyas, the Puraniks, and the Saivas,
make Kal, or time, one of the twenty-seven, or thirty, or thirty-
six component essences or phenomena of the universe of matter
and mind, and thus give it distinct functions, or a separate
existence.

[2] A passage of Nanak's in the supplement to the *Adi-
Granth*, after saying that there have been multitudes of prophets, teachers, and holy men, concludes thus:

The Lord of Lords is the One God, the Almighty God himself;

Oh Nanak! his qualities are beyond comprehension.'

[3] See the *Adi-Granth*, towards the end of the portion called *Asa*.

looks with favour.[1]  Yet the extension of grace is  1469-1539.
linked with the exercise of our will and the beneficent  Faith, grace,
use of our faculties.  God, said Nanak, places salvation  and good
in good works and uprightness of conduct: the Lord  works all
will ask of man, 'What has he done?' [2]—and the teacher  necessary.
further required timely repentance of men, saying, 'If
not until the day of reckoning the sinner abaseth himself, punishment shall overtake him'.[3]

Nanak adopted the philosophical system of his  Nanak
countrymen, and regarded bliss as the dwelling of the  adopts the
soul with God after its punitory transmigrations should  Brahma-
have ceased.  Life, he says, is as the shadow of the  nical philo-
passing bird, but the soul of man is, as the potter's  sophy; but
wheel, ever circling on its pivot.[4]  He makes the same  in a popu-
uses of the current language or notions of the time on  lar sense,
other subjects, and thus says, he who remains bright  or by way
amid darkness (Anjan), unmoved amid deceit (Maya),  of illustra-
that is, perfect amid temptation, should attain happi-  tion only.
ness.[5]  But it would be idle to suppose that he speculated upon being, or upon the material world, after
the manner of Plato or Vyasa; [6] and it would be
unreasonable to condemn him because he preferred the
doctrine of a succession of habiliments, and the possible
purification of the most sinful soul, to the resurrection
of the same body, and the pains of everlasting fire.[7]

[1] See the Adi-Granth, end of the Asa Rag, and in the supplementary portion called the Ratan Mala.

[2] The Adi-Granth, Prabhati Ragni, Cf. Malcolm (Sketch,
p. 161) and Wilkins (As. Res., i. 289, &c.).

[3] See the Nasihat Nama, or admonition of Nanak to Karon,
a fabulous monarch, which, however, is not admitted into the
Granth, perhaps because its personal or particular application
is not in keeping with the abstract and general nature of that
book. Neither, indeed, is it certainly known to be Nanak's composition, although it embodies many of his notions.

[4] Adi-Granth, end of the Asa Rag.

[5] Adi-Granth. in the Suhi and Ramkali portions.

[6] See Appendix VIII.

[7] The usual objection of the Muhammadans to the Hindu
doctrine of transmigration is, that the wicked soul of this present world has no remembrance of its past-condition and bygone punishments, and does not, therefore, bring with it any
inherent incentive to holiness. The Muhammadans, however, do
not show that a knowledge of the sin of Adam, and consequent
corruption of his posterity, is instinctive to a follower of Christ
or to a disciple of their own prophet; and, metaphysically, an
impartial thinker will perhaps prefer the Brahman doctrine of
a soul finally separated from the changeable matter of our
senses, to the Egyptian scheme of the resurrection of the cor-
ruptible body,—a notion which seems to have impressed itself
on the Israelites, notwithstanding the silence of Moses, and
which resisted for centuries the action of other systems, and
which was at length revived with increased force in connexion
with the popular belief in miracles. See also note 2, p. 24 ante.

1469-1539.

Nanak ad-
mits the
mission of
Muhammad
as well as
the Hindu-
incarna-
tions.

Nanak also referred to the Arabian prophet, and to the Hindu incarnations, not as impostors and the diffusers of evil, but as having truly been sent by God to instruct mankind, and he lamented that sin should nevertheless prevail. He asserted no special divinity, although he may possibly have considered himself, as he came to be considered by others, the successor of these inspired teachers of his belief, sent to reclaim fallen mortals of all creeds and countries within the limits of his knowledge. He rendered his mission applicable to all times and places, yet he declared himself to be but the slave, the humble messenger of the Almighty, making use of universal truth as his sole instrument.[1] He did not claim for his writings, replete as they were with wisdom and devotion,[2] the merit of a direct transcription of the words of God; nor did he say that his own preaching required or would be sanctioned by miracles.[3] 'Fight with no weapon,' said he, 'save the word of God; a holy teacher hath no means save the purity of his doctrine.'[4] He taught that asceticism or abandonment of the world was unnecessary, the pious hermit and the devout householder being equal in the eyes of the Almighty; but he did not, like his contemporary Vallabh, express any invidious preference for married teachers, although his own example showed that he considered every one should fulfil the functions

Disclaims
miraculous
powers.

Discour-
ages asce-
ticism.

[1] The whole scope of Nanak's teaching is that God is all in all, and that purity of mind is the first of objects. He urges all men to practise devotion, and he refers to past prophets and dispensations as being now of no avail, but he nowhere attributes to himself any superiority over others. He was a man among men, calling upon his fellow creatures to live a holy life. (Cf. the *Dabistan*, ii. 249, 250, 253; and see Wilson, *As. Res.*, xvii. 234, for the expression 'Nanak thy slave is a freewill offering unto thee'.)

[2] The Muhammadan writers are loud in their praises of Nanak's writings. (Cf. the *Siar ul Mutakharin*, i. 110, 111, and the *Dabistan*, ii. 251, 252.)

With these sober views of the Orientals may be contrasted the opinion of the European, Baron Hugel, who says (*Travels*, p. 283) that the *Granth* is 'a compound of mystical absurdities'. He admits, however, that the Sikhs worship one God, abhor images, and reject caste, at least in theory.

[3] See particularly the *Sri Rag* chapter of the *Adi-Granth*. In 'the Maj Var portion Nanak says to a pretender to miracles, 'Dwell thou in flame uninjured, remain unharmed amid eternal ice, make blocks of stone thy food, spurn the solid earth before thee with thy foot, weigh the heavens in a balance, and then ask thou that Nanak perform wonders!'

Strauss (*Life of Jesus*, ii. 237) points out that Christ censured the seeking for miracles (John 48), and observes that the apostles in their letters do not mention miracles at all.

[4] Malcolm, *Sketch*, pp. 20, 21, 165.

of his nature.[1] In treating the two prominent external observances of Hindus and Muhammadans, veneration for the cow and abhorrence of the hog, he was equally wise and conciliatory, yielding perhaps something to the prejudices of his education as well as to the gentleness of his disposition. 'The rights of strangers,' said he, 'are the one the ox, and the other the swine, but "Pirs" and "Gurus" will praise those who partake not of that which hath enjoyed life.' [2]

Thus Nanak extricated his followers from the accumulated errors of ages, and enjoined upon them devotion of thought and excellence of conduct as the first of duties. He left them, erect and free, unbiassed in mind and unfettered by rules, to become an increasing body of truthful worshippers. His reform was in its immediate effect religious and moral only; believers were regarded as 'Sikhs' or disciples, not as subjects; and it is neither probable, nor is it necessary to suppose, that he possessed any clear and sagacious views of social amelioration or of political advancement. He left the progress of his people to the operation of time: for his congregation was too limited, and the state or society too artificial, to render it either requisite or

*(margin notes:)* 1469-1539.

Conciliatory between Muhammadans and Hindus.

Nanak fully extricates his followers from error.

But his reformation necessarily religious and moral only.

Nanak left his Sikhs or disciples without

---

[1] Adi-Granth, particularly the Asa Ragni and Ramkali Ragni. (Cf. the Dabistan, ii. 271.)

[2] Adi-Granth, Maj chapter. Cf. Malcolm (Sketch, p. 36, note, and p. 137), where it is said Nanak prohibited swine's flesh; but, indeed, the flesh of the tame hog had always been forbidden to Hindus. (Manu's Institutes. v. 19.) The Dabistan (ii. 248) states that Nanak prohibited wine and pork, and himself abstained from all flesh but, in truth, contradictory passages about food may be quoted, and thus Ward (The Hindoos, iii. 466) shows that Nanak defended those who eat flesh, and declared that the infant which drew nurture from its mother lived virtually upon flesh. The author of the Gur Ratnavali pursues the idea, in a somewhat trivial manner indeed, by asking whether man does not take woman to wife, and whether the holiest of books are not bound with the skins of animals !

The general injunctions of Nanak have sometimes been misinterpreted by sectarian followers and learned strangers, to mean 'great chariness of animal life', almost in a mere ceremonial sense. (Wilson, As. Res., xvii. 233.) But the Sikhs have no such feeling, although the Jains and others carry a pious regard for worms and flies to a ludicrous extent—a practice which has reacted upon at least some families of Roman Catholic Christians in India. Those in Bhopal reject, during Lent, the use of unrefined sugar, an article of daily consumption, because, in its manufacture, the lives of many insects are necessarily sacrificed ! [It is curious that the Greeks and Romans believed the life of the ox to have been held sacred during the golden age: and Cicero quotes Aratus, to show that it was only during the iron age the flesh of cattle began to be eaten. (On the Nature of the Gods, Francklin's translation, p. 154.)—J.D.C.]

1469-1539.

new social
laws as a
separate
people.

But guard-
ed against
their nar-
rowing into
a sect.

possible for him to become a municipal law-giver, to subvert the legislation of Manu, or to change the immemorial usages of tribes or races.[1] His care was rather to prevent his followers contracting into a sect, and his comprehensive principles narrowing into monastic distinctions. This he effected by excluding his son, a meditative and perhaps bigoted ascetic, from the ministry when he should himself be no more; and, as his end approached, he is stated to have made a trial of the obedience or merits of his chosen disciples, and to have preferred the simple and sincere Lahna. As they journeyed along, the body of a man was seen lying by the wayside. Nanak said, 'Ye who trust in me, eat of this food.' All hesitated save Lahna; he knelt and uncovered the dead, and touched without tasting the flesh of man; but, behold! the corpse had disappeared and Nanak was in its place. The Guru embraced his faithful follower, saying he was as him-

Nanak de-
clares
Angad to

self, and that his spirit would dwell within him.[2] .The name of Lahna was changed to Angi-Khud, or Angad, or own body,[3] and whatever may be the foundation

---

[1] Malcolm (*Sketch*, pp. 44, 147) says Nanak made little or no alteration in the civil institutions of the Hindus, and Ward (*The Hindoos*, iii. 463) says, the Sikhs have no written civil or criminal laws. Similar observations of dispraise or applause might be made with regard to the code of the early Christians, and we know the difficulties under which the apostles laboured, owing to the want of a new declaratory law, or owing to the scruples and prejudices of their disciples. (Acts xv. 20, 28, 29, and other passages.) The seventh of the articles of the Church of England, and the nineteenth chapter of the Scottish Confession of Faith, show the existing perplexity of modern divines, and, doubtless, it will long continue to be disputed how far Christians are amenable to some portions of the Jewish law, and whether Sikhs should wholly reject the institutions of Manu and the usages of race. There were Judaizing Christians and there are Brahmanizing Sikhs; the swine was a difficulty with one, the cow is a difficulty with the other; and yet the greatest obstacle, perhaps, to a complete obliteration of caste, is the root-feeling that marriages should properly take place only between people of the same origin or nation, without much reference to faith. (Cf. Ward on *The Hindoos*, ii. 459; Malcolm, *Sketch* p. 157 note; and Forster's *Travels*, i. 293, 295, 308.)

[2] This story is related by various Punjabi compilers, an l it is given with one of the variations by Dr. Macgregor, in his *History of the Sikhs* (i. 48). In the Dabistan (ii. 268, 269) there is a story of a similar kind about the successive sacrifice in the four ages of a cow, a horse, an elephant, and a man. The pious partakers of the flesh of the last offering were declared to be saved, and the victim himself again appeared in his bodily shape.

[3] Cf. Malcolm, *Sketch of the Sikhs*, p. 24 note. [Angad, however, is an old Hindu name, and the ambassador of Rama to Ravan was so called. (Kennedy, *Res. Hind. Mythol.*, p. 438.) —J.D.C.]

of the story or the truth of the etymology, it is certain that the Sikhs fully believe the spirit of Nanak to have been incarnate in each succeeding Guru.[1] Angad was acknowledged as the teacher of the Sikhs, and Sri Chand, the son of Nanak, justified his father's fears, and became the founder of the Hindu sect of 'Udasis', a community indifferent to the concerns of this world.[2]

1469-1539:
be his suc-
cessor as a
teacher of
men

[1] This belief is an article of faith with the Sikhs. Cf. the *Dabistan* (ii. 253, 281). The Guru Har Gobind signed himself 'Nanak' in a letter to Muhsin Fani, the author of that work.

[2] For some account of the Udasis, see Wilson, *Asiatic Researches*, xvii. 232. The sect is widely diffused; its members are proud of their connexion with the Sikhs, and all reverence, and most possess and use, the *Granth* of Nanak.

NOTE.—For many stories regarding Nanak himself, which it has not been thought necessary to introduce into the text or notes, the curious reader may refer with profit to Malcolm's *Sketch*, to the second *volume* of the *Dabistan*, and to the first volume of Dr. Macgregor's recently published *History*.

# CHAPTER III

## THE SIKH GURUS OR TEACHERS, AND THE MOIDIFICATION OF SIKHISM UNDER GOBIND
### 1539-1716

Guru Angad—Guru Amar Das and the Udasi Sect—Guru Ram Das—Guru Arjun—The First Granth and Civil Organisation of the Sikhs—Guru Har Gobind and the Military Ordering of the Sikhs—Guru Har Rai—Guru Har Kishan —Guru Tegh Bahadur—Guru Gobind, and the Political Establishment of the Sikhs—Banda Bairagi the Temporal Successor of Gobind—The Dispersion of the Sikhs.

**1539-52.**

**Angad upholds the broad principles of Nanak. Dies 1552.**

NANAK died in 1539, and he was succeeded by the Angad of his choice, a Kshattriya of the Tihan subdivision of the race, who himself died in 1552, at Kadur, near Goindwal, on the Beas river. Little is related of his ministry, except that he committed to writing much of what he had heard about Nanak from the Guru's ancient companion, Bala Sindhu, as well as some devotional observations of his own, which were afterwards incorporated in the *Granth*. But Angad was true to the principles of his great teacher, and, not deeming either of his own sons worthy to succeed him, he bestowed his apostolic blessing upon Amar Das, an assiduous follower.[1]

**Amar Das succeeds.**

Amar Das was likewise a Kshattriya, but of the Bhalla subdivision. He was active in preaching, and successful in obtaining converts, and it is said that he found an attentive listener in the tolerant Akbar. The immediate followers of Sri Chand, the son of Nanak, had hitherto been regarded as almost equally the disciples of the first teacher with the direct adherents of Angad; but Amar Das declared passive and recluse 'Udasis' to be wholly separate from active and domestic 'Sikhs', and thus finally preserved the infant church

**Separates the Sikhs from the Udasis.**

[1] Angad was born, according to most accounts, in 1561 Sambat, or A.D. 1504, but according to others in 1567 (or A.D. 1510). His death is usually placed in 1609 Sambat (A.D. 1552), but sometimes it is dated a year earlier, and the Sikh accounts affect a precision as to days and months which can never gain credence. Foster (*Travels*, i. 296) gives 1542, perhaps a misprint for 1552, as the period of his death.

or state from disappearing as one of many sects.[1] In 1552-74.
the spirit of Nanak he likewise pronounced that the
'true Sati was she whom grief and not flame consumed, His views
and that the afflicted should seek consolation with the with regard
Lord'; thus mildly discountenancing a perverse custom, to 'Sati'.
and leading the way to amendment by persuasion Dies 1574.
rather than by positive enactment.[2] Amar Das died in
1574, after a ministration of about twenty-two years
and a half.[3] He had a son and a daughter, and it is
said that his delight with the uniform filial love and
obedience of the latter led him to prefer her husband
before other disciples, and to bestow upon him his
'Barkat' or apostolic virtue. The fond mother, or
ambitious woman, is further stated to have obtained
an assurance from the Guru that the succession should
remain with her posterity.

Ram Das, the son-in-law of Amar Das, was a Ram Das
Kshattriya of the Sodhi subdivision, and he was worthy succeeds
of his master's choice and of his wife's affection. He is and esta-<br>blishes him-
said to have been held in esteem by Akbar, and to have self at
received from him a piece of land, within the limits of Amritsar.
which he dug a reservoir, since well known as Amritsar, or the pool of immortality; but the temples and
surrounding huts were at first named Ramdaspur, from
the founder.[4] Ram Das is among the most revered of
the Gurus, but no precepts of wide application, or
rules of great practical value or force, are attributed to

[1] Malcolm (Sketch, p. 27) says distinctly that Amar Das
made this separation. The Dabistan (ii. 271) states generally
that the Gurus had effected it, and in the present day some
educated Sikhs think that Arjun first authoritatively laid down
the difference between an Udasi and a genuine follower of
Nanak.

[2] The Adi-Granth, in that part of the Suhi chapter which
is by Amar Das. Forster (Travels, i. 309) considers that
Nanak prohibited Sati, and allowed widows to marry; but
Nanak did not make positive laws of the kind, and perhaps
self-sacrifice was not authoritatively interfered with until first
Akbar and Jahangir (Memoirs of Jahangir, p. 28), and afterwards the English, endeavoured to put an end to it.

[3] The accounts agree as to the date of Amar Das's birth,
placing it in 1566 Sambat, or A.D. 1509. The period of his
death, 1631 Sambat, or A.D. 1574, seems likewise certain,
although one places it as late as A.D. 1580.

[4] Malcolm, Sketch, p. 29; Forster, Travels, i. 297; the
Dabistan, ii. 275. The Sikh accounts state that the possession
of Akbar's gift was disputed by a Bairagi, who claimed the
land as the site of an ancient pool dedicated to Ram Chandra,
the tutelary deity of his order; but the Sikh Guru said haught-
ily he was himself the truer representative of the hero. The
Bairagi could produce no proof; but Ram Das dug deep into the
earth, and displayed to numerous admirers the ancient steps
of the demi-god's reservoir!

1574-81.

Dies 1581.

Arjun suc-
ceeds and
fairly
grasps the
idea of
Nanak.

Makes
Amritsar
the 'Holy
City' of
the Sikhs

Compiles
the Adi-
Granth.

him. His own ministry did not extend beyond seven years, and the slow progress of the faith of Nanak seems apparent from the statement that at the end of forty-two years his successor had not more than double that number of disciples or instructed followers.[1]

Arjun succeeded his father in 1581, and the wishes of his mother, the daughter of Amar Das, were thus accomplished.[2] Arjun was perhaps the first who clearly understood the wide import of the teachings of Nanak, or who perceived how applicable they were to every state of life and to every condition of society. He made Amritsar the proper seat of his followers, the centre which should attract their worldly longings for a material bond of union; and the obscure hamlet, with its little pool, has become a populous city and the great place of pilgrimage of the Sikh people.[3] Arjun next arranged the various writings of his predecessors;[4] he added to them the best known, or the most suitable, compositions of some other religious reformers of the few preceding centuries, and completing the whole with a prayer and some exhortations of his own, he declared the compilation to be pre-eminently the 'Granth' or Book; and he gave to his followers their fixed rule of religious and moral conduct, with an assu-

[1] Such seems to be the meaning of the expression. 'He held holy converse with eighty-four Sikhs,' used by Bhai Kanh Singh in a manuscript compilation of the beginning of this century.
Ram Das's birth is placed in 1581 Sambat, or A. D. 1524, his marriage in A. D. 1542, the founding of Amritsar in A. D. 1577, and his death in A. D. 1581.

[2] It seems doubtful whether Ram Das had two or three sons, Pirthi Chand (or Bharut Mal or Dhi Mal), Arjun, and Mahadev, and also whether Arjun was older or younger than Pirthi Chand. It is more certain, however, that Pirthi Chand claimed the succession on the death of his brother, if not on the death of his father, and he was also indeed accused of endeavouring to poison Arjun. (Cf. Malcom, Sketch, p. 30, and the Dabistan, ii. 273.) The descendants of Pirthi Chand are still to be found in the neighbourhood of the Sutlej, especially at Kot Har Sahai, south of Ferozepore.

[3] The ordinary Sikh accounts represent Arjun to have taken up his residence at Amritsar; but he lived for some time at least at Taran Taran, which lies between that city and the junction of the Beas and Sutlej. (Cf. the Dabistan, ii. 275.)

[4] Malcolm, Sketch, p. 30. General tradition and most writers attribute the arrangement of the First Granth to Arjun; but Angad is understood to have preserved many observations of Nanak, and Forster (Travels, i. 297) states that Ram Das compiled the histories and precepts of his predecessors, and annexed a commentary to the work. The same author, indeed (Travels, i. 296 note), also contradictorily assigns the compilation to Angad.

rance that multitudes even of divine Brahmans had
wearied themselves with reading the Vedas, and had
found not the value of an oil-seed within them.[1] The Reduces
Guru next reduced to a systematic tax the customary customary
offerings of his converts or adherents, who, under his offerings to
ascendancy, were to be found in every city and pro- a systema-
vince. The Sikhs were bound by social usage, and tic tax or
disposed from reverential feelings, to make such pre- tithe;
sents to their spiritual guide; but the agents of Arjun
were spread over the country to demand and receive
the contributions of the faithful, which they proceeded
to deliver to the Guru in person at an annual assembly.
Thus the Sikhs, says the almost contemporary Muhsin
Fani, became accustomed to a regular government.[2]
Nor was Arjun heedless of other means of acquiring and engages
wealth and influence; he dispatched his followers into in traffic.
foreign countries to be as keen in traffic as they were
zealous in belief, and it is probable that his transactions
as a merchant were extensive, although confined to the
purchase of horses in Turkestan.[3]

Arjun became famous among pious devotees, and
his biographers dwell on the number of saints and holy
men who were edified by his instructions. Nor was he
unheeded by those in high station, for he is said to
have refused to betroth his son to the daughter of Arjun pro-
Chandu Shah, the finance administrator of the Lahore vokes the
province;[4] and he further appears to have been sought enmity of
as a political partisan, and to have offered up prayers Chandu
for Khusru, the son of Jahnagir, when in rebellion and Shah.
in temporary possession of the Punjab. The Guru was Becomes a

[1] Adi-Granth, in that portion of the Suhi chapter written
by Arjun. For some account of the Adi, or First Granth,
see Appendix I.
[2] The Dabistan, ii. 270, &c. Cf. Malcolm, Sketch, p. 30.
[3] The ordinary Sikh accounts are to this effect. Cf. the
Dabistan, ii. 271.
[4] Cf. Forster, Travels, i. 298. The Sikh accounts represent
that the son of Arjun was mentioned to Chandu as a suitable
match for his daughter, and that Chandu slightingly objected,
saying, Arjun, although a man of name and wealth, was still
a beggar, or one who received alms. This was reported to
Arjun; he resented the taunt, and would not be reconciled to
the match, notwithstanding the personal endeavours of
Chandu to appease him and bring about the union.
Shah is a corrupted suffix to names, extensively adopted
in India. It is a Persian word signifying a king, but applied
to Muhammadan Fakirs as Maharaja is used by or towards
Hindu devotees. It is also used to denote a principal merchant,
or as a corruption of Sahu or Sahukar, and it is further used
as a name or title, as a corruption of Sah or Sahai. The Gond
converts to Muhammadanism on the Narbada all add the word
Shah to their names.

**1581-1606**
**partisan of Prince Khusru in rebellion.**
**Imprisonment and death of Arjun, 1606.**

summoned to the emperor's presence, and fined and imprisoned at the instigation chiefly, it is said, of Chandu Shah, whose alliance he had rejected, and who represented him as a man of a dangerous ambition.[1] Arjun died in 1606, and his death is believed to have been hastened by the rigours of his confinement; but his followers piously assert that, having obtained leave to bathe in the river Ravi, he vanished in the shallow stream, to the fear and wonder of those guarding him.[2]

**Diffusion of Sikhism.**
**The writings of Gur Das Bhulleh.**

During the ministry of Arjun the principles of Nanak took a firm hold on the minds of his followers,[3] and a disciple named Gur Das gives a lofty and imaginative view of the mission of that teacher. He regards him as the successor of Vyasa and Muhammad, and as the destined restorer of purity and sanctity; the regenerator of a world afflicted with the increasing wickedness of men, and with the savage contentions of numerous sects. He declaims against the bigotry of the Muhammadans and their ready resort to violence; he denounces the asceticism of the Hindus, and he urges all men to abandon their evil ways, to live peacefully and virtuously, and to call upon the name of the one true God to whom Nanak had borne witness. Arjun is commonly said to have refused to give these writings of his stern but fervid disciple a place in the *Granth*, perhaps as unsuited to the tenor of Nanak's exhortations, which scarcely condemn or threaten others. The writings of Gur Das are, indeed, rather figurative descriptions of actual affairs than simple hymns in praise

[1] *Dabistan*, ii. 272, 273. The Sikh accounts correspond sufficiently as to the fact of the Guru's arraignment, while they are silent about his treason. They declare the emperor to have been satisfied of his sanctity and innocence (generally), and attribute his continued imprisonment to Chandu's malignity and disobedience of orders. (Cf. Malcolm, *Sketch*, p. 32.) Muhsin Fani also states that a Muhammadan saint of Thanesar was banished by Jahangir for aiding Khusru with his prayers. (*Dabistan*, ii. 273.) The emperor himself simply states (*Memoirs*, p. 88) that at Lahore he impaled seven hundred of the rebels, and on his way to that city he appears (*Memoirs*, p. 81) to have bestowed a present on Shaikh Nizam of Thanesar; but he may have subsequently become aware of his hostility.

[2] Cf. Malcolm, *Sketch*, p. 33; the *Dabistan*, ii. 272—3; and Forster *Travels*, i. 298.

A. D. 1553 seems the most probable date of Arjun's birth, although one account places it as late as A. D. 1565. Similarly 1663 Sambat, or 1015 Hijri, or A. D. 1606, seems the most certain date of his death.

[3] Muhsin Fani observes (*Dabistan*, ii. 270) that in the time of Arjun Sikhs were to be found everywhere throughout the country.

of God; but they deserve attention as expounding Nanak's object of a gradual fusion of Muhammadans and Hindus into common observers of a new and a better creed, and as an almost contemporary instance of the conversion of the noble but obscure idea of an individual into the active principle of a multitude, and of the gradual investiture of a simple fact with the gorgeous mythism of memory and imagination. The unpretending Nanak, the deplorer of human frailty and the lover of his fellow men, becomes, in the mind of Gur Das and of the Sikh people, the first of heavenly powers and emanations, and the proclaimed instrument of God for the redemption of the world; and every hope and feeling of the Indian races is appealed to in proof or in illustration of the reality and the splendour of his mission.[1]

1581-1606.

*The conceptions of Nanak become the moving impulses of a people; and his real history a mythical narrative.*

On the death of Arjun, his brother Pirthi Chand made some attempts to be recognized as Guru, for the only son of the deceased teacher was young, and ecclesiastical usage has everywhere admitted a latitude of succession. But some suspicion of treachery towards Arjun appears to have attached to him, and his nephew soon became the acknowledged leader of the Sikhs, although Pirthi Chand himself continued to retain a few followers, and thus sowed the first fertile seeds of dissent, or elements of dispute or of change, which ever increase with the growth of a sect or a system.[2]

*Har Gobind becomes Guru after a disputed succession.*

[1] The work of Bhai Gur Das Bhulleh, simply known as such, or as the Gyan Ratnavali (Malcolm, *Sketch*, p. 30, note), is much read by the Sikhs. It consists of forty chapters, and is written in different kinds of verse. Some extracts may be seen in Appendix XIX, and in Malcolm, *Sketch*, p. 152, &c. Gur Das was the scribe of Arjun, but his pride and haughtiness are said to have displeased his master, and his compositions were refused a place in the sacred book. Time and reflection—and the Sikhs add a miracle—made him sensible of his failings and inferiority, and Arjun perceiving his contrition, said he would include his writings in the *Granth*. But the final meekness of Gur Das was such, that he himself declared them to be unworthy of such association; whereupon Arjun enjoined that all Sikhs should nevertheless read them. He describes Arjun (Malcolm, *Sketch*, p. 30, note) to have become Guru without any formal investiture or consecration by his father, which may further mark the commanding character of that teacher.

Malcolm (*Sketch*, p. 32) appears to confound Chandu Shah (or Dhani Chand) with Gur Das.

[2] Malcolm, *Sketch*, p. 30, and *Dabistan*, ii. 273. These sectaries were called *Mina*, a term commonly used in the Punjab, and which is expressive of contempt or opprobrium, as stated by Muhsin Fani. The proneness to sectarianism among the first Christians was noticed and deprecated by Paul (1 Cor. i. 10-13.

1606-45.

Chandu
Shah slain
or put to
death.
Har Gobind
arms the
Sikhs and
becomes a
military
leader.

Har Gobind was not, perhaps, more than eleven years
of age at his father's death, but he was moved by his
followers to resent the enmity of Chandu Shah, and
he is represented either to have procured his condemnation by the emperor, or to have slain him by open
force without reference to authority.[1] Whatever may
be the truth about the death of Chandu and the first
years of Har Gobind's ministry, it is certain that, in a
short time, he became a military leader as well as a
spiritual teacher. Nanak had sanctioned or enjoined
secular occupations, Arjun carried the injunction into
practice, and the impulse thus given speedily extended
and became general. The temper and the circumstances of Har Gobind both prompted him to innovation;
he had his father's death to move his feelings, and in
surpassing the example of his parent, even the jealous
dogma of the Hindu law, which allows the most lowly
to arm in self-defence, may not have been without its
influence on a mind acquainted with the precepts of
Manu.[2] Arjun trafficked as a merchant, and played
his part as a priest in affairs of policy; but Har Gobind
grasped a sword, and marched with his devoted followers among the troops of the empire, or boldly led
them to oppose and overcome provincial governors or

The gra-
dual modi-
fication of
Sikhism;

personal enemies. Nanak had himself abstained from
animal food, and the prudent Arjun endeavoured to
add to his saintly merit or influence by a similar moderation; but the adventurous Har Gobind became a
hunter and an eater of flesh, and his disciples imitated
him in these robust practices.[3] The genial disposition
of the martial apostle led him to rejoice in the compa-
nionship of a camp, in the dangers of war, and in the
excitements of the chase, nor is it improbable that the
policy of a temporal chief mingled with the feelings
of an injured son and with the duties of a religious
guide, so as to shape his acts to the ends of his ambition, although *that* may not have aimed at more than
a partial independence under the mild supremacy of
the son of Akbar. Har Gobind appears to have admitted criminals and fugitives among his followers, and
where a principle of antagonism had already arisen,
they may have served him zealously without greatly
reforming the practice of their lives; and, indeed, they
are stated to have believed that the faithful Sikh would

[1] Cf. Forster, *Travels*, i. 298.
[2] For this last supposition, see Malcolm, *Sketch*, pp. 44.,
189. There is perhaps some straining after nicety of reason
in the notion, as Manu's injunction had long become obsolete
in such matters, especially under the Muhammadan supremacy.
[3] The *Dabistan*, ii. 248, and Malcolm Sketch, p. 36.

pass unquestioned into heaven.[1]  He had a stable of 1606-45.
eight hundred horses; three hundred mounted followers were constantly in attendance upon him, and a
guard of sixty matchlock-men secured the safety of
his person, had he ever feared or thought of assassination.[2]  The impulse which he gave to the Sikhs was *and com-*
such as to separate them a long way from all Hindu *plete sepa-*
*ration of the*
sects, and after the time of Har Gobind the 'disciples' *Sikhs from*
were in little danger of relapsing into the limited merit *Hindu dis-*
or utility of monks and mendicants.[3] *senters.*

Har Gobind became a follower of the Emperor *Har Gobind*
Jahangir, and to the end of his life his conduct partook *falls under*
*the dis-*
as much of the military adventurer as of the enthu- *pleasure of*
siastic zealot.  He accompanied the imperial camp to *Jahangir;*
Kashmir, and he is at one time represented as in holy
colloquy with the religious guide of the Mughal, and
at another as involved in difficulties with the emperor
about retaining for himself that money which he should
have disbursed to his troops. He had, too, a multitude
of followers, and his passion for the chase, and fancied
independence as a teacher of men, may have led him
to offend against the sylvan laws of the court.  The
emperor was displeased, the fine imposed on Arjun had
never been paid, and Har Gobind was placed as a pri- *is impri-*
soner on scanty food in the fort of Gwalior.  But the *soned,*
faithful Sikhs continued to revere the mysterious
virtues or the real merits of their leader.  They flocked
to Gwalior, and bowed themselves before the walls
which restrained their persecuted Guru, till at last the *and re-*
prince, moved, perhaps, as much by superstition as by *leased.*
pity, released him from confinement.[4]

On the death of Jahangir in 1628, Har Gobind con- *Jahangir*
tinued in the employ of the Muhammadan Government, *dies 1628,*
*and Har*
but he appears soon to have been led into a course of *Gobind en-*
armed resistance to the imperial officers in the Punjab. *gages in a*
A disciple brought some valuable horses from Turke- *petty war-*
stan; they were seized, as was said, for the emperor, *fare.*

---

[1] The *Dabistan*, ii. 284, 286.    [2] The *Dabistan*, ii. 277.
[3] See Appendix IX.
[4] Cf. the *Dabistan*, ii. 273, 274, and Forster, *Travels*, i.
298, 299.  But the journey to Kashmir, and the controversy
with Muhammadan saints or Mullas, are given on the authority
of the native chronicles. Muhsin Fani represents Har Gobind
to have been imprisoned for twelve years, and Forster attributes his release to the intervention of a Muhammadan leader,
who had originally induced him to submit to the emperor.

The Emperor Jahangir, in his *Memoirs*, gives more than
one instance of his credulity and superstitious reverence for
reputed saints and magicians.  See particularly his *Memoirs*,
p. 129, &c., where his visit to a worker of wonders is narrated.

and one was conferred as a gift on the Kazi or Judge of Lahore. The Guru recovered this one animal by pretending to purchase it; the judge was deceived, and his anger was further roused by the abduction of, the Sikhs say his daughter, the Muhammadans his favourite concubine, who had become enamoured of the Guru. Other things may have rendered Har Gobind obnoxious, and it was resolved to seize him and to disperse his followers. He was assailed by one Mukhlis Khan, but he defeated the imperial troops near Amritsar, fighting, it is idly said, with five thousand men against seven thousand. Afterwards a Sikh, a converted robber, stole two of the emperor's prime horses from Lahore, and the Guru was again attacked by the provincial levies, but the detachment was routed and its leaders slain. Har Gobind now deemed it prudent to retire for a time to the wastes of Bhatinda, south of the Sutlej, where it might be useless or dangerous to follow him; but he watched his opportunity and speedily returned to the Punjab, only, however, to become engaged in fresh contentions. The mother of one Painda Khan, who had subsequently risen to some local eminence, had been the nurse of Har Gobind, and the Guru had ever been liberal to his foster brother. Painda Khan was moved to keep to himself a valuable hawk, belonging to the Guru's eldest son, which had flown to his house by chance: he was taxed with the detention of the bird; he equivocated before the Guru, and became soon after his avowed enemy. The presence of Har Gobind seems ever to have raised a commotion, and Painda Khan was fixed upon as a suitable leader to coerce him. He was attacked; but the warlike apostle slew the friend of his youth with his own hand, and proved again a victor. In this action a soldier rushed furiously upon the Guru; but he warded the blow and laid the man dead at his feet, exclaiming, 'Not so, but thus, is the sword used'; an observation from which the author of the *Dabistan* draws the inference 'that Har Gobind struck not in anger, but deliberately and to give instruction; for the function of a Guru is to teach.'[1]

Har Gobind
retires to
the wastes
of Hariana.

Returns to
the Punjab.

Slays in
fight one
Painda
Khan, his
friend.

Har Gobind appears to have had other difficulties and adventures of a similar kind, and occasionally to have been reduced to great straits; but the Sikhs always rallied round him, his religious reputation in-

[1] See the *Dabistan*, ii. 275; but native accounts, Sikh and Muhammadan, have been mainly followed in narrating the sequence of events. Compare, however, the *Dabistan*, ii. 284. for the seizure of horses belonging to a disciple of the Guru.

creased daily, and immediately before his death he was
visited by a famous saint of the ancient Persian faith.[1]
He died in peace in 1645, at Kiratpur on the Sutlej, a
place bestowed upon him by the hill chief of Kahlur,
and the veneration of his followers took the terrible
form of self-sacrifice. A Rajput convert threw himself
amid the flames of the funeral pyre, and walked several
paces till he died at the feet of his master.   A Jat
disciple did the same, and others, wrought upon by
these examples, were ready to follow, when Har
Rai, the succeeding Guru, interfered and forbade them.[2]

During the ministry of Har Gobind, the Sikhs
increased greatly in numbers, and the fiscal policy of
Arjun, and the armed system of his son, had already
formed them into a kind of separate state within the
empire. The Guru was, perhaps, not unconscious of
his latent influence, when he played with the credulity
or rebuked the vanity of his Muhammadan friend. 'A
Raja of the north', said he, 'has sent an ambassador to
ask about a place called Delhi, and the name and
parentage of its king. I was astonished that he had
not heard of the commander of the faithful, the lord
of the ascendant, Jahangir.'[3] But during his busy life
he never forgot his genuine character, and always
styled himself 'Nanak', in deference to the firm belief
of the Sikhs, that the soul of their great teacher ani-

*Margin notes:* 1606-45. Death of Har Gobind A.D. 1645. Self-sacrifice of disciples on his pyre. The body of Sikhs forms a separate establishment within the empire. Some anecdotes of Har Gobind.

[1] The *Dabistan,* ii. 280.

[2] This is related on the authority of the *Dabistan,* ii. 280,
281. Har Gobind's death is also given agreeably to the text
of the *Dabistan* as having occurred on the 3rd Mohurrum,
1055 Hijri, or on the 19th Feb., A. D. 1645. Malcolm, *Sketch,*
p. 37, and Forster, *Travels,* i. 299, give A. D. 1644 as the exact
cr probable date, obviously from regarding 1701 Sambat (which
Malcolm also quotes) as identical throughout, instead of for
about the first nine months only, with A. D. 1644, an error which
may similarly apply to several conversions of dates in this
history.   The manuscript accounts consulted place the Guru's
death variously in A. D. 1637, 1638, and 1639; but they lean to
the middle term. All, however, must be too early, as Muhsin
Fani (*Dabistan,* ii. 281) says he saw Har Gobind in A. D. 1643.
Har Gobind's birth is placed by the native accounts in the
early part of 1652 Sambat, corresponding with the middle of
A. D. 1595.

[3] See the *Dabistan,* ii. 276, 277. The friend being Muhsin
Fani himself. The story perhaps shows that the Sikh truly
considered the Muhammadan to be a gossiping and somewhat
credulous person. The dates would rather point to Shah
Jahan as the emperor alluded to than Jahangir, as given
parenthetically in the translated text of the *Dabistan.* Jahangir
died in A. D. 1628, and Muhsin Fani's acquaintance with Har
Gobind appears not to have taken place till towards the last
years of the Guru's life, or till after A. D. 1640.

1606-45.

His philo-
sophical
views.

mated each of his successors.[1] So far as Har Gobind knew or thought of philosophy as a science, he fell into the prevailing views of the period: God, he said, is one, and the world is an illusion, an appearance without a reality; or he would adopt the more Pantheistic notion, and regard the universe as composing the one Being. But such reflections did not occupy his mind or engage his heart, and the rebuke of a Brahman that if the world was the same as God, he, the Guru, was one with the ass grazing hard by, provoked a laugh only from the tolerant Har Gobind.[2] That he thought conscience and understanding our only divine guides, may probably be inferred from his reply to one who declared the marriage of a brother with a sister to be forbidden by the Almighty. Had God prohibited it, said he; it would be impossible for man to accomplish it.[3] His contempt for idolatry, and his occasional wide departure from the mild and conciliatory ways of Nanak, may be judged from the following anecdote: One of his followers smote the nose off an image; the several neighbouring chiefs complained to the Guru, who summoned the Sikh to his presence; the culprit denied the act, but said ironically, that if the god bore witness against him, he would die willingly. 'Oh, fool !' said the Rajas, 'how should the god speak?' 'It is plain', answered the Sikh, 'who is the fool; if the god cannot save his own head, how will he avail you?'[4]

Har Rai
succeeds as
Guru, 1645.

Gurdit, the eldest son of Har Gobind, had acquired a high reputation, but he died before his father, leaving two sons, one of whom succeeded to the apostleship.[5]

---

[1] Cf. the *Dabistan*, ii. 281.

[2] Cf. the *Dabistan*, ii. 277, 279, 280.

[3] The *Dabistan*, ii. 280. [Cicero seems to have almost as high an opinion of the functions of conscience. It points out to us, he says, without Divine assistance, the difference between virtue and vice. (*Nature of the Gods*, Francklin's translation, p. 213.)—J.D.C.]

[4] The *Dabistan*, ii. 276.

[5] For some allusions to Gurdit or Gurditta, see the *Dabistan*, ii. 281, 282. His memory is yet fondly preserved, and many anecdotes are current of his personal strength and dexterity. His tomb is at Kiratpur, on the Sutlej, and it has now become a place of pilgrimage. In connexion with his death, a story is told, which at least serves to mark the aversion of the Sikh teachers to claim the obedience of the multitude by an assumption of miraculous powers. Gurditta had raised a slaughtered cow to life, on the prayer, some say, of a poor man the owner, and his father was displeased that he should so endeavour to glorify himself. Gurditta said that as a life was required by God, and as he had withheld one, he would yield his own; whereupon he lay down and gave up his spirit. A similar story is told of Atal Rai, the youngest son of Har Gobind, who had raised the child of a sorrowing widow

Har Rai, the new Guru, remained at Kiratpur for a time, until the march of troops to reduce the Kahlur Raja to obedience induced him to remove eastward into the district of Sarmor.[1]  There he also remained in peace until he was induced, in 1658-9, to take part, of a nature not distinctly laid down, with Dara Shikoh, in the struggle between him and his brothers for the empire of India.  Dara failed, his adherents became rebels, and Har Rai had to surrender his elder son as a hostage. The youth was treated with distinction and soon released, and the favour of the politic Aurangzeb is believed to have roused the jealousy of the father.[2] But the end of Har Rai was at hand, and he died at Kiratpur in the year 1661.[3]  His ministry was mild, yet such as won for him general respect; and many of the 'Bhais', or brethren, the descendants of the chosen companions of a Guru, trace their descent to one disciple or other distinguished by Har Rai.[4]  Some sects, also of Sikhs, who affect more than ordinary precision, had their origin during the peaceful supremacy of this Guru.[5]

*1645-61.*

*Becomes a political partisan.*

*Dies A. D. 1661.*

to life.  His father reproved him, saying Gurus should display their powers in purity of doctrine and holiness of living. The youth, or child as some say, replied as Gurditta had done, and died.  His tomb is in Amritsar, and is likewise a place deemed sacred.

Gurditta's younger son was named Dhirmal, and his descendants are still to be found at Kartarpur, in the Jullundur Doab.

[1] See the *Dabistan*, ii. 282. The place meant seems to be Taksal or Tangsal, near the present British station of Kasauli to the northward of Ambala.

The important work of Muhsin Fani brings down the history of the Sikhs to this point only.

[2] The Guru's leaning towards Dara is given on the authority of native accounts only, it is highly probable in itself, considering Dara's personal character and religious principles.

[3] The authorities mostly agree as to the date of Har Rai's death, but one account places it in A. D. 1662. The Guru's birth is differently placed in 1628 and 1629.

[4] Of these Bhai Bhagtu, the founder of the Kaithal family, useful partisans of Lord Lake, but now reduced to comparative insignificance under the operation of the British system of escheat, was one of the best known.  Dharam Singh, the ancestor of the respectable Bhais of Bagrian, a place between the Sutlej and Jumna, was likewise a follower of Har Rai.

Nowadays the title of Bhai is in practice frequently given to any Sikh of eminent sanctity, whether his ancestor were the companion of a Guru or not.  The Bedis and Sodhis, however, confine themselves to the distinctive names of their tribes, or the Bedis call themselves Baba or father, and the Sodhis sometimes arrogate to themselves the title of Guru, as the representatives of Gobind and Ram Das.

[5] Of these sects the Suthris or the Suthra-Shahis are the best known.  Their founder was one Sucha, a Brahman, and

Har Rai left two sons, Ram Rai, about fifteen, and Har Kishan, about six years of age; but the elder was the offspring of a handmaiden, and not of a wife of equal degree, and Har Rai is further said to have declared the younger his successor. The disputes between the partisans of the two brothers ran high, and the decision was at last referred to the emperor. Aurangzeb .nay have been willing to allow the Sikhs to choose their own Guru, as some accounts have it, but the more cherished tradition relates that, being struck with the child's instant recognition of the empress among a number of ladies similarly arrayed, he declared the right of Har Kishan to be indisputable, and he was accordingly recognized as head of the Sikhs: but before the infant apostle could leave Delhi, he was attacked

with small-pox, and died, in 1664, at that place.[1]

When Har Kishan was about to expire, he is stated to have signified that his successor would be found in the village of Bakala, near Goindwal, on the Beas river. In this village there were many of Har Gobind's relatives, and his son, Tegh Bahadur, after many wanderings and a long sojourn at Patna, on the Ganges, had taken up his residence at the same place. Ram Rai

continued to assert his claims, but he never formed a large party, and Tegh Bahadur was generally acknowledged as the leader of the Sikhs. The son of Har Gobind was rejoiced, but he said he was unworthy to wear his father's sword, and in a short time his supremacy and his life were both endangered by the machinations of Ram Rai, and perhaps by his own suspicious proceedings.[2] He was summoned to Delhi as a pre-

---

they have a *st'han* or *dera*, or place under the walls of the citadel of Lahore. (Cf. Wilson, *As. Res.*, xvii. 236.) The name, or designation, means simply the pure. Another follower of Har Rai was a Khattri trader, named Fattu, who got the title, or adopted the name of Bhai P'hiru, and who, according to the belief of some people, became the real founder of the Udasis.

[1] Cf. Malcolm, *Sketch*, p. 38, and Forster, *Travels*, i. 299. One native account places Har Kishan's death in A. D. 1666, but 1664 seems the preferable date. His birth took place in A. D. 1656.

[2] Cf., generally, Malcolm, *Sketch*, p. 38; Forster, *Travels*, i. 299; and Browne's *India Tracts*, ii. 3, 4. Tegh Bahadur's refusal to wear the sword of his father is given, however, on the authority of manuscript native accounts, which likewise furnish a story, showing the particular act which led to his recognition as Guru. A follower of the sect, named Makhan Sah (or Shah), who was passing through Bakala, wished to make an offering to the Guru of his faith, but he was perplexed by the number of claimants. His offering was to be 525 rupees in all, but the amount was known to him alone, and he silently resolved to

tender to power and as a disturber of the peace, but
he had found a listener in the chief of Jaipur; the
Rajput advocated his cause, saying such holy men
rather went on pilgrimages than aspired to sovereignty,
and he would take him with him on his approaching
march to Bengal.[1] Tegh Bahadur accompanied the
Raja to the eastward. He again resided for a time at   Tegh Baha-
Patna, but afterwards joined the army, to bring suc-   dur retires
cess, says the chronicler, to the expedition against the   for a time
chiefs of Assam. He meditated on the banks of the   to Bengal.
Brahmaputra, and he is stated to have convinced the
heart of the Raja of Kamrup, and to have made him a
believer in his mission.[2]

After a time Tegh Bahadur returned to the Pun-   Tegh Baha-
jab, and bought a piece of ground, now known as   dur re-
Makhowal, on the banks of the Sutlej, and close to   turns to
Kiratpur, the chosen residence of his father. But the   the Punjab.
hostility and the influence of Ram Rai still pursued
him, and the ordinary Sikh accounts represent him, a
pious and innocent instructor of men, as once more
arraigned at Delhi in the character of a criminal; but
the truth seems to be that Tegh Bahadur followed the
example of his father with unequal footsteps, and that,
choosing for his haunts the wastes between Hansi and   Leads a life
the Sutlej, he subsisted himself and his disciples by   of violence;
plunder, in a way, indeed, that rendered him not un-   and is con-
popular with the peasantry. He is further credibly   strained to
represented to have leagued with a Muhammadan   appear at
zealot, named Adam Hafiz, and to have levied contri-   Delhi.
butions upon rich Hindus, while his confederate did
the same upon wealthy Musalmans. They gave a

give a rupee to each, and to hail him as Guru who should (from
intuition) claim the remainder. Tegh Bahadur demanded the
balance, and so on.

[1] Forster and Malcolm, who follow native Indian accounts,
both give Jai Singh, as the name of the prince who countenanced Tegh Bahadur, and who went to Bengal on an expedition;
but one manuscript account refers to Bir Singh as the friendly
chief. Tod (Rajasthan, ii. 355) says Ram Singh, the son of the
first Jai Singh, went to Assam, but he is silent about his actions.
It is not unusual in India to talk of eminent men as living,
although long since dead, as a Sikh will now say he is Ranjit
Singh's soldier; and it is probable that Ram Singh was nominally forgotten, owing to the fame of his father, the 'Mirza
Raja', and even that the Sikh chroniclers of the early part of
the last century confounded the first with the second of the
name, their contemporary Sawai Jai Singh, the noted astrono-
mer and patron of the learned. Malcolm (Sketch, p. 39) who,
perhaps, copies Forster (Travels, i. 299, 300), says Tegh Bahadur was, at this time, imprisoned for two years.

[2] These last two clauses are almost wholly on the authority
of a manuscript Gurmukhi summary of Tegh Bahadur's life.

ready asylum to all fugitives, and their power interfered with the prosperity of the country; the imperial
troops marched against them, and they were at last
defeated and made prisoners. The Muhammadan saint
was banished, but Aurangzeb determined that the Sikh
should be put to death.[1]

When Tegh Bahadur was on his way to Delhi, he
sent for his youthful son, and girding upon him the
sword of Har Gobind, he hailed him as the Guru of
the Sikhs. He told him he was himself being led to
death, he counselled him not to leave his body a prey
to dogs, and he enjoined upon him the necessity and
the merit of revenge. At Delhi, the story continues,
he was summoned before the emperor, and half-insult-
ingly, half-credulously, told to exhibit miracles in proof
of the alleged divinity of his mission. Tegh Bahadur
answered that the duty of man was to pray to the Lord;
yet he would do one thing, he would write a charm,
and the sword should fall harmless on the neck around
which it was hung. He placed it around his own neck
and inclined his head to the executioner: a blow
severed it, to the surprise of a court tinged with superstition, and upon the paper was found written, "Sir Dia,
Sirr na dia,'—he had given his head but not his secret;
his life was gone, but his inspiration or apostolic virtue
still remained in the world. Such is the narrative of
a rude and wonder-loving people; yet it is more certain

that Tegh Bahadur was put to death as a rebel in 1675,
and that the stern and bigoted Aurangzeb had the
body of the unbeliever publicly exposed in the streets
of Delhi.[2]

[1] The author of the *Siar ul Mutakharin* (i. 112, 113) mentions these predatory or insurrectionary proceedings of Tegh
Bahadur, and the ordinary manuscript compilations admit that
such charges were made, but deprecate a belief in them. For
Makhowal the Guru is said to have paid 500 rupees to the Raja
of Kahlur.

[2] All the accounts agree that Tegh Bahadur was ignomi-
niously put to death. The end of the year A.D. 1675—as Maugsar
is sometimes given as the month—seems the most certain date
of his execution. His birth is differently placed in A.D. 1612 and
1621. [It was on this occasion that the famous prophecy on the
ultimate sovereignty of the white race in Delhi is said to have
been uttered (though some modern critics consider it a later
invention). 'I see', he said dauntlessly to the emperor, 'a power
rising in the West which will sweep your empire into the dust.'
His body was quartered and hung before the city gates; but the
Sikhs never forgot his prophetic words. They have accounted
largely for Sikh loyalty to British rule; and they were on the
lips of the gallant Punjab regiments before Delhi in 1857 when
at last they avenged in blood the martyrdom of their leader
(Rawlinson, *Indian Historical Studies*, p. 177, and Macauliffe,

Tegh Bahadur seems to have been of a character hard and moody, and to have wanted both the genial temper of his father and the lofty mind of his son. Yet his own example powerfully aided in making the disciples of Nanak a martial as well as a devotional people. His reverence for the sword of his father, and his repeated injunction that his disciples should obey the bearer of his arrows, show more of the kingly than of the priestly spirit; and, indeed, about this time the Sikh Gurus came to talk of themselves, and to be regarded by their followers as 'Sachcha Padshahs', or as 'veritable kings', meaning, perhaps, that they governed by just influence and not by the force of arms, or that they guided men to salvation, while others controlled their worldly actions. But the expression could be adapted to any circumstances, and its mystic application seems to have preyed upon and perplexed the minds of the Mughal princes, while it illustrates the assertion of an intelligent Muhammadan writer, that Tegh Bahadur, being at the head of many thousand men, aspired to sovereign power.[1]

*1675-1708.*

*Tegh Bahadur's character and influence.*

*The title 'True king' applied to the Gurus*

When Tegh Bahadur was put to death, his only son was in his fifteenth year. The violent end and the last injunction of the martyr Guru made a deep impression on the mind of Gobind, and in brooding over his own loss and the fallen condition of his country, he became the irreconcilable foe of the Muhammadan name, and conceived the noble idea of moulding the vanquished Hindus into a new and aspiring people. But Gobind was yet young, the government was suspicious of his followers, and among the Sikhs themselves there were parties inimical to the son of Tegh Bahadur. His friends were therefore satisfied that the mutilated body of the departed Guru was recovered by the zeal and dexterity of some humble disciples,[2] and that the son

*Gobind succeeds to the apostleship, 1675*

vol. i, Preface, pp. xiii–xviii and vol. iv, 381). The story is related by two Sikh authors.—ED.]

[1] Saiyid Ghulam Husain, the author of the *Siar ul Mutakharin* (i. 112), is the writer referred to.

Browne, in his *India Tracts* ·(ii. 2, 3), and who uses· a compilation, attributes Aurangzeb's resolution to put Tegh Bahadur to death, to his assumption of the character of a 'true king', and to his use of the title of 'Bahadur', expressive of *valour, birth, and dignity.* The Guru, in the narrative referred to, disavows all claim to miraculous powers. For some remarks on the term 'Sachcha Padshah', see Appendix XIII.

Tegh Bahadur's objections to wear his father's sword, and his injunction to reverence. his arrows, that is, to heed what the bearer of them should say, are given on native authority.

? Certain men of the unclean and despised caste of Sweepers were dispatched to Delhi to bring away the dispersed limbs

But lives in ret.rement for several years.

himself performed the funeral rites so essential to the welfare of the living and the peace of the dead. Gobind was placed in retirement amid the lower hills on either side of the Jumna, and for a series of years he occupied himself in hunting the tiger and wild boar, in acquiring a knowledge of the Persian language, and in storing his mind with those ancient legends which describe the mythic glories of his race.[1]

Gobind's character becomes developed.

In this obscurity Gobind remained perhaps twenty years;[2] but his youthful promise gathered round him the disciples of Nanak, he was acknowledged as the head of the Sikhs, the adherents of Ram Rai declined into a sect of dissenters, and the neighbouring chiefs became impressed with a high sense of the Guru s superiority and a vague dread of his ambition. But

Her resolves on modifying the system of Nanak, and on combating the Muhammadan faith and power.

Gobind's views and motives;

Gobind ever dwelt upon the fate of his father, and the oppressive bigotry of Aurangzeb; study and reflection had enlarged his mind, experience of the world had matured his judgement, and, under the mixed impulse of avenging his own and his country's wrongs, he resolved upon awakening his followers to a new life, and upon giving precision and aim to the broad and general institutions of Nanak. In the heart of a powerful empire he set himself to the task of subverting it, and from the midst of social degradation and religious corruption, he called up simplicity of manners, singleness of purpose, and enthusiasm of desire.[3]

of Tegh Bahadur, and it is said they partly owed their success to the exertions of that Makhan Shah, who had been the first to hail the deceased as Guru.

[1] The accounts mostly agree as to this seclusion and occupation of Gobind during his early manhood; but Forster (Travels, i. 301) and also some Gurumukhi accounts, state that he was taken to Patna in the first instance, and that he lived there for some time before he retired to the Srinagar hills.

[2] The period is nowhere definitely given by English or Indian writers; but from a comparison of dates and circumstances, it seems probable that Gobind did not take upon himself a new and special character as a teacher of men until about the thirty-fifth year, or until the year 1695 of Christ. A Sikh author, indeed, quoted by Malcolm (Sketch, p. 186, note) makes Gobind's reforms date from A.D. 1696; but contradictorily one or more of Gobind's sayings or writings are made to date about the same period from the south of India, whither he proceeded only just before his death.

[3] The ordinary accounts represent Gobind, as they represent his grandfather, to have been mainly moved to wage war against Muhammadans by a desire of avenging the death of his parent. It would be unreasonable to deny to Gobind the merit of other motives likewise; but, doubtless, the fierce feeling in question strongly impelled him in the prosecution of his lofty and comprehensive design. The sentiment is indeed common to all times and places : it is as common in the present Indian as

Gobind was equally bold, systematic, and sanguine; but it is not necessary to suppose him either an unscrupulous impostor or a self-deluded enthusiast. He thought that the minds of men might be wrought upon to great purposes, he deplored the corruption of the world, he resented the tyranny which endangered his own life, and he believed the time had come for another teacher to arouse the latent energies of the human will. His memory was filled with the deeds of primaeval seers and heroes; his imagination dwelt on successive dispensations for the instruction of the world, and his mind was not perhaps untinged with a superstitious belief in his own earthly destiny.[1] In an extant and authentic composition,[2] he traces his mortal *and mode* descent to ancient kings, and he extols the piety of his *of present-* immediate parents which rendered them acceptable to *ing his* God. But his own unembodied soul, he says, reposed *mission.* in bliss, wrapt in meditation, and it murmured that it should appear on earth even as the chosen messenger of the Lord—the inheritor of the spirit of Nanak, transmitted to him as one lamp imparts its flame to another.[3]

it was in the ancient European world; and even the 'most Christian of poets' has used it without rebuke to justify the anger of a shade in Hades, and his own sympathy as a mortal man yet dwelling in the world :

'Oh guide beloved !
His violent death yet unavenged, said I,
By any who are partners in his shame
Made him contemptuous; therefore, as I think,
He passed me speechless by, and doing so
Hath made me more compassionate his fate.'
Dante, *Hell*, xxix. Cary's translation.

[1] The persuasion of being moved by something more than the mere human will and reason, does not necessarily imply delusion or insanity in the ordinary sense of the term, and the belief is everywhere traceable as one of the phenomena of 'mind', both in the creation of the poet and in the recorded experience of actual life. Thus the reader will remember the 'unaccustomed spirit' of Romeo, and the 'rebuked genius' of Macbeth, as well as the 'star' of Napoleon; and he will call to mind the 'martial transports' of Ajax infused by Neptune, as well as the 'daemon' of Socrates and the 'inspiration' of the holy men of Israel.

[2] The *Vichitr Natak*, or Wondrous Tale, which forms a portion of the *Daswin Padshah ka Granth*, or Book of the Tenth King.

[3] The reader will contrast what Virgil says of the shade of Rome's 'great emperor', with the devoted Quietism of the Indian reformer :

'There mighty Caesar waits his vital hour,
Impatient for the world, and grasps his promised power.'
*Aeneid*, vi.
He will also call to mind the sentiment of Milton, which the more ardent Gobind has greatly heightened.

The religions
of the world
held to be
corrupt,
and a new
dispensa-
tion to have
been vou-
chsafed.

The legend
regarding
Gobind's
reforma-
tion of the
sect of
Nanak.

He describes how the 'Daityas' had been vainly sent to reprove the wickedness of man, and how the succeeding 'Devtas' procured worship for themselves as Siva and Brahma and Vishnu. How the Siddhs had established diverse sects, how Gorakhnath and Ramanand introduced other modes, and how Muhan mad had required men to repeat his own name when beseeching the Almighty. Each perversely, continues Gobind, established ways of his own and misled the world, but he himself had come to declare a perfect faith, to extend virtue, and to destroy evil. Thus, he said, had he been manifested, but *he* was only as other men, the servant of the supreme, a beholder of the wonders of creation, and whosoever worshipped *him* as the Lord should assuredly burn in everlasting flame. The practices of Muhammadans and Hindus he declared to be of no avail, the reading of Korans and Purans was all in vain, and the votaries of idols and the worshippers of the dead could never attain to bliss. God, he said, was not to be found in texts or in modes, but in humility and sincerity.[1]

Such is Gobind's mode of presenting his mission; but his followers have extended the allegory, and have variously given an earthly close to his celestial vision. He is stated to have performed the most austere devotions at the fane of the goddess-mother of mankind on the summit of the hill named Naina, and to have asked how in the olden times the heroic Arjun transpierced multitudes with an arrow. He was told that by prayer and sacrifice the power had been attained. He invited from Benares a Brahman of great fame for piety and for power over the unseen world. He himself carefully consulted the Vedas, and he called upon his numerous disciples to aid in the awful ceremony he was about to perform. Before all he makes successful trial of the virtue of the magician, and an ample altar is labouriously prepared for the *Hom,* or burnt offering. He is told that the goddess will appear to him, an armed shade, and that, undaunted, he should hail her and ask for fortune. The Guru, terror-struck, could but advance his sword, as if in salutation to the

'He asked, but all the heavenly quire stood mute.
And silence was in heaven: on man's behalf,
Patron or intercessor none appeared.'
Until Christ himself said—
'Account me man, I for his sake will leave
Thy bosom, and this glory next to thee
Freely put off.'—*Paradise Lost,* iii.

[1] Cf. the extracts given by Malcolm from the *Vichitr Natak* (*Sketch,* p. 173, &c.)

dread appearance. The goddess touched it in token of 1675-1708.
acceptance, and a divine weapon, an axe of iron, was
seen amid the flames. The sign was declared to be
propitious, but fear had rendered the sacrifice incomplete, and Gobind must die himself, or devote to death
one dear to him, to ensure the triumph of his faith.
The Guru smiled sadly; he said *he* had yet much to
accomplish in this world. and that his father's spirit
was still unappeased. He looked towards his children,
but maternal affection withdrew them: twenty-five
disciples then sprang forward and declared their readiness to perish; one was gladdened by being chosen.
and the fates were satisfied.[1]

Gobind is next represented to have again assem-  The prin-
bled his followers, and made known to them the great  ciples in-
objects of his mission. A new faith had been declared,  culcated by
and henceforth the 'Khalsa', the saved or liberated,[2]  Gobind.
should alone prevail. God must be worshipped in  The 'Khalsa'
truthfulness and sincerity, but no material resemblance  Old forms
must degrade the Omnipotent; the Lord could only be  useless.
beheld by the eye of faith in the general body of the  God is one.
Khalsa.[3] All, he said, must become as one; the lowest  All men are
were equal with the hignest; caste must be forgotten;  equal.
they must accept the 'Pahul' or initiation from him,[4]  Idolatry to
and the four races must eat as one out of one vessel.  be contem-
The Turks must be destroyed, and the graves of those  ned, and
called saints neglected. The ways of the Hindus must

---

[1] This legend is given with several variations, and one may
be seen in Malcolm (*Sketch*, p. 53, note) and another in Macgregor's *History of the Sikhs* (i. 71). Perhaps the true origin of
the myth is to be found in Gobind's reputed vision during sleep
of the great goddess. (Malcolm, p. 187.) The occurrence is
placed in the year A.D. 1696. (Malcolm, *Sketch*, p. 86.)

[2] Khalsa, or Khalisa, is of Arabic derivation, and has such
original or secondary meanings as pure, special, free, &c. It is
commonly used in India to denote the immediate territories of
any chief or state as distinguished from the lands of tributaries
and feudal followers. Khalsa can thus be held either to denote
the *kingdom of Gobind, or that the Sikhs are the chosen people.*

[3] This assurance is given in the Rehet Nameh, or Rule of
Life of Gobind, which, however, is not included in the *Granth*.
In the same composition he says, or is held to have said, that
the believer who wishes to see the Guru shall behold him in
the Khalsa.

Those who object to such similitudes, or to such struggles
of the mind after precision, should remember that Abelard
likened the Trinity to a syllogism with its three terms; and that
Wallis, with admitted orthodoxy, compared the Godhead to a
mathematical cube with its three dimensions. (Bayle's *Dictionary*, art. 'Abelard'.)

[4] Pahul (pronounced nearly as *Powl*), means literally a
gate, a door, and thence initiation. The word may have the
same origin as the Greek word.

be abandoned, their temples viewed as holy and their
rivers looked upon as sacred; the Brahman's thread
must be broken; by means of the Khalsa alone could
salvation be attained. They must surrender themselves wholly to their faith and to him their guide.
Their words must be 'Kritnash, Kulnash, Dharmnash,
Karmnash,' the forsaking of occupation and family, of
belief and ceremonies. 'Do thus,' said Gobind, 'and the
world is yours.' [1] Many Brahman and Kshattriya followers murmured, but the contemned races rejoiced;
they reminded Gobind of their devotion and services,
and asked that *they* also should be allowed to bathe
in the sacred pool, and offer up prayers in the temple
of Amritsar. The murmurings of the twice-born increased, and many took their departure, but Gobind
exclaimed that the lowly should be raised, and that
hereafter the despised should dwell next to himself.[2]

[1] The text gives the substance and usually the very words
of the numerous accounts to the same purport. (Cf. also Malcolm, *Sketch*, pp. 148, 151.)

[2] Churhas, or men of the Sweeper caste, brought away the
remains of Tegh Bahadur from Delhi, as has been mentioned
(*ante*, pp. 59-60, note 2). Many of that despised, but no oppressed race, have adopted the Sikh faith in the Punjab, and they
are commonly known as Ranghrheta Sikhs. *Ranghar* is a term
applied to the Rajputs about Delhi who have become Muhammadans; but in Malwa the predatory Hindu Rajputs are similarly styled, perhaps from *Rank*, a poor man, in opposition to *Rana*,
one of high degree. Ranghrheta seems thus rather a diminutive
of Rangghar than a derivative of *rang* (colour) as commonly
understood. The Ranghrheta Sikhs are sometimes styled
*Mazhabi*, or of the (Muhammadan) faith, from the circumstance
that the converts from Islam are so called, and that many
Sweepers throughout India have become Muhammadans.

[These Mazhabis in the past have proved themselves, and
are at the present time, extremely good soldiers. The Pioneer
regiments—23rd, 32nd, 34th—into which they are recruited
have a proud record of service in many campaigns. Mr. Candler,
in an article in *Blackwood's Magazine*, September 1909,
observes: 'The general reluctance of the low-caste Hindu to
elevate himself by becoming a Sikh may perhaps be explained
by the historical exception of the Mazhabis. These Sikhs, the
descendants of converts from the despised Sweeper caste, were
welcomed by the Khalsa at a time when they were engaged
in a desperate struggle with the forces of Islam. But when the
Sikhs dominated the Punjab they found that the equality their
religion promised them existed in theory rather than in fact.
They occupied much the same position among the Jat and
Khalsa descended Sikhs as their ancestors, the Sweepers, enjoyed among Hindus They were debarred from all privileges
and were, at one time excluded from the army.'

According to the census Report of 1912 the Mazhabi population now numbers 21,691. 'They have taken to husbandry
and have been declared as a separate agricultural tribe in the
districts of Gujranwala and Lyallpur.' (*Census Report*, 1912.)
—Ed.]

Gobind then poured water into a vessel and stirred it with the sacrificial axe, or with the sword rendered divine by the touch of the goddess. His wife passed by, as it were by chance, bearing confections of five kinds: he hailed the omen as propitious, for the coming of woman denoted an offspring to the Khalsa numerous as the leaves of the forest. He mingled the sugars with the water, and then sprinkled a portion of it upon five faithful disciples, a Brahman, a Kshattriya, and three Sudras. He hailed them as 'Singhs', and declared them to be the Khalsa. He himself received from them the 'Pahul' of his faith, and became Gobind Singh, saying, that hereafter, whenever five Sikhs should be assembled together, there he also would be present.[1]

Gobind thus abolished social distinctions,[2] and took away from his followers each ancient solace of superstition; but he felt that he must engage the heart as well as satisfy the reason, and that he must give the Sikhs some common bonds of union which should remind the weak of their new life, and add fervour to

In allusion to the design of inspiring the Hindus with a new life, Gobind is reported to have said that he 'would teach the sparrow to strike the eagle.' (See Malcolm, *Sketch*, p. 74, where it is used with reference to Aurangzeb, but the saying is attributed to Gobind under various circumstances by different authors.)

[1] The Brahman novitiate is stated to have been an inhabitant of the Deccan, and the Kshattriya of the Punjab; one Sudra, a Jhinwar (Kahar), was of Jaganath, the second, a Jat, was of Hastinapur, and the third, a Chhimba or cloth printer, was of Dwarka in Gujrat.

For the declaration about five Sikhs forming a congregation, or about the assembly of five men ensuring the presence or the grace of the Guru, cf. Malcolm, *Sketch*, p. 186. [Five is also the number of the necessary attributes of the true follower of Gobind Singh, viz. Kes, Khanda, Kangha, Kara, Kach—long hair, dagger, comb, bangle, breeches.—ED.]

Gobind had originally the cognomen, or titular name, of 'Rai', one in common use among Hindus, and largely adopted under the variation of 'Rao' by the military Marathas; but on declaring the comprehensive nature of his reform, the Guru adopted for himself and followers the distinctive appellation of 'Singh', meaning literally a lion, and metaphorically a champion or warrior. It is the most common of the distinctive names in use among Rajputs, and it is now the invariable termination of every proper name among the disciples of Gobind. It is sometimes used alone, as Khan is used among the Muhammadans, to denote pre-eminence. Thus Sikh chiefs would talk of Ranjit Singh, as ordinary Sikhs will talk of their own immediate leaders, as the 'Singh Sahib', almost equivalent to 'Sir King', or 'Sir Knight', in English. Strangers likewise often address any Sikh respectfully as 'Singhji'.

[2] See Appendix X.

1675-1708.

Lustration
by water.
Reverence
for Nanak.

The excla-
mation,
Hail Guru !

Unshorn
locks; the
title of
Singh;
and devo-
tion to
arms.

the devotion of the sincere. They should have one form of initiation, he said, the sprinkling of water by five of the faithful;[1] they should worship the One Invisible God; they should honour the memory of Nanak and of his transanimate successors;[2] their watchword should be, Hail Guru![3] but they should revere and bow to nought visible save the *Granth*, the book of their belief.[4] They should bathe, from time to time, in the pool of Amritsar; their locks should remain unshorn; they should all name themselves 'Singhs', or soldiers, and of material things they should devote their finite energies to steel alone.[5] Arms should dignify their person; they should be ever waging war, and great would be his merit who fought in the van, who slew an enemy, and who despaired not although overcome. He cut off the three sects of dissenters from all intercourse: the Dhirmalis, who had laboured to destroy Arjun; the Ram Rais, who had compassed the death of his father; and the Masandis, who had resisted his own authority. He denounced the 'shaven', meaning, perhaps, all Muhammadans and Hindus; and for no reason which bears clearly on the worldly scope of his mission, he held up to reprobation those slaves of a perverse custom, who impiously take the lives of their infant daughters.[6]

Gobind had achieved one victory, he had made himself master of the imagination of his followers; but a more laborious task remained, the destruction of the empire of unbelieving oppressors. He had established the Khalsa, the theocracy of Singhs, in the midst of Hindu delusion and Muhammadan error; he had confounded Pirs and Mullas, Sadhs and Pandits, but he had yet to vanquish the armies of a great emperor, and to subdue the multitudes whose faith he impugned. The design of Gobind may seem wild and senseless to those accustomed to consider the firm sway and regular policy of ancient Rome, and who daily witness the power and resources of the well-ordered governments

[1] See Appendix XI.
[2] The use of the word 'transanimate' may perhaps be allowed. The Sikh belief in the descent of the individual spirit of Nanak upon each of his successors, is compared by Gobind in the *Vichitr Natak* to the imparting of flame from one lamp to another.
[3] See Appendix XII.
[4] Obeisance to the *Granth* alone is inculcated in the Rahat Nama or Rule of Life of Gobind, and he endeavoured to guard against being himself made an object of future idolatry, by denouncing (in the *Vichitr Natak*) all who should regard him as a god.
[5] See Appendix XIII.          [6] See Appendix XIV.

of modern Europe.  But the extensive empires of the 1675-1708.
East, as of semi-barbarism in the West, have never The cha-
been based on the sober convictions of a numerous racter and
people; they have been mere dynasties of single tribes, condition
rendered triumphant by the rapid development of of the
warlike energy, and by the comprehensive genius of Mughal em-
eminent leaders.  Race has succeeded race in dominion, Gobind re-
and what Cyrus did with his Persians and Charle- solved to
magne with his Franks, Babar began and Akbar com- assail it.
pleted with a few Tartars their personal followers.  The
Mughals had even a less firm hold of empire than the
Achaemenides or the Carlovingians; the devoted clans-
men of Babar were not numerous, his son was driven
from his throne, and Akbar became the master of Akbar.
India as much by political sagacity, and the generous
sympathy of his nature, as by military enterprise and
the courage of his partisans.  He perceived the want
of the times, and his commanding genius enabled him
to reconcile the conflicting interests and prejudices of
Muhammadans and Hindus, of Rajputs, Turks, and
Pathans.  At the end of fifty years he left his heir a
broad and well-regulated dominion; yet one son of
Jahangir contested the empire with his father, and
Shah Jahan first saw his children waging war with one
another for the possession of the crown which he himself still wore, and at length became the prisoner of
the ablest and most successful of the combatants.
Aurangzeb ever feared the influence of his own exam- Aurangzeb.
ple: his temper was cold; his policy towards Muhammadans was one of suspicion, while his bigotry and
persecutions rendered him hateful to his Hindu subjects.  In his old age his wearied spirit could find no
solace; no tribe of brave and confiding men gathered
round him: yet his vigorous intellect kept *him* an
emperor to the last, and the hollowness of his sway
was not apparent to the careless observer until he was
laid in his grave.  The empire of the Mughals wanted
political fusion, and its fair degree of administrative
order and subordination was vitiated by the doubt
which hung about the succession.[1]  It comprised a
number of petty states which rendered an unwilling

[1] Notwithstanding this defect, the English themselves have
yet to do much before they can establish a system which shall
last so long and work so well as Akbar's organization of Par-
gana Chaudris and Qanungos, who may be likened to hereditary
county sheriffs, and registrars of landed property and holdings.
The objectionable hereditary law was modified in practice by
the adoption of the most able or the most upright as the representative of the family.  [A somewhat pessimistic statement
viewing the way in which modern administrators have dealt
with the land questions.—ED.]

1675-1708.

obedience to the sovereign power; it was also studded
over with feudal retainers, and all these hereditary
princes and mercenary 'Jagirdars' were ever ready to
resist, or to pervert, the measures of the central government. They considered then, as they do now, that a
monarch exercised sway for his own interests only,
without reference to the general welfare of the country; no public opinion of an intelligent people systematically governed controlled them, and applause always
awaited the successful aspirant to power. Akbar did
something to remove this antagonism between the
rulers and the ruled, but his successors were less wise
than himself, and religious discontent was soon added
to the love of political independence. The southern
portions of India, too, were at this time recent conquests, and Aurangzeb had been long absent,[1] hopelessly endeavouring to consolidate his sway in that
distant quarter. The Himalayas had scarcely been
penetrated by the Mughals, except in the direction of
Kashmir, and rebellion might rear its head almost
unheeded amid their wild recesses. Lastly, during this

Sivaji the
Maratha.

period, Sivaji had roused the slumbering spirit of the
Maratha tribes. He had converted rude herdsmen into
successful soldiers, and had become a territorial chief

Guru
Gobind.

in the very neighbourhood of the emperor. Gobind
added religious fervour to warlike temper, and his
design of founding a kingdom of Jat upon the waning
glories of Aurangzeb's dominion does not appear to
have been idly conceived or rashly undertaken.

Gobind's
plans of
active op-
position,
(about)
1695.

Yet it is not easy to place the actions of Gobind
in due order, or to understand the particular object of
each of his proceedings. He is stated by a credible
Muhammadan author to have organized his followers
into troops and bands, and to have placed them under
the command of trustworthy disciples.[2] He appears
to have entertained a body of Pathans, who are everywhere the soldiers of fortune,[3] and it is certain that
he established two or three forts along the skirts of the

His mili-
tary posts;

hills between the Sutlej and Jumna. He had a post at
Paunta in the Kirda vale near Nahan, a place long
afterwards the scene of a severe struggle between the

[1 A reference to the conquest by Aurangzeb of the kingdom of Bijapur (1686) and Golconda (1687). From 1681 to
his death in 1707 the Emperor was almost incessantly engaged
in a series of campaigns against these kingdoms and the rising
power of the Marathas.—Ed.]

[2] *Siar ul Mutakharin*, i. 113.

[3] The Maratha histories show that Sivaji likewise hired
bands of Pathans, who had lost service in the declining kingdom
of Bijapur. (Grant Duff, *Hist. of the Marathas*, i. 165.)

Gurkhas and the English. He had likewise a retreat at Anandpur-Makhowal, which had been established by his father,[1] and a third at Chamkaur, fairly in the plains and lower down the Sutlej than the chosen haunt of Tegh Bahadur. He had thus got strongholds which secured him against any attempts of his hill neighbours, and he would next seem to have endeavoured to mix himself up with the affairs of these half-independent chiefs, and to obtain a commanding influence over them, so as by degrees to establish a virtual principality amid mountain fastnesses to serve as the basis of his operations against the Mughal government. As a religious teacher he drew contributions and procured followers from all parts of India, but as a leader he perceived the necessity of a military pivot, and as a rebel he was not insensible to the value of a secure retreat. 1675-1708. *and leagues with the chiefs of the Lower Himalayas.*

*His influence as a religious teacher.*

Gobind has himself described the several actions in which he was engaged, either as a principal or as an ally.[2] His pictures are animated; they are of some value as historical records, and their sequence seems more probable than that of any other narrative. His first contest was with his old friend the chief of Nahan, aided by the Raja of Hindur, to whom he had given offence, and by the mercenary Pathans in his own service, who claimed arrears of pay, and who may have hoped to satisfy all demands by the destruction of Gobind and the plunder of his establishments. But the Guru was victorious, some of the Pathan leaders fell, and Gobind slew the young warrior, Hari Chand of Nalagarh, with his own hand. The Guru nevertheless deemed it prudent to move to the Sutlej; he strengthened Anandpur, and became the ally of Bhim Chand of Kuhlur, who was in resistance to the imperial authorities of Kot Kangra. The Muhammadan commander was joined by various hill chiefs, but in the end he was routed, and Bhim Chand's rebellion

*Gobind quarrels with the Rajas of Nahan and Nalagarh.*

*Aids the Raja of Kuhlur and other chiefs against the imperial forces.*

---

[1] Anandpur is situated close to Makhowal. The first name was given by Gobind to his own particular residence at Makhowal, as distinguished from the abode of his father, and it signified the place of happiness. A knoll, with a seat upon it, is here pointed out, whence it is said Gobind was wont to discharge an arrow a coss and a quarter—about a mile and two-thirds English, the Punjabi coss being small.

[2] Namely, in the *Vichitr Natak*, already quoted as a portion of the Second *Granth*. The *Guru Bilas*, by Sukha Singh, corroborates Gobind's account, and adds many details. Malcolm (*Sketch*, p. 58, &c.) may be referred to for translations of some portions of the *Vichitr Natak* bearing on the period, but Malcolm's own general narrative of the events is obviously contradictory and inaccurate.

seemed justified by success. A period of rest ensued, during which, says Gobind, he punished such of his followers as were lukewarm or disorderly. But the aid which he rendered to the chief of Kuhlur was not forgotten, and a body of Muhammadan troops made an unsuccessful attack upon his position. Again an imperial commander took the field, partly to coerce Gobind, and partly to reduce the hill rajas, who, profiting by the example of Bhim Chand, had refused to pay their usual tribute. A desultory warfare ensued; some attempts at accommodation were made by the hill chiefs but these were broken off, and the expedition ended in the rout of the Muhammadans.

Gobind's proceedings excite the suspicions of the hill chiefs, and cause the emperor some anxiety, (about) 1701.

The success of Gobind, for all was attributed to him, caused the Muhammadans some anxiety, and his designs appear likewise to have alarmed the hill chiefs, for they loudly claimed the imperial aid against one who announced himself as the True King. Aurangzeb directed the governors of Lahore and Sirhind to march against the Guru, and it was rumoured that the emperor's son, Bahadur Shah, would himself take the field in their support.[1] Gobind was surrounded at Anandpur by the forces of the empire. His own resolution

Gobind reduced to straits at Anandpur.

was equal to any emergency, but numbers of his followers deserted him. He cursed them in this world and in the world to come, and others who wavered he caused to renounce their faith, and then dismissed them with ignominy. But his difficulties increased, desertions continued to take place, and at last he found himself at the head of no more than forty devoted followers.

His children escape; but are subsequently put to death.

His mother, his wives, and his two youngest children effected their escape to Sirhind, but the boys were there betrayed to the Muhammadans and put to death.[2] The faithful forty said they were ready to die with their priest and king, and they prayed him to recall his curse upon their weaker-hearted brethren, and to restore to them the hope of salvation. Gobind said that

[1] Malcolm (Sketch, p. 60, note) says that this allusion would place the warfare in A. D. 1701, as Bahadur Shah was at that time sent from the Deccan towards Kabul. Some Sikh traditions, indeed, represent Gobind as having gained the goodwill of, or as they put it, as having shown favour to, Bahadur Shah; and Gobind himself, in the Vichitr Natak, says that a son of the emperor came to suppress the disturbances, but no name is given. Neither does Mr. Elphinstone (History, ii. 545) specify Bahadur Shah; and, indeed, he merely seems to conjecture that a prince of the blood, who was sent to put down disturbances near Multan, was really employed against the Sikhs near Sirhind.

[2] The most detailed account of this murder of Gobind's children is given in Browne's India Tracts, ii. 6, 7.

his wrath would not endure. But he still clung to temporal success; the fort of Chamkaur remained in his
possession, and he fled during the night and reached
the place in safety.

*1675-1708.*

He himself
flies to
Chamkaur.

At Chamkaur Gobind was again besieged.[1] He was
called upon to surrender his person and to renounce
his faith, but Ajit Singh, his son, indignantly silenced
the bearer of the message. The troops pressed upon
the Sikhs; the Guru was himself everywhere present,
but his two surviving sons fell before his eyes, and his
little band was nearly destroyed. He at last resolved
upon escape, and taking advantage of a dark night, he
treaded his way to the outskirts of the camp, but
there he was recognized and stopped by two Pathans.
These men, it is said, had in former times received
kindness at the hands of the Guru, and they now assisted him in reaching the town of Bahlolpur, where
he trusted his person to a third follower of Islam, one
Pir Muhammad, with whom it is further said the Guru
had once studied the Koran. Here he ate food from
Muhammadans, and declared that such might be done
by Sikhs under pressing circumstances. He further
disguised himself in the blue dress of a Musalman
Dervish, and speedily reached the wastes of Bhatinda.
His disciples again rallied round him, and he succeeded
in repulsing his pursuers at a place since called
'Muktsar', or the Pool of Salvation. He continued his
flight to Dam-Dama, or the Breathing Place, half way
between Hansi and Ferozepore; the imperial authorities thought his strength sufficiently broken, and they
did not follow him further into a parched and barren
country.

Gobind
escapes
from Cham-
kaur,
1705-6.

Success-
fully resists
his pursuers
at Muktsar;

and rests
at Dam-
Dama, near
Bhatinda.

At Dam-Dama Gobind remained for some time
and he occupied himself in composing the supplemental
*Granth*, 'the Book of the Tenth King', to rouse the
energies and sustain the hopes of the faithful. This
comprises the *Vichitr Natak*, or 'Wondrous Tale', the
only historical portion of either *Granth*, and which he
concludes by a hymn in praise of God, who had ever
assisted him. He would, he says, make known in another book the things which he had himself accomplished, the glories of the Lord which he had witnessed,

Gobind
composes
the **Vichitr
Natak.**

At Chamkaur. in one of the towers of the small brick
fort, is still shown the tomb of a distinguished warrior, a Sikh
of the Sweeper caste, named Jiwan Singh, who fell during the
siege. The bastion itself is known as that of the Martyr. A
temple now stands where Ajit Singh and Jujhar Singh, the
eldest sons of Gobind, are reputed to have fallen.
Gobind's defeat and flight are placed by the Sikhs in A. D.
1705-6.

Summoned
by Aurang-
zeb to his
presence.

Replies to
the em-
peror in a
denuncia-
tory strain.

Aurangzeb
dies, and
Bahadur
Shah suc-
ceeds, A. D.
1707.

Gobind
proceeds to
the south
of India.

Enters the
imperial
service.

and his recollections or visions of his antecedent existence. All he had done, he said, had been done with
the aid of the Almighty; and to 'Loh', or the mysterious virtue of iron, he attributed his preservation.
While thus living in retirement, messengers arrived
to summon him to the emperor's presence, but Gobind
replied to Aurangzeb in a series of parables admonitory
of kings, partly in which, and partly in a letter which
accompanied them, he remonstrates rather than humbles himself. He denounces the wrath of God upon
the monarch, rather than deprecates the imperial anger
against himself; he tells the emperor that he puts no
trust in him, and that the 'Khalsa' will avenge him. He
refers to Nanak's religious reform, and he briefly
alludes to the death of Arjun and of Tegh Bahadur.
He describes his own wrongs and his childless condition. He was, as one without earthly link, patiently
awaiting death, and fearing none but the sole Emperor, the King of Kings. Nor, said he, are the prayers
of the poor ineffectual; and on the day of reckoning it
would be seen how the emperor would justify his
manifold cruelties and oppressions. The Guru was
again desired to repair to Aurangzeb's presence, and
he really appears to have proceeded to the south some
time before the aged monarch was removed by death.[1]

Aurangzeb died in the beginning of 1707, and his
eldest son, Bahadur Shah, hastened from Kabul to
secure the succession. He vanquished and slew one
brother near Agra, and, marching to the south, he
defeated a second, Kambakhsh, who died of his
wounds. While engaged in this last campaign, Bahadur
Shah summoned Gobind to his camp. The Guru went;
he was treated with respect, and he received a military
command in the valley of the Godavari. The emperor
perhaps thought that the leader of insurrectionary
Jats might be usefully employed in opposing rebellious
Marathas, and Gobind perhaps saw in the imperial
service a ready way of disarming suspicion and of
reorganizing his followers.[2] At Dam-Dama he had

---

[1] In this narrative of Gobind's warlike actions, reference
has been mainly had to the *Vichitr Natak* of the Guru, to the
*Guru Bilas* of Sukha Singh, and to the ordinary modern compilations in Persian and Gurmukhi; transcripts, imperfect
apparently, of some of which latter have been put into English
by Dr. Macgregor (*History of the Sikhs*, pp. 79-99).

[2] The Sikh writers seem unanimous in giving to their great
teacher a military command in the Deccan, while some recent
Muhammadan compilers assert that he died at Patna. But the
liberal conduct of Bahadur Shah is confirmed by the contemporary historian, Khafi Khan, who states that he received rank
in the Mughal army (see Elphinstone, *Hist. of India*, ii. 566

again denounced evil upon all who should thenceforward desert him; in the south he selected the daring
Banda as an instrument, and the Sikhs speedily reap-
peared in overwhelming force upon the banks of the
Sutlej. But Gobind's race was run, and he was not
himself fated to achieve aught more in person. He had
engaged the services of an Afghan, half-adventurer,
half-merchant, and he had procured from him a considerable number of horses.[1] The merchant, or servant, pleaded his own necessities, and urged the payment of large sums due to him. Impatient with delay,
he used an angry gesture, and his mutterings of
violence provoked Gobind to strike him dead. The
body of the slain Pathan was removed and buried, and
his family seemed reconciled to the fate of its head.
But his sons nursed their revenge, and awaited an
opportunity of fulfilling it. They succeeded in stealing Gobind
upon the Guru's retirement, and stabbed him mortally wounded by
when asleep or unguarded. Gobind sprang up and the assassins.
assassins were seized; but a sardonic smile played upon
their features, and they justified their act of retribution. The Guru heard: he remembered the fate of
their father, and he perhaps called to mind his own
unavenged parent. He said to the youths that they had
done well, and he directed that they should be released
uninjured.[2] The expiring Guru was childless, and the

note), and it is in a degree corroborated by the undoubted fact
of the Guru's death on the banks of the Godavari. The traditions
preserved at Nader give Kartik, 1765 (Sambat), or towards the
end of A. D. 1703, as the date of Gobind's arrival at that place.

[1] It would be curious to trace how far India was colonized
in the intervals of great invasions by petty Afghan and Turkoman leaders, who defrayed their first or occasional expenses by
the sale of horses. Tradition represents that both the destroyer
of Manikiala in the Punjab, and the founder of Bhatnair in
Hariana, were emigrants so circumstanced; and Amir Khan,
the recent Indian adventurer, was similarly reduced to sell his
steeds for food. (*Memoirs of Amir Khan*, p. 16.)

[2] All the common accounts narrate the death of Gobind
as given in the text, but with slight differences of detail, while
some add that the widow of the slain Pathan continually urged
her sons to seek revenge. Many accounts, and especially those
by Muhammadans, likewise represent Gobind to have become
deranged in his mind, and a story told by some Sikh writers
gives a degree of countenance to such a belief. They say that
the heart of the Guru inclined towards the youths whose father
he had slain, that he was wont to play simple games of skill
with them, and that he took opportunities of inculcating upon
them the merit of revenge, as if he was himself weary of life,
and wished to fall by their hands. The *Siar ul Mutakharin*
(i. 114) simply says that Gobind died of grief on account of
the loss of his children. (Cf. Malcolm, *Sketch*, p. 70, &c.: and
Elphinstone, *History*, ii. 564.) The accounts now furnished by

1675-1708.

and dies,
A. D. 1708,
declaring
his mission
to be ful-
filled, and
the Khalsa
to be com-
mitted to
God.

Gobind's
end un-
timely, but
labours not
fruitless.

assembled disciples asked in sorrow who should inspire them with truth and lead them to victory when he was no more. Gobind bade them be of good cheer; the appointed Ten had indeed fulfilled their mission, but he was about to deliver the Khalsa to God, the never-dying. 'He who wishes to behold the Guru, let him search the *Granth* of Nanak. The Guru will dwell with the Khalsa; be firm and be faithful: wherever five Sikhs are gathered together there will I also be present.' [1]

Gobind was killed in 1708, at Nader, on the banks of the Godavari.[2] He was in his forty-eighth year, and if it be thought by any that his obscure end belied the promise of his whole life, it should be remembered that—

> 'The hand of man
> Is but a tardy servant of the brain,
> And follows, with its leaden diligence,
> The fiery steps of fancy';[3]

the priests of the temple at Nader, represent the *one* assassin of the Guru to have been the grandson of the Painda Khan, slain by Har Gobind, and they do not give him any further cause of quarrel with Gobind himself.

[1] Such is the usual account given of the Guru's dying injunctions; and the belief that Gobind consummated the mission or dispensation of Nanak seems to have been agreeable to the feelings of the times, while it now forms a main article of faith. The mother, and one wife of Gobind, are represented to have survived him some years; but each, when dying, declared the Guruship to rest in the general body of the Khalsa, and not in any one mortal; and hence the Sikhs do not give such a designation even to the most revered of their holy men, their highest religious title being 'Bhai', literally 'brother', but corresponding in significance with the English term 'elder'.

[2] Gobind is stated to have been born in the month of Poh, 1718 (Sambat), which may be the end of A. D. 1661 or beginning of 1662, and all accounts agree in placing his death about the middle of 1765 (Sambat), or towards the end of A. D. 1708.

At Nader there is a large religious establishment, partly supported by the produce of landed estates, partly by voluntary contributions, and partly by sums levied annually, agreeably to the mode organized by Arjun. The principal of the establishment dispatches a person to show his requisition to the faithful, and all give according to their means. Thus the common horsemen in the employ of Bhopal give a rupee and a quarter each a year, besides offerings on occasions of pilgrimage.

Ranjit Singh sent considerable sums to Nader, but the buildings commenced with the means which he provided have not been completed.

Nader is also called Apchalanagar, and in Southern and Central India it is termed pre-eminently 'the Gurudwara', that is, 'the house of the Gurus.'

[3] *Sir Marmaduke Maxwell,* a dramatic poem, Act iv. scene 6.

that when Muhammad was a fugitive from Mecca, 'the
lance of an Arab might have changed the history of
the world'; [1] and that the Achilles of poetry, the
reflexion of truth, left Troy untaken. The lord of the
Myrmidons, destined to a short life and immortal glory,
met an end almost as base as that which he dreaded
when struggling with Simois and Scamander; and the
heroic Richard, of eastern and western fame, whose
whole soul was bent upon the deliverance of Jerusalem,
veiled his face in shame and sorrow that God's holy
city should be left in the possession of infidels: he would
not behold that which he could not redeem, and he
descended from the Mount to retire to captivity and a
premature grave. [2] Success is thus not always the
measure of greatness. The last apostle of the Sikhs
did not live to see his own ends accomplished, but he
effectually roused the dormant energies of a vanqui- A new
shed people, and filled them with a lofty although character
fitful longing for social freedom and national ascen- impressed
dancy, the proper adjuncts of that purity of worship upon the
which had been preached by Nanak. Gobind saw what reformed
was yet vital, and he relumed it with Promethean fire. Hindus;
A living spirit possesses the whole Sikh people, and the
impress of Gobind has not only elevated and altered
the constitution of their minds, but has operated materially and given amplitude to their physical frames.
The features and external form of a whole people
have been modified, and a Sikh chief is not more dis-
tinguishable by his stately person and free and manly
bearing, than a minister of his faith is by a lofty
thoughtfulness of look, which marks the fervour of his
soul, and his persuasion of the near presence of the
Divinity. [3] Notwithstanding these changes it has

---

[1] Gibbon, *Decline and Fall of the Roman Empire*, ix. 285.

[2] For this story of the lion-like king, see Gibbon (*Decline
and Fall*, xi. 143). See also Turner's comparison of the characters of Achilles and Richard (*History of England*, p. 300), and
Hallam's assent to its superior justness relatively to his own
parallel of the Cid and the English hero (*Middle Ages*, iii. 482).

[3] This physical change has been noticed by Sir Alexander
Burnes (*Travels*, i. 285, and ii. 39), by Elphinstone (*History
of India*, ii. 564), and it also slightly struck Malcolm (*Sketch*,
p. 129). Similarly a change of aspect, as well as of dress, &c.,
may be observed in the descendants of such members of Hindu
families as became Muhammadans one or two centuries ago,
and whose personal appearance may yet be readily compared
with that of their undoubted Brahmanical cousins in many
parts of Malwa and Upper India. That Prichard (*Physical
History of Mankind*, i. 183 and i. 191) notices no such change
in the features, although he does in the characters, of the
Hottentots and Esquimaux who have been converted to Christianity, may either show that the attention of our observers

although
not fully
apparent to
strangers,
if so to
Indians.

been usual to regard the Sikhs as essentially Hindu, and they doubtless are so in language and everyday customs, for Gobind did not fetter his disciples with political systems or codes of municipal laws; yet, in religious faith and worldly aspirations, they are wholly different from other Indians, and they are bound together by a community of inward sentiment and of outward object unknown elsewhere. But the misapprehension need not surprise the public nor condemn our scholars,[1] when it is remembered that the learned of Greece and Rome misunderstood the spirit of those humble men who obtained a new life by baptism. Tacitus and Suetonius regarded the early Christians as a mere Jewish sect, they failed to perceive the fundamental difference, and to appreciate the latent energy and real excellence, of that doctrine, which has added dignity and purity to modern civilization.[2]

and inquirers has not been directed to the subject, or that the savages in question have embraced a new faith with little of living ardour and absorbing enthusiasm.

[1] The author alludes chiefly to Professor H. H. Wilson, whose learning and industry are doing so much for Indian history. (See *Asiatic Researches*, xvii. 237, 238; and continuation of Mill's *History*, vii. 101, 102.) Malcolm holds similar views in one place (*Sketch*, pp. 144, 148, 150), but somewhat contradicts himself in another (*Sketch*, p. 43). With these opinions, however, may be compared the more correct views of Elphinstone (*History of India*, ii. 562, 564) and Sir Alexander Burnes (*Travels*, i. 284, 285), and also Major Browne's observation (*India Tracts*, ii. 4) that the Sikh doctrine bore the same relation to the Hindus as the Protestant does to the Romish.

[2] See the *Annals of Tacitus*, Murphy's translation (book xv, sect. 44, note 15). Tacitus calls Christianity a dangerous superstition, and regards its professors as moved by 'a sullen hatred of the whole human race'—the Judaic characteristic of the period. Suetonius talks of the *Jews* raising disturbances in the reign of Claudius, at the instigation of 'one Chrestus', thus evidently mistaking the whole of the facts, and further making a Latin name, genuine indeed, but misapplied, of the Greek term for anointed.

Again, the obscure historian, Vopiscus, preserves a letter, written by the Emperor Hadrian, in which the Christians are confounded with the adorers of Serapis, and in which the *bishops* are said to be especially devoted to the worship of that strange god, who was introduced into Egypt by the Ptolemies (Waddington, *History of the Church*, p. 37); and even Eusebius himself did not properly distinguish between Christians and the Essenic Therapeutae (Strauss, *Life of Jesus*, i. 294), although the latter formed essentially a mere sect, or order, affecting asceticism and mystery.

It is proper to add that Mr. Newman quotes the descriptions of Tacitus and others as referring really to Christians and not to Jews (*On the Development of Christian Doctrine*, p. 205, &c.). He may be right, but the grounds of his dissent from the views of preceding scholars are not given.

Banda, the chosen disciple of Gobind, was a native of the South of India, and an ascetic of the Bairagi order;[1] and the extent of the deceased Guru's preparations and means will be best understood from the narrative of the career of his followers, when his own commanding spirit was no more. The Sikhs gathered in numbers round Banda when he reached the north-west, bearing with him the arrows of Gobind as the pledge of victory. Banda put to flight the Mughal authorities in the neighbourhood of Sirhind, and then attacked, defeated, and slew the governor of the province. Sirhind was plundered, and the Hindu betrayer and Musalman destroyer of Gobind's children were themselves put to death by the avenging Sikhs.[2] Banda next established a stronghold below the hills of Sirmur,[3] he occupied the country between the Sutlej and Jumna, and he laid waste the district of Saharanpur.[4]

Bahadur Shah, the emperor, had subdued his rebellious brother Kambakhsh, he had come to terms with the Marathas, and he was desirous of reducing the princes of Rajputana to their old dependence, when he heard of the defeat of his troops and the sack of his city by the hitherto unknown Banda.[5] He hastened towards the Punjab, and he did not pause to enter his capital after his southern successes; but in the meantime his generals had defeated a body of Sikhs near Panipat, and Banda was surrounded in his new stronghold. A zealous convert, disguised like his leader.

*1708-16.*

*Banda succeeds Gobind as a temporal leader.*

*Proceeds to the north, and captures Sirhind.*
*1709-10.*

*The emperor marches towards Lahore.*

*But Banda is in the meantime driven towards Jammu.*

---

[1] Some accounts represent Banda to have been a native of Northern India, and the writer, followed by Major Browne (*India Tracts*, ii. 9), says he was born in the Jullundur Doab.

'Banda' signifies *the slave*, and Sarup Chand, the author of the *Gur-Ratnavali*, states that the Bairagi took the name or title when he met Gobind in the south, and found that the powers of his tutelary god Vishnu were ineffectual in the presence of the Guru. Thenceforward, he said, he would be the slave of Gobind.

[2] For several particulars, true or fanciful, relating to the capture of Sirhind, see Browne, *India Tracts*, ii. 9, 10. See also Elphinstone, *History of India*, ii. 565, 566. Wazir Khan was clearly the name of the governor, and not Faujdar Khan, as mentioned by Malcolm (*Sketch*, pp. 77, 78). Wazir Khan was indeed the 'Faujdar', or military commander in the province, and the word is as often used as a proper name as to denote an office.

[3] This was at Mukhlispur, near Sadowra, which lies north-east from Ambala, and it appears to be the 'Lohgarh', that is, the iron or strong fort, of the *Siar ul Mutakharin* (i. 115).

[4] Forster, *Travels*, i. 304.

[5] Cf. Elphinstone, *History of India*, ii. 561, and Forster, *Travels*, i. 304. This was in A. D. 1709-10.

Bahadaur
Shah dies
at Lahore.
1712.

Jahandar
Shah slain
by Far-
rukhsiyar,
who
becomes
emperor.
1713.

The Sikhs
reappear
under Ban-
da, and the
province of
Sirhind is
plundered.

Banda
reduced
eventually
and taken
pr.soner.
A. D. 1716;

allowed himself to be captured during a sally of the
besieged, and Banda withdrew with all his followers.[1]
After some successful skirmishes he established himself near Jammu in the hills north of Lahore, and laid
the fairest part of the Punjab under contribution.
Bahadur Shah had by this time advanced to Lahore
in person, and he died there in the month of February,
1712.[2]

The death of the emperor brought on another
contest for the throne. His eldest son, Jahandar Shah,
retained power for a year, but in February 1713 he was
defeated and put to death by his nephew Farrukhsiyar.
These commotions were favourable to the Sikhs; they
again became united and formidable, and they built
for themselves a considerable fort, named Gurdaspur,
between the Beas and Ravi.[3] The viceroy of Lahore
marched against Banda, but he was defeated in a
pitched battle and the Sikhs sent forward a party towards Sirhind, the governor of which, Bayazid Khan,
advanced to oppose them. A fanatic crept under his
tent and mortally wounded him; the Muhammadans
dispersed, but the city does not seem to have fallen a
second time a prey to the exulting Sikhs.[4] The emperor now ordered Abdus Samad Khan, the governor
of Kashmir, a Turani noble and a skilful general, to
assume the command in the Punjab, and he sent to his
aid some chosen troops from the eastward. Abdus
Samad Khan brought with him some thousands of his
own warlike countrymen, and as soon as he was in
possession of a train of artillery he left Lahore, and
falling upon the Sikh army he defeated it, after a
fierce resistance on the part of Banda. The success
was followed up, and Banda retreated from post to
post, fighting valiantly and inflicting heavy losses on
his victors; but he was at length compelled to shelter
himself in the fort of Gurdaspur. He was closely besieged; nothing could be conveyed to him from without; and after consuming all his provisions, and eating

---

[1] Cf. Elphinstone, *History*, ii. 566, and Forster, *Travels*,
i. 305. The zeal of the devotee was applauded without being
pardoned by the emperor.

[2] Cf. the *Siar ul Mutakharin*, i. 109, 112.

[3] *Gurdaspur* is near Kalanaur, where Akbar was saluted
as emperor, and it appears to be the Lohgarh of the ordinary
accounts followed by Forster, Malcolm, and others. It now
contains a monastery of Sarsut Brahmans, who have adopted
many of the Sikh modes and tenets.

[4] Some accounts nevertheless represent Banda to have
again possessed himself of Sirhind.

horses, asses, and even the forbidden ox, he was 1708-16.
reduced to submit.[1] Some of the Sikhs were put to
death, and their heads were borne on pikes before
Banda and others as they were marched to Delhi with
all the signs of ignominy usual with bigots, and common
among barbarous or half-civilized conquerors.[2]    A
hundred Sikhs were put to death daily, contending
among themselves for priority of martyrdom, and on
the eighth day Banda himself was arraigned before his
judges. A Muhammadan noble asked the ascetic from
conviction, how one of his knowledge and understanding could commit crimes which would dash him into
hell; but Banda answered that he had been as a mere
scourge in the hands of God for the chastisement of
the wicked, and that he was now receiving the meed
of his own crimes against the Almighty. His son was
placed upon his knees, a knife was put into his hands,
and he was required to take the life of his child. He    and put to
did so, silent and unmoved; his own flesh was then torn    death at
with red-hot pincers, and amid these torments he    Delhi.
expired, his dark soul, say the Muhammadans, winging
its way to the regions of the damned.[3]

The memory of Banda is not held in much esteem    The views
by the Sikhs; he appears to have been of a gloomy    of Banda
disposition, and he was obeyed as an energetic and    confined
daring leader, without being able to engage the per-    and his
sonal sympathies of his followers. He did not perhaps    memory
comprehend the general nature of Nanak's and    not revered.
Gobind's reforms; the spirit of sectarianism possessed
him, and he endeavoured to introduce changes into
the modes and practices enjoined by these teachers,
which should be more in accordance with his own
ascetic and Hindu notions. These unwise innovations

[1] Cf. Malcolm, *Sketch*, pp. 79, 80; Forster, *Travels*, i. 306
and note; and the *Siar ul Mutakharin*, i. 116, 117. The ordinary accounts make the Sikh army amount to 35,000 men
(Forster says 20,000); they also detain Abdus Samad a year at
Lahore before he undertook anything, and they bring down
all the hill chiefs to his aid, both of which circumstances are
probable enough.

[2] *Siar ul Mutakharin*, i. 118, 120. Elphinstone (*History*, ii.
574, 575), quoting the contemporary Khafi Khan, says the
prisoners amounted to 740. The *Siar ul Mutakharin* relates
how the old mother of Bayazid Khan killed the assassin of her
son, by letting fall a stone on his head, as he and the other
prisoners were being led through the streets of Lahore.

[3] Malcolm (*Sketch*, p. 82,) who quotes the *Siar ul Mutakharin*. The defeat and death of Banda are placed by the *Siar
ul Mutakharin* (i. 109), by Orme (*History*, ii. 22), and
apparently by Elphinstone (*History*, ii. 564), in the year A. D.
1716; but Forster (*Travels*, i. 306 note) has the date 1714.

and restrictions were resisted by the more zealou
Sikhs, and they may have caused the memory of a
able and enterprising leader to be generally neglected.

**The Sikhs
generally
much de-
pressed
after the
death of
Banda.**

After the death of Banda an active persecutioi
was kept up against the Sikhs, whose losses in battl
had been great and depressing. All who could b
seized had to suffer death, or to renounce their faith
A price, indeed, was put upon their heads, and so vigo
rously were the measures of prudence, or of vengeance
followed up, that many conformed to Hinduism; other;
abandoned the outward signs of their belief, and tho
more sincere had to seek a refuge among the recesse;
of the hills, or in the woods to the south of the Sutlej
The Sikhs were scarcely again heard of in history foi
the period of a generation.[2]

**Recapitu-
lation.

Nanak.**

Thus, at the end of two centuries, had the Sikh
faith become established as a prevailing sentiment anc
guiding principle to work its way in the world. Nanak
disengaged his little society of worshippers from Hindu
idolatry and Muhammadan superstition, and placed
them free on a broad basis of religious and moral

**Amar Das.
Arjun.**

purity; Amar Das preserved the infant community
from declining into a sect of quietists or ascetics; Arjun
gave his increasing followers a written rule of conduct

**Har Gobind.
Gobind
Singh.**

and a civil organization; Har Gobind added the use of
arms and a military system; and Gobind Singh bestowed upon them a distinct political existence, and inspired them with the desire of being socially free and
nationally independent. No further legislation was
required; a firm persuasion had been elaborated, and
a vague feeling had acquired consistence as an active
principle. The operation of this faith become a fact,
is only now in progress, and the fruit it may yet bear
cannot be foreseen. Sikhism arose where fallen and
corrupt Brahmanical doctrines were most strongly
acted on by the vital and spreading Muhammadan
belief. It has now come into contact with the civiliza-

---

[1] Cf. Malcolm, *Sketch*, pp. 83, 84. But Banda is sometimes
styled Guru by Indians, as in the *Siar ul Mutakharin* (i. 114),
and there is still an order of half-conformist Sikhs which regards him as its founder. Banda, it is reported, wished to
establish a sect of his own, saying that of Gobind could not
endure; and he is further declared to have wished to change
the exclamation or salutation, 'Wah Guru ke Fateh!' which had
been used or ordained by Gobind, into 'Fateh Dharam!' and
'Fateh Darsan!' (Victory to faith! Victory to the sect!). Cf.
Malcolm, *Sketch*, pp. 83, 84.

[2] Cf. Forster (*Travels*, i. 312, 313), and Browne (*India
Tracts*, ii. 13), and also Malcolm (*Sketch*, pp. 85, 86).

tion and Christianity of Europe, and the result can only be known to a distant posterity.[1]

[1] There are also elements of change within Sikhism itself, and dissent is everywhere a source of weakness and decay, although sometimes it denotes a temporary increase of strength and energy. Sikh sects, at least of quietists, are already numerous, although the great development of the tenets of Guru Gobind has thrown other denominations into the shade. Thus the prominent division into 'Khulasa', meaning 'of Nanak', and 'Khalsa', meaning 'of Gobind', which is noticed by Forster (*Travels*, i. 309), is no longer in force. The former term, Khulasa, is almost indeed unknown in the present day, while all claim membership with the Khalsa. Nevertheless the peaceful Sikhs of the first teacher are still to be everywhere met with in the cities of India, although the warlike Singhs of the tenth king have become predominant in the Punjab, and have scattered themselves as soldiers from Kabul to the south of India.

---

Note.—The reader is referred to Appendices I, II, III, and IV for some account of the *Granths of the Sikhs*, for some illustrations of principles and practices taken from the writings of the Gurus, and for abstracts of certain letters attributed to Nanak and Gobind, and which are descriptive of some views and modes of the Sikh people. Appendix V may also be referred to for a list of some Sikh sects or denominations.

# CHAPTER IV

## THE ESTABLISHMENT OF SIKH INDEPENDENCE
### 1716—64

Decline of the Mughal Empire—Gradual reappearance of the
Sikhs—The Sikhs coerced by Mir Mannu, and persecuted
by Taimur the son of Ahmad Shah—The Army of the
'Khalsa' and the State of the 'Khalsa' proclaimed to be
substantive Powers—Adina Beg Khan and the Marathas
under Raghuba—Ahmad Shah's incursions and victories—
The provinces of Sirhind and Lahore possessed in sovereignty by the Sikhs—The political organization of the
Sikhs as a feudal confederacy—The Order of Akalis.

1716-38.

The Mughal
empire ra-
pidly de-
clines.
Nadir Shah,
the Mara-
thas, &c.

AURANGZEB was the last of the race of Taimur who
possessed a genius for command, and in governing a
large empire of incoherent parts and conflicting principles, his weak successors had to lean upon the doubtful
loyalty of selfish and jealous ministers, and to prolong
a nominal rule by opposing insurrectionary subjects to
rebellious dependents. Within a generation Muhammadan adventurers had established separate dominations
in Bengal, Lucknow, and Hyderabad; the Maratha
Peshwa had startled the Muslims of India by suddenly
appearing in arms before the imperial city,[1] and the
stern usurping Nadir had scornfully hailed the long
descended Muhammad Shah as a brother Turk in the
heart of his blood-stained capital.[2] The Afghan colo-
nists of Rohilkhand and the Hindu Jats of Bharatpur
had raised themselves to importance as substantive
powers,[3] and when the Persian conqueror departed

[1] This was in A. D. 1737, when Baji Rao, the Peshwa, made
an incursion from Agra towards Delhi. (See Elphinstone,
History, ii. 609, and Grant Duff, History of the Mahrattas, i.
533, 534.)

[2] See Nadir Shah's letter to his son, relating his successful
invasion of India. (Asiatic Researches, x. 545, 546.)

[3] A valuable account of the Rohillas may be found in
Forster's Travels (i. 115, &c.), and the public is indebted to
the Oriental Translation Committee of London for the memoirs
of Hafiz Rahmat Khan, one of the most eminent of their leaders.

The Jats of Bhartpur and Dholpur, and of Hathras and
other minor places, deserve a separate history.

with the spoils of Delhi,[1] the government was weaker, 1716-38. and society was more disorganized, than when the fugitive Babar entered India in search of a throne worthy of his lineage and his personal merits.

These commotions were favourable to the reappearance of a depressed sect; but the delegated rule of Abdus Samad in Lahore was vigorous, and, both under him and his weaker successor,[2] the Sikhs comported themselves as peaceful subjects in their villages, or lurked in woods and valleys to obtain a precarious livelihood as robbers.[3] The tenets of Nanak and Gobind had nevertheless taken root in the hearts of the people; the peasant and the mechanic nursed their faith in secret, and the more ardent clung to the hope of ample revenge and speedy victory. The departed Guru had declared himself the last of the prophets; the believers were without a temporal guide, and rude untutored men, accustomed to defer to their teacher as divine, were left to work their way to greatness, without an ordained method, and without any other bond of union than the sincerity of their common faith. The progress of the new religion, and the ascendancy of its votaries, had thus been trusted to the pregnancy of the truths announced, and to the fitness of the Indian mind for their reception. The general acknowledgement of the most simple and comprehensive principle is sometimes uncertain, and is usually slow and irregular, and this fact should be held in view in considering the history of the Sikhs from the death of Gobind to the present time.

*The weakness of the Muhammadan government favourable to the Sikhs, 1716-38.*

*The Sikhs kept together by the fervour of their belief.*

During the invasion of Nadir Shah, the Sikhs collected in small bands, and plundered both the stragglers of the Persian army and the wealthy inhabitants who fled towards the hills on the first appearance of the conqueror, or when the massacre at Delhi became generally known.[4] The impunity which

*The Sikhs form bands of plunderers, 1738-9.*

---

[1] [ These included the famous peacock throne of Shah Jahan and the celebrated Koh-i-Nur. The subsequent history of the latter is too well known to need repetition.—ED. ]

[2] He was likewise the son of the conqueror of Banda. His name was Zakariya Khan, and his title Khan Bahadur.

[3] Cf. Forster's *Travels*. i. 313, and Browne's *India Tracts*, ii. 13.

[4] Browne, *India Tracts*, ii. 13, 14. Nadir acquired from the Mughal emperor the provinces of Sindh and Kabul, and four districts of the province of Lahore, lying near the Jhelum river.
Zakariya Khan, son of Abdul Samad, was viceroy of Lahore at the time.
The defeat of the Delhi sovereign, and Nadir's entry into the capital, took place on the 13th of February and early in March, 1739, respectively, but were not known in London until

1737-46.

attended these efforts encouraged them to bolder attempts, and they began to visit Amritsar openly instead of in secrecy and disguise. The Sikh horseman, says a Muhammadan author, might be seen riding at full gallop to pay his devotions at that holy shrine. Some might be slain, and some might be captured, but none were ever known to abjure their creed, when thus taken on their way to that sacred place.[1] Some Sikhs next succeeded in establishing a small fort at Dalhwal on the Ravi, and they were unknown or disregarded, until considerable numbers assembled and proceeded to levy contributions around Eminabad, which lies to the north of Lahore. The marauders were attacked, but the detachment of troops was repulsed and its leader slain. A larger force pursued and defeated them; many prisoners were brought to Lahore, and the scene of their execution is now known as 'Shahid Ganj', or the place of martyrs.[2] It is further marked by the tomb of Bhai Taru Singh, who was required to cut his hair and to renounce his faith; but the old companion of Guru Gobind would yield neither his conscience nor the symbol of his conviction, and his real or pretended answer is preserved to the present day. The hair, the scalp, and the skull, said he, have a mutual connexion; the head of man is linked with life, and *he* was prepared to yield his breath with cheerfulness.

Establish a fort at Dalhwal on the Ravi:

but are at last dispersed. (about) 1745-6.

Ahmad Shah's first invasion of India. 1747-8.

The viceroyalty of Lahore was about this time contested between the two sons of Zakariya Khan, the successor of Abdus Samad, who defeated Banda. The younger, Shah Nawaz Khan, displaced the elder, and to strengthen himself in his usurpation, he opened a correspondence with Ahmad Shah Abdali, who became master of Afghanistan on the assassination of Nadir Shah, in June 1747. The Durrani king soon collected round his standard numbers of the hardy tribes of Central Asia, who delight in distant inroads and successful rapine. He necessarily looked to India as the most productive field of conquest or incursion, and he could cloak his ambition under the double pretext of the tendered allegiance of the governor of Lahore, and

the 1st of October, so slow were the communications, and of so little importance was Delhi to Englishmen, three generations ago. (Wade's *Chronological British History,* p. 417.)

[1] The author is quoted, but not named by Malcolm, *Sketch,* p. 88.

[2] Cf. Browne, *India Tracts,* ii. 13; Malcolm, *Sketch,* p. 86; and Murray's *Ranjit Singh,* by Prinsep, p. 4. Yahya Khan, the elder son of Zakariya Khan, was governor of the Punjab at the time.

of the favourable reception at Delhi of *his* enemy, 1747-8. Nadir Shah's fugitive governor of Kabul.[1] Ahmad Shah crossed the Indus: but the usurping viceroy of Lahore had been taunted with his treason; generosity prevailed over policy, and he resolved upon opposing the advance of the Afghans. He was defeated, and the Abdali became master of the Punjab. The Shah pursued his march to Sirhind, where he was met by the Wazir of the declining empire. Some desultory skirmishing and one more decisive action took place, but the result of the whole was so unfavourable to the invader that he precipitately recrossed the Punjab, and gave an opportunity to the watchful Sikhs of harassing his rear and of gaining confidence in their own prowess. The minister of Delhi was killed by a cannon ball during the short campaign, but the gallantry and the services of his son, Mir Mannu, had been conspicuous, and he became the viceroy of Lahore and Multan, under the title of Muin-ul-mulk.[2]

Retires from Sirhind. and is harassed by the Sikhs, March 1748.

Mir Mannu governor of the Punjab.

The new governor was a man of vigour and ability, but his object was rather to advance his own interests than to serve the emperor; and in the administration of his provinces he could trust to no feelings save those which he personally inspired. He judiciously retained the services of two experienced men, Kaura Mal and Adina Beg Khan, the one as his immediate deputy, and the other as the manager of the Jullundur Doab. Both had dealt skilfully for the times with the insurrectionary Sikhs, who continued to press themselves more and more on the attention of their unloyal governors.[3] During the invasion of Ahmad Shah they had thrown up a fort close to Amritsar, called the Ram Rauni, and one of their most able leaders had arisen, Jassa Singh Kalal, a brewer or distiller, who boldly proclaimed the birth of a new power in the state—the 'Dal' of the 'Khalsa,' or army of the theocracy of 'Singhs'.[4] As soon

Mir Mannu rules vigorously, and employs Kaura Mal and Adina Beg Khan, 1748.

But the Sikhs reappear and Jassa Singh Kalal proclaims the existence of

---

[1] Cf. Murray's *Ranjit Singh*, by Prinsep, p. 9, and Browne, *India Tracts*, ii. 15. Nasir Khan, the governor, hesitated about marrying his daughter to Ahmad Shah; one of another race, as well as about rendering obedience to him as sovereign. Cf., however, Elphinstone (*Account of Kabul*, ii. 285), who makes no mention of these particulars.

[2] Cf. Elphinstone, *Kabul*, ii. 285, 286, and Murray's *Ranjit Singh*, pp. 6-8.

[3] Kaura Mal was himself a follower of Nanak, without having adopted the tenets of Gobind. (Forster, *Travels*, i. 314.) Adina Beg Khan was appointed manager of the Jullundur Doab by Zakariya Khan, with orders to coerce the Sikhs after Nadir Shah's retirement. (Browne, *India Tracts*, ii. 14.)

[4] Cf. Browne, *India Tracts*, ii. 16, who gives Charsa Singh,

1748.
the 'Dal'
or army of
the Khalsa.

Mannu dis-
perses the
Sikhs, and
comes to
terms with
Ahmad
Shah, who
had again
crossed the
Indus, end
of 1748.

Mir Mannu
breaks with
Delhi by
resisting
his super-
cession in
Multan;

as Mir Mannu had established his authority, he marched against the insurgents, captured their fort, dispersed their troops, and took measures for the general preservation of good order.[1] His plans were interrupted by the rumoured approach of a second Afghan invasion; he marched to the Chenab to repel the danger, and he dispatched agents to the Durrani camp to avert it by promises and concessions. Ahmad Shah's own rule was scarcely consolidated, he respected the ability of the youth who had checked him at Sirhind, and he retired across the Indus on the stipulation that the revenues of four fruitful districts should be paid to him as they had been paid to Nadir Shah, from whom he pretended to derive his title.[2]

Mir Mannu gained applause at Delhi for the success of his measures, but his ambition was justly dreaded by the Wazir Safdar Jang, who knew his own designs on Oudh, and felt that the example would not be lost on the son of his predecessor. It was proposed to reduce his power by conferring the province of Multan on Shah Nawaz Khan, whom Mir Mannu himself had supplanted in Lahore;[3] but Mannu had an accurate knowledge of the imperial power and of his own resources, and he sent his deputy, Kaura Mal, to resist the new governor. Shah Nawaz Khan was defeated and slain, and the elated viceroy conferred the title of Maharaja on his successful follower.[4] This virtual independence of Delhi, and the suppression of Sikh disturbances, emboldened Mannu to persevere in his probably original design, and to withhold the pro-

Tuka Singh, and Kirwar Singh, as the confederates of Jassa Kalal.

[1] Both Kaura Mal and Adina Beg, but especially the former, the one from predilection, and the other from policy, are understood to have dissuaded Mir Mannu from proceeding to extremities against the Sikhs. Cf. Browne, *Tracts*, ii. 16, and Forster, *Travels*, i. 314, 315, 327, 328, which latter, however, justly observes that Mannu had objects in view of greater moment to himself than the suppression of an infant sect.

[2] The Afghans state that Mir Mannu also became the Shah's tributary for the whole of the Punjab and, doubtless, he *promised* anything to get the invader away and to be left alone. (Cf. Elphinstone, *Kabul*, ii. 286, and Murray, *Ranjit Singh*, pp. 910.)

[3] Hayatulla Khan, the younger son of Zakariya Khan, is stated in local Multan chronicles to have held that province when Nadir Shah entered Sind, in 1739-40, to fairly settle and subdue it, and to have then tendered his allegiance to the Persian conqueror, from whom he received the title of Shah Nawaz Khan.

[4] Cf. Murray's *Ranjit Singh*, p. 10.

mised tribute from Ahmad Shah. A pretence of demanding it was made, and the payment of all arrears was offered, but neither party felt that the other could be trusted, and the Afghan king marched towards Lahore. Mannu made a show of meeting him on the frontier, but finally he took up an entrenched position under the walls of the city. Had he remained on the defensive the Abdali might probably have been foiled, but, after a four months' beleaguer, he was tempted to risk an action. Kaura Mal was killed; Adina Beg scarcely exerted himself; Mannu saw that a prolonged contest would be ruinous, and he prudently retired to the citadel and gave in his adhesion to the conqueror. The Shah was satisfied with the surrender of a considerable treasure and with the annexation of Lahore and Multan to his dominions. He expressed his admiration of Mannu's spirit as a leader, and efficiency as a manager, and he continued him as his own delegate in the new acquisitions. The Shah took measuers to bring Kashmir also under his sway, and then retired towards his native country.[1]

This second capture of Lahore by strangers necessarily weakened the administration of the province, and the Sikhs, ever ready to rise, again became troublesome; but Adina Beg found it advisable at the time to do away with the suspicions which attached to his inaction at Lahore, and to the belief that he temporized with insurgent peasantry for purposes of his own. He was required to bring the Sikhs to order, for they had virtually possessed themselves of the country lying between Amritsar and the hills. He fell suddenly upon them during a day of festival at Makhowal, and gave them a total defeat. But his object was still to be thought their friend, and he came to an understanding with them that their payment of their own rents should be nominal or limited, and their exactions from others moderate or systematic. He took also many of them into his pay; one of the number being Jassa Singh, a carpenter, who afterwards became a chief of consideration.[2]

Mir Mannu died a few months after the re-establishment of his authority as the deputy of a new master.[3] His widcw succeeded in procuring the

*Side notes:*

1749-52.
and withholds tribute from Ahmad Shah, who crosses the Indus for the third time.

1749-51. Abdali reaches Lahore.

1752, and defeats Mannu; but retains him as governor of the Punjab. April 1752.

The Sikhs gradually increase in strength;

but are defeated by Adina Beg, who nevertheless gives them favourable terms, A. D. 1752.

Jassa the carpenter.

Mir Mannu dies, and Lahore is

---

[1] Cf. Elphinstone, *Kabul*, ii. 288, and Murray's *Ranjit Singh*, pp. 10, 13.

[2] Cf. Browne, *India Tracts*, ii. 17, and Malcolm, *Sketch*, p. 82.

[3] Forster (*Travels*, i. 315) and Malcolm (*Sketch*, p. 92), say 1752. Browne (*Tracts*, ii. 18) gives the Hijri year, 1165,

1756-3.

reannexed
to Delhi,
end of
1752.

Ahmad
Shah's
fourth in-
vasion.
Prince Tai-
mur, go-
vernor of
the Punjab,
and Najib-
ud-daula
placed at
the head of
the Delhi
army, 1755-6.

Taimur
expels the
Sikhs :rom
Amritsar.

acknowledgement of his infant son as viceroy under
her own guardianship, and she endeavoured to stand
equally well with the court of Delhi and with the
Durrani king. She professed submission to both, and
she betrothed her daughter to Ghazi-ud-din, the grandson of the first Nizam of the Deccan, who had supplanted the viceroy of Oudh as the minister of the
enfeebled empire of India.[1] But the Wazir wished to
recover a province for his sovereign, as well as to
obtain a bride for himself. He proceeded to Lahore
and removed his enraged mother-in-law; and the Punjab remained for a time under the nominal rule of
Adina Beg Khan, until Ahmad Shah again marched
and made it his own. The Durrani king passed through
Lahore in the winter of 1755-6, leaving his son Taimur
under the tutelage of a chief, named Jahan Khan, as
governor. The Shah likewise annexed Sirhind to his
territories, and although he extended his pardon to
Ghazi-ud-din personally, he did not return to Kandahar until he had plundered Delhi and Mathura, and
placed Najib-ud-daula, a Rohilla leader, near the person of the Wazir's puppet king, as the titular commander of the forces of the Delhi empire, and as the
efficient representative of Abdali interests.[2]

Prince Taimur's first object was to thoroughly
disperse the insurgent Sikhs, and to punish Adina Beg
for the support which he had given to the Delhi
minister in recovering Lahore. Jassa, the carpenter,
had restored the Ram Rauni of Amritsar; that place
was accordingly attacked, the fort was levelled, the
buildings were demolished, and the sacred reservoir
was filled with the ruins. Adina Beg would not trust
the prince, and retired to the hills, secretly aiding and
encouraging the Sikhs in their desire for revenge. They
assembled in great numbers, for the faith of Gobind

which corresponds with A. D. 1751, 1752. Murray (Ranjit Singh,
p. 13) simply says Mannu did not long survive his submission,
but Elphinstone (Kabul, ii. 288) gives 1756 as the date of the
viceroy's death.

[1] The original name of Ghazi-ud-din was Shahab-ud-din,
corrupted into Sahoodeen and Shaodeen by the Marathas.

[2] Cf. Forster, Travels, i. 316, 317; Browne, Tracts, ii. 48;
Malcolm, Sketch, pp. 92, 94; Elphinstone, Kabul, ii. 288, 289;
and Murray, Ranjit Singh, pp. 14, 15.

During the nominal viceroyalty of Mir Mannu's widow,
one Bikari Khan played a conspicuous part as her deputy. He
was finally put to death by the lady as one who designed to
supplant her authority; but he was, nevertheless, supposed to
have been her paramour. (Cf. Browne, ii. 18, and Murray,
p. 14.) The gilt mosque at Lahore was built by this Bikari
Khan.

was the living conviction of hardy single-minded **1758-61.**
villagers, rather than the ceremonial belief of busy
citizens, with thoughts diverted by the opposing interests and conventional usages of artificial society. The
country around Lahore swarmed with horsemen; the **But the**
prince and his guardian were wearied with their cum- **Afghans**
brous efforts to scatter them, and they found it prudent **eventually**
to retire towards the Chenab. Lahore was temporarily **retire, and**
occupied by the triumphant Sikhs, and the same Jassa **the Sikhs**
Singh, who had proclaimed the 'Khalsa' to be a state **Lahore**
and to possess an army, now gave it another symbol **and coin**
of substantive power. He used the mint of the Mughals **money,**
to strike a rupee bearing the inscription, 'Coined by **1756-8.**
the grace of the "Khalsa" in the country of Ahmad,
conquered by Jessa the Kalal.' [1]

The Delhi minister had about this time called in **The Mara-**
the Marathas to enable him to expel Najib-ud-daula, **thas at**
who, by his own address and power, and as the agent **Delhi, 1758.**
of Ahmad Shah Abdali, had become paramount in the
imperial councils. Ghazi-ud-din easily induced Raghuba,
the Peshwa's brother, to advance; Delhi was occupied
by the Marathas, and Najib-ud-daula escaped with
difficulty. Adina Beg found the Sikhs less willing to
defer to him than he had hoped; they were, moreover,
not powerful enough to enable him to govern the Punjab unaided, and he accordingly invited the Marathas **Maratha**
to extend their arms to the Indus. He had also a body **aid against**
of Sikh followers, and he marched from the Jumna in **the Afghans**
company with Raghuba. Ahmad Shah's governor of **sought by**
Sirhind was expelled, but Adina Beg's Sikh allies **Adina Beg**
incensed the Marathas by anticipating them in the **Khan.**
plunder of the town, which, after two generations of **Raghuba**
rapine, they considered as peculiarly their right. The **enters La-**
Sikhs evacuated Lahore, and the several Afghan gar- **hore, and**
risons retired and left the Marathas masters of Multan **appoints**
and of Attock, as well as of the capital itself. Adina **Adina Beg**
Beg became the governor of the Punjab, but his vision **viceroy of**
of complete independence was arrested by death, and **the Punjab.**
a few months after he had established his authority he **May 1758.**
was laid in his grave.[2] The Marathas seemed to see all **Adina Beg**
**dies, end**
**of 1758.**

[1] Cf. Browne, *Tracts*, ii. 19: Malcolm, *Sketch*, p. 93, &c.;
Elphinstone, *Kabul*, ii. 289; and Murray, *Ranjit Singh*, p. 15.

Elphinstone, using Afghan accounts, says Adina Beg defeated a body of Taimur troops; and Murray, using apparently
the accounts of Punjab Muhammadans, omits the occupation
of Lahore by the Sikhs.

[2] Cf. Browne, *India Tracts* ii. 19, 20; Forster, *Travels*, i.
317, 318; Elphinstone, *Kabul*, ii. 290; and Grant Duff, *History of
the Marathas*, ii. 132. Adina Beg appears to have died before
the end of 1758.

India at their feet, and they concerted with Ghazi-ud-din a scheme pleasing to both, the reduction of Oudh and the expulsion of the Rohillas.[1] But the loss of the Punjab brought Ahmad Shah a second time to the banks of the Jumna, and dissipated for ever the Maratha dreams of supremacy.[2]

**Ahmad Shah's fifth expedition, 1759-61.**

The Durrani king marched from Baluchistan up the Indus to Peshawar, and thence across the Punjab. His presence caused Multan and Lahore to be evacuated by the Marathas, and his approach induced the Wazir Ghazi-ud-din to take the life of the emperor. while the young prince, afterwards Shah Alam, was absent endeavouring to gain strength by an alliance with the English, the new masters of Bengal. The Maratha commanders, Sindhia and Holkar, were separately overpowered; the Afghan king occupied Delhi, and then advanced towards the Ganges to engage Shuja-ud-daula, of Oudh, in the general confederacy against the southern Hindus, who were about to make an effort for the final extinction of the Muhammadan rule. A new commander, untried in the northern wars, but accompanied by the Peshwa's heir and by all the Maratha chiefs of name. was advancing from Poona, confident in his fortune and in his superior numbers. Sedasheo Rao easily expelled the Afghan detachment from Delhi, while the main body was occupied in the Doab, and he vainly talked of proclaiming young Wiswas Rao to be the paramount of India. But Ahmad Shah gained his great victory of Panipat in the beginning of 1761, and both the influence of the Peshwa among his own people, and the power of the Marathas in Hindustan, received a blow, from which neither fully recovered, and which, indirectly, aided the accomplishment of *their* desires by almost unheeded foreigners.[3]

**Delhi occupied by the Afghans, but afterwards taken by the Marathas, 1760.**

**The Marathas signally defeated at Panipat, and expelled temporarily from Upper India, 7th Jan., 1761.**

The Afghan king returned to Kabul immediately after the battle, leaving deputies in Sirhind and Lahore,[4] and the Sikhs only appeared, during this cam-

---

[1] Cf. Elphinstone, *History of India*, ii. 669, 670.

[2] Najib-ud-daula, and the Rohillas likewise, urged Ahmad to return, when they saw their villages set on flames by the Marathas. (Elphinstone, *India*, ii. 670, and Browne, *Tracts*, ii. 20.)

[3] Browne, *India Tracts*, ii. 20, 21; Elphinstone, *History of India*, ii. 670, &c.; and Murray, *Ranjit Singh*, pp. 17, 20.
Elphinstone says the Maratha leader only delayed to proclaim Wiswas the paramount of Hindustan until the Durranis should be driven across the Indus. See also Grant Duff, *History of the Marathas*, ii. 142 and note.

[4] Baland Khan in Lahore, and Zain Khan in Sirhind, according to Browne, *India Tracts*, ii. 21, 23.

paign, as predatory bands hovering round the Durrani army; but the absence of all regular government gave them additional strength, and they became not only masters of their own villages, but began to erect forts for the purpose of keeping stranger communities in check. Among others Charat Singh, the grandfather of Ranjit Singh, established a stronghold of the kind in his wife's village of Gujrnauli (or Gujranwala), to the northward of Lahore. The Durrani governor, or his deputy, Khwaja Obed, went to reduce it in the beginning of 1762,[1] and the Sikhs assembled for its relief. The Afghan was repulsed, he left his baggage to be plundered, and fled to shut himself up within the walls of Lahore.[2] The governor of Sirhind held his ground better, for he was assisted by an active Muhammadan leader of the country, Hinghan Khan of Maler Kotla; but the Sikhs resented this hostility of an Indian Pathan as they did the treason of a Hindu religionist of Jindiala, who wore a sword like themselves, and yet adhered to Ahmad Shah. The 'army of the Khalsa' assembled at Amritsar, the faithful performed their ablutions in the restored pool, and perhaps the first regular 'Gurumatta', or diet for conclave, was held on this occasion. The possessions of Hinghan Khan were ravaged, and Jindiala was invested, preparatory to attempts of greater moment.[3]

But the restless Ahmad Shah was again at hand. This prince, the very ideal of the Afghan genius, hardy and enterprising, fitted for conquest, yet incapable of empire, seemed but to exist for the sake of losing and recovering provinces. He reached Lahore towards the end of 1762, and the Sikhs retired to the South of the Sutlej, perhaps with some design of joining their brethren who were watching Sirhind, and of overpowering Zain Khan the governor, before they should be engaged with Ahmad Shah himself; but in two long and rapid marches from Lahore, by way of Ludhiana, the king came up with the Sikhs when they were about to enter into action with his lieutenant. He gave them a total defeat, and the Muhammadans were as active in the

*Marginal notes:*
1761-2
The Sikhs unrestrained in the open country

Gujranwala successfully defended by Charat Singh, and the Durranis confined to Lahore, 1761-2.
The Sikhs assemble at Amritsar, and ravage the country on either side of the Sutlej.
Ahmad Shah's sixth invasion, 1762.

The 'Ghulu Ghara', or

---

[1] Murray (*Ranjit Singh*, p. 21) makes Khwaja Obed the governor, and he may have succeeded or represented Baland Khan, whom other accounts show to have occasionally resided at Rohtas. Gujranwala is the more common, if less ancient, form of the name of the village attacked. It was also the place of Ranjit Singh's birth, and is now a fair-sized and thriving town. (Cf Munshi Shahamat Ali's *Sikhs and Afghans*, p. 51.)

[2] Murray, *Ranjit Singh*, pp. 22, 23.

[3] Cf. Browne, *India Tracts*, ii. 22, 23; and Murray, *Ranjit Singh*, p. 23.

1762-3.

great defeat
of the Sikhs
near Ludhi-
ana, Feb.
1762.

Alha Singh
of Patiala.

pursuit as they had been ardent in the attack. The Sikhs are variously reported to have lost from twelve to twenty-five thousand men, and the rout is still familiarly known as the 'Ghulu Ghara', or great disaster.[1] Alha Singh, the founder of the present family of Patiala, was among the prisoners, but his manly deportment pleased the warlike king, and the conqueror may not have been insensible to the policy of widening the difference between a *Malwa* and a *Manjha* Singh. He was declared a raja of the state and dismissed with honour. The Shah had an interview at Sirhind with

Kabuli Mal
governor of
Lahore.

Ahmad
Shah re-
t res after
committing
various ex-
cesses, end
of 1762.

his ally or dependent, Najib-ud-daula; he made a Hindu, named Kabuli Mal, his governor of Lahore, and then hastened towards Kandahar to suppress an insurrection in that distant quarter; but he first gratified his own resentment, and indulged the savage bigotry of his followers, by destroying the renewed temples of Amritsar, by polluting the pool with slaughtered cows, by encasing numerous pyramids with the heads of decapitated Sikhs, and by cleansing the walls of desecrated mosques with the blood of his infidel enemies.[2]

The Sikhs
continue to
increase in
strength.

The Sikhs were not cast down; they received daily accessions to their numbers; a vague feeling that they were a people had arisen among them; all were bent on revenge, and their leaders were ambitious of dominion and of fame. Their first efforts were directed against the Pathan colony of Kasur, which place they took and

Kasur
plundered.

plundered, and they then fell upon and slew their old enemy Hinghan Khan of Maler Kotla. They next marched towards Sirhind, and the court of Delhi was incapable of raising an arm in support of Muhammadanism. Zain Khan, the Afghan governor, gave battle

The
Afghans
defeated,
Dec. 1763.

to the true or probable number of 40,000 Sikhs in the month of December 1763, but he was defeated and slain, and the plains of Sirhind, from the Sutlej to the Jumna, were occupied by the victors without further opposition. Tradition still describes how the Sikhs dispersed as soon as the battle was won, and how, riding day and night, each horseman would throw his belt and scabbard, his articles of dress and accoutrement, until he was almost naked, into successive

[1] The scene of the fight lay between Gujerwal and Bernala, perhaps twenty miles south from Ludhiana. Hingham Khan, of Maler Kotla, seems to have guided the Shah. Cf. Browne, *Tracts*, ii. 23; Forster, *Travels*, i. 319; and Murray, *Ranjit Singh*, pp. 23, 25. The action appears to have been fought in February 1762.

[2] Cf. Forster, *Travels*, i. 320; and Murray, *Ranjit Singh*, p. 25.

villages, to mark them as his. Sirhind itself was totally
destroyed, and the feeling still lingers which makes it
meritorious to carry away a brick from the place which
witnessed the death of the mother and children of
Gobind Singh. The impulse of victory swept the Sikhs
across the Jumna, and their presence in Saharanpur
recalled Najib-ud-daula from his contests with the Jats,
under Suraj Mal, to protect his own principality, and
he found it prudent to use negotiation as well as force,
to induce the invaders to retire.[1]

Najib-ud-daula was successful against the Jats, and
Suraj Mal was killed in fight; but the wazir, or regent,
was himself besieged in Delhi, in 1764, by the son of
the deceased chief, and the heir of Bhartpur was aided
by a large body of Sikhs, as well as of Marathas more
accustomed to defy the imperial power.[2] The loss of
Sirhind had brought Ahmad Shah a seventh time
across the Indus, and the danger of Najib-ud-daula led
him onwards to the neighbourhood of the Jumna; but
the siege of Delhi being raised—partly through the
mediation or the defection of the Maratha chief,
Holkar, and the Shah having perhaps rebellions to
suppress in his native provinces, hastened back without
making any effective attempt to recover Sirhind. He
was content with acknowledging Alha Singh of Patiala
as governor of the province on his part, that chief having opportunely procured the town itself in exchange
from the descendant of an old companion of the Guru's,
to whom the confederates had assigned it. The Sikh
accounts do not allow that the Shah retired unmolested,
but describe a long and arduous contest in the vicinity
of Amritsar, which ended without either party being
able to claim a victory, although it precipitated the
already hurried retirement of the Afghans. The Sikhs
found little difficulty in ejecting Kabuli Mal, the governor of Lahore, and the whole country, from the
Jhelum to the Sutlej, was partitioned among chiefs and
their followers, as the plains of Sirhind had been
divided in the year previous. Numerous mosques were
demolished, and Afghans in chains were made to wash
the foundations with the blood of hogs. The chiefs
then assembled at Amritsar, and proclaimed their own
sway and the prevalence of their faith, by striking a

*Margin notes:*
1763-4.

Sirhind taken and destroyed, and the province permanently occupied by the Sikhs.

The Sikhs aid the Jats of Bhartpur in besieging Delhi, 1764

Ahmad Shah's seventh expedition and speedy retirement.

The Sikhs become masters of Lahore.

A general assembly held at Amritsar, and the

---

[1] Cf. Browne, *India Tracts*, ii. 24, and Murray, *Ranjit Singh*,
pp. 26, 27. Some accounts represent the Sikhs to have also become temporarily possessed of Lahore at this period.

[2] Cf. Browne, *Tracts*, ii. 24. Sikh tradition still preserves
the names of the chiefs who plundered the vegetable market
at Delhi on this occasion.

1764.

sect esta-
blished as a
rul.ng people.

The Sikhs
form or fall
into a poli-
tical system,

which may
be termed a
theocratic
confederate
feudalism.

Their Gu-
rumattas,
or diets.

coin with an inscription to the effect that Guru Gobind had received from Nanak 'Deg, Tegh, and Fath', or Grace, Power, and Rapid Victory.[1]

The Sikhs were not interfered with for two years, and the short interval was employed in ascertaining their actual possessions, and in determining their mutual relations in their unaccustomed condition of liberty and power. Every Sikh was free, and each was a substantive member of the commonwealth; but their means, their abilities, and their opportunities were various and unequal, and it was soon found that all could not lead, and that there were even then masters as well as servants. Their system naturally resolved itself into a theocratic confederate feudalism, with all the confusion and uncertainty attendant upon a triple alliance of the kind in a society half-barbarous. God was their helper and only judge, community of faith or object was their moving principle, and warlike array, the devotion to steel of Gobind, was their material instrument. Year by year the 'Sarbat Khalsa', or whole Sikh people, met once at least at Amritsar, on the occasion of the festival of the mythological Rama, when the cessation of the periodical rains rendered military operations practicable. It was perhaps hoped that the performance of religious duties, and the awe inspired by so holy a place, might cause selfishness to yield to a regard for the general welfare, and the assembly of chiefs was termed a 'Gurumatta', to denote that, in conformity with Gobind's injunction, they sought wisdom and unanimity of counsel from their teacher and the book of his word.[2] The leaders who

---

[1] Cf. Browne, *India Tracts*, ii. 25, 27; Forster, *Travels*, i. 321, 323; Elphinstone, *Kabul*, ii. 296, 297; and Murray, *Ranjit Singh*, pp. 26, 27.

The rupees struck were called 'Gobindsnahi', and the use of the emperor's name was rejected (Browne, *Tracts*, ii. 28), although existing coins show that it was afterwards occasionally inserted by petty chiefs. On most coins struck by Ranjit Singh is the inscription,

'Deg, tegh, wa fath, wa nasrat be darang
Yaft az Nanak Guru Gobind Singh',

that is literally, 'Grace, power, and victory, victory without pause, Guru Gobind Singh obtained from Nanak.' For some observations on the words Deg and Tegh, and Fath, see Appendices IX and XII. Browne (*Tracts*, ii. Introd. vii) gives no typical import to 'Deg', and therefore leaves it meaningless; but he is perhaps more prudent than Col. Sleeman, who writes o: 'the sword, the *pot* victory, and conquest being quickly found' &c. &c. (See *Rambles of An Indian Official*, ii. 233, note.)

[2] 'Mat' means understanding, and 'Matta' counsel or wis-

thus piously met, owned no subjection to one another,
and they were imperfectly obeyed by the majority of
their followers; but the obvious feudal, or military
notion of a chain of dependence, was acknowledged as
the law, and the federate chiefs partitioned their joint
conquests equally among themselves, and divided their
respective shares in the same manner among their own
leaders of bands, while these again subdivided their
portions among their own dependents, agreeably to
the general custom of subinfeudation.[1] This positive
or understood rule was not, however, always applicable
to actual conditions, for the Sikhs were in part of their
possessions 'earthborn', or many held lands in which
the mere withdrawal of a central authority had left
them wholly independent of control. In theory such
men were neither the subjects nor the retainers of any
feudal chiefs, and they could transfer their services to
whom they pleased, or they could themselves become
leaders, and acquire new lands for their own use in
the name of the Khalsa or commonwealth.[2] It would
be idle to call an everchanging state of alliance and
dependence by the name of a constitution, and we
must look for the existence of the faint outline of a
system, among the emancipated Sikhs, rather in the

*The system not devised, or knowingly adopted, and therefore*

dom. Hence Gurumatta becomes, literally, 'the advice of the
Guru.'

Malcolm (*Sketch*, p. 52) considers, and Browne (*Tracts*, ii.
vii) leaves it to be implied, that Gobind directed the assemblage
of Gurumatta; but there is no authority for believing that he
ordained any formal or particular institution, although, doubtless, the general scope of his injunctions, and the peculiar
political circumstances of the times, gave additional force to
the practice of holding diets or conclaves—a practice common
to mankind everywhere, and systematized in India from time
immemorial. Cf. Forster, *Travels*, i. 328, &c., for some observations on the transient Sikh government of the time, and on
the more enduring characteristics of the people. See also Malcolm, *Sketch*, p. 120, for the ceremonial forms of a Gurumatta.

[1] Cf. Murray, *Ranjit Singh*, pp. 33—37. From tracts of
country which the Sikhs subdued but did not occupy. 'Rakhi'
(literally, protection money) was regularly levied. The Rakhi
varied in amount from perhaps a fifth to a half of the rental
or government share of the produce. It corresponded with
the Maratha 'Chowt', or fourth, and both terms meant 'black-
mail', or, in a higher sense, tribute. Cf. Browne, *India Tracts*,
ii. viii, and Murray, *Ranjit Singh*, p. 32. The subdivisions of
property were sometimes so minute that two, or three, or ten
Sikhs might become co-partners in the rental of one village,
or in the house tax of one street of a town, while the fact that
jurisdiction accompanied such right increased the confusion.

[2] Hallam shows that the Anglo-Saxon freeholder had a
similar latitude of choice with regard to a lord or superior.
(*Middle Ages*, Supplemental Notes, p. 210.)

incomplete
and tempo-
rary.

dictates of our common nature, than in the enactments of assemblies, or in the injunctions of their religious guides. It was soon apparent that the strong were ever ready to make themselves obeyed, and ever anxious to appropriate all within their power, and that unity of creed or of race nowhere deters men from preying upon one another. A full persuasion of God's grace was nevertheless present to the mind of a Sikh, and every member of that faith continues to defer to the mystic Khalsa; but it requires the touch of genius, or the operation of peculiar circumstances, to give direction and complete effect to the enthusiastic belief of a multitude.

The con-
federacies
called
Misals.

The confederacies into which the Sikhs resolved themselves have been usually recorded as twelve in number, and the term used to denote such a union was the Arabic word 'Misal', alike or equal.[1] Each Misal obeyed or followed a 'Sirdar', that is simply, a chief or leader; but so general a title was as applicable to the head of a small band as to the commander of a large host of the free and equal 'Singhs' of the system. The confederacies did not all exist in their full strength at the same time, but one 'Misal' gave birth to another; for the federative principle necessarily pervaded the union, and an aspiring chief could separate himself from his immediate party, to form, perhaps, a greater

Their
names and
particular
origin.

one of his own. The Misals were again distinguished by titles derived from the name, the village, the district, or the progenitor of the first or most eminent chief, or from some peculiarity of custom or of leadership. Thus, of the twelve : (1) the *Bhangis* were so called from the real or fancied fondness of its members for the use of an intoxicating drug;[2] (2) the *Nishanias* followed the standard bearers of the united army; (3) the *Shahids* and *Nihangs* were headed by the descendants of honoured martyrs and zealots; (4) the *Ramgarhias* took their name from the Ram Rauni, or Fortalice of God, at Amritsar, enlarged into Ramgarh, or Fort of the Lord, by Jassa the Carpenter; (5) the *Nakkais* arose in a tract of country to the south of Lahore so-called; (6) the *Ahluwalias* derived their title

[1] Notwithstanding this usual derivation of the term, it may be remembered that the Arabic term 'Musluhut' (spelt with another s than that in 'misal') means armed men and warlike people. 'Misal', moreover, means, in India, a file of papers, or indeed anything serried or placed in ranks.

[2] Bhang is a product of the hemp plant, and it is to the Sikhs what opium is to Rajputs, and strong liquor to Europeans. Its qualities are abused to an extent prejudicial to the health and understanding.

from the village in which Jassa, who first proclaimed <sup>1764.</sup> the existence of the army of the new theocracy, had helped his father to distil spirits; (7) the *Ghanais* or *Kanhayas;* (8) the *Feizulapurias* or *Singhpurias;* (9) the *Sukerchukias,* and (10), perhaps, the *Dallehwalas,* were similarly so denominated from the villages of their chiefs; (11)· the *Krora Singhias* took the name of their third leader, but they were sometimes called *Punjgurhias,* from the village of their first chief; and (12) the *Phulkias* went back to the common ancestor of Alha Singh and other Sirdars of his family.¹

Of the Misals, all save that of Phulkia arose in the Punjab or to the north of the Sutlej, and they were termed *Manjha* Singhs, from the name of the country around Lahore, and in contradistinction to the *Malwa* Singhs, so called from the general appellation of the districts lying between Sirhind and Sirsa. The Feizula-purias, the Ahluwalias, and the Ramgarhias, were the first who arose to distinction in Manjha, but the Bhangis soon became so predominant as almost to be supreme; they were succeeded to some extent in this pre-eminence by the Ghanais, an offshoot of the Feizu-lapurias, until all fell before Ranjit Singh and the Sukerchukias. In Malwa the Phulkias always admitted the superior merit of the Patiala branch; this dignity was confirmed by Ahmad Shah's bestowal of a title on Alha Singh, and the real strength of the confederacy made it perhaps inferior to the Bhangis alone. The Nishanias and Shahids scarcely formed Misals in the conventional meaning of the term, but complementary bodies set apart and honoured by all for particular reasons.² The Nakkais never achieved a high power or

*The relative pre-eminence of the Misals or confe-deracies.*

---

¹ Capt. Murray (*Ranjit Singh*, pp. 29, &c.) seems to have been the first who perceived and pointed out the Sikh system of 'Misals'. Neither the organization nor the term is mentioned specifically by Forster, or Browne, or Malcolm, and at first Sir David Ochterlony considered and acted as if 'misal' meant tribe or race, instead of party or confederacy. (Sir D. Ochterlony to the Government of India, December 30, 1809.) The succession to the leadership of the Krora Singhia confederacy may be mentioned as an instance of the uncertainty and irregularity natural to the system of 'Misals', and indeed to all powers in process of change or development. The founder was succeeded by his nephew, but that nephew left his authority to Krora Singh, a petty personal follower, who again bequeathed the command to Baghel Singh, his own menial servant. The reader will remember the parallel instance of Alfteghin and Sebekteghin, and it is curious that Mr. Macaulay notices a similar kind of descent among the English admirals of the seventeenth century, viz. from chief to cabin-boy, in the cases of Myngs, Narborough, and Shovel (*History of England,* i. 306).

² Perhaps Capt. Murray is scarcely warranted in making

1764.

name, and the Dallehwalas and Krora Singhias, an
offshoot of the Feizulapurias, acquired nearly all their
possessions by the capture of Sirhind; and although
the last obtained a great reputation, it never became
predominant over others.

The original and acquired possessions of the Misals.

The native possessions of the Bhangis extended
north, from their cities of Lahore and Amritsar to the
Jhelum, and then down that river. The Ghanais dwelt
between Amritsar and the hills. The Sukerchukias
lived south of the Bhangis, between the Chenab and
Ravi. The Nakkais held along the Ravi, south-west of
Lahore. The Feizulapurias possessed tracts along the
right bank of the Beas and of the Sutlej, below its
junction. The Ahluwalias similarly occupied the left
bank of the former river. The Dallehwalas possessed
themselves of the right bank of the Upper Sutlej, and
the Ramgarhias lay in between these last two, but
towards the hills. The Krora Singhias also held lands
in the Jullundur Doab. The Phulkias were native to
the country about Sunam and Bhatinda, to the south
of the Sutlej, and the Shahids and Nishanias do not
seem to have possessed any villages which they did not
hold by conquest; and thus these two Misals, along
with those of Manjha, who captured Sirhind, viz. the
Bhangis, the Ahluwalias, the Dallehwalas, the Ramgarhias, and the Krora Singhias, divided among themselves the plains lying south of the Sutlej and under
the hills from Ferozepore to Karnal, leaving to their
allies, the Phulkias, the lands between Sirhind and
Delhi, which adjoined their own possessions in Malwa.[1]

The gross forces of the Sikhs, and the relative

The number of horsemen which the Sikhs could
muster have been variously estimated from seventy
thousand to four times that amount, and the relative
strength of each confederacy is equally a subject to
doubt.[2] All that is certain is the great superiority of

the Nishanias and Shahids regular Misals. Other bodies, especially to the westward of the Jhelum, might, with equal reason,
have been held to represent separate confederacies. Capt.
Murray, indeed, in such matters of detail, merely expresses the
local opinions of the neighbourhood of the Sutlej.

1 Dr. Macgregor, in his *History of the Sikhs* (i. 28, &c.),
gives an abstract of some of the ordinary accounts of a few
of the Misals.

2 Forster, in 1783 (*Tarvels*, i. 333), said the Sikh forces
were estimated at 300,000, but might be taken at 200,000.
Browne (*Tracts*, Illustrative Map) about the same period
enumerates 73,000 horsemen and 25,000 foot. Twenty years
afterwards Col. Francklin said, in one work (*Life of Shah Alam*,
note, p. 75), that the Sikhs mustered 248,000 cavalry, and in
another book (*Life of George Thomas*, p. 68 note) that they
could not lead into action more than 64,000. George Thomas

1764.
strength of
the Misals.

the Bhangis, and the low position of the Nakkais and Sukerchukias. The first could perhaps assemble 20,000 men, in its widely scattered possessions, and the last about a tenth of that number; and the most moderate estimate of the total force of the nation may likewise be assumed to be the truest. All the Sikhs were horsemen, and among a half-barbarous people dwelling on plains, or in action with undisciplined forces, cavalry must ever be the most formidable arm. The Sikhs speedily became famous for the effective use of the matchlock when mounted, and this skill is said to have descended to them from their ancestors, in whose hands the bow was a fatal weapon. Infantry were almost solely used to garrison forts, or a man followed a misal on foot, until plunder gave him a horse or the means of buying one. Cannon was not used by the early Sikhs, and its introduction was very gradual, for its possession implies wealth, or an organization both civil and military.[1]

The order
of Akalis.

Their origin
and prin-
ciples of
action.

Besides the regular confederacies, with their moderate degree of subordination, there was a body of men who threw off all subjection to earthly governors, and who peculiarly represented the religious element of Sikhism. These were the 'Akalis', the immortals, or rather the soldiers of God, who, with their blue dress and bracelets of steel, claimed for themselves a direct institution by Gobind Singh. The Guru had called upon men to sacrifice everything for their faith, to leave their homes and to follow the profession of arms; but he and all his predecessors had likewise denounced the inert asceticism of the Hindu sects, and thus the fanatical feeling of a Sikh took a destructive turn. The Akalis formed themselves in their struggle to reconcile warlike activity with the relinquishment of the world The meek and humble were satisfied with the assiduous performance of menial offices in temples, but the fierce enthusiasm of others prompted them to act from time to time as the armed guardians of Amritsar, or suddenly to go where blind impulse might lead them, and to win their daily bread, even single-handed, at the point of the sword.[2] They also took upon themselves

himself estimated their strength at 60,000 horse and 5,000 foot. (*Life*, by Francklin, p. 274.)

[1] George Thomas, giving the supposed status of A. D. 1800, says the Sikhs had 40 pieces of field artillery. (*Life*, by Francklin, .p. 274.)

[2] Cf. Malcolm (*Sketch*, p. 116), who repeats, and apparently acquiesces in, the opinion, that the Akalis were instituted as an order by Guru Gobind. There is not, however, any writing of Gobind's on record, which shows that he

something of the authority of censors, and, although no leader appears to have fallen by their hands for defection to the Khalsa, they inspired awe as well as respect, and would sometimes plunder those who had offended them or had injured the commonwealth. The passions of the Akalis had full play until Ranjit Singh became supreme, and it cost that able and resolute chief much time and trouble, at once to suppress them, and to preserve his own reputation with the people.

wished the Sikh faith to be represented by mere zealots, and it seems clear that the class of men arose as stated in the text.

So strong is the feeling that a Sikh should work, or have an occupation, that one who abandons the world, and is not of a warlike turn, will still employ himself in some way for the benefit of the community. Thus the author once found an Akali repairing, or rather making, a road, among precipitous ravines, from the plain of the Sutlej to the petty town of Kiratpur. He avoided intercourse with the world generally. He was highly esteemed by the people, who left food and clothing at particular places for him, and his earnest persevering character had made an evident impression on a Hindu shepherd boy, who had adopted part of the Akali dress, and spoke with awe of the devotee.

# CHAPTER V

## FROM THE INDEPENDENCE OF THE SIKHS TO THE ASCENDANCY OF RANJIT SINGH AND THE ALLIANCE WITH THE ENGLISH
### 1765—1808-9

Ahmad Shah's last Invasion of India—The Pre-eminence of the Bhangi Confederacy among the Sikhs—Taimur Shah's Expeditions—The Phulkia Sikhs in Hariana—Zabita Khan —The Kanhaya Confederacy paramount among the Sikhs —Mahan Singh Sukerchukia becomes conspicuous—Shah Zaman's Invasions and Ranjit Singh's rise—The Marathas under Sindhia Predominant in Northern India—General Perron and George Thomas—Alliances of the Marathas and Sikhs—Intercourse of the English with the Sikhs—Lord Lake's Campaigns against Sindhia and Holkar—First Treaty of the English with the Sikhs—Preparations against a French Invasion of India—Treaty of Alliance with Ranjit Singh, and of Protection with Cis-Sutlej Sikh Chiefs.

THE Sikhs had mastered the upper plains from Karnal and Hansi to the banks of the Jhelum. The necessity of union was no longer paramount, and rude untaught men are ever prone to give the rein to their passions, and to prefer their own interests to the welfare of the community. Some dwelt on real or fancied injuries, and thought the time had come for ample vengeance; others were moved by local associations to grasp at neighbouring towns and districts; and the truer Sikh alone at once resolved to extend his faith, and to add to the general domain of the Khalsa, by complete conquest or by the imposition of tribute. When thus about to arise, after their short repose, refreshed and variously inclined, they were again awed into unanimity by the final descent of Ahmad Shah. That monarch, whose activity and power declined with increase of years and the progress of disease, made yet another attempt to recover the Punjab, the most fertile of his provinces. He crossed the Indus in 1767, but he avoided Lahore and advanced no farther than the Sutlej. He endeavoured to conciliate when he could no longer overcome, and he bestowed the title of Maharaja, and the office of military commander in Sirhind, upon the warlike Amar Singh, who had succeeded his grandfather as chief of Patiala, or

1767
___
The Sikhs
hurried into
activity by
Ahmad
Shah's final
descent,
A. D. 1767.

Amar
Singh of

1767-8.

Patiala, and the Rajput chief of Katotch, appointed to command under the Abdali.

Ahmad Shah retires. Rohtas taken by the Sikhs, 1768.

The Sikhs ravage the Lower Punjab;

and enter into terms with Bhawalpur;

threaten Kashmir, and press Najib-ud-

of the Malwa Sikhs. He likewise saw a promising ally in the Rajput chief of Katotch, and he made him his deputy in the Jullundur Doab and adjoining hills. His measures were interrupted by the defection of his own troops; twelve thousand men marched back towards Kabul, and the Shah found it prudent to follow them. He was harassed in his retreat, and he had scarcely crossed the Indus before Sher Shah's mountain stronghold of Rohtas was blockaded by the Sukerchukias, under the grandfather of Ranjit Singh, aided by a detachment of the neighbouring Bhangi confederacy. The place fell in 1768, and the Bhangis almost immediately afterwards occupied the country as far as Rawalpindi and the vale of Khanpur, the Gakhars showing but little of that ancient hardihood which distinguished them in their contests with invading Mughals.[1]

The Bhangis, under Hari Singh, next marched towards Multan, but they were met by the Muhammadan Daudputras, who had migrated from Sind on learning Nadir Shah's intention of transplanting them to Ghazni, and had established the principality now known as Bhawalpur.[2] The chief, Mobarik Khan, after a parley with Hari Singh, arranged that the neutral town of Pakpattan, held by a Musalman saint of eminence, should be the common boundary. Hari Singh then swept towards Dera Ghazi Khan and the Indus, and while thus employed, his feudatory of Gujrat, who had recently taken Rawalpindi, made an attempt to penetrate into Kashmir by the ordinary road, but was repulsed with loss. On the Jumna, and in the great Doab, the old Najib-ud-daula was so hard pressed by Rai Singh Bhangi, who emulated him as a paternal

[1] Forster, *Travels*, i. 323; Elphinstone, *Kabul*, ii. 297; Murray, *Ranjit Singh*, p. 27; Moorcroft, *Travels*, i. 127; and manuscript accounts consulted by the author.

[2] When Nadir Shah proceeded to establish his authority in Sindh, he found the ancestor of the Bhawalpur family a man of reputation in his native district of Shikarpur. The Shah made him the deputy of the upper third of the province; but, becoming suspicious of the whole clan, he resolved on removing it to Ghazni. The tribe then migrated up the Sutlej, and seized lands by force. The Daudputras are so called from Daud (David), the first of the family who acquired a name. They fabulously trace their origin to the Caliph Abbas; but they may be regarded as Sindian Baluchis, or as Baluchis changed by a long residence in Sind. In establishing themselves on the Sutlej, they reduced the remains of the ancient Langahs and Johiyas to further insignificance; but they introduced the Sindian system of canals of irrigation, and both banks of the river below Pakpattan bear witness to their original industry and love of agriculture.

governor in his neighbouring town and district of
Jagadhri, and by Baghel Singh Krora Singhia, that he
proposed to the Marathas a joint expedition against
these new lords. His death, in 1770, put an end to the
plan, for his succeeding son had other views, and encouraged the Sikhs as useful allies upon an emergency.[1]

Hari Singh Bhangi died, and he was succeeded by
Jhanda Singh, who carried the power of the Misal to
its height. He rendered Jammu tributary, and the
place was then of considerable importance, for the
repeated Afghan invasions, and the continued insurrections of the Sikhs, had driven the transit trade of the
plans to the circuitous but safe route of the hills; and
the character of the Rajput chief, Ranjit Deo, was such
as gave confidence to traders, and induced them to flock
to his capital for protection. The Pathans of Kasur
were next rendered tributary, and Jhanda Singh then
deputed his lieutenant, Mujja Singh, against Multan;
but that leader was repulsed and slain by the united
forces of the joint Afghan governors and of the Bhawalpur chief. Next year, or in 1772, these joint
managers quarrelled, and as one of them asked the
assistance of Jhanda Singh, that unscrupulous leader
was enabled to possess himself of the citadel. On his
return to the northward, he found that a rival claimant
of the Jammu chiefship had obtained the aid of Charat
Singh Sukerchukia, and of Jai Singh, the rising leader
of the Kanhaya Misal. Charat Singh was killed by the
bursting of his own matchlock, and Jai Singh was then
so base as to procure the assassination of Jhanda Singh.
Being satisfied with the removal of this powerful chief,
the Kanhaya left the Jammu claimant to prosecute his
cause alone, and entered into a league with the old
Jassa Singh Ahluwalia, for the expulsion of the other
Jassa Singh the Carpenter, who had rendered Ahmad
Shah's nominal deputy, Ghamand Chand of Katotch,
and other Rajputs of the hills, his tributaries. The
Ramgarhia Jassa Singh was at last beaten, and he
retired to the wastes of Hariana to live by plunder. At
this time, or about 1774, died the Muhammadan governor of Kangra. He had contrived to maintain himself
in independence, or in reserved subjection to Delhi or
Kabul, although the rising chief of Katotch had long
desired to possess so famous a stronghold. Jai Singh
Kanhaya was prevailed on to assist him, and the place
fell; but the Sikh chose to keep it to himself, and the
possession of the imperial fort aided him in his usurpa-

*Side notes:* 1770. daula on the Jumna and Ganges, 1770. — Jhanda Singh of the Bhangi Misal pre-eminent, 1770. — Jammu rendered tributary. — Kasur reduced to submission. — and Multan occupied, 1772. — Jhanda Singh assassinated by Jai Singh Kanhaya, 1774. — Jai Singh Kanhaya and Jassa Singh Kalal expel Jassa the Carpenter. — Kangra falls to the Kanhaya Misal about 1774.

---

[1] The memoirs of the Bhawalpur family, and manuscript
Sikh histories. Cf. also Forster, *Travels*, i. 148.

tion of Jassa Singh's authority over the surrounding Rajas and Thakurs.[1]

Taimur Shah of Kabul recovers Multan, 1779.

In the south of the Punjab the Bhangi Sikhs continued predominant; they seem to have possessed the strong fort of Mankera as well as Multan, and to have levied exactions from Kalabagh downwards. They made an attempt to carry Shujabad, a place built by the Afghans on losing Multan, but seem to have failed. Taimur Shah, who succeeded his father in 1773, was at last induced or enabled to cross the Indus, but his views were directed towards Sind, Bhawalpur, and the Lower Punjab, and he seems to have had no thought of a reconquest of Lahore. In the course of 1777-8, two detachments of the Kabul army unsuccessfully endeavoured to dislodge the Sikhs from Multan, but in the season of 1778-9 the Shah marched in person against the place. Ghanda Singh, the new leader of the Bhangis, was embroiled with other Sikh chiefs, and his lieutenant surrendered the citadel after a show of resistance. Taimur Shah reigned until 1793, but he was fully occupied with Sindian, Kashmiri, and Uzbeg rebellions; the Sikhs were even unmolested in their possession of Rawalpindi, and their predatory horse traversed the plains of Chach up to the walls of Attock.[2]

Taimur Shah dies, leaving the Sikhs masters of the Upper Punjab as far as Attock, 1793.

The Phulkias master Hariana, 1768-78.

In the direction of Hariana and Delhi, the young Amar Singh Phulkia began systematically to extend and consolidate his authority. He acquired Sirsa and Fatehabad, his territories marched with those of Bikaner and Bhawalpur, and his feudatories of Jind and Kaithal possessed the open country around Hansi and Rohtak. He was recalled to his capital of Patiala by a final effort of the Delhi court to re-establish its authority in the province of Sirhind. An army, headed by the minister of the day, and by Farkhunda Bukht, one of the imperial family, marched in the season 1779-80. Karnal was recovered; some payments were promised; and the eminent Krora-Singhia leader, Baghel Singh,

An expedition sent from Delhi against the Malwa Sikhs, 1779-80.

---

[1] The memoirs of the Bhawalpur chief and manuscript Sikh accounts. Cf. Murray, *Ranjit Singh*, p. 38, &c.; and Forster, *Travels*, i. 283, 286, 336.

Ranjit Deo, of Jammu, died in A.D. 1770.

Charat Singh was killed accidentally, and Jhanda Singh was assassinated, in 1774.

Hari Singh Bhangi appears to have been killed in battle with Amar Singh of Patiala, about 1770.

[2] Memoirs of the Bhawalpur chief, and other manuscript histories. Cf. Browne, *India Tracts*, ii. 28, and Forster, *Travels*, i. 324; Elphinstone (*Kabul*, ii. 303) makes 1781, and not 1779, the date of the recovery of Multan from the Sikhs.

tendered his submission. Dehsu Singh, of Kaithal, 1781-5.
was seized and heavily mulcted, and the army approached Patiala. Amar Singh promised fealty and tribute, and Baghel Singh seemed sincere in his mediation; but suddenly it was learnt that a large body of Sikhs had marched from Lahore, and the Mughal troops retired Succeeds in with precipitation to Pañipat, not without a suspicion part only. that the cupidity of the minister had been gratified with Sikh gold, and had induced him to betray his master's interests. Amar Singh died in 1781, leaving a minor Amar son of imbecile mind. Two years afterwards a famine Singh of Patiala desolated Hariana; the people perished or sought other dies, 1781. homes; Sirsa was deserted, and a large tract of country passed at the time from under regular sway, and could not afterwards be recovered by the Sikhs.[1]

In the Doab of the Ganges and Jumna, the Sikhs Zabita Khan, son rather subsidized Zabita Khan, the son of Najib-ud- of Najib-daula, than became his deferential allies. That chief ud-daula, had designs, perhaps, upon the titular ministry of the aided in his empire, and having obtained a partial success over the designs on imperial troops, he proceeded, in 1776, towards Delhi, the minis-with the intention of laying siege to the city. But try by the Sikhs, 1776. when the time for action arrived he mistrusted his power; the emperor, on his part, did not care to provoke him too far; a compromise was effected, and he was confirmed in his possession of Saharanpur. On this occasion Zabita Khan was accompanied by a body of Sikhs, and he was so desirous of conciliating them, that he is credibly said to have adopted their dress, to have received the Pahul, or initiatory rite, and to have taken the new name of Dharam Singh.[2]

Jassa Singh Ramgarhia, when compelled to fly to the The ravages of the Sikhs Punjab by the Kanhaya and Ahluwalia confederacies, in the Doab was aided by Amar Singh Phulkia in establishing him- and Rohil-self in the country near Hissar, whence he proceeded khand to levy exactions up to the walls of Delhi. In 1781 a under Ba-body of Phulkia and other Sikhs marched down the ghel Singh Doab, but they were successfully attacked under the Krora Singhia, walls of Meerut by the imperial commander Mirza 1781-5. Shafi Beg, and Gajpat Singh of Jind was taken pri- The Sikhs soner. Nevertheless, in 1783, Baghel Singh and other defeated at commanders were strong enough to propose crossing Meerut, the Ganges, but they were deterred by the watchful- 1783.

[1] Manuscript histories, and Mr. Ross Bell's report of 1836, on the Bhattiana boundary. Cf. Francklin, *Shah Alam*, pp. 86, 90, and Shah Nawaz Khan's Epitome of Indian History, called *Mirrit-i-Aftab Numa*.

[2] Cf. Forster, *Travels*, i. 325; *Browne*, India Tracts; ii. 29; and Francklin, *Shah Alam*, p. 72.

ness of the Oudh troops on the opposite bank. The destructive famine already alluded to seems to have compelled Jassa Singh to move into the Doab, and, in

1785, Rohilkhand was entered by the confederates and plundered as far as Chandosi, which is within forty miles of Bareilly. At this period Zabita Khan was almost confined to the walls of his fort of Ghausgarh, and the hill raja of Garhwal, whose ancestor had received Dara as a refugee in defiance of Aurangzeb, had been rendered tributary, equally with all his brother Rajputs, in the lower hills westward to the Chenab.

The Sikhs were predominant from the frontiers of Oudh to the Indus, and the traveller Forster amusingly describes the alarm caused to a little chief and his people by the appearance of *two* Sikh horsemen under the walls of their fort, and the assiduous services and respectful attention which the like number of troopers met with from the local authorities of Garhwal, and from the assembled wayfarers at a place of public reception.[1]

In the Punjab itself Jai Singh Kanhaya continued to retain a paramount influence. He had taken Mahan Singh, the son of Charat Singh Sukerchukia, under his protection, and he aided the young chief in capturing

Russulnaggar on the Chenab, from a Muhammadan family. Mahan Singh's reputation continued to increase, and, about 1784-5, he so far threw off his dependence upon Jai Singh as to interfere in the affairs of Jammu on his own account. His interference is understood to have ended in the plunder of the place; but the wealth he had obtained and the independence he had shown both roused the anger of Jai Singh, who rudely repelled Mahan Singh's apologies and offers of atonement, and the spirit of the young chief being fired, he went away resolved to appeal to arms. He sent to Jassa Singh Ramgarhia, and that leader was glad of an opportunity of recovering his lost possessions. He joined Mahan Singh, and easily procured the aid of Sansar Chand, the grandson of Ghamand Chand of

Katotch. The Kanhayas were attacked and defeated; Gurbakhsh Singh, the eldest son of Jai Singh, was killed, and the spirit of the old man was effectually

humbled by this double sorrow. Jassa Singh was restored to his territories, and Sansar Chand obtained the fort of Kangra, which his father and grandfather had been so desirous of possessing. Mahan Singh now

---

[1] Forster, *Travels*, i. 228, 229, 262, 326 and note. Cf. also Francklin. *Shah Alam*, pp. 93, 94, and the Persian epitome *Mirrit-i-Aftab Numa*.

became the most influential chief in the Punjab, and he gladly assented to the proposition of Sudda Kour, the widow of Jai Singh's son, that the alliance of the two families should be cemented by the union of her infant daughter with Ranjit Singh, the only son of Mahan Singh, and who was born to him about 1780. Mahan Singh next proceeded to attack Gujrat, the old Bhangi chief of which, Gujar Singh, his father's confederate, died in 1791; but he was himself taken ill during the siege, and expired in the beginning of the following year at the early age of twenty-seven.[1]

1793-7. made over to Sansar Chand of Katotch. Mahan Singh pre-eminent among the Sikhs 1785-92. Mahan Singh dies, 1792.

Shah Zaman succeeded to the throne of Kabul in the year 1793, and his mind seems always to have been filled with idle hopes of an Indian empire. In the end of 1795 he moved to Hassan Abdal, and sent forward a party which is said to have recovered the fort of Rohtas; but the exposed state of his western dominions induced him to return to Kabul. The rumours of another Durrani invasion do not seem to have been unheeded by the princes of Upper India, then pressed by the Marathas and the English. Ghulam Muhammad, the defeated usurper of Rohilkhand, crossed the Punjab in 1795-6, with the view of inducing Shah Zaman to prosecute his designs, and he was followed by agents on the part of Asaf-ud-daula of Oudh, partly to counteract, perhaps, the presumed machinations of his enemy, but mainly to urge upon his majesty that all Muhammadans would gladly hail him as a deliverer. The Shah reached Lahore, in the beginning of 1797, with thirty thousand men, and he endeavoured to conciliate the Sikhs and to render his visionary supremacy an agreeable burden. Several chiefs joined him, but the proceedings of his brother Mahmud recalled him before he had time to make any progress in settling the country, even had the Sikhs been disposed to submit without a struggle; but the Sikhs were perhaps less dismayed than the beaten Marathas and the ill-informed English. The latter lamented, with the Wazir of Oudh, the danger to which his dominions were exposed; they prudently cantoned a force at Anupshahr in the Doab, and their apprehensions led them to depute a mission to Teheran, with the view of insti-

Shah Zaman succeeds to the throne of Kabul, 1793.

Invited to enter India by the Rohillas and the Wazir of Oudh, 1795-6.

Shah Zaman at Lahore, 1797.

[1] Manuscript histories and chronicles. Cf. Forster, *Travels*, i. 288; Murray, *Ranjit Singh*, pp. 42, 48; and Moorcroft, *Travels*, i. 127. The date of 1785-6, for the reduction of the Kanhayas and the restoration of Jassa Singh, &c., is preferred to 1782, which is given by Murray, partly because the expedition to Rohilkhand took place in 1785, as related by Forster (*Travels*, i. 326 note), and Jassa Singh is generally admitted to have been engaged in it, being then in banishment.

1798-9.
The Shah's
second
march to
Lahore,
1798-9.

gating the Shah of Persia to invade the Afghan territories. Shah Zaman renewed his invasion in 1798; a body of five thousand men, sent far in advance, was attacked and dispersed on the Jhelum, but he entered Lahore without opposition, and renewed his measures of mixed conciliation and threat. He found an able leader, but doubtful partisan, in Nizam-ud-din Khan, a Pathan of Kasur, who had acquired a high local reputation, and he was employed to coerce such of the Sikhs, including the youthful Ranjit Singh, as pertinaciously kept aloof. *They* distrusted the Shah's honour; but Nizam-ud-din distrusted the permanence of his power, and he prudently forbore to proceed to extremities against neighbours to whom he might soon be left a prey. Some resultless skirmishing took place, but the designs of Mahmud, who had obtained the support of Persia, again withdrew the ill-fated king to the west, and he quitted Lahore in the beginning of 1799.

Ranjit
Singh
rises to
eminence,

During this second invasion the character of Ranjit Singh seems to have impressed itself, not only on other Sikh leaders, but on the Durrani Shah. He coveted Lahore, which was associated in the minds of men with the possession of power, and, as the king was unable to cross his heavy artillery over the flooded Jhelum, he made it known to the aspiring chief that their transmission would be an acceptable service. As

and obtains
a cession of
Lahore
from the
Afghan
king, 1799.

many pieces of cannon as could be readily extricated were sent after the Shah, and Ranjit Singh procured what he wanted, a royal investiture of the capital of the Punjab. Thenceforward the history of the Sikhs gradually centres in their great Maharaja; but the revival of the Maratha power in Upper India, and the appearance of the English on the scene, require that the narrative of his achievements should be somewhat interrupted.[1]

1785-8.
The power

The abilities of Madhagi Sindhia restored the

---

[1] Elphinstone (*Kabul*, ii. 308) states that Shah Zaman was exhorted to undertake his expedition of 1795 by a refugee prince of Delhi, and encouraged in it by Tipu Sultan. The journey of Ghulam Muhammad, the defeated Rohilla chief, and the mission of the Wazir of Oudh, are given on the authority of the Bhawalpur family annals, and from the same source may be added an interchange of deputations on the part of Shah Zaman and Sindhia, the envoys, as in the other instance, having passed through Bhawalpur town. A suspicion of the complicity of Asaf-ud-daula, of Lucknow, does not seem to have occurred to the English historians, who rather dilate on the exertions made by their government to protect their pledged ally from the northern invaders. Nevertheless, the statements of the Bhawalpur chronicles on the subject seem in every way credible.

power of the Marathas in Northern India, and the discipline of his regular brigades seemed to place his administration on a firm and lasting basis. He mastered
Agra in 1785, and was made deputy vicegerent of the
empire by the titular emperor, Shah Alam. He entered
at the same time into an engagement with the confederate Sikh chiefs, to the effect that of all their joint
conquests on either side of the Jumna, he should have
two-thirds and the 'Khalsa' the remainder.[1]  This
alliance was considered to clearly point at the kingdom
of Oudh, which the English were bound to defend, and
perhaps to affect the authority of Delhi, which they
wished to see strong; but the schemes of the Maratha
were for a time interrupted by the Rohilla Ghulam
Kadir.  This chief succeeded his father, Zabita Khan,
in 1785, and had contrived, by an adventurous step, to
become the master of the emperor's person a little more
than a year afterwards. He was led on from one
excess to another, till at last, in 1788, he put out the
eyes of his unfortunate sovereign, plundered the palace
in search of imaginary treasures, and declared an unheeded youth to be the successor of Akbar and
Aurangzeb. These proceedings facilitated Sindhia's
views, nor was his supremacy unwelcome in Delhi
after the atrocities of Ghulam Kadir and the savage
Afghans.  His regular administration soon curbed the
predatory Sikhs, and instead of being received as allies
they found that they would merely be tolerated as
dependants or as servants.  Rai Singh, the patriarchal
chief of Jagadhri, was retained for the time as farmer
of considerable districts in the Doab, and, during ten
years, three expeditions of exaction were directed
against Patiala and other states in the province of
Sirhind.  Patiala was managed with some degree of
prudence by Nanu Mal, the Hindu Diwan of the
deceased Amar Singh; but he seems to have trusted
for military support to Baghel Singh, the leader of the
Krora Singhias, who contrived to maintain a large
body of horse, partly as a judicious mediator, and
partly by helping Patiala in levying contributions on
weaker brethren, in aid of the Mughal and Maratha
demands, which could neither be readily met nor
prudently resisted.[2]

General Perron succeeded his countryman, De
Boigne, in the command of Daulat Rao Sindhia's
largest regular force, in the year 1797, and he was soon

---

[1] Browne, *India Tracts*, ii. 29.
[2] Manuscript accounts. Cf. Francklin, *Shah Alam*, pp.
179-85.

1787-1800

Sindhia's
deputy in
Northern
India, 1797.

Sindhia's
and Per-
ron's views
crossed by
Holkar and
George
Thomas,
1787-97.

George
Thomas
establishes
himself at
Hansi.
1798.

after appointed the Maharaja's deputy in Northern India. His ambition surpassed his powers; but his plans were nevertheless systematic, and might have temporarily extended his own, or the Maratha, authority to Lahore, had not Sindhia's influence been endangered by Holkar, and had not Perron's own purposes been crossed by the hostility and success of the adventurer George Thomas.[1] This Englishman was bred to the sea, but an eccentricity of character, or a restless love of change, caused him to desert from a vessel of war at Madras in 1781-2, and to take military service with the petty chiefs of that presidency. He wandered to the north of India, and in 1787 he was employed by the well-known Begum Samru,[2] and soon rose high in favour with that lady. In six years he became dissatisfied, and entered the service of Appa Khande Rao, one of Sindhia's principal officers, and under whom De Boigne had formed his first regiments. While in the Maratha employ, Thomas defeated a party of Sikhs at Karnal, and he performed various other services; but seeing the distracted state of the country, he formed the not impracticable scheme of establishing a separate authority of his own. He repaired the crumbling walls of the once important Hansi, he assembled soldiers about him, cast guns, and deliberately proceeded to acquire territory. Perron was apprehensive of his power—the more so, perhaps, as Thomas was encouraged by Holkar, and supported by Lakwa Dada and other Marathas, who entertained a great jealousy of the French commandant.[3]

[1] [For an excellent sketch of the life of this adventurer see the article 'A Free Lance from Tipperary' in *Strangers within the Gates,* by G. Festing. Edinburgh, and London, 1914. —ED.]

[2] [This remarkable woman, whose origin is wrapped in mystery, was said to have been a dancing-girl in Delhi. She subsequently married 'Somru', a European adventurer, who had entered the service of the Emperor and had received the Jagir of Sardhana, a few miles from Delhi. 'Somru'—whose real name was Reinhard—was a man of the foulest antecedents, and among his other exploits he had been principally concerned in the murder of the English prisoners at Patna in 1763. Upon her husband's death the Begum succeeded to his estate and to the leadership of the disreputable band of cut-throats who formed his army. After the battle of Assaye she submitted to the English, embraced Christianity about 1781, and was publicly embraced by Lord Lake, to the great horror of the spectators. She ended her days in great sanctity, and was buried in the Roman Catholic Cathedral at Sardhana which she herself had built. See also Sleeman, *Rambles and Recollections,* ed. V. A. Smith, chap. 75. Oxford University Press, 1915.—ED.]

[3] Francklin, *Life of George Thomas,* pp. 1, 79, 107, &c.,

In 1799 Thomas invested the town of Jind, belonging to Bhag Singh, of the Phulkia confederacy. The old chief, Baghel Singh Krora Singhia, and the Amazonian sister of the imbecile Raja of Patiala, relieved the place, but they were repulsed when they attacked Thomas on his retreat to Hansi. In 1800 Thomas took Fatehabad, which had been deserted during the famine of 1783, and subsequently occupied by the predatory Bhattis of Hariana, then rising into local repute, notwithstanding the efforts of the Patiala chief, who, however, affected to consider them as his subjects, and gave them some aid against Thomas. Patiala was the next object of Thomas's ambition, and he was encouraged by the temporary secession of the sister of the chief; but the aged Tara Singh, of the Dallehwala confederacy, interfered, and Thomas had to act with caution. He obtained, nevertheless, a partial success over Tara Singh, he received the submission of the Pathans of Maler Kotla, and he was welcomed as a deliverer by the converted Muhammadans of Raikot, who had held Ludhiana for some time, and all of whom were equally jealous of the Sikhs. At this time Sahib Singh, a Bedi of the race of Nanak, pretended to religious inspiration, and, having collected a large force, he invested Ludhiana, took the town of Maler Kotla, and called on the English adventurer to obey him as the true representative of the Sikh prophet. But Sahib Singh could not long impose even on his countrymen, and he had to retire across the Sutlej. Thomas's situation was not greatly improved by the absence of the Bedi, for the combination against him was general, and he retired from the neighbourhood of Ludhiana towards his stronghold of Hansi. He again took the field, and attacked Safidon, an old town belonging to the chief of Jind. He was repulsed, but the place not appearing tenable, it was evacuated, and he obtained possession of it. At this time he is said to have had ten battalions and sixty guns, and to have possessed a territory yielding about 450,000 rupees, two-thirds of which he held by right of seizure, and one-third as a Maratha feudatory; but he had rejected all Perron's overtures with suspicion, and Perron was resolved to crush him. Thomas was thus forced to come to terms with the Sikhs, and he wished it to appear that he had engaged them on his side against Perron; but they were really desirous of getting rid of one who plainly designed their ruin, or at least their subjection, and the alacrity

*1787-1800 and engages in hostilities with the Sikhs, 1799.*

*Thomas marches towards Ludhiana, 1800.*

*Opposed by Sahib Singh Bedi.*

*Retires to Hansi, but afterwards masters Safidon near Delhi.*

*Thomas rejects Perron's overtures and resorts to arms, 1801.*

and Major Smith, *Account of Regular Corps in the Service of Indian Princes*, p. 118, &c.

of Patiala in the Maratha service induced a promise, on the part of the French commander, of the restitution of the conquests of Amar Singh in Hariana. After twice beating back Perron's troops at points sixty miles distant, Thomas was compelled to surrender in the beginning of 1802, and he retired into the British provinces, where he died in the course of the same year.[1]

Perron had thus far succeeded. His lieutenant, by name Bourquin, made a progress through the Cis-Sutlej states to levy contributions, and the commander himself dreamt of a dominion reaching to the Afghan hills, and of becoming as independent of Sindhia as that chief was of the Peshwa.[2] He formed an engagement with Ranjit Singh for a joint expedition to the Indus, and for a partition of the country south of Lahore;[3] but Holkar had given a rude shock to Sindhia's power, and Perron had long evaded a compliance with the Maharaja's urgent calls for troops to aid him where support was most essential. Sindhia became involved with the English, and the interested hesitation of Perron was punished by his supersession. He was not able, or he did not try, to recover his authority by vigorous military operations; he knew he had committed himself, and he effected his escape from the suspicious Marathas to the safety and repose of the British territories, which were then about to be extended by the victories of Delhi and Laswari, of Assaye and Argaon.[4]

In the beginning of the eighteenth century the agents of the infant company of English merchants were vexatiously detained at the imperial court by the insurrection of the Sikhs under Banda, and the discreet 'factors', who were petitioning for some trading privileges, perhaps witnessed the heroic death of the national *Singhs*, the soldiers of the 'Khalsa', without comprehending the spirit evoked by the genius of Gobind, and without dreaming of the broad fabric of

1 See generally Francklin, *Life of George Thomas,* and Major Smith, *Account of Regular Corps in Indian States,* p. 21, &c. The Sikh accounts attribute many exploits to the sister of the Raja of Patiala, and among them an expedition into the hill territory of Nahan, the state from which Patiala wrested the vale of Pinjaur, with its hanging gardens, not, however, without the aid of Bourquin, the deputy of Perron.

2 Malcolm (*Sketch,* p. 106) considers that Perron could easily have reduced the Sikhs, and mastered the Punjab.

3 This alliance is given on the authority of a representation made to the Resident at Delhi, agreeably to his letter to Sir David Ochterlony of July 5, 1814.

4 Cf. Major Smith, *Account of Regular Corps in Indian States,* p. 31, &c.

empire about to be reared on their own patient labours.[1] Forty years afterwards, the merchant Omichand played a conspicuous part in the revolution which was crowned by the battle of Plassey; but the sectarian Sikh, the worldly votary of Nanak, who used religion as a garb of outward decorum, was outwitted by the audacious falsehood of Clive; he quailed before the stern scorn of the English conqueror, and he perished the victim of his own base avarice.[2] In 1784 the progress of the genuine Sikhs attracted the notice of Hastings, and he seems to have thought that the presence of a British agent at the court of Delhi might help to deter them from molesting the Wazir of Oudh.[3] But the Sikhs had learnt to dread others as well as to be a cause of fear, and shortly afterwards they asked the British Resident to enter into a defensive alliance against the Marathas, and to accept the services of thirty thousand horsemen, who had posted themselves near Delhi to watch the motions of Sindhia.[4] The

*1957-88.*

the campaign against Banda. 1715-17.

Clive and Omichand. 1757.

Warren Hastings tries to guard Oudh against the Sikhs. 1784

The Sikhs ask English aid against the Marathas 1788.

[1] See Orme, *History*, ii. 22, &c., and Mill, Wilson's edition, iii. 34, &c. The mission was two years at Delhi during 1715, 1716, 1717, and the genuine patriotism of Mr. Hamilton, the surgeon of the deputation, mainly contributed to procure the cession of thirty-seven villages near Calcutta, and the exemption from duty of goods protected by English passes. This latter privilege was a turning-point in the history of the English in India, for it gave an impulse to trade, which vastly increased the importance of British subjects, if it added little to the profits of the associated merchants. [It may be added that a dispute about the issue of those passes brought about an open rupture between the East India Company and Mir Kasim, Nawab of Bengal, in 1763. The latter was utterly defeated at the Battle of Bunar in 1764 and as one of the terms of peace in the following year—the year of Clive's return to India--the Diwani (fiscal administration) of Bengal, Bihar and Orissa was granted by the Emperor Shah Alam to the Company, in return for a yearly payment of 26 lakhs, while the Nawab, the successor of Mir Kasim, was deprived of all power and pensioned.—ED.]

In the *Granth* of Guru Gobind there are at least four allusions to Europeans, the last referring specially to an Englishman. First, in the *Akal Stut*, Europeans are enumerated among the tribes inhabiting India, second and third, in the *Kalki* chapters of the 24 *Autars*, apparently in praise of the systematic modes of Europeans; and fourth, in the Persian *Hikayats*, where both a European and an Englishman appear as champions for the hand of a royal damsel, to be vanquished, of course, by the hero of the tale.

[2] That Omichand was a Sikh is given on the authority of Forster, *Travels*, i. 337. That he died of a broken heart is doubted by Professor Wilson. (Mill, *India*, iii. 192 note, ed, 1840.)

[3] Browne, *India Tracts*, ii 29, 30; and Francklin, *Shah Alam.* pp. 115, 116.

[4] Auber, *Rise and Progress of the British Power in India.*

8 (45-68/1975)

English had then a slight knowledge of a new and distant people, and an estimate, two generations old, may provoke a smile from the protectors of Lahore. 'The Sikhs', says Col. Francklin, 'are in their persons tall. ... their aspect is ferocious, and their eyes piercing; ... they resemble the Arabs of the Euphrates, but they speak the language of the Afghans; ... their collected army amounts to 250,000 men, a terrific force, yet from want of union not much to be dreaded.'[1] The judicious and observing Forster put some confidence in similar statements of their vast array, but he estimated more surely than any other early writer the real character of the Sikhs, and the remark of 1783, that an able chief would probably attain to absolute power on the ruins of the rude commonwealth, and become the terror of his neighbours, has been amply borne out by the carrer of Ranjit Singh.[2]

The battle of Delhi[3] was fought on the 11th Septemeber, 1803, and five thousand Sikhs swelled an army which the speedy capture of Aligarh had taken by surprise.[4] The Marathas were overthrown, and the Sikhs dispersed; but the latter soon afterwards tendered their allegiance to the British commander. Among the more important chiefs whose alliance or whose occasional services were accepted were Bhai Lal Singh of Kaithal, who had witnessed the success of Lord Lake, Bhag Singh, the patriarchal chief of Jind, and, after a time, Bhanga Singh, the savage master of Tha-

---

ii. 26, 27. The chief who made the overtures was Dulcha Singh of Rudaur on the Jumna, who afterwards entered Sindhia's service. Cf. Francklin, *Shah Alam,* p. 78 note.

[1] Francklin, *Shah Alam,* pp. 75, 77, 78.

[2] Forster's *Travels,* ii. 340. See also p. 324, where he says the Sikhs had raised in the Punjab a solid structure of religion. The remark of the historian Robertson may also be quoted as apposite, and with the greater reason as prominence has lately been given to it in the House of Commons on the occasion of thanking the army for its services during the Sikh campaign of 1848-9. He says that the enterprising commercial spirit of the English, and the martial ardour of the Sikhs, who possess the energy natural to men in the earlier stages of society, can hardly fail to lead sooner or later to open hostility. (*Disquisition Concerning Ancient India,* note iv, sect. 1, written in 1789-90.)

[3] [For an interesting discussion as to the exact site of this battle, the result of which was the occupation of Delhi by the English and the placing of the Emperor Shah Alam under their protection, the reader is referred to an article by Sir Edward Maclagan, in the *Journal of the Punjab Historical Society,* vol. iii.—ED.]

[4] Major Smith, *Account of Regular Corps in Indian States,* p. 34.

nesar.[1] The victory of Laswari was won within two months, and the Maratha power seemed to be annihilated in Northern India. The old blind emperor Shah Alam was again flattered with the semblance of kingly power, his pride was soothed by the demeanour of the conqueror, and, as the Mughal name was still imposing, the feelings of the free but loyal soldier were doubtless gratified by the bestowal of a title which declared an English nobleman to be 'the sword of the state' of the great Tamerlane.[2]

1803-5.

of Jind and Kaithal.

Shah Alam freed from Maratha thraldom.

The enterprising Jaswant Rao Holkar had by this time determined on the invasion of Upper India, and the retreat of Col. Monson[3] buoyed him up with hopes of victory and dominion. Delhi was invested, and the Doab was filled with troops; but the successful defence of the capital by Sir David Ochterlony, and the reverse of Dig, drove the great marauder back into Rajputana. During these operations a British detachment, under Col. Burn, was hard pressed at Shamli, near Saharanpur, and the opportune assistance of Lal Singh of Kaithal and Bhag Singh of Jind contributed to its ultimate relief.[4] The same Sikh chiefs deserved and received the thanks of Lord Lake for attacking and killing one Ika Rao, a Maratha commander who had taken up a position between Delhi and Panipat; but others were disposed to adhere to their sometime allies, and Sher Singh of Buriya fell in action with Col. Burn, and the conduct of Gurdit Singh of Ladwa induced the British general to deprive him of his villages in the Doab, and of the town of Karnal.[5]

The English wars with Holkar, 1804-5.

The Sikhs mostly side with the English and render good service.

In 1805 Holkar and Amir Khan again moved northward, and proclaimed that they would be joined by the Sikhs, and even by the Afghans; but the rapid movements of Lord Lake converted their advance into a retreat or a flight. They delayed some time at Patiala, and they did not fail to make a pecuniary profit out of

Holkar retires towards the Sutlej, 1805.

Delays at Patiala.

---

[1] Manuscript memoranda of personal inquiries.

[2] Mill, *History of British India*, Wilson's ed., vi. 510.

[3] [He had made a rash advance into Holkar's territory in July 1804, to unite with another English force under Col. Murray. Lack of supplies caused him to retreat, and he only reached Agra at the end of August, after losing the major part of his army. However, he took his revenge at Dig, as that victory was mainly his work.—Ed.]

[4] Manuscript memoranda. Both this aid in 1804, and the opposition of the Sikhs at Delhi, in 1803, seem to have escaped the notice of English observers, or to have been thought undeserving of record by English historians. (Mill, *History*, vi. 503, 592, ed. 1840.)

[5] Manuscript memoranda of written documents and of personal inquiries.

1803-8.

the differences then existing between the imbecile Raja and his wife;[1] but when the English army reached the neighbourhood of Karnal, Holkar continued his retreat towards the north, levying contributions where he could, but without being joined by any of the Sikh chiefs of the Cis-Sutlej states. In the Punjab itself he is represented to have induced some to adopt his cause, but Ranjit Singh long kept aloof, and when at last he met Holkar at Amritsar, the astute young chief wanted aid in reducing the Pathans of Kasur before he would give the Marathas any assistance against the English. Amir Khan would wish it to be believed, that *he* was unwilling to be a party to an attack upon good Muhammadans, and it is certain that the perplexed Jaswant Rao talked of hurrying on to Peshawar; but Lord Lake was in force on the banks of the Beas, the political demands of the British commander were moderate, and, on the 24th December, 1805, an arrangement was come to, which allowed Holkar to return quietly to Central India.[2]

Lord Lake was joined on his advance by the two chiefs, Lal Singh and Bhag Singh, whose services have already been mentioned, and at Patiala he was welcomed by the weak and inoffensive Sahib Singh, who presented the keys of his citadel, ar expatiated on his devotion to the British Governmer   Bhag Singh was the maternal uncle of Ranjit Sing , and his services were not unimportant in determining that calculating leader to avoid an encounter with disciplined battalions and a trained artillery. Ranjit Singh is believed to have visited the British camp in disguise, that he might himself witness the military array of a leader who had successively vanquished both Sindhia and Holkar,[3] and he was, moreover, too acute to see any permanent advantage in linking his fortunes with those of men reduced to the condition of fugitives. Fateh Singh Ahluwalia, the grand-nephew of Jassa Singh Kalal, and the chosen companion of the future Maharaja, was the medium of intercourse, and an arrangement was soon entered into with 'Sardars' Ranjit Singh and Fateh Singh jointly, which provided that Holkar

*Side notes:*

**Halts at Amritsar, but fails in gaining over Ranjit Singh.**

**Holkar comes to terms with the English and marches to the south. 1805-6.**

**Friendly relations of the English with the Sikhs of Sirhind. 1803-8.**

**Formal engagement entered into with Ranjit Singh and Fateh Singh Ahluwalia. 1806.**

---

[1] Amir Khan, in his *Memoirs* (p. 276), says characteristically, that Holkar remarked to him, on observing the silly differences between the Raja and the Rani, 'God has assuredly sent us these two pigeons to pluck; do you espouse the cause of the one, while I take up with the other.'

[2] Cf. Amir Khan, *Memoirs*, pp. 276, 285: and Murray. *Ranjit Singh*, p. 57, &c.

[3] See Moorcroft, *Travels*. i. 102.

should be compelled to retire from Amritsar, and that 1804.
so long as the two chiefs conducted themselves as
friends the English Government would never form any
plans for the seizure of their territories.[1]  Lord Lake The Eng-
entered into a friendly correspondence with Sansar lish correspond with
Chand, of Katotch, who was imitating Ranjit Singh by Sansar
bringing the petty hill chiefs under subjection; but no Chand of
engagement was entered into, and the British com- Katotch.
mander returned to the provinces by the road of
Ambala and Karnal.[2]

The connexion of Lord Lake with many of the The Sikhs
Sikh chiefs of Sirhind had been intimate, and the ser- of Sirhind
regarded as
vices of some had been opportune and valuable.  Imme- virtually
diately after the battle of Delhi, Bhag Singh of Jind dependants
was upheld in a jagir which he possessed near that city, of the Eng-
and in 1804 another estate was conferred jointly on him lish by
and his friend Lal Singh of Kaithal.  In 1806 these Lord Lake.
leaders were further rewarded with life grants, yielding about £11,000 a year, and Lord Lake was understood to be willing to give them the districts of Hansi
and Hissar on the same terms; but these almost desert
tracts were objected to as unprofitable.  Other petty
chiefs received rewards corresponding with their
services, and all were assured that they should continue to enjoy the territorial possessions which they
held at the time of British interference without being
liable to the payment of tribute.  These declarations But the
or arrangements were made when the policy of Lord connection
not regu-
Wellesley was suffering under condemnation; the reign larly de-
of the English was to be limited by the Jumna, a for- clared, or
mal treaty with Jaipur was abrogated, the relations of made bind-
the Indian Government with Bhartpur were left ing in form.
doubtful, and, although nothing was made known to
the Sikh chiefs of Sirhind, their connexion with the
English came virtually to an end, so far as regarded
the reciprocal benefits of alliance.[3]

It is now necessary to return to Ranjit Singh, Retrospect
whose authority had gradually become predominant with reference to

[1] See the treaty itself, Appendix XXIII.
[2] The public records show that a newswriter was maintained for some time in Katotch, and the correspondence
about Sansar Chand leaves the impression that Ranjit Singh
could never wholly forget the Raja's original superiority, nor
the English divest themselves of a feeling that he was
independent of Lahore.
[3] The original grants to Jind, Kaithal, and others, and
also similar papers of assurance, are carefully preserved by
the several families; and the various English documents show
that Bhag Singh, of Jind, was always regarded with much
kindliness by Lord Lake, Sir John Malcolm, and Sir David
Ochterlony.

1799-1804.

Ranjit
Singh's rise.

Ranjit
Singh mas-
ters Lahore.
1799.

Reduces
the Bhangi
Misal and
the Pathans
of Kasur,
1801-2.

Allies him-
self with
Fateh
Singh
Ahluwalia.

Ranjit
Singh ac-
quires Am-
ritsar, 1802;

and con-
fines San-
sar Chand
to the hills,
1803-4,

who be-
comes in-
volver'
with the
Gurkhas.

among the Sikh people. His first object was to master Lahore from the incapable chiefs of the Bhangi confederacy who possessed it, and before Shah Zaman had been many months gone, effect was given to his grant by a dexterous mixture of force and artifice. Ranjit Singh made Lahore his capital, and, with the aid of the Kanhayas (or Ghani) confederacy, he easily reduced the whole of the Bhangis to submission, although they were aided by Nizam-ud-din Khan of Kasur. In 1801-2 the Pathan had to repent his rashness; his strongholds were difficult to capture, but he found it prudent to become a feudatory, and to send his best men to follow a new master. After this success Ranjit Singh went to bathe in the holy pool of Taran Taran, and, meeting with Fateh Singh Ahluwalia, he conceived a friendship for him, as has been mentioned, and went through a formal exchange of turbans, symbolical of brotherhood. During 1802 the allies took Amritsar from the widow of the last Bhangi leader of note, and, of their joint spoil, it fell to the share of the master of the other capital of the Sikh country. In 1803 Sansar Chand, of Katotch, in prosecution of his schemes of aggrandizement, made two attempts to occupy portions of the fertile Doab of Jullundur, but he was repulsed by Ranjit Singh and his confederate. In 1804 Sansar Chand again quitted his hills, and captured Hoshiarpur and Bajwara; but Ranjit Singh's approach once more compelled him to retreat, and he soon afterwards became involved with the Gurkhas, a new people in search of an empire which should comprise the whole range of Himalayas.[1]

---

[1] Cf. Murray, *Ranjit Singh*, pp. 51, 55.

Capt. Murray, the political agent at Ambala, and Capt. Wade, the political agent at Ludhiana, each wrote a narrative of the life of Ranjit Singh, and that of the former was printed in 1834, with a few corrections and additions, and some notes, by Mr. Thoby Prinsep, secretary to the Indian Government. The author has not seen Capt. Wade's report, or narrative, but he believes that it, even in a greater degree than Capt. Murray's, was founded on personal recollections and on oral report, rather than on contemporary English documents, which reflected the opinions of the times, and which existed in sufficient abundance after 1803 especially. The two narratives in question were, indeed, mainly prepared from accounts drawn up by intelligent Indians, at the requisition of the English functionaries, and of these the chronicles of Buta Shah, a Muhammadan, and Sohan Lal, a Hindu, are the best known, and may be had for purchase. The inquiries of Capt. Wade, in especial, were extensive, and to both officers the public is indebted for the preservation of a continuous narrative of Ranjit Singh's actions.

The latter portion of the present chapter, and also chapters

In little more than a year after Shah Zaman quitted the Punjab, he was deposed and blinded by his brother Mahmud, who was in his turn supplanted by a third brother, Shah Shuja, in the year 1803. These revolutions hastened the fall of the exotic empire of Ahmad Shah, and Ranjit Singh was not slow to try his arms against the weakened Durrani governors of districts and provinces. In 1804-5 he marched to the westward; he received homage and presents from the Muhammadans of Jhang and Sahiwal, and Muzaffar Khan of Multan, successfully deprecated an attack by rich offerings. Ranjit Singh had felt his way and was satisfied; he returned to Lahore, celebrated the festival of the Holi in his capital, and then went to bathe in the Ganges at Hardwar, or to observe personally the aspect of affairs to the eastward of the Punjab. Towards the close of 1805 he made another western inroad, and added weight to the fetters already imposed on the proprietor of Jhang; but the approach of Holkar and Amir Khan recalled, first Fateh Singh, and afterwards himself, to the proper city of the whole Sikh people. The danger seemed imminent, for a famed leader of the dominant Marathas was desirous of bringing down an Afghan host, and the English army, exact in discipline, and representing a power of unknown views and resources, had reached the neighbourhood of Amritsar.[1]

*1803-5.*

*Shah Zaman deposed by Shah Mahmud and the Durrani empire weakened; wherefore Ranjit Singh proceeds to the south-west of the Punjab, 1805.*

*Returns to the north on Holkar's approach, 1805.*

A formal council was held by the Sikhs, but a portion only of their leaders were present. The singleness of purpose, the confident belief in the aid of God, which had animated mechanics and shepherds to resent persecution, and to triumph over Ahmad Shah, no longer possessed the minds of their descendants, born to comparative power and affluence, and who, like rude and ignorant men broken loose from all law, gave the rein to their grosser passions. Their ambition was personal and their desire was for worldly enjoyment. The genuine spirit of Sikhism had again sought the dwelling of the peasant to reproduce itself in another form; the rude system of mixed independence and confederacy was unsuited to an extended dominion; it had served its ends of immediate agglomeration, and the 'Misals' were in effect dissolved. The mass of the people remained satisfied with their village freedom, to

*A Sikh Gurumatta, or national council, held;*

*but the confederate system found decayed and lifeless.*

VI and VII, follow very closely the author's narratives of the British connexion with the Sikhs, drawn up for Government, a [literary] use which he trusts may be made, without any impropriety, of an unprinted paper of his own writing.

[1] See Elphinstone, *Kabul*, ii. 325; and Murray, *Ranjit Singh*, pp. 56, 57.

which taxation and inquisition were unknown; but the petty chiefs and their paid followers, to whom their faith was the mere expression of a conventional custom, were anxious for predatory licence, and for additions to their temporal power. Some were willing to join the English, others were ready to link their fortunes with the Marathas, and all had become jealous of Ranjit Singh, who alone was desirous of excluding the stranger invaders, as the great obstacles to his own ambition of founding a military monarchy which should ensure to the people the congenial occupation of conquest. In truth, Ranjit Singh laboured, with more or less of intelligent design, to give unity and coherence to diverse atoms and scattered elements; to mould the increasing Sikh nation into a well-ordered state or commonwealth, as Gobind had developed a sect into a people, and had given application and purpose to the general institutions of Nanak.[1]

*and a single temporal authority virtually admitted in the person of Ranjit Singh.*

*Ranjit Singh interferes in the affairs of the Sikhs of Sirhind 1806.*

Holkar retired, and Ranjit Singh, as has been mentioned, entered into a vague but friendly alliance with the British Government. Towards the close of the same year he was invited to interfere in a quarrel between the chief of Nabha and the Raja of Patiala, and it would be curious to trace whether the English authorities had first refused to mediate in the dispute in consequence of the repeated instructions to avoid all connexion with powers beyond the Jumna. Ranjit Singh crossed the Sutlej, and took Ludhiana from the declining Muhammadan family which had sought the protection of the adventurer George Thomas. The place was bestowed upon his uncle, Bhag Singh of Jind, and as both Jaswant Singh of Nabha, whom he had gone to aid, and Sahib Singh of Patiala, whom he had gone to coerce, were glad to be rid of his destructive arbitration, he retired with the present of a piece of artillery and some treasure, and went towards the hills of Kangra, partly that he might pay his superstitious devotions at the natural flames of Juala Mukhi.[2]

*Takes Ludhiana, 1806;*

*and receives offerings from Patiala.*

*Sansar Chand and*

At this time the unscrupulous ambition of Sansar Chand of Katotch had brought him into fatal collision

---

[1] Malcolm (*Sketch*, pp. 106, 107) remarks on the want of unanimity among the Sikhs at the time of Lord Lake's expedition. Cf. Murray, *Ranjit Singh*, pp. 57, 58.

[2] See Murray, *Ranjit Singh*, pp. 59, 60. The letter of Sir Charles Metcalfe to Government, of June 17, 1809, shows that Ranjit Singh was not strong enough at the time in question, 1806, to interfere, by open force, in the affairs of the Malwa Sikhs, and the letters of Sir David Ochterlony, of February 14, March 7, 1809 and July 30, 1811, show that the English engagements of 1805, with the Patiala and other chiefs, were virtually at an end, so far as regarded the reciprocal benefits of alliance.

with the Gurkhas. That able chief might have given
life to a confederacy against the common enemies of
all the old mountain principalities, who were already
levying tribute in Garhwal : but Sansar Chand in his
desire for supremacy had reduced the chief of Kahlur,
or Belaspur, to the desperate expedient of throwing
himself on the support of the Nepal commander. Amar
Singh Thappa gladly advanced, and, notwithstanding
the gallant resistance offered by the young chief of
Nalagarh, Sansar Chand's coadjutor in his own aggressions, the Gurkha authority was introduced between
the Sutlej and Jumna before the end of 1805, during
which year Amar Singh crossed the former river and
laid siege to Kangra. At the period of Ranjit Singh's
visit to Juala Mukhi, Sansar Chand was willing to
obtain his aid; but, as the fort was strong and the
sacrifices required considerable, he was induced to
trust to his own resources, and no arrangement was
then come to for the expulsion of the new enemy.[1]

1806.
the Gur-
khas, 1805.
Sansar
Chand and
h.s con-
federate of
Nalagarh
driven to
the north
of the Sut
lej. 1805;

and the
Gurkhas
invest
Kangra.

In 1807 Ranjit Singh first directed his attention to
Kasur, which was again rebellious, and the relative
independence of which caused him disquietude,
although its able chief, Nizam-ud-din, had been dead
for some time; nor was he, perhaps, without a feeling
that the reduction of a large colony of Pathans, and
the annexation of the mythological rival of Lahore,
would add to his own merit and importance. The
place was invested by Ranjit Singh, and by Jodh Singh
Ramgarhia, the son of his father's old ally, Jassa the
Carpenter. Want of unity weakened the resistance of
the then chief, Kutb-ud-din, and at the end of a month
he surrendered at discretion, and received a tract of
land on the opposite side of the Sutlej for his maintenance. Ranjit Singh afterwards proceeded towards
Multan, and succeeded in capturing the walled town;
but the citadel resisted such efforts as he was able to
make, and he was perhaps glad that the payment of a
sum of money enabled him to retire with credit; he
was, nevertheless, unwilling to admit his failure, and,

Ranjit
Singh ex-
pels the
Pathan
chief of Ka-
sur. 1807;

and partial-
ly succeeds
against
Multan.

[2] Cf. Murray, *Ranjit Singh*, p. 60; and Moorcroft, *Travels*,
i. 127, &c.

Sansar Chand attributed his overthrow by the Gurkhas
to his dismissal of his old Rajput troops and employment of
Afghans, at the instigation of the fugitive Rohilla chief, Ghulam
Muhammad, who had sought an asylum with him.

The Gurkhas crossed the Jumna to aid the chief of Nahan
against his subjects, and they crossed the Sutlej to aid one
Rajput prince against another—paths always open to new and
united races. References in public records show that the latter
river was crossed in A.D. 1805.

1807.

in the communications which he then held with the
Nawab of Bahawalpur, the ready improver of opportunities endeavoured to impress that chief with the
belief that a regard for him alone had caused the
Afghan governor to be left in possession of his stronghold.[1]

Ranjit
Singh em-
ploys
Mokham
Chand,
1807.

During the same year, 1807, Ranjit Singh took into
his employ a Kshattriya, named Mohkam Chand, an
able man, who fully justified the confidence reposed in
him. With this new servant in his train he proceeded
to interfere in the dissensions between the Raja of
Patiala and his intriguing wife, which were as lucrative
to the master of Lahore as they had before been to
Holkar and Amir Khan. The Rani wished to force
from the weak husband a large assignment for the
support of her infant son, and she tempted Ranjit
Singh, by the offer of a necklace of diamonds and a
piece of brass ordnance, to espouse her cause. He

Crosses the
Sutlej for
the second
time;

crossed the Sutlej, and decreed to the boy a maintenance of 50,000 rupees per annum. He then attacked
Naraingarh, between Ambala and the hills, and held
by a family of Rajputs, but he only secured it after
a repulse and a heavy loss. Tara Singh, the old chief
of the Dallehwala confederacy, who was with the
Lahore force on this occasion, died before Naraingarh,

and returns
to seize the
territories
of the
deceased
Dallehwala
chief.

and Ranjit Singh hastened back to secure his possessions in the Jullundur Doab. The widow of the aged
leader equalled the sister of the Raja of Patiala in
spirit, and she is described to have girded up her gar-
ments, and to have fought, sword in hand, on the
battered walls of the fort of Rahon.[2]

The Sikhs
of Sirhind
become ap-
prehensive
of Ranjit
Singh.

In the beginning of 1808 various places in the
Upper Punjab were taken from their independent Sikh
proprietors, and brought under the direct management
of the new kingdom of Lahore, and Mohkam Chand
was at the same time employed in effecting a settlement of the territories which had been seized on the
left bank of the Sutlej. But Ranjit Singh's systematic
aggressions had begun to excite fear in the minds of
the Sikhs of Sirhind, and a formal deputation, consist-

British
protection
asked,
1808;

ing of the chiefs of Jind and Kaithal, and the Diwan,
or minister, of Patiala, proceeded to Delhi, in March
1808, to ask for British protection. The communications

---

[1] Murray, *Ranjit Singh*, pp. 60, 61, and the manuscript
memoirs of the Bahawalpur family.

[2] Cf. Murray, *Ranjit Singh*, pp. 61, 63. The gun obtained
by Ranjit Singh from Patiala on this occasion was named Karri
Khan, and was captured by the English during the campaign
of 1845-6.

of the English Government with the chiefs of the
Cis-Sutlej states had not been altogether broken off,
and the Governor-General had at this time assured the
Muhammadan Khan of Kunjpura, near Karnal,[1] that
he need be under no apprehensions with regard to his
hereditary possessions, while the petty Sikh chief of
Sikri had performed some services which were deemed
worthy of a pension.[2] But the deputies of the collective
states could obtain no positive assurances from the
British authorities at Delhi, although they were led to
hope that, in the hour of need, they would not be
deserted. This was scarcely sufficient to save them
from loss, and perhaps from ruin; and, as Ranjit Singh
had sent messengers to calm their apprehensions, and
to urge them to join his camp, they left Delhi for the
purpose of making their own terms with the acknowledged Raja of Lahore.[3]

    The Governor-General of 1805,[4] who dissolved or
deprecated treaties with princes beyond the Jumna,
and declared that river to be the limit of British dominion, had no personal knowledge of the hopes and
fears with which the invasions of Shah Zaman agitated
the minds of men for the period of three or four years;
and had the Sikhs of Sirhind sought protection from
Lord Cornwallis, they would doubtless have received
a decisive answer in the negative. But the reply of
encouragement given in the beginning of 1808 was
prompted by renewed danger; and the belief that the
French, the Turkish, and the Persian emperors meditated the subjugation of India led another new Governor-General to seek alliances, not only beyond the
Jumna, but beyond the Indus.[5] The designs or the
desires of Napoleon appeared to render a defensive
alliance with the Afghans and with the Sikhs impera-
tive; Mr. Elphinstone was deputed to the court of Shah
Shuja, and in September 1808 Mr. Metcalfe was sent
on a mission to Ranjit Singh for the purpose of bring-

Marginal notes:
1808-9

but not
distinctly
acceded.

Whereupon
the chiefs
repair to
Ranjit
Singh.

The under-
stood de-
signs of the
French on
India
modify the
pol.cy of
the English
towards
the Sikhs
1808-9.

---

[1] In a document dated 18th January, 1808.

[2] Mr. Clerk of Ambala to the agent at Delhi, 19th May,
1837.

[3] See Murray, Ranjit Singh, pp. 64, 65.

[4] [Lord Cornwallis had been sent out in 1805 with strict
orders to pursue a pacific and economizing policy, as the
Directors were alarmed at the expense of the wars waged by
his predecessor—Lord Wellesley. But Cornwallis died two
months after his arrival, and was temporarily succeeded by
Sir G. Barlow.—Ed.]

[5] Mr. Auber (Rise and Progress of the British Power in
India, ii. 461), notices the triple alliance which threatened
Hindustan [Lord Minto had arrived as Governor-General in
1807.—Ed.]

1808-9.
The chiefs
of Sirhind
tak .;
under
protection,
and a close
alliance
sought
with Ranjit
Singh.

Mr. Met-
calfe sent
as envoy to
Lahore,
1808-9.
Aversion
of Ranjit
Singh to a
restrictive
treaty, and
his th.rd
expedition
across the
Sutlej.

British
troops
moved to
the Sutlej,
1809.

ing about the desired confederation.[1] The chiefs of Patiala, Jind, and Kaithal were also verbally assured that they had become dependent princes of the British Government; for the progress of Ranjit Singh seemed to render the interposition of some friendly states, between his military domination and the peaceful sway of the English, a measure of prudence and foresight.[2]

Mr. Metcalfe was received by Ranjit Singh at his newly conquered town of Kasur, but the chief affected to consider himself as the head of the whole Sikh people, and to regard the possession of Lahore as giving him an additional claim to supremacy over Sirhind. He did not, perhaps, see that a French invasion would be ruinous to *his* interests; he rather feared the colossal power on his borders, and he resented the intention of confining him to the Sutlej.[3] He suddenly broke off negotiations, and made his third inroad to the south of the Sutlej. He seized Faridkot and Ambala, levied exactions in Maler Kotla and Thanesar, and entered into a symbolical brotherhood or alliance with the Raja of Patiala. The British envoy remonstrated against these virtual acts of hostility, and he remained on the banks of the Sutlej until Ranjit Singh recrossed that river.[4]

The proceedings of the ruler of Lahore determined the Governor-General, if doubtful before, to advance a detachment of troops to the Sutlej, to support Mr. Metcalfe in his negotiations, and to effectually confine Ranjit Singh to the northward of that river.[5] Provision would also be thus made, it was said, for possible warlike operations of a more extensive character, and the British frontier would be covered by a confederacy of friendly chiefs, instead of threatened by a hostile military government. A body of troops was accordingly moved across the Jumna in January 1809, under the command of Sir David Ochterlony. The General

---

[1] [Col. Malcolm was dispatched on a similar mission to Persia at the same time, and concluded a treaty (1809) which did away with the possibility of French interference in that quarter.—Ed.]

[2] Government to Sir David Ochterlony, 14th Nov., 1808. Cf. Murray, *Ranjit Singh*, pp. 65, 66.

[3] Moorcroft ascertained (*Travels*, i. 94) that Ranjit Singh had serious thoughts of appealing to the sword, so unpalatable was English interference. The well-known Fakir Uziz-ud-din was one of the two persons who dissuaded him from war.

[4] Murray, *Ranjit Singh* p. 66.

[5] Government to Sir David Ochterlony, 14th Nov. and 29th Dec., 1808.

advanced, by way of Buriya and Patiala, towards <sub>1809.</sub> Ludhiana; he was welcomed by all the Sirhind chiefs, save Jodh Singh Kalsia, the nominal head of the Krora-Singhia confederacy : but during his march he was not without apprehensions that Ranjit Singh might openly break with his government, and, after an interview with certain agents whom that chief had sent to him with the view of opening a double negotiation, he made a detour and a halt, in order to be near his supplies should hostilities take place.[1]

Ranjit Singh was somewhat discomposed by the near presence of a British force but he continued to evade compliance with the propositions of the envoy, and he complained that Mr. Metcalfe was needlessly reserved about his acquisitions on the south banks of the Sutlej, with regard to which the Government had only declared that the restoration of his last conquests, and the absolute withdrawal of his troops to the northward of the river, must form the indispensable basis of further negotiations.[2] Affairs were in this way when intelligence from Europe induced the Governor-General to believe that Napoleon must abandon his designs upon India, or at least so far suspend them as to render defensive precautions unnecessary.[3] It was therefore made known that the object of the English Government had become limited to the security of the country south of the Sutlej from the encroachments of Ranjit Singh; for that, independent of the possible approach of a European enemy, it was considered advisable on

*The views of the English become somewhat modified; but Ranjit Singh still required to keep to the north of the Sutlej.*

[1] Sir David Ochterlony to Government, 20th Jan., and 4th, 9th, and 14th Feb., 1809, with Government to Sir David Ochterlony, of 13th March, 1809. Government by no means approved of what Sir David Ochterlony had done, and he, feeling aggrieved, virtually tendered his resignation of his command. (Sir David Ochterlony to Government, 19th April, 1809.)

[2] Sir David Ochterlony to Government, 14th Feb., 1809, and Government to Sir David Ochterlony, 30th July, 1809. Lieut.-Col. Lawrence (*Adventures in the Punjab*, p. 131, note g) makes Sir Charles Metcalfe sufficiently communicative on this occasion with regard to other territories, for he is declared to have told the Maharaja that by a compliance with the then demands of the English, he would ensure their neutrality with respect to encroachments elsewhere.

[3] Government to Sir David Ochterlony, 30th Jan., 1809. [Probably the altered relations between Napoleon and Turkey were the main cause of this. The Franco-Turkish alliance of 1807 had come to an end with the deposition of Mustapha IV and accession of Mahmud II—July 1808—and the improved relations of England and Turkey led to the signature by the latter powers of the Treaty of the Dardanelles (January 1809). —Ed.]

1809.

other grounds to afford protection to the southern Sikhs. Ranjit Singh must still, nevertheless, withdraw his troops to the right bank of the Sutlej, his last usurpations must also be restored, but the restitution of his first conquests would not be insisted on; while, to remove all cause of suspicion, the detachment under Sir David Ochterlony could fall back from Ludhiana to Karnal, and take up its permanent position at the latter place.[1] But the British commander represented the advantage of keeping the force where it was; his Government assented to its detention, at least for a time, and Ludhiana thus continued uninterruptedly to form a station for British troops.[2]

Ranjit Singh yields;

In the beginning of February 1809, Sir David Ochterlony had issued a proclamation declaring the Cis-Sutlej states to be under British protection, and that any aggressions of the Chief of Lahore would be resisted with arms.[3] Ranjit Singh then perceived that the British authorities were in earnest, and the fear struck him that the still independent leaders of the Punjab might likewise tender their allegiance and have it accepted. All chance of empire would thus be lost, and he prudently made up his mind without further delay. He withdrew his troops as required, he relinquished his last acquisitions, and at Amritsar, on the 25th April, 1809, the now single Chief of Lahore signed a treaty which left him the master of the tracts he had originally occupied to the south of the Sutlej, but confined his ambition for the future to the north and westward of that river.[4]

and enters into a formal treaty, 25th April, 1809.

The terms of Sikh dependence and of English supremacy in Sirhind.

The Sikh, and the few included Hindu and Muhammadan chiefs, between the Sutlej and Jumna, having been taken under British protection, it became necessary to define the terms on which they were secured from foreign danger. Sir David Ochterlony observed,[5] that when the chiefs first sought protection, their jealousy of the English would have yielded to their fears of Ranjit Singh, and they would have agreed to any conditions proposed, including a regular tribute. But their first overtures had been rejected, and the mission to Lahore had taught them to regard *their* defence as a secondary object, and to think that *English*

[1] Government to Sir David Ochterlony, 30th Jan., 6th Feb., and 13th March, 1809.

[2] Sir David Ochterlony to Government, 6th May, 1809, and Government to Sir David Ochterlony, 13th June, 1809.

[3] See Appendix XXIV.

[4] See the treaty itself, Appendix XXV. Cf. Murray, *Ranjit Singh*, pp. 67, 68.

[5] Sir David Ochterlony to Government, 17th March, 1809

1809.

Sir David
Ochter-
lony
shows that
the English
regarded
themselves
alone in
offering
protection.

apprehensions of remote foreigners had saved *them* from the arbiter of the Punjab. Protection, indeed, had become no longer a matter of choice; they must have accepted it, or they would have been treated as enemies.[1] Wherefore, continued Sir David, the chiefs expected that the protection would be gratuitous. The Government, on its part, was inclined to be liberal to its new dependants, and finally a proclamation was issued on the 3rd May, 1809, guaranteeing the chiefs of 'Sirhind and Malwa' against the power of Ranjit Singh, leaving them absolute in their own territories exempting them from tribute, but requiring assistance in time of war, and making some minor provisions which need not be recapitulated.[2]

The rela-
tions of the
protected
chiefs
among
themselves.

No sooner were the chiefs relieved of their fears of Ranjit Singh, than the more turbulent began to prey upon one another, or upon their weaker neighbours; and, although the Governor-General had not wished them to consider themselves as in absolute subjection to the British power,[3] Mr. Metcalfe pointed out [4] that it was necessary to declare the chiefs to be protected singly against one another, as well as collectively against Ranjit Singh; for, if such a degree of security were not guaranteed, the oppressed would necessarily have recourse to the only other person who could use coercion with effect, viz. to the Raja of Lahore. The justness of these views was admitted, and, on the 22nd August, 1811, a second proclamation was issued, warning the chiefs against attempts at usurpation, and reassuring them of independence and of protection against Ranjit Singh.[5]   Nevertheless, encroachments did not at once cease, and the Jodh Singh Kalsia, who avoided giving in his adhesion to the British Government on the advance of Sir David Ochterlony, required to have troops sent against him in 1818 to compel the surrender of tracts which he had forcibly seized.[6]

[1] See also Government to Resident at Delhi, 26th Dec., 1808.  Baron Hugel (*Travels,* p. 279) likewise attributes the interference of the English, in part at least, to selfishness, but with him the motive was the petty desire of benefiting by escheats, which the dissipated character of the chiefs was likely to render speedy and numerous! This appetite for morsels of territory, however, really arose at a subsequent date, and did not move the English in 1809.

[2] See Appendix XXVI.

[3] Government to Sir David Ochterlony, 10th April, 1809.

[4] Mr. Metcalfe to Government, 17th June, 1809.

[5] See the proclamation, Appendix XXVII.

[6] Resident at Delhi to Agent at Ambala, 27th Oct., 1818, mulcting the chief in the military expenses incurred, 65,000

1809-18.

Perplexi-
ties of
British
authorities
regarding
the rights
of supre-
macy, and
the opera-
tion of in-
ternational
laws.

The history of the southern or Malwa Sikhs need
not be continued, although it presents many points of
interest to the general reader, as well as to the student
and to those concerned in the administration of India.
The British functionaries soon became involved in
intricate questions about interference between equal
chiefs, and between chiefs and their confederates or
dependants; they laboured to reconcile the Hindu laws
of inheritance with the varied customs of different
races, and with the alleged family usages of peasants
suddenly become princes. They had to decide on
questions of escheat, and being strongly impressed with
the superiority of British municipal rule, and with the
undoubted claim of the paramount to some benefit in
return for the protection it afforded, they strove to
prove that collateral heirs had a limited right only, and
that exemption from tribute necessarily implied an
enlarged liability to confiscation. They had to define
the common boundary of the Sikh states and of British
rule, and they were prone to show, after the manner
of Ranjit Singh, that the present possession of a principal town gave a right to all the villages which had
ever been attached to it as the seat of a local authority,
and that all waste lands belonged to the supreme
power, although the dependant might have last possessed them in sovereignty and intermediately brought
them under the plough. They had to exercise a paramount municipal control, and in the surrender of
criminals, and in the demand for compensation for
property stolen from British subjects, the original
arbitrary nature of the decisions enforced has not yet
been entirely replaced by rules of reciprocity. But the
government of a large empire will always be open to
obloquy, and liable to misconception, from the acts of
officious and ill-judging servants, who think that they
best serve the complicated interests of their own rulers
by lessening the material power of others, and that
any advantage they may seem to have gained for the
state they obey will surely promote their own objects.
Nor, in such matters, are servants alone to blame, and
the whole system of internal government in India

rupees. The head of the family, Jodh Singh, had recently
returned with Ranjit Singh's army from the capture of Multan,
and he was always treated with consideration by the Maharaja;
and, bearing in mind the different views taken by dependent
Sikhs and governing English, of rights of succession, he had
fair grounds of dissatisfaction. He claimed to be the head of
the 'Krora Singhia' Misal, and to be the heir of all childless
feudatories. The British Government, however, made itself the
valid or efficient head of the confederacy.

requires to be remodelled and made the subject of a
legislation at once wise, considerate, and comprehensive.  In the Sikh states ignorance has been the main
cause of mistakes and heart-burnings, and in 1818 Sir
David Ochterlony frankly owned to the Marquis of
Hastings[1] that his proclamation of 1809 had been
based on an erroneous idea.  He thought that a few
great chiefs only existed between the Sutlej and
Jumna, and that on them would devolve the maintenance of order; whereas he found that the dissolution
of the 'Misals', faulty as was their formation, had
almost thrown the Sikhs back upon the individual
independence of the times of Ahmad Shah.  Both in
considering the relation of the chiefs to one another,
and their relation collectively to the British Government, too little regard was perhaps had to the
peculiar circumstances of the Sikh people.  They were
in a state of progression among races as barbarous as
themselves, when suddenly the colossal power of England arrested them, and required the exercise of political moderation and the practice of a just morality
from men ignorant alike of despotic control and of
regulated freedom.[2]

*1809-18.*

*Sir David Ochter-lony's frank admission of the false basis of his original policy.*

[1] In a private communication, dated 17th May, 1818.
[2] In the Sikh States on either side of the Sutlej, the British
Government was long fortunate in being represented by such
men as Capt. Murray and Mr. Clerk, Sir David Ochterlony, and
Lieut.-Col. Wade—so different from one another, and yet so
useful to one common purpose of good for the English power.
These men, by their personal character or influence, added to
the general reputation of their countrymen, and they gave
adaptation and flexibility to the rigid unsympathizing nature
of a foreign and civilized supremacy. Sir David Ochterlony will
long live in the memory of the people of Northern India as one
of the greatest of the conquering English chiefs; and he was
among the very last of the British leaders who endeared himself both to the army which followed him and to the princes
who bowed before the colossal power of his race.
    Nevertheless, the best of subordinate authorities, immersed
in details and occupied with local affairs, are liable to be
biassed by views which promise immediate and special
advantage. They can seldom be more than upright or dexterous
administrators, and they can still more rarely be men whose
minds have been enlarged by study and reflexion as well as
by actual experience of the world. Thus the ablest but too
often resemble merely the practical man of the moment; while
the supreme authority, especially when absent from his
councillors and intent upon some great undertaking, is of
necessity dependent mainly upon the local representatives of
the Government, whose notions must inevitably be partial or
one-sided, for good, indeed, as well as for evil. The author has
thus, even during his short service, seen many reasons to be
thankful that there is a remote deliberative or corrective body,
which can survey things through an atmosphere cleared of

mists, and which can judge of measures with reference both to the universal principles of justice and statesmanship, and to their particular bearing on the English supremacy in India, which should be characterized by certainty and consistency of operation, and tempered by a spirit of forbearance and adaptation.

# CHAPTER VI

## FROM THE SUPREMACY OF RANJIT SINGH TO THE REDUCTION OF MULTAN, KASHMIR, AND PESHAWAR

### 1809-1823-4

Mutual distrust of Ranjit Singh and the English gradually removed—Ranjit Singh and the Gurkhas—Ranjit Singh and the ex-kings of Kabul—Ranjit Singh and Fateh Khan, the Kabul Wazir—Ranjit Singh and Shah Shuja each fail against Kashmir—Fateh Khan put to death—Ranjit Singh captures Multan, overruns Peshawar, occupies Kashmir, and annexes the 'Derajat' of the Indus to his dominions—The Afghans defeated, and Peshawar brought regularly under tribute—Death of Muhammad Azim Khan of Kabul, and, of Sansar Chand of Katotch—Ranjit Singh's power consolidated—Shah .Shuja's expedition of 1818-21—Appa Sahib of Nagpur—The traveller Moorcroft—Ranjit Singh's Government—The Sikh Army—The Sikhs and other military tribes—French officers—Ranjit Singh's family—Ranjit Singh's failings and Sikh vices—Ranjit Singh's personal favourites and trusted servants.

A TREATY of peace and friendship was thus formed between Ranjit Singh and the English Government; but confidence is a plant of slow growth, and doubt and suspicion are not always removed by formal protestations. While arrangements were pending with the Maharaja, the British authorities were assured that he had made propositions to Sindhia;[1] agents from Gwalior, from Holkar, and from Amir Khan,[2] continued to show themselves for years at Lahore, and their masters long dwelt on the hope that the tribes of the Punjab and of the Deccan might yet be united against the stranger conquerors. It was further believed by the English rulers that Ranjit Singh was anxiously trying to induce the Sikhs of Sirhind to throw off their allegiance, and to join him and Holkar against their protectors.[3] Other special instances might also be quoted,

[1] Resident at Delhi to Sir David Ochterlony, 28th June, 1809.

[2] Sir D. Ochterlony to Government, 15th Oct., 1809; 5th, 6th, and 7th Dec., 1809; and 5th and 30th Jan., and 22nd Aug., 1810.

[3] Sir D. Ochterlony to Government, 5th Jan. 1810.

1809-11.

and Ranjit
Singh
equally
doubtful on
his part:

but distrust
gradually
vanishes on
either side.

and Sir David Ochterlony even thought it prudent to lay in supplies and to throw up defensive lines at Ludhiana.[1] Ranjit Singh had likewise *his* suspicions, but they were necessarily expressed in ambiguous terms, and were rather to be deduced from his acts and correspondence, and from a consideration of his position, than to be looked for in overt statements or remonstrances. By degrees the apprehensions of the two governments mutually vanished, and, while Ranjit Singh felt he could freely exercise his ambition beyond the Sutlej, the English were persuaded he would not embroil himself with its restless allies in the south, so long as he had occupation elsewhere. In 1811 presents were exchanged between the Governor-General and the Maharaja,[2] and during the following year Sir David Ochterlony became his guest at the marriage of his son, Kharak Singh,[3] and from that period until within a year of the late war, the rumours of a Sikh invasion served to amuse the idle and to alarm the credulous, without causing uneasiness to the British viceroy.

Ranjit
Singh
acquires
Kangra,
and con-
fines the
Gurkhas to
the left of
the Sutlej.
1809.

On the departure of Mr. Metcalfe, the first care of Ranjit Singh was to strengthen both his frontier post of Phillaur opposite Ludhiana, and Gobindgarh the citadel of Amritsar, which he had begun to build as soon as he got possession of the religious capital of his people.[4] He was invited, almost at the same time, by Sansar Chand of Katotch, to aid in resisting the Gurkhas, who were still pressing their long-continued siege of Kangra, and who had effectually dispelled the Rajput prince's dreams of a supremacy reaching from the Jumna to the Jhelum. The stronghold was offered to the Sikh ruler as the price of his assistance, but Sansar Chand hoped, in the meantime, to gain admittance himself, by showing to the Gurkhas the futility of resisting Ranjit Singh, and by promising to surrender the fort to the Nepal commander, if allowed to withdraw his family. The Maharaja saw through the schemes of Sansar Chand, and he made the son of his ally a prisoner, while he dexterously cajoled the Khatmandu general, Amar Singh Thappa, who proposed a joint warfare against the Rajput mountaineers, and to take, or receive, in the meantime, the fort of Kangra

---

[1] Sir D. Ochterlony to Government, 31st Dec., 1809, and 7th Sept., 1810.

[2] A carriage was at this time sent to Lahore. See, further, Resident of Delhi to Sir D. Ochterlony, 25th Feb., 1811, and Sir D. Ochterlony to Government, 15th Nov., 1811.

[3] Sir D. Ochterlony to Government, 18th July, 1811 and 23rd Jan., 1812.

[4] Cf. Murray, *Ranjit Singh*. p. 76.

as part of the *Gurkha* share of the general spoil. The
Sikhs got possession of the place by suddenly demanding admittance as the expected relief. Sansar Chand
was foiled, and Amar Singh retreated across the Sutlej,
loudly exclaiming that he had been grossly duped.[1]
The active Nepalese commander soon put down some
disorders which had arisen in his rear, but the disgrace
of his failure before Kangra rankled in his mind, and
he made preparations for another expedition against
it. He proposed to Sir David Ochterlony a joint march
to the Indus, and a separate appropriation of the plains
and the hills;[2] and Ranjit Singh, ignorant alike of
English moderation and of international law, became
apprehensive lest the allies of Nepal should be glad of
a pretext for coercing one who had so unwillingly
acceded to their limitation of his ambition. He made
known that *he* was desirous of meeting Amar Singh
Thappa on his own ground; and the reply of the Governor-General that he might not only himself cross the
Sutlej to chastise the invading Gurkhas in the hills,
but that, if they descended into the plains of Sirhind,
he would receive English assistance, gave him another
proof that the river of the treaty was really to be an
impassable barrier. He had got the assurance he
wanted, and he talked no more of carrying his horsemen into mountain recesses.[3] But Amar Singh long
brooded over his reverse, and tried in various ways to
induce the British authorities to join him in assailing
the Punjab. The treaty with Nepal, he would say,
made all strangers the mutual friends or enemies of
the two governments, and Ranjit Singh had wantonly
attacked the Gurkha possessions in Katotch. Besides,
he would argue, to advance is the safest policy, and
what could have brought the English to the Sutlej but
the intention of going beyond it?[4] The Nepal war of
1814 followed, and the English became the neighbours
of the Sikhs in the hills as well as in the plains, and
the Gurkhas, instead of grasping Kashmir, trembled
for their homes in Khatmandu. Ranjit Singh was not
then asked to give his assistance, but Sansar Chand
was directly called upon by the English representative

*Marginal notes:*
1809.

The Gur-
khas urge
the English
to effect a
joint con-
quest of the
Punjab,
1809.

But Ranjit
Singh told
he may
cross the
Sutlej to
resist the
Nepal
leader,
1811.

Amar Singh
Thappa
again
presses an
alliance
against the
Sikhs, 1813.

War be-
tween the
English
and Gur-
khas,
1814-15.

Sansar
Chand of
Katotch,

---

[1] Murray, *Ranjit Singh*, pp. 76, 77. The Maharaja told
Capt. Wade that the Gurkhas wanted to share Kashmir with
him, but that he thought it best to keep them out of the Punjab
altogether. (Capt. Wade to Government, 25th May, 1831.)
[2] Sir D. Ochterlony to Government, 16th and 30th Dec.,
1809.
[3] Sir D. Ochterlony to Government, 12th Sept., 1811, and
Government to Sir D. Ochterlony, 4th Oct. and 22nd Nov., 1811.
[4] Sir D. Ochterlony to Government, 20th December, 1813.

1811-15.

Ranjit
Singh and
the English.

to attack the Gurkhas and their allies,—a hasty requisition, which produced a remonstrance from the
Maharaja, and an admission, on the part of Sir David
Ochterlony, that his supremacy was not questioned;
while the experienced Hindu chief had forborne to
commit himself with either state, by promising much
and doing little.[1]

Shah Shuja
expelled
from Af-
ghanistan.
1809-10.

Ranjit Singh felt secure on the Upper Sutlej, but
a new danger assailed him in the beginning of 1810,
and again set him to work to dive to the bottom of
British counsels. Mr. Elphinstone had scarcely concluded a treaty with Shah Shuja against the Persians
and French, before that prince was driven out of his
kingdom by the brother whom he had himself supplanted, and who had placed his affairs in the hands of
the able minister, Fateh Khan. The Maharaja was at
Wazirabad, sequestering that place from the family of
a deceased Sikh chief, when he heard of Shah Shuja's
progress to the eastward with vague hopes of procuring
assistance from one friendly power or another. Ranjit

Ranjit
Singh's
suspicions
and plans.

Singh remembered the use he had himself made of
Shah Zaman's grant of Lahore, he feared the whole
Punjab might similarly be surrendered to the English
in return for a few battalions, and he desired to keep
a representative of imperial power within his own
grasp.[2] He amused the ex-king with the offer of co-
operation in the recovery of Multan and Kashmir, and
he said he would himself proceed to meet the Shah to

The Maha-
raja meets
the Shah,

save him further journeying, towards Hindustan.[3] They
saw one another at Sahiwal, but no determinate
arrangement was come to, for some prospects of suc-

[1] Government to Sir D. Ochterlony, 1st and 20th Oct.,
1814. Resident at Delhi to Sir D. Ochterlony, 11th Oct., 1814,
and Sir David's letter to Ranjit Singh, dated 29th Nov., 1814.

During the war of 1814 Sir David Ochterlony sometimes
almost despaired of success; and, amid his vexations, he once
at least recorded his opinion that the Sepoys of the Indian army
were unequal to such mountain warfare as was being waged.
(Sir D. Ochterlony to Government, 22nd Dec., 1814.) The most
active and useful ally of the English during the war was Raja
Ram Saran of Hindur (or Nalagarh), the descendant of the
Hari Chand slain by Guru Gobind and who was himself the
ready coadjutor of Sansar Chand in many aggressions upon
others, as well as in resistance to the Gurkhas. The venerable
chief was still alive in 1846, and he continued to talk with
admiration of Sir David Ochterlony and his 'eighteen pounders',
and to expatiate upon the aid he himself rendered in dragging
them up the steeps of the Himalayas.

[2] Sir D. Ochterlony to Government, 10th and 30th Dec.,
1809.

[3] Sir D. Ochterlony to Government, 7th, 10th, 17th, and
30th Dec., 1809, and 30th Jan., 1810.

cess dawned upon the Shah, and he felt reason to 1809-10.
distrust Ranjit Singh's sincerity.[1] The conferences but no ar-
were broken off; but the Maharaja hastened, while rangement
there was yet an appearance of union, to demand the come to,
surrender of Multan for himself in the name of the 1810.
king. The great gun called 'Zamzam',[2] or the 'Bhangi Ranjit Singh
Top', was brought from Lahore to batter the walls of attempts
the citadel; but all his efforts were in vain, and he Multan, but<br>fails, Feb.-
retired, foiled, in the month of April, with no more April, 1810;
than 180,000 rupees to soothe his mortified vanity. The
Governor, Muzaffar Khan, was by this time in correspondence with the British viceroy in Calcutta, and
Ranjit Singh feared that a tender of allegiance might
not only be made but accepted.[3] He therefore proposed and pro-
to Sir David Ochterlony that the two "allied powers" poses to the
should march against Multan and divide the conquest English a
equally.[4] It was surmised that he wanted the siege joint expe-<br>dition
train of the English, but he may likewise have wished against it.
to know whether the Sutlej was to be as good a boundary in the south as in the north. He was told
reprovingly that the English committed aggressions
upon no one, but otherwise the tenor of the correspondence was such as to lead him to believe that he
would not be interfered with in his designs upon
Multan.[5]

Shah Shuja proceeded towards Attock after his Shah
interview with Ranjit Singh, and having procured Shuja's
some aid from the rebellious brother of the Governor Peshawar<br>and Multan
of Kashmir, he crossed the Indus, and, in March 1810, campaign,
made himself master of Peshawar. He retained posses- and subse-
sion of the place for about six months, when he was quent im-
compelled to retreat southward by the Wazir's brother, prisonment
Muhammad Azim Khan. He made an attempt to gain in Kashmir,<br>1810-12.
over the Governor of Multan, but he was refused
admittance within its walls, and was barely treated
with courtesy, even when he encamped a few miles

---

[1] Shah Shuja's 'Autobiography', chap. xxii, published in
the *Calcutta Monthly Journal* for 1839.The original was undoubtedly revised, if not really written, by the Shah.

[2] [Known to all the world as 'Kim's' gun, it now reposes
in its last resting-place outside the Central Museum in Lahore.
—ED.]

[3] Sir D. Ochterlony to Government, 29th March and 23rd
May, 1810. In the latter it is stated that 250,000 rupees were
paid, and the sum of 180,000 is given on Capt. Murray's authority. (*Life of Ranjit Singh*, p. 81.)

[4] Sir D. Ochterlony to Government, 23rd July and 13th
Aug., 1810.

[5] Sir D. Ochterlony to Government, 29th March and 17th
Sept., 1810, and Government to Sir D. Ochterlony, 25th Sept.,
1840. (Cf. Murray, *Ranjit Singh*, pp. 80, 81.)

distant. He again moved northward, and, as the enemies of Mahmud were numerous, he succeeded in mastering Peshawar a second time, after two actions, one a reverse and the other a victory. But those who had aided him became suspicious that he was in secret league with Fateh Khan the Wazir, or, like Ranjit Singh, they wished to possess his person; and, in the course of 1812, he was seized in Peshawar by Jahan Dad Khan, Governor of Attock, and removed, first to that fort, and afterwards to Kashmir, where he remained as a prisoner for more than twelve months.[1]

After the failure before Multan, Ranjit Singh and his minister, Mohkam Chand, were employed in bringing more fully under subjection various Sikh and Muhammadan chiefs in the plains, and also the hill Rajas of Bhimbar, Rajaori, and other places. In the month of February 1811, the Maharaja had reached the salt mines between the Jhelum and Indus, and hearing that Shah Mahmud had crossed the latter river, he moved in force to Rawalpindi, and sent to ascertain his intentions. The Shah had already deputed agents to state that his object was to punish or overawe the Governor of Kashmir, who had sided with his brother, Shah Shuja, then in the neighbourhood of Multan; and

Ranjit Singh meets Shah Mahmud. 1811.

the two princes being satisfied, they had a meeting of ceremony before the Maharaja returned to Lahore, to renew his confiscation of lands held by the many petty chiefs who had achieved independence or sovereignty while the country was without a general controlling power, but who now fell unresistingly before the systematic activity of the young Maharaja.[2]

The blind Shah Zaman repairs for a time to Lahore, 1811.

In the year 1811, the blind Shah Zaman crossed the Punjab, and was visited by Ranjit Singh. He took up his residence in Lahore for a time, and deputed his son Eunus to Ludhiana, where he was received with attention by Sir David Ochterlony; but as the prince perceived that he was not a welcome guest, his father

---

[1] Sir. D. Ochterlony to Government, 10th Jan. and 26th Feb., 1816, and 27th April, 1812. Shah Shuja's 'Autobiography' chaps. xxiii-xxv, in the *Calcutta Monthly Journal* for 1839, and Murray, *Ranjit Singh*, pp. 79, 87, 92.

Shah Shuja's second appearance before Multan in 1810-11 is given mainly on Capt. Murray's authority, and the attempt is not mentioned in the Shah's memoirs although it is admitted that he went into the Derajat of the Indus, i.e. to Dera Ismail Khan, &c.

[2] Murray, *Ranjit Singh*, p. 83, &c. The principal of the chiefs whose territories were usurped was Budh Singh, of the Singhpuria or Feizulapuria Misal. See also Sir D. Ochterlony to Government, 15th Oct., 1811.

quitted Ranjit Singh's city, and became a wanderer for a time in Central Asia.[1] In the following year the families of the two ex-kings took up their abode at Lahore, and as the Maharaja was preparing to bring the hill chiefs south of Kashmir under his power, with a view to the reduction of the valley itself, and as he always endeavoured to make success more complete or more easy by appearing to labour in the cause of others, he professed to the wife of Shah Shuja that he would release her husband and replace Kashmir under the Shah's sway; but he hoped the gratitude of the distressed lady would make the great diamond, Koh-i-nur, the reward of his chivalrous labours when they should be crowned with success. His principal object was doubtless the possession of the Shah's person, and when, after his preliminary successes against the hill chiefs, including the capture of Jammu by his newly married son, Kharak Singh, he heard, towards the end of 1812, that Fateh Khan the Kabul Wazir had crossed the Indus with the design of marching against Kashmir, he sought an interview with him, and said he would assist in bringing to punishment both the rebel, who detained the king's brother, and likewise the Governor of Multan, who had refused obedience to Mahmud. Fateh Khan had been equally desirous of an interview, for he felt that he could not take Kashmir if opposed by Ranjit Singh, and he readily promised anything to facilitate his immediate object. The Maharaja and the Wazir each hoped to use the other as a tool, yet the success of neither was complete. Kashmir was occupied in February 1813; but Fateh Khan outstripped the Sikhs under Mohkam Chand, and he maintained that as he alone had achieved the conquest, the Maharaja could not share in the spoils. The only advantage which accrued to Ranjit Singh was the possession of Shah Shuja's person, for the ill-fated king was allowed by Fateh Khan to go whither he pleased, and he preferred joining the Sikh army, which he accompanied to Lahore, to becoming

*Side notes:*
1811-12.

The family of Shah Shuja repairs to Lahore, 1812.

Ranjit Singh uses the Shah's name for purposes of his own

Ranjit Singh meets Fateh Khan, the Kabul Wazir, 1812;

and a joint enterprise against Kashmir resolved on.

Fateh Khan outstrips the Sikhs, and holds the valley for Mahmud, 1813.

Shah Shuja joins Ranjit Singh who acquires Attock;

---

[1] Murray, *Ranjit Singh*, p. 87. The visit of the prince was considered very embarrassing with reference to Ranjit Singh: for Shah Shuja might follow, and he was one who claimed British aid under the treaty of 1809. It was regretted that the 'obligations of political necessity should supersede the dictates of compassion'; it was argued that the treaty referred to defence against the French, and not against a brother; and the loyal-hearted Sir David Ochterlony was chidden for the reception he gave to the distressed Shahzada. (Government to Sir D. Ochterlony; 19th Jan., 1811, and the correspondence generally of Dec. 1810 and Jan. 1811.)

1813-14.

virtually a prisoner in Kabul.[1] But the Maharaja's expedients did not entirely fail him, and as the rebel Governor of Attock was alarmed by the success of Shah Mahmud's party in Kashmir, he was easily persuaded to yield the fort to Ranjit Singh. This unlooked-for stroke incensed Fateh Khan, who accused the Maharaja of barefaced treachery, and endeavoured further to intimidate him by pretending to make over-

while Moh-kam Chand defeats the Kabul Wazir in a pitched battle.

tures to Shah Shuja; but the Maharaja felt confident of his strength, and a battle was fought on the 13th July, 1813, near Attock, in which the Kabul Wazir, and his brother Dost Muhammad Khan, were defeated by Mohkam Chand and the Sikhs.[2]

Ranjit Singh ob-tains the Koh-i-nur diamond. 1813-14;

Ranjit Singh was equally desirous of detaining Shah Shuja in Lahore, and of securing the great diamond which had adorned the throne of the Mughals. The king evaded a compliance with all demands for a time, and rejected even the actual offer of moderate sums of money; but at last the Maharaja visited the Shah in person, mutual friendship was declared, an exchange of turbans took place, the diamond was sur-

and pro-mises aid to Shah Shuja.

rendered,[3] and the king received the assignment of a jagir in the Punjab for his maintenance, and a pro-mise of aid in recovering Kabul. Ranjit Singh then

Makes a movement towards the Indus.

moved towards the Indus to watch the proceedings of Fateh Khan, who was gradually consolidating the power of Mahmud, and he required Shah Shuja to join him, perhaps with some design of making an attempt on Kashmir; but Fateh Khan was likewise watchful, the season was advanced, and the Maharaja

Shah Shuja's distresses.

suddenly returned. Shah Shuja followed slowly, and on the way he was plundered of many valuables, by ordinary robbers, as the Sikhs said, but by the Sikhs themselves, as the Shah believed. The inferior agents of Ranjit Singh may not have been very scrupulous, but the Shah had traitors in his own household, and the high officer who had been sent to conduct Mr. Elphinstone to Peshawar, embezzled much of the

[1] Murray, *Ranjit Singh*, pp. 92, 95; Sir D. Ochterlony to Government, 4th March, 1813; and Shah Shuja's 'Autobiogra-phy', chap. xxv.

[2] Murray, *Ranjit Singh*, pp. 95, 100; Sir D. Ochterlony to Government, 1st July, 1813.

[3] Murray, *Ranjit Singh*, p. 96, &c.: Shah Shuja's 'Autobio-graphy', chap. xxv; Sir D. Ochterlony to Government, 16th and 23rd April, 1813, and to the Resident at Delhi, 15th Oct., 1813 The Shah's own account of the methods practised to get pos-session of the diamond is more favourable than Capt. Murray's to Ranjit Singh. The Shah wanted a jagir of 100,000 rupees, and one of 50,000 was assigned to him; but effect to the assign-ment was never given, nor perhaps expected.

Shah's property when misfortune overtook him. This *1814-16.*
Mir Abdul Hassan had originally informed the Sikh
chief of the safety of the Koh-i-nur and other valuables, he plotted when in Lahore to make it appear
the king was in league with the Governor of Kashmir,
and he finally threw difficulties in the way of the
escape of his master's family from the Sikh capital.
The flight of the Begums to Ludhiana was at last *The flight of*
effected in December 1814; for Shah Shuja perceived *his family*
the design of the Maharaja to detain him a prisoner, *from Lahore*
and to make use of his name for purposes of his own. *1814;*
A few months afterwards the Shah himself escaped to
the hills; he was joined by some Sikhs discontented *April, 1815;*
with Ranjit Singh, and he was aided by the chief of *and his own*
Kishtwar in an attack upon Kashmir. He penetrated *escape to*
into the valley, but he had to retreat, and, after resid- *Kishtwar.*
ing for some time longer with his simple, but zealous, *Fails against*
mountain host, he marched through Kulu, crossed the *Kashmir,*
Sutlej, and joined his family at Ludhiana in Septem- *and retires*
ber 1816.[1]  His presence on the frontier was regarded *to Ludhiana,*
as embarrassing by the British Government, which *1816.*
desired that he should be urged to retire to Karnal or
Saharanpur, and Sir David Ochterlony was further
discretionally authorized to tell Ranjit Singh that the
ex-king of Kabul was not a welcome guest within the
limits of Hindustan. Nevertheless the annual sum of
18,000 rupees, which had been assigned for the support
of his family, was raised to 50,000 on his arrival, and
personally he was treated with becoming respect and
consideration.[2]

Shah Shuja thus slipped from the hands of the *Ranjit Singh*
Maharaja, and no use could be made of his name in *attempts*
further attempts upon Kashmir; but Ranjit Singh con- *Kashmir*
tinued as anxious as ever to obtain possession of the *and is repul-*
valley, although the Governor had, in the meantime, *sed, 1814.*
put himself in communication with the English.[3]  The
chiefs south of the Pir Panjal range having been
brought under subjection, military operations were
commenced towards the middle of the year 1814 Sickness detained the experienced Mohkam Chand at the

[1] Murray, *Ranjit Singh*, pp. 102, 103; Shah Shuja's 'Autobiography', chaps. xxv, xxvi.

[2] Government to Sir D. Ochterlony, 2nd and 20th Aug.,
1815, and 14th, 21st, and 28th Sept., 1816. The Wafa Begam
had before been told that the Shah's family had no claims to
British protection or intervention. (Government to Resident
at Delhi, 19th Dec., 1812, and 1st July, 1813.)

[3] Government to Sir D. Ochterlony, 29th Oct. and 23rd
Nov., 1813.

capital, but he warned the Maharaja of the difficulties which would beset him as soon as the rains set in, and he almost urged the postponement of the expedition. But the necessary arrangements had been completed, and the approach was made in two columns. The more advanced division surmounted the lofty barrier, a detachment of the Afghan force was repulsed, and the town of Supain was attacked; but the assault failed, and the Sikhs retired to the mountain passes. Muhammad Azim Khan, the Governor, then fell on the main body of Ranjit Singh, which had been long in view on the skirts of the valley, and compelled the Maharaja to retreat with precipitation. The rainy season had fairly set in, the army became disorganized, a brave chief, Mit'h Singh Behrania, was slain, and Ranjit Singh reached his capital almost alone about the middle of August. The advanced detachment was spared by Muhammad Azim Khan, out of regard, he said, for Mohkam Chand, the grandfather of its commander; and as doubtless the aspiring brother of the Wazir Fateh Khan had views of his own amid the struggles then going on for power, he may have thought it prudent to improve every opportunity to the advantage of his own reputation.[1]

Various chiefs in the hills, and various places towards the Indus, reduced, 1815-16.

The efforts made during the expedition to Kashmir had been great, and the Maharaja took some time to reorganize his means. Towards the middle of 1815 he sent detachments of troops to levy exactions around Multan, but he himself remained at Adinanagar, busy with internal arrangements, and perhaps intent upon the war then in progress between the British and the Nepalese, which, for a period of six months, was scarcely worthy of the English name. The end of the same year was employed in again reducing the Muhammadan tribes south-east of Kashmir, who had thrown off their allegiance during the retreat of the Sikhs. In the beginning of 1816 the refractory hill Raja of Nurpur sought poverty and an asylum in the British dominions, rather than resign his territories and accept a maintenance. The Muhammadan chiefship of Jhang was next finally confiscated, and Leiah, a dependency of Dera Ismail Khan, was laid under contribution. Uch on the Chenab, the seat of families of Saiyids, was temporarily occupied by Fateh Singh Ahluwalia, and the possessions of Jodh Singh Ramgarhia, lately deceased, the son of Jassa the Carpenter

[1] Murray, *Ranjit Singh*, pp. 104, 108, and Sir D. Ochterlony to Government, 13th Aug., 1814. Diwan Mohkam Chand died soon after Ranjit Singh's return.

(the confederate of the Maharaja's father), were seized and annexed to the territories of the Lahore government. Sansar Chand was honoured and alarmed by a visit from his old ally, and the year 1816 terminated with the Maharaja's triumphant return to Amritsar.[1]

The northern plains and lower hills of the Punjab had been fairly reduced to obedience and order, and Ranjit Singh's territories were bounded on the south and west by the real or nominal dependencies of Kabul, but the Maharaja's meditated attacks upon them were postponed for a year by impaired health. His first object was Multan, and early in 1818 an army marched to attack it, under the nominal command of his son, Kharak Singh, the titular reducer of Jammu. To ask what were the Maharaja's reasons for attacking Multan would be futile; he thought the Sikhs had as good a right as the Afghans to take what they could, and the actual possessor of Multan had rather asserted his own independence than faithfully served the heirs of Ahmad Shah. A large sum of money was demanded and refused. In the course of February, the city was in possession of he Sikhs, but the fort held out until the beginning of June, and chance had then some share in its capture. An Akali, named Sadhu Singh, went forth to do battle for the 'Khalsa', and the very suddenness of the onset of his small band led to success. The Sikhs, seeing the impression thus strangely made, arose together, carried the outwork, and found an easy entry through the breaches of a four months' batter. Muzaffar Khan, the governor, and two of his sons, were slain in the assault, and two others were made prisoners. A considerable booty fell to the share of the soldiery, but when the army reached Lahore, the Maharaja directed that the plunder should be restored. He may have felt some pride that his commands were not altogether unheeded, but he complained that they were not so productive as he had expected.[2]

1816-18.

Ranjit Singh captures Multan, 1818.

---

[1] Cf. Murray, *Ranjit Singh*, pp. 108, 111.

[2] The place fell on the 2nd June, 1818. See Murray, *Ranjit Singh*, p. 114, &c. The Maharaja told Mr. Moorcroft that he got very little of the booty he attempted to recover. (Moorcroft, *Travels*, i. 102.) Muhammad Muzaffar Khan, the governor, had held Multan from the time of the expulsion of the Sikhs of the Bhangi 'Misal', in 1779. In 1807 he went on a pilgrimage to Mecca, and, although he returned in two years, he left the nominal control of affairs with his son, Sarafraz Khan. On the last approach of Ranjit Singh, the old man refused, according to the Bahawalpur annals, to send his family to the south of the Sutlej, as on other occasions of siege; but whether he did so in the confidence, or in the despair, of a successful resistance is not clear.

1818-19.

Fateh
Khan, Wazir
of Kabul,
put to
death, 1818.

During the same year, 1818, Fateh Khan, the Kabul Wazir, was put to death by Kamran, the son of Mahmud, the nominal ruler. He had gone to Herat to repel an attack of the Persians, and he was accompanied by his brother, Dost Muhammad, who again had among his followers a Sikh chief, Jai Singh Atariwala, who had left the Punjab in displeasure. Fateh Khan was successful, and applause was freely bestowed upon his measures; but he wished to place Herat, then held by a member of Ahmad Shah's family, within his own grasp, and Dost Muhammad and his Sikh ally were employed to eject and despoil the prince-governor. Dost Muhammad effected his purpose somewhat rudely, the person of a royal lady was touched in the eagerness of the riflers to secure her jewels, and Kamran made this affront offered to a sister a pretext for getting rid of the man who from the stay had become the tyrant of his family. Fateh Khan was first blinded and then murdered; and the crime saved Herat, indeed, to Ahmad Shah's heirs, but deprived them for a time, and now perhaps for ever, of the rest of his possessions. Muhammad Azim Khan hastened from Kashmir, which he left in charge of Jabbar Khan, another of the many brothers. He at first thought of reinstating Shah Shuja, but he at last proclaimed Shah Ayub as king, and in a few months he was master of Peshawar and Ghazni, of Kabul and Kandahar. This change of rulers favoured, if it did not justify, the views of Ranjit Singh, and towards the end of 1818 he crossed the Indus and entered Peshawar, which was evacuated on his approach. But it did not suit his purposes, at the time, to endeavour to retain the district; he garrisoned Khairabad, which lies on the right bank of the river, so as to command the passage for the future, and then retired, placing Jahan Dad Khan, his old ally of Attock, in possession of Peshawar itself, to hold it as he could by his own means. The Barakzai governor, Yar Muhammad Khan, returned as soon as Ranjit Singh had gone, and the powerless Jahan Dad made no attempt to defend his gift.[1]

Muhammad
Azim pro-
claims Shah
Ayub.

Ranjit Singh
marches to
Peshawar,

which he
makes over
to Jahan
Dad Khan,
1818.

Ranjit Singh
intent upon
Kashmir.

Ranjit Singh's thoughts were now directed towards the annexation of Kashmir, the garrison of which had been reduced by the withdrawal of some good troops

[1] Cf. Murray, *Ranjit Singh*, pp. 117, 120; Shah Shuja's 'Autobiography', chap. xxvii; and Munshi Mohan Lal, *Life of Dost Muhammad*, i. 99, 104.

Capt. Murray (p. 131) places the defection of Jai Singh of Atari in the year 1822; but cf. also Mr. Masson, *Travels*, iii. 21, 32, in support of the earlier date assigned.

by Muhammad Azim Khan; but the proceedings of Desa Singh Majithia and Sansar Chand for a moment changed his designs upon others into fears for himself. These chiefs were employed on an expedition in the hills to collect the tribute due to the Maharaja; and the Raja of Kahlur, who held territories on both sides of the Sutlej, ventured to resist the demands made. Sansar Chand rejoiced in this opportunity of revenge upon the friend of the Gurkhas; the river was crossed, but the British authorities were prompt, and a detachment of troops stood ready to oppose force to force. Ranjit Singh directed the immediate recall of his men, and he desired Sirdar Desa Singh to go in person, and offer his apologies to the English agent.[1] This alarm being over, the Maharaja proceeded with his preparations against Kashmir, the troops occupying which had, in the meantime, been reinforced by a detachment from Kabul. The Brahman, Diwan Chand, who had exercised the real command at Multan, was placed in advance, the Prince Kharak Singh headed a supporting column, and Ranjit Singh himself remained behind with a reserve and for the purpose of expediting the transit of the various munitions of war. The choice of the Sikh cavalry marched on foot over the mountains along with the infantry soldiers, and they dragged with them a few light guns; the passes were scaled on the 5th July 1819, but Jabbar Khan was found ready to receive them. The Afghans repulsed the invaders, and mastered two guns; but they did not improve their success, and the rallied Sikhs again attacked them, and won an almost bloodless victory.[2]

*1818-19.*

*Delayed by a discussion with the English. March 1819.*

*But finally annexes the valley to his dominions. 1819*

A few months after Kashmir had been added to the Lahore dominions, Ranjit Singh moved in person to the south of the Punjab, and Dera Ghazi Khan on the Indus, another dependency of Kabul, was seized by the victorious Sikhs. The Nawab of Bahawalpur, who held lands under Ranjit Singh in the fork of the Indus and Chenab, had two years before made a successful attack on the Durrani chief of the place, and it was now transferred to him in form, although his Cis-Sutlej possessions had virtually, but not formally, been taken under British protection in the year 1815, and he had thus become, in a measure, independent of the Maharaja's power.[3] During the year 1820 partial attempts

*The Dera-jat of the Indus annexed to Lahore. 1819-20.*

---

[1] Cf. Murray, *Ranjit Singh*, pp. 121, 122, and Moorcroft, *Travels*, 110, for the duration of the Maharaja's displeasure with Desa Singh.

[2] Cf. Murray, *Ranjit Singh*, pp. 122-4.

[3] Government to Superintendent Ambala, 15th Jan., 1815.

were made to reduce the turbulent Muhammadan tribes to the south-west of Kashmir, and, in 1821, Ranjit Singh proceeded to complete his conquests on the Central Indus by the reduction of Dera Ismail Khan. The strong fort of Mankera, situated between the two westernmost rivers of the Punjab, was held out for a time by Hafiz Ahmad Khan, the father of the titular governor, who scarcely owned a nominal subjection to Kabul; but the promise of honourable terms induced him to surrender before the end of the year, and the country on the right bank of the Indus, including Dera Ismail Khan, was left to him as a feudatory of Lahore.[1]

Muhammad Azim had succeeded to the power of his brother, Fateh Khan, and, being desirous of keeping Ranjit Singh to the left bank of the Indus, he moved to Peshawar in the year 1822, accompanied by Jai Singh, the fugitive Sikh chief, with the intention of attacking Khairabad opposite Attock. Other matters caused him hastily to retrace his steps, but his proceedings had brought the Maharaja to the westward, who sent to Yar Muhammad Khan, the governor of Peshawar, and demanded tribute. This leader, who apprehended the designs of his brother, Muhammad Azim Khan, almost as much as he dreaded Ranjit Singh, made an offering of some valuable horses.[2] The Maharaja was satisfied and withdrew perhaps the more readily, as some differences had arisen with the British authorities regarding the right to a place named Whadni, to the south of the Sutlej, which had been transferred by Ranjit Singh to his intriguing and ambitious mother-in-law, Sada Kaur, in the year 1808. The lady was regarded by the English agents as being the independent representative of the interests of the Kanhaya (or Ghani) confederacy of Sikhs on *their* side of the river, and therefore as having a right to their protection. But Ranjit Singh had quarrelled with and imprisoned his mother-in-law, and had taken possession of the fort of Whadni. It was resolved to eject him by force, and a detachment of troops marched from Ludhiana and restored the authority of the captive widow. Ranjit Singh prudently made no attempt to resist the British agent, but he was

and Sir D. Ochterlony to Government, 23rd July, 1815.  Cf. Murray, *Ranjit Singh*, p. 124.  The Bahawalpur Memoirs state that Ranjit Singh came down the Sutlej as far as Pakpattan, with the view of seizing Bahawalpur, but that show of resistance having been made, and some presents offered, the Maharaja moved westward.

[1] Cf. Murray, *Ranjit Singh*, pp. 129, 130, and Sir A. Burnes' *Kabul*. p. 92.

[2] Cf. Murray, *Ranjit Singh*, pp. 134-7.

not without apprehensions that his occupation of the 1823. place would be construed into a breach of the treaty, and he busied himself with defensive preparations. A friendly letter from the superior authorities at Delhi relieved him of his fears, and allowed him to prosecute his designs against Peshawar without further interruption.[1]

Muhammad Azim Khan disapproved of the presentation of horses to Ranjit Singh by Yar Muhammad Khan, and he repaired to Peshawar in January 1823. Yar Muhammad fled into the Usufzai hills rather than meet his brother, and the province seemed lost to one branch of the numerous family; but the chief of the Sikhs was at hand, resolved to assert his equality of right or his superiority of power. The Indus was forded on the 13th March, the guns being carried across on elephants. The territory of the Khattaks bordering the river was occupied, and at Akora the Maharaja received and pardoned the fugitive Jai Singh Atariwala. A religious war had been preached, and twenty thousand men, of the Khattak and Usufzai tribes, had been assembled by their priests and devotees to fight for their faith against the unbelieving invaders. This body of men was posted on and around heights near Noshahra, but on the left bank of the Kabul river, while Muhammad Azim Khan, distrustful of his influence over the independent militia, and of the fidelity of his brothers, occupied a position higher up on the right bank of the stream. Ranjit Singh detached a force to keep the Wazir in check, and crossed the river to attack the armed peasantry. The Sikh 'Akalis' at once rushed upon the Muhammadan 'Ghazis', but Phula Singh, the wild leader of the fanatics of Amritsar, was slain, and his horsemen made no impression on masses

*The Sikhs march against Peshawar, 1823.*

*The battle of Noshahra, 14th March, 1823.*

[1] Cf. Murray, *Ranjit Singh*, p. 134, where the proceedings are given very briefly, and scarcely with accuracy. Capt. Murray's and Capt. Ross's letters to the Resident at Delhi, from Feb. to Sept. 1822, give details, and other information is obtainable from the letters of Sir D. Ochterlony to Capt. Ross, dated 7th Nov., 1821, and of the Governor-General's Agent at Delhi to Capt. Murray, of 22nd June, and to Government of the 23rd Aug. 1822; and from those of Government to the Governor-General's Agent, 24th April, 13th July, and 18th Oct., 1822. On this occasion the Akali Phula Singh is reported by Capt. Murray to have offered to retake Whadni single-handed, and Ranjit Singh to have commissioned him to embody a thousand of his brethren. Sir Claude Wade (*Narrative of Personal Services*, p. 10 note) represents Sir Charles Metcalfe to have considered the proceedings of the English with regard to Whadni as unwarranted—for with the domestic concerns of the Maharaja they had no political concern.

1823-4.

of footmen advantageously posted. The Afghans then exultingly advanced, and threw the drilled infantry of the Lahore ruler into confusion. They were checked by the fire of the rallying battalions, and by the play of the artillery drawn up on the opposite bank of the river, and at length Ranjit Singh's personal exertions with his cavalry converted the check into a victory. The brave and believing mountaineers reassembled after their rout, and next day they were willing to renew the fight under their 'Pirzada', Muhammad Akbar; but the Kabul Wazir had fled with percipitation, and they were without countenance or support.

**Peshawar reduced, but left as a dependency with Yar Muhammad Khan.**

Peshawar was sacked, and the country plundered up to the Khaibar Pass; but the hostile spirit of the population rendered the province of difficult retention, and the prudent Maharaja gladly accepted Yar Muhammad's tender of submission. Muhammad Azim Khan died shortly afterwards, and with him expired all show of unanimity among the bands of brothers who possessed the three capitals of Peshawar, Kabul, and Kandahar; while Shah Mahmud and his son Kamran exercised a precarious authority in Herat, and Shah Ayub, who had been proclaimed titular monarch of Afghanistan, remained a cipher in his chief city.[1]

**Death of Muhammad Azim Khan. 1823.**

**Ranjit Singh feels his way towards Sind. 1823-4.**

Towards the end of the year 1823, Ranjit Singh marched to the south-west corner of his territories, to reduce refractory Muhammadan Jagirdars, and to create an impression of his power on the frontiers of

[1] Cf. Murray, *Ranjit Singh*, p. 137, &c.; Moorcroft, *Travels*, ii. 333, 334; and Masson, *Journeys*, iii. 58-60. Ranjit Singh told Capt. Wade that, of his disciplined troops, his Gurkhas alone stood firm under the assault of the Muhammadans. (Capt. Wade to Resident at Delhi, 3rd April, 1839.)

The fanatic, Phula Singh, already referred to in the preceding note, was a man of some notoriety. In 1809 he attacked Sir Charles Metcalfe's camp, and afterwards the party of a British officer employed in surveying the Cis-Sutlej states. In 1814-15 he fortified himself in Abohar (between Ferozepur and Bhatnair), since construed into a British possession (Capt. Murray to Agent, Delhi, 15th May, 1823); and in 1820 he told Mr. Moorcroft that he was dissatisfied with Ranjit Singh, that he was ready to join the English, and that, indeed, he would carry fire and sword wherever Mr. Moorcroft might desire. (*Travels*, i. 110.)

With regard to Dost Muhammad Khan it is well known, and Mr. Masson (*Journeys*, iii. 59, 60) and Munshi Mohan Lal (*Life of Dost Muhammad*, i. 127, 128) both show the extent to which he was an intriguer on this occasion. This circumstance was subsequently lost sight of by the British negotiators and the British public; and Sikh and Afghan leaders were regarded as essentially antagonistic, instead of as ready to coalesce for their selfish ends under any of several probable contingencies.

Sind—to tribute from the Amirs of which country he had already advanced some claims.[1] He likewise pretended to regard Shikarpur as a usurpation of the Talpur dynasty; but his plans were not yet matured, and he returned to his capital to learn of the death of Sansar Chand. He gave his consent to the succession of the son of a chief whose power once surpassed his own, and the Prince Kharak Singh exchanged turbans, in token of brotherhood, with the heir of tributary Katotch.[2]

1824

Sansar Chand of Katotch dies, end of 1824.

Ranjit Singh had now brought under his sway the three Muhammadan provinces of Kashmir, Multan, and Peshawar : he was supreme in the hills and plains of the Punjab proper; the mass of his dominion had been acquired; and although his designs on Ladakh and Sind were obvious, a pause in the narrative of his actions may conveniently take place, for the purpose of relating other matters necessary to a right understanding of his character, and which intimately bear on the general history of the country.

Ranjit Singh's power consolidated, and the mass of his dominion acquired.

Shah Shuja reached Ludhiana, as has been mentioned, in the year 1816, and secured for himself an honoured repose : but his thoughts were intent on Kabul and Kandahar; he disliked the British notion that he had tamely sought an asylum, and he wished to be regarded as a prince in distress, seeking for aid to enable him to recover his crown. He had hopes held out to him by the Amirs of Sind when hard pressed, perhaps, by Fateh Khan, and he conceived that an invasion of Afghanistan might be successfully prosecuted from the southward. He made offers of advantage to the English, but he was told that they had no concern with the affairs of strangers, and desired to live in peace with all their neighbours. He was thus casting about for means when Fateh Khan was murdered, and the tenders of allegiance which he received from Muhammad Azim Khan at once induced him to quit Ludhiana. He left that place in October 1818: with the aid of the Nawab of Bahawalpur, he mastered Dera Ghazi Khan; he sent his son Timur to occupy Shikarpur, and he proceeded in person towards Peshawar, to become, as he believed, the king of the Durranis. But Muhammad Azim Khan had, in the meantime, seen fit to proclaim himself the

Miscellaneous transactions. Shah Shuja's expedition against Shikarpur and Peshawar, 1818-21.

[1] Capt. Murray to the Governor-General's Agent, Delhi, 15th Dec. 1825, and Capt. Wade to the same, 7th Aug. 1823.
[2] Murray, *Ranjit Singh*, p. 141. For an interesting account of Sansar Chand, his family, and his country, see Moorcroft, *Travels*, i. 126-46.

1821-2.

Wazir of Ayub, and Shah Shuja, hard pressed, sought safety among some friendly clans in the Khaibar hills. He was driven thence at the end of two months, and had scarcely entered Shikarpur when Muhammad Azim Khan's approach compelled him to retire. He went first to Khairpur, and afterwards to Hyderabad, and, having procured some money from the Sindians, he returned and recovered Shikarpur, where he resided for a year. But Muhammad Azim Khan again approached, the Hyderabad chiefs pretended that the Shah was plotting to bring in the English, and their money was this time paid for his expulsion. The ex-king, finding his position untenable, retired through Rajputana to Delhi, and eventually took up his residence a second time at Ludhiana, in June 1821. His brother, the blind Shah Zaman, after visiting Persia, and perhaps Arabia, arrived at the same place about the same time and nearly by the same road. Shah Shuja's stipend had all along been drawn by his family, represented by the able and faithful Wafa Begum, and an allowance, first of 18,000, and afterwards of 24,000 rupees a year, was assigned for the support of Shah Zaman, when he also became a petitioner to the English Government.[1]

*The Shah returns to Ludhiana, 1821; and is followed by Shah Zaman, who takes up his abode at the same place.*

In the year 1820, Appa Sahib, the deposed Raja of the Maratha kingdom of Nagpur, escaped from the custody of the British' authorities and repaired to Amritsar. He would seem to have had the command of large sums of money, and he endeavoured to engage Ranjit Singh in his cause; but the Maharaja had been told the fugitive was the violent enemy of his English allies, and he ordered him to quit his territories. The chief took up his abode for a time in Sansar Chand's principality of Katotch, and while there he would appear to have entered into some idle schemes with Prince Haidar, a son of Shah Zaman, for the subjugation of India south and east of the Sutlej. The Durrani was to be monarch of the whole, from Delhi to Cape Comorin; but the Maratha was to be Wazir of the empire, and to hold the Deccan as a dependent sovereign.

*Appa Sahib, ex-Raja of Nagpur, 1820-2.*

*His idle schemes with the son of Shah Zaman.*

[1] Cf. Shah Shuja's 'Autobiography', chaps. xxvii, xxviii, xxix, in the *Calcutta Monthly Journal* for 1839, and the *Bahawalpur Family Annals* (Manuscript). Capt. Murray (*History of Ranjit Singh,* p. 103) merely states that Shah Shuja made an unsuccessful attempt to recover his throne; but the following letters may be referred to in support of all that is included in the paragraph : Government to Resident, Delhi, 10th May and 7th June 1817; Capt. Murray to Resident, Delhi, 22nd Sept. and 10th Oct. 1818, and 1st April 1825; and Capt. Murray to Sir D. Ochterlony, 29th April, 30th June, and 27th Aug. 1821.

The Punjab was not included; but it did not transpire
that either Ranjit Singh, or Sansar Chand, or the two
ex-kings of Kabul, were privy to the design, and, as
soon as the circumstance became known, Sansar Chand
compelled his guest to proceed elsewhere. Appa Sahib
repaired, in 1822, to Mandi, which lies between Kangra
and the Sutlej; but he wandered to Amritsar about
1828, and only finally quitted the country during the
following year; to find an asylum with the Raja of
Jodhpur. That state had become an English dependency, and the ex-Raja's surrender was required; but
the strong objections of the Rajput induced the Government to be satisfied with a promise of his safe
custody, and he died almost forgotten in the year 1840.[1]

As has been mentioned, the Raja Bir Singh, of
Nurpur, in the hills, had been dispossessed of his chiefship in the year 1816. He sought refuge to the south
of the Sutlej, and immediately made proposals to Shah
Shuja, who had just reached Ludhiana, to enter into a
combination against Ranjit Singh. The Maharaja had
not altogether despised similar tenders of allegiance
from various discontented chiefs, when the Shah was
his prisoner-guest in Lahore; he remembered the treaty
between the Shah and the English, and he knew how
readily dethroned kings might be made use of by the
ambitious. He wished to ascertain the views of the
English authorities, but he veiled his suspicions of
*them* in terms of apprehension of the Nurpur Raja. His
troops, he said, were absent in the neighbourhood of
Multan, and Bir Singh might cross the Sutlej and raise
disturbances. The reception of emissaries by Shah
Shuja was then discountenanced, and the residence of
the exiled Raja at Ludhiana was discouraged; but
Ranjit Singh was told that his right to attempt the
recovery of his chiefship was admitted, although he
would not be allowed to organize the means of doing
so within the British limits. The Maharaja seemed
satisfied that Lahore would be safe while he was
absent in the south or west, and he said no more.[2]

*The petty
ex-chief of
Nurpur
causes Ran-
jit Singh
some
anxiety
owing to
his resort
to the
English.*

---

[1] Cf. Murray, *Ranjit Singh* p. 126; Moorcroft, *Travels*. i.
109; and the quasi-official authority, the *Bengal and Agra
Gazetteer* for 1841, 1842 (articles 'Nagpur' and 'Jodhpur'). See
also Capt. Murray, letters to Resident at Delhi, 24th Nov. and
22nd Dec. 1821, the 13th Jan. 1822, and 16th June 1824; and
likewise Capt. Wade to Resident at Delhi, 15th March 1828.

[2] The public correspondence generally of 1816—17 has
here been referred to, and especially the letter of Government
to Resident at Delhi, dated 11th April 1817. In 1826 Bir Singh
made another attempt to recover his principality; but he was
seized and imprisoned. (Murray, *Ranjit Singh*, p. 145, and

1819-20.

The travel-
ler Moor-
croft in the
Punjab,
1820.

In the year 1819 the able and adventurous traveller, Moorcroft, left the plains of India in the hope
of reaching Yarkand and Bukhara. In the hills of the
Punjab he experienced difficulties, and he was induced
to repair to Lahore to wait upon Ranjit Singh. He was
honourably received, and any lurking suspicions of his
own designs, or of the views of his Government, were
soon dispelled. The Maharaja conversed with frankness of the events of his life; he showed the traveller
his bands of horsemen and battalions of infantry, and
encouraged him to visit any part of the capital without
hesitation, and at his own leisure. Mr. Moorcroft's
medical skill and general knowledge, his candid manner and personal activity, produced an impression
favourable to himself and advantageous to his countrymen; but his proposition that British merchandise
should be admitted into the Punjab at a fixed scale
of duties was received with evasion. The Maharaja's
revenues might be affected, it was said, and his principal officers, whose advice was necessary, were absent
on distant expeditions. Every facility was afforded to
Mr. Moorcroft in prosecuting his journey, and it was
arranged that, if he could not reach Yarkand from
Tibet, he might proceed through Kashmir to Kabul
and Bukhara, the route which it was eventually found
necessary to pursue. Mr. Moorcroft reached Ladakh
in safety, and in 1821 he became possessed of a letter
from the Russian minister, Price Nesselrode, recom-
mending a merchant to the good offices of Ranjit Singh
and assuring him that the traders of the Punjab would
be well received in the Russian dominions—for the
emperor was himself a benign ruler, he earnestly
desired the prosperity of other countries, and he was
especially the well-wisher of that reigned over by the
King of the Sikhs. The person recommended had died
on his way southward from Russia; and it appeared
that, six years previously, he had been the bearer of
similar communications for the Maharaja of Lahore,
and the Raja of Ladakh.[1]

Ranjit
Singh's
general
system of
govern-
ment, and
view of his

Ranjit Singh now possessed a broad dominion, and
an instructed intellect might have rejoiced in the opportunity accorded for wise legislation, and for consolidating aggregated provinces into one harmonious
empire. But such a task neither suited the Maharaja's
genius nor that of the Sikh nation; nor is it, perhaps,

Capt. Murray to Resident at Delhi, 25th Feb. 1827.) He was
subsequently released, and was alive, but unheeded, in 1844.
   [1] Moorcroft, Travels, i. 99, 103; and see also pp. 383, 387,
with respect to a previous letter to Ranjit Singh.

agreeable to the constitution of any political society,
that its limits shall be fixed, or that the pervading
spirit of a people shall rest, until its expansive force is
destroyed and becomes obnoxious to change and decay.
Ranjit Singh grasped the more obvious characteristics
of the impulse given by Nanak and Gobind; he dexterously turned them to the purposes of his own material
ambition, and he appeared to be an absolute monarch
in the midst of willing and obedient subjects. But he
knew that he merely directed into a particular channel
a power which he could neither destroy nor control,
and that, to prevent the Sikhs turning upon himself, or
contending with one another, he must regularly engage
them in conquest and remote warfare. The first political system of the emancipated Sikhs had crumbled to
pieces, partly through its own defects, partly owing
to its contact with a well-ordered and civilized government, and partly in consequence of the ascendancy of
one superior mind. The 'Misals' had vanished, or were
only represented by Ahluwalia and Patiala (or Phulkia), the one depending on the personal friendship of
Ranjit Singh for its chief, and the other upheld in
separate portions by the expediency of the English.
But Ranjit Singh never thought his own or the Sikh
sway was to be confined to the Punjab, and his only
wish was to lead armies as far as faith in the Khalsa
and confidence in his skill would take brave and
believing men. He troubled himself not at all with the
theory or the practical niceties of administration, and
he would rather have added a province to his rule than
have received the assurances of his English neighbours
that he legislated with discrimination in commercial
affairs and with a just regard for the amelioration of
his ignorant and fanatical subjects of various persuasions. He took from the land as much as it could
readily yield, and he took from merchants as much as
they could profitably give; he put down open marauding; the Sikh peasantry enjoyed a light assessment; no
local officer dared to oppress a member of the Khalsa;
and if elsewhere the farmers of revenue were resisted
in their tyrannical proceedings, they were more likely
to be changed than to be supported by battalions. He
did not ordinarily punish men who took redress into
their own hands, for which, indeed his subordi ates
were prepared, and which they guarded against as they
could. The whole wealth and the whole energies of
the people were devoted to war, and to the preparation
of military means and equipment. The system is that
common to all feudal governments, and it gives much

scope to individual ambition, and tends to produce independence of character. It suited the mass of the Sikh population; they had ample employment, they loved contention, and they were pleased that city after city admitted the supremacy of the Khalsa and enabled them to enrich their families. But Ranjit Singh never arrogated to himself the title or the powers of despot or tyrant. He was assiduous in his devotions; he honoured men of reputed sanctity, and enabled them to practise an enlarged charity; he attributed every success to the favour of God, and he styled himself and people collectively the 'Khalsa', or commonwealth of Gobind. Whether in walking barefooted to make his obeisance to a collateral representative of his prophets, or in rewarding a soldier distinguished by that symbol of his faith, a long and ample beard, or in restraining the excesses of the fanatical Akalis, or in beating an army and acquiring a province, his own name and his own motives were kept carefully concealed, and everything was done for the sake of the Guru, for the advantage of the Khalsa, and in the name of the Lord.[1]

[1] Ranjit Singh, in writing or in talking of his government, always used the term 'Khalsa'. On his seal he wrote, as any Sikh usually writes, his name, with the prefix 'Akal Sahai', that is, for instance, 'God the helper, Ranjit Singh'—an inscription strongly resembling the 'God with us' of the Commonwealth of England. Professor Wilson (*Journal Royal Asiatic Society*. No. xvii, p. 51) thus seems scarcely justified in saying that Ranjit Singh deposed Nanak and Gobind, and the supreme ruler of the universe, and held himself to be the impersonation of the Khalsa !

With respect to the abstract excellence or moderation, or the practical efficiency or suitableness of the Sikh government, opinions will always differ, as they will about all other governments. It is not simply an unmeaning truism to say that the Sikh government suited the Sikhs well, for such a degree of fitness is one of the ends of all governments of ruling classes, and the adaptation has thus a degree of positive merit. In judging of *individuals*, moreover, the extent and the peculiarities of the civilization of their times should be remembered, and the present condition of the Punjab shows a combination of the characteristics of rising mediaeval Europe and of the decaying Byzantine empire—semi-barbarous in either light, but possessed at once of a native youthful vigour, and of an extraneous knowledge of many of the arts which adorn life in the most advanced stages of society.

The fact, again, that a city like Amritsar is the creation of the Sikhs at once refutes many charges of oppression or misgovernment, and Col. Francklin only repeats the general opinion of the time when he says (*Life of Shah Alam*, p. 77) that the lands under Sikh rule were cultivated with great assiduity. Mr. Masson could hear of no complaints in Multan (*Journeys*, i. 30, 398), and although Moorcroft notices the depressed condition of the Kashmiris (*Travels*, i. 123) he does

In the year 1822 the French Generals, Ventura and Allard, reached Lahore by way of Persia and Afghanistan, and, after some little hesitation, they were employed and treated with distinction.[1] It has been usual to attribute the superiority of the Sikh army to the labours of these two officers, and of their subsequent coadjutors, the Generals Court and Avitabile; but, in truth, the Sikh owes his excellence as a soldier to his own hardihood of character, to that spirit of adaptation which distinguishes every new people, and to that feeling of a common interest and destiny implanted in him by his great teachers. The Rajputs and Pathans are valiant and high-minded warriors: but their pride and their courage are personal only, and concern them as men of ancient family and noble lineage; they will do nothing unworthy of their birth, but they are indifferent to the political advancement of their race. The efforts of the Marathas, in emancipating themselves from a foreign yoke, were neither guided nor strengthened by any distinct hope or desire. They became free, but knew not how to remain independent, and they allowed a crafty Brahman[2] to turn their

1822.
The Sikh army.

Arrival of French officers at Lahore, 1822

Excellences of the Sikhs as soldiers.

Characteristics of Rajputs and Pathans, of Marathas.

not notice the circumstance of a grievous famine having occurred shortly before his visit, which drove thousands of the people to the plains of India, and he forgets that the valley had been under the sway of Afghan adventurers for many years, the severity of whose rule is noticed by Forster (*Travels*, ii. 26, &c.). The ancestors of the numerous families of Kashmiri Brahmans, now settled in Delhi, Lucknow, &c., were likewise refugees from Afghan oppression: and it is curious that the consolidation of Ranjit Singh's power should have induced several of these families to repair to the Punjab, and even to return to their original country. This, notwithstanding the Hinduism of the Sikh faith, is still somewhat in favour of Sikh rule.

[1] Murray, *Ranjit Singh*, p. 131, &c.

[2] [The reference is to Nana Farnavis, who became Prime Minister of the Peshwa in 1775 and who died in 1800, having exercised an extraordinary influence over Maratha politics during his years of ascendancy. 'He had consistently been opposed to the political progress of the English as subversive of Maratha power, and he objected to the employment of foreign troops under any conditions; but he was faithful to his political engagements, and his devotion to the maintenance of the honour of his own nation is attested by the respect of all his contemporaries. The faithless materials with which he had to deal at the close of his life threw him into intrigues and combinations for his own preservation which would otherwise have been avoided and left him at liberty to continue the able administration he had conducted for twenty-five years' (Meadows Taylor). On the occasion of his death the English Resident at Poona wrote: 'With him has departed all the wisdom and moderation of the Maratha Government.' See Grant Duff, *History of the Marathas*, ed. 1826, p. 188.—ED.]

aimless aspirations to his own profit, and to found a dynasty of 'Peshwas' on the achievements of unlettered Sudras. Ambitious soldiers took a further advantage of the spirit called up by Sivaji, but as it was not sustained by any pervading religious principle of action, a few generations saw the race yield to the expiring efforts of Muhammadanism, and the Marathas owe their present position, as rulers, to the intervention of European strangers. The genuine Maratha can scarcely be said to exist, and the two hundred thousand spearmen of the last century are once more shepherds and tillers of the ground. Similar remarks apply to the Gurkhas, that other Indian people which has risen to greatness in latter times by its own innate power, unmingled with religious hope. They became masters, but no peculiar institution formed the landmark of their thoughts, and the vitality of the original impulse seems fast waning before the superstition of an ignorant priesthood and the turbulence of a feudal nobility. The difference between these races and the fifth tribe of Indian warriors will be at once apparent. The Sikh looks before him only, the ductility of his youthful intellect readily receives the most useful impression, or takes the most advantageous form, and religious faith is ever present to sustain him under any adversity, and to assure him of an ultimate triumph.

The Rajput and Pathan will fight as Pirthi Raj and Jenghiz Khan waged war; they will ride on horses in tumultuous array, and they will wield a sword and spear with individual dexterity : but neither of these cavaliers will deign to stand in regular ranks and to handle the musket of the infantry soldier, although the Muhammadan has always been a brave and skilful server of heavy cannon. The Maratha is equally averse to the European system of warfare, and the less stiffened Gurkha has only had the power or the opportunity of forming battalions of footmen, unsupported by an active cavalry and a trained artillery. The early force of the Sikhs was composed of horsemen, but they seem intuitively to have adopted the new and formidable matchlock of recent times, instead of their ancestral bows, and the spear common to every nation. Mr. Forster noticed this peculiarity in 1783, and the advantage it gave in desultory warfare.[1] In 1805, Sir John Malcolm did not think the Sikh was better mounted than the Maratha;[2] but, in 1810, Sir David Ochterlony considered that, in the confidence of un-

Aversion of the older military tribes of India to regular discipline, with the exception of the Gurkhas, and partially of the Muhammadans.

The Sikh forces originally composed of horsemen armed with matchlocks. Notices of the Sikh troops, by Forster, 1783;

[1] Forster, *Travels*, i. 332.
[2] Malcolm, *Sketch of the Sikhs*, pp. 150, 151.

tried strength, his great native courage would show
him more formidable than a follower of Sindhia or
Holkar, and readily lead him to face a battery of well-
served guns.[1] The peculiar arm of the contending
nations of the last century passed into a proverb, and
the phrase, the Maratha spear, the Afghan sword, the
Sikh matchlock, and the English cannon, is still of
common repetition; nor does it gratify the pride of the
present masters of India to hear their success attributed
rather to the number and excellence of their artillery,
than to that dauntless courage and firm array which
have enabled the humble footmen to win most of those
distant victories which add glory to the English name.
Nevertheless it has always been the object of rival
powers to obtain a numerous artillery; the battalions
of De Boigne would never separate themselves from
their cannon, and the presence of that formidable arm
is yet, perhaps, essential to the full confidence of the
British Sepoy.[2]

Ranjit Singh said that, in 1805, he went to see the
order of Lord Lake's army,[3] and it is known that in
1809 he admired and praised the discipline of Mr.
Metcalfe's small escort, who repulsed the sudden onset

*1822.
by Malcolm, 1805;
and by Ochterlony, 1810.
Characteristic arms of different races, including the English.
The general importance given to artillery by the Indians.
a· consequence of the victories of the English.
Ranjit Singh labours to introduce discipline;*

---

[1] Sir D. Ochterlony to Government, 1st Dec. 1810.

[2] This feeling is well known to all who have had any
experience of Indian troops. A gunner is a prouder man than
a musketeer: when battalions are mutinous, they will not allow
strangers to approach their guns, and the best-dispositioned
regiments will scarcely leave them in the rear to go into action
unencumbered, an instance of which happened in Perron's
warfare with George Thomas. (Major Smith, *Regular Corps in
Indian Employ*, p. 24.)

The ranks of the British Army are indeed filled with
Rajputs and Pathans so called, and also with Brahmans; but
nearly all are from the provinces of tne Upper Ganges, the
inhabitants of which have become greatly modified in character
by complete conquest and mixture with strangers; and, while
they retain some of the distinguishing marks of their races,
they are, as soldiers, the merest mercenaries, and do not
possess the ardent and restless feeling, or that spirit of clanship,
which characterize the more genuine descendants of Kshattriyas and Afghans. The remarks in the text thus refer
especially to the Pathans of Rohilkhand and Hariana and
similar scattered colonies, and to the yeomanry and little
proprietors of Rajputana. [Much of this is of course incorrect
and refers to the pre-Mutiny conditions of the Army. With the
exception of a few mountain batteries the artillery is now
entirely in the hands of British troops. The Brahman element
in the Army has also been greatly reduced. At the present
time 63 per cent. of the efficient fighting forces of the Indian
Army came from the Punjab.—Ed.]

[3] Moorcroft, *Travels*, i. 102. [The fact of this visit having
been made is also borne out by a passage in the Diary of
L. Sohan Lal. The latter was Court Vakil to Ranjit Singh.—Ed]

of a body of enraged Akalis.[1] He began, after that period, to give his attention to the formation of regular infantry, and in 1812 Sir David Ochterlony saw two regiments of Sikhs, besides several of Hindustanis, drilled by men who had resigned or deserted the British service.[2] The next year the Maharaja talked of raising twenty-five battalions,[3] and his confidence in discipline was increased by the resistance which the Gurkhas offered to the British arms. He enlisted people of that nation, but his attention was chiefly given to the instruction of his own countrymen, and in 1820 Mr. Moorcroft noticed with approbation the appearance of the Sikh foot-soldier.[4] Ranjit Singh had not got his people to resign their customary weapons and order of battle without some trouble. He encouraged them by good pay, by personal attention to their drill and equipment, and by himself wearing the strange dress, and going through the formal exercise.[5] The old chiefs disliked the innovation, and Desa Singh Majithia, the father of the present mechanic and disciplinarian Lahna Singh, assured the companions of Mr. Moorcroft that Multan and Peshawar and Kashmir had all been won by the free Khalsa cavalier.[6] By degrees the infantry service came to be preferred, and, before Ranjit Singh died, he saw it regarded as the proper warlike array of his people. Nor did they give their heart to the musket alone, but were perhaps more readily brought to serve guns than to stand in even ranks as footmen.

Such was the state of change of the Sikh army, and such were the views of Ranjit Singh, when Generals Allard and Ventura obtained service in the Punjab.

[1] Murray, *Ranjit Singh*, p. 68.

[2] Sir D. Ochterlony to Government, 27th Feb. 1812.

[3] Sir D. Ochterlony to Government, 4th March 1813.

[4] Moorcroft, *Travels*. i. 98. There were at. that time, as there are still, Gurkhas in the service of Lahore.

[5] The author owes this anecdote to Munshi Shahamat Ali, otherwise favourably known to the public by his book on the Sikhs and Afghans.

[6] Moorcroft, *Travels*, i. 98. Ranjit Singh usually required his feudatories to provide for constant service, a horseman for every 500 rupees which they held in land, besides being ready with other fighting-men on an emergency. This proportion left the Jagirdar one-half only of his estate untaxed, as an efficient horseman cost about 250 rupees annually. The Turks (Ranke, *Ottoman Empire*, ed. 1843, Introd., p. 5) required a horseman for the first 3,000 *aspers*, or 50 dollars, or say 125 rupees, and an additional one for every other 5,000 aspers, or 208 rupees. In England, in the seventeenth century, a horseman was assessed on every five hundred pounds of income. (Maçaulay, *History of England*. i. 29.)

They were fortunate in having an excellent material to work with, and, like skilful officers, they made a good use of their means and opportunities. They gave a moderate degree of precision and completeness to a system already introduced; but their labours are more conspicuous in French words of command, in treble ranks, and in squares salient with guns, than in the ardent courage, the alert obedience, and the long endurance of fatigue, which distinguished the Sikh horsemen sixty years ago, and which pre-eminently characterize the Sikh footman of the present day among the other soldiers of India.[1] Neither did Generals Ventura and Allard, Court and Avitabile, ever assume to themselves the merit of having created the Sikh army, and perhaps their ability and independence of character added more to the general belief in European superiority, than all their instructions to the real efficiency of the Sikhs as soldiers.

1820.

Punjab before the arrival of French officers; whose services were yet of value to Ranjit Singh, and honourable to themselves.

When a boy, Ranjit Singh was betrothed, as has been related, to Mehtab Kaur, the daughter of Gurbakhsh Singh, the young heir of the Kanhaya (or Ghani) chiefship, who fell in battle with his father Mahan Singh. Sada Kaur, the mother of the girl, possessed a high spirit and was ambitious of power, and, on the death of the Kanhaya leader, Jai Singh, about 1793, her influence in the affairs of the confede-

---

[1] For notices of this endurance of fatigue, see Forster, *Travels*, i. 332, 333; Malcolm, *Sketch*, p. 141; Mr. Masson, *Journeys*, i. 433; and Col. Steinbach, *Punjab*, pp. 63, 64.

The general constitution of a Sikh regiment was a commandant and adjutant, with subordinate officers to each company. The men were paid by deputies of the 'Bakshi', or paymaster; but the rolls were checked by 'Mutasaddis', or clerks, who daily noted down whether the men were absent or present. To each regiment at least one 'Granthi', or reader of the scriptures, was attached, who, when not paid by the government, was sure of being supported by the men. The Granth was usually deposited near the 'jhanda', or flag, which belonged to the regiment, and which represented its headquarters. Light tents and beasts of burden were allowed in fixed proportions to each battalion, and the state also provided two cooks, or rather bakers, for each company, who baked the men's cakes after they had themselves kneaded them, or who, in some instances, provided unleavened loaves for those of their own or an inferior race. In cantonments the Sikh soldiers lived to some extent in barracks, and not each man in a separate hut, a custom which should be introduced into the British service. [The barrack system has been introduced. The whole organization of the Sikh army under Ranjit Singh is of much interest. Quite recently some research has been initiated and is still in progress upon the Sikh records in the Secretariat at Lahore. The result of this, as far as it concerns the army, will be found in the Appendix, section XXXIX.—ED.]

racy became paramount. She encouraged her young son-in-law to set aside the authority of his own widow mother, and at the age of seventeen the future Maharaja is not only said to have taken upon himself the management of his affairs, but to have had his mother put to death as an adultress. The support of Sada Kaur was of great use to Ranjit Singh in the beginning of his career, and the cooperation of the Kanhaya Misal mainly enabled him to master Lahore and Amritsar. Her hope seems to have been that, as the grandmother of the chosen heir of Ranjit Singh, and as a chieftainess in her own right, she would be able to exercise a commanding influence in the affairs of the Sikhs; but her daughter was childless, and Ranjit Singh himself was equally able and wary. In 1807 it was understood that Mehtab Kaur was pregnant, and it is believed that she was really delivered of a daughter; but, on Ranjit Singh's return from an expedition, he was presented with two boys as his offspring. The Maharaja doubted :

and perhaps he always gave credence to the report that Sher Singh was the son of a carpenter, and Tara Singh the child of a weaver, yet they continued to be brought up under the care of their reputed grandmother, as if their parentage had been admitted. But Sada Kaur perceived that she could obtain no power in the names of the children, and the disappointed woman addressed the English authorities in 1810, and denounced her son-in-law as having usurped her rights, and as resolved on war with his new allies. Her communications received some attention, but she was unable to organize an insurrection, and she became in a manner reconciled to her position. In 1820, Sher Singh was virtually adopted by the Maharaja, with the apparent object of finally setting aside the power of his mother-in-law. She was required to assign half of the lands of the Kanhaya chiefship for the maintenance of the youth; but she refused, and she was in consequence seized and imprisoned, and her whole possessions confiscated. The little estate of Whadni, to the south of the Sutlej, was however restored to her through British intervention, as has already been mentioned.[1]

Ranjit Singh was also betrothed, when a boy, to the daughter of Khazan Singh, a chief of the Nakkais confederacy, and by her he had a son in the year 1802, who was named Kharak Singh, and brought up as his

[1] Cf. Murray, *Ranjit Singh*, pp. 46-51, 63, 127, 128, 134, 135. See also Sir D. Ochterlony to Government, 1st and 10th Dec. 1810, and p. 144 of this volume.

heir. The youth was married, in the year 1812, to the 1802-21.
daughter of a Kanhaya leader, and the nuptials were
celebrated amid many rejoicings. In 1816 the Maharaja
placed the mother under some degree of restraint
owing to her mismanagement of the estates assigned
for the maintenance of the prince, and he endeavoured
to rouse the spirit of his son to exertion and enterprise;
but he was of a weak and indolent character, and the Nau Nihal
attempt was vain. In the year 1821 a son was born to Singh born
Kharak Singh, and the child, Nau Nihal Singh, soon to Kharak
came to be regarded as the heir of the Punjab.[1] Singh, 1821.

Such were the domestic relations of Ranjit Singh, Ranjit
but he shared largely in the opprobrium heaped upon Singh's per-
his countrymen as the practisers of every immorality, sonal licen-
and he is not only represented to have frequently tiousness
indulged in strong drink, but to have occasionally out- and intem-
raged decency by appearing in public inebriated, and perance, in
surrounded with courtesans.[2] In his earlier days one connexion
of these women, named Mohra, obtained a great ascen- with the
dancy over him, and, in 1811, he caused coins or medals vices
to be struck bearing her name; but it would be idle to vaguely
regard Ranjit Singh as an habitual drunkard or as one attributed
greatly devoted to sensual pleasures; and it would be to the mass
equally unreasonable to believe the mass of the Sikh of the Sikh
people as wholly lost to shame, and as revellers in people.
every vice which disgraces humanity. Doubtless the
sense of personal honour and of female purity is less
high among the rude and ignorant of every age, than
among the informed and the civilized; and when the
whole peasantry of a country suddenly attain to power
and wealth, and are freed from many of the restraints
of society, an unusual proportion will necessarily
resign themselves to the seductions of pleasure, and
freely give way to their most depraved appetites. But
such excesses are nevertheless exceptional to the general usage, and those who vilify the Sikhs at one time,
and describe their long and rapid marches at another,
should remember the contradiction, and reflect that
what common-sense and the better feelings of our
nature have always condemned, can never be the
ordinary practice of a nation. The armed defenders of
a country cannot be kept under the same degree of
moral restraint as ordinary citizens, with quiet habits,
fixed abodes, and watchful pastors, and it is illogical
to apply the character of a few dissolute chiefs and
licentious soldiers to the thousands of hardy peasants
and industrious mechanics, and even generally to that

[1] Cf. Murray, *Ranjit Singh*, pp. 48, 53, 90, 91, 112, 129.
[2] Cf. Murray, *Ranjit Singh*, p. 85.

body of brave and banded men which furnishes the
most obvious examples of degradation.[1] The husbandman of the Punjab, as of other provinces in Upper
India, is confined to his cakes of millet or wheat and
to a draught of water from the well; the soldier fares
not much better, and neither indulge in strong liquors,
except upon occasions of rejoicing. The indolent man
of wealth or station, or the more idle religious fanatic,
may seek excitement, or a refuge from the vacancy of
his mind, in drugs and drink; but expensiveness of diet
is rather a Muhammadan than an Indian characteristic,
and the Europeans carry their potations and the pleasures of the table to an excess unknown to the Turk
and Persian, and which greatly scandalize the frugal
Hindu.[2]

Ranjit Singh's favourites.

Yet Ranjit Singh not only yielded more than was
becoming to the promptings of his appetites, but, like
all despots and solitary authorities, he laid himself
open to the charge of extravagant partiality and favouritism. He had placed himself in some degree in
opposition to the whole Sikh people; the free followers
of Gobind could not be the observant slaves of an
equal member of the Khalsa, and he sought for
strangers whose applause would be more ready if less
sincere, and in whom he could repose some confidence
as the creatures of his favour. The first who thus rose
to distinction was Khushal Singh, a Brahman from
near Saharanpur, who enlisted in one of the first raised
regiments, and next became a runner or footman on
the Maharaja's establishment. He attracted Ranjit
Singh's notice, and was made Jamadar of the Devni,

Khushal Singh, a Brahman, 1811-20.

[1] Col. Steinbach (Punjab, pp. 76, 77) admits general
simplicity of diet, but he also makes some revolting practices
universal. Capt. Murray (Ranjit Singh, p. 85) and Mr. Masson
(Journeys, i. 435) are likewise somewhat sweeping in their
condemnations, and even Mr. Elphinstone (History of India,
ii. 565) makes the charge of culpable devotion to sensual
pleasures very comprehensive. The morals, or the manners, of
a people, however, should not be deduced from a few examples
of profligacy; but the Indians equally exaggerate with regard
to Europeans, and, in pictorial or pantomimic pieces, they
usually represent Englishmen drinking and swearing in the
society of courtesans, and as equally prompt to use their
weapons with or without a reason.

[2] Forster (Travels, i. 333) notices the temperance of the
Sikhs, and their forbearance from many enervating sensual
pleasures, and he quotes, he thinks, Col. Polier to a similar
effect. Malcolm (Sketch, p. 141) likewise describes the Sikhs
as hardy and simple; but, doubtless, as the power of the
nation has increased since these times, luxuries and vicious
pleasures have, in numerous instances, followed wealth and
indolence.

or master of the entry, about the year 1811. His brother seemed likely to supplant him, but his refusal
to become a Sikh favoured Khushal Singh's continuance in power, until both yielded to the Jammu Rajputs in the year 1820. Gulab Singh, the eldest of three
sons, claimed that his grandfather was the brother of
the well-known Ranjit Deo; but the family was perhaps
illegitimate, and had become impoverished, and Gulab
Singh took service as a horseman in a band commanded
by Jamadar Khushal Singh. He sent for his second
brother, Dhian Singh, and then, again like the reigning
favourite, they both became running footmen under
Ranjit Singh's eye. Their joint assiduity, and the
graceful bearing of the younger man, again attracted
the Maharaja's notice, and Dhian Singh speedily took
the place of the Brahman chamberlain, without, however, consigning him to neglect, for he retained his
estates and his position as a noble. Gulab Singh
obtained a petty command and signalized himself by
the seizure of the turbulent Muhammadan Chief of
Rajauri. Jammu was then conferred in jagir or fief
upon the family, and the youngest brother, Suchet
Singh, as well as the two elder, were one by one raised
to the rank of Raja, and rapidly obtained an engrossing
and prejudicial influence in the counsels of the Maharaja, excepting, perhaps, in connexion with his English relations, the importance of which required and
obtained the exercise of his own unbiassed opinion.
The smooth and crafty Gulab Singh ordinarily remained in the hills, using Sikh means to extend his
own authority over his brother Rajputs, and eventually
into Ladakh; the less able, but more polished, Dhian
Singh, remained continually in attendance upon the
Maharaja, ever on the watch, in order that he might
anticipate his wishes; while the elegant Suchet Singh
fluttered as a gay courtier and gallant soldier, without
grasping at power or creating enemies. The nominal
fakir or devotee, the Muhammadan Aziz-ud-din, never
held the place of an ordinary favourite, but he attached
himself at an early period to Ranjit Singh's person, and
was honoured and trusted as one equally prudent and
faithful; and, during the ascendancy both of Khushal
Singh and Dhian Singh, he was always consulted, and
invariably made the medium of communication with
the British authorities. The above were the most
conspicuous persons in the Lahore court; but the mind
of Ranjit Singh was never prostrate before that of
others, and he conferred the government of Multan
on the discreet Sawan Mal, and rewarded the military

1802-21.

Hari Singh
Nalwa.
Fateh
Singh Ah-
luwalia.
Desa Singh
Majithia.

talents and genuine Sikh feelings of Hari Singh Nalwa by giving him the command on the Peshawar frontier; while his ancient companion, Fateh Singh Ahluwalia, remained, with increased wealth, the only representative of the original 'Misals', and Desa Singh Majithia enjoyed the Maharaja's esteem and confidence as governor of Amritsar and of the Jullundur Doab.[1]

[1] Cf. Murray, *Ranjit Singh*, pp. 84, 113, 125, 147; Munshi Shahamat Ali's *Sikhs and Afghans*, chaps. iv and vii; and, with regard to Aziz-ud-din and Desa Singh, see Moorcroft, *Travels*, i. 94, 98, 110, &c. Lieut.-Col. Lawrence's work, *The Adventurer in the Punjab*, and Capt. Osborne's *Court and Camp of Ranjit Singh*, likewise contain some curious information about the Maharaja's chiefs and favourites; and the author has had the further advantage of referring to a memorandum on the subject, drawn up by Mr. Clerk for Lord Ellenborough. Mohkam Chand has already been alluded to (see *ante*, p. 136), and the Brahman Diwan Chand may also be mentioned. He was the real commander when Multan was stormed, and he led the advance when Kashmir was at last seized. Of genuine Sikhs, too, Mit'h Singh Behrania was distinguished as a brave and generous soldier.

# CHAPTER VII

## FROM THE ACQUISITION OF MULTAN, KASHMIR, AND PESHAWAR, TO THE DEATH OF RANJIT SINGH

### 1824-39

Changed Relations of the English and Sikhs—Miscellaneous Transactions—Capt. Wade, the Political Agent for Sikh Affairs—The Jammu Rajas—Syed Ahmad Shah's Insurrection at Peshawar—The Fame of Ranjit Singh—The Meeting at Rupar with Lord William Bentinck—Ranjit Singh's views on Sindh, and the English Scheme of Navigating the Indus—Shah Shuja's Expedition of 1833-5, and Ranjit Singh's Regular Occupation of Peshawar—Ladakh reduced by Raja Gulab Singh—Ranjit Singh's Claims on Shikarpur and designs on Sindh crossed by the Commercial Policy of the English—The connexion of the English with the Barakzais of Afghanistan—Dost Muhammad retires before Ranjit Singh—The Sikhs defeated by the Afghans—The Marriage of Nau Nihal Singh—Sir Henry Fane—The English, Dost Muhammad, and the Russians, and the Restoration of Shah Shuja—Ranjit Singh feels curbed by the English—The Death of Ranjit Singh.

RANJIT SINGH had brought Peshawar under his sway, but the complete reduction of the province was yet to cost him an arduous warfare of many years. He had become master of the Punjab almost unheeded by the English; but the position and views of that people had changed since they asked his aid against the armies of Napoleon. The Jumna and the sea-coast of Bombay were no longer the proclaimed limits of their empire; the Narbada had been crossed, the states of Rajputana had been rendered tributary, and, with the laudable design of diffusing wealth and of linking remote provinces together in the strong and useful bonds of commerce, they were about to enter upon schemes of navigation and of trade, which caused them to deprecate the ambition of the king of the Sikhs, and led them, by sure yet unforeseen steps, to absorb his dominion in their own, and to grasp, perhaps inscrutably to chasten, with the cold unfeeling hand of worldly rule, the youthful spirit of social change and religious reformation evoked by the genius of Nanak and Gobind.

1823

Change in the position of the Sikhs relatively to the English after the year 1823.

1824-5.

Miscel-
laneous
trans-
actions,
1824-5

Peshawar.

Nepal.

Sind.

Bharatpur.

Fateh
Singh the
Ahluwalia
chief.

In the year 1824, the turbulent Muhammadan tribes on either side of the Indus above Attock arose in rebellion, and the Sikh General, Hari Singh, received a severe check. The Maharaja hastened by forced marches to that quarter, and again forded the rapid, stony-bedded Indus; but the mountaineers dispersed at his approach, and his display of power was hardly rewarded by Yar Muhammad Khan's renewed protestations of allegiance.[1] In 1825 Ranjit Singh's attention was amused with overtures from the Gurkhas, who forgot his former rivalry in the overwhelming greatness of the English; but the precise object of the Nepalese did not transpire, and the restless spirit of the Sikh chief soon led him to the Chenab, with the design of seizing Shikarpur.[2] The occurrence of a scarcity in Sind, and perhaps the rumours of the hostile preparations of the English against Bharatpur,[3] induced him to return to his capital before the end of the year. The *Jat* usurper of the Jumna asked his brother *Jat* of the Ravi to aid him; but the Maharaja acted to discredit the mission, and so satisfied the British authorities without compromising himself with the master of a fortress which had successfully resisted the disciplined troops and the dreaded artillery of his neighbours.[4] But about the same time Ranjit Singh likewise found reason to distrust the possessors of strongholds; and Fateh Singh Ahluwalia was constrained by his old brother in arms to leave a masonry citadel unfinished, and was further induced by his own fears to fly to the south of the Sutlej. He was assured of English protection in his ancestral estates in the Sirhind province, but Ranjit Singh, remembering perhaps the joint treaty with Lord Lake, earnestly endeavoured to allay the fears of the fugitive, and to recall a chief so dangerous in the hands of his allies. Fateh Singh

---

[1] Capt. Murray, *Ranjit Singh*, pp. 141, 142.

[2] Agent at Delhi to Capt. Murray, 18th March 1825, and Capt. Murray in reply, 28th March. Cf. also Murray, *Ranjit Singh*, p. 144.

[3] [This famous fortress was besieged by the English forces (20,000 men and 100 guns) on 10th Dec. 1825, and fell on 18th Jan. 1826. Its capture made a great impression, as it had been deemed impregnable. The operations were under the direction of Lord Combermere, the Commander-in-Chief who, as Sir Stapleton Cotton, had fought under Wellington in the Peninsula.—Ed.]

[4] Capt. Murray to the Resident at Delhi, 1st and 3rd Oct. 1825, and Capt. Wade to Capt. Murray, 5th Oct. 1825. Capt. Wade, however, in the printed *Narrative of his Services*, p. 7, represents Ranjit Singh as pausing to take advantage of any disasters which might befall the English.

returned to Lahore in 1827; he was received with
marked honour, and he was confirmed in nearly all his
possessions.[1]

Towards the end of 1826, Ranjit Singh was attacked with sickness, and he sought the aid of European
skill. Dr. Murray, a surgeon in the British-Indian army,
was sent to attend him, and he remained at Lahore for
some time, although the Maharaja was more disposed
to trust to time and abstinence, or to the empirical
remedies of his own physicians, than to the prescribers
of unknown drugs and the practisers of new ways.
Ranjit Singh, nevertheless, liked to have his foreign
medical adviser near him, as one from whom information could be gained, and whom it might be advantageous to please. He seemed anxious about the proposed visit of Lord Amherst, the Governor-General,
to the northern provinces; he asked about the qualities
of the Burmese troops,[2] and the amount of money
demanded by the English victors at the end of the war
with that people; he was inquisitive about the mutiny
of a regiment of Sepoys at Barrackpore, and he wished
to know whether native troops had been employed
in quelling it.[3] On the arrival of Lord Amherst at
Simla, in 1827, a further degree of intimacy became
inevitable, a mission of welcome and inquiry was sent
to wait upon his lordship, and the compliment was

*Margin notes: 1827. Ranjit Singh falls sick, and is attended by an English surgeon, 1826. Anecdotes. Lord Amherst, the British Governor-General, 1827.*

[1] Resident at Delhi to Capt. Murray, 13th Jan. 1826, and
Capt. Murray, *Ranjit Singh*, p. 144. The old chief had, as early
as 1811, desired to be regarded as separately connected with
the English, so fearful had he become of his 'turban-brother'
(Government to Sir D. Ochterlony, 4th Oct. 1811.)
  The Cis-Sutlej Muhammadan Chief of Mamdot, formerly
of Kasur, fled and returned about the same time as Fateh
Singh, for similar reasons, and after making similar endeavours to be recognized as an English dependant. (Government
to Resident at Delhi, 28th April 1827, with correspondence to
which it relates, and cf. Murray, *Ranjit Singh*, p. 145.)
[2] [The Burmese War broke out on 24th Feb. 1824 as the
result of disturbed relations going back as far as 1818. It lasted
till 24th Feb. 1826, when, by the Treaty of Yandabu, the
Burmese Government ceded the provinces of Tenasserim,
Aracan, and Assam, and paid an indemnity of one million
sterling.—ED.]
[3] Capt. Wade to the Resident at Delhi, 24th Sept. and 30th
Nov. 1826, and 1st Jan. 1827. Cf. Murray, *Ranjit Singh*,. p. 145.
[The mutiny at Barrackpore was the result of the disinclination
of the troops to go on service in Burma. There were three
native regiments at this station—26th, 47th, and 62nd—and all
of them became disaffected. On 1st Nov. 1824, the 47th broke
into open mutiny. English troops were sent to the station, and
the 47th were dispersed by artillery and the regiment was struck
off the army list. The other two regiments escaped without
punishment.—ED.]

**1827-8.**

Lord Combermere, the British Commander-in-Chief.

Capt. Wade made the immediate agent for the affairs of Lahore, 1827.

Discussions about rights to districts south of the Sutlej, 1827-8. Anandpur, Whadni, Ferozepore, &c.

returned by the deputation of Capt. Wade, the British frontier authority, to the Maharaja's court.[1] During the following year the English Commander-in-Chief arrived at Ludhiana, and Ranjit Singh sent an agent to convey to him his good wishes; but an expected invitation to visit the strongholds of the Punjab was not given to the captor of Bharatpur.[2]

The little business to be transacted between the British and Sikh governments was entrusted to the management of the Resident at Delhi, who gave his orders to Capt. Murray, the political agent at Ambala, who again had under him an assistant, Capt. Wade, at Ludhiana, mainly in connexion with the affairs of the garrison of that place. When Capt. Wade was at Lahore, the Maharaja expressed a wish that, for the sake of dispatch in business, the agency for his Cis-Sutlej possessions should be vested in the officer at Ludhiana subordinate to the resident at Delhi, but independent of the officer at Ambala.[3] This wish was complied with;[4] but in attempting to define the extent of the territories in question, it was found that there were several doubtful points to be settled. Ranjit Singh claimed supremacy over Chamkaur, and Anandpur Makhowal, and other places belonging to the Sodhis, or collateral representatives of Guru Gobind. He also claimed Whadni,which, a few years before, had been wrested from him on the plea that it was his mother-in-law's; and he claimed Ferozepore, then held

[1] Government to Capt. Wade, 2nd May, 1827.
[2] Murray, *Ranjit Ranjit*, p. 147. About this time the journeyings and studies of the enthusiastic scholar Csoma de Koros, and the establishment of Simla as a British post, had made the Chinese of Tibet as curious about the English in one way as Ranjit Singh was in another. Thus the authorities at Garo appear to have addressed the authorities of Bissehir, an English dependency, saying, 'that in ancient times there was no mention of the "Filingha" (i.e. Faranghis or Franks), a bad and small people, whereas now many visited the upper countries every year, and had caused the chief of Bissehir to make preparations for their movements. The Great Lama was displeased, and armies had been ordered to be watched. The English should be urged to keep within their own limits, or, if they wanted an alliance, they could go by sea to Pekin. The people of Bissehir should not rely on the wealth and the expertness in warfaring of the English: the emperor was 30 *paktsat* (120 miles) higher than they; he ruled over the four elements; a war would involve the six nations of Asia in calamities; the English should remain within their boundaries;' —and so on, in a strain of deprecation and hyperbole. (Political Agent. Sabathu, to Resident at Delhi, 26th March 1827.)
[3] Capt. Wade to Resident at Delhi, 20th June 1827.
[4] Government to Resident at Delhi, 4th Oct. 1827.

by a childless widow, and also all the Ahluwalia districts, besides others which need not be particularized.[1]
The claims of the Maharaja over Ferozepore and the
ancestral possessions of Fateh Singh Ahluwalia were
rejected; but the British title to supremacy over
Whadni could no longer, it was found, be maintained.
The claims of Lahore to Chamkaur and Anandpur
Makhowal were expediently admitted, for the British
right did not seem worth maintaining, and the affairs
of the priestly class of Sikhs could be best managed by
a ruler of their own faith.[2] Ranjit Singh disliked the
loss of Ferozepore, which the English long continued
to admire as a commanding position;[3] but the settlement generally was such as seemed to lessen the
chances of future collision between the two governments.

Ranjit Singh's connexion with the English thus
became more and more close, and about the same time
he began to resign himself in many instances to the
views of his new favourites of Jammu. The Maharaja
had begun to notice the boyish promise of Hira Singh,
the son of Dhian Singh, and he may have been equally
pleased with the native simplicity, and with the tutored
deference, of the child. He gave him the title of Raja,
and his father, true to the Indian feeling, was desirous
of establishing the purity of his descent by marrying
his son into a family of local power and of spotless
genealogy. The betrothal of a daughter of the deceased Sansar Chand of Kangra was demanded in the year
1828, and the reluctant consent of the new chief,
Anrudh Chand, was obtained when he unwittingly had
put himself wholly in the power of Dhian Singh by

Gradual
ascendancy
of Dhian
Singh, his
brothers,
and his son.
1820-8.

Proposed
marriage of
Hira Singh
into the
family of
Sansar
Chand, 1828.

---

[1] Capt. Wade to the Resident at Delhi, 20th Jan. 1828, and
Capt. Murray to the same, 19th Feb. 1828.

In the case of Ferozepore, Government subsequently
decided (Government to Agent at Delhi, 24th Nov. 1838) that
certain collateral heirs (who had put in a claim) could not
succeed, as, according to Hindu law and Sikh usage, no right
of descent existed after a division had taken place. So
uncertain, however, is the practice of the English, that one or
more precedents in favour of the Ferozepore claimants might
readily be found within the range of cases connected with the
Sikh states.

[2] Government to the Resident at Delhi, 14th Nov. 1828.

[3] In 1823 Capt. Murray talked of the 'strong and important
fortress' of Ferozepore having been recovered by Ranjit Singh,
for the widow proprietress from whom it had been seized by
a claimant (Capt. Murray to the Agent at Delhi, 20th July
1823), and the supreme authorities similarly talked (Government to Agent at Delhi, 30th Jan. 1824) of the political and
military advantages of Ferozepore over Ludhiana.

1829.

Flight of
Sansar
Chand's
widow and
son.

Raja Hira
Singh's
marriage.
1829.

Insurruc-
tion at
Peshawar
under Sai-
yid Ahmad
Shah
Ghazi.  1827.
History of
the Saiyid.

His doc-
trines of
religious
reform.

visiting Lahore with his sisters for the purpose of joining in the nuptial ceremonies of the son of Fateh Singh Ahluwalia. The proposed degradation rendered the mother of the girls more indignant perhaps than the head of the family, and she contrived to escape with them to the south of the Sutlej. Anrudh Chand was required to bring them back, but he himself also fled, and his possessions were seized. The mother died of grief and vexation, and the son followed her to the grave, after idly attempting to induce the English to restore him by force of arms to his little principality. Sansar Chand had left several illegitimate children, and in 1829 the disappointed Maharaja endeavoured to obtain some revenge by marrying two of the daughters himself, and by elevating a son to the rank of Raja, and investing him with an estate out of his father's chief-ship. The marriage of Hira Singh to a maiden of his own degree was celebrated during the same year with much splendour, and the greatness of Ranjit Singh's name induced even the chiefs living under British pro-tection to offer their congratulations and their presents on the occasion.[1]

In the meanwhile a formidable insurrection had been organized in the neighbourhood of Peshawar, by an unheeded person and in an unlooked-for manner. One Ahmad Shah, a Muhammadan of a family of Saiyids of Bareilly in Upper India, had been a follower of the great mercenary leader, Amir Khan, but he lost his employment when the military force of his chief was broken up on the successful termination of the campaign against the joint Maratha and Pindari powers, and after Amir Khan's own recognition by the English as a dependent prince. The Saiyid went to Delhi, and a preacher of that city, named Abdul Aziz, declared himself greatly edified by the superior sanc-tity of Ahmad, who denounced the corrupt forms of worship then prevalent, and endeavoured to enforce attention to the precepts of the Koran alone, without reference to the expositions of the early Fathers. His reputation increased, and two Maulais, Ismail and Abdul Hai, of some learning, but doubtful views, attached themselves to the Saiyid as his humble dis-ciples and devoted followers.[2] A pilgrimage was

[1] Murray, *Ranjit Singh*, pp. 147, 148, and Resident at Delhi to Government, 28th Oct. 1828.

[2] A book was composed by Mauli Ismail, on the part of Saiyid Ahmad, in the Urdu, or vernacular language of Upper India, at once exhortative and justificatory of his views. It is called the *Takvia-ul-Iman*, or 'Basis of the Faith', and it was

preached as a suitable beginning for all undertakings, 1822-6.
and Ahmad's journey to Calcutta. in 1822, for the purpose of embarkation, was one of triumph, although his
proceedings were little noticed until his presence in a
large city gave him numerous congregations. He set H.s pilgri-
sail for Mecca and Medina, and he is commonly be- mage.
lieved, but without reason, to have visited Constantinople. After an absence of four years he returned to
Delhi, and called upon the faithful to follow him in a
war against infidels. He acted as if he meant by unbelievers the Sikhs alone, but his precise objects are
imperfectly understood. He was careful not to offend
the English; but the mere *supremacy* of a remote
nation over a wide and populous country gave him
ample opportunities for unheeded agitation. In 1826 His journey
he left Delhi with perhaps five hundred attendants, through
and it was arranged that other bands should follow in Rajputana
and Sind,
succession under appointed leaders. He made some to Kanda-
stay at Tonk, the residence of his old master, Amir har and
Khan, and the son of the chief, the present Nawab, was Peshawar.
enrolled among the disciples of the new saint. He
obtained considerable assistance, at least in money,

printed in Calcutta. It is divided into two portions, of which
the first only is understood to be the work of Ismail, the second
part being inferior, and the production of another person.

In the preface the writer deprecates the opinion 'that the
wise and learned alone can comprehend God's word. God himself had said a prophet had been raised up among the rude
and ignorant for their instruction, and that He, the Lord, had
rendered obedience easy. There were two things essential : a
belief in the unity of God, which was to know no other, and
a knowledge of the Prophet, which was obedience to the law.
Many held the sayings of the saints to be their guide; but the
word of God was alone to be attended to, although the writings
of the pious, which agreed with the Scriptures, might be read
for edification.'

The first chapter treats of the unity of God, and in it the
writer deprecates the supplication of saints, angels, &c., as
impious. He declares the reasons given for such worship to be
futile, and to show an utter ignorance of God's word. 'The
ancient idolaters had likewise said that they merely venerated
powers and divinities, and did not regard them as the equal
of the Almighty; but God himself had answered these heathens. Likewise the Christians had been admonished for giving
to dead monks and friars the honour due to the Lord. God is
alone, and companion he has none; prostration and adoration
are due to him, and to no other.' The writer proceeds in a
similar strain, but assumes some doubtful positions, as that
Muhammad says God is one, and man learns from his parents
that he was born; he believes his mother, and yet he distrusts
the apostle: or that an evil-doer who has faith is a better man
than the most pious idolater.

The printed Urdu Korans are eagerly bought by all who
can afford the money, and who know of their existence.

1827-9.

Rouses the
Usufzais to
a religious
war.

Saiyid Ah-
mad Shah
fails
against
the Sikhs
at Akora.
1827.

from the youthful convert, and he proceeded through
the desert to Khairpur in Sind, where he was well
received by Mir Rustam Khan, and where he awaited
the junction of the 'Ghazis', or fighters for the faith,
who were following him. Ahmad marched to Kandahar, but his projects were mistrusted or misunderstood; he received no encouragement from the Barakzai
brothers in possession, and he proceeded northward
through the Ghilzai country, and in the beginning of
1827 he crossed the Kabul river to Panjtar in the
Usufzai hills, between Peshawar and the Indus.[1]

The Panjtar family is of some consequence among
the warlike Usufzais, and as the tribe had become
apprehensive of the designs of Yar Muhammad Khan,
whose dependence on Ranjit Singh secured him from
danger on the side of Kabul, the Saiyid and his 'Ghazis'
were hailed as deliverers, and the authority or supremacy of Ahmad was generally admitted. He led his
ill-equipped host to attack a detachment of Sikhs, which
had been moved forward to Akora, a few miles above
Attock, under the command of Budh Singh Sindhan-
wala, of the same family as the Maharaja. The Sikh
commander entrenched his position, and repulsed the
tumultuous assault of the mountaineers with considerable loss, but as he could not follow up his success,
the fame and the strength of the Saiyid continued to
increase, and Yar Muhammad deemed it prudent to
enter into an agreement obliging him to respect the
territories of the Usufzais. The curbed governor of
Peshawar is accused of a base attempt to remove
Ahmad by poison, and, in the year 1829, the fact or the
report was made use of by the Saiyid as a reason for
appealing to arms. Yar Muhammad was defeated and
mortally wounded, and Peshawar was perhaps saved

[1] Cf. Murray, *Ranjit Singh*, pp. 145, 146. About Saiyid
Ahmad, the author has learnt much from the 'Ghazi's' brother-
in-law, and from a respectable Mauli, who likewise followed
his fortunes, and both of whom are now in honourable employ
in the chiefship of Tonk. He has likewise learnt many particulars from Munshi Shahamat Ali, and especially from Pir
Ibrahim Khan, a straightforward and intelligent Pathan of
Kasur, in the British service, who thinks Ahmad right, notwithstanding the holy neighbourhood of Pakpattan, Multan,
and Utch! Indeed, most educated Muhammadans admit the
reasonableness of his doctrines, and the able Regent-Begum of
Bhopal is not indisposed to emulate the strictness of the Chief
of Tonk, as an abhorrer of vain ceremonies. Among humbler
people the Saiyid likewise obtained many admirers, and it is
said that his exhortations generally were so efficacious, that
even the tailors of Delhi were moved to scrupulously return
remnants of cloth to their employers!

to his brother, Sultan Muhammad, by the presence of a Sikh force under the Prince Sher. Singh and General Ventura, which had been moved to that quarter under pretence of securing for the Maharaja a long-promised horse of famous breed named Laila, the match of one of equal renown named Kahar, which Ranjit Singh had already prided himself on obtaining from the Barakzai brothers.[1]

The Sikh troops withdrew to the Indus, leaving Sultan Muhammad Khan and his brothers to guard their fief or dependency as they could, and it would even seem that Ranjit Singh hoped the difficulties of their position, and the insecurity of the province, would justify its complete reduction.[2] But the influence of Saiyid Ahmad reached to Kashmir, and the mountaineers between that valley and the Indus were unwilling subjects of Lahore. Ahmad crossed the river in June 1830, and planned an attack upon the Sikh force commanded by Hari Singh Nalwa and General Allard; but he was beaten off, and forced to retire to the west of the river. In a few months he was strong enough to attack Sultan Muhammad Khan; the Barakzai was defeated, and Peshawar was occupied by the Saiyid and his 'Ghazis'. His elation kept pace with his success, and, according to tradition, already busy with his career, he proclaimed. himself Khalif, and struck a coin in the name of 'Ahmad the Just, the defender of the faith, the glitter of whose sword scattereth destruction among infidels'. The fall of Peshawar caused some alarm in Lahore, and the force on the Indus was strengthened, and placed under the command of Prince Sher Singh. The petty Muhammadan chiefs generally, with whom self-interest overcame faith, were averse to the domination of the Indian adventurer, and the imprudence of Saiyid Ahmad gave umbrage to his Usufzai adherents. He had levied from the peasants a tithe of their goods, and this measure caused little or no dissatisfaction, for it agreed

Saiyid Ahmad Shah crosses the Indus, 1830.

He is compelled to retire, but falls upon and routs Sultan Muhammad Khan, and occupies Peshawar, 1830.

The Saiyid's influence decreases.

[1] Cf. Murray, *Ranjit Singh,* pp. 146, 149. The followers of Saiyid Ahmad believe that poison was administered, and describe the 'Ghazi' as suffering much from its effects.

General Ventura at last succeeded in obtaining *a* Laila, but that the real horse, so named, was transferred, is doubtful, and at one time it was declared to be dead. (Capt. Wade to the Resident, Delhi, 17th May 1829.)

[2] Capt. Wade to the Resident, Delhi, 13th Sept. 1830. The Maharaja also reserved a cause of quarrel with the Barakzais, on account of their reduction of the Khattaks, a tribe which Ranjit Singh said Fateh Khan, the Wazir, had agreed to leave independent. (Capt. Wade to Government, 9th Dec. 1831.)

1831.

with their notion of the rights of a religious teacher; but his decree that all the young women of marriageable age should be at once wedded, interfered with the profits of Afghan parents, proverbially avaricious, and who usually disposed of their daughters to the wealthiest bridegrooms. But when Saiyid Ahmad was accused, perhaps unjustly, of assigning the maidens one by one to his needy Indian followers, his motives were impugned, and the discontent was loud. Early in November 1830 he was constrained to relinquish Peshawar to Sultan Muhammad at a fixed tribute, and he proceeded to the left bank of the Indus to give battle to the Sikhs. The Saiyid depended chiefly on the few 'Ghazis' who had followed his fortunes throughout, and on the insurrectionary spirit of the Muzaffarabad and other chiefs, for his Usufzai adherents had greatly decreased. The hill 'khans' were soon brought under subjection by the efforts of Sher Singh and the governor of Kashmir; yet Ahmad continued active, and, in a desultory warfare amid rugged mountains, success for a time attended him; but, during a cessation of the frequent conflicts, he was surprised, early in May 1831, at a place called Balakot, and fallen upon and slain. The Usufzais at once expelled his deputies, the 'Ghazis' dispersed in disguise, and the family of the Saiyid hastened to Hindustan to find an honourable asylum with their friend the Nawab of Tonk.[1]

The fame of Ranjit Singh was now at its height, and his friendship was sought by distant sovereigns. In 1829, agents from Baluchistan brought horses to the Sikh ruler, and hoped that the frontier posts of Harrand and Dajal, westward of the Indus, which his feudatory of Bahawalpur had usurped, would be restored to the Khan.[2] The Maharaja was likewise in communication with Shah Mahmud of Herat,[3] and in 1830 he was

He relinquishes Peshawar, 1830;

and retires towards Kashmir, and is surprised and slain, May 1831.

Ranjit Singh courted by various parties.

The Baluchs.

Shah Mahmud.

[1] Capt. Wade to Resident at Delhi, 21st March 1831, and other dates in that and the previous year. Cf. Murray, *Ranjit Singh*, p. 150. The followers of the Saiyid strenuously deny his assumption of the title of Khalif, his new coinage, and his bestowal of Usufzai maidens on his Indian followers.

[2] Capt. Wade to the Resident at Delhi, 3rd May 1829, and 29th April 1830. Harrand was once a place of considerable repute. (See Munshi Mohan Lal, *Journal*, under date 3rd March 1836.) The Bahawalpur Memoirs show that the Nawab was aided by the treachery of others in acquiring it. The place had to be retaken by General Ventura (as the author learnt from that officer), when Bahawal Khan was deprived of his territories west of the Sutlej.

[3] Capt. Wade to Resident at Delhi, 21st Jan. 1829, and 3rd Dec. 1830.

invited, by the Baiza Bai of Gwalior, to honour the nuptials of the young Sindhia with his presence.[1] The English were at the same time not without a suspicion that he had opened a correspondence with Russia,[2] and they were themselves about to flatter him as one necessary to the fulfilment of their expanding views of just influence and profitable commerce.

In the beginning of 1831, Lord William Bentinck, the Governor-General of India, arrived at Simla, and a Sikh deputation waited upon his Lordship to convey to him Ranjit Singh's complimentary wishes for his own welfare and the prosperity of his Government. The increasing warmth of the season prevented the dispatch of a formal return mission, but Capt. Wade, the political agent at Ludhiana, was made the bearer of a letter to the Maharaja, thanking him for his attention. The principal duty of the agent was, however, to ascertain whether Ranjit Singh wished, and would propose, to have an interview with Lord William Bentinck, for it was a matter in which it was thought the English Viceroy could not take the initiative.[3] The object of the Governor-General was mainly to give the world an impression of complete unanimity between the two states; but the Maharaja wished to strengthen his own authority, and to lead the Sikh public to believe his dynasty was acknowledged as the proper head of the 'Khalsa', by the predominant English rulers. The able chief, Hari Singh, was one of those most averse to the recognition of the right of the Prince Kharak Singh, and the heir apparent himself would seem to have been aware of the feelings of the Sikh people, for he had the year before opened a correspondence with the Governor of Bombay, as if to derive hope from the vague terms of a complimentary reply.[4] Ranjit Singh thus

Lord Bentinck, the Governor-General, at Simla, 1831.

A meeting proposed with Ranjit Singh, and desired by both parties for different reasons.

---

[1] Capt. Wade to Resident at Delhi, 7th April 1830.  The Maharaja declined the invitation, saying Sindhia was not at Lahore when his son was married.

[2] Capt. Wade to Resident at Delhi, 24th August 1830.

[3] Government to Capt. Wade, 28th April 1831, and Murray, *Ranjit Singh*, p. 162.

[4] With regard to this interchange of letters, see the Persian Secretary to the Political Secretary at Bombay, 6th July 1830.
That Ranjit Singh was jealous, personally, of Hari Singh, or that the servant would have proved a traitor to the living master, is not probable : but Hari Singh was a zealous Sikh and an ambitious man, and Kharak Singh was always full of doubts and apprehensions with respect to his succession and even his safety. Ranjit Singh's anxiety with regard to the meeting at Rupar, exaggerated, perhaps, by Mr. Allard, may be learnt from Mr. Prinsep's account in Murray, *Ranjit Singh*, p. 162. Col. Wade has informed the author that the whole of

1831.

The meeting at Rupar, 17th July 1831.

31st Oct. 1831.

Ranjit Singh's anx.ety about Sind.

The scheme of opening the Indus to commerce.

readily proposed a meeting, and one took place at Rupar, on the banks of the Sutlej, in the month of October (1831). A present of horses from the King of England had, in the meantime, reached Lahore, by the Indus and Ravi rivers, under the escort of Lieut. Burnes, and during one of the several interviews with the Governor-General, Ranjit Singh had sought for and obtained a written assurance of perpetual friendship.[1] The impression went abroad that his family would be supported by the English Government, and ostensibly Ranjit Singh's objects seemed wholly, as they had been partly, gained. But his mind was not set at ease about Sind: vague accounts had reached him of some design with regard to that country; he plainly hinted his own schemes, and observed the Amirs had no efficient troops, and that they could not be well disposed towards the English, as they had thrown difficulties in the way of Lieut. Burnes's progress.[2] But the Governor-General would not divulge to his inquiring guest and ally the tenor of propositions already on their way to the chiefs of Sind, confessedly lest the Maharaja should at once endeavour to counteract his peaceful and beneficial intentions.[3] Ranjit Singh may or may not have felt that he was distrusted, but as he was to be a party to the opening of the navigation of the Indus, and as the project had been matured, it would have better suited the character and the position of the British Government had no concealment been attempted.

The traveller Moorcroft had been impressed with the use which might be made of the Indus as a channel of British commerce,[4] and the scheme of navigating that river and its tributaries was eagerly adopted by the Indian Government, and by the advocates of material utilitarianism. One object of sending King William's presents for Ranjit Singh by water was to ascertain, as if undesignedly, the trading value of the

the Sikh chiefs were said by Ranjit Singh himself to be averse to the meeting with the British Governor-General.
[1] Murray, *Ranjit Singh*, p. 166.
[2] Murray, *Ranjit Singh*, p. 167. This opinion of Ranjit Singh about Sindian troops may not be pleasing to the victors of Dabo and Miani, although the Maharaja impugned not their courage, but their discipline and equipment. Shah Shuja's expedition of 1834, nevertheless, served to show the fairness of Ranjit Singh's conclusions.
[3] Murray, *Ranjit Singh*, pp. 167, 168. The whole of the tenth chapter of Capt. Murray's book, which includes the meeting at Rupar, may be regarded as the composition of Mr. Prinsep, the Secretary to Government, with the Governor-General.
[4] Moorcroft, *Travels*, ii. 338.

classical stream,[1] and the result of Lieut. Burnes's 1831. observations convinced Lord William Bentinck of its superiority over the Ganges. There seemed also, in his Lordship's opinion, good reason to believe that the great western valley had at one time been as populous as that of the east, and it was thought that the judicious exercise of the paramount influence of the British Government might remove those political obstacles which had banished commerce from the rivers of Alexander.[2] It was therefore resolved, in the current language of the day, to open the Indus to the navigation of the world.

Before the Governor-General met Ranjit Singh, he had directed Col. Pottinger [3] to proceed to Hyderabad, to negotiate with the Amirs of Sind the opening of the lower portion of the river to all boats on the payment of a fixed toll; [4] and, two months afterwards, or towards the end of 1831, he wrote to the Maharaja that the desire he had formerly expressed to see a steamboat, was a proof of his enlightened understanding, and was likely to be gratified before long, as it was wished to draw closer the commercial relations of the two states. Capt. Wade was at the same time sent to explain, in person, the object of Col. Pottinger's mission to Sind, to propose the free navigation of the Sutlej in continuation of that of the Lower Indus, and to assure the Maharaja that, by the extension of British commerce, was not meant the extension of the British power.[5] But Ranjit Singh, also, had his views and his suspicions.[6] In the south of the Punjab he had wrought by indirect means, as long as it was necessary to do so among a newly conquered people. The Nawab of Bahawalpur, his manager of the country across to Dera Ghazi Khan, was less regular in his payments than he should have been, and his expulsion from the Punjab Proper would be profitable, and unaccompanied with danger, if the English remained neutral. Again, Baha-

*Marginal notes:* Proposal made to the Sindians and the Sikhs. 19th Dec. 1831. Ranjit Singh's views and suspicions.

---

[1] Government to Col. Pottinger, 22nd Oct. 1831, and Murray, *Ranjit Singh*, p. 153.

[2] Government to Col. Pottinger, 22nd Oct. 1831.

[3] [Afterwards Sir H. E. Pottinger, Bart., first Governor of Hong Kong.—Ed. ]

[4] Murray, *Ranjit Singh*, p. 168.

[5] Government to Capt. Wade, 19th Dec. 1831. It is admitted that the mission, or the schemes, had a political reference to Russia and her designs, but the Governor-General would not avow his motives. (Murray, *Ranjit Singh*, p. 168.)

[6] Ranjit Singh's attention was mainly directed to Sind, and a rumoured matrimonial alliance between one of the Amirs, or the son of one of them, and a Persian princess, caused him some anxiety. (Capt. Wade to Government, 5th Aug. 1831.)

1831-2.

He repels
the Daud-
putras from
the Lower
Punjab,
1831,
and declares
his superior
right to
Shikarpur.

wal Khan was virtually a chief protected by the British Government on the left bank of the Sutlej, and Lieut. Burnes was on his way up the Indus. The Maharaja, ever mistrustful, conceived that the politcial status of that officer's observation would be referred to and upheld by his Government as the true and permanent one,[1] and hence the envoy found affairs in process of change when he left the main stream of the Indus, and previous to the interview at Rupar, General Ventura had dispossessed Bahawal Khan both of his Lahore farms and of his ancestral territories on the right bank of the Sutlej.[2] Further, Shikarpur formed no part of the Sind of the Kalhoras or Talpurs; it had only fallen to the latter usurpers after the death of Muhammad Azim Khan, the wazir of the titular king, Shah Ayub, and it continued to be held jointly by the three families of Khairpur, Mirpur, and Hyderabad, as a fortuitous possession. Ranjit Singh considered that he, as the paramount of the Barakzais of the Indus, had a better right to the district than the Amirs of south-eastern Sind, and he was bent upon annexing it to his dominions.[3]

Ranjit
Singh
yields to
the English
demands,
1832.

Such was Ranjit Singh's temper of mind when visited by Capt. Wade to negotiate the opening of the Sutlej to British traders. The Maharaja avowed himself well pleased, but he had hoped that the English were about to force their way through Sind; he asked how many regiments Col. Pottinger had with him, and he urged his readiness to march and coerce the Amirs.[4] It was further ascertained that he had made propositions to Mir Ali Murad of Mirpur, to farm Dera Ghazi Khan, as if to sow dissensions among the Talpurs, and to gain friends for Lahore, while Col. Pottinger was winning allies for the English.[5] But he perceived that the Governor-General had resolved upon his course, and he gave his assent to the common use of the Sutlej and Indus, and to the residence of a British officer at Mithankot to superintend the navigation.[6] He did not

---

[1] This view appears to have subsequently occurred to Capt. Wade as having influenced the Maharaja. See his letter. to Government, 18th Oct. 1836.

[2] Capt. Wade to Government, 5th Nov. 1831.

[3] This argument was continually used by Ranjit Singh. See, for instance, Capt. Wade to Government, 15th Jan. 1837.

[4] Capt. Wade to Government, 1st and 13th Feb. 1832.

[5] Capt. Wade to Government, 21st Dec. 1831; and Col. Pottinger to Government, 23rd Sept. 1837.

[6] See Appendices XXVIII and XXIX. A tariff on goods was at first talked of, but subsequently a toll on boats was preferred. From the Himalayas to the sea the whole toll was

desire to appear as if in opposition to his allies of many years, but he did not seek to conceal from Capt. Wade his opinion that the commercial measures of the English had really abridged his political power, when he gave up for the time the intention of seizing Shikarpur.[1]

The connexion of the English with the nations of the Indus was about to be rendered more complicated by the revived hopes of Shah Shuja. That ill-fated king had taken up his abode, as before related, at Ludhiana, in the year 1821, and he brooded at his leisure over schemes for the reconquest of Khorasan. In 1826 he was in correspondence with Ranjit Singh, who ever regretted that the Shah was not his guest or his prisoner.[2] In 1827 he made propositions to the British Government, and he was told that he was welcome to recover his kingdom with the aid of Ranjit Singh or of the Sindians, but that, if he failed, his present hosts might not again receive him.[3] In 1829 the Shah was induced, by the strange state of affairs in Peshawar consequent on Saiyid Ahmad's ascendancy, to suggest to Ranjit Singh that, with Sikh aid, he could readily master it, and reign once more an independent sovereign. The Maharaja amused him with vain hopes, but the English repeated their warning, and the ex-king's hopes soon fell.[4] In 1831 they again rose, for the Talpur Amirs disliked the approach of English envoys, and they gave encouragement to the tenders of their titular monarch.[5] Negotiations were reopened with Ranjit Singh, who was likewise out of humour with the English about Sind, and he was not unwilling to aid the Shah in the recovery of his rightful throne; but the views of the Sikh reached to the Persian frontier as well as to the shores of the ocean, and he suggested that it would be well if the slaughter of kine were prohibited throughout Afghanistan, and if the gates of Somnath were restored to their original temple. The Shah was not prepared for these concessions, and he evaded them by reminding the Maharaja that his chosen allies, the English, freely took the lives of

*Margin notes:*
1833-5. Declaring however, that their commerce interfered with his policy.

Shah Shuja's second expedition to Afghanistan. 1833-5.

The Shah's overtures to the English. 1827.

His negotiations with the Sindians. 1831; and with Ranjit Singh. 1831.

The gates of Somnath and the slaughter of kine.

fixed at 570 rupees, of which the Lahore Government got Rs. 155, 4, 0 for territories on the right bank, and Rs. 39, 5, 1 for territories on the left bank of the Sutlej. (Government to Capt. Wade, 9th June 1834, and Capt. Wade to Government, 13th Dec. 1835.)

[1] Capt. Wade to Government, 13th Feb. 1832.
[2] Capt. Wade to the Resident at Delhi, 25th July 1826.
[3] Resident at Delhi to Capt. Wade, 25th July 1827.
[4] Government to Resident at Delhi, 12th June 1829.
[5] Capt. Wade to Government, 9th Sept. 1831.

1832.

cows, and that a prophecy foreboded the downfall of the Sikh empire on the removal of the gates from Ghazni.[1]

**Further negotiations with the Sikhs and Sindians, 1832.**

In 1832 a rumoured advance of the Persians against Herat gave further encouragement to Shah Shuja in his designs.[2] The perplexed Amirs of Sind offered him assistance if he would relinquish his supremacy, and the Shah promised acquiescence if he succeeded.[3] To Ranjit Singh the Shah offered to waive his right to Peshawar and other districts beyond the Indus, and also to give an acquittance for the Koh-i-nur diamond, in return for assistance in men and money. The Maharaja was doubtful what to do; he was willing to secure an additional title to Peshawar, but he was apprehensive of the Shah's designs, should the expedition be successful.[4] He wished, moreover, to know the precise views of the English, and he therefore proposed that they should be parties to any engagement entered into, for he had no confidence, he said, in Afghans.[5] Each of the three parties had distinct and incompatible objects. Ranjit Singh wished to get rid of the English *commercial* objections to disturbing the Amirs of Sind, by offering to aid the rightful *political* paramount in its recovery. The ex-king thought the Maharaja really wished to get him into his power, and the project of dividing Sind fell to the ground.[6] The Talpur Amirs, on their part, thought that they would save Shikarpur by playing into the Shah's hands, and they therefore endeavoured to prevent a coalition between him and the Sikh ruler.[7]

**The English indifferent about the Shah's attempts:**

The Shah could not come to any satisfactory terms with Ranjit Singh, but as his neutrality was essential, especially with regard to Shikarpur, a treaty of alliance

[1] Capt. Wade to Government, 21st Nov. 1831.—Considering the ridicule occasioned by the subsequent removal by the English of these traditional gates, it may gratify the approvers and originators of the measure to know that they *were* of some local importance. When the author was at Bahawalpur in 1845, a number of Afghan merchants came to ask him whether their restoration could be brought about—for the repute of the fane (a tomb made a temple by superstition), and the income of its pir or saint, had much declined. They would carefully convey them back, they said, and they added that they understood the Hindus did not want them, and that of course they could be of no value to the Christians!
[2] Government to Capt. Wade, 19th Oct. 1832.
[3] Capt. Wade to Government, 15th Sept. 1832.
[4] Capt. Wade to Government, 13th Dec. 1832.
[5] Capt. Wade to Government 31st Dec. 1832.
[6] Capt. Wade to Government. 9th April 1833.
[7] Capt. Wade to Government. 27th March 1833.

was entered into by which the districts beyond the Indus, and in the possession of the Sikhs, were formally ceded to the Maharaja.[1] The English had also become less averse to his attempt, and he was assured that his annual stipend would be continued to his family, and no warning was held out to him against returning, as had before been done.[2] A third of his yearly allowance was even advanced to him: but the political agent was at the same time desired to impress upon all people, that the British Government had no interest in the Shah's proceedings, that its policy was one of complete neutrality, and it was added that Dost Muhammad could be so assured in reply to a letter received from him.[3] Dost Muhammad had mastered Kabul shortly after Muhammad Azim Khan's death, and he soon learnt to become apprehensive of the English. In 1832 he cautioned the Amirs of Sind against allowing them to establish a commercial factory in Shikarpur, as Shah Shuja would certainly soon follow to guard it with an army,[4] and he next sought, in the usual way, to ascertain the views of the paramounts of India by entering into a correspondence with them.

*1832.*

*but Dost Muhammad Khan is alarmed, and courts their friendship.*

Shah Shuja left Ludhiana in the middle of February 1833. He had with him about 200,000 rupees in treasure, and nearly 3,000 armed followers.[5] He got a gun and some camels from Bahawal Khan, he crossed the Indus towards the middle of May, and he entered Shikarpur without opposition. The Sindians did not oppose him, but they rendered him no assistance, and they at last thought it better to break with him at once than to put *their* means into *his* hands for their own

*The Shah sets out, Feb. 1833.*

---

[1] This treaty, which became the foundation of the Tripartite Treaty of 1838, was drawn up in March 1833, and finally agreed to in August of that year. (Capt. Wade to Government, 17th June 1834.)

[2] Government to Capt. Wade, 19th Dec. 1832.

[3] Government to Capt. Faithful, Acting Political Agent, 13th Dec. 1832, and to Capt. Wade, 5th and 9th of March 1833.

[4] The Bahawalpur Memoirs state that such a recommendation was pressed by Dost Muhammad on the Amirs; the belief in the gradual conversion of 'Kothis', or residencies or commercial houses, into 'Chaonis', or military cantonments, having, it may be inferred, become notorious as far as Kabul. Dost Muhammad's main object, however, was to keep Shah Shuja at a distance; and he always seems to have held that he was safe from the English themselves so long as Lahore remained unshaken. For another instance of the extent to which the English were thought to be identified with Shah Shuja, see the *Asiatic Journal*, xix. 38, as quoted by Professor Wilson in Moorcroft's *Travels*, p. 340 *n.*, vol. ii.

[5] Capt. Wade to Government, 9th April 1833.

more assured destruction.[1] But they were signally defeated near Shikarpur on the 9th January 1834, and they willingly paid 500,000 rupees in cash, and gave a promise of tribute for Shikarpur, to get rid of the victor's presence.[2] The Shah proceeded towards Kandahar, and he maintained himself in the neighbourhood of that city for a few months; but, on the 1st July, he was brought to action by Dost Muhammad Khan and his brothers, and fairly routed.[3] After many wanderings, and an appeal to Persia and to Shah Kamran of Herat, and also an attempt upon Shikarpur,[4] he returned to his old asylum at Ludhiana in March 1835, bringing with him about 250,000 rupees in money and valuables.[5]

Ranjit Singh, on his part, was apprehensive that Shah Shuja might set aside their treaty of alliance, so he resolved to guard against the possible consequences of the ex-king's probable success, and to seize Peshawar before his tributaries could tender their allegiance to Kabul.[6] A large force, under the nominal command of the Maharaja's grandson, Nau Nihal Singh, but really led by Sirdar Hari Singh, crossed the Indus, and an increased tribute of horses was demanded on the plea of the prince's presence, for the first time, at the head of an army. The demand would seem to have been complied with, but the citadel of Peshawar was nevertheless assaulted and taken on the 6th May 1834.[7] The hollow negotiations with Sultan Muhammad Khan are understood to have been precipitated by the impetuous Hari Singh, who openly expressed his contempt for all Afghans, and did not conceal his design to carry the Sikh arms beyond Peshawar.[8]

The Sikhs were, in the meantime, busy elsewhere as well as in Peshawar itself. In 1832 Hari Singh had finally routed the Muhammadan tribes above Attock, and to better ensure their obedience, he built a fort on the right side of the Indus.[9] In 1834 a

[1] Capt. Wade to Government, 25th Aug. 1833, and the Memoirs of the Bahawalpur Family.

[2] Capt. Wade to Government, 30th Jan. 1834.

[3] Capt. Wade to Government, 25th July 1834.

[4] Capt. Wade to Government, 21st Oct. and 29th Dec. 1834, and 6th Feb. 1845.

[5] Capt. Wade to Government, 19th March 1835.

[6] Capt. Wade to Government, 17th June 1834.

[7] Capt. Wade to Government, 19th May 1834.

[8] These views of Hari Singh's were sufficiently notorious in the Punjab some years ago, when that chief was a person before the public.

[9] Capt. Wade to Government, 7th Aug. 1832.

force was employed against the Afghans of Tak and Bannu, beyond Dera Ismail Khan; but a considerable detachment signally failed in an attack upon a mountain stronghold, and a chief of rank and upwards of 300 men were slain. The ill success vexed the Maharaja, and he desired his agent to explain to the British authorities the several particulars; but lest they should still be disposed to reflect upon the quality of his troops, he reminded Capt. Wade that such things had happened before, that his rash officers did not wait until a breach had been effected, and that, indeed, the instance of General Gillespie and the Gurkhas at Kalanga afforded an exact illustration of what had taken place![1] In 1833 the grandson of Sansar Chand, of Katotch, was induced to return to his country, and on his way through Ludhiana he was received with considerable ceremony by the British authorities, for the fame of Sansar Chand gave to his posterity some semblance of power and regal dignity. A jagir or fief of 50,000 rupees was conferred upon the young chief, for the Maharaja was not disposed from nature to be wantonly harsh, nor from policy to drive any one to desperation.[2] During the same year Ranjit Singh proposed to send a chief to Calcutta with presents for the King of England, and not improbably with the view of ascertaining the general opinion about his designs on Sind. The mission, under Gujar Singh Majithia, finally took its departure in September 1834, and was absent a year and a half.[3]

When Mr. Moorcroft was in Ladakh (in 1821, &c.), the fear of Ranjit Singh was general in that country, and the Sikh governor of Kashmir had already demanded the payment of tribute;[4] but the weak and distant state was little molested until the new Rajas of Jammu had obtained the government of the hill principalities between the Ravi and Jhelum, and felt that their influence with Ranjit Singh was secure and commanding. In 1834 Zorawar Singh, Raja Gulab Singh's commander in Kishtwar, took advantage of internal disorders in Leh, and declared that an estate, anciently held by the Kishtwar chief, must be restored.

*Margin notes:* 1832-6. / Sansar Chand's grandson returns, 1833. / Ranjit Singh sends a mission to Calcutta, 1834-6. / Ranjit Singh and Ladakh, 1821. / Ladakh reduced by the Jammu Rajas, 1834-5.

[1] Capt. Wade to Government, 10th May 1834. Dera Ismail Khan and the country about it was not fairly brought into order until two years afterwards. (Capt. Wade to Government, 7th and 13th July 1836.)

[2] Capt. Wade to Government, 9th Oct. 1833, and 3rd Jan. 1835.

[3] Capt. Wade to Government, 11th Sept. 1834, and 4th April 1836.

[4] Moorcroft, *Travels*, i. 420.

He crossed into the southern districts, but did not reach the capital until early in 1835. He sided with one of the contending parties, deposed the reigning Raja and set up his rebellious minister in his stead. He fixed a tribute of 30,000 rupees, he placed a garrison in·the fort, he retained some districts along the northern slopes of the Himalayas, and reached Jammu with his spoils towards the close of 1835. The dispossessed Raja complained to the Chinese authorities in Lassa; but, as the tribute continued to be regularly paid by his successor, no notice was taken of the usurpation. The Governor of Kashmir complained that Gulab Sing.'s commercial regulations interfered with the regular supply of shawl wool, and that matter was at once adjusted; yet the grasping ambition of the favourites nevertheless caused Ranjit Singh some misgivings amid all their protestations of devotion and loyalty.[1]

But Ranjit Singh's main apprehensions were on the side of Peshawar, and his fondest hopes in the direction of Sind. The defeat which the Amirs had sustained diminished their confidence in themselves, and when Shah Shuja returned beaten from Kandahar,. Nur Muhammad of Hyderabad was understood to be willing to surrender Shikarpur to the Maharaja, on condition of his guarantee against the attempts of the ex-king.[2] But this pretext would not get rid of the English objections; and Ranjit Singh, moreover, had little confidence in the Sindians. He kept, as a check over them, a representative of the expelled Kalhoras, as a pensioner on his bounty, in Rajanpur beyond the Indus;[3] and, at once to overawe both them and the Barakzais, he again opened a negotiation with Shah Shuja as soon as he returned to Ludhiana.[4] But his

[1] Capt. Wade to Government, 27th Jan. 1835, and Mr. Vigne, *Travels in Kashmir and Tibet*, ii. 352; their statements being corrected or amplified from the author's manuscript notes. The Prince Kharak Singh became especially apprehensive of the designs of the Jammu family. (Capt. Wade to Government, 10th Aug. 1836.)

[2] Capt. Wade to Government, 6th Feb. 1835.

[3] Capt. Wade to Government, 17th June 1834. Sarafraz Khan, otherwise called Ghulam Shah, was the Kalhora expelled by the Talpurs. He received Rajanpur in jagir from Kabul, and was maintained in it by Ranjit Singh. The place was held to yield 100,000 rupees, including certain rents reserved by the state, but the district was not really worth 30,000 rupees.

[4] Capt. Wade to Government, 17th April 1835, and other letters of the same year. The Maharaja still urged that the English should guarantee, as it were, Shah Shuja's moderation in success; partly, perhaps, because the greatness of the dynasty

main difficulty was with his British allies; and, to prove
to them the reasonableness of his discontent, he would
instance the secret aid which the Mazari freebooters
received from the Amirs; [1] he would again insist that
Shikarpur was a dependency of the chiefs of Khoras-
san,[2] and he would hint that the river below Mithankot
was not the Indus but the Sutlej, the river of the treaty,
—the stream which had so long given freshness and
beauty to the emblematic garden of their friendship,
and which continued its fertilizing way to the ocean,
separating, yet uniting, the realms of the two brotherly
powers of the East! [3]

But the English had formed a treaty of navigation
with Sind, and the designs of Ranjit Singh were displeasing to them. They said they could not view without regret and disapprobation the prosecution of plans
of unprovoked hostility against states to which they
were bound by ties of interest and goodwill.[4] They
therefore wished to dissuade Ranjit Singh against any
attempt on Shikarpur; but they felt that this must be
done discreetly, for their object was to remain on
terms of friendship with every one, and to make their
influence available for the preservation of the general
peace.[5] Such were the sentiments of the English; but,
in the meantime, the border disputes between the
Sikhs and Sindians were fast tending to produce a
rupture. In 1833 the predatory tribe of Mazaris, lying
along the right bank of the Indus, below Mithankot,
had been chastised by the Governor of Multan, who
proposed to put a garrison in their stronghold of
Rojhan, but was restrained by the Maharaja from so
doing.[6] In 1835 the Amirs of Khairpur were believed
to be instigating the Mazaris in their attacks on the
Sikh posts; and as the tribe was regarded by the English as dependent on Sind, although possessed of such
a degree of separate existence as to warrant its mention
in the commercial arrangements as being entitled to a
fixed portion of the whole toll, the Amirs were inform-

*Ranjit Singh's ambition displeasing to the English.*

of Ahmad Shah still dwelt in the mind of the first paramount
of the Sikhs, but partly also with the view of sounding his
European allies as to *their* real intentions.

[1] Capt. Wade to Government, 5th Oct. 1836.
[2] Capt. Wade to Government, 15th Jan. 1837.
[3] Capt. Wade to Government, 5th Oct. 1836.

[4] Government to Capt. Wade, 22nd Aug. 1836.—This plea
will recall to mind the usual argument of the Romans for
interference, viz. that *their* friends were not to be molested by
strangers.

[5] Government to Capt. Wade, 22nd Aug. 1836.
[6] Capt. Wade to Government, 27th May 1835.

1835-6.

The Maha-
raja never-
theless
keeps in
view his
plans of
aggrandize-
ment.

The objects
of the Eng-
ish become
political as
well as com-
mercial,
1836.

and they
resolve on
mediating
between
Ranjit
Singh and
the Sindians.

The
English
desire
to restrain
Ranjit
Singh
without
threaten-
ing him.

ed that the English looked to them to restrain the Mazaris, so as to deprive Ranjit Singh of all pretext for interference.[1] The aggressions nevertheless continued, or were alleged to be continued; and in August 1836, the Multan Governor took formal possession of Rojhan.[2] In the October following the Mazaris were brought to action and defeated, and the Sikhs occupied a fort called Ken, to the south of Rojhan, and beyond the proper limit of that tribe.[3]

Thus was Ranjit Singh gradually feeling his way by force; but the English had, in the meantime, resolved to go far beyond him in diplomacy. It had been determined that Capt. Burnes should proceed on a commercial mission to the countries bordering on the Indus, with the view of completing the reopening of that river to the traffic of the world.[4] But the Maharaja, it was said, should understand that their objects were purely mercantile, and that, indeed, his aid was looked for in establishing somewhere a great entrepot of trade, such as, it had once been hoped, might have been commenced at Mithankot.[5] Yet the views of the British authorities with regard to Sind were inevitably becoming political as well as commercial. The condition of that country, said the Governor-General, had been much thought about, and the result was a conviction that the connexion with it should be drawn closer.[6] The Amirs, he continued, might desire the protection of the English against Ranjit Singh, and previous negotiations, which their fears or their hostility had broken off, might be renewed with a view to giving them assistance; and, finally, it was determined that the English Government should mediate between Ranjit Singh and the Sindians, and afterwards adjust the other external relations of the Amirs when a Resident should be stationed at Hyderabad.

With regard to Ranjit Singh, the English rulers observed that they were bound by the strongest considerations of political interest to prevent the extension of the Sikh power along the course of the Indus, and that, although they would respect the acknowledged territories of the Maharaja, they desired that his existing relations of peace should not be disturbed; for, if

[1] Government to Capt. Wade, 27th May 1835, and 5th Sept. 1836; and Government to Col. Pottinger, 19th Sept. 1836.
[2] Capt. Wade to Government, 29th Aug. 1836.
[3] Capt. Wade to Government, 2nd Nov. 1836.
[4] Government to Capt. Wade, 5th Sept. 1836.
[5] Government to Capt. Wade, 5th Sept. 1836.
[6] Government to Col. Pottinger, 26th Sept. 1836.

war took place, the Indus would never be opened to 1836.
commerce. The political agent was directed to use
every means short of menace to induce Ranjit Singh
to abandon his designs against Shikarpur; and Shah
Shuja, whose hopes were still great, and whose negotiations were still talked of, was to be told that if he
left Ludhiana he must not return, and that the maintenance for his family would be at once discontinued.
With regard to the Mazaris, whose lands had been
actually occupied by the Sikhs, it was said that their
reduction had effected an object of general benefit; and
that the question of their permanent control could be
determined at a future period.[1]

The Sindians, on their part, complained that the The Sindians
fort of Ken had been occupied, and in reply to Ranjit impatient,
Singh's demand that their annual complimentary or and ready
prudential offerings should be increased, or that a to resort
large sum should be paid for the restoration of their to arms.
captured fort, they avowed their determination to
resort to arms.[2] Nor can there be any doubt that Sind
would have been invaded by the Sikhs, had not Col.
Pottinger's negotiations for their protection deterred
the Maharaja from an act which he apprehended the
English might seize upon to declare *their* alliance at
an end. The princes Kahrak Singh and Nau Nihal
Singh were each on the Indus, at the head of considerable armies, and the remonstrances of the Britisn
political agent alone detained the Maharaja himself at Ranjit
Lahore. Nevertheless, so evenly were peace and war Singh
balanced in Ranjit Singh's mind, that Capt. Wade equally
thought it advisable to proceed to his capital to ex- ready;
plain to him in person the risks he would incur by
acting in open opposition to the British Government.
He listened, and at last yielded. His deference, he said, but yields
to the wishes of his allies took place of every other to the re-
consideration; he would let his relations with the presenta-
Amirs of Sind remain on their old footing, he would tions of
destroy the fort of Ken, but he would continue to the English,
occupy Rojhan and the Mazari territory.[3] Ranjit Dec. 1836.
Singh was urged by his chiefs not to yield to the demands of the English, for to their understanding it was
not clear where such demands would stop; but he shook
his head, and asked them what had become of the two
hundred thousand spears of the Marathas![4]—and, as

[1] Government to Capt. Wade, 26th Sept. 1836.
[2] Capt. Wade to Government, 2nd Nov. and 13th Dec. 1836.
[3] Capt. Wade to Government, 3rd Jan. 1837.
[4] Cf. Capt. Wade to Government, 11th Jan. 1837. Ranjit
Sihgh not unfrequently referred to the overthrow of the Mara-

1836.

Yet continues to hold Rojhan with ulterior views.

Retrospect. The English and Barakza.s. 1829-36.

Sultan Muhammad Khan solicits the

if to show how completely he professed to forget or forgive the check imposed on him, he invited the Governor-General to be present at Lahore on the occasion of the marriage of the grandson whom he had hoped to hail as the conqueror of Sind.[1] Nevertheless he continued to entertain a hope that his objects might one day be attained; he avoided a distinct settlement of the boundary with the Amirs, and of the question of supremacy over the Mazaris.[2] Neither was he disposed to relinquish Rojhan; the place remained a Sikh possession, and it may be regarded to have become formally such by the submission of the chief of the tribe in the year 1838.[3]

It is now necessary to go back for some years to trace the connexion of the English Government with the Barakzai rulers of Afghanistan. Muhammad Azim Khan died in 1823, as has been mentioned, immediately after Peshawar became tributary to the Sikhs. His son Habib-ullah nominally succeeded to the supremacy which Fateh Khan and Muhammad Azim had both exercised; but it soon became evident that the mind of the youth was unsettled, and his violent proceedings enabled his crafty and unscrupulous uncle, Dost Muhammad Khan, to seize Kabul, Ghazni, and Jalalabad as his own, while a second set of his brothers held Kandahar in virtual independence, and a third governed Peshawar as the tributaries of Ranjit Singh.[4] In the year 1824 Mr. Moorcroft, the traveller, was upon the whole well satisfied with the treatment he received from the Barakzais, although their patronage cost him money.[5] A few years afterwards Sultan Muhammad Khan of Peshawar, who had most to fear from strangers, opened a communication with the political agent at Ludhiana,[6] and in 1829 he wished to negotiate as an

tha power as a reason for remaining, under all and any circumstances, on good terms with his European allies. See also Col. Wade's *Narrative of Personal Services*, p. 44, note. [Though the Maharaja kept loyally to his treaty of friendship with the English, he occasionally manifested some suspicion of their victorious advance in India. On one occasion he was shown a map of the country in which the English possessions were marked in red. The Maharaja asked what the red portions indicated, and on being told tossed the map aside with the impatient remark, *Sab lal hojaega* (All will become red).—ED.]

[1] Capt. Wade to Government, 5th Jan. 1837.
[2] Capt. Wade to Government, 13th and 15th Feb., 8th July, and 10th Aug. 1837.
[3] Capt. Wade to Government, 9th Jan. 1838.
[4] Cf. Moorcroft, *Travels*, ii. 345, &c, and Munshi Mohan Lal, *Life of Dost Muhammad Khan*, i. 130, 153, &c.
[5] Moorcroft, *Travels*, ii. 346, 347.
[6] Capt. Wade to the Resident at Delhi, 21st April 1828.

independent chief with the British Government.[1]  But
the several brothers were jealous of one another, many
desired separate principalities, Dost Muhammad aimed
at supremacy, rumours of Persian designs alarmed
them on the west, the aggressive policy of Ranjit Singh
gave them greater cause of fear on the east, and the
chance presence of English travellers in Afghanistan
again led them to hope that the foreign masters of
India might be induced to give them stability between
contending powers.[2]  In 1832 Sultan Muhammad Khan
again attempted to open a negotiation, if only for the
release of his son, who was a hostage with Ranjit
Singh.[3]  The Nawab, Jabbar Khan of Kabul, likewise
addressed letters to the British frontier authority, and
in 1832 Dost Muhammad himself directly asked for the
friendship of the English.[4]  All these communications
were politely acknowledged, but at the time it was
held desirable to avoid all intimacy of connexion with
rulers so remote.[5]

In 1834 new dangers threatened the usurping Barakzais.  Shah Shuja had defeated the Sindians and
had arrived in force at Kandahar, and the brothers
once again endeavoured to bring themselves within the
verge of British supremacy.  They had heard of English arts as well as of English arms; they knew that
all were accessible of flattery, and Jabbar Khan suddenly proposed to send his son to Ludhiana, in order,
he said, that his mind might be improved by European
science and civilization.[6]  But Jabbar Khan, while he

*1829-32.*
*friendship or protection of the English against the Sikhs, 1829.*

*Dost Muhammad Khan does the same, 1832.*

*The Barakzais, apprehensive of Shah Shuja, again press for an alliance with the English; and Jabbar Khan sends his son to Ludhiana, 6th May 1834.*

---

[1] Capt. Wade to Government, 19th May 1832. The brothers
had already (1823, 1824) made similar proposals through Mr.
Moorcroft. (See *Travels,* ii. 340.)

[2] Mr. Fraser and Mr. Stirling, of the Bengal Civil Service,
were in Afghanistan, the former in 1826, apparently, and the
latter in 1828.  Mr. Masson also entered the country by way of
the Lower Punjab in 1827, and the American, Dr. Harlan,
followed him in a year by the same route.  Dr. Harlan came
to Lahore in 1929, after leading the English authorities to believe that he desired to constitute himself an agent between
their Government and Shah Shuja, with reference doubtless
to the ex-king's designs on Kabul.  (Resident at Delhi to Capt.
Wade, 3rd Feb. 1829.)  The Rev. Mr. Wolff should be included
among the travellers in Central Asia at the time in question.

[3] Capt. Wade to Government, 19th May and 3rd July 1832.

[4] Capt. Wade to Government, 9th July 1832, and 17th Jan.
1833. Col. Wade in the *Narrative of Personal Services,* p. 23,
note, regards these overtures of Dost Muhammad, and also
the increased interest of Russia and Persia in Afghan affairs,
to Lieut. Burnes's Journey (to Bokhara, in 1832) and to Shah
Shuja's designs.

[5] Government to Capt. Wade, 28th Feb. 1833.

[6] Capt. Wade to Government, 9th March 1834.

1834.

appeared to adhere to Dost Muhammad rather than to others, had nevertheless an ambition of his own, and he was more than suspected of a wish to make his admiration of the amenities of English life the means of acquiring political power.[1]  Thus, doubtful of all about him, Dost Muhammad left Kabul to oppose Shah Shuja, but the Sikhs had, in the meantime, occupied Peshawar, and the perplexed ruler grasped once more at British aid as his only sure resource.[2]  He tendered his submission as a dependent of Great Britain, and having thus endeavoured to put his dominions in trust, he gave Shah Shuja battle.  But the Shah was defeated, and the rejoicing victor forgot his difficulties.  He declared war against the Sikhs on account of their capture of Peshawar and he endeavoured to make it a religious contest by rousing the population generally to destroy infidel invaders.[3]  He assumed the proud distinction of 'Ghazi', or champion of the faith, and the vague title of 'Amir', which he interpreted 'the noble', for he did not care to wholly offend his brothers, whose submission he desired, and whose assistance was necessary to him.[4]

*Dost Muhammad formally tenders his allegiance to the English, 1st July 1834;*

*but defeats Shah Shuja and recovers confidence.*

Dost Muhammad Khan, amid all his exultation, was still willing to use the intervention of unbelievers as well as the arms of the faithful, and he asked the English masters of India to help him in recovering Peshawar.[5]  The youth who had been sent to Ludhiana to become a student, was invested with the powers of a diplomatist, and the Amir sought to prejudice the British authorities against the Sikhs, by urging that *his* nephew and *their* guest had been treated with suspicion, and had suffered restraint on his way across the Punjab.  But the English had not yet thought of requiring him to be an ally for purposes of their own, and Dost Muhammad was simply assured that the son of Nawab Jabbar Khan should be well taken care of on the eastern side of the Sutlej.  A direct reply to his solicitation was avoided, by enlarging on the partial truth that the Afghans were a commercial people equally with the English, and on the favourite scheme of the great traffickers of the world, the opening of the Indus to commerce.  It was hoped, it was added, that the new impulse given to trade would better help the

*Dost Muhammad attempts to recover Peshawar.*

*The English decline interfering.*

[1] Capt. Wade to Government, 17th May 1834. Cf. Masson, *Journeys*, iii. 218, 220.

[2] Capt. Wade to Government, 17th June 1834.

[3] Capt. Wade to Government, 25th Sept. 1834.

[4] Capt. Wade to Government, 27th Jan. 1835.

[5] Capt. Wade to Government, 4th Jan. and 13th Feb. 1835.

two governments to cultivate a profitable friendship, 1835. and the wondering Amir, full of warlike schemes, was naively asked, whether he had any suggestions to offer about a direct route for merchandise between Kabul and the great boundary river of the Afghans![1] The English rulers had also to reply to Ranjit Singh, who was naturally suspicious of the increasing intimacy between his allies and his enemies, and who desired that the European lords might appear rather as his than as Dost Muhammad's supporters; but the Governor-General observed that any endeavours to mediate would lead to consequences seriously embarrassing, and that Dost Muhammad would seem to have interpreted general professions of amity into promises of assistance.[2]

The two parties were thus left to their own means. Ranjit Singh began by detaching Sultan Muhammad Khan from the Amir, with whom he had sought a refuge on the occupation of Peshawar by the Sikhs; and the ejected tributary listened the more readily to the Maharaja's propositions, as he apprehended that Dost Muhammad would retain Peshawar for himself, should Ranjit Singh be beaten. Dost Muhammad came to the eastern entrance of the Khaibar Pass, and Ranjit Singh amused him with proposals until he had concentrated his forces. On the 11th of May 1835, the Amir was almost surrounded. He was to have been attacked on the 12th, but he thought it prudent to retreat, which he did with the loss of two guns and some baggage. He had designed to carry off the Sikh envoys, and to profit by their presence as hostages or as prisoners; but his brother, Sultan Muhammad Khan, to whom the execution of the project had been entrusted, had determined on joining Ranjit Singh, and the rescue of the agents gave him a favourable introduction to the victor. Sultan Muhammad and his brothers had considerable jagirs conferred on them in the Peshawar district, but the military control and civil management of the province was vested solely in an officer appointed from Lahore.[3]

*Ranjit Singh and Dost Muhammad in force at Peshawar, 1835.*

*Dost Muhammad retires rather than risk a battle, 11th May 1835.*

[1] Government to Capt. Wade, 19th April 1834, and 11th Feb. 1835. Abdul Ghias Khan, the son of Jabbar Khan, reached Ludhiana in June 1834, and the original intention of sending him to study at Delhi was abandoned.

[2] Government to Capt. Wade, 20th April 1835.

[3] Capt. Wade to Government, 25th April, and 1st, 15th, and 19th May 1835. Cf. Masson, *Journeys*, iii. 342, &c.; Mohan Lal, *Life of Dost Muhammad*, i. 172, &c.; and also Dr. Harlan's *India and Afghanistan*, pp. 124, 158. Dr. Harlan himself was one of

1835-6.

Dost Mu-
hammad
looks to-
wards
Persia, but
still prefers
an English
alliance.
1836.

The Kanda-
har chiefs
desirous of
English a,d.
Ranjit
Singh en-
deavours to
gain over
Dost Mu-
hammad.

But the
Amir pre-
fers war.
1836-7.

Hari
Singh's
designs.

Battle of
Jamrud.
30th April
1837.

Dost Muhammad suffered much in general estimation by withdrawing from an encounter with the Sikhs. His hopes in the English had not borne fruit, and he was disposed to court Persia; [1] but the connexion was of less political credit and utility than one with the English, and he tried once more to move the Governor-General in his favour. The Sikhs, he said, were faithless, and he was wholly devoted to the interests of the British Government.[2] The Kandahar brothers, also, being pressed by Shah Kamran of Herat, and unable to obtain aid from Dost Muhammad, made propositions to the English authorities; but Kamran's own apprehensions of Persia soon relieved them of their fears, and they did not press their solicitations for European aid.[3] Ranjit Singh, on his part, disliked an English and Afghan alliance, and sought to draw Dost Muhammad within the vortex of his own influence. He gave the Amir vague hopes of obtaining Peshawar, and he asked him to send him some horses, which he had learnt was a sure way of leading others to believe they had won his favour. Dost Muhammad was not unwilling to obtain a hold on Peshawar, even as a tributary, but he felt that the presentation of horses would be declared by the Sikh to refer to Kabul and not to that province.[4] The disgrace of his retreat rankled in his mind, and he at last said that a battle must be fought at all risks.[5] He was the more inclined to resort to arms, as the Sikhs had sounded his brother, Jabbar Khan, and as Sirdar Hari Singh had occupied the entrance of the Khaibar Pass and entrenched a position at Jamrud, as the basis of his scheme for getting through the formidable defile.[6] The Kabul troops marched and assembled on the eastern side of Khaibar, under the command of Muhammad Akbar Khan,[7] the most warlike of the Amir's sons. An attack was made on the post at Jamrud, on the 30th of April 1837; but the Afghans could not carry it, although they threw

the envoys sent to Dost Muhammad on the occasion.
The Sikhs are commonly said to have had 80,000 men in the Peshawar valley at this time.
[1] Capt. Wade to Government, 23rd Feb. 1836. Dost Muhammad's overtures to Persia seem to have commenced in Sept. 1835.
[2] Capt. Wade to Government, 19th July 1836.
[3] Capt. Wade to Government, 9th March 1836.
[4] Capt. Wade to Government, 12th April 1837.
[5] Capt. Wade to Government, 1st May 1837.
[6] Capt. Wade to Government, 13th Jan. 1837.
[7] [Afterwards the murderer of Sir W. Macnaghten and the chief actor in the tragedy of the retreat from Kabul (1842). —Ed.]

the Sikhs into disorder. Hari Singh, by feigning a retreat, drew the enemy more fully into the plains; the brave leader was present everywhere amid his retiring and rallying masses, but he fell mortally wounded, and the opportune arrival of another portion of the Kabul forces converted the confusion of the Sikhs into a total defeat. But two guns only were lost; the Afghans could not master Jamrud or Peshawar itself, and, after plundering the valley for a few days, they retreated rather than risk a second battle with the reinforced army of Lahore.[1]

1836-7.

The Sikhs defeated, and Hari Singh k.lled; but the Afghans retire.

The death of Hari Singh and the defeat of his army caused some anxiety in Lahore; but the Maharaja promptly roused his people to exertion, and all readily responded to his call. It is stated that field guns were dragged from Ramnagar, on the Chenab, to Peshawar in six days, a distance by road of more than two hundred miles.[2] Ranjit Singh advanced in person to Rohtas, and the active Dhian Singh hastened to the frontier, and set an example of devotion and labour by working with his own hands on the foundations of a regular fort at Jamrud.[3] Dost Muhammad was buoyed up by his fruitless victory, and he became more than ever desirous of recovering a province so wholly Afghan; but Ranjit Singh contrived to amuse him, and the Maharaja was found to be again in treaty with the Amir, and again in treaty with Shah Shuja, and with both at the same time.[4] But the commercial envoy of the English had gradually sailed high up the Indus of their imaginary commerce, and to his Government the time seemed to have come when political interference

Ranjit Singh's efforts to retrieve his affairs at Peshawar.

His nego- tiations with Dost Muham- mad and Shah Shuja.

The English resolve on mediating between the Sikhs and Afghans, 1837:

---

[1] Capt. Wade to Government, 13th and 23rd May and 5th July 1837. Cf. Masson, *Journeys*, iii. 382, 387, and Mohan Lal, *Life of Dost Muhammad*, i. 226, &c.

It seems that the Afghans were at first routed or repulsed with the loss of some guns, but that the opportune arrival of Shams-ud-din Khan, a relation of the Amir, with a considerable detachment, turned the battle in their favour. It is neverthe- less believed that had not Hari Singh been killed, the Sikhs would have retrieved the day. The troops in the Peshawar valley had been considerably reduced by the withdrawal of large parties to Lahore, to make a display on the occasion of Nau Nihal Singh's marriage, and of the expected visit of the English Governor-General and Commander-in-Chief.

[2] Lieut.-Col. Steinbach (*Punjab*, pp. 64, 68) mentions that he had himself marched with his Sikh regiment 300 miles in twelve days, and that the distance had been performed by others in eleven.

[3] Mr. Clerk's Memorandum of 1842, regarding the Sikh chiefs, drawn up for Lord Ellenborough.

[4] Cf. Capt. Wade to Government, 3rd June 1837, and Government to Capt. Wade, 7th Aug. 1837.

1837.

would no longer be embarrassing, but, on the contrary, highly advantageous to schemes of peaceful trade and beneficial intercourse. It was made known that the British rulers would be glad to be the means of negotiating a peace honourable to both parties, yet the scale was turned in favour of the Afghan, by the simultaneous admission that Peshawar was a place to which Dost Muhammad could scarcely be expected to resign all claim.[1] Nevertheless, it was said, the wishes of Ranjit Singh could be ascertained by Capt. Wade, and Capt. Burnes could similarly inquire about the views of the Amir. The latter officer was formally invested with diplomatic powers,[2] and the idle designs or restless intrigues, of Persians and Russians, soon caused the disputes of Sikhs and Afghans to merge in the British scheme of reseating Shah Shuja on the throne of Kabul. At the end of a generation the repose of the English masters of India was again disturbed by the rumoured march of European armies,[3] and their suspicions were further roused by the conduct of the French General, Allard. That officer after a residence of several years in the Punjab, had been enabled to visit his native country, and he returned by way of Calcutta in the year 1836. While in France he had induced his Government to give him a document, accrediting him to Ranjit Singh, in case his life should be endangered, or in case he should be refused permission to quit the Lahore dominions. It was understood by the English that the paper was only to be produced to the *Maharaja* in an extremity of the kind mentioned; but General Allard himself considered that it was only to be so laid in form before the *English authorities*, in support of a demand for aid when he might chance to be straitened. He at once delivered his credentials to the Sikh ruler; it was rumoured that General Allard had become a French ambassador, and it was some time before the British authorities forgave the fancied deceit, or the vain effrontery of their guest [4]

*the more especially as they are apprehensive of Russia,*

*and are further dissatisfied with the proceedings of General Allard.*

[1] Government to Capt. Wade, 31st July 1837.

[2] Government to Capt. Wade, 11th Sept. 1837.

[3] The idea of Russian designs on India engaged the attention of the British viceroy in 1831 (see Murray, *Ranjit Singh*, by Prinsep, p. 168), and it at the same time possessed the inquiring but sanguine mind of Capt. Burnes, who afterwards gave the notion so much notoriety. (See Capt. Wade to Government, 3rd Aug. 1831.)

[4] The author gives what the French officers held to be the intended use of the credentials, on the competent authority of General Ventura, with whom he formerly had conversations on the subject. The English view, however, is that which was

Ranjit Singh had invited the Governor-General of
India, the Governor of Agra (Sir Charles Metcalfe),
and the Commander-in-Chief of the British forces to
be present at the nuptials of his grandson, which he
designed to celebrate with much splendour. The prince
was wedded to a daughter of the Sikh chief, Sham
Singh Atariwala, in the beginning of March 1837, but
of the English authorities Sir Henry Fane alone was
able to attend. That able commander was ever a careful observer of military means and of soldierly qualities; he formed an estimate of the force which would
be required for the complete subjugation of the Punjab,
but at the same time he laid it down as a principle, that
the Sutlej and the wastes of Rajputana and Sind were
the best boundaries which the English could have in
the east.[1] The prospect of a war with the Sikhs was
then remote, and hostile designs could not with honour

1837.

The mar-
riage of
Nau Nihal
Singh, 1837

Sir Henry
Fane at
Lahore.

taken by the British ambassador in Paris, as well as by the
authorities in Calcutta, with whom General Allard was in personal communication. (Government to Capt. Wade, 16th Jan.
and 3rd April 1837.)

Of the two views, that of the English is the less honourable,
with reference to their duty towards Ranjit Singh, who might
have justly resented any attempt on the part of a servant to
put himself beyond the power of his master, and any interference in that servant's behalf on the part of the British
Government.

In the letter to Ranjit Singh, Louis Philippe is styled, in
French, 'Empereur' (Capt. Wade to Government, 15th Sept.
1837); a title which, at the time, may have pleased the vanity
of the French, although it could not have informed the understandings of the Sikhs, as, agreeably to Persian and Indian
practice, king or queen is always translated 'Padshah' equally
with emperor. Sir Claude Wade seems to think that the real
design of the French was to open a regular intercourse with
Ranjit Singh, and to obtain a political influence in the Punjab.
The Maharaja, however, after consulting the British Agent,
decided on not taking any notice of the overtures. (Sir Claude
Wade, Narrative, p. 38, note.) [A piece of diplomacy on the
part of the French Government, typical of the chicanery of
Louis Philippe and his advisers. The monarch who could
perpetrate the sordid scandal of the Spanish marriage was
equally capable of an underhand intrigue with Ranjit Singh.
—Ed.]

[1] These views of Sir Henry Fane's may not be on record,
but they were well known to those about his Excellency. His
estimate was, as I remember to have heard from Capt. Wade,
67,000 men, and he thought there might be a two years' active
warfare.

This visit to Lahore was perhaps mainly useful in
enabling Lieut.-Col. Garden, the indefatigable quarter-
master-general of the Bengal Army, to compile a detailed
map of that part of the country, and which formed the
groundwork of all the maps used when hostilities did at last
break out with the Sikhs.

1837.

The Sikh
military
Order of
the Star.

Ranjit
Singh's
object the
gratifica-
tion of his
guests and
allies.

Anecdotes
showing a
similar
purpose.

be entertained by a guest. Sir Henry Fane, therefore, entered heartily into the marriage festivities of Lahore, and his active mind was amused with giving shape to a scheme, which the intuitive sagacity of Ranjit Singh had acquiesced in as pleasing to the just pride or useful vanity of English soldiers. The project of establishing an Order of merit similar to those dying exponents of warlike skill and chivalrous fraternity among European nations, had been for some time entertained, and although such a system of distinction can be adapted to the genius of any people, the object of the Maharaja was simply to gratify his English neighbours, and advantage was accordingly taken of Sir Henry Fane's presence to establish the 'Order of the auspicious Star of the Punjab' on a purely British model.[1] This method of pleasing, or occupying the attention of the English authorities, was not unusual with Ranjit Singh, and he was always ready to inquire concerning matters which interested them, or which might be turned to account by himself. He would ask for specimens of, and for information about, the manufacture of Sambhar salt and Malwa opium.[2] So early as 1812 he had made trial of the sincerity of his new allies, or had shown his admiration of their skill, by asking for five hundred muskets. These were at once furnished to him, but a subsequent request for a supply of fifty thousand such weapons excited a passing suspicion.[3] He readily entered into a scheme of freighting a number of boats with merchandise for Bombay, and he was praised for the interest he took in commerce, until it was known that he wished the return cargo to consist of arms for his infantry.[4] He would have his artillerymen learn gunnery at Ludhiana,[5] and he would send shells of zinc to be inspected in the hope that he might receive some hints about the manufacture of iron shrapnels.[6]

---

[1] Capt. Wade to Government, 7th April 1837. [On the occasion of this visit the Maharaja displayed considerable interest in the great wars of Europe. He was particularly interested in the career of Napoleon. Col. Wallis, one of Sir Henry's staff, had fortunately been at Waterloo, and the Maharaja asked him many questions concerning the battle. —ED.]

[2] Capt. Wade to the Resident at Delhi, 2nd Jan. 1831, and to Government, 25th Dec. 1835.

[3] Capt. Wade to Government, 22nd July 1836.

[4] Cf. Government to Capt. Wade, 11th Sept. 1837.

[5] Capt. Wade to Government, 7th Dec. 1831.

[6] When the restoration of Shah Shuja was resolved on, Ranjit Singh sent shells to Ludhiana to be looked at and commented on, as if, being engaged in one political cause there should not be any reserve about military secrets!

He would inquire about the details of European war- 1837.
fare, and he sought for copies of the pay regulations of
the Indian army and of the English practice of courts
martial, and bestowed dresses of honour on the trans-
lator of these complicated and inapplicable systems;[1]
while, to further satisfy himself, he would ask what
punishment had been found an efficient substitute for
flogging.[2] He sent a lad, the relation of one of his
chiefs, to learn English at the Ludhiana school, in
order, he said, that the youth might aid him in his correspondence with the British Government, which Lord
William Bentinck had wished to carry on in the English
tongue instead of in Persian;[3] and he sent a number
of young men to learn something of medicine at the
Ludhiana dispensary, which had been set on foot by
the political agent—but in order, the Maharaja said,
that they might be useful in his battalions.[4] In such
ways, half-serious, half-idle, did Ranjit Singh endeavour to ingratiate himself with the representatives of
a power he could not withstand and never wholly
trusted.

Ranjit Singh's rejoicings over the marriage and
youthful promise of his grandson were rudely interrupted by the success of the Afghans at Jamrud, and
the death of his able leader Hari Singh, as has been
already related. The old man was moved to tears
when he heard of the fate of the only genuine Sikh
chief of his creation;[5] and he had scarcely vindicated
his supremacy on the frontier, by filling the valley of
Peshawar with troops, when the English interfered to
embitter the short remainder of his life, and to set
bounds to his ambition on the west, as they had already
done on the east and south. The commercial policy of

The British
scheme of
opening the
Indus to
commerce
ends in the
project of
restoring
Shah Shuja.

---

[1] Major Hough, who has added to the reputation of the
Indian army by his useful publications, put the practice of
courts martial into a Sikh dress for Ranjit Singh. (Government to Capt. Wade, 21st November 1834.)

[2] Government to Capt. Wade, 18th May 1835, intimating
that solitary confinement had been found a good substitute.

[3] Capt. Wade to Government, 11th April 1835. Some of
the princes of India, all of whom are ever pron    suspicion,
were not without a belief that, by writing in English, it was
designed to keep them in ignorance of the real views and
declarations of their paramount.

[4] Some of these young men were employed with the
force raised at Peshawar, in 1839, to enable Prince Taimur
to march through Khaibar.

[5] Capt. Wade to Government, 13th May 1837, quoting
Dr. Wood, a surgeon in the British army, temporarily deputed
to attend on Ranjit Singh, and who was with his camp at
Rohtas on this occasion.

1837.

Sir Alex.
Burnes at
Kabul,
1837-8.

the British people required that peace and industry should at once be introduced among the half-barbarous tribes of Sind, Khorasan, and the Punjab; and it was vainly sought to give fixed limits to newly-founded feudal governments, and to impress moderation of desire upon grasping military sovereigns. It was wished that Ranjit Singh should be content with his past achievements; that the Amirs of Sindh, and the chiefs of Herat, Kandahar, and Kabul should feel themselves secure in what they held, but incapable of obtaining more; and that the restless Shah Shuja should quietly abandon all hope of regaining the crown of his daily dreams.[1] These were the views which the English viceroy required his agents to impress on Talpurs, Barakzais, and Sikhs; and their impracticability might have quietly and harmlessly become apparent, had not Russia found reason and opportunity to push her intrigues, through Persia and Turkestan, to the banks of the Indus.[2] The desire of effecting a reconciliation between Ranjit Singh and Dost Muhammad induced the British Government to offer its mediation;[3] the predilections of its frank and enterprising envoy led him to seize upon the admission that the Amir could scarcely be expected to resign all pretensions to Peshawar.[4] The crafty chief made use of this partiality,

[1] Cf. Government to Capt. Wade, 1? ৷৷ Nov. 1837, and to Capt. Burnes and Capt. Wade, both of tl  ৽ 20th January 1838. With regard to Sind, also, the views of Ranjit Singh were not held to be pleasing, and the terms of his communication with the Amirs were thought equivocal, or denotative of a reservation, or of the expression of a right he did not possess. (Government to Capt. Wade, 25th Sept. and 13th Nov. 1837.)

[2] Without reference to the settled policy of Russia, or to what she may always have thought of the virtual support which England gives to Persia and Turkey against her power, the presence of inquiring agents in Khorasan and Turkestan, and the progressive extension of the British Indian dominion, must have put her on the alert, if they did not fill her with reasonable suspicions.

[3] Government to Capt. Wade, 31st July 1837.

[4] These predilections of Sir Alex. Burnes, and the hopes founded on them by Dost Muhammad, were sufficiently notorious to those in personal communication with that valuable pioneer of the English; and his strong wish to recover Peshawar, at least for Sultan Muhammad Khan, is distinctly stated in his own words, in Masson, *Journeys*, iii. 423. The idea of taking the district from the Sikhs, either for Dost Muhammad or his brothers, is moreover apparent from Sir Alex. Burnes's published letters of 5th Oct. 1837, and 26th Jan. and 13th March 1838 (Parliamentary Papers, 1839), from the Government replies of remark and caution, dated 20th Jan., and especially of 27th April 1838, and from Mr. Masson's statement (*Journeys*, iii. 423, 448). Mr. Masson

and of the fact that his friendship was courted, to try and secure himself against the only power he really feared, viz. that of the Sikhs; and he renewed his overtures to Persia and welcomed a Russian emissary, with the view of intimidating the English into the surrender of Peshawar, and into a guarantee against Ranjit Singh. Friendly assurances to the Kandahar brothers, and a hint that the Sikhs were at liberty to march on Kabul, would have given Dost Muhammad a proper sense of his insignificance;[1] but the truth and the importance of his hostile designs were both believed or assumed by the British Government, while the rumours of a northern invasion were eagerly received and industriously spread by the vanquished princes of India, and the whole country vibrated with the hope that the uncongenial domination of the English was about to yield to the ascendancy of another and less dissimilar race.[2] The recall of Capt. Burnes from Kabul gave speciousness to the wildest statements; the advantage of striking some great blow became more and more obvious; for the sake of consistency it was necessary to maintain peace on the Indus, and it was wisely resolved to make a triumphant progress through Central Asia, and to leave Shah Shuja as a dependent prince on his ancestral throne. The conception was bold and perfect; and had it been steadily adhered to, the whole project would have eminently answered the ends intended, and would have been, in every way, worthy of the English name.[3]

In the beginning of 1838 the Governor-General did not contemplate the restoration of Shah Shuja;[4] but in

*1837-8.*

*Dost Muhammad eventually falls into the views of Persia and Russia. The original policy of the English erroneous.*

*But, under the circumstances brought about, the expedition to Kabul wisely and boldly conceived.*

*Negotiations regarding the*

himself thought it would be but justice to restore the district to Sultan Muhammad Khan, while Munshi Mohan Lal (*Life of Dost Muhammad*, i. 257, &c.) represents the Amir to have thought that the surrender of Peshawar to his brother would have been more prejudicial to his interests than its retention by the Sikhs.

[1] Such were Capt. Wade's views, and they are sketched in his letters of the 15th May and 28th Oct. 1837, with reference to commercial objects, although the line of policy may not have been steadily adhered to, or fully developed.

[2] The extent to which this feeling was prevalent is known to those who were observers of Indian affairs at the time, and it is dwelt upon in the Governor-General's minute of the 20th Aug. 1839.

[3] The Governor-General's minute of 12th May 1838, and his declaration of the 1st October of the same year, may be referred to as summing up the views which moved the British Government on the occasion. Both were published by order of Parliament in March 1839.

[4] Government to Capt. Wade, 20th Jan. 1838.

1838.

restoration
of Shah
Shuja,
May, July,
1838.

Ranjit
Singh dis-
satisfied;
but finally
assents.

four months the scheme was adopted, and in May of
that year Sir William Macnaghten was sent to Ranjit
Singh to unfold the views of the British Government.[1]
The Maharaja grasped at the first idea which presented
itself, of making use of the Shah at the head of *his*
armies, with the proclaimed support of the paramount
power in India; but he disliked the complete view of
the scheme, and the active co-operation of his old allies.
It chafed him that he was to resign all hope of Shikarpur, and that he was to be enclosed within the iron
arms of the English rule. He suddenly broke up his
camp at Dinanagar, leaving the British envoys to
follow at their leisure, or to return, if they pleased,
to Simla; and it was not until he was told the expedition would be undertaken whether he chose to share
in it or not, that he assented to a modification of his
own treaty with Shah Shuja, and that the triple alliance was formed for the subversion of the power of
the Barakzais.[2] The English, on their part, insisted
on a double invasion of Afghanistan : first, because the
Amirs of Sind disliked a proffered treaty of alliance or
dependence, and they could conveniently be coerced as
tributaries by Shah Shuja on his way to Kandahar;

[1] The proximate cause of the resolution to restore Shah
Shuja was, of course, the preference given by Dost
Muhammad to a Persian and Russian over a British alliance,
and the immediate object of deputing Sir W. Macnaghten to
Lahore was to make Ranjit Singh as much as possible a party
to the policy adopted. (See, among other letters, Government to Capt. Wade, 15th May 1838.) The deputation crossed
into the Punjab at Rupar on the 20th May. It remained some
time at Dinanagar, and afterwards went to Lahore. The first
interview with Ranjit Singh was on the 31st May, the last
on the 13th July. Sir William Macnaghten recrossed the
Sutlej at Ludhiana on the 15th July, and on that and the
following day he arranged with Shah Shuja in person the
terms of his restoration.

Two months before the deputation waited upon Ranjit
Singh, he had visited Jammu for apparently the first time in
his life, and the same may be regarded as the last in which
the worn-out prince tasted of unalloyed happiness. Gulab
Singh received his sovereign with every demonstration of
loyalty, and, bowing to the Maharaja's feet, he laid before
him presents worth nearly forty thousand pounds, saying he
was the humblest of his slaves, and the most grateful of those
on whom he had heaped favours. Ranjit Singh shed tears,
but afterwards pertinently observed that, in Jammu, gold
might be seen where formerly there was naught but stones.
(Major Mackeson's letter to Capt. Wade of 31st March 1838.)

[2] That Ranjit Singh was told he would be left out if he
did not choose to come in, does not appear on public record.
It was, however, the only convincing argument used during
the long discussions, and I think Major Mackeson was made
the bearer of the message to that effect.

and, secondly, because it was not deemed prudent to
place the ex-king in the hands of Ranjit Singh, who
might be tempted to use him for Sikh rather than for
British objects.[1]    It was therefore arranged that the
Shah himself should march by way of Shikarpur and
Quetta, while his son moved on Kabul by the road of
Peshawar, and at the head of a force provided by the
Maharaja of the Punjab.    The British force assembled
at Ferozepore towards the close of 1838, and further
eclat was given to the opening of a memorable campaign, by an interchange of hospitalities between the
English viceroy and the Sikh ruler.[2]   Ostensibly Ranjit    *Ranjit*
Singh had reached the summit of his ambition; he was    *Singh ap-*
acknowledged to be an arbiter in the fate of that em-    *parently at*
*the height*
pire which had tyrannized over his peasant forefathers,    *of great-*
and he was treated with the greatest distinction by the    *ness;*
foreign paramounts of India: but his health had become seriously impaired; he felt that he was in truth

[1] Cf. the Governor-General's minute of 12th of May 1838,
and his instructions to Sir William Macnaghten of the 15th
of the same month. Ranjit Singh was anxious to get something lasting and tangible as his share of the profit of the
expedition, and he wanted Jalalabad, as there seemed to be
a difficulty about Shikarpur. The Maharaja got, indeed, a
subsidy of two hundred thousand rupees a year from the
Shah for the use of his troops; a concession which did not
altogether satisfy the Governor-General (see letter to Sir
William Macnaghten, 2nd July, 1838), and the article became,
in fact, a dead letter.
    The idea of creating a friendly power in Afghanistan, by
guiding Ranjit Singh upon Kabul, seems to have been
seriously entertained, and it was a scheme which promised
many solid advantages. Cf. the Governor-General's minute,
12th May 1838, the author's abstract of which differs somewhat from the copy printed by order of Parliament in 1839,
and Mr. Masson (*Journeys*, iii. 487, 488) who refers to a
communication from Sir William Macnaghten on the subject.
For the treaty about the restoration of Shah Shuja, see
Appendix XXX.
    [2] At one of the several meetings which took place on
this occasion, there was an interchange of compliments, which
may be noticed. Ranjit Singh likened the friendship of the
two states to an apple, the red and yellow colours of which
were, he said, so blended, that although the semblance was
twofold the reality was one. Lord Auckland replied that the
Maharaja's simile was very happy, inasmuch as red and
yellow were the national colours of the English and Sikhs
respectively; to which Ranjit Singh rejoined in the same
strain that the comparison was indeed in every way appropriate, for the friendship of the two powers was, like the
apple, fair and delicious. The translations were given in
English and Urdu with elegance and emphasis by Sir William
Macnaghten and Fakir Aziz-ud-din, both of whom were
masters, although in different ways, of language, whether
written or spoken.

fairly in collision with the English, and he became indifferent about the careful fulfilment of the engagements into which he had entered. Shahzada Taimur marched from Lahore in January 1839, accompanied by Col. Wade as the British representative; but it was with difficulty the stipulated auxiliary force was got together at Peshawar, and although a considerable army at last encamped in the valley, the commander, the Maharaja's grandson, thwarted the negotiations of Prince Taimur and the English agent, by endeavouring to gain friends for Lahore rather than for the proclaimed sovereign of the Afghans.[1] Ranjit Singh's health continued to decline. He heard of the fall of Kandahar in April, and the delay at that place may have served to cheer his vexed spirit with the hope

that the English would yet be baffled; but he died on the 27th of June, at the age of fifty-nine, before the capture of Ghazni and the occupation of Kabul, and the forcing of the Khaibar Pass with the aid of his own troops, placed the seal of success on a campaign in which he was an unwilling sharer.

Ranjit Singh found the Punjab a waning confederacy, a prey to the factions of its chiefs, pressed by the Afghans and the Marathas, and ready to submit to English supremacy. He consolidated the numerous petty states into a kingdom, he wrested from Kabul the fairest of its provinces, and he gave the potent English no cause for interference. He found the military array of his country a mass of horsemen, brave indeed, but ignorant of war as an art, and he left it mustering fifty thousand disciplined soldiers, fifty thousand well-armed yeomanry and militia, and more than three hundred pieces of cannon for the field. His rule was founded on the feelings of a people, but it involved the joint action of the necessary principles of military order and territorial extension; and when a limit had been set to Sikh dominion, and his own commanding genius was no more, the vital spirit of his race began to consume itself in domestic contentions.'

[1] See, among other letters, Capt. Wade to Government, 18th Aug. 1839. For some interesting details regarding Capt. Wade's military proceedings, see Lieut. Barr's published *Journal;* and for the diplomatic history, so to speak, of his mission, see Munshi Shahamat Ali, *Sikhs and Afghans.*

[2] In 1831, Capt. Murray estimated the Sikh revenue at little more than 2½ millions sterling, and the army at 82,000 men, including 15,000 regular infantry and 376 guns. (Murray, *Ranjit Singh,* by Prinsep, pp. 185, 186.) In the same year Capt. Burnes (*Travels,* i. 289, 291) gives the revenue at 2¼ millions, and the army at 75,000, including 25,000 regular

1839.

When Ranjit Singh was Lord Auckland's host at
Lahore and Amritsar, his utterance was difficult, and
the powers of his body feeble; he gradually lost the use
of his speech, and of the faculties of his mind; and,
before his death, the Rajas of Jammu had usurped to
themselves the whole of the functions of government,
which the absence of Nau Nihal Singh enabled them
to do with little difficulty. The army was assembled,
and a litter, said to contain the dying Maharaja, was
carried along the extended line. Dhian Singh was
assiduous in his mournful attentions; he seemed to take
orders as if from his departing sovereign, and from
time to time, during the solemn procession, he made
known that Ranjit Singh declared the Prince Kharak
Singh his successor, and himself, Dhian Singh, the
wazir or minister of the kingdom.[1] The soldiery
acquiesced in silence, and the British Government was
perhaps more sincere than the Sikh people in the congratulations offered, agreeably to custom, to the new
and unworthy master of the Punjab.

The artifices
of Dhian
Singh to
bring about
the quiet
succession
of Karak
Singh.

infantry. Mr. Masson (*Journeys*. i. 430) gives the same
revenue; but fixes the army at 70,000 men, of whom 20,000
were disciplined. This may be assumed as an estimate of 1838,
when Mr. Masson returned from Kabul. In 1845, Lieut.-Col.
Steinbach (*Punjab*, p. 58) states the army to have amounted
to 110,000 men, of whom 70,000 were regulars. The returns
procured for Government in 1844, and which cannot be far
wrong, show that there were upwards of 40,000 regularly
drilled infantry, and a force of about 125,000 men in all,
maintained with about 375 guns or field carriages. Cf. the
*Calcutta Review*, iii. 176; Dr. Macgregor, *Sikhs*, ii. 86, and
Major Smith, *Reigning Family of Lahore*, appendices,
p. xxxvii, for estimates, · correct in some particulars, and
moderate in others.
   For a statement of the Lahore revenues, see Appendix
XXXVIII; and for a list of the Lahore army, see Appendix
XXXIX.
   Many descriptions of Ranjit Singh's person and manners
have been written, of which the fullest is perhaps
that in Prinsep's edition of Murray, *Life*, p. 187, &c.; while
Capt. Osborne's *Court and Camp*, and Col. Lawrence's
*Adventurer in the Punjab,* contain many illustrative touches
and anecdotes. The only good likeness of the Maharaja which
has been published is that taken by the Hon. Miss Eden; and
it, especially in the original drawing, is true and expressive.
Ranjit Singh was of small stature. When young he was dexterous in all manly exercises, but in his old age he became
weak and inclined to corpulency. He lost an eye when a child
by the small-pox, and the most marked characteristic of his
mental powers was a broad and massive forehead, which the
ordinary portraits do not show.
   [1] Mr. Clerk's memorandum of 1842 for Lord Ellenborough.

# CHAPTER VIII

## FROM THE DEATH OF MAHARAJA RANJIT SINGH TO THE DEATH OF WAZIR JAWAHIR SINGH

### 1839—45

Kharak Singh's power usurped by his son Nau Nihal Singh—Lieut.-Col. Wade and Mr. Clerk—Nau Nihal Singh and the Rajas of Jammu—The death of Kharak Singh—The death of Nau Nihal Singh—Sher Singh proclaimed Maharaja, but the authority of sovereign assumed by the mother of Nau Nihal Singh—Sher Singh gains over the troops and succeeds to power—The army assumes a voice in affairs, and becomes an organized political body—The English willing to interfere—The English undervalue the Sikhs—The Sikhs in Tibet:—opposed by the Chinese, and restrained by the English—The English in Kabul—General Pollock's campaign—The Sindhianwala and Jammu families—The death of Sher Singh—The death of Raja Dhian Singh—Dalip Singh proclaimed Maharaja with Hira Singh as Wazir—Unsuccessful insurrections—Pandit Jall's proceedings and views—Hira Singh expelled and slain—Jawahir Singh nominated Wazir—Gulab Singh submits — Pishaura Singh in rebellion — Jawahir Singh put to death by the army.

1839.

Sher Singh claims the succession, June-July 1839; but Nau Nihal Singh assumes all real power, and temporarily allies himself with the Jammu Rajas.

THE imbecile Kharak Singh was acknowledged as the master of the Punjab; but Sher Singh, the reputed son of the deceased king, at once urged *his* superior claims or merits on the attention of the British viceroy; [1] and Nau Nihal Singh, the real offspring of the titular sovereign, hastened from Peshawar to take upon himself the duties of ruler. The prince, a youth of eighteen, was in his heart opposed to the proclaimed minister and the Rajas of Jammu; but the ascendancy of one Chet Singh over the weak mind of the Maharaja, and Kharak Singh s own desire of resting upon the influence of the British agent, induced the two parties to coalesce, first for the destruction of the minion, and

[1] Government to Mr. Clerk, 12th July 1839. Mr. Clerk, who was acting for Col. Wade while absent at Peshawar, seems to have detained Sher Singh's messenger, and to have sent his letter to the Governor-General somewhat in that ordinary spirit of Indian correspondence, which 'transmits' everything 'for information and for such orders as may seem necessary'. Lord Auckland hastily desired Sher Singh to be told Kharak Singh was his master.

afterwards for the removal of Col. Wade. That officer 1839. had stood high with Ranjit Singh as a liberal construer of Sikh rights, or as one who would carefully show how a collision with the English was to be avoided; he had steadily refused to make Dhian Singh the medium of his communications with the old Maharaja; he had offended the heir-apparent by unceremoniously accusing him of machinations with Afghan chiefs; and in the eyes of the Sikhs he was pledged to Kharak Singh at all hazards, by the prominent part he had taken in the meeting at Rupar before noticed. His presence was thus disliked, and his interference dreaded, by men not inclined to wholly yield themselves to English counsels, and yet accustomed to see the suggestions of the Governor-General regularly carried into effect by the sovereign of Lahore.

The privacy of the Maharaja's household was The favou-rudely violated by the prince and minister at daybreak rite, Chet on the 8th of October 1839, and Chet Singh was awak- Singh, put ened from his slumbers to be put to death, within a 8th Oct. few paces of his terrified master.[1] The removal of Col. 1839. Wade was mixed up with the passage of British troops across the Punjab, and had to be effected in another manner.

The Governor-General had designed that the Mr. Clerk Anglo-Indian army which accompanied Shah Shuja succeeds Lieut.-Col. should return by way of Peshawar, instead of retracing Wade as its steps through the Bolan Pass; and when his lord- Agent, ship visited Ranjit Singh at Lahore, the proposition 1st April. was verbally conceded, although not definitively set- 1840. tled by an interchange of letters.[2] In September 1839, Mr. Clerk was sent on a mission of condolence and con-gratulation to the new Maharaja, and to finally arrange about the return of Lord Keane with the stormers of Ghazni.[3] The prince and minister were each conscious

[1] Gulab Singh was perhaps the most prominent and resolute actor in this tragedy, although his brother and Nau Nihal Singh were both present. Col. Wade was desired to express to the Lahore Court the regret of the British Govern-ment that such a scene of violence should have occurred (Government to Col. Wade, 28th Oct. 1839); and similarly Mr. Clerk had been directed to explain to Kharak Singh the disapprobation with which the English viewed the practice of sati, with reference to what had taken place at his father's funeral. (Government to Mr. Clerk, 20th Aug. 1839.) [For a detailed account of this sati the reader is referred to Latif, History of the Punjab, pp. 492-6—Ed.].

[2] Government to Mr. Clerk, 20th Aug. 1839.

[3] [Kandahar had been entered by the English and. Shah Shuja proclaimed Amir on May 8th, 1839. Ghazni was stormed in July. Kabul was entered in August, and it was then arranged

of their mutual enmity and secret design of grasping supremacy, but they were even more averse to the presence of a British army in the heart of the Punjab than to one hovering on a distant frontier. It might be used to take part with one or other claimant, or it might be turned against both in favour of the contemned Kharak Singh : but the passage of the troops could not be wholly refused, and they therefore urged a march by the difficult route of Dera Ismail Khan, and they succeeded in fixing upon a line which prudently avoided the capital, and also in obtaining a premature assurance that an English force should not again march through the Sikh country.[1] The chiefs were pleased with the new English negotiator, as all have ever been with that prompt and approved functionary. Something is always expected from a change, and when a return mission was deputed to Simla, it was whispered that Col. Wade had made himself personally objectionable to those who exercised sway at Lahore; and the complaint was repeated to Lord Keane, when he quitted his army for a few days to visit the Maharaja.[2] In the month of November (1839), Col. Wade was himself at the Sikh metropolis on his way from Kabul, but Kharak Singh was kept at a distance on pretence of devotional observances, lest he should throw himself on the protection of one believed to be ill-disposed towards those who sought his life, or his virtual relinquishment of power.[3]

The relief of the British troops in Kabul.

A portion of the British army of invasion had eventually to be left in Afghanistan, as it was thought that Shah Shuja could not maintain himself without support. The wants of regular forces are manifold, that the bulk of the army should return to India, leaving an army of occupation to maintain Shah Shuja upon his throne. —Ed.]

[1] Mr. Clerk to Government, 14th Sept. 1839. The Governor-General was not satisfied that a kind of pledge had been given that British troops should not again cross the Punjab. (Government to Mr. Clerk, 14th Oct. 1839.)

[2] See, particularly, Government to Col. Wade, 29th Jan. 1840, and Col. Wade to Government, 1st April 1840.

[3] Cf. Munshi Shahamat Ali, *Sikhs and Afghans*, p. 543, &c., and some remarks in a note, p. 545, about the English policy generally towards Kharak Singh, which note may safely be held to be Col. Wade's own. Doubtless had Col. Wade continued to enjoy the complete confidence or support of the Governor-General, the subsequent history of the Punjab would have been different from, if not better than, that which all have witnessed. So much may the British representative effect at an Indian court, without directly interfering, provided he is at once, firm, judicious, and well-informed.

and a supply of stores and ammunition had to be col-  1840.
lected for transmission to Kabul on Col. Wade's
resumption of his duties at Ludhiana, towards the end
of 1839. It was desired to send a regiment of Sepoys
as a guard with the convoy, but the Sikh minister and
heir apparent urged that such could not be done under
the terms of the agreement concluded a few months
previously. Their aversion to their old English representative was mixed up with the general objection to
making their country a common highway for foreign
armies, and they thus ventured to offer obstructions to
the speedy equipment of the isolated British forces,
mainly with the view of discrediting Col. Wade. The
Governor-General was justly impressed with the
necessity of keeping open the straight road to Kabul,
and he yielded to the wishes of the Lahore factions
and removed his agent, but not before Dhian Singh
and the prince had despaired of effecting their object,
and had allowed the convoy bristling with bayonets,
to proceed on its way.[1] In the beginning of April 1840,
Mr. Clerk succeeded to the charge of the British relations with the Punjab; and, independent of his general
qualifications, he was the person best suited to the
requirements of the time; for the very reason which
rendered the agency of Col. Wade invaluable when it
was desired to preserve Sind and to invade Afghanistan, now rendered that of Mr. Clerk equally beneficial
to the indeterminate policy of the English in India.
Both officers had the confidence of the *de facto* Sikh
rulers of the time, and all their recommendations were
held to be given in a spirit of goodwill towards the
Government of the Punjab, as well as in obedience to
the dictates of British interests.

The Sikh prince and the English viceroy had thus  English ne-
each accomplished the objects of the moment. On the  gotiations
one hand, the Maharaja was overawed by the vigour  about trade.
and success of his aspiring son, and, on the other, the
Punjab was freely opened to the passage of British
troops, in support of a policy which connected the west
of Europe with the south of Asia by an unbroken chain
of alliances. The attention of each party was next
turned to other matters of near concern, and the English recurred to their favourite scheme of navigating
the Indus, and of forming an entrepot on that river,

[1] The Governor-General was about to proceed to Calcutta,
which made him the more desirous of having an agent on the
frontier, at once approved of by himself and agreeable to the
Sikhs, i.e. to the influential parties for the time being at
Lahore. (Government to Col. Wade, 29th Jan. 1840.)

which should at once become the centre of a vast traffic.[1] The treaty of 1834 had placed a toll on boats which used the channels of the Indus and Sutlej, and in 1839 the Sikhs deferred to the changing views of their allies, and put the duty on the goods themselves, according to an assumed *ad valorem* scale, instead of on the containing vessels.[2] This scheme inevitably gave rise to a system of search and detention, and in June 1840 the tolls upon the *boats* were again reimposed, but at reduced rates, and with the omission of such as contained grain, wood, and limestone.[3] B t in spite of every government endeavour, and of the adventitious aid of large consuming armies, the expectation of creating an active and valuable commerce by the Indus has not yet been fulfilled; partly because Sind and Afghanistan are, in truth, unproductive countries on the whole, and are inhabited by half-savage races, with few wants and scanty means; and partly because a large capital has for ages been embarked in the land trade which connects the north of India with the south, which traverses the old principalities of Rajputana and the fertile plains of Malwa, and which gives a livelihood to the owners of numerous herds of camels and black cattle. To change the established economy of prudent merchants must be the work of time in a country long subject to political commotion, and the idea of forming an emporium by proclamation savours more of Eastern vanity than of English sense and soberness.[4]

[1] Government to Mr. Clerk, 4th May 1840. The establishment of a great entrepot of trade was a main feature of the scheme for opening the navigation of the Indus. (Government to Capt. Wade, 5th Sept. 1836.)

[2] Mr. Clerk to Government, 19th May and 18th Sept. 1839, and Government to Mr. Clerk, 20th Aug. 1839. For the agreement itself, see Appendix XXXI.

[3] Mr. Clerk to Government, 5th May and 15th July 1840. For the agreement itself, see Appendix XXXII. Subsequently, idle discussions occasionally arose with local authorities, as to whether lime was included under limestone, whether bamboos were wood, and whether rice was comprehended under the technical term 'grain', which it is not in India. Similarly the limited meaning of 'corn' in England has, perhaps, given rise to the modern phrase 'bread-stuffs'.

[4] Nevertheless the experiment was repeated in 1846, on the annexation of the Jullundur Doab, when it was hoped, but equally in vain, that Hoshiarpur might suddenly become a centre of exchange. Every part of India bears various marks of the unrealized hopes of sanguine individuals with reference to the expected benefits of English sway, which diffuses, indeed, some moral as well as material blessings, but which must effect its work by slow and laborious means.

Nau Nihal Singh's great aim to destroy, or to reduce to insignificance, the potent Rajas of Jammu, who wished to engross the whole power of the state, and who jointly held Ladakh and the hill principalities between the Ravi and Jhelum in fief, besides numerous estates in various parts of the Punjab. He took advantage of the repeated dilatoriness of the Mandi and other Rajput chiefs around Kangra in paying their stipulated tribute, to move a large force into the eastern hills, and the resistance his troops experienced amid mountain fastnesses seemed fully to justify the continuous dispatch of reinforcements. His design was, to place a considerable army immediately to the north-east of Jammu, to be ready to co-operate with the troops which could reach that place in a few marches from Lahore. The commanders chosen were the skilful General Ventura and the ardent young chief Ajit Singh Sindhianwala, neither of whom bore goodwill towards Raja Dhian Singh.[1] The plans of the youthful prince thus seemed in every way well devised for placing the rajas in his grasp, but his attention was distracted by disputes with the English authorities about the limits of the expanding dominion of Lahore and of the restored empire of Kabul, and by a direct accusation not only of encouraging turbulent refugees from Shah Shuja's power, but of giving friendly assurances to Dost Muhammad Khan, who was then preparing for that inroad which fluttered the English authorities in Khorasan, and yet paved the way for the surrender of their dreaded enemy. Shah Shuja claimed all places not specified in the treaty, or not directly held by Lahore; nor can it be denied that the English functionaries about the Shah were disposed to consider old Durrani claims as more valid than the new rights of Sikh conquerors; and thus the *province* of Peshawar, which the Punjab Government further maintained to have been ceded in form by the Shah separately in 1834, as well as by the treaty of 1838, was proposed to be reduced to strips of land along the banks of its dividing river.[2] Intercepted papers were produced, bearing the seals of Nau Nihal Singh, and promising pecuniary aid to Dost Muhammad; but the charge of treachery was calmly repelled. the seals were alleged to be forgeries, and the British agent for the Punjab admitted that it was not the character of the free and confident Sikhs to resort to secret and traitorous cor-

1843.

Nau Nihal Singh's schemes against the Rajas of Jammu.

Interrupted by discussions with the English about Afghanistan.

[1] Cf. Mr. Clerk to Government, 6th Sept. 1840.
[2] See particularly Sir William Macnagthen to Government, 28th Feb. and 12th March 1840.

1840.

respondence.[1] The Barakzai chief, Sultan Muhammad Khan, was, however, made to lead as prisoners to Ludhiana the Ghilzai rebels who had sought an asylum in his fief of Kohat, near Peshawar, and whose near presence disturbed the antagonistic rule of the arbitrary Shah and his moderate English allies.[2]

Nau Nihal Singh thus seemed to have overcome the danger which threatened him on the side of England, and to be on the eve of reducing the overgrown power of his grandfather's favourites. At the same time the end of the Maharaja's life was evidently approaching; and although his decline was credibly declared to have been hastened by drugs as well as by unfilial harshness, there were none who cared for a ruler so feeble and unworthy. Karak Singh at last died on the 5th November 1840, prematurely old and care-worn, at the age of thirty-eight, and Nau Nihal Singh became a king in name as well as in power; but the same day dazzled him with a crown and deprived him of life. He had performed the last rites at the funeral pyre of his father, and he was passing under a covered gateway with the eldest son of Gulab Singh by his side, when a portion of the structure fell, and killed the minister's nephew on the spot, and so seriously injured the prince that he became senseless at the time, and expired during the night. It is not positively known that the Rajas of Jammu thus designed to remove Nau Nihal Singh; but it is difficult to acquit them of the crime, and it is certain that they were capable of committing it. Self-defence is the only palliation, for it is equally certain that the prince was compassing their degradation, and, perhaps, their destruction.[3] Nau Nihal Singh was killed in his twentieth

*Death of Maharaja Kharak Singh, 5th Nov. 1840.*

*Death of the Prince Nau Nihal Singh, 5th Nov. 1840.*

[1] Government to Mr. Clerk, 1st Oct. 1840, and Mr. Clerk to Government, 9th Dec. 1840. Cf., however, Col. Steinbach (*Punjab*, p. 23), who states that the prince was rousing Nepal as well as Kabul to aid him in expelling the English; forgetful that Nau Nihal Singh's first object was to make himself master of the Punjab by destroying the Jammu Rajas.

[2] Government to Mr. Clerk, 12th Oct., and Mr. Clerk to Government, 14th May, 10th Sept., and 24th Oct. 1840.

[3] Cf. Mr. Clerk to Government, 6th, 7th, and 10th Nov. 1840, who, further, in his memorandum of 1842, drawn up for Lord Ellenborough, mentions Gen. Ventura's opinion that the fall of the gateway was accidental. Lieut.-Col. Steinbach, *Punjab* (p. 24), and Major Smith, *Reigning Family of Lahore* (p. 35, &c.) may be quoted as giving some particulars, the latter on the authority of an eye-witness, a European adventurer, known as Capt. Gardner, who was present a part of the time, and whose testimony is unfavourable to Raja Dhian Singh. [The scene of this tragedy was the gateway in the fort

year; he promised to be an able and vigorous ruler; 1840.
and had his life been spared, and had not English policy
partly forestalled him, he would have found an ample
field for his ambition in Sind, in Afghanistan, and
beyond the Hindu Kush; and he might, perhaps, at last
have boasted that the inroads of Mahmud and of
Taimur had been fully avenged by the aroused peasants
of India.

The good-natured voluptuary, Sher Singh, was Sher Singh
regarded by the Sikh minister and by the British agent proclaimed
as the only person who could succeed to the sovereignty sovereign;
of the Punjab; and as he was absent from Lahore when
the Maharaja died and his son was killed, Dhian Singh
concealed the latter circumstance as long as possible,
to give Sher Singh time to collect his immediate
friends; and the English representative urged him by
message to maintain good order along the frontier, as
men's minds were likely to be excited by what had
taken place.[1]   But Sher Singh's paternity was more
than doubtful; he possessed no commanding and few
popular qualities; the Rajas of Jammu were odious to
the majority of the Sikh chiefs; and thus Chand Kaur, but Chand
the widow of Kharak Singh, and the mother of the Kaur, the
slain prince, assumed to herself the functions of regent widow of
or ruler, somewhat unexpectedly indeed, but still Kharak
unopposed at the moment by those whom she had sur- assumes
prised.   She was supported by several men of reputa- power, and
tion, but mainly by the Sindhianwala family, which Sher Singh
traced to a near and common ancestor with Ranjit retires.
Singh.   The lady herself talked of adding to the claims
of the youthful Hira Singh, by adopting him, as he
had really, if not formally, been adopted by the old
Maharaja.   She further distracted the factions by declaring that her daughter-in-law was pregnant; and
one party tried to gain her over by suggesting a
marriage with Sher Singh, an alliance which she spur-
ned, and the other more reasonably proposed Atar Singh
Sindhianwala as a suitable partner, for she might have
taken an honoured station in his household agreeably
to the latitude of village custom in the north-west of
India.   But the widow of the Maharaja loudly asserted
her own right to supreme power, and after a few weeks
the government was stated to be composed, 1st, of the
'Mai', or 'Mother', pre-eminently as sovereign, or as

at Lahore facing the Hazuri Bagh and the Badshahi Musjid.
It is now closed, but may be easily recognised by its prominent
towers.—ED.]

[1] Cf. Mr. Clerk to Government, 7th Nov. 1840, and also
Mr Clerk's Memorandum of 1842.

regent for the expected offspring of Nau Nihal Singh;
2nd, of Sher Singh as vicegerent, or ·as president of
the council of state; and, 3rd, of Dhian Singh as wazir,
or executive minister.  The compromise was a mere
temporary expedient, and Dhian Singh and Sher Singh
soon afterwards began to absent themselves for varying periods from Lahore : the one partly in the hope
that the mass of business which had arisen with the
English, and with which he was familiar, would show
to all that his aid was essential to the government; and
the other, or indeed both of them, to silently take
measures for gaining over the army with promises of
donatives and increased pay, so that force might be
resorted to at a fitting time.  But the scorn with which
Sher Singh's hereditary claim was treated made the
minister doubtful whether a more suitable instrument
might not be necessary, and the English authorities
were accordingly reminded of what perhaps they had
never known, viz. that Rani Jindan, a favourite wife
or concubine of Ranjit Singh, had borne to him a son
named Dalip, a few months before the conferences took
place about reseating Shah Shuja on the throne of
Kabul.[1]

The British viceroy did not acknowledge Mai
Chand Kaur as the undoubted successor of her husband and son, or as the sovereign of the country; but
he treated her government as one *de facto*, so far as
to carry on business as usual through the accredited
agents of either power.  The Governor-General's
anxiety for the preservation of order in the Punjab
was nevertheless considerable; and it was increased by
the state of affairs in Afghanistan, for the attempts of
Dost Muhammad and the resolution of meeting him
with English means alone, rendered the dispatch of
additional troops necessary, and before Kharak Singh's
death three thousand men had reached Ferozepore on
their way to Kabul.[2]  The progress of this strong brigade was not delayed by the contentions at Lahore; it
pursued its march without interruption, and on its
arrival at Peshawar it found Dost Muhammad a prisoner instead of a victor.  The ex-Amir journeyed
through the Punjab escorted by a relieved brigade;
and although Sher Singh was then laying siege to the

Dalip Singh's
birth and
pretensions
made known.

The English
remain
neutral at
the time.

Dost
Muhammad
Khan at-
tempts
Kabul, but
eventually
surrenders
to the
English.

[1] Cf. Mr. Clerk to Government, of dates between the 10th
Nov. 1840, and 2nd Jan. 1841, inclusive, particularly of the 11th
and 24th Nov. and 11th Dec., besides those specified. It seems
almost certain that the existence of the boy Dalip was not
before known to the British authorities.

[2] Government to Mr. Clerk, 1st and 2nd Nov. 1840, and
other letters to and from that functionary.

citadel of Lahore, the original prudence of fixing a 1840.
route for British troops clear of the Sikh capital, and
the complete subjugation of the Muhammadan tribes,
left the English commander unaware of the struggle
going on, except from ordinary reports and news-
writers.[1]

The English Government made, indeed, no de- Sher Singh
claration with regard to the Lahore succession; but it gains over
was believed by all that Sher Singh was looked upon with Dhian
as the proper representative of the kingdom, and the Singh's aid.
advisers of Mai Chand Kaur soon found that they could
not withstand the specious claims of the prince, and
the commanding influence of the British name, without
throwing themselves wholly on the support of Raja
Dhian Singh.  That chief was at one time not unwilling
to be the sole minister of the Maharani, and the more
sagacious Gulab Singh saw advantages to his family
amid the complex modes necessary in a female rule,
which might not attend the direct sway of a prince of
average understanding, inclined to favouritism, and
pledged to Sikh principles.  But the Mai's councillors
would not consent to be thrown wholly into the shade,
and Dhian Singh thus kept aloof, and secretly assured
Sher Singh of his support at a fitting time.  The prince,
on his part, endeavoured to sound the English agent
as to his eventual recognition, and he was satisfied with
the reply, although he merely received an assurance
that the allies of thirty-two years wished to see a strong
government in the Punjab.[2]

Sher Singh had, with the minister's aid, gained Sher Singh
over some divisions of the army, and he believed that attacks
all would declare for him if he boldly put himself at Lahore,
their head.  The eagerness of the prince, or of his im- 14th-18th
mediate followers, somewhat precipitated measures; Jan. 1841.
and when he suddenly appeared at Lahore, on the
14th January 1841, he found that Dhian Singh had not
arrived from Jammu, and that Gulab Singh would
rather fight for the Maharani, the acknowledged head
of the state, than tamely become a party on compul-
sion to his ill-arranged schemes.  But Sher Singh was
no longer his own master, and the impetuous soldiery
at once proceeded to breach the citadel.  Gulab Singh

---

[1] The returning brigade was commanded by the veteran
Col. Wheeler [afterwards Sir Hugh Wheeler, the ill-fated
commander of the garrison of Cawnpore—Ed.], whose name is
familiar to the public in connexion both with Afghan and
Sikh wars.

[2] See Mr. Clerk's letters to Government of Dec. 1840 and
Jan. 1841, generally, particularly that of the 9th Jan.

Chand Kaur
yields, and
Sher Singh
proclaimed
Maharaja.

The Sind-
hianwala
family.

The army
becomes
uncontrol-
lable.

Sher Singh
alarmed.

in vain urged some delay, or a suspension of hostilities; but on the 18th January Dhian Singh and most of the principal chiefs had arrived and ranged themselves on one side or the other. A compromise took place; the Mai was outwardly treated with every honour, and large estates were conferred upon her; but Sher Singh was proclaimed Maharaja of the Punjab, Dhian Singh was declared once more to be wazir of the state, and the pay of the soldiery was permanently raised by one rupee *per mensem*. The Sindhianwalas felt that they must be obnoxious to the new ruler; and Atar Singh and Ajit Singh took early measures to effect their escape from the capital, and eventually into the British territories; but Lehna Singh, the other principal member, remained with the division of the army which he commanded in the hills of Kulu and Mandi.[1]

Sher Singh had induced the troops of the state to make him a king, but he was unable to command them as soldiers, or to sway them as men, and they took advantage of his incapacity and of their own strength to wreak their vengeance upon various officers who had offended them, and upon various regimental accountants and muster-masters who may have defrauded them of their pay. Some houses were plundered, and several individuals were seized and slain. A few Europeans had likewise rendered themselves obnoxious; and General Court, a moderate and high-minded man, had to fly for his life, and a brave young Englishman named Foulkes was cruelly put to death. Nor was this spirit of violence confined to the troops at the capital, or to those in the eastern hills, but it spread to Kashmir and Peshawar; and in the former place Mian Singh, the governor, was killed by the soldiery; and in the latter, General Avitabile was so hard pressed that he was ready to abandon his post and to seek safety in Jalalabad.[2] It was believed at the time, that the army would not rest satisfied with avenging what it considered its own injuries; it was thought it might proceed to a general plunder or confiscation of property; the population of either side of the Sutlej was prepared for an extensive commotion, and the wealthy merchants of Amritsar prophesied the pillage of their warehouses, and were clamorous for British protection. Sher Singh shrank within himself appalled, and he seemed timorously to resort to the English agent for support against

[1] See Mr. Clerk's letters, of dates from 17th to 30th Jan. 1841.
[2] Cf. Mr. Clerk to Government, 26th Jan., 8th and 14th Feb., 28th April, and 30th May 1841.

the fierce spirit he had roused and could not control; or he doubtfully endeavoured to learn whether such disorders would be held equally to end his reign and the British alliance. The English watched the confusion with much interest and some anxiety, and when cities seemed about to be plundered, and provinces ravaged, the question of the duty of a civilized and powerful neighbour naturally suggested itself, and was answered by a cry for interference, but the shapes which the wish took were various and contradictory. Nevertheless, the natural desire for aggrandizement, added to the apparently disorganized state of the army, contributed to strengthen a willing belief in the inferiority of the Sikhs as soldiers, and in the great excellence of the mountain levies of the chiefs of Jammu, who alone seemed to remain the masters of their own servants. To the apprehension of the English authorities, the Sikhs were mere upstart peasants of doubtful courage, except when maddened by religious persecution; but the ancient name of Rajput was sufficient to invest the motley followers of a few valiant chiefs with every warlike quality. This erroneous estimate of the Sikhs tainted British counsels until the day of P'heerooshuhur.[1]

1841.

The English anxious about the general tranquillity.

undervalue the Sikhs,

The English seemed thus called upon to do something, and their agent in Kabul, who was committed to make Shah Shuja a monarch in means as well as in rank, grasped at the death of Ranjit Singh's last representative; he pronounced the treaties with Lahore to be at an end, and he wanted to annex Peshawar to the Afghan sway. The British Government in Calcutta rebuked this hasty conclusion, but cheered itself with the prospect of eventually adding the Derajat of the Indus, as well as Peshawar, to the unproductive Durrani kingdom, without any breach of faith towards the Sikhs; for it was considered that their dominions might soon be rent in two by the Sindhianwala Sirdars and the

and are ready to interfere by force of arms, Feb. 1841.

---

[1] This erroneous estimate of the troops of the Jammu Rajas and other hill chiefs of the Punjab relatively to the Sikhs, may be seen insisted on in Mr. Clerk's letters to Government of the 2nd Jan. and 13th April 1841, and especially in those of the 8th and 10th Dec. of that year, and of the 15th Jan., 10th Feb., and 23rd April, 1842. Mr. Clerk's expressions are very decided, such as that the Sikhs feared the hill-men, who were braver, and that Rajputs might hold Afghans in check, which Sikhs could not do; but he seems to have forgotten that the ancient Rajputs had, during the century gone by, yielded on either side to the new and aspiring Gurkhas and Marathas, and even that the Sikhs themselves had laid the twice-born princes of the Himalayas under contribution from the Ganges to Kashmir.

Jammu Rajas.[1]  The British agent on the Sutlej did
not think the Lahore empire so near its dissolution in
that mode, and confident in his own dexterity, in the
superiority of his troops, and in the greatness of the
English name, he proposed to march to the Sikh capital with 12,000 men, to beat and disperse a rebel army
four times more numerous, to restore order, to strengthen the sovereignty of Sher Singh, and take the cis-
Sutlej districts and forty lakhs of rupees in coin as the
price of his aid.[2]  This promptitude made the Maharaja
think himself in danger of his life at the hands of his
subjects, and of his kingdom at the hands of his allies;[3]
nor was the Governor-General prepared for a virtual
invasion, although he was ready to use force if a large
majority of the Sikhs as well as the Maharaja himself

*The mili-
tary dis-
orders sub-
side, but
the people
become
suspicious
of the
English.*

desired such intervention.[4]  After this, the disorders
in the army near Lahore gradually subsided; but the
opinion got abroad that overtures had been made to
the eager English; and so far were the Sikh soldiery
from desiring foreign assistance, that Lehna Singh
Sindhianwala was imprisoned by his own men, in the
Mandi hills, on a charge of conspiracy with his refugee
brother to introduce the supremacy of strangers.[5]

*Major
Broadfoot's
passage
across the
Punjab.*

The suspicions and hatred of the Sikhs were further roused by the proceedings of an officer, afterwards
nominated to represent British friendship and moderation.  Major Broadfoot had been appointed to recruit
a corps of Sappers and Miners for the service of Shah
Shuja, and as the family of that sovereign, and also
the blind Shah Zaman with his wives and children,
were about to proceed to Kabul, he was charged with
the care of the large and motley convoy. He entered the

---

[1] See especially Government to Sir William Macnaghten,
of 28th Dec. 1840, in reply to his proposals of the 26th Nov.
The Governor-General justly observed that the treaty was not
formed with an individual chief, but with the Sikh state, so
long as it might last and fulfil the obligations of its alliance.

[2] Mr. Clerk to Government, of the 26th March 1841.

[3] When Sher Singh became aware of Mr. Clerk's propositions, he is said simply to have drawn his finger across his
throat, meaning that the Sikhs would at once take his life
if he assented to such measures. The readiness of the English
to co-operate was first propounded to Fakir Aziz-ud-din, and
that wary negotiator said the matter could not be trusted to
paper; he would himself go and tell Sher Singh of it. He went,
but he did not return, his object being to keep clear of schemes
so hazardous.

[4] Government to Mr. Clerk, 18th Feb. and 29th March
-1841. The Governor-General truly remarked that Mr. Clerk,
rather than the Maharaja, had proposed an armed interference.

[5] Mr. Clerk to Government, 25th March 1841.

Punjab in April 1841, when the mutinous spirit of the 1841 Sikh army was spreading from the capital to the provinces. A body of mixed or Muhammadan troops had been directed by the Lahore Government to accompany the royal families as an escort of protection, but Major Broadfoot became suspicious of the good faith of this detachment, and on the banks of the Ravi he prepared to resist, with his newly recruited regiment, an attack on the part of those who had been sent to conduct him in safety. On his way to the Indus he was even more suspicious of other bodies of troops which he met or passed; he believed them to be intent on plundering his camp, and he considered that he only avoided collisions by dexterous negotiations and by timely demonstrations of force. On crossing the river at Attock, his persuasion of the hostile designs of the battalions in that neighbourhood and towards Peshawar was so strong, that he put his camp in a complete state of defence, broke up the bridge of boats, and called upon the Afghan population to rise and aid him against the troops of their government. But it does not appear that his apprehensions had even a plausible foundation, until at this time he seized certain deputies from a mutinous regiment when on their way back from a conference with their commander, and who appear to have come within the limits of the British pickets. This proceeding alarmed both General Avitabile, the governor of Peshawar, and the British agent at that place; and a brigade, already warned, was hurried from Jalalabad to overawe the Sikh forces encamped near the Indus. But the Shah's families and their numerous followers had passed on unmolested before the auxiliary troops had cleared the Khaibar Pass, and the whole proceeding merely served to irritate and excite the distrust of the Sikhs generally, *The Sikhs* and to give Sher Singh an opportunity of pointing out *further* to his tumultuous soldiers that the Punjab was sur- *irritated* rounded by English armies, both ready and willing to *against the* make war upon them.[1] *English.*

Before the middle of 1841 the more violent pro- *The* ceedings of the Lahore troops had ceased, but the *changed* relation of the army to the state had become wholly *relation of* altered; it was no longer the willing instrument of an *the Lahore* arbitrary and genial government, but it looked upon *army to* itself. and was regarded by others, as the representa- *the state.* tive body of the Sikh people, as the 'Khalsa' itself *Its mili-* assembled by tribes or centuries to take its part in *tary orga-* *nization*

[1] Cf. Mr. Clerk to Government, 25th May and 10th June 1841.

1841.

enables it
to become
the repre-
sentative
body of the
Khalsa.

public affairs. The efficiency of the army as a disciplined force was not much impaired, for a higher
feeling possessed the men, and increased alacrity and
resolution supplied the place of exact training. They
were sensible of the advantages of systematic union,
and they were proud of their armed array as the visible
body of Gobind's commonwealth. As a general rule,
the troops were obedient to their appointed officers, so
far as concerned their ordinary military duties, but
the position of a regiment, of a brigade, of a division,
or of the whole army, relatively to the executive government of the country, was determined by a committee or assemblage of committees, termed a 'Panch' or
'Panchayat', i.e. a jury or committee of five, composed
of men selected from each battalion, or each company,
in consideration of their general character as faithful
*Sikh* soldiers, or from their particular influence in
their native villages.[1] The system of Panchayats is
common throughout India, and every tribe, or section
of a tribe, or trade, or calling, readily submits to the
decisions of its elders or superiors seated together in
consultation. In the Punjab the custom received a
further development from the organization necessary
to an army; and even in the crude form of representation thus achieved, the Sikh people were enabled to
interfere with effect, and with some degree of consistency, in the nomination and in the removal of their
rulers. But these large assemblies sometimes added
military licence to popular tumult, and the corrupt
spirit of mercenaries to the barbarous ignorance of
ploughmen. Their resolutions were often unstable or
unwise, and the representatives of different divisions
might take opposite sides from sober conviction or
self-willed prejudice, or they might be bribed and
cajoled by such able and unscrupulous men as Raja
Gulab Singh.[2]

Negotia-
tions with
the English
about in-
land trade.
1841.

The partial repose in the autumn of 1841 was
taken advantage of to recur to those mercantile objects,
of which the British Government never lost sight.
The facilities of navigating the Indus and Sutlej had

[1] One is strongly reminded of the organization of the
Parliamentary army under Cromwell, with its regimental
'elders', &c.—ED.]

[2] See Mr. Clerk's letter of the 14th March 1841, for Fakir
Aziz-ud-din's admission, that even then the army was united
and ruled by its panchayats. With reference to the Panchayats
of India, it may be observed that Hallam shows, chiefly from
Palgrave, that English juries likewise were originally as much
arbitrators as investigators of facts. *Middle Ages*, Notes to
Chap. VIII.)

been increased, and it was now sought to extend cor- 1841.
responding advantages to the land trade of the Punjab.
Twenty years before, Mr. Moorcroft had, of his own
instance, made proposals to Ranjit Singh for the admission of British goods into the Lahore dominions at
fixed rates of duty.[1]  In 1832, Col. Wade again brought
forward the subject of a general tariff for the Punjab,
and the Maharaja appeared to be not indisposed to
meet the views of his allies; but he really disliked to
make arrangements of which he did not fully see the
scope and tendency, and he thus tried to evade even
a settlement of the river tolls, by saying that the
prosperity of Amritsar would be affected, and by
recurring to that ever ready objection, the slaughter
of kine. Cows, he said, might be used as food by those
who traversed the Punjab under a British guarantee,[2]
In 1840, when Afghanistan was garrisoned by Indian
troops, the Governor-General pressed the subject a
second time on the notice of the Lahore authorities; and after a delay of more than a year, Sher
Singh assented to a reduced scale and to a fixed rate of
duty, and also to levy the whole sum at one place; but
the charges still appeared excessive, and the British
viceroy lamented the ignorance displayed by the Sikh
Maharaja, and the disregard which he evinced for the
true interests of his subjects.[3]

The Lahore Government was convulsed at its Zorawar
centre, but its spirit of progress and aggrandizement Singh. the
was active on the frontiers, where not hemmed in by deputy of
British armies. The deputies in Kashmir had always the Jammu
been jealous of the usurpations of Gulab Singh in Rajas. takes
been jealous of the usurpations of Gulab Singh in Iskardo.
Tibet, but Mian Singh, a rude soldier, the governor of 1840.
the valley during the commotions at Lahore, was
alarmed into concessions by the powerful and ambitious Rajas of Jammu, and he left Iskardo, and the whole
valley of the Upper Indus, a free field for the aggressions of their lieutenants.[4]  Ahmad Shah, the reigning

[1] Moorcroft, *Travels*, i. 103.

[2] Cf. Col. Wade to Government, 7th Nov. and 5th Dec.
1832. These objections are often urged in India, not because
they are felt to be reasonable in themselves, or applicable to
the point at issue, but because religion is always a strong
ground to stand on, and because it is the only thing which the
English do not virtually profess a desire to change. Religion
is thus brought in upon all occasions of apprehension or
disinclination.

[3] Government to Mr. Clerk, 4th May 1840 and 11th Oct.
1841, and Mr. Clerk to Government of 20th Sept. 1841.

[4] Sir Claude Wade (*Narrative of Services*, p. 33, note)
represents the Jammu family to have obtained from the British

chief of Balti, had differences with his family, and he proposed to pass over his eldest son in favour of a younger one, in fixing the succession. The natural heir would seem to have endeavoured to interest the Governor of Kashmir, and also Zorawar Singh, the Jammu deputy in Ladakh, in his favour; and in 1840 he fled from his father and sought refuge and assistance in Leh. Gnodup Tanzin, the puppet king of Ladakh, had conceived the idea of throwing off the Jammu authority; he had been trying to engage Ahmad Shah in the design; the absence of Zorawar Singh was opportune, and he allowed a party of Iskardo troops to march on Leh, and to carry off the son of their chief. Zorawar Singh made this inroad a pretext for war; and before the middle of the year 1840 he was master of Little Tibet, but he left the chiefship in the family of Ahmad Shah, on the payment of a petty yearly tribute of seven thousand rupees, so barren are the rocky principalities between Imaus and Emodus.[1] Zorawar Singh was emboldened by his own success and by the dissensions at Lahore; he claimed fealty from Gilgit; he was understood to be desirous of quarrelling with the Chinese governor of Yarkand; and he renewed antiquated claims of Ladakh supremacy, and demanded the surrender of Rohtak, Garo, and the lakes of Mansarowar, from the priestly king of Lhasa.[2]

Zorawar Singh seizes Garo from the Chinese of Lassa. 1841.

Zorawar Singh was desirous of acquiring territory, and he was also intent on monopolizing the trade in shawl-wool, a considerable branch of which followed the Sutlej and more eastern roads to Ludhiana and Delhi, and added nothing to the treasury of Jammu.[3] In May and June 1841, he occupied the valleys of the Indus and Sutlej, to the sources of those rivers, and he fixed a garrison close to the frontiers of Nepal, and on the opposite side of the snowy range from the British post of Almora. The petty Rajput princes between the Kali and Sutlej suffered in their revenues, and trembled for their territories; the Nepal Govern-

Government an assurance that the limitations put upon Sikh conquests to the west and south by the Tripartite Treaty of 1839 would not be held to apply to the north or Tibetan side, in which direction, it was said, the Sikhs were free to act as they might please.

[1] Cf. Mr. Clerk to Government, 26th April, 9th and 31st May, and 25th Aug. 1840.
[2] Cf. Mr. Clerk to Government, 25th Aug. and 8th Oct. 1840, and 2nd Jan. and 5th June 1841.
[3] Cf. Mr. Clerk to Government, 5th and 22nd June, 1841.

ment had renewed intrigues set on foot in 1838, and 1841.
was in correspondence with the crafty minister of
Lahore, and with the disaffected Sindhianwala chiefs; [1]
and the English Government itself was at war with
China, at the distance of half the earth's circumfer-
ence.[2] It was held that the trade of British Indian subjects must not be interfered with by Jammu conquests
in Chinese Tibet; it was deemed unadvisable to allow
the Lahore and Nepal dominions to march with one
another behind the Himalayas; and it was thought the
Emperor of Pekin might confound independent Sikhs
with the predominant English, and throw additional
difficulties in the way of pending or probable negotiations.[3] It was, therefore, decided that Sher Singh    The English
should require his feudatories to evacuate the Lassa    interfere.
territories; a day, the 10th of December 1841, was fixed
for the surrender of Garo; and a British officer was sent
to see that the Grand Lama's authority was fully re-
established. The Maharaja and his tributaries yielded,
and Zorawar Singh was recalled; but before the order
could reach him, or be acted on, he was surrounded
in the depth of winter, and at a height of twelve

[1] Cf. Mr. Clerk to Government, 16th Aug. and 23rd Nov.
1840, and 17th Jan. 1841; and Government to Mr. Clerk, 19th
Oct. 1840. The correspondence of Nepal with the Sikhs, or
rather with the Jammu faction, doubtless arose in part from
the presence of Matabar Singh, an eminent Gurkha, as a
refugee in the Punjab. He crossed the Sutlej in 1838, and soon
got a high command in the Lahore service, or rather; perhaps,
a high position at the court. His success in this way, and his
necessary correspondence with British functionaries, made the
Nepal Government apprehensive of him, and at last he became
so important in the eyes of the English themselves, that in 1840,
when differences with Katmandu seemed likely to lead to
hostilities, overtures were virtually made to him, and he was
kept in hand, as it were, to be supported as a claimant for
power, or as a partisan leader, should active measures be
necessary. He was thus induced to quit the Punjab, where his
presence, indeed, was not otherwise satisfactory; but the
differences with the Gurkhas were composed, and Matabar
Singh was cast aside with an allowance of a thousand rupees
a month from the potent government which had demeaned
itself by using him as a tool. (Cf. particularly Government to
Mr. Clerk, 4th May and 26th Oct. 1840; and Mr. Clerk to
Government, 22nd Oct. 1840.)
[2] The first China or Opium War ended by the Treaty of
Nankin (1842), which resulted in the cession of Hong Kong
and the opening of the first five treaty ports.—Ed.]
[3] Cf. Government to Mr. Clerk, 16th Aug. and 6th and 20th
Sept. 1841. The Sikhs, too, had their views with regard to
China, and naively proposed co-operation with the English, or
a diversion in Tartary in favour of the war then in progress
on the sea coast! (Mr. Clerk to Government, 18th Aug. and
20th Oct. 1841.)

1841.

The Sikhs defeated by a force from Lassa.

thousand feet or more above the sea, by a superior force from Lassa inured to frost and snow. The men of the Indian plains and southern Himalayas were straitened for fuel—as necessary as food in such a climate and at such a season; some even burnt the stocks of their muskets to warm their hands; and on the day of battle, in the middle of December, they were benumbed in their ranks during a fatal pause; their leader was slain, a few principal men were reserved as prisoners, but the mass was left to perish, huddled in heaps behind rocks, or at the bottoms of ravines. The neighbouring garrison on the Nepal frontier fled on hearing of the defeat; the men were not pursued, but in passing over ranges sixteen thousand feet high, on their way to Almora, the deadly cold reduced them to half their numbers, and left a moiety of the remainder maimed for life.[1]

The Chinese recover Garo.

During the spring of 1842 the victorious Chinese advanced along the Indus, and not only recovered their own province, but occupied Ladakh and laid siege to the citadel of Leh. The Kalmaks and the ancient Sokpos, or Sacae, talked of another invasion of Kashmir, and the Tartars of the Greater and Lesser Tibet were elate with the prospect of revenge and plunder : but troops were poured across the Himalayas; the swordsmen and cannoneers of the south were dreaded by the unwarlike Bhotias; the siege of Leh was raised and in the month of September (1842) Gulab Singh's commander seized the Lassa Wazir by treachery, and dislodged his troops by stratagem from a position between Leh and Rohtak, where they had proposed to await the return of winter. An arrangement was then come to between the Lassa and Lahore authorities, which placed matters on their old footing, agreeably to the desire of the English; and as the shawl-wool trade to the British provinces was also revived, no further intervention was considered necessary between the jealous Chinese and the restrained Sikhs.[2]

Peace between the Chinese and Sikhs.

[1] In this rapid sketch of Ladakh affairs, the author has necessarily depended for the most part on his own personal knowledge. After the battle on the Mansarowar Lake, the western passes remained closed for five weeks, and the defeat of the Sikhs was thus made known in Calcutta and Peshawar, through the reports of the fugitives to Almora, before it was heard of in the neighbouring Garo. From the observations of Lieut. H. Strachey it would appear that the height of the Mansarowar Lake is 15,250 feet. (*Jour. As. Soc.*, Bengal, Aug. 1848, p. 155.)

[2] At Amritsar in March 1846. when Gulab Singh was formally inaugurated as Maharaja of Jammu, he exhibited

When, in April 1841, the troops in Kashmir put their governor to death, Raja Gulab Singh was sent to restore order, and to place the authority of the new manager, Ghulam Muhi-ud-din, on a firm footing. The mutinous regiments were overpowered by numbers and punished with severity, and it was soon apparent that Gulab Singh had made the governor whom he was aiding a creature of his own, and had become the virtual master of the valley.[1] Neither the minister nor his brother had ever been thought well pleased with English interference in the affairs of the Punjab; they were at the time in suspicious communication with Nepal; and they were held to be bound to Sultan Muhammad Khan, whose real or presumed intrigues with the enemies of Shah Shuja had occasioned his removal to Lahore a year previously.[2] General Avitabile had become more and more urgent to be relieved from his dangerous post at Peshawar; the influence of Dhian Singh was predominant in Sikh counsels; and the English opinion of the ability of the Jammu Rajas and of the excellence of their troops was well known, and induced a belief in partiality to be presumed.[3] It was therefore proposed by Sher Singh to bestow the Afghan province on the restorer of order in Kashmir. But this arrangement would have placed the hills from the neighbourhood of Kangra to the Kaibar Pass in the hands of men averse to the English and hostile to Shah Shuja; and as their troublesome ambition had been checked in Tibet, so it was resolved that their more dangerous establishment on the Kabul river should be prevented. In the autumn of 1841, therefore,

*1841*

*The ambitious views of the Jammu Rajas towards the Indus.*

*Clash with the policy of the English.*

the engagements with the Lama of Lassa, drawn out on his part in yellow, and on the part of the Chinese in red ink, and each impressed with the open hand of the negotiators dipped in either colour instead of a regular seal or written signature. The 'Panja', or *hand*, seems in general use in Asia as typical of a covenant, and it is, moreover, a common emblem on the standards of the eastern Afghans.

[1] Cf. Mr. Clerk to Government, 13th May, 9th July, and 3rd Sept. 1840.

[2] For this presumed understanding between the Jammu Rajas and the Barakzais of Peshawar, Mr. Clerk's letter of the 8th Oct. 1840, may be referred to among others.

[3] Mr. Clerk leant upon and perhaps much overrated Dhian Singh's capacity, 'his military talents, and aptitude for business.' (Mr. Clerk to Government, 7th Nov. 1840, and 13th May 1841.) General Ventura, for instance, considered the Raja to possess a very slender understanding, and in such a matter he may be held to be a fair as well as a competent judge, although personally averse to the minister.

the veto of the English agent was put upon Raja Gulab Singh's nomination to Peshawar.[1]

About two months afterwards, or on the 2nd November (1841), that insurrection broke out in Kabul which forms so painful a passage in British history. No valiant youth arose superior to the fatal influence of military subordination, to render illustrious the retreat of a handful of Englishmen, or, more illustrious still, the successful defence of their position.[2] The brave spirit of Sir William Macnaghten laboured perseveringly, but in vain, against the unworthy fear which possessed the highest officers of the army; and the dismay of the distant commanders imparted some of its poison to the supreme authorities in India, who were weary of the useless and burdensome occupation of Khorasan. The first generous impulse was awed into a desire of annulling the Durrani alliance, and of collecting a force on the Indus, or even so far back as the Sutlej, there to fight for the empire of Hindustan with the torrents of exulting Afghans which the startled imaginations of Englishmen readily conjured up.[3] No confidence was placed in the efficiency or the friendship of the Sikhs;[4] and although their aid was always considered of importance, the mode in which

[1] Government to Mr. Clerk, 2nd Aug., and Mr. Clerk to Government, 20th Aug..1841.

[2] There was no want of gallant and capable men in the subordinate ranks of the army, and it is known that the lamented Major Pottinger recorded his disapprobation of the retreat so fatuously commenced and so fatally ended, although, to give validity to documents, or an appearance of unanimity to counsels, he unfortunately put his name to the orders requiring the surrender of Kandahar and Jalalabad.

[3] Cf. Government to the Commander-in-Chief, 2nd Dec. 1841, and 10th Feb. 1842; Government to Mr. Clerk, 10th Feb. 1842; and Government to General Pollock, 24th Feb. 1842. Of those who recorded their opinions about the policy to be followed at the moment, it may be mentioned that Mr. Robertson, the Lieutenant-Governor of Agra, and Sir Herbert Maddock, the Political Secretary, advised a stand at Peshawar; and that Mr. Prinsep, a member of council, and Mr. Colvin, the Governor-General's private secretary, recommended a withdrawal to the Sutlej. All, however, contemplated ulterior operations.

The Commander-in-Chief, it is well known, thought the means of the *English* for defending India itself somewhat scanty, and Mr. Clerk thought the *Sikhs* would be unable to check the invasion of mountaineers, which would assuredly take place were Jalalabad to fall. (Mr. Clerk to Government, 15th Jan. 1842.)

[4] Government to the Commander-in-Chief, 15th March 1842.

it was asked and used only served to sink the Lahore army lower than before in British estimation.[1]

Four regiments of sepoys marched from Ferozepore without guns, and unsupported by cavalry, to vainly endeavour to force the Pass of Khaibar; and the Sikh troops at Peshawar were urged by the local British authorities in their praiseworthy ardour, rather than deliberately ordered by their own government at the instance of its ally, to co-operate in the attempt, or indeed to march alone to Jalalabad. The fact that the English had been beaten was notorious, and the belief in their alarm was welcome : the Sikh governor was obliged, in the absence of orders, to take the sense of the regimental 'punches' or committees; and the hasty requisition to march was rejected, through fear alone, as the English said, but really with feelings in which contempt, distrust, and apprehension were all mixed. The district Governor-General, Avitabile, who fortunately still retained his province, freely gave what aid he could; some pieces of artillery were furnished as well as abundance of ordinary supplies, and the British detachment effected the relief of Ali Musjid. But the unpardonable neglect of going to the fort without the food which had been provided, obliged the garrison to retreat after a few days, and the disinclination of the Sikhs to fight the battles of strangers communicated itself to the mercenary soldiers of the English, and thus added to the Governor-General's dislike of the Afghan connexion.[2]

*1841.*

*The English distrustful of the Sikhs, but yet urged upon them for aid.*

[1] Mr. Colvin, in the minute referred to in the preceding note, grounds his proposition for withdrawing to the Sutlej partly on Mr. Clerk's low estimate of the Sikhs, and their presumed inability to resist the Afghans. Col. Wade seems to have had a somewhat similar opinion of the comparative prowess of the two races, on the fair presumption that the note (p. 535) of Munshi Shahamat Ali's *Sikhs and Afghans* is his. He says the Sikhs always dreaded the Khaibaris; and, indeed, General Avitabile could also take up the notion with some reason, in one sense, as the magistrate of a district surrounded by marauding highlanders, and with sufficient adroitness in another when he did not desire to see Sikh regiments hurried into mountain defiles at the instance of the English authorities. (Cf. the *Calcutta Review*, No. III, p. 182.)

[2] The statements in this paragraph are mainly taken from the author's notes of official and demi-official correspondence. The letter of Government to Mr. Clerk, of the 7th Feb. 1842, may also be referred to about the failure to hold Ali Musjid; and, further, it may be mentioned that Mr. Clerk, in his letter of the 10th February, pointed out, that although the Sikhs might not willingly co-operate in any sudden assault planned by the English, they would be found ready to give assistance

The necessity of at least relieving the garrison of Jalalabad was paramount, and in the spring of 1842 a well-equipped British force arrived at Peshawar; but the active co-operation of the Sikhs was still desirable, and it was sought for under the terms of an obsolete article of the tripartite treaty with Shah Shuja, which gave Lahore a subsidy of two lakhs of rupees in exchange for the services of 5,000 men.[1] Sher Singh was willing to assist beyond this limited degree; he greatly facilitated the purchase of grain and the hire of carriage cattle in the Punjab, and his auxiliaries could be made to outnumber the troops of his allies; but he felt uneasy about the proceedings of the Sindhianwala chiefs, one of whom had gone to Calcutta to urge his own claims, or those of Mai Chand Kaur, and all of whom retained influence in the Sikh ranks. He was assured that the refugees should not be allowed to disturb his reign, and there thus seemed to be no obstacle in the way of his full co-operation.[2] But the genuine Sikhs were held by the English to be both mutinous in disposition and inferior in warlike spirit; the soldiers of Jammu were preferred, and Gulab Singh was required to proceed to Peshawar to repress the insubordinate 'Khalsa', and to give General Pollock the assurance of efficient aid.[3] The Raja was at the time completing the reduction of some insurgent tribes between Kashmir and Attock, and his heart was in Tibet, where he had himself lost an army and a kingdom. He went, but he knew the temper of his own hill levies : he was naturally unwilling to run any

during the campaign in the ways their experience taught them to be the most likely to lead to success.

[1] See Government to Mr. Clerk, 3rd May and 23rd July 1842. The English agents, however, rather tauntingly and imploringly reminded the Sikh authorities that they were bound to have such a force ready by agreement as well as by friendship, than formally revived the demand for its production under the stipulations of the treaty.

[2] Cf. Mr. Clerk to Government, 2nd Jan. and 31st March 1842, and Government to Mr. Clerk, 17th Jan. and 12th May 1842. With regard to assistance rendered by the Sikhs during the Afghan War in furnishing escorts, grain, and carriage for the British troops, Mr. Clerk's letters of the 15th Jan., 18th May, and 14th June 1842 may be quoted. In the last it is stated that 17,381 camels had been procured through Sikh agency between 1839 and 1842.

[3] Cf. Mr. Clerk to Government, 15th Jan., 10th Feb., and 6th May, 1842. Government at first seemed indifferent whether Gulab Singh went or not; and, indeed, Mr. Clerk himself rather suggested than required the Raja's employment; but suggestions or wishes could not, under the circumstances, be misconstrued.

risk by following the modes of strangers to which he 1842. was unused, and he failed in rendering the Sikh battalions as decorous and orderly as English regiments. His prudence and ill success were looked upon as collusion and insincerity, and he was thought to be in league with Akbar Khan for the destruction of the army of an obnoxious European power.[1] Still his aid was held to be essential, and the local British officers proposed to bribe him by the offer of Jalalabad, independent of his sovereign Sher Singh. The scheme was justly condemned by Mr. Clerk,[2] the Khaibar Pass was forced in the month of April, and the auxiliary Sikhs acquitted themselves to the satisfaction of the English general, without any promise having been made to the Raja of Jammu, who gladly hurried to the Ladakh frontier to look after interests dearer to him than the success or the vengeance of foreigners. It was designed by General Pollock to leave the whole of the Sikh division at Jalalabad, to assist in holding that district, while the main English army went to Kabul; but the proper interposition of Col. Lawrence[3] enabled a portion of the Lahore troops to share in that retributive march, as they had before shared in the first invasion, and fully shown their fitness for meeting difficulties when left to do so in their own way.

*Kabul retaken.*

The proposition of conferring Jalalabad on Gulab Singh was taken up in a modified form by the new Governor-General, Lord Ellenborough. As his lordship's views became formed, he laid it down as a principle that neither the English nor the Sikh Government should hold dominion beyond the Himalayas and the 'Safed Koh' of Kabul; and as the Durrani alliance seemed to be severed, there was little to apprehend from Jammu and Barakzai intrigues. It was, therefore, urged that Gulab Singh should be required by the Maharaja to relinquish Ladakh, and to accept Jalalabad on equal terms of dependency on the Punjab.[4]

*Discussions regarding Jalalabad, and the limits of Sikh dominion.*

[1] Cf. Mr. Clerk to Government, 19th March 1842.

[2] Mr. Clerk to Government, 13th Feb. 1842. The officers referred to are Major Mackeson and Lieut.-Col. Sir Henry Lawrence, whose names are so intimately, and in so many ways honourably, identified with the career of the English in the north-west of India.

[3] Lieut.-Col. Lawrence to Major Mackeson, 23rd Aug. 1842. Lieut.-Col. Lawrence's article in the *Calcutta Review* (No. III, p. 180) may also be advantageously referred to about the proceedings at Peshawar under Col., Wild, Sir George Pollock, and Raja Gulab Singh.

[4] Government to Mr. Clerk, 27th April 1842.

The Sikhs were sufficiently desirous of adding to their dominion another Afghan district; but the terms did not satisfy Gulab Singh, nor did Sher Singh see fit to come to any conclusion until he should know the final views of the English with regard to the recognition of a government in Kabul.[1] The death of Shah Shuja and his suspicious proceedings were held to render the re-occupation of the country unnecessary, and the tripartite treaty was declared to be at an end,[2] but the policy of a march on the Afghan capital was strongly urged and wisely adopted.[3] There seemed to be a prospect of wintering in Kabul, and it was not until the victorious troops were on their return to India that it was believed the English would ever forgo the possession of an empire. The Sikhs then consented to take Jalalabad, but before the order transferring it could reach General Pollock,[4] that commander had destroyed the fortifications, and nominally abandoned the place to the king whom he had expediently set up in the Bala Hisar.[5] It is probable that Sher Singh was not unwilling to be relieved of the invidious gift, for his own sway in Lahore was distracted, and Dost

[1] Mr. Clerk to Government, 18th May 1842.

[2] Government to Mr. Clerk, 27th May and 29th July 1842. In the treaty drafted by the Sikhs to take the place of the tripartite one, they put forward a claim of superiority over Sind, and somewhat evaded the question of being parties only, instead of principals, to the acknowledgement of a ruler in Kabul. The treaty, however, never took a definite shape.

[3] Even the Sikhs talked of the impolicy, or, at least, the disgrace, of suddenly and wholly withdrawing from Afghanistan in the manner proposed. (Mr. Clerk to Government, 19th July 1842.) Mr. Clerk himself was among the most prominent of those who at first modestly urged a march on Kabul, and afterwards manfully remonstrated against a hasty abandonment of the country. (See his letter above quoted and also that of the 23rd April 1842.)

[4] The order was dated the 18th Oct. 1942. Lord Ellenborough himself was not without a suspicion that the victorious generals might frame excuses for wintering in Kabul, and the expedition of Sir John M'Caskill into the Kohistan was less pleasing to him on that account than it would otherwise have been.

[5] The Calcutta Review for June 1849 (p. 539) points out that the king, viz. Shahpur, son of Shah.Shuja, was rather set up solely by the chiefs at Kabul than in any way by Sir George Pollock, who had no authority to recognise any sovereign in Afghanistan. My expression has, indeed, reference mainly to the prudent countenance afforded to a native prince by a foreign conqueror about to retrace his steps through a difficult country, inhabited by a warlike people; but as it may mislead, as to Sir George Pollock's actual proceedings, I gladly insert this note.

Muhammad was about to be released under the pledge 1842.
of a safe passage through the Punjab dominions; and
it may have been thought prudent to conciliate the
father of Akbar Khan, so famous for his successes
against the English, by the surrender of a possession
it was inconvenient to hold.[1]

The Governor-General had prudently resolved to The
assemble an army at Ferozepore, as a reserve in case Governor-
of further disasters in Afghanistan, and to make known General
to the princes of India that their English masters had meets the
the ready means of beating any who might rebel.[2] minister
Lord Ellenborough was also desirous of an interview and heir-
with Sher Singh, and as gratitude was uppermost for apparent at
the time, and added a grace even to success, it was Ferozepore,
proposed to thank the Maharaja in person for the 1842.
proofs which he had afforded of his continued friendship.  To invest the scene with greater eclat, it was
further determined, in the spirit of the moment, to
give expression to British sincerity and moderation at

[1] The Sikhs were not unwilling to acquire territory, but
they wished to see their way clearly, and they were unable
to do so until the English had determined on their own line
of policy.  The Sikhs knew, indeed, of the resolution of the
Governor-General to sever all connexion with Afghanistan,
but they also knew the sentiments of the majority of Englishmen about at least temporarily retaining it.  They saw, moreover, that recruited armies were still in possession of every
stronghold, and the policy was new to them of voluntarily relin-
quishing dominion.  They therefore paused, and the subsequent
release of Dost Muhammad again fettered them when the
retirement of the troops seemed to leave them free to act,
for they were bound to escort the Amir safely across the
Punjab, and could not therefore make terms with him.  The
Sikhs would have worked through Sultan Muhammad Khan
and other chiefs until they were in a condition to use the frequent plea of the English, of being able to govern better than
dependants. (Cf. Mr. Clerk to Government, 2nd Sept. 1842.)

[2] Lord Auckland had likewise thought that such a demonstration might be advisable. (Government to Mr. Clerk, 3rd
Dec. 1841.)  Of measures practically identified with Lord
Ellenborough's administration, Lord Auckland may further
claim the merit of giving the generals commanding in
Afghanistan supreme authority (Resolution of Government,
6th Jan. 1842), and of directing Sir William Nott to act without
reference to previous instructions, and as *he* might deem best
for the safety of his troops and the honour of the British name.
(Government to Sir William Nott, 10th Feb. 1842.) To Lord
Auckland, however, is due the *doubtful* praise of suggesting the
release of Dost Muhammad (Government to Mr. Clerk, 24th
Feb. 1842); and he must certainly bear a share of the blame
attached to the exaggerated estimate formed of the dangers
which threatened the English after the retreat from Kabul, and
to the timorous rather than prudent design of falling back on
the Indus, or even on the Sutlej.

the head of the two armies returning victorious from Kabul, with their numbers increased to nearly forty thousand men by the force assembled on the Sutlej. The native English portion of this array was considerable, and perhaps so many Europeans had never stood together under arms on Indian ground since Alexander and his Greeks made the Punjab a province of Macedon. The Sikhs generally were pleased with one cause of this assemblage, and they were glad to be relieved of the presence of the English on their western frontier; but Sher Singh himself did not look forward to his visit to Lord Ellenborough without some misgivings, although under other circumstances his vanity would have been gratified by the opportunity of displaying his power and magnificence. He felt his incapacity as a ruler, and he needlessly feared that he might be called to account for Sikh excesses and for a suspected intercourse with the hostile Amirs of Sind then trembling for their fate, and even that the subjugation of the Punjab was to be made the stepping-stone to the complete reduction of Afghanistan. He had no confidence in himself; and he dreaded the vengeance of his followers, who believed him capable of sacrificing the Khalsa to his own interests. Nor was Dhian Singh supposed to be willing that the Maharaja should meet the Governor-General, and his suspicious temper made him apprehensive that his sovereign might induce the English viceroy to accede to his ruin, or to the reduction of his exotic influence. Thus both Sher Singh and his minister perhaps rejoiced that a misunderstanding which prevented the reception at Ludhiana of Lahna Singh Majithia, was seized hold of by the English to render a meeting doubtful or impossible.[1]

[1] On several occasions Raja Dhian Singh expressed his apprehensions of an English invasion, as also did Maharaja Sher Singh. (See, for instance, Mr. Clerk to Government, 2nd Jan. 1842.) The writer of the article in the *Calcutta Review* (No. II, p. 493), who is believed to be Lieut.-Col. Lawrence, admits Dhian Singh's aversion to a meeting between his sovereign and the British Governor-General. The reviewer likewise describes Sher Singh's anxiety at the time, but considers him to have been desirous of throwing himself unreservedly on English protection, as doubtless he might have been, had he thought himself secure from assassination, and that Lord Ellenborough would have kept *him* seated on the throne of Lahore at all hazards.

About the suspected hostile intercourse with the Amirs of Sind, see Thornton's *History of India* vi. 447 The Sikhs, however, were never required to give any explanation of the charges.

The misunderstanding to which Sardar Lahna Singh w

Lord Ellenborough justly took offence at a slight
which, however unwittingly, had been really offered
to him; he was not easily appeased; and when the personal
apologies of the minister, accompanied by the
young heir-apparent, had removed every ground of
displeasure, the appointed time, the beginning of January
1843, for the breaking-up of the large army had
arrived, and the Governor-General did not care to
detain his war-worn regiments any longer from their
distant stations. No interview thus took place with
Sher Singh; but the boy prince, Pertab Singh, was
visited by Lord Ellenborough; and the rapidity with
which a large escort of Sikh troops was crossed over
the Sutlej when swollen with rain, and the alacrity
and precision with which they manoeuvred, deserved
to have been well noted by the English captains, proud
as they had reason to be of the numbers and achievements
of their own troops. The prince likewise reviewed
the Anglo-Indian forces, and the Sikh chiefs
looked with interest upon the defenders of Jalalabad,
and with unmixed admiration upon General Nott followed
by his valiant and compact band. At last the
armed host broke up; the plains of Ferozepore were
no longer white with numerous camps; and the relieved
Sher Singh hastened, or was hurried, to Amritsar to
return thanks to God that a great danger had passed
away. This being over, he received Dost Muhammad Dost Mu-
Khan with distinction at Lahore, and in February hammad
(1843) entered into a formal treaty of friendship with returns to
the released Amir, which said nothing about the Eng- Kabul,
lish gift of Jalalabad.[1] 1843.

a party was simply as follows: The Sardar had been sent to
wait upon the Governor-General on his arrival on the frontier,
according to ordinary ceremonial. It was arranged that the
Sardar should be received by his lordship at Ludhiana, and
the day and hour were fixed, and preparations duly made. Mr.
Clerk went in person to meet the chief, and conduct him to the
Governor-General's presence, his understanding being that he
was to go half the distance or so towards the Sikh encampment.
The Sardar understood or held that Mr. Clerk should or would
come to his tent, and thus he sat still while Mr. Clerk rested
half-way for two hours or more. Lord Ellenborough thought
the excuse of the Sardar frivolous, and that offence was wantonly
given, and he accordingly required an explanation to be
afforded. (Government to Mr. Clerk, 15th Dec. 1842.) There
is some reason to believe that the Lahore Vakil, who was in
the interest of Raja Dhian Singh, misled the obnoxious Lahna
Singh about the arrangements for conducting him to the
Governor-General's tents, with the view of discrediting him
both with his own master and with the English.

[1] Government to Mr. Clerk, 15th Feb. and 17th Mar. 1843.

Anxieties
of Sher
Singh.

The Sind-
hianwala
chiefs and
the Jammu
Rajas
coalesce.

But Sher Singh principally feared his own chiefs and subjects, and although the designed or fortuitous murder of Mai Chand Kaur, in June 1842,[1] relieved him of some of his apprehensions, he felt uneasy under the jealous domination of Dhian Singh, and began to listen readily to the smooth suggestions of Bhai Gurmukh Singh, his priest so to speak, and who was himself of some religious reputation, as well as the son of a man of acknowledged sanctity and influence.[2] The English Government, in its well-meant but impracticable desire to unite all parties in the country, had urged the restoration to favour of the Sindhianwala chiefs, who kept its own agents on the alert, and the Maharaja himself in a state of doubt or alarm.[3] Sher Singh, from his easiness of nature, was not averse to a reconciliation, and by degrees he even became not unwilling to have the family about him as some counterpoise to the Rajas of Jammu. Neither was Dhian Singh opposed to their return, for he thought they might be made some use of since Mai Chand Kaur was no more, and thus Ajit Singh and his uncles again took their accustomed places in the court of Lahore. Nevertheless, during the summer of 1843, Dhian Singh perceived that his influence over the Maharaja was fairly on the wane; and he had good reason to dread the machinations of Gurmukh Singh and the passions of the multitude when roused by a man of his character. The minister then again began to talk of the boy, Dalip Singh, and to endeavour to possess the minds of the Sindhianwala

[1] Mr. Clerk to Government, 15th June 1842. The widow of Maharaja Kharak Singh was so severely beaten, as was said by her female attendants, that she almost immediately expired. The only explanation offered, was that she had chidden the servants in question for some fault, and the public was naturally unwilling to believe Sher Singh, at least, guiltless of instigating the murder.

[2] In the beginning of his reign Sher Singh had leant much upon an active and ambitious follower, named Jawala Singh, whose bravery was conspicuous during the attack on Lahore. This petty leader hoped to supplant both the Sindhianwala chiefs and the Jammu Rajas as leading courtiers, but he proceeded too hastily; he was seized and imprisoned by Dhian Singh in May 1841, and died by foul means immediately afterwards. (Cf. Mr. Clerk to Government, 7th May and 10th June 1841.)

[3] Mr. Clerk to Government, 7th April 1842, and Government to Mr. Clerk, 12th May 1842; see also Lieut.-Col. Richmond to Government, 5th Sept. 1843. Mr. Clerk became Lieutenant-Governor of Agra in June 1843, and he was succeeded as Agent on the frontier by Lieut.-Col. Richmond, an officer of repute, who had recently distinguished himself under Sir George Pollock.

chiefs with the belief that they had been inveigled to
Lahore for their more assured destruction. Ajit Singh
had by this time become the boon companion of the
Maharaja; but he was himself ambitious of power, and
he and his uncle Lahna Singh grasped at the idea of
making the minister a party to their own designs. They
appeared to fall wholly into his views; and they would,
they said, take Sher Singh's life to save their own. On
the 15th September (1843), Ajit Singh induced the
Maharaja to inspect some levies he had newly raised;
he approached, as if to make an offering of a choice
carbine, and to receive the commendations usual on
such occasions, but he raised the weapon and shot his
sovereign dead. The remorseless Lahna Singh took
the life of the boy Pertab Singh, at the same time, and
the kinsmen then joined Dhian Singh, and proceeded
with him to the citadel to proclaim a new king. The
hitherto wary minister was now caught in his own toils,
and he became the dupe of his accomplices. He was
separated from his immediate attendants, as if for the
sake of greater privacy, and shot by the same audacious
chief who had just imbrued his hands in the blood of
their common master.[1] The conspirators were thus far
successful in their daring and in their crimes, but they
neglected to slay o imprison the son of their last
victim; and the minds of the soldiers do not seem to
have been prepared for the death of Dhian Singh, as
they were for that of the Maharaja. The youthful Hira
Singh was roused by his own danger and his filial
duty; he could plausibly accuse the Sindhianwalas of
being alone guilty of the treble murder which had
taken place, and he largely promised rewards to the
troops if they would avenge the death of *their* friend
and *his* father. The army generally responded to his
call, and the citadel was immediately assaulted; yet so
strong was the feeling of aversion to Jammu ascendancy among the Sikh people, that could the feeble
garrison have held out for three or four days, until the
first impulse of anger and surprise had passed away, it
is almost certain that Hira Singh must have fled for his
life. But the place was entered on the second evening;
the wounded Lahna Singh was at once slain; and Ajit
Singh, in attempting to boldly escape over the lofty
walls, fell and was also killed.[2] Dalip Singh was then
proclaimed Maharaja, and Hira Singh was raised to

*Marginal notes:*

1843.

Sher Singh asasssinated by Ajit Singh, Sept. 15, 1843;

who likewise puts Dhian Singh to death, Sept. 15, 1843.

Hira Singh avenges his father.

---

[1] Lieut.-Col. Richmond to Government, 17th and 18th
Sept. 1843.

[2] Lieut.-Col. Richmond to Government, 20th Sept. 1843.

the high and fatal office of Wazir; but he was all-powerful for the moment; the Sindhianwala possessions were confiscated, and their dwellings razed to the ground : nor did the youthful avenger stay until he had found out and put to death Bhai Gurmukh Singh and Missar Beli Ram, the former of whom was believed to have connived at the death of his confiding master, and to have instigated the assassination of the minister; and the latter of whom had always stood high in the favour of the great Maharaja, although strongly opposed to the aggrandizement of the Jammu family. Sardar Atar Singh Sindhianwala, who was hurrying to Lahore when he heard of the capture of the citadel, made a hasty attempt to rouse the village population in his favour through the influence of Bhai Bir Singh, a devotee of great repute; but the 'Khalsa' was almost wholly represented by the army, and he crossed at once into the British territories to avoid the emissaries of Hira Singh.[1]

The power
of the army
increases.

The new minister added two rupees and a half, or five shillings a month, to the pay of the common soldiers, and he also discharged some arrears due to them. The army felt that it had become the master of the state, and it endeavoured to procure donatives, or to place itself right in public estimation, by threatening to eject the Jammu faction, and to make the Bhai Bir Singh, already mentioned, a king as well as a priest.[2] Jawahir Singh, the maternal uncle of the boy Maharaja, already grasped the highest post he could occupy; nor was the minister's family united within itself. Suchet Singh's vanity was mortified by the ascendancy of his nephew, a stripling, unacquainted with war, and inexperienced in business; and he endeavoured to form a party which should place him in power.[3] The youthful Wazir naturally turned to his other uncle, Gulab Singh, for support, and that astute chief cared not who held titles so long as he was deferred to and left unrestrained; but the Sikhs were still averse to him personally, and jealous lest he should attempt to garrison every stronghold with his own followers. Gulab Singh was, therefore, cautious in his proceedings, and before he reached Lahore, on the 10th of November, he had sought to ingratiate himself with all parties, save Jawahir Singh, whom he may have despised as of no

Raja Gulab
Singh.

[1] Lieut.-Col. Richmond's letters from 21st Sept. to 2nd Oct. 1843.

[2] Lieut.-Col. Richmond to Government, 26th Sept. 1843.

[3] Lieut.-Col. Richmond to Government, 16th and 22nd Oct. 1843.

capacity.[1] Jawahir Singh resented this conduct, and, taking advantage of the ready access to the Maharaja's person which his relationship gave him, he went with the child in his arms, on the occasion of a review of some troops, and urged the assembled regiments to depose the Jammu Rajas, otherwise he would fly with his nephew, their acknowledged prince, into the British territories. But the design of procuring aid from the English was displeasing to the Sikhs, both as an independent people and as a licentious soldiery, and Jawahir Singh was immediately made a prisoner, and thus received a lesson which influenced his conduct during the short remainder of his life.[2]

Nevertheless, Hira Singh continued to be beset with difficulties. There was one Fateh Khan Tiwana, a personal follower of Dhian Singh, who was supposed to have been privy to the intended assassination of his master, and to have designedly held back when Ajit Singh took the Raja to one side. This petty leader fled as soon as the army attacked the citadel, and endeavoured to raise an insurrection in his native province of Dera Ismail Khan, which caused the greater anxiety, as the attempt was supposed to be countenanced by the able and hostile Governor of Multan.[3] Scarcely had measures been adopted for reducing the petty rebellion, when Kashmira Singh and Peshawara Singh, sons born to, or adopted by, Ranjit Singh at the period of his conquest of the two Afghan provinces from which they were named, started up as the rivals of the child Dalip, and endeavoured to form a party by appearing in open opposition at Sialkot. Some regiments ordered to Peshawar joined the two princes; the Muhammadan regiments at Lahore refused to march against them unless a pure Sikh force did the same; and it was with difficulty, and only with the aid of Raja Gulab Singh, that the siege of Sialkot was formed. The two young men soon showed themselves to be incapable of heading a party; Hira Singh relaxed in his efforts against them; and towards the end of March he raised the siege, and allowed them to go at large.[4] The minister had, however, less reason to be satisfied with the success of Jawahir Singh, who, about the same

*Margin notes:*
1843-4.

Sardar Jawahir Singh, Nov. 24, 1843.

Fateh Khan Tiwana.

The insurrection of Kashmira Singh and Peshawara Singh, 1843-4.

Jawahir Singh.

---

[1] Cf. Lieut.-Col. Richmond to Government, 26th Sept. and 16th Nov. 1843.

[2] Lieut.-Col. Richmond to Government, 28th Nov. 1843.

[3] Lieut.-Col. Richmond to Government, 12th Dec. 1843.

[4] Lieut.-Col. Richmond to Government, 23rd and 27th March 1844.

The
attempt of
Raja
Suchet
Singh,
March
1844.

time, induced his guards to release him, and he was unwillingly allowed to assume his place in the court as the uncle of the child to whose sovereignty in the abstract all nominally deferred.[1]

Raja Suchet Singh was believed to have been a secret party to the attempts of Kashmira Singh, and the release of Jawahir Singh was also probably effected with his cognizance. The Raja believed himself to be popular with the army, and especially with the cavalry portion of it, which, having an inferior organization, began to show some jealousy of the systematic proceedings of the regular infantry and artillery. He had retired to the hills with great reluctance; he continued intent upon supplanting his nephew; and suddenly, on the evening of the 26th of March 1844, he appeared at Lahore with a few followers; but he appealed in vain to the mass of the troops, partly because Hira Singh had been liberal in gifts and profuse in promises, and partly because the shrewd deputies who formed the Panchayats of the regiments had a sense of their own importance, and were not to be won for purposes of mere faction, without diligent and judicious seeking. Hence, on the morning after the arrival of the sanguine and hasty Raja, a large force marched against him without demur; but the chief was brave : he endeavoured to make a stand in a ruinous building, and he died fighting to the last, although his little band was almost destroyed by the fire of a numerous artillery before the assailants could reach the enclosure.[2]

The insurrection of
Sardar
Atar Singh
and Bhai
Bir Singh,
May 1844.

Within two months after this rash undertaking, Atar Singh Sindhianwala, who had been residing at Thanesar, made a similar ill-judged attempt to gain over the army, and to expel Hira Singh. He crossed the Sutlej on the 2nd May, but instead of moving to a distance, so as to avoid premature collisions, and to enable him to appeal to the feelings of the Sikhs, he at once joined Bhai Bir Singh, whose religious repute attracted numbers of the agricultural population and took up a position almost opposite Ferozepore, and within forty miles of the capital. The disaffected Kashmira Singh joined the chief, but Hira Singh stood as a suppliant before the assembled Khalsa, and roused the feelings of the troops by reminding them that the Sindhianwalas looked to the English for support. A large force promptly marched from Lahore, but it was wished to detach Bhai Bir Singh from the rebel, for

[1] Lieut.-Col. Richmond to Government, 27th March 1844.
[2] Lieut.-Col. Richmond to Government, 29th March 1844.

to assail so holy a man was held to be sacrilege by the
soldiers, and on the seventh of the month deputies were
sent to induce the Bhai to retire. Some expressions
moved the anger of Sardar Atar Singh, and he slew
one of the deputies with his own hand. This act led
to an immediate attack. Atar Singh and Kashmira
Singh were both killed, and it was found that a can-
non-shot had likewise numbered Bhai Bir Singh with
the slain. The commander on this occasion was Labh
Singh, a Rajput of Jammu, and the possession of the
family of Kashmira Singh seemed to render his success more complete; but the Sikh infantry refused to
allow the women and children to be removed to
Lahore; and Labh Singh, alarmed by this proceeding
and by the lamentations over the death of Bir Singh,
hastened to the capital to ensure his own safety.[1]

Hira Singh was thus successful against two main
enemies of his rule, and as he had also come to an
understanding with the Governor of Multan, the proceedings of Fateh Khan Tiwana gave him little uneasiness.[2] The army itself was his great cause of anxiety,
not lest the Sikh dominion should be contracted, but
lest he should be rejected as its master; for the Panchayats, although bent on retaining their own power,
and on acquiring additional pay and privileges for their
constituents the soldiers, were equally resolved on
maintaining the integrity of the empire, and they
arranged among themselves about the relief. of the
troops in the provinces. On the frontiers, indeed, the
Sikhs continued to exhibit their innate vigour, and
towards the end of 1843 the secluded principality of
Gilgit was overrun and annexed to Kashmir. The
Panchayats likewise felt that it was the design of the
Raja and his advisers to disperse the Sikh army over
the country, and to raise additional corps of hill men,
but the committees would not allow a single regiment
to quit Lahore without satisfying themselves of the
necessity of the measure; and thus Hira Singh was
induced to take advantage of a projected relief of the
British troops in Sind, and the consequent march of
several battalions towards the Sutlej. to heighten or
give a colour to his own actual suspicions, and to hint
that a near danger threatened the Sikhs on the side of
the English. The 'Khalsa' was most willing to encoun-

*The Governor of Multan submits.*

*Gilgit reduced. 1843*

*Hira Singh professes suspicions of the English.*

---

[1] Lieut.-Col. Richmond to Government, 10th, 11th, and
12th May 1844.

[2] Cf. Lieut.-Col. Richmond to Government, 29th April 1844.

The
mutiny of
the British
Sepoys
ordered to
Sind.

Discussions
with the
English
about the
village
Moran.

ter *that* neighbour, and a brigade was induced to move
to Kasur, and others to shorter distances from the capital, under the plea, as avowed to the British authorities, of procuring forage and supplies with greater
facility.[1] Such had indeed been Ranjit Singh's occasional practice when no assemblage of British forces
could add to his ever present fears;[2] but Hira Singh's
apprehensions of his own army and of his English allies
were lessened by his rapid successes, and by the disgraceful spirit which then animated the regular regiments in the British service. The Sepoys refused to
proceed to Sind, and the Sikhs watched the progress of
the mutiny with a pleased surprise. It was new to
them to see these renowned soldiers in opposition to
their government; but any glimmering hopes of fatal
embarrassment to the colossal power of the foreigners
were dispelled by the march of European troops, by
the good example of the irregular cavalry, and by the
returning sense of obedience of the sepoys themselves.
The British forces proceeded to Sind, and the Lahore
detachment was withdrawn from Kasur.[3]

Nevertheless there were not wanting causes of real
or alleged dissatisfaction with the British Government, which at last served the useful purpose of
engaging the attention of the Lahore soldiery. The
protected Sikh Raja of Nabha had given a village,
named Moran, to Ranjit Singh at the Maharaja's request, in order that it might be bestowed on Dhanna
Singh, a Nabha subject, but who stood high in favour
with the master of the Punjab. The village was so
given in 1819, or after the introduction of the English
supremacy, but without the knowledge of the English
authorities, which circumstance rendered the aliena-
tion invalid, if it were argued that the village had
become separated from the British sovereignty. The
Raja of Nabha became displeased with Dhanna Singh,
and he resumed his gift in the year 1843; but in so
doing his soldiers wantonly plundered the property of
the feudatory, and thus gave the Lahore Government
a ground of complaint, of which advantage was taken
for party purposes.[4] But Hira Singh and his advisers

[1] Cf. Lieut.-Col. Richmond to Government, 20th Dec. 1843,
and 23rd March 1844.
[2] See, for instance, Sir David Ochterlony to Government,
16th Oct. 1812.
[3] Cf. Lieut.-Col. Richmond to Government, 29th April
1844.
[4] Lieut.-Col. Richmond to Government, 18th and 28th
May 1844.

took greater exception still to the decision of the British Government with regard to a quantity of coin and bullion which Raja Suchet Singh had secretly deposited in Ferozepore, and which his servants were detected in endeavouring to remove after his death. The treasure was estimated at 1,500,000 rupees, and it was understood to have been sent to Ferozepore during the recent Afghan War, for the purpose of being offered as part of an ingratiatory loan to the English Government, which was borrowing money at the time from the protected Sikh chiefs. The Lahore minister claimed the treasure both as the escheated property of a feudatory without male heirs of his body, and as the confiscated property of a rebel killed in arms against his sovereign; but the British Government considered the right to the property to be unaffected by the owner's treason, and required that the title to it, according to the laws of Jammu or of the Punjab, should be regularly pleaded and proved in a British court. It was argued in favour of Lahore that no British subject or dependent claimed the treasure, and that it might be expediently made over to the ruler of the Punjab for surrender to the legal or customary owner; but the supreme British authorities would not relax further from the conventional law of Europe than to say that if the Maharaja would write that the Rajas Gulab Singh and Hira Singh assented to the delivery of the treasure to the Sikh state for the purpose of being transferred to the rightful owners, it would no longer be detained. This proposal was not agreed to, partly because differences had in the meantime arisen between the uncle and nephew, and partly because the Lahore councillors considered their original grounds of claim to be irrefragable, according to Indian law and usage, and thus the money remained a source of dissatisfaction, until the English stood masters in Lahore, and accepted it as part of the price of Kashmir, when the valley was alienated to Raja Gulab Singh.[1]

1844.
and about
treasure
buried by
Suchet
Singh.

[1] For the discussions about the surrender or the detention of the treasure, see the letters of Lieut.-Col. Richmond to Government of the 7th April, 3rd and 27th May, 25th July, 10th Sept., and 5th and 25th Oct. 1844; and of Government to Lieut.-Col. Richmond of the 19th and 22nd April, 17th May, and 10th Aug. of the same year.

The principle laid down of deciding the claim to the treasure at a British tribunal, and according to the laws of Lahore or of Jammu, does not distinguish between public and individual right of heirship; or rather it decides the question with reference solely to the law in private cases. Throughout India, the practical rule has ever been that such property shall

1844.

Hira Singh
guided by
Pandit
Jalla, his
preceptor.

Hira Singh had, in his acts and successes, surpassed the general expectation, and the manner in which
affairs were carried on seemed to argue unlooked-for
abilities of a high order; but the Raja himself had little
more than a noble presence and a conciliatory address
to recommend him, and the person who directed every
measure was a Brahman Pandit, named Jalla, the
family priest, so to speak, of the Jammu brothers, and
the tutor of Dhian Singh's sons. This crafty and ambitious man retained all the influence over the youthful
minister which he had exercised over the boyish pupil
on whom Ranjit Singh lavished favours. Armies had
marched, and chiefs had been vanquished, as if at the
bidding of the preceptor become councillor. His views
expanded, and he seems to have entertained the idea

be administered agreeably to the customs of the tribe or
province to which the deceased belonged; and very frequently,
when the only litigants are subjects of one and the same foreign
state, it is expediently made over to the sovereign of that state
for adjudication, on the plea that the rights of the parties can
be best ascertained on the spot, and that every ruler is a
renderer of justice.

In the present instance the imperfection of the International Law of Europe may be more to blame than the
Government of India and the legal authorities of Calcutta, for
refusing to acknowledge the right of an allied and friendly
state to the property of a childless rebel; to which property,
moreover, no British subject or dependent preferred a claim.
Vattel lays it down that a stranger's property remains a part
of the aggregate wealth of his nation, and that the right to it
is to be determined according to the laws of his own country
(Book II, chap. viii, §§ 109 and 110); but in the section in
question reference is solely had to cases in which subjects or
private parties are litigants; although Mr. Chitty, in his note to
§ 103 (ed. 1834), shows that foreign sovereigns can in England
sue, at least, British subjects.

The oriental customary law with regard to the estates and
property of Jagirdars (feudal beneficiaries) may be seen in
Bernier's *Travels* (p. 181), and it almost seems identical with
that anciently in force among the Anglo-Saxons with reference to 'nobles by service', the followers of a lord or king. (See
Kemble's *Saxons in England*, i. 178, &c.) The right of the
Government is full, and it is based on the feeling or principle
that a beneficiary has only the use during life of estates or
offices, and that all he may have accumulated, through parsi-
mony or oppression, is the property of the state. It may be
difficult to decide between a people and an expelled sovereign,
about his guilt or his tyranny, but there can be none in deciding between an allied state and its subject about treason or
rebellion. Neither refugee traitors nor patriots are allowed to
abuse their asylum by plotting against the Government which
has cast them out; and an extension of the principle would
prevent desperate adventurers defrauding the state which has
reared and heaped favours on them, by removing their
property previc s to engaging in rash and criminal enterprises.

of founding a dynasty of 'Peshwas' among the rude Jats 1844. of the Punjab, as had been done by one of his tribe among the equally rude Marathas of the south.  He fully perceived that the Sikh army must be conciliated, and also that it must be employed.  He despised, and with some reason, the spirit and capacity of most of the titular chiefs of the country; and he felt that Raja Gulab Singh absorbed a large proportion of the revenues of the country, and seriously embarrassed the central government by his overgrown power and influence.  It was primarily requisite to keep the army well and regularly paid, and hence the Pandit proceeded without scruple to sequester several of the fiefs of the sirdars, and gradually to inspire the soldiery with the necessity of a march against Jammu.  Nor was he without a pretext for denouncing Gulab Singh, as that unscrupulous chief had lately taken possession of the estates of Raja Suchet Singh, to which he regarded himself as the only heir.[1]

Jalla showed vigour and capacity in all he did, but he proceeded too hastily in some matters, and he attempted too much at one time.  He did not, perhaps, understand the Sikh character in all its depths and ramifications, and he probably undervalued the subtlety of Gulab Singh.  The Raja, indeed, was induced to divide the Jagirs of Suchet Singh with his nephew,[2] but Fateh Khan Tiwana again excited an insurrection in the Derajat;[3] Chattar Singh Atariwala took up arms near Rawalpindi,[4] and the Muhammadan tribes southwest of Kashmir were encouraged in rebellion by the dexterous and experienced chief whom Pandit Jalla sought to crush.[5]  Peshawara Singh again aspired to the sovereignty of the Punjab; he was supported by Gulab Singh, and Jalla at last perceived the necessity of coming to terms with one so formidable.[6]  A reconciliation was accordingly patched up, and the Raja sent his son Sohan Singh to Lahore.[7]  The hopes of Peshawara Singh then vanished, and he fled for safety to the south of the Sutlej.[8]

*Pandit Jalla and Gulab Singh.*

[1] Cf. Lieut.-Col. Richmond to Government, 13th Aug. and 10th Oct. 1844.

[2] Lieut.-Col. Richmond to Government, 30th Oct. 1844.

[3] Lieut.-Col. Richmond to Government, 14th June 1844.

[4] Lieut.-Col. Richmond to Government, 16th Oct. 1844.

[5] Major Broadfoot to Government, 24th Nov. 1844.

[6] Lieut.-Col. Richmond to Government, 16th Oct. 1844, and Major Broadfoot to Government, 24th Nov. 1844.

[7] Lieut.-Col. Richmond to Government, 30th Oct. 1844, and Major Broadfoot to Government, 13th Nov. and 16th Dec. 1844.

[8] Major Broadfoot to Government, 14th and 18th Nov.

1844.

Pandit
Jalla irri-
tates the
Sikhs, and
offends the
Queen-
mother.

Pandit Jalla made the additional mistake of forgetting that the Sikhs were not jealous of Gulab Singh alone, but of all strangers to their faith and race; and in trying to crush the chiefs, he had forgotten that they were Sikhs equally with the soldiers, and that the 'Khalsa' was a word which could be used to unite the high and low. He showed no respect even to sardars of ability and means. Lahna Singh Majithia quitted the Punjab, on pretence of a pilgrimage, in the month of March 1844,[1] and the only person who was raised to any distinction was the unworthy Lal Singh, a Brahman, and a follower of the Rajas of Jammu, but who was understood to have gained a disgraceful influence over the impure mind of Rani Jindan. The Pandit again, in his arrogance, had ventured to use some expressions of impatience and disrespect towards the mother of the Maharaja, and he had habitually treated Jawahir Singh, her brother, with neglect and contempt. The impulsive soldiery was wrought upon by the incensed woman and ambitious man; the relict of the great Maharaja appealed to the children of the Khalsa, already excited by the proscribed chiefs, and Hira Singh and Pandit Jalla perceived that their rule was at an end. On the 21st December 1844 they endeavoured to avoid the wrath of the Sikh soldiery by a sudden flight from the capital, but they were overtaken and slain before they could reach Jammu, along with Sohan Singh, the cousin of the minister, and Labh Singh, so lately hailed as a victorious commander. The memory of Pandit Jalla continued to be execrated, but the fate of Hira Singh excited some few regrets, for he had well avenged the death of his father, and he had borne his dignities with grace and modesty.[2]

Hira Singh
and Pandit
Jalla fly,
but are
overtaken
and put to
death, 21st
Dec. 1844.

Jawahir
Singh and
Lal Singh
attain
power.

The sudden breaking up of Hira Singh's government caused some confusion for a time, and the state seemed to be without a responsible head; but it was gradually perceived that Jawahir Singh, the brother, and Lal Singh, the favourite of the Rani, would form the most influential members of the administration.[2]

1844. Major Broadfoot, who succeeded Lieut.-Col. Richmond as agent on the frontier on the 1st Nov. 1844, received Peshawara Singh with civilities unusual under the circumstances, and proposed to assign him an allowance of a thousand rupees a month.

[1] Lahna Singh went first to Hardwar and afterwards to Benares. He next visited Gaya and Jagannath and Calcutta, and he was residing in the last-named place when hostilities broke out with the Sikhs.

[2] Cf. Major Broadfoot to Government, 24th and 28th Dec. 1844.

Peshawara Singh, indeed, escaped from the custody of 1844.
the British authorities, by whom he had been placed
under surveillance, when he fled across the Sutlej; but
he made no attempt at the moment to become supreme,
and he seemed to adhere to those who had so signally
avenged him on Hira Singh.[1] The services of the troops
were rewarded by the addition of half a rupee a month
to the pay of the common soldier, many fiefs were
restored, and the cupidity of all parties in the state was
excited by a renewal of the designs against Gulab
Singh.[2] The disturbances in the mountains of Kashmir
were put down, the insurgent Fateh Khan was taken
into favour, Peshawar was secure against the power of
all the Afghans, although it was known that Gulab
Singh encouraged the reduced Barakzais with promises
of support;[3] but it was essential to the government
that the troops should be employed : it was pleasing
to the men to be able to gratify their avarice or their
vengeance, and they therefore marched against Jammu
with alacrity.[4]

Gulab Singh, who knew the relative inferiority of The Sikh
his soldiers, brought all his arts into play. He distri- army
buted his money freely among the Panchayats of regi- moves
ments, he gratified the members of these committees against Jammu
by his personal attentions, and he again inspired
Peshawara Singh with designs upon the sovereignty
itself. He promised a gratuity to the army which had Feb. to
marched to urge upon him the propriety of submission, March
he agreed to surrender certain portions of the general 1845.
possessions of the family, and to pay to the state a fine
of 3,500,000 rupees.[5] But an altercation arose between
the Lahore and Jammu followers when the promised
donative was being removed, which ended in a fatal
affray; and afterwards an old Sikh chief, Fateh Singh
Man, and one Bachna, who had deserted Gulab Singh's
service, were waylaid and slain.[6] The Raja protested
against the accusation of connivance or treachery; nor

---

[1] Cf. Major Broadfoot to Government, 28th Dec. 1844, and
4th Jan. 1845. As Major Broadfoot, however, points out, the
prince seemed ready enough to grasp at power even so early
as January.

[2] Cf. Major Broadfoot to Government, 28th Dec. 1844, and
2nd Jan. 1845.

[3] Major Broadfoot to Government, 16th Jan. 1845.

[4] The troops further rejected the terms to which the
Lahore court seemed inclined to come with Gulab Singh.
(Major Broadfoot to Government, 22nd Jan. 1845.)

[5] Major Broadfoot to Government, 18th March 1845.

[6] Major Broadfoot to Government, 3rd March 1845.

Gulab
Singh sub-
mits and
repairs to
Lahore,
April 1845.

is it probable that at the time he desired to take the life
of any one except Bachna, who had been variously
employed by him, and who knew the extent of his resources. The act nevertheless greatly excited the Sikh
soldiery, and Gulab Singh perceived that submission
alone would save Jammu from being sacked. He succeeded in partially gaining over two brigades, he joined
their camp, and he arrived at Lahore early in April
1845, half a prisoner, and yet not without a reasonable
prospect of becoming the minister of the country; for
the mass of the Sikh soldiery thought that one so great
had been sufficiently humbled, the Panchayats had
been won by his money and his blandishments, and
many of the old servants of Ranjit Singh had confidence in his ability and in his goodwill towards the state
generally.[1]   There yet, however, existed some remnants of the animosity which had proved fatal to Hira
Singh; the representatives of many expelled hill chiefs
were ready to compass the death of their greatest
enemy; and an Akali fanatic could take the life of the
'Dogra' Raja with applause and impunity.   Jawahir
Singh plainly aimed at the office of Wazir, and Lal
Singh's own ambition prompted him to use his influence with the mother of the Maharaja to resist the
growing feeling in favour of the chief whose capacity
for affairs all envied and dreaded.   Hence Gulab Singh
deemed it prudent to avoid a contest for power at that
time, and to remove from Lahore to a place of greater
safety.   He agreed to pay in all a fine of 6,800,000
rupees, to yield up nearly all the districts which
had been held by his family, excepting his own
proper fiefs, and to renew his lease of the salt mines
between the Indus and Jhelum, on terms which virtually deprived him of a large profit, and of the political superiority in the hills of Rohtas.[2]  He was present
at the installation of Jawahir Singh as Wazir on the
14th May,[3] and at the betrothal of the Maharaja to a
daughter of the Atari chief Chattar Singh on the 10th
July; [4] and towards the end of the following month
he retired to Jammu, shorn of much real power, but
become acceptable to the troops by his humility, and
to the final conviction of the English authorities, that

Jawahir
Singh for-
mally ap-
pointed
Wazir,
May 14.
1845.

1 Cf. Major Broadfoot to Government, 8th and 9th April
and 5th May 1845.

2 Major Broadfoot to Government, 5th May 1845.

3 Major Broadfoot to Government, 24th May 1845.

4 Major Broadfoot to Government, 14th July 1845.

the levies of the mountain Rajputs were unequal to a contest even with the Sikh soldiery.[1]

The able Governor of Multan was assassinated in the month of September 1844 by a man accused of marauding, and yet imprudently allowed a considerable degree of liberty.[2]  Mulraj, the son of the Diwan, had been appointed or permitted to succeed his father by the declining government of Hira Singh, and he showed more aptitude for affairs than was expected. He suppressed a mutiny among the provincial troops, partly composed of Sikhs, with vigour and success; and he was equally prompt in dealing with a younger brother, who desired to have half the province assigned to him as the equal heir of the deceased Diwan. Mulraj put his brother in prison, and thus freed himself from all local dangers; but he had steadily evaded the demands of the Lahore court for an increased farm or contract, and he had likewise objected to the large 'Nazarana', or relief, which was required as the usual condition of succession. As soon, therefore, as Gulab Singh had been reduced to obedience, it v s proposed to dispatch a force against Multan, and the 'Khalsa' approved of the measure through the assembled Panchayats of regiments and brigades. This resolution induced the new governor to yield, and in September (1845) it was arranged that he should pay a fine of 1,800,000 rupees. He escaped an addition to his contract sum, but he was deprived of some petty districts to satisfy in a measure the letter of the original demand.[3]

The proceedings of Peshawara Singh caused more disquietude to the new Wazir personally than the hostility of Gulab Singh, or the resistance of the Gov-

1845.

Sawan Mal, of Multan, assassinated, Sept. 1844.

Mulraj, his son, succeeds:

and agrees to the terms of the Lahore court, 1845.

The rebellion of Peshawara Singh;

[1] Major Broadfoot confessed that 'late events had shown the Raja's weakness in the hills', where he should have been strongest, had his followers been brave and trusty. (Major Broadfoot to Government, 5th May 1845.)

[2] Lieut.-Col. Richmond to Government, 10th Oct. 1844.

[3] In this paragraph the author has followed mainly his own notes of occurrences. The mutiny of the Multan troops took place in Nov. 1844. The Governor at once surrounded them, and demanded the ringleaders, and on their surrender being refused, he opened a fire upon their whole body, and killed, as was said, nearly 400 of them. Diwan Mulraj seized and confined his brother in Aug. 1845, and in the following month the terms of his succession were settled with the Lahore court. [Mulraj never paid his fine. In April 1848, when threatened with force, he resigned, and Kahn Singh was sent from Lahore to relieve him, accompanied by Mr. Vans Agnew and Lieut. Anderson. The murder of these officers on their arrival at Multan led to the second Sikh War and the final extinction of Sikh independence.—ED.]

1845.

ernor of Multan. The prince was vain and of slender capacity, but his relationship to Ranjit Singh gave him some hold upon the minds of the Sikhs. He was encouraged by Gulab Singh, then safe in the hills, and he was assured of support by the brigade of troops which had made Jawahir Singh a prisoner when that chief threatened to fly with the Maharaja into the British territories. Jawahir Singh had not heeded the value to the state of the prudence of the soldiers in restraining him; he thought only of the personal indignity, and soon after his accession to power he barbarously mutilated the commander of the offending divi-

March 1845;

sion, by depriving him of his nose and ears. Peshawara Singh felt himself countenanced, and he endeavoured to rally a party around him at Sialkot, which he held in fief. But the Sikhs were not disposed to thus suddenly admit his pretensions; he was reduced to straits; and in the month of June he fled, and lived at large on the country, until towards the end of July, when he surprised the fort of Attock, proclaimed himself Maharaja, and entered into a correspondence with Dost Muhammad Khan. Sardar Chattar Singh of Atari was sent against the pretender, and troops were moved from Dera Ismail Khan to aid in reducing him. The prince was beleaguered in his fort, and became aware

who submits, but is put to death Aug.-Sept. 1845.

of his insignificance; he submitted on the 30th August, and was directed to be removed to Lahore, but he was secretly put to death at the instigation of Jawahir Singh, and through the instrumentality, as understood, of Fateh Khan Tiwana, who sought by rendering an important service to further ingratiate himself with that master for the time being who had restored him to favour, and who had appointed him to the management of the upper Derajat of the Indus.[1]

The Sikh soldiery displeased and distrustful.

This last triumph was fatal to Jawahir Singh, and anger was added to the contempt in which he had always been held. He had sometimes displayed both energy and perseverance, but his vigour was the impulse of personal resentment, and it was never characterized by judgement or by superior intelligence. His original design of flying to the English had displeased the Sikhs, and rendered them suspicious of his good faith as a member of the Khalsa; and no sooner had his revenge been gratified by the expulsion of Hira Singh and Pandit Jalla, than he found himself the mere sport and plaything of the army, which had only united

[1] Cf. Major Broadfoot to Government, 14th and 26th July and 8th and 18th Sept. 1845.

with him for the attainment of a common object. The 1845.
so' diery began to talk of themselves as pre-eminently
the 'Panth Khalsagi', or congregation of believers;[1]
and Jawahir Singh was overawed by the spirit which **The per-**
animated the armed host. In the midst of the successes **plexity of**
against Jammu, he trembled for his fate, and he twice **Jawahir**
laid plans for escaping to the south of the Sutlej; but **Singh.**
the troops were jealous of such a step on the part of
their nominal master. He felt that he was watched,
and he abandoned the hope of escape to seek relief in
dissipation, in the levy of Muhammadan regiments,
and in idle or desperate threats of war with his British
allies.[2] Jawahir Singh was thus despised and distrusted by the Sikhs themselves; their enmity to him was
fomented by Lal Singh, who aimed at the post of
wazir; and the murder of Peshawara Singh added to
the general exasperation, for the act was condemned
as insulting to the people, and it was held up to reprobation by the chiefs as one which would compromise
their own safety, if allowed to pass with impunity.[3]
The Panchayats of regiments met in council, and they **The army**
resolved that Jawahir Singh should die as a traitor to **condemns**
the commonwealth, for death is almost the only mode **him and**
by which tumultuous, half-barbarous governments can **puts him to**
remove an obnoxious minister. He was accordingly **death,**
required to appear on the 21st September before the **Sept. 21,**
assembled Khalsa to answer for his misdeeds. He went, **1845.**
seated upon an elephant; but fearing his fate, he took
with him the young Maharaja and a quantity of gold
and jewels. On his arrival in front of the troops, he
endeavoured to gain over some influential deputies
and officers by present donatives and by lavish promises, but he was sternly desired to let the Maharaja
be removed from his side, and to be himself silent.
The boy was placed in a tent near at hand, and a party
of soldiers advanced and put the wazir to death by a
discharge of musketry.[4] Two other persons, the syco-
phants of the minister, were killed at the same time.

[1] Or, as the 'Sarbat Khalsa', the body of the elect. Major
Broadfoot (letter of 2nd Feb. 1845) thought this title, which
the soldiers arrogated to themselves, was new in correspondence; but Government pointed out, in reply, that it was an old
term according to the Calcutta records.
[2] Cf. Major Broadfoot to Government, 23rd and 28th Feb.,
5th April (a demi-official letter), and 15th and 18th Sept. 1845.
[3] Cf. Major Broadfoot to Government, 22nd Sept. 1845.
[4] Cf. Major Broadfoot to Government, 26th Sept. 1845. It
may be added that the Sik's generally regarded Jawahir Singh
as one ready to bring in the English, and as faithless to the
Khalsa.

but no pillage or massacre occurred; the act partook of the solemnity and moderation of a judicial process, ordained and witnessed by a whole people; and the body of Jawahir Singh was allowed to be removed and burnt with the dreadful honours of the Sati sacrifice, among the last, perhaps, which will take place in India.

The army all-powerful.

For some time after the death of Jawahir Singh, no one seemed willing to become the supreme administrative authority in the state, or to place himself at the head of that self-dependent army, which in a few months had led captive the formidable chief of Jammu, reduced to submission the powerful governor of Multan, put down the rebellion of one recognized as the brother of the Maharaja, and pronounced and executed judgement on the highest functionary in the kingdom, and which had also without effort contrived to keep the famed Afghans in check at Peshawar and along the frontier. Raja Gulab Singh was urged to repair to the capital, but he and all others were overawed, and the Rani Jindan held herself for a time a regular court, in the absence of a wazir. The army was partly satisfied with this arrangement, for the committees considered that they could keep the provinces obedient, and they reposed confidence in the talents or the integrity of the accountant Dina Nath, of the paymaster Bhagat Ram, and of Nur-ud-din, almost as familiar as his old and infirm brother Aziz-ud-din, with the particulars of the treaties and engagements with the English. The army had formerly required that these three men should be consulted by Jawahir Singh; but the advantage of a responsible head was, nevertheless, apparent, and as the soldiers were by degrees wrought upon to wage war with their European neighbours, Raja Lal Singh was nominated wazir, and Sardar Tej Singh was reconfirmed in his office of Commander-in-Chief. These appointments were made early in November 1845.[1]

Lal Singh made wazir, and Tej Singh Commander-in-Chief, in expectation of an English war.

[1] In this paragraph the author has followed mainly his own notes of occurrences.

# CHAPTER IX

## THE WAR WITH THE ENGLISH
### 1845—6

Causes leading to a war between the Sikhs and English—The
English, being apprehensive of frontier disturbances, adopt
defensive measures on a scale opposed to the spirit of the
policy of 1809—The Sikhs, being prone to suspicion,
consider themselves in danger of invasion—And are
further moved by their want of confidence in the English
representative—The Sikhs resolve to anticipate the English,
and wage war by crossing the Sutlej—The tactics of the
Sikhs—The views of the Sikh leaders—Ferozepore
purposely spared—The Battle of Mudki—The Battle of
P'heerooshuhur, and retreat of the Sikhs—The effect of
these barren victories upon the Indians and the English
themselves—The Sikhs again cross the Sutlej—The
Skirmish of Badowal—The Battle of Aliwal—Negotiations
through Raja Gulab Singh—The Battle of Sobraon—The
submission of the Sikh Chiefs, and the occupation of
Lahore—The partition of the Punjab—The Treaty with
Dalip Singh—The Treaty with Gulab Singh—Conclusion,
relative to the position of the English in India.

THE English Government had long expected that
it would be forced into a war with the overbearing
soldiery of the Punjab : the Indian public, which considered only the fact of the progressive aggrandizement of the strangers, was prepared to hear of the
annexation of another kingdom without minutely
inquiring or caring about the causes which led to it;
and the more selfish chiefs of the Sikhs had always
desired that such a degree of interference should be
exercised in the affairs of their country as would
guarantee to them the easy enjoyment of their possessions. These wealthy and incapable men stood rebuked
before the superior genius of Ranjit Singh, and before
the mysterious spirit which animated the people
arrayed in arms, and they thus fondly hoped that a
change would give them all they could desire; but it
is doubtful whether the Sikh soldiery ever seriously
thought, although they often vauntingly boasted, of
fighting with the paramount power of Hindustan, until
within two or three months of the first battles, and
even then the rude and illiterate yeomen considered

1845-6.
The Indian
public pre-
pared for
a war
between
the Sikhs
and
English.

that they were about to enter upon a war purely defensive, although one in every way congenial to their feelings of youthful pride and national jealousy.

**The apprehensions of the English.** From the moment the Sikh army became predominant in the state, the English authorities had been persuaded that the machinery of government would be broken up, that bands of plunderers would everywhere arise, and that the duty of a civilized people to society generally, and of a governing power to its own subjects, would all combine to bring on a collision; and thus measures which seemed sufficient were adopted for strengthening the frontier posts, and for having a force at hand which might prevent aggression, or which would at least exact retribution and vindicate the supremacy of the English name.[1] These were the fair and moderate objects of the British Government; **The fears of the Sikhs.** but the Sikhs took a different view of the relative conditions of the two states; they feared the ambition of their great and growing neighbour, they did not understand why they should be dreaded when intestine commotions had reduced their comparative inferiority still lower; or why inefficiency of rule should be construed into hostility of purpose; defensive measures took in their eyes the form of aggressive preparations, and they came to the conclusion that their country was to be invaded. Nor does this conviction of the weaker and less intelligent power appear to be strange or unreasonable, although erroneous—for it is always to be borne in mind that India is far behind Europe in civilization, and that political morality or moderation is as little appreciated in the East in these days as it was in Christendom in the Middle Ages. Hindustan, moreover, from Kabul to the valley of Assam and the island of Ceylon, is regarded as one country, and dominion in it is associated in the minds of the people with the predominance of one monarch or of one race. The supremacy of Vikramajit and Chandra Gupta, of the Turkomans and Mughals, is familiar to all, and thus on hearing of further acquisitions by the English, a Hindu or Muhammadan will simply observe that the destiny of the nation is great, or that its cannon is irresistible. A prince may chafe that he loses a province or is rendered tributary; but the public will never accuse the conquerors of unjust aggression, or at least of unrighteous and unprincipled ambition.

[1] Cf. Minute by the Governor-General, of the 16th June 1845, and the Governor-General to the Secret Committee, 1st October 1845. (Parliamentary Paper, 1846.)

To this general persuasion of the Sikhs, in common
with other Indian nations, that the English were and
are ever ready to extend their power, is to be added
the particular bearing of the British Government towards the Punjab itself.  In 1809, when the apprehensions of a French invasion of the East had subsided,
when the resolution of making the Jumna a boundary
was still approved, and when the policy of forming
the province of Sirhind into a neutral or separating
tract between two dissimilar powers had been wisely
adopted, the English Viceroy had said that rather than
irritate Ranjit Singh, the detachment of troops which
had been advanced to Ludhiana might be withdrawn
to Karnal.[1]  It was not indeed thought advisable to
carry out the proposition; but up to the period of the
Afghan war of 1838, the garrison of Ludhiana formed
the only body of armed men near the Sikh frontier,
excepting the provincial regiment raised at Sabathu
for the police of the hills after the Gurkha war.  The
advanced post on the Sutlej was of little military or
political use; but it served as the most conspicuous
symbol of the compact with the Sikhs; and they, as the
inferior power, were always disposed to lean upon old
engagements as those which warranted the least degree
of intimacy or dictation.  In 1835 the petty chiefship of
Ferozepore, seventy miles lower down the Sutlej than
Ludhiana, was occupied by the English as an escheat
due to their protection of all Sikh lordships save that
of Lahore.  The advantages of the place in a military
point of view had been perseveringly extolled, and its
proximity to the capital of the Punjab made Ranjit
Singh, in his prophetic fear, claim it as a dependency
of his own.[2]  In 1838 the Maharaja's apprehensions
that the insignificant town would become a cantonment
were fully realized; for twelve thousand men assembled at Ferozepore to march to Khorasan; and as it was
learnt, before the date fixed for the departure of the
army, that the Persians had raised the siege of Herat,
it was determined that a small division should be left
behind, until the success of the projected invasion
rendered its presence no longer necessary.[3]  But the
succeeding warfare in Afghanistan and Sind gave the

[1] Government to Sir David Ochterlony, 30th Jan. 1809.

[2] See chap. vii.

[3] This was the understanding at the time, but no document
appears to have been drawn up to that effect. It was indeed
expected that Shah Shuja would be seated on his throne, and
the British army withdrawn, all within a twelvemonth.

new cantonment a character of permanency, and in 1842 the remoteness from support of the *two* posts on the Sutlej was one of the arguments used for advancing a considerable body of troops to Ambala as a reserve, and for placing European regiments in the hills still closer to the Sikh frontier.[1] The relations of 1809 were nevertheless cherished by the Sikhs, although they may have been little heeded by the English amid the multifarious considerations attendant on their changed position in India, and who, assured of the rectitude of their intentions, persuaded of the general advantage of their measures, and conscious of their overwhelming power, are naturally prone to disregard the less obvious feelings of their dependants, and to be careless of the light in which their acts may be viewed by those whose aims and apprehensions are totally different from their own.

The English views about Peshawar, and their offer to support Sher Singh, all weigh with the Sikhs.

It had never been concealed from the Sikh authorities, that the helpless condition of the acknowledged government of the country was held to justify such additions to the troops at Ludhiana and Ferozepore as would give confidence to the inhabitants of these districts, and ensure the successful defence of the posts themselves against predatory bands.[2] Nor did the Sikhs deny the abstract right of the English to make what military arrangements they pleased for the security of their proper territories : but that any danger was to be apprehended from Lahore was not admitted by men conscious of their weakness; and thus by every process of reasoning employed, the Sikhs still came to the same conclusion that they were threatened. Many circumstances, unheeded or undervalued by the English, gave further strength to this conviction. It had not indeed been made known to the Sikhs that Sir William Macnaghten and others had proposed to dis-

[1] The author cannot refer to any written record of these reasons, but he knows that they were used. When the step in advance was resolved on, it is only to be regretted that the cantonment was not formed at Sirhind, the advantages of which as a military post with reference to the Punjab, as being central to all the principal passages of the Sutlej, Sir David Ochterlony had long before pointed out. (Sir D. Ochterlony to Government, 3rd May 1810.) Some delicacy, however, was felt towards the Sikhs of Patiala, to whom Sirhind belonged; although the more important and less defensible step of alarming the Sikhs of Lahore had been taken without heed or hesitation.

[2] Cf. the Governor-General to the Secret Committee. 2nd Dec. 1845, (Parliamentary Papers, 1846); and also his dispatch of the 31st Dec. 1845 (Parliamentary Papers, p. 28).

member their kingdom by bestowing Peshawar on
Shah Shuja, when Ranjit Singh's line was held to end
with the death of his grandson; but it would be idle
to suppose the Lahore government ignorant of a
scheme which was discussed in official correspondence,
and doubtless in private society, or of the previous
desire of Sir Alexander Burnes to bestow the same
tract on Dost Muhammad Khan, which was equally a
topic of conversation; and the Sikh authorities must
at least have had a lively remembrance of the English
offer of 1843, to march upon their capital, and to disperse their army. Again, in 1844 and 1845, the facts
were whispered abroad and treasured up, that the
English were preparing boats at Bombay to make
bridges across the Sutlej, that troops in Sind were
being equipped for a march on Multan,[1] and that the
various garrisons of the north-west provinces were
being gradually reinforced, while some of them were
being abundantly supplied with the munitions of war
as well as with troops.[2]   None of these things were
communicated to the Sikh government, but they were
nevertheless believed by all parties, and they were

[1] The collection of ordnance and ammunition at Sakhar
for the equipment of a force of five thousand men, to march
towards Multan, was a subject of ordinary official correspondence in 1844-5, as, for instance, between the Military Board in
Calcutta and the officers of departments under its control. Sir
Charles Napier assures the author that he, although Governor,
had no cognizance of the correspondence in question, and made
no preparations for equipping a force for service. Of the fact
of the correspondence the author has no doubt; but the expression 'collection of the means', used in the first edition, can be
held to imply too much, and the meaning is now correctly
restored to 'ordnance and ammunition'. The object of the
Supreme Government was not to march on Multan at that
time, but to be prepared, at least in part, for future hostilities.

[2] The details of the preparations made by Lords Ellenborough and Hardinge may be seen in an article on the
administration of the latter nobleman, in the *Calcutta Review*,
which is understood to be the production of Lieut.-Col.
Lawrence.

Up to 1838 the troops on the frontier amounted to one
regiment at Sabathu, and two at Ludhiana, with six pieces of
artillery, equalling in all little more than 2,500 men. Lord
Auckland made the total about 8,000, by increasing Ludhiana
and creating Ferozepore. Lord Ellenborough formed further
new stations at Ambala, Kasauli, and Simla, and placed in all
about 14,000 men and 48 field guns on the frontier. Lord
Hardinge increased the aggregate force to about 32,000 men,
with 68 field guns, besides having 10,000 men with artillery at
Meerut. After 1843, however, the station of Karnal, on the
Jumna, was abandoned, which in 1838 and preceding years
may have mustered about 4,000 men.

1845-6.

The Sikhs
further
moved by
their esti-
mate of the
British
Agent of
the day.

held to denote a campaign, not of defence, but of aggression.[1]

The Sikhs thus considered that the fixed policy of the English was territorial aggrandizement, and that the immediate object of their ambition was the conquest of Lahore. This persuasion of the people was brought home to them by the acts of the British representative for the time, and by the opinion which they had preformed of his views. Mr. Clerk became Lieutenant-Governor of Agra in June 1843, and he was succeeded as Agent for the affairs of the Sikhs by Lieut.-Col. Richmond, whose place again was taken by Major Broadfoot, a man of undoubted energy and ability, in November of the following year. In India the views of the British Government are, by custom, made known to allies and dependants through one channel only, namely that of an accredited English officer. The personal character of such a functionary gives a colour to all he does and says; the policy of the government is indeed judged of by the bearing of its representative, and it is certain that the Sikh authorities did not derive any assurance of an increasing desire for peace, from the nomination of an officer who, thirty months before, had made so stormy a passage through their country.[2]

Major
Broadfoot's
views and
overt acts
equally dis-
pleasing to
the Sikhs.

One of Major Broadfoot's [3] first acts was to declare the Cis-Sutlej possessions of Lahore to be under British protection equally with Patiala and other chiefships, and also to be liable to escheat on the death or deposition of Maharaja Dalip Singh.[4] This view was not formally announced to the Sikh government, but it was notorious, and Major Broadfoot acted on it when he proceeded to interfere authoritatively, and by a display

[1] Cf. the Governor-General to the Secret Committee, Dec. 2, 1845.

[2] Sir Claude Wade. in his *Narrative of Services* (p. 19, note), well observes it to be essential to the preservation of the English system of alliances in India, that political representatives should be regarded as friends by the chiefs with whom they reside, rather than as the mere instruments of conveying the orders or of enforcing the policy of foreign masters.

[3] See p. 214, with regard to Major Broadfoot's passage of the Punjab in 1841.

[4] Major Broadfoot's letters to Government, of the 7th Dec. 1844, 80th Jan. and 28th Feb. 1845, may be referred to as explanatory of his views. In the last letter he distinctly says that if the young Maharaja Dalip Singh, who was then ill of the small-pox, should die he would direct the reports regarding the Cis-Sutlej districts to be made to himself (through the Lahore vakil or agent indeed), and not to any one in the Punjab.

of force, in the affairs of the priest-like Sodhis of Anandpur-Makhowal, a fief to which some years before it had been declared to be expedient to waive all claim, especially as Ranjit Singh could best deal with the privileged proprietors.[1] Again, a troop of horse had crossed the Sutlej near Ferozepore, to proceed to Kot Kapura, a Lahore town, to relieve or strengthen the mounted police ordinarily stationed there; but the party had crossed without the previous sanction of the British Agent having been obtained, agreeably to an understanding between the two governments, based on an article of the treaty of 1809, but which modified arrangement was scarcely applicable to so small a body of men proceeding for such a purpose. Major Broad-foot nevertheless required the horsemen to recross; and as he considered them dialtory in their obedience, he followed them with his escort, and overtook them as they were about to ford the river. A shot was fired by the English party, and the extreme desire of the Sikh commandant to avoid doing anything which might be held to compromise his government, alone prevented a collision.[2] Further, the bridge-boats which had been prepared at Bombay were dispatched towards Feroze-pore in the autumn of 1845, and Major Broadfoot almost avowed that hostilities had broken out when he manifested an apprehension of danger to these armed vessels, by ordering strong guards of soldiers to escort them safely to their destination, and when he began to exercise their crews in the formation of bridges after their arrival at Ferozepore.[3]

[1] With regard to Anandpur, see chap. vii.    About the particular dispute noticed in the text, Major Broadfoot's letter to Government of the 13th Sept. 1845 may be referred to. It labours in a halting way to justify his proceedings and his assumption of jurisdiction under ordinary circumstances.

[2] Cf. Major Broadfoot to Government, 27th March 1845. It is understood that the Government disapproved of these proceedings.

The *Calcutta Review* for June 1849 (p. 547) states that the Governor-General did not, as represented, disapprove, but, on the contrary, entirely approved, of Major Broadfoot's proceed-ings in this matter. The Reviewer writes like one possessed of official knowledge, but I am nevertheless unwilling to believe that the Governor-General could have been pleased with the violent and unbecoming act of his agent, although his lordship may have desired to see the irregular conduct of the Sikhs firmly checked.

[3] A detachment of troops under a European officer was required to be sent with each batch of boats, owing to the state of the Punjab. Nevertheless, small iron steamers were allowed to navigate the Sutlej at the time without guards, and one lay

1845-6.

Major
Broadfoot's
proceed-
ings held to
virtually
denote war.

The views held by Major Broadfoot, and virtually adopted by the supreme government, with respect to the Cis-Sutlej districts, and also the measures followed in particular instances, may all be defended to a certain extent, as they indeed were, on specious grounds, as on the vague declarations of Sir David Ochterlony or on the deferential injunctions of Ranjit Singh.[1] It is even believed that if the cession of the tracts in question had been desired, their relinquishment might have been effected without a resort to arms; but every act of Major Broadfoot was considered to denote a foregone resolution, and to be conceived

under the guns of Phillaur for several days without meeting aught except civility on the part of the Sikhs.

[1] Major Broadfoot is understood to have quoted to the Sikhs a letter of Sir David Ochterlony's, dated the 7th May 1809, to Mohkam Chand, Ranjit Singh's representative, to the effect that the Cis-Sutlej Lahore states were equally under British protection with other states; and also an order of April 1824, from Ranjit Singh, requiring his authorities south of the Sutlej to obey the English Agent, on pain of having their noses slit. It is not improbable that Sir David Ochterlony may, at the early date quoted, have so understood the nature of the British connexion with reference to some particular case then before him, but that the Cis-Sutlej states of Lahore were held under feudal obligations to the English seems scarcely tenable, for the following reasons : (1) The protection extended by the English to the chiefs of Sirhind was declared to mean protection to them against Ranjit Singh, and therefore not protection of the whole country between the Sutlej and Jumna, a portion of which belonged to Lahore. (See the Treaty of 1809, and Article I of the declaration of the 3rd May 1809: and also Government to Sir David Ochterlony, 10th April 1809.) Further, when convenient, the British Government could even maintain, that although the Treaty of 1809 was binding on Ranjit Singh, with reference to Cis-Sutlej states, it was not binding on the English, whom it simply authorized to interfere at their discretion. (Government to Capt. Wade, 23rd April 1833.) This was indeed written with reference to Bahawalpur, but the application was made general. (2) The protection accorded to the chiefs of Sirhind was afterwards extended so as to give them security in the plains, but not in the hills, against the Gurkhas as well as against Ranjit Singh (Government to Sir David Ochterlony, 23rd Jan. 1810); while with regard to Ranjit Singh's own Cis-Sutlej possessions, it was declared that he himself must defend them (against Nepal), leaving it a question of policy as to whether he should or should not be aided in their defence. It was further added, that he might march through his Cis-Sutlej districts, to enable him to attack the Gurkhas in the hills near the Jumna, in defence of the districts in question, should he so wish. (Government to Sir David Ochterlony, 4th Oct. and 22nd Nov. 1811.) The opinion of Sir Charles Metcalfe, about the proceedings of the English with regard to Whadni (see ante, p. 163, note), may also be quoted as bearing on the case in a way adverse to Major Broadfoot.

in a spirit of enmity rather than of goodwill.[1] Nor did
the Sikhs seem to be menaced by their allies on one
side only.  In the summer of 1845 some horsemen from
Multan crossed a few miles into the Sind territory in

[1] It was generally held by the English in India that Major
Broadfoot's appointment greatly increased the probabilities of
a war with the Sikhs; and the impression was equally strong
that had Mr. Clerk, for instance, remained as Agent, there
would have been no war. Had Mr. Clerk again, or Col. Wade,
been the British representative in 1845, either would have gone
to Lahore in person, and would have remonstrated against the
selfish and unscrupulous proceedings of the managers of
affairs as obviously tending to bring on a rupture. They would
also have taken measures to show to the troops that the British
Government would *not* be aggressors; they would have told
the chiefs that a war would compromise them with the English,
nor would they have come away until every personal risk had
been run, and every exertion used to avert a resort to arms.
That Major Broadfoot was regarded as hostile to the Sikhs may,
perhaps, almost be gathered from his own letters. On the 19th
March 1845 he wrote that the Governor of Multan had asked
what course he, the Governor, should pursue, if the Lahore
troops marched against him, to enforce obedience to demands
made. The question does not seem one which a recusant
servant would put under ordinary circumstances to the
preserver of friendship between his master and the English.
Major Broadfoot, however, would appear to have recurred
to the virtual overtures of Diwan Mulraj, for on the 20th Nov.
1845, when he wrote to all authorities in any way connected
with the Punjab, that the British provinces were threatened
with invasion, he told the Major-General at Sakhar that the
Governor of Multan would defend *Sind* with *his* provincials
against the Sikhs!—thus leading to the belief that he had
succeeded in detaching the Governor from his allegiance to
Lahore. When this note was originally written, the author
thought that Major Broadfoot's warning in question had been
addressed to Sir Charles Napier himself, but he has subsequently ascertained that the letter was sent to his Excellency's
deputy in the upper portion of the country, and that Sir Charles
Napier has no recollection of receiving a similar communication.
    Some allusion may also be made to a falsified speech of
Sir Charles Napier's, which ran the round of the papers at the
time, about the British army being called on to move into the
Punjab, especially as Major Broadfoot considered the Sikh
leaders to be moved in a greater degree by the Indian news-
papers than is implied in a passing attention to reiterated
paragraphs about invasion. He thought, for instance, that
Pandit Jalla understood the extent to which Government
deferred to public opinion, and that the Brahman himself
designed to make use of the press as an instrument. (Major
Broadfoot to Government, 30th Jan. 1845.)
    In the first edition of this history the speech of Sir Charles
Napier was referred to as if it had really been made in the terms
reported, but the author has now learnt from his Excellency
that nothing whatever was said about leading troops into the
Punjab, or about engaging in war with the Sikhs. The author
has likewise ascertained from Sir Charles Napier, that the

1845-6.

Sir Charles
Napier's
acts con-
sidered
further
proof of
hostile
views.

pursuit of certain marauders, and in seizing them, the
Lahore soldiers were reported to have used needless
violence, and perhaps to have committed other excesses. Nevertheless, the object of the troopers was
evident; and the boundary of the two provinces between the Indus and the hills is nowhere defined, but
the governor, Sir Charles Napier, immediately ordered
the wing of a regiment to Kashmor, a few miles below
Rojhan, to preserve the integrity of his frontier from
violation. The Lahore authorities were thus indeed
put upon their guard, but the motives of Sir Charles
Napier were not appreciated, and the prompt measures
of the conqueror of Sind were mistakenly looked
upon as one more proof of a desire to bring about a
war with the Punjab.

The Lahore
chiefs make
use of the
persuasion
of the
people for
their own
ends.

The Sikh army, and the population generally, were
convinced that war was inevitable; but the better informed members of the government knew that no
interference was likely to be exercised without an
overt act of hostility on their part.[1] When moved as
much by jealousy of one another as by a common dread
of the army, the chiefs of the Punjab had clung to
wealth and ease rather than to honour and independence, and thus Maharaja Sher Singh, the Sindhianwalas, and others, had been ready to become tributary,
and to lean for support upon foreigners. As the
authority of the army began to predominate, and to
derive force from its system of committees, a new
danger threatened the territorial chiefs and the adventurers in the employ of the government. They
might successively fall before the cupidity of the
organized body which none could control, or an able
leader might arise who would absorb the power of all
others, and gratify his followers by the sacrifice of the
rich, the selfish, and the feeble. Even the Raja of

mention made in the first edition about a proposal to station
a considerable force at Kashmor having been disapproved by
the Supreme Government is incorrect, and he offers his apologies to the distinguished leader misrepresented for giving
original or additional currency to the errors in question.

[1] Cf. Enclosure No. 6 of the Governor-General's letter to
the Secret Committee of the 2nd Dec. 1845. (Parliamentary
Papers, 26th Feb. 1846, p. 21.) Major Broadfoot, however,
states of Gulab Singh, what was doubtless true of many others,
viz. that he believed the English had designs on the Punjab.
(Major Broadfoot to Government, 5th May 1845.) It is indeed
notorious that Sikhs and Afghans commonly said the English
abandoned Kabul because they did not hold Lahore, and that
having once established themselves in the Punjab, they would
soon set about the regular reduction of Khorasan.

Jammu, always so reasonably averse to a close connexion with the English, began to despair of safety as
a feudatory in the hills, or of authority as a minister
at Lahore without the aid of the British name, and
Lal Singh, Tej Singh, and many others, all equally
felt their incapacity to control the troops. These men
considered that their only chance of retaining power
was to have the army removed by inducing it to
engage in a contest which they believed would end in
its dispersion, and pave the way for their recognition
as ministers more surely than if they did their duty by
the people, and earnestly deprecated a war which must
destroy the independence of the Punjab.[1]    Had the
shrewd committees of the armies observed no military
preparations on the part of the English, they would
not have heeded the insidious exhortations of such
mercenary men as Lal Singh and Tej Singh, although
in former days they would have marched uninquiringly
towards Delhi at the bidding of their great Maharaja.
But the views of the government functionaries coin-

1845-6.

and urge
the army
against the
English, in
order that
it may be
destroyed.

[1] Cf. Enclosures to the Governor-General's letter to the
Secret Committee of the 31st Dec. 1845. (Parliamentary Papers,
26th Feb. 1846, p. 29.) It has not been thought necessary to
refer to the intemperance of the desperate Jawahir Singh, or
to the amours of the Maharani, which, in the papers laid before
the British Parliament, have been used to heighten the folly
and worthlessness of the Lahore court. Jawahir Singh may have
sometimes been seen intoxicated, and the Maharani may have
attempted little concealment for her debaucheries, but decency
was seldom violated in public; and the essential forms of a court
were preserved to the last, especially when strangers were present. The private life of princes may be scandalous enough,
while the moral tone of the people is high, and is, moreover,
applauded and upheld by the transgressors themselves, in their
capacity of magistrates. Hence the domestic vices of the powerful have, comparatively, little influence on public affairs. Further, the proneness of news-mongers to enlarge upon such personal failings is sufficiently notorious; and the diplomatic service
of India has been often reproached for dwelling pruriently or
maliciously on such matters. Finally, it is well known that the
native servants of the English in Hindustan, who in too many
instances are hirelings of little education or respectability,
think they best please their employers, or chime in with their
notions, when they traduce all others, and especially those with
whom there may be a rivalry or a collision. So inveterate is
the habit of flattery, and so strong is the belief that Englishmen
love to be themselves praised and to hear others slighted,
that even petty local authorities scarcely refer to allied or
dependent princes, their neighbours, in verbal or in written
reports, without using some terms of disparagement towards
them. Hence the scenes of debauchery described by the Lahore
news-writer are partly due to his professional character, and
partly to his belief that he was saying what the English wanted
to hear.

1845-6.

cided with the belief of the impulsive soldiery; and when the men were tauntingly asked whether they would quietly look on while the limits of the Khalsa dominion were being reduced, and the plains of Lahore occupied by the remote strangers of Europe, they answered that they would defend with their lives all belonging to the commonwealth of Gobind, and that they would march and give battle to the invaders on their own ground.[1] At the time in question, or early in November, two Sikh villages near Ludhiana were placed under sequestration, on the plea that criminals concealed in them had not been surrendered.[2] The measure was an unusual one, even when the Sikhs and the English were equally at their ease with regard to one another; and the circumstance, added to the rapid approach of the Governor-General to the frontier, re-moved any doubts which may have lingered in the minds of the Panchayats. The men would assemble in groups and talk of the great battle they must soon wage, and they would meet round the tomb of Ranjit Singh and vow fidelity to the Khalsa.[3] Thus wrought upon, war with the English was virtually declared on the 17th November; a few days afterwards the troops began to move in detachments from Lahore; they commenced crossing the Sutlej between Hariki and Kasur on the 11th December, and on the 14th of that month a portion of the army took up a position within a few miles of Ferozepore.[4]

The Sikhs cross the Sutlej. 11th Dec. 1845.

The initiative was thus taken by the Sikhs, who by an overt act broke a solemn treaty, and invaded the territories of their allies. It is further certain that the English people had all along been sincerely desir-ous of living at peace with the Punjab, and to a casual observer the aggression of the Sikhs may thus appear as unaccountable as it was fatal; yet further inquiry will show that the policy pursued by the English them-selves for several years was not in reality well calcu-lated to ensure a continuance of pacific relations, and that they cannot therefore be held wholly blameless

[1] The ordinary private correspondence of the period contained many statements of the kind given in the text.
[2] Major Broadfoot's official correspondence seems to have ceased after the 21st Nov. 1845; and there is no report on this affair among his recorded letters.
[3] The Lahore news-letters of the 24th Nov. 1845, prepared for Government.
[4] Cf. the Governor-General to the Secret Committee, 2nd and 31st Dec. 1845, with enclosures. (Parliamentary Papers, 1846.)

for a war which they expected and deprecated, and 1845-6. which they knew could only tend to their own aggrandizement. The proceedings of the English, indeed, do not exhibit that punctilious adherence to the spirit of first relations which allows no change of circumstances to cause a departure from arrangements which had, in the progress of time, come to be regarded by a weaker power as essentially bound up with its independence. Neither do the acts of the English seem marked by that high wisdom and sure foresight, which should distinguish the career of intelligent rulers acquainted with actual life, and the examples of history. Treaties of commerce and navigation had been urged upon the Sikhs, notwithstanding their dislike to such bonds of unequal union; they were chafed that they had been withheld from Sind, from Afghanistan, and from Tibet, merely, they would argue, that these countries might be left open to the ambition of the English; and they were rendered suspicious by the formation of new military posts on their frontier contrary to prescriptive usage, and for reasons of which they did not perceive the force or admit the validity. The English looked upon these measures with reference to *their own* schemes of amelioration; and they did not heed the conclusions which the Sikhs might draw from them, although such conclusions, how erroneous soever, would necessarily become motives of action to a rude and warlike race. Thus, at the last, regard was mainly had to the chance of predatory inroads, or to the possibility that sovereign and nobles and people, all combined, would fatuitously court destruction by assailing their gigantic neighbour, and little thought was given to the selfish views of factious Sikh chiefs, or to the natural effects of the suspicions of the Sikh commonalty when wrought upon by base men for their own ends. Thus, too, the original agreement which left the province of Sirhind free of troops and of British subjects, and which provided a confederacy of dependent states to soften the mutual action of a half-barbarous military dominion and of a humane and civilized government, had been set aside by the English for objects which seemed urgent and expedient, but which were good in their motive rather than wise in their scope. The measure was misconstrued by the Sikhs to denote a gradual but settled plan of conquest; and hence the *subjective* mode of reasoning employed was not only vicious in logic, but, being met by arguments even more narrow and one-sided, became faulty in

1845-6.

policy, and, in truth, tended to bring about that collision which it was so much desired to avoid.

A corresponding singleness of apprehension also led the confident English to persevere in despising or misunderstanding the spirit of the disciples of Gobind. The unity and depth of feeling, derived from a young and fervid faith, were hardly recognized, and no historical associations exalted the Sikhs to the dignity of Rajputs and Pathans.

In 1842 they were held, as has been mentioned, to be unequal to cope with the Afghans, and even to be inferior in martial qualities to the population of the Jammu hills. In 1845 the Lahore soldiery was called a 'rabble' in sober official dispatches, and although subsequent descriptions allowed the regiments to be composed of the yeomanry of the country, the army was still declared to be daily deteriorating as a military body.[1] It is, indeed, certain that English officers and Indian sepoys equally believed they were about to win battles by marching steadily and by the discharge of a few artillery shots, rather than by skilful dispositions hard fighting, and a prolonged contest.[2]

The English unprepared for a campaign.

The English not only undervalued their enemy, but, as has been hinted, they likewise mistook the form which the long-expected aggressions of the Sikhs would assume.[3] It was scarcely thought that the

[1] Major Broadfoot to Government, 18th and 25th Jan. 1845. A year before, Lieut.-Col. Lawrence (*Calcutta Review*, No. III, pp. 176, 177) considered the Sikh army as good as that of any other Indian power, and not inferior, indeed, to the Gwalior troops which fought at Maharajpur. The Lahore artillery, however, he held to be very bad, although he was of opinion that in position the guns would be well served. In his *Adventurer in the Punjab* (p. 47, note k) he had previously given a decided preference to the Maratha artillery.

[2] Major Smyth is, however, of opinion that the sepoys in the British service had a high opinion of the Sikh troops, although the English themselves talked of them as boasters and cowards. (Major Smyth, *Reigning Family of Lahore*, Introduction, pp. xxiv and xxv.) Cf. Dr. Macgregor, *History of the Sikhs*, ii. 89, 90.

[3] Cf. the Governor-General to the Secret Committee, 31st Dec. 1845 (Parliamentary Papers, 1846), and the *Calcutta Review*, No. XVI. p. 475. A few words may here be said on a subject which occasioned some discussion in India at the time, viz. Major Broadfoot's reputed persevering disbelief that the Sikhs would cross the Sutlej, although his assistant, Capt. Nicolson, stationed at Ferozepore, had repeatedly said they would. The matter was taken up by the Indian public as if Capt. Nicolson had for several months, or for a year and more, held that the British provinces would assuredly be in-

ministry, or even that the army, would have the courage to cross the river in force, and to court an equal contest; the known treasonable views of the chiefs, and the unity and depth of feeling which possessed the troops, were not fully appreciated, and it continued to be believed that a desultory warfare would sooner or later ensue, which would indeed require the British to interfere, but which would still enable them to do so at their own convenience. Thus boats for bridges, and regiments and guns, the natural and undesigned provocatives to a war, were sufficiently numerous; but food and ammunition, and carriage and hospital stores, such as were necessary for a campaign, were all behind at Delhi or Agra, or still remained to be collected; for the desire of the English was, it is said, peace, and they had hoped that an assemblage of troops would prevent predatory aggression, or deter the Sikhs from engaging in suicidal hostilities.[1]

vaded within a definite period; whereas. with regard to what the Sikh army might eventually do, Capt. Nicolson was as uncertain as others, up to within a week or so of the passage of the Sutlej in December 1845. The truth seems to be, that Major Broadfoot affected to disbelieve Capt. Nicolson's report of the actual march and near approach of the Lahore army, of its encampment on the Sutlej, and of its evident resolution to cross the river, giving the preference to intelligence of a contrary nature received direct from the Sikh capital, and which tallied with his own views of what the Sikhs would finally do. That such was the case, may indeed be gathered from the Governor-General's dispatch to the Secret Committee of the 31st Dec. 1845. (Parliamentary Papers, 1846, pp. 26, 27.)

The writer of the article in the *Calcutta Review*, No. XVI, endeavours to justify Major Broadfoot's views by showing that all the officers on the frontier held similar opinions. The point really at issue, however, is not whether, generally speaking, invasion were probable, but whether in the beginning of December 1845 Major Broadfoot should not have held that the Sutlej would be crossed. The Reviewer forgets to add that of the local officers Major Broadfoot alone knew at the time the extent of provocation which the Sikhs had received; and that the officers wrote with no later news before them than that of the 17th of November. Hence all, save Major Broadfoot himself had very imperfect means of forming a judgement of what was likely to take place. With regard to what the English should have been prepared against, Lieut.-Col. Richmond's letter of the 3rd April 1844, to the address of the Commander-in-Chief, may be referred to as in favour of having stations strong if they were to be kept up at all.

[1] It was a common and a just remark at the time, that although the Indian Government was fortunate in having a practical and approved soldier like Lord Hardinge at its head, under the circumstances of a war in progress, yet that had Lord Ellenborough remained Governor-General, the army would have taken the field better equipped than it did.

1845-6.

The
English
nasten to
oppose
the Sikhs.

The Governor-General [1] joined the Commander-in-Chief at Ambala early in December 1845, and as soon as it seemed certain that the Sikhs were marching in force towards the Sutlej, the English troops in the upper provinces were all put in motion. The nearest divisions were those of Ambala, Ludhiana, and Ferozepore, which numbered in all about 17,000 available men, with 69 field guns; and as the last-mentioned force was the most exposed, the Ambala troops were moved straight to its support, and Lord Hardinge further prudently resolved to leave Ludhiana with a mere garrison for its petty fort, and to give Lord Gough as large a force as possible, with which to meet the Sikhs, should they cross the Sutlej as they threatened.[2]

The
numbers of
the Sikhs.

The Lahore army of invasion may have equalled 35,000 or 40,000 men, with a hundred and fifty pieces of artillery, exclusive of a force detached towards Ludhiana to act as circumstances might render advantageous. The numbers of the Sikhs were understood at the time to greatly exceed those given, but the strength of armies is usually exaggerated both by the victors and the vanquished; and there is no satisfactory proof that the regular troops of the Sikhs exceeded those of the English by more than a half, although numerous bodies of undisciplined horse swelled the army of the invaders to more than double that of their opponents.[3]

[1] Sir Henry Hardinge had succeeded Lord Ellenborough as Governor-General in July 1844. The Commander-in-Chief was Sir Hugh Gough.—Ed.]

[2] The effective force at Ferozeshah was 17,727 men, according to the *Calcutta Review* (No. XVI, p. 472), and 16,700 according to Lord Hardinge's dispatch of the 31st Dec. 1845. This was the available force, out of 32,479 men in all, posted from Ambala to the Sutlej. The author has learnt that Lord Gough is satisfied the number of the enemy at Ferozeshah and the other battles of the campaign have been underestimated in this narrative. There cannot, indeed, be any statements of decisive authority referred to, but the settled conviction of the Commander-in-Chief is of primary consideration, and requires to be recorded in this new edition; especially as, with a characteristic singleness of heart, his lordship, in noticing the probable error, had regard rather to the reputation of the army he led than to his own fame.

[3] The Governor-General, in his dispatch of the 31st Dec. 1845, estimates the Sikhs at from 48,000 to 60,000 men: but with regard to efficient troops, it may be observed that the whole regular army of the country did not exceed 42,000 infantry, including the regiments at Lahore, Multan, Pesnawar, and Kashmir, as well as those forming the main army of invasion. Perhaps an estimate of 30,000 *embodied* troops of all kinds would be nearer the truth than any other.

The Sikh leaders threatened Ferozepore, but no attack was made upon its seven thousand defenders, which with a proper spirit were led out by their commander, Sir John Littler, and showed a bold front to the overwhelming force of the enemy. The object, indeed, of Lal Singh and Tej Singh was not to compromise themselves with the English by destroying an isolated division, but to get their own troops dispersed by the converging forces of their opponents. Their desire was to be upheld as the ministers of a dependent kingdom by grateful conquerors, and they thus deprecated an attack on Ferozepore, and assured the local British authorities of their secret and efficient goodwill. But these men had also to keep up an appearance of devotion to the interests of their country, and they urged the necessity of leaving the easy prey of a cantonment untouched, until the leaders cf the English should be attacked, and the fame of the Khalsa exalted by the captivity or death of a Governor-General.[1] The Sikh army itself understood the necessity of unity of counsel in the affairs of war, and the power of the regimental and other committees was temporarily suspended by an agreement with the executive heads of the state, which enabled these unworthy men to effect their base objects with comparative ease.[2] Nevertheless, in the ordinary military arrangements of occupying positions and distributing infantry and cavalry, the generals and inferior commanders acted for them-

*1845-6.*

*Ferozepore threatened, but purposely not attacked.*

*The objects of Lal Singh and Tej Singh.*

*The tactics of the Sikhs.*

[1] It was sufficiently certain and notorious at the time that Lal Singh was in communication with Capt. Nicolson, the British Agent at Ferozepore, but, owing to the untimely death of that officer, the details of the overtures made, and expectations held out, cannot now be satisfactorily known. (Cf. Dr. Macgregor's *History of the Sikhs*, ii. 80.)

The *Calcutta Review* for June 1849 (p. 549), while doubting the fact, or at least the extent and importance, of Lal Singh's and Tej Singh's treachery, admits that the former was not only in communication with Capt. Nicolson, as stated, but that on the 7th Feb. 1846 he was understood to have sent a plan of the Sikh position at Sobraon to Col. Lawrence, and that on the 19th Dec. 1845, the day after the battle of Mudki, Lal Singh's agent came to Major Broadfoot, and was dismissed with a rebuke. [As regards Tej Singh's treachery it may be stated that, according to a reliable tradition, that officer discovered early in the operations that his artillery ammunition had been tampered with and much of it rendered useless. Such treachery on the part of his own side doubtless had considerable effect upon his subsequent conduct. -ED.]

[2] Lal Singh was appointed wazir, and Tej Singh commander-in-chief of the army on or about the 8th Nov. 1845, according to the *Lahore News-Letter* of that date, prepared for Government.

selves, and all had to pay some respect to the spirit
which animated the private soldiers in their readiness
to do battle for the commonwealth of Gobind. The
effects of this enthusiastic unity of purpose in an army,
headed by men not only ignorant of warfare, but
studiously treacherous towards their followers, was
conspicuously visible in the speediness with whicn
numerous heavy guns and abundance of grain and
ammunition were brought across a large river. Every
Sikh considered the cause as his own, and he would
work as a labourer as well as carry a musket; he would
drag guns, drive bullocks, lead camels, and load and
unload boats with a cheerful alacrity, which contrasted
strongly with the inapt and sluggish obedience of mere
mercenaries, drilled, indeed, and fed with skill and
care, but unwarmed by one generous feeling for their
country or their foreign employers. The youthful
Khalsa was active and strong of heart, but the soldiers
had never before met so great a foe, and their tactics
were modified by involuntary awe of the British army,
renowned in the East for achievements in war. The
river had been crossed, and the treaty broken; but
the Sikhs were startled at their own audacity, and
they partially entrenched one portion of their forces,
while they timorously kept the other as a reserve out
of danger's way. Thus the valiant Swedes, when they
threw themselves into Germany under their king, the
great Gustavus, revived the castrametation of Roman
armies in the presence of the experienced commanders
of Austria; [1] and thus the young Telemachus, tremu-
lously bold, hurled his unaccustomed spear against the
princes of Ithaca, and sprang for shelter behind the
shield of his heroic father! [2]

The battle
of Mudki.
18th Dec.
1845.

The Ambala and Ludhiana divisions of the British
army arrived at Mudki, twenty miles from Ferozepore,
on the 18th December; and they had scarcely taken up

[1] As at Werben. before the battle of Leipzig. Col. Mitchell
says Gustavus owed his success almost as much to the spade
as to the sword. (*Life of Wallenstein*, p. 210.)

[2] *Odyssey*. xxii. The practice of the Sikhs would probably
have resolved itself into the system of fortified camps of the
Romans at night and during halts, and into the Greek custom
of impenetrable phalanxes on the battle-field. while it almost
anticipates the European tendencies of the day about future
warfare—which are, to mass artillery, and make it overwhelming. The Sikhs would have moved with their infantry and
guns together, while they swept the country with their cavalry;
and it is clear that no troops in India or in Southern Asia, save
the movable brigades of the English, could have successfully
assailed them.

their ground before they were attacked by a detach- 1845-6.
ment of the Sikh army, believed at the time to be
upwards of thirty thousand strong, but which really
seems to have consisted of less than two thousand
infantry, supported by about twenty-two pieces of
artillery, and eight or ten thousand horsemen.[1]  Lal
Singh headed the attack, but, in accordance with his
original design, he involved his followers in an engagement, and then left them to fight as their
undirected valour might prompt.  The Sikhs were repulsed with the loss of seventeen guns,[2] but the success
of the English was not so complete as should have
been achieved by the victors in so many battles; and
it was wisely determined to effect a junction with the
division of Sir John Littler before assailing the advanced wing of the Sikh army, which was encamped
in a deep horse-shoe form around the village of
P'heerooshuhur, about ten miles both from Mudki and
from Ferozepore.[3]  This position was strengthened by
more than a hundred pieces of artillery, and its slight
and imperfect entrenchments had, here and there, been
raised almost waist high since the action at Mudki.  It
was believed at the time to contain about fifty
thousand men, but subsequent inquiries reduced the
infantry to twelve regiments, and the cavalry to the

[1] See Lord Gough's dispatch of the 19th December 1845
for the estimate of 30,000 men, with 40 guns.  Capt. Nicolson
in his private correspondence of the period, and writing from
Ferozepore, gives the Sikh force at about 3,500 only, which is
doubtless too low, although subsequent inquiries all tended
to show that the infantry portion was weak, having been
composed of small detachments from each of the regiments in
position at Ferozeshah.  The *Calcutta Review*, No. XVI, p. 489,
estimates the guns at 22 only, and, the estimate being moderate,
it is probably correct.

[2] The British loss in the action was 215 killed and 657
wounded.  (See Lord Gough's dispatch of the 19th Dec. 1845.)
The force under Lord Gough at the time amounted to about
11,000 men.  In this action the English may, in a military sense,
be said to have been surprised.  Their defective system of
spies left them ignorant of the general position and probable
objects of the enemy; and the little use their commanders have
usually made of cavalry left the near approach of the Sikhs
unknown, and therefore unchecked.  [Among the killed was
Sir Robert Sale, the defender of Jalalabad.—ED.]

[3] The correct name of the place, which has become identified with an important battle, is as given in the text:—
'P'heeroo' being the not uncommon name of a man, and 'shuhur'
an ordinary termination, signifying place or city.  The name
'Ferozeshah' is erroneous, but it is one likely to be taken up
on hearing 'P'heerooshuhur' badly pronounced by peasants and
others.  The Sikhs call the battle 'P'heeroo ka larai', or the
fight of P'heeroo simply, without the addition of 'shuhur'.

eight or ten thousand which had before been engaged. The wing of the Sikh army attacked did not, therefore, greatly surpass its assailants, except in the number and size of its guns, the English artillery consisting almost wholly of six and nine pounders.[1] But the belief in the fortune of the British arms was strong, and the Sepoys would then have marched with alacrity against ten times their own numbers.

The
battle of
P'heeroo-
shuhur, and
retreat of
the Sikhs,
21st and
22nd Dec.
1845.

A junction was effected with Sir John Littler's division about midday on the 21st December, and at a distance of four miles from the enemy's position. Considerable delay occurred in arranging the details of the assault, which was not commenced until within an hour of sunset. The confident English had at last got the field they wanted; they marched in even array, and their famed artillery opened its steady fire. But the guns of the Sikhs were served with rapidity and precision, and the foot-soldiers stood between and behind the batteries, firm in their order, and active with their muskets. The resistance met was wholly unexpected, and all started with astonishment. Guns were dismounted, and their ammunition was blown into the air; squadrons were checked in mid career; battalion after battalion was hurled back with shattered ranks, and it was not until after sunset that portions of the enemy's position were finally carried. Darkness, and the obstinacy of the contest, threw the English into confusion; men of all regiments and arms were mixed together; generals were doubtful of the fact or of the extent of their own success, and colonels knew not what had become of the regiments they commanded, or of the army of which they formed a part. Some portions of the enemy's line had not been broken, and

---

[1] Both the Sikhs and the European officers in the Lahore service agree in saying that there were only twelve battalions in the lines of P'heerooshuhur, and such indeed seems to have been the truth. The Governor-General and Commander-in-Chief vaguely estimated the whole Sikh army on the left bank of the Sutlej at 60,000 strong, and Lord Gough makes Tej Singh bring 30,000 horse, *besides* fresh battalions, and a large park of artillery into action on the 22nd December, which would leave but a small remainder for the previous defence of P'heerooshuhur. (See the dispatches of the 22nd and 31st Dec. 1845.) The author has learnt that, after the war, Lord Gough ascertained, through the British authorities at Lahore, that the Sikhs esimated their numbers at P'heerooshuhur at 46,808 men, of all kinds, with 88 guns, 'including those brought up and taken away by Tej Singh'. This low estimate of the strength of the Sikhs in artillery is in favour of the credibility of the statement, and if Tej Singh's men are likewise included in the numbers given, the estimate may perhaps be fully trusted.

the uncaptured guns were turned by the Sikhs upon masses of soldiers, oppressed with cold and thirst and fatigue, and who attracted the attention of the watchful enemy by lighting fires of brushwood to warm their stiffened limbs. The position of the English was one of real danger and great perplexity; their mercenaries had proved themselves good soldiers in foreign countries as well as in India itself, when discipline was little known, or while success was continuous; but in a few hours the five thousand children of a distant land found that their art had been learnt, and that an emergency had arisen which would tax their energies to the utmost. On that memorable night the English were hardly masters of the ground on which they stood; they had no reserve at hand, while the enemy had fallen back upon a second army, and could renew the fight with increased numbers. The not imprudent thought occurred of retiring upon Ferozepore; but Lord Gough's dauntless spirit counselled otherwise, and his own and Lord Hardinge's personal intrepidity in storming batteries, at the head of troops of English gentlemen and bands of hardy yeomen, eventually achieved a partial success and a temporary repose. On the morning of the 22nd December, the last remnants of the Sikhs were driven from their camp; but as the day advanced the second wing of their army approached in battle-array, and the wearied and famished English saw before them a desperate and, perhaps, useless struggle. This reserve was commanded by Tej Singh; he had been urged by his zealous and sincere soldiery to fall upon the English at daybreak, but *his* object was to have the dreaded army of the Khalsa overcome and dispersed, and he delayed until Lal Singh's force was everywhere put to flight, and until his opponents had again ranged themselves round their colours. Even at the last moment he rather skirmished and made feints than led his men to a resolute attack, and after a time he precipitately fled, leaving his subordinates without orders and without an object, at a moment when the artillery ammunition of the English had failed, when a portion of their force was retiring upon Ferozepore, and when no exertions could have prevented the remainder from retreating likewise, if the Sikhs had boldly pressed forward.[1]

---

[1] For the battle of P'heerooshuhur, see Lord Gough's dispatch of the 22nd, and Lord Hardinge's of the 31st Dec. 1845. The Governor-General notices in especial the exertions of the infantry soldiers; and one of the charges made by the

1845-6.

The diffi-
culties and
apprehen-
sions of the
English.

A battle had thus been won, and more than seventy pieces of artillery and some conquered or confiscated territories graced the success; but the victors had lost a seventh of their numbers, they were paralysed after their prodigious exertions and intense excitement, and

3rd Light Dragoons has been a theme of general admiration. The loss sustained was 694 killed, and 1,721 wounded. [The casualties among the officers were very heavy—103 in all. Among them was the political officer, Major Broadfoot, who has figured so prominently in previous pages.—ED.]

After the war, Lord Gough learnt that the loss of the Sikhs in killed probably amounted to 2,000 in all, as the heirs of 1,782 men of the regular troops alone claimed balances of pay due to relatives slain. This argues a great slaughter; and yet it was a common remark at the time, that very few dead bodies were to be seen on the field after the action.

The statements of the *Quarterly Review* for June 1846, pp. 203-6, and of the *Calcutta Review* for Dec. 1847, p. 498, may be referred to about certain points still but imperfectly known, and which it is only necessary to allude to in a general way in this history. Two of the points are: (1) the proposal to fall back on Ferozepore during the night of the 21st December; and (2) the actual movement of a considerable portion of the British army towards that place on the forenoon of the following day.

Had the Sikhs been efficiently commanded, a retirement on Ferozepore would have been judicious in a military point of view, but as the enemy was led by traitors, it was best to fearlessly keep the field. Perhaps neither the incapacity nor the treason of Lal Singh and Tej Singh were fully perceived or credited by the English chiefs, and hence the anxiety of the one on whom the maintenance of the British dominion intact mainly depended.

At P'heerooshuhur the larger calibre and greater weight of metal of the mass of the Sikh artillery, and consequently the superiority of practice relatively to that of the field guns of the English, was markedly apparent in the condition of the two parks after the battle. The captured cannon showed scarcely any marks of round shot or shells, while nearly a third of the British guns were disabled in their carriages or tumbrils.

With regard to this battle it may be observed that the English had not that exact knowledge of the Sikh strength and position which might have been obtained even by means of reconnoitring; and it may also *perhaps* be said that the attack should have been made in column rather than in line, and after the long flanks of the enemy's position had been enfiladed by artillery. The extent, indeed, to which the English were unprepared for a campaign, and the manner in which their forces were commanded in most of the actions of the war, should be carefully borne in mind; for it was defective tactics and the absolute want of ammunition, as much as the native valour and aptitude of the Sikhs, which gave for a time a character of equality to the struggle, and which in this history seems to make a comparatively petty power dispute with the English supremacy in Northern India. Had the English been better led and better equipped, the fame of the Sikhs would not have been so great as it is, and the British chronicler would have been spared the ungracious task of declaring unpleasing truths.

the Sikhs were allowed to cross the Sutlej at their leisure to prepare for fresh contests. The sepoy mercenaries had for the first time met an equal antagonist with their own weapons—even ranks and the fire of artillery. They loudly complained of the inferiority of their cannon; they magnified banks two and three feet high into formidable ramparts, and exploding tumbrils and stores of powder became, in their imaginations, designed and deadly mines. Nor was this feeling of respect and exaggeration confined to the Indians alone; the European soldiers partook of it; and the British public, as well as the dignitaries of the church and the heads of the state, became impressed with the immensity of the danger which had threatened the peace, and perhaps the safety, of their exotic dominion.[1] Regiments of men, and numerous single officers variously employed, were summoned from the most distant provinces to aid in vindicating the military renown of

No one, however, can be insensible to the claims which the veteran chief of the army has established to his country's gratitude, by his cheering hardihood under every circumstance of danger, and by his great successes over all opponents. The robust character of Lord Gough has on many occasions stood England in good stead.

[1] The alarm of the English about the occupation of Delhi and the passage of the Jumna, may be likened to the nervous dread of Augustus, when he heard of the defeat of Varus and the destruction of his legions; and that one so astute, and so familiar with the sources of Roman power and the causes of Roman weakness, should have feared the consequences of a German invasion of Italy, at once palliates the apprehensions of the English in India and shows upon what slight foundations and undreamt-of chances the mightiest fabrics of dominion sometimes rest. Yet it is not clear that Augustus was not alarmed rather for himself than for Rome. He may have thought that a successful inroad of barbarians would encourage domestic enemies, and so lead to his own downfall, without sensibly affecting the real power of his country. Similarly, the apprehensions of the English after P'heerooshuhur may be said to have had a personal as much as a national reference, and there is no good reason for believing that one or two or even three defeats on the Sutlej would have shaken the stability of the British rule to the east and south of Delhi. All the chiefs of India, indeed, are willing enough to be independent but no union for any such purpose yet exists among them, and only one or two are at any moment ready to take up arms; whereas the resources of the English are vast, obedience among them is perfect, and victory would soon return to valour and unanimity. Still, an unsuccessful warfare on the part of the English of three or four consecutive years, might justly be regarded as the commencement of their decline; although it is very doubtful whether any combination of the present powers of India could drive them from Bengal, or from the coasts of the Deccan.

1845-6.

the English race, and the political supremacy of three generations. All longed for retribution, and all were cheered amid their difficulties by the genial temper and lofty bearing of one chief; and by the systematic industry and full knowledge of military requirements possessed by the other. But joy and gratitude were yet uppermost for the moment; the hope of revenge was disturbed by the remembrance of danger; and, unmindful of the rebuke of the wise Ulysses, a partial Divinity was praised by proclamation, for the deliverance *he* had vouchsafed to *his* votaries.

Unholy is the voice
Of loud thanksgiving over slaughtered men.[1]

The Sikhs
recross the
Sutlej, and
threaten
Ludhiana,
Jan. 1846.

The British army was gradually reinforced, and it took up a position stretching from Ferozepore towards Hariki, and parallel to that held by the Sikhs on the right bank of the Sutlej. But the want of ammunition and heavy guns reduced the English to inactivity, and delay produced negligence on their part and emboldened the enemy to fresh acts of daring. The Cis-Sutlej feudatories kept aloof from their new masters, or they excited disturbances; and the Raja of Ladwa, a petty prince dependent on the English, but who had been denounced as a traitor for a year past,[2] openly pro-

---

[1] *Odyssey*, xxii. The Governor-General's notification of the 25th December 1845 calls upon the troops to render acknowledgements to God, and the ecclesiastical authorities in Calcutta subsequently circulated a form of thanksgiving. The anxiety of the Governor-General may be further inferred from his proclamation, encouraging desertion from the Sikh ranks, with the assurance of present rewards and future pensions, *and the immediate decision of any lawsuits in which the deserters might be engaged in the British provinces!* (Major Smith, *Reigning Family of Lahore,* Introduction, p. xxvi *n.*)

The feeling which prompted the troops of Cromwell or Gustavus to kneel and return thanks to God on the field of victory must ever be admired and honoured; for it was genuine, and pervaded all ranks, from the leader downwards, and it would equally have moved the soldiers to reproaches and humiliation had they been beaten. But such tokens of reverence and abasement come coldly and without a vital meaning in the guise of a 'general order' or 'circular memorandum'; and perhaps a civilized and intelligent government might with advantage refrain from such tame and passionless assurances of devotion and gratitude, while it gave more attention to religious exercises in its regimental regulations. God should rather be kept ever present to the minds of the armed servants of the state by daily worship and instruction, than ostentatiously lauded on the rare occasion of a victory.

[2] Major Broadfoot to Government, 13th Dec. 1844. This chief received the title of Raja from Lord Auckland, partly as a compliment to Ranjit Singh, to whom he was related, and

1845-6.

ceeded from the neighbourhood of Karnal, and joined the division of the Sikh army under Ranjor Singh, which had crossed the Jullundur Doab, to the neighbourhood of Ludhiana. This important town had been denuded of its troops to swell the first army of defence, and it was but slowly and partially garrisoned by fresh regiments arriving from the eastward, although it covered the several lines of approach from the Jumna towards Ferozepore.[1]    Early in January the Raja of Ladwa returned to withdraw his family from his fief of Badowal near Ludhiana, and he took the opportunity of burning a portion of the cantonment at the latter place, which the paucity of infantry and the want of cavalry on the spot enabled him to do with impunity. About the same time, the main army of the Sikhs, observing the supineness of their opponents, began to recross the Sutlej and to construct a bridge-head to secure the freedom of their passage. The English were unwillingly induced to let the Sikhs labour at this work, for it was feared that an attack would bring on a general engagement, and that the want of ammunition would prevent a battle being won or a victory being completed. The Sikhs naturally exulted, and they proclaimed that they would again fall upon the hated foreigners. Nor were their boasts altogether disbelieved; the disadvantages of Ferozepore as a frontier post became more and more apparent, and the English began to experience difficulty in obtaining

partly in approbation of his liberality in providing the means of throwing a bridge across the classical Sarsuti, at Thanesar. He was a reckless, dissipated man, of moderate capacity; but he inherited the unsettled disposition of his father, Gurdut Singh, who once held Karnal and some villages to the east of the Jumna, and who caused the English some trouble between 1803 and 1809.

[1] It is not clear why Ludhiana was not adequately garrisoned, or rather covered, by the troops which marched from Meerut after the battle of P'heerooshuhur. The Governor-General's attention was, indeed, chiefly given to strengthening the main army in its unsupported position of Ferozepore—the real military disadvantage of which he had ample reason to deplore; while amidst his difficulties it may possibly have occurred to his Lordship, that the original policy of 1809—of being strong on the Jumna rather than on the Sutlej—was a truly wise one with reference to the *avoidance* of a war with the Sikhs.

The desire of being in force near the capitals of the Punjab and the main army of the Sikhs likewise induced Lord Hardinge to direct Sir Charles Napier to march from Sind, without heeding Multan, although, as his Lordship publicly acknowledged, that victorious commander had been sent for when it was thought the campaign might become a series of sieges.

supplies from the country they had annexed by the pen without having secured by the sword. The petty fort of Muktsar, where Gobind repulsed his Mughal pursuers after his flight from Chamkaur, was successfully defended for a time against some provincial companies and the auxiliaries of Bikanir, which, like the legionaries themselves, were deficient in artillery ammunition. The equally petty fort of Dharmkot was held, in defiance of the near presence of the right wing of the English army; and other defensible places towards Sirhind overawed the population, and interfered with the peaceful march of convoys and detachments.[1]

The skirmish of Badowal, Jan. 21, 1846.

On the 17th January 1846, Major-General Sir Harry Smith[2] was sent with a brigade to capture Dharmkot, which was surrendered without bloodshed, and the transit of grain to the army was thus rendered more secure. The original object of Sir Harry Smith's diversion was to cover the march of the large convoy of guns, ammunition, and treasure in progress to Ferozepore, as well as to clear the country of partisan troops which restricted the freedom of traffic; but when it became known that Ranjor Singh had crossed the Sutlej in force and threatened Ludhiana, the General was ordered to proceed to the relief of that place. On the 20th of January he encamped at the trading town of Jugraon, within twenty-five miles of his destination, and the authorities of the son of Fateh Singh Ahluwalia, of the treaty of 1805, to whom the place belonged, readily allowed him to occupy its well-built fort. It was known on that day that Ranjor Singh was in position immediately to the westward of Ludhiana, and that he had thrown a small garrison into Badowal, which lay about eighteen miles distant on the direct road from Jugraon. The British detachment, which

[1] The hill station of Simla, where many English families reside, and which is near the Sutlej, and the equally accessible posts of Kasauli and Sabathu, were at this time likewise threatened by the Lahore feudatory of Mandi, and some Sikh partisans; and as the regiments usually stationed at these places had been wholly withdrawn, it would not have been difficult to have destroyed them. But the local British authorities were active in collecting the quotas of the hill Rajputs, and judicious in making use of their means; and no actual incursion took place, although a turbulent sharer in the sequestered Anandpur-Makhowal had to be called to account.

[2] This distinguished officer, who fought through the Peninsular War, afterwards served in South Africa, where his memory is commemorated by the towns of Aliway and Harrismith. His wife, a Spanish lady, who accompanied him through the Peninsular campaigns, also gave her name to a South African town, 'Ladysmith',—a place not without fame.—ED.]

had been swelled by reinforcements to four regiments 1845-6.
of infantry, three regiments of cavalry, and eighteen
guns, marched soon after midnight; and early on the
morning of the 21st January it was learnt that the
whole Sikh army, estimated at ten thousand men, had
moved to Badowal during the preceding day. That
place was then distant eight miles from the head of
the column, and Sir Harry Smith considered that if he
had made a detour to the right, so as to leave the
Sikhs about three miles on his other flank, he would
be able to effect his junction with the Ludhiana
brigade without molestation. A short halt took place to
enable the baggage to get somewhat ahead, and it was
arranged that the long strings of animals should move
parallel to the troops and on the right flank, so as to
be covered by the column. As Badowal was approached, the Sikhs were seen to be in motion likewise, and
apparently to be bent on intercepting the English; but
as it was not wished to give them battle, Sir Harry
Smith continued his march, inclining however still
more to his right, and making occasional halts with the
cavalry to enable the infantry to close up, it having
fallen behind owing to the heavy nature of the ground.
But the Sikhs were resolved on fighting, and they commenced a fire of artillery on the British horse, which
obtained a partial cover under sand-banks, while the
guns of the detachment opened upon the Sikhs and
served to keep their line in check. By the time that
the British infantry and small rear-guard of cavalry
had closed up, the fire of the Sikhs had begun to tell,
and it was thought that a steady charge by the infantry would throw them into disorder, and would allow
the baggage to pass on, and give time to the Ludhiana
troops to come to the aid of their comrades. A close
contest was indeed the prompting of every one's heart
at the moment; but as the regiments of foot were being
formed into line, it was found that the active Sikhs
had dragged guns, unperceived, behind sand hillocks to
the rear of the column—or, as matters then stood, that
they had turned their enemy's left flank. These guns
threw their enfilading shot with great rapidity and
precision, and whole sections of men were seen to fall
at a time without an audible groan amid the hissing of the iron storm. The ground was heavy, the men
were wearied with a march of nine hours and eighteen
miles, and it became evident that a charge might prove
fatal to the exhausted victors. The infantry once more
resumed its march, and its retirement or retreat upon

18  (45-68/1975)

**1845-6.**

Ludhiana was covered with skill and steadiness by the cavalry.[1] The Sikhs did not pursue, for they were without a leader, or without one who wished to see the English beaten. Ranjor Singh let his soldiers engage in battle, but that he accompanied them into the fight is more than doubtful, and it is certain that he did not essay the easy task of improving the success of his own men into the complete reverse of his enemy. The mass of the British baggage was at hand, and the temptation to plunder could not be resisted by men who were without orders to conquer. Every beast of burden which had not got within sight of Ludhiana, or which had not, timorously but prudently, been taken back to Jugraon, when the firing was heard, fell into the hands of the Sikhs, and they were enabled boastfully to exhibit artillery store carts as if they had captured British cannon.[2]

*The Sikhs encouraged, and Gulab Singh induced to repair to Lahore.*

Ludhiana was relieved, but an unsuccessful skirmish added to the belief so pleasing to the prostrate princes of India, that the dreaded army of their foreign maste s had at last been foiled by the skill and valour of the disciples of Gobind, the kindred children of their own soil. The British sepoys glanced furtively at one another, or looked towards the east, their home; and the brows of Englishmen themselves grew darker as they thought of struggles rather than triumphs. The Governor-General and Commander-in-Chief trembled for the safety of that siege train and convoy of ammunition, so necessary to the efficiency of an army which they had launched in haste against aggressors and received back shattered by the shock of opposing arms. The leader of the beaten brigades saw before him a tarnished name after the labours of a life, nor was he met by many encouraging hopes of rapid retribution. The Sikhs on their side were correspondingly elated; the presence of European prisoners added to their triumph; Lal Singh and Tej Singh shrank within themselves with fear, and Gulab Singh, who had been spontaneously hailed as minister and leader, began to think that the Khalsa was really formidable to one

[1 Under Col. Cureton.—ED.]

2 Cf. the Governor-General to the Secret Committee, 19th Jan. and 3rd Feb., and Lord Gough's dispatch of the 1st Feb. 1845. After the skirmish of the 21st January there were found to be sixty-nine killed, sixty-eight wounded, and seventy-seven missing; of which last, several were taken prisoners, while others rejoined their corps in a day or two. Of the prisoners, Mr. Barron, an assistant-surgeon, and some European soldiers were taken to Lahore.

greater far than himself, and he arrived at Lahore on 1845-6.
the 27th of January, to give unity and vigour to the
counsels of the Sikhs.[1] The army under Tej Singh had
recrossed the Sutlej in force; it had enlarged the
bridge-head before alluded to, and so entrenched a
strong position in the face of the British divisions. The
Sikhs seemed again to be about to carry the war into
the country of their enemy; but Gulab Singh came too
late—their fame had reached its height, and defeat and
subjection speedily overtook them.

During the night of the 22nd January, Ranjor The battle
Singh marched from Badowal to a place on the Sutlej of Aliwal,
about fifteen miles below Ludhiana, where he imme- 28th Jan.
diately collected a number of boats as if to secure the 1846.
passage of the river. The object of this movement is
not known; but it may have been caused by a want of
confidence on the part of the Sikhs themselves, as there
were few regular regiments among them, until joined
by a brigade of four battalions and some guns from
the main army, which gave them a force of not less
than fifteen thousand combatants. Sir Harry Smith
immediately occupied the deserted position of the
enemy, and he was himself reinforced simultaneously
with the Sikhs by a brigade from the main army of
the English. On the 28th January the General marched
with his eleven thousand men, to give the enemy battle, or to reconnoitre his position and assail it in some
degree of form, should circumstances render such a
course the most prudent. The Sikhs were nearly ten
miles distant, and midway it was learnt that they were
about to move with the avowed object of proceeding
with a part or the whole of their force to relieve the
fort of Gungrana or to occupy the neighbouring town
of Jugraon, both of which posts were close to the line
of the British communications with the Jumna. On
reaching the edge of the table-land, bounding the sun-
ken belt of many miles in breadth within which the
narrower channel of the Sutlej proper winds irregu-
larly, a portion of the Sikhs were observed to be in
motion in a direction which would take them clear of
the left of the British approach; but as soon as they saw
that they were liable to be attacked in flank, they faced
towards their enemy and occupied with their right the
village of Bundri, and with their left the little hamlet
of Aliwal, while with that activity necessary to their
system, and characteristic of the spirit of the common

[1] Cf. the Governor-General to the Secret Committee, 3rd
Feb. 1846.

soldiers, they immediately began to throw up banks of earth before their guns, where not otherwise protected, such as would afford some cover to themselves and offer some impediment to their assailants. An immediate collision was inevitable, and the British commander promptly gave the order for battle. The regiments of cavalry which headed the advance opened their glittering ranks to the right and left, and made apparent the serried battalions of infantry and the frowning batteries of cannon. The scene was magnificent and yet overawing : the eye included the whole field, and glanced approvingly from the steady order of one foe to the even array of the other; all bespoke gladness of mind and strength of heart; but beneath the elate looks of the advancing warriors there lurked that fierce desire for the death of his fellows which must ever impel the valiant soldier. When thus deployed, the lines of battle were not truly parallel. The Sikh line inclined towards and extended beyond the British right, while the other flanks were, for a time, comparatively distant. The English had scarcely halted during their march of eight miles, even to form their line; but the Sikhs nevertheless commenced the action. It was perceived by Sir Harry Smith that the capture of the village of Aliwal was of the first importance, and the right of the infantry was led against it. A deadly struggle seemed impending; for the Sikh ranks were steady and the play of their guns incessant; but the holders of the post were battalions of hill-men, raised because their demeanour was sober, and their hearts indifferent to the Khalsa, and after firing a straggling volley, they fled in confusion, headed by Ranjor Singh, their immediate leader, and leaving the brave Sikh artillerymen to be slaughtered by the conquerors. The British cavalry of the right made at the same time a sweeping and successful charge, and one-half of the opposing army was fairly broken and dispersed; but the Sikhs on their own right seemed to be outflanking their opponents in spite of the exertions of the English infantry and artillery; for there the more regular battalions were in line, and the true Sikh was not easily cowed. A prompt and powerful effort was necessary, and a regiment of European lancers,[1] supported by one of Indian cavalry, was launched against the even ranks of the Lahore infantry. The Sikhs knelt to receive the orderly but impetuous charge of the English warriors, moved alike by noble

[1 H.M.'s 16th Lancers, under Col. Cureton.—Ed.]

recollections of their country, by military emulation, 1845-6. and by personal feelings of revenge; but at the critical moment, the unaccustomed discipline of many of Gobind's champions failed them. They rose, yet they reserved their fire, and delivered it together at the distance of a spear's throw; nor was it until the mass had been three times ridden· through that the Sikhs dispersed. The charge was timely and bold; but the ground was more thickly strewn with the bodies of victorious horsemen than of beaten infantry. An attempt was made to rally behind Bundri; but all resistance was unavailing, the Sikhs were driven across the Sutlej, more than fifty pieces [1] of cannon were taken, and the General forgot his sorrows, and the soldiers their sufferings and indignities, in the fullness of their common triumph over a worthy enemy, in a well-planned and bravely fought battle.[2]

[1] Sixty-seven is the official number given.—ED.]
[2] Cf. Sir Harry Smith's dispatch of the 30th January, and Lord Gough's dispatch of the 1st February 1846. (Parliamentary Papers, 1846.) The loss sustained was 151 killed, 413 wounded, and 25 missing.

The *Calcutta Review,* No. XVI, p. 499, states that Sir Harry Smith required some pressing before he would engage the Sikhs, after his reverse at Badowal. That active leader, however, was in no need of such promptings, and had adequate reinforcements reached him sooner than they did, the battle of Aliwal would have been sooner fought. It may likewise be here mentioned, that neither does the reviewer throughout his article do fair justice to Lord Gough. nor, in a particular instance, to the commissariat department of the army. Thus, with regard to the Commander-in-Chief, it is more than hinted (see p. 497), that Lord Hardinge was in no way to blame—that is, that Lord Gough *was* to blame—for the delay which occurred in attacking the Sikhs at P'heerooshuhur. It may be difficult to ascertain the causes, or to apportion the blame, but the Governor-General can proudly stand on his acknowledged merits and services, and wants no support at the expense of an ancient comrade-in-arms. Again, with regard to the commissariat, it is stated, at p. 488, that supplies, which the head of the department in the field asked six weeks to furnish, were procured by Major Broadfoot in six days. The commissariat department could only use money and effect purchases by contract, or in the open market; but Major Broadfoot could summarily require 'protected chiefs', on pain of confiscation, to meet all his demands; and thé writer of the article might have learnt, or must have been aware, that the requisitions in question led to one chief being disgraced by the imposition of a fine, and had some share in the subsequent deposal of another. Had the British magistrates of Delhi, Saharanpur, Bareilly, and other places, been similarly empowered to seize by force the grain and carriage within their limits, there would have been no occasion to disparage the commissariat department. Further, it is known to many, and it is in itself plain, that had the military authorities been required, or allowed, to

1845-6.

The Sikh
chiefs
anxious to
treat, and
the English
desirous of
ending the
war.

The victory was equally important and opportune, and the time-serving Gulab Singh, whose skill and capacity might have protracted the war, first reproached the vanquished Sikhs for rashly engaging in hostilities with their colossal neighbour, and then entered into negotiations with the English leaders.[1] The Governor-General was not displeased that the Lahore authorities should be ready to yield; for he truly felt that to subjugate the Punjab in one season, to defeat an army as numerous as his own, to take two capitals, ard to lay siege to Multan, and Jammu, and Peshawar— all within a few months—was a task of difficult achievement and full of imminent risks. The dominion of the English in India hinges mainly upon the number and efficiency of the troops of their own race which they can bring into the field; and a campaign in the hot weather would have thinned the ranks of the European regiments under the most favourable circumstances, and the ordinary recurrence of an epidemic disease would have proved as fatal to the officers of every corps present as to the common soldiers. But besides this important consideration, it was felt that the minds of men throughout India were agitated, and that protracted hostilities would not only jeopardize the communications with the Jumna, but might disturb the whole of the north-western provinces, swarming with a military population which is ready to follow any standard affording pay or allowing plunder, and which already sighs for the end of a dull reign of peace. Bright visions of standing triumphant on the Indus and of numbering the remotest conquests of Alexander among the provinces of Britain, doubtless warmed the imagination of the Governor-General; but the first object was to drive the Sikhs across the Sutlej by force of arms, or to have them withdrawn to their own side of the river by the unconditional submission of the chiefs and the

prepare themselves as they wished, they as simple soldiers, who had no financial difficulties to consider, would have been amply prepared with all that an army of invasion or defence could have required, long before the Sikhs crossed the Sutlej. Lord Hardinge was chiefly responsible for the timely and adequate equipment of the army, in anticipation of a probable war; and with the Governor-General in the field, possessed of superior and anomalous powers, the Commander-in-Chief could only be held responsible—and that but to a limited extent—for the strategy of a campaign or the conduct of a battle.

[1] Cf. the Governor-General to the Secret Committee, of the 19th Feb. 1846.

delegates of the army; for, until that were done, no 1845-6.
progress could be said to have been made in the war,
and every petty chief in Hindustan would have silently
prepared for asserting his independence, or for enlarging his territory on the first opportunity.  But the total
dispersion of so large and so well equipped a body of
brave men, as that which lay within sight of the available force of the British Government, could not be
accomplished by one defeat, if the chiefs of the country
were to be rendered desperate, and if all were to place
their valour and unanimity under the direction of one
able man.  The English, therefore, intimated to Gulab
Singh their readiness to acknowledge a Sikh sovereignty in Lahore after the army should have been
disbanded; but the Raja declared his inability to deal
with the troops, which still overawed him and other
well-wishers to the family of Ranjit Singh.  This help-
lessness was partly exaggerated for selfish objects; but
time pressed; the speedy dictation of a treaty under
the walls of Lahore was essential to the British reputation; and the views of either party were in some
sort met by an understanding that the Sikh army
should be attacked by the English, and that when
beaten it should be openly abandoned by its own government; and further, that the passage of the Sutlej
should be unopposed and the road to the capital laid
open to the victors.  Under such circumstances of discreet policy and shameless treason was the battle of
Sobraon fought.[1]

An understanding come to, that the Sikh army shall be attacked by the one and deserted by the other.

The Sikhs had gradually brought the greater part
of their force into the entrenchment on the left bank
of the Sutlej, which had been enlarged as impulse
prompted or as opportunity seemed to offer.  They
placed sixty-seven pieces of artillery in battery, and
their strength was estimated at thirty-five thousand
fighting men; but it is probable that twenty thousand
would exceed the truth; and of that reduced number,
it is certain that all were not regular troops.  The entrenchment likewise showed a fatal want of unity of
command and of design; and at Sobraon, as in the
other battles of the campaign, the soldiers did every-

The defensive position of the Sikhs.

[1] Cf. the Governor-General's letter to the Secret Committee, of the 19th Feb. 1846; from which, however, those only
who were mixed up with the negotiations can extract aught
indicative of the understandng with Gulab Singh which is
alluded to in the text. It was for this note chiefly, if not
entirely, that the author was removed from political employment by the East India Company. This was the author's own
conviction, from careful inquiries made in India; and has been
the result of equally careful inquiries made by men in England.

thing and the leaders nothing. Hearts to dare and hands to execute were numerous; but there was no mind to guide and animate the whole : each inferior commander defended his front according to his skill and his means, and the centre and left, where the disciplined battalions were mainly stationed, had batteries and salient points as high as the stature of a man, and ditches which an armed soldier could not leap without exertion; but a considerable part of the line exhibited at intervals the petty obstacles of a succession of such banks and trenches as would shelter a crouching marksman or help him to sleep in security when no longer a watcher. This was especially the case on the right flank, where the looseness of the river sand rendered it impossible to throw up parapets without art and labour, and where irregular troops, the least able to remedy such disadvantages, had been allowed or compelled to take up their position. The flank in question was mainly guarded by a line of two hundred 'zamburuks' or falconets; [1] but it derived some support from a salient battery, and from the heavy guns retained on the opposite bank of the river.[2] Tej Singh commanded in this entrenchment, and Lal Singh lay with his horse in loose order higher up the stream, watched by a body of British cavalry. The Sikhs, generally, were somewhat cast down by the defeat at

[1] These were light swivel guns—usually mounted on camels. In the muster-rolls of the Sikh army they are shown as organized into regular batteries like field artillery. Specimens of these guns may be seen in the Armoury in the Fort at Lahore.—Ed.]

[2] The ordinary belief that the entrenchments of Sobraon were jointly planned and executed by a French and a Spanish colonel, is as devoid of foundation as that the Sikh army was rendered effective solely by the labours and skill of French and Italian generals. Hurbon the brave Spaniard, and Moutor the Frenchman, who were at Sobraon, doubtless exerted themselves where they could, but their authority or their influence did not extend beyond a regiment or a brigade, and the lines showed no trace whatever of scientific skill or of unity of design. [This note is typical of the author's belittling style. The works were really of an extremely strong nature. 'For some weeks the Sikhs under the direction of a Spanish officer named *Huerba* had been employed in constructing a remarkably powerful *tete de pont* at the village of Sobraon to cover a bridge of boats which they had thrown across the river Sutlej .... and it was now completed in a series of half-moon bastions, connected by curtains, and covered by a ditch in front, both flanks resting on the river. This great work, two and a half miles in length, was protected by batteries on the right bank of the river, so as to command the passage, and manned by 35,000 of the best of the Sikh troops with 67 guns.' (Meadows Taylor.)—Ed.]

Aliwal, and by the sight of the unhonoured remains of their comrades floating down the Sutlej; but the self-confidence of a multitude soon returns : they had been cheered by the capture of a post of observation established by the English and left unoccupied at night, and they resumed their vaunting practice of performing their military exercises almost within hail of the British pickets. Yet the judgement of the old and experienced could not be deceived; the dangers which threatened the Sikh people pressed upon their minds; they saw no escape from domestic anarchy or from foreign subjection, and the grey-headed chief Sham Singh of Atari made known his resolution to die in the first conflict with the enemies of his race, and so to offer himself up as a sacrifice of propitiation to the spirit of Gobind and to the genius of his mystic commonwealth.

1845-6.

In the British camp the confidence of the soldiery was likewise great, and 'none there despaired of the fortune of England. The spirits of the men had been raised by the victory of Aliwal, and early in February a formidable siege train and ample stores of ammunition arrived from Delhi. The sepoys looked with delight upon the long array of stately elephants dragging the huge and heavy ordnance of their predilections, and the heart of the Englishman himself swelled with pride as he beheld these dread symbols of the wide dominion of his race. It was determined that the Sikh position should be attacked on the 10th February, and various plans were laid down for making victory sure, and for the speedy gratification of a burning resentment. The officers of artillery naturally desired that their guns, the representatives of a high art, should be used agreeably to the established rules of the engineer, or that ramparts should be breached in front and swept in flank before they were stormed by defenceless battalions; but such deliberate tediousness of process did not satisfy the judgement or the impatience of the commanders, and it was arranged that the whole of the heavy ordnance should be planted in masses opposite particular points of the enemy's entrenchment, and that when the Sikhs had been shaken by a continuous storm of shot and shell, the right or weakest part of the position should be assaulted in line by the strongest of the three investing divisions, which together mustered nearly fifteen thousand men. A large body of British cavalry was likewise placed to watch the movements of Lal Singh-

The English plan of attack.

and the two divisions which lay near Ferozepore were held ready to push across the Sutlej as soon as victory should declare itself. The precise mode of attack was not divulged, or indeed finally settled, until noon of the preceding day, for it was desired to surprise the commanding post of observation, which indifference or negligence had allowed to fall into the hands of the Sikhs a short time before. The evening and the early hours of darkness of the 9th February were thus occupied with busy preparations; the hitherto silent camp poured all its numbers abroad; soldiers stood in groups, talking of the task to be achieved by their valour; officers rode hastily along to receive or deliver orders; and on that night what Englishman passed battalion after battalion to seek a short repose, or a moment's solitary communion, and listened as he went to the hammering of shells and the piling of iron shot, or beheld the sentinel pacing silently along by the gleam of renewed fires, without recalling to mind his heroic king and the eve of Agincourt, rendered doubly immortal by the genius of Shakespeare?

The British divisions advanced in silence, amid the darkness of night and the additional gloom of a thick haze. The coveted post was found unoccupied; the Sikhs seemed everywhere taken by surprise, and they beat clamorously to arms when they saw themselves about to be assailed. The English batteries opened at sunrise, and for upwards of three hours an incessant play of artillery was kept up upon the general mass of the enemy. The round shot exploded tumbrils, or dashed heaps of sand into the air; the hollow shells cast their fatal contents fully before them, and the devious rockets sprang aloft with fury to fall hissing amid a flood of men; but all was in vain, the Sikhs stood unappalled, and 'flash for flash returned, and fire for fire'. The field was resplendent with embattled warriors, one moment umbered in volumes of sulphurous smoke, and another brightly apparent amid the splendour of beaming brass and the cold and piercing rays of polished steel. The roar and loud reverberation of the ponderous ordnance added to the impressive interest of the scene, and fell gratefully upon the ear of the intent and enduring soldier. But as the sun rose higher, it was felt that a distant and aimless cannonade would still leave the strife to be begun, and victory to be achieved by the valiant hearts of the close-fighting infantry. The guns ceased for a time, and each warrior addressed himself in silence to the coming conflict—

a glimmering eye and a firmer grasp of his weapon alone telling of the mighty spirit which wrought within him. The left division of the British army advanced in even order and with a light step to the attack, but the original error of forming the regiments in line instead of in column rendered the contest more unequal than such assaults need necessarily be. Every shot from the enemy's lines told upon the expanse of men, and the greater part of the division was driven back by the deadly fire of muskets and swivels and enfilading artillery. On the extreme left, the regiments effected an entrance amid the advanced banks and trenches of petty outworks where possession could be of little avail; but their comrades on the right were animated by the partial success; they chafed under the disgrace of repulse, and forming themselves instinctively into wedges and masses, and headed by an old and fearless leader, they rushed forward in wrath.[1] With a shout they leaped the ditch, and upswarming, they mounted the rampart, and stood victorious amid captured cannon. But the effort was great; the Sikhs fought with steadiness and resolution; guns in the interior were turned upon the exhausted assailants, and the line cf trench alone was gained. Nor was this achievement the work of a moment. The repulse of the first assailants required that the central division should be brought forward, and these supporting regiments also moved in line against ramparts higher and more continuous than the barriers which had foiled the first efforts of their comrades. They too recoiled in confusion before the fire of the exulting Sikhs; but at the distance of a furlong they showed both their innate valour and habitual discipline by rallying and returning to the charge. Their second assault was aided on the left by the presence, in the trenches of that flank, of the victorious first division; and thus the regiments of the centre likewise became, after a fierce struggle on their own right, possessed of as many of the enemy's batteries as lay to their immediate front. The unlooked-for repulse of the second division, and the arduous contest in which the first was engaged, might have led a casual witness of the strife to ponder on the multitude of varying circumstances which determine success in war; but the leaders were collected and prompt, and the battalions on the right, the victors of Aliwal, were impelled against the opposite flank of the

[1] Sir Robert Dick was mortally wounded close to the trenches while cheering on his ardent followers.

Sikhs; but there, as on all other points attacked, destruction awaited brave men. They fell in heaps, and the first line was thrown back upon the second, which, nothing daunted, moved rapidly to the assault. The two lines mingled their ranks and rushed forward in masses, just as the second division had retrieved its fame, and as a body of cavalry had been poured into the camp from the left to form that line of advance which surpassed the strength of the exhausted infantry.

Openings were thus everywhere effected in the Sikh entrenchments, but single batteries still held out; the interior was filled with courageous men, who took advantage of every obstacle, and fought fiercely for every spot of ground. The traitor, Tej Singh, indeed, instead of leading fresh men to sustain the failing strength of the troops on his right, fled on the first assault, and, either accidentally or by design, sank a boat in the middle of the bridge of communication. But the ancient Sham Singh remembered his vow; he clothed himself in simple white attire, as one devoted to death, and calling on all around him to fight for the Guru, who had promised everlasting bliss to the brave, he repeatedly rallied his shattered ranks, and at last fell a martyr on a heap of his slain countrymen. Others might be seen standing on the ramparts amid showers of balls, waving defiance with their swords, or telling the gunners where the fair-haired English pressed thickest together. Along the stronger half of the battlements, and for the period of half an hour, the conflict raged sublime in all its terrors. The trenches were filled with the dead and the dying. Amid the deafening roar of cannon, and the multitudinous fire of musketry, the shouts of triumph or of scorn were yet heard, and the flashing of innumerable swords was yet visible; or from time to time exploding magazines of powder threw bursting shells and beams of wood and banks of earth high above the agitated sea of smoke and flame which enveloped the host of combatants, and for a moment arrested the attention amid all the din and tumult of the tremendous conflict. But gradually each defensible position was captured, and the enemy was pressed towards the scarcely fordable river; yet, although assailed on either side by squadrons of horse and battalions of foot, no Sikh offered to submit, and no disciple of Gobind asked for quarter. They everywhere showed a front to the victors, and stalked slowly and sullenly away, while many rushed singly forth to meet assured death by contending with a multitude.

The victors looked with stolid wonderment upon the 1845-6. indomitable courage of the vanquished, and forbore to strike where the helpless and the dying frowned unavailing hatred. But the necessities of war pressed upon the commanders, and *they* had effectually to disperse that army which had so long scorned their power. The fire of batteries and battalions precipitated the flight of the Sikhs through the waters of the Sutlej, and the triumph of the English became full and manifest. The troops, defiled with dust and smoke and carnage, thus stood mute indeed for a moment, until the glory of their success rushing upon their minds, they gave expression to their feelings, and hailed their victorious commanders with reiterated shouts of triumph and congratulation.[1]

On the night of the victory some regiments were The pushed across the Sutlej opposite Ferozepore; no passage of enemy was visible; and on the 12th February the fort the Sutlej, of Kasur was occupied without opposition. On the following day the army encamped under the walls of that Maharaja.

[1] Cf. Lord Gough's dispatch of the 13th Feb. 1846, and Macgregor, *History of the Sikhs*, ii. 154, &c. The casualties on the side of the British were 320 killed, and 2,083 wounded. The loss of the Sikhs, perhaps, exceeded 5,000, and possibly amounted to 8,000, the lower estimate of the English dispatches.

The Commander-in-Chief estimated the force of the Sikhs at 30,000 men, and it was frequently said they had 36 regiments in position; but it is nevertheless doubtful whether there were so many as 20,000 *armed men* in the trenches. The numbers of the actual assailants may be estimated at 15,000 effective soldiers. After the war, Lord Gough ascertained, through the British authorities at Lahore, that the Sikhs admitted their strength at Sobraon to have been 42,626 men. Perhaps, however, this estimate includes all the troops on the right bank of the river, as well as those in the entrenched position on the opposite side. If so, the statement seems in every way credible. Similarly, Lord Gough learnt that 3,125 heirs of soldiers killed claimed arrears of pay, from which fact and other circumstances which came to his knowledge, his Lordship thinks the Sikhs may have lost from 12,000 to 15,000 men in this decisive victory.

Sobraon, or correctly Subrahan, the name by which the battle is known, is taken from that of a small village, or rather two small villages, in the neighbourhood. The villages in question were inhabited by the subdivision of a tribe called Subrah, or, in the plural, Subrahan; and hence the name became applied to their place of residence, and has at last become identified with a great and important victory. This mode of designating villages by means of the plural form of a patronymic is common in India, and it was once frequent in our own country, as noticed by Mr. Kemble (*Saxons in England*, i. 59 *n.*, and Appendix A, p. 478) in 1.329 instances, such as Tooting in Surrey, Malling in Kent, &c., from the Totingas, Meallingas, and other families or clans.

1845-6.

and the
occupation
of Lahore.

ancient town, and it was ascertained that the Sikhs
still held together to the number of twenty thousand
men in the direction of Amritsar. But the power of
the armed representatives of the Khalsa was gone; the
holders of treasure and food, and all the munitions of
war, had first passively helped to defeat them, and
then openly joined the enemy; and the soldiery readily
assented to the requisition of the court that Gulab
Singh, their chosen minister, should have full powers
to treat with the English on the already admitted basis
of recognizing a Sikh government in Lahore. On the
15th of the month the Raja and several other chiefs
were received by the Governor-General at Kasur, and
they were told that Dalip Singh would continue to be
regarded as a friendly sovereign, but that the country
between the Beas and Sutlej would be retained by the
conquerors, and that a million and a half sterling must
be paid as some indemnity for the expenses of the war,
in order, it was said, that all might hear of the punishment which had overtaken aggressors, and become
fully aware that inevitable loss followed vain hostilities
with the unoffending English. After a long discussion
the terms were reluctantly agreed to, the young Maharaja came and tendered his submission in person, and
on the 20th February the British army arrived at the
Sikh capital. Two days afterwards a portion of the
citadel was garrisoned by English regiments, to mark
more plainly to the Indian world that a vaunting
enemy had been effectually humbled; for throughout
the breadth of the land the chiefs talked, in the bit-
terness of their hearts, of the approaching downfall of
the stern unharmonizing foreigners.[1]

Negotia-
tions.

The Governor-General desired not only to chastise
the Sikhs for their past aggressions, but to overawe
them for the future, and he had thus chosen the Beas,
as offering more commanding positions with reference
to Lahore than the old boundary of the Sutlej. With
the same object in view, he had originally thought Raja
Gulab
Singh.
Gulab Singh might advantageously be made independent in the hills of Jammu.[2] Such a recognition by the
British Government had, indeed, always been one of
the wishes of that ambitious family; but it was not,
perhaps, remembered that Gulab Singh was still more
desirous of becoming the acknowledged minister of the

[1] Cf. the Governor-General to the Secret Committee,
under dates the 19th Feb. and 4th March 1846.
[2] Cf. the Governor-General to the Secret Committee, of
3rd and 19th Feb. 1846.

dependent Punjab; [1] nor was it perhaps thought that the 1845-6. overtures of the Raja—after the battle of Aliwal had foreboded the total rout of the Sikh army—were all made in the hope of assuring to himself a virtual vice-royalty over the whole dominion of Lahore.  Gulab Singh had been appointed Wazir by the chiefs and people when danger pressed them, and he had been formally treated with as minister by the English when the Governor-General thought time was short, and his own resources distant; [2] but when Lal Singh saw that Lal Singh. after four pitched battles the English viceroy was content or compelled to leave Lahore a dependent ally, he rejoiced that his undiminished influence with the mother of the Maharaja would soon enable him to supplant the obnoxious chief of Jammu.  The base sycophant thus congratulated himself on the approaching success of all his treasons, which had simply for their object his own personal aggrandizement at the expense of Sikh independence.  Gulab Singh felt his inability to support himself without the countenance of the English; but they had offered no assurance of support as minister, and he suddenly perplexed the Governor-General by asking what *he* was to get for all he had done to bring about a speedy peace, and to render the army an easy prey.  It was remembered that at Kasur he had said the way to carry on a war with the English was to leave the sturdy infantry entrenched and watched, and to sweep the open country with cavalry to

---

[1] This had been the aim of the family for many years; or, at least, from the time that Dhian Singh exerted himself to remove Col. Wade, in the hope that a British representative might be appointed who would be well disposed towards himself, which he thought Col. Wade was not. Mr. Clerk was aware of both schemes of the Lahore minister, although the greater prominence was naturally given to the project of rendering the Jammu chiefs independent, owing to the aversion with which they were regarded after Nau Nihal Singh's death.

Had the English said that they desired to see Gulab Singh remain minister, and had they been careless whether Lal Singh lived or was put to death, it is highly probable that a fair and vigorous government would have been formed, and also that the occupation of Lahore, and perhaps the second treaty of 1846, need never have taken place.

[2] Cf. the Governor-General's letter to the Secret Committee, of the 3rd and 19th Feb. 1846. In both of these dispatches Lord Hardinge indicates that he intended to do something for Gulab Singh, but he does not state that he designed to make him independent of Lahore, nor does he say that he told the Sikh chiefs the arrangements then on foot might include the separation of Jammu; and the truth would seem to be, that in the first joy of success the scheme of conciliating the powerful Raja remained in a manner forgotten.

the gates of Delhi; and while negotiations were still pending, and the season advancing, it was desired to conciliate one who might render himself formidable in a day, by joining the remains of the Sikh forces, and by opening his treasures and arsenals to a warlike population.

**The partition of the Punjab, and independence of Gulab Singh.** The low state of the Lahore treasury, and the anxiety of Lal Singh to get a dreaded rival out of the way, enabled the Governor-General to appease Gulab Singh in a manner sufficiently agreeable to the Raja himself, and which still further reduced the importance of the successor of Ranjit Singh. The Raja of Jammu did not care to be simply the master of his native mountains, but as two-thirds of the pecuniary indemnity required from Lahore could not be made good, territory was taken instead of money, and Kashmir and the hill states from the Beas to the Indus were cut off from the Punjab Proper, and transferred to Gulab Singh as a separate sovereign for a million of pounds sterling. The arrangement was a dexterous one, if reference be only had to the policy of reducing the power of the Sikhs; but the transaction scarcely seems worthy of the British name and greatness, and the objections become stronger when it is considered that Gulab Singh had agreed to pay sixty-eight lakhs of rupees (£680 000), as a fine to his paramount, before the war broke out,[1] and that the custom of the East as well as of the West requires the feudatory to aid his lord in foreign war and domestic strife. Gulab Singh ought thus to have paid the deficient million of money as a Lahore subject, instead of being put in possession of Lahore provinces as an independent prince. The succession of the Raja was displeasing to the Sikhs generally, and his separation was les n accordance with his own aspirations than the ministry of Ranjit Singh's empire; but his rise to sovereign power excited nevertheless the ambition of others, and Tej Singh, who knew his own wealth, and was fully persuaded of the potency of gold, offered twenty-five lakhs of rupees for a princely crown and another dismembered province. He was chid for his presumptuous misinterpretation of English principles of action; the arrangement with Gulab Singh was the only one of the kind which took place, and the new ally was formally invested with the title of Maharaja at Amritsar

[1] Major Broadfoot to Government, 5th May 1845. The author never heard, and does not believe, that this money was paid by Gulab Singh.

on the 15th March 1846.[1] But a portion of the territory at first proposed to be made over to him was reserved by his masters, the payments required from him were reduced by a fourth, and they were rendered still more easy of liquidation by considering him to be the heir to the money which his brother Suchet Singh had buried in Ferozepore.[2]

Lal Singh became minister once more; but he and all the traitorous chiefs knew that they could not maintain themselves, even against the reduced army, when the English should have fairly left the country, and thus the separation of Gulab Singh led to a further departure from the original scheme. It was agreed that a British force should remain at the capital until the last day of December 1846, to enable the chiefs to feel secure while they reorganized the army and introduced order and efficiency into the administration. The end of the year came; but the chiefs were still helpless; they clung to their foreign support, and gladly assented to an arrangement which leaves the English in immediate possession of the reduced dominion of Ranjit Singh, until his reputed son and feeble successor shall attain the age of manhood.[3]

While the Governor-General and Commander-in-Chief remained at Lahore at the head of twenty thousand men, portions of the Sikh army came to the capital to be paid up and disbanded. The soldiers showed neither the despondency of mutinous rebels nor the effrontery and indifference of mercenaries, and their manly deportment added lustre to that valour which the victors had dearly felt and generously extolled. The men talked of their defeat as the chance of war,

*Margin notes:*
1845-6.

Supplementary arrangements of 1846. placing Dalip Singh under British tutelage during his minority.

The Sikhs not disheartened by their reverses.

---

[1] On this occasion 'Maharaja' Gulab Singh stood up, and with joined hands, expressed his gratitude to the British viceroy—adding, without however any ironical meaning, that he was indeed his 'Zurkharid', or gold-boughten slave!

In the course of this history there has, more than once, been occasion to allude to the unscrupulous character of Raja Gulab Singh; but it must not therefore be supposed that he is a man malevolently evil. He will, indeed, deceive an enemy and take his life without hesitation, and in the accumulation of money he will exercise many oppressions; but he must be judged with reference to the morality of his age and race, and to the necessities of his own position. If these allowances be made, Gulab Singh will be found an able and moderate man, who does little in an idle or wanton spirit, and who is not without some traits both of good humour and generosity of temper.

[2] See Appendices XXXIV, XXXV, and XXXVI, for the treaties with Lahore and Jammu.

[3] See Appendix XXXVII for the second treaty with Lahore.

or they would say that *they* were mere imitators of unapproachable masters. But, amid all their humiliation, they inwardly dwelt upon their future destiny with unabated confidence; and while gaily calling themselves inapt and youthful scholars, they would sometimes add, with a significant and sardonic smile, that the 'Khalsa' itself was yet a child, and that as the commonwealth of Sikhs grew in stature, Gobind would clothe his disciples with irresistible might and guide them with unequalled skill. Thus brave men sought consolation, and the spirit of progress which collectively animated them yielded with a murmur to the superior genius of England and civilization, to be chastened by the rough hand of power, and perhaps to be moulded to noblest purposes by the informing touch of knowledge and philosophy.[1]

Conclusion. —The position of the English in India.

The separate sway of the Sikhs and the independence of the Punjab have come to an end, and England reigns the undisputed mistress of the broad and classic land of India. Her political supremacy is more regular and systematic than the antique rule of the Brahmans and Kshattriyas, and it is less assailable from without than the imperfect dominion of the Muhammadans; for in disciplined power and vastness of resources, in unity of action and intelligence of design, her government surpasses the experience of the East, and emulates the magnificent prototype of Rome. But the Hindus made the country wholly their own, and from sea to sea, from the snowy mountains almost to the fabled bridge of Rama, the language of the peasant is still that of the twice-born races; the speech of the wild foresters and mountaineers of the centre and south has been permanently tinged by the old predominance of the Kshattriyas, and the hopes and fears and daily habits of myriads of men still vividly represent the genial myths and deep philosophy of the Brahmans, which more than two thousand years ago arrested the attention of the Greeks. The Muhammadans entered the country to destroy, but they remained

[1] In March 1846, or immediately after the war, the author visited the Sikh temples and establishments at Kiratpur and Anandpur-Makhowal. At the latter place, the chosen seat of Gobind, reliance upon the future was likewise strong; and the grave priests or ministers said, by way of assurance, that the pure faith of the Khalsa was intended for all countries and times; and added, by way of compliment, that the disciples of Nanak would ever be grateful for the aid which the stranger English had rendered in subverting the empire of the intolerant and oppressive Muhammadans!

to colonize, and swarms of the victorious races long 1845-6.
continued to pour themselves over its rich plains,
modifying the language and ideas of the vanquished,
and becoming themselves altered by the contact, until,
in the time of Akbar, the 'Islam' of India was a national
system, and until, in the present day, the Hindu and
Muhammadan do not practically differ more from one
another than did the Brahmans and Kshattriyas and
Veisyas of the time of Manu and Alexander. They are
different races with different religious systems, but
harmonizing together in social life, and mutually
understanding and respecting and taking a part in
each other's modes and ways and doings. They are
thus silently but surely removing one another's differences and peculiarities, so that a new element results
from the common destruction, to become developed
into a faith or a fact in future ages. The rise to power
of contemned Sudra tribes, in the persons of Marathas,
Gurkhas, and Sikhs, has brought about a further mixture of the rural population and of the lower orders
in towns and cities, and has thus given another blow
to the reverence for antiquity. The religious creed of
the people seems to be even more indeterminate than
their spoken dialects, and neither the religion of the
Arabian prophet, nor the theology of the Vedas and
Purans, is to be found pure except among professed
Mullas and educated Brahmans, or among the rich and
great of either persuasion. Over this seething and
fusing mass, the power of England has been extended
and her spirit sits brooding. Her pre-eminence in the
modern world may well excite the envy of the nations;
but it behoves her to ponder well upon the mighty
task which her adventurous children have set her in
the East, and to be certain that her sympathizing labours in the cause of humanity are guided by intelligence towards a true and attainable end. She rules
supreme as the welcome composer of political troubles;
but the thin superficies of her dominion rests tremblingly upon the convulsed ocean of social change and
mental revolution. Her own high civilization and the
circumstances of her intervention isolate her in all her
greatness; she can appeal to the reason only of her
subjects, and can never lean upon the enthusiasm of
their gratitude or predilections.[1]  To preserve her poli-

[1] Mr. Macaulay's comparison (*History of England*, i. 364,
&c.) between the manners of the earlier Georges and Charles
II, as bearing on the kingly office, is peculiarly applicable to the
British rule in India. The English, like their own stranger sovereigns of the last century, govern in the East according to law,

tical ascendancy she must be ever prudent and circumspect; and to leave a lasting impress she must do more than erect palaces and temples, the mere material monuments of dominion. Like Greece and Rome, she may rear edifices of surpassing beauty, she may bridge gulfs and pierce mountains with the wand of wealth ar d science. Like these ancient peoples, she may even give birth in strange lands to such kings as Herod the Great and to such historians as Flavius Josephus; but, like imperial Rome, she may live to behold a Vortigern call in a Hengist, and a Syagrius yield to a Clovis. She may teach another Cymbeline the amenities of civilized life, and she may move another Attalus to bequeath to her another Pergamus. These are tasks of easy achievement; but she must also endeavour to give her poets and her sages an immortality among nations unborn, to introduce laws which shall still be in force at the end of sixty generations, and to tinge the faith and the minds of the people with her sober science and just morality, as Christianity was affected by the adoptive policy of Rome and by the plastic philosophy of Greece. Of all these things England must sow the seeds and lay the foundations befor: she can hope to equal or surpass her great exemplars[1]

But England can do nothing un' . she has rendered her dominion secure, and hithertc all her thoughts have been given to the extension of her supremacy. Up to this time she has been a rising power, the welcome supplanter of Mughals and Marathas, and the ally which the remote weak sought against the neighbouring strong. But her greatness is at its height : it has come to *her* turn to be feared instead of courted, and the hopes of men are about to be built on her

but they cannot give themselves a place in the hearts of their subjects, while those whom reason can convince are neither numerous nor influential in political affairs. Sir H. M. Elliot, in the Introduction (p. xxix) to his important and interesting volume on the Muhammadan Historians of India, admits 'the many defects inherent in a system of foreign administration, in which language, colour, religion, customs, and laws preclude all natural sympathy between sovereign and subject : but he at the same time declares the English have, nevertheless, done more in fifty years for the substantial benefit of the people, at least of Upper India, than the Musalmans did in ten times that period—an opinion that requires to be supported to a more extended comparison of material works than is given by the learned writer. [The author's gloomy prognostications have been rudely shaken by the events of 1914-15, and tne spontaneous loyalty shown by all classes during the great European War.--ED.]

[1] See Appendix XV.

wished-for destruction. The princes of India can no longer acquire fame or territory by preying upon one another. Under the exact sway of their new paramount, they must divest themselves of ambition and of all the violent passions of their nature, and they must try to remain kings without exercising the most loved of the functions of rulers. The Indians, indeed, will themselves politely liken England and her dependent sovereigns to the benignant moon accompanied by hosts of rejoicing stars in her nightly progress, rather than to the fierce sun which rides the heavens in solitude scarcely visible amidst intolerable brightness; but men covet power as well as ease, and crave distinction as well as wealth; and thus it is with those who endeavour to jest with adversity. England has immediately to make her attendant princes feel, that while resistance is vain, they are themselves honoured, and hold a substantive position in the economy of the imperial government, instead of being merely tolerated as bad rulers or regarded with contempt and aversion as half-barbarous men. Her rule has hitherto mainly tended to the benefit of the trading community; men of family name find no place in the society of their masters, and no employment in the service of the state; and while the peasants have been freed from occasional ruinous exaction, and from more rare personal torture, they are oppressed and impoverished by a well-meant but cumbrous and inefficient law,[1] and by an excessive and partial taxation, which looks almost wholly to the land for the necessary revenue of a government.[2] The husbandman is sullen and indifferent,[3] the gentleman nurses his wrath in secrecy,

[1 I have removed a footnote here inserted by the author in elaboration of this statement. The note is quite untrue under modern conditions and has ceased to have any practical value. The views of both the author and of Sleeman, whom he quotes (*Rambles and Recollections of an Indian Official*, Oxford Edition, p. 544), are typical of a point of view which has now happily passed away.—ED.]

2 See Appendix XVI.

3 Lieut.-Col. Sleeman considers (*Rambles and Recollections of an Indian Official*, p. 432) that neither have the English gained, nor did other rulers possess, the goodwill of the peasantry and landholders of the country.

In considering the position of the English, or of any ruling power, in Inida, it should always be borne in mind that no bodies of peasantry, excepting perhaps the Sikhs and, in a lesser degree, the Rajputs of the west, and no classes of men, excepting perhaps the Muhammadans and, in a lesser degree, the Brahmans, take any interest in the government of their country, or have collectively any wish to be dominant. The

kings idly chafe and intrigue, and all are ready to hope
for everything from a change of masters. The merchant alone sits partly happy in the reflection, that if
he is not honoured with titles and office, the path to
wealth has been made smooth, and its enjoyment
rendered secure.

Princes and nobles and yeomen can all be kept in
obedience for generations by overwhelming means,
and by a more complete military system than at present
sent obtains. Numerous forts and citadels,[1] the occasional assemblage of armies, and the formation of
regiments separately composed of different tribes and
races,[2] will long serve to ensure supremacy and to

masses of the population, whether of towns or villages, are
ready to submit to any master, native 'or foreign; and the
multitudes of submissive subjects possessed by England con-
tribute nothing to her strength except as tax-payers, and,
during an insurrection or after a conquest, would at once give
the 'government share of the produce' to the wielder of power
for the time being, and would thereby consider themselves freed
from all obligations and liabilities. England must be just and
generous towards these tame myriads; but the men whom she
has pre-eminently to keep employed, honoured, and overawed
are the turbulent military classes, who are ever ready to rebel
and ever desirous of acquiring power.

[1] The fewness of places of strength, and indeed of places
of ordinary security, for magazines of arms and ammunition
is a radical defect in the military system of the English in
India. The want of extensive granaries is also much felt, both
as a measure of the most ordinary prudence in case of insurrection or any military operation, and as some check upon
prices on the common recurrence of droughts in a country in
which capitalists do not yet go hand in hand with the government, and are but little amenable to public opinion beyond
their order. Such was, and is, the custom of the native princes,
and no practice exists without a reason. [The first defect was
realised and remedied as one of the lessons of the Mutiny,
while the question of the check on prices is one of the common-
places of a modern administration.—ED.]

[2] The English have not succeeded in making their well-
ordered army a separate caste or section of the community,
except very partially in the Madras presidency, where a
sepoy's home is his regiment. It is, moreover, but too apparent
that the active military spirit of the sepoys, when on service
in India, is not now what it was when the system of the
'Company' was new and the fortune of the Strangers beginning.
This is partly due to the general pacification of the country,
partly to the practice of largely enlisting tame-spirited men of
inferior caste because they are well behaved, or pliant intriguing Brahmans because they can write and are intelligent; and
partly because the system of central or rather single management has been carried too far. The Indian is eminently a
partisan, and his predilection for his immediate superior should
be encouraged, the more especially as there can be no doubt
of the loyalty of the English commandant. The clannish, or
feudal, or mercenary, attachment do not in India yield to

crush the efforts of individuals; but England has care- 1845-(
fully to watch the progress of that change in social
relations and religious feelings of which Sikhism is
the most marked exponent.  Among all ranks of men
there is a spirit at work which rejects as vain the
ancient forms and ideas whether of Brahmanism or
Muhammadanism,[1] and which clings for present solace

rational conviction or political principle, and colonels of battalions should have very large powers.  Regiments separately
composed of men of one or other of the military classes might
sometimes give trouble within themselves, and sometimes come
into collision with other regiments; but a high warlike feeling
would be engendered; and unless England chooses to identify
herself with some of the inferior races, and to evoke a new
spirit by becoming a religious reformer, she must keep the
empire she has won by working upon the feelings she finds
prevalent in the country.  [The suggestion in the text has long
since been dismissed as impracticable by modern military
administrators.—ED.]

[1] The following remark of the Hindus, regarding some
of their most sacred persons, has now a wider application than
smart sayings commonly possess.  They describe Purs-Ram,
Vyasa, Rama, and Krishna as 'Sirree, Siftee, Dana, and Dee-
wana'—or Purs-Ram as hasty, heedless; because, for the fault
of one ruler, he proceeded to slay a whole generation of men;
Vyasa, as wordy, or a flatterer, because he would make all to
resemble gods; Rama, alone, as wise, or politic, because all his
actions denoted forethought; and Krishna, as eminently silly
or trivial, because all he did was of that character.  That names
still revered are sometimes so treated denotes a readiness for
change.  [The most common phenomenon now apparent in
both Hindu and Muhammadan worlds is somewhat akin to
that which inspired the Reformation in Europe—a movement
on the part of certain sections of the community in favour of
the removal of accretions and the reversion to the more simple,
patriarchal, and puritanical regime of an earlier epoch.  To
such a conception is due such a movement, in the Hindu world,
as that of the Arya Somaj, which has so many supporters and
so wide an influence in India to-day.  This movement has for
its primary object a return to the Vedas—as alone sufficient for
the salvation of man—and to the simple existence of the
earlier days.  Space does not permit of a detailed examination
of the whole history and progress of the Arya Somaj movement
and of the life and teaching of its founder Swami Dayananda
Saraswati.  For a further study of the subject the reader is
referred to the recently published history of the Arya Somaj
by L. Lajpat Rai.
    Another modern development has been that of the Brahmo
Somaj—a body of Unitarian tendency and teaching.  In the
Muhammadan world the same tendency towards reform may
be noticed.  In modern times the most extensive reform movement within the borders of Islam has been the Senussi movement.  But while this has become a distinct force among the
Muhammadans of Africa it has had little or no effect upon
India.  Many intelligent Muhammadans in India have assured
me that they consider the position of their Church in India
to-day very analogous to that of the Church of England on the

and future happiness to new intercessors and to another manifestation of divine power and mercy. This
labouring spirit has developed itself most strongly on
the confines of the two antagonist creeds; but the feeling pervades the Indian world, and the extension of
Sikh arms would speedily lead to the recognition of
Nanak and Gobind as the long-looked-for Comforters.[1]
The Sikhs have now been struck by the petrific hand

eve of the Reformation. The 'dead hand' of mediaeval England
has in their judgement its counterpart in India to-day. Isolation
and environment have both played their part in bringing about
this state of affairs. As regards the first of these factors one
may take the analogy a little farther back historically. It may
be taken as an admitted fact that the Church in England ante-
rior to the Norman Conquest suffered considerably from its
isolation, and that one of the benefits of that conquest was the
removal of that barrier. Cut off from the religious life of the
rest of the Continent, except in so far as the rather uncertain
link of pilgrimage maintained the connexion, the Saxon Church
became local, formalized, perhaps indifferent. And when we
turn to Muhammadan India we find a similar state of things.
The link of pilgrimage exists—made stronger by modern
facilities for travel—but in the main the isolation exists. This
isolation has resulted in the gradual growth of a host of local
traditions and local cults. And here the second factor—environment—comes into play. Living in close association with
Hinduism, drawing at an earlier period a number of converts
from that religion, the followers of Islam in India have been
profoundly affected. To take a single instance, caste. The
Muhammadan of to-day of Rajput descent cannot, in many
cases, forget his original caste. Despite the democratic nature
of the religion to which he now belongs, his whole life is largely
influenced by the traditions of the creed of his ancestors. One
could give many instances of this from one's own experience.
They are common phenomena of India to-day in the face of
modern development. The intelligent Muhammadan of to-day
view the state of his religion with the feelings of an Englishman just before the Reformation. He is fully conscious of
imperfections, of accretions, of a departure from the pure
tenets of his religion. Islam in modern India is looking for a
Luther, but the desire for internal reform is not associated
with any feeling of hostility towards other creeds. The idea is
rather that it is because of its imperfections that Islam stands
now where it does, and that reform is necessary to enable it
to hold its place successfully amid other organised religions of
to-day. A detailed description of the various reformed sects
which do exist among the Punjabi Muhammadans to-day may
be found in the Census Report of 1912.—ED.]

[1] Widely spread notions, how erroneous soever they be, in
one sense, always deserve attention, as based on some truth
or conviction. Thus the Hindus quote an altered or spurious
passage of the Bhagavat, describing the successive rulers of
India as follows: (1) the Yavvans (Greeks), eight kings;
(2) the Tooshkurs (Turks or Muhammadans), fourteen kings;
(3) the Gurand (the fair, i.e. the English), ten kings; and
(4) the Mowna (or silent, i.e. the disciples of Nanak the Seer),
eleven kings.

of material power, and the ascendancy of a third race has everywhere infused new ideas, and modified the aspirations of the people. The confusion has thus been increased for a time; but the pregnant fermentation of mind must eventually body itself forth in new shapes; and a prophet of name unknown may arise to diffuse a system which shall consign the Vedas and Koran to the oblivion of the Zendavest and the Sibylline Leaves, and which may not perhaps absorb one ray of light from the wisdom and morality of that faith which adorns the civilization of the Christian rulers of the country. But England must hope that she is not to exercise an unfruitful sway; and she will add fresh lustre to her renown, and derive an additional claim to the gratitude of posterity, if she can seize upon the essential principles of that element which disturbs her multitudes of Indian subjects, and imbue the mental agitation with new qualities of beneficent fertility, so as to give to it an impulse and a direction, which shall surely lead to the prevalence of a religion of truth and to the adoption of a government of freedom and progress.

# APPENDIXES

## APPENDIX I

### THE JATS AND JATS OF UPPER INDIA

ACCORDING to the dictionaries *Jat* means a race, a tribe, or a particular race so called, while *Jat* means manner, kind, and likewise matted hair. But throughout Punjab *Jat* also implies a fleece, a fell of hair; and in Upper Sind *a Jat* now means a rearer of camels or of black cattle, or a shepherd in opposition to a husbandman. In the Punjab generally *a Jat* means still a villager, a rustic *par excellence*, as one of the race by far the most numerous, and as opposed to one engaged in trade or handicraft. This was observed by the author of the *Dabistan* nearly two centuries ago (*Dabistan*, ii. 252); but since the *Jats* of Lahore and the *Jats* of the Jumna have acquired power, the term is becoming more restricted, and is occasionally employed to mean simply one of that particular race.

The Jats merge on one side into the Rajputs, and on the other into the Afghans, the names of the Jat subdivisions being the same with those of Rajputs in the east, and again with those of Afghans, and even Baluchis, in the west, and many obscure tribes being able to show plausibly that at least they are as likely to be Rajputs or Afghans as to be Jats. The Jats are indeed enumerated among the arbitrary or conventional thirty-six royal races of the local bards of Rajputana (Tod's *Rajasthan*, i. 106), and they themselves claim affinity with the Bhotias, and aspire to a lunar origin, as is done by the Raja of Patiala. As instances of the narrow and confused state of our knowledge regarding the people of India, it may be mentioned that the Birks (or Virks), one of the most distinguished tribes of Jats, is admitted among the Chaluk Rajputs by Tod (i. 100), and that there are *Kukker* and *Kakar* Jats, *Kukker Kokur*, and *Kakar* Afghans, besides Gakhars, not included in any of the three races. Further, the family of Umarkot in Sind is stated by Tod (*Rajasthan*, i. 92, 93) to be Framar' (or Powar), while the

Emperor Humayun's chronicler talks of the followers (i.e. brethren) of that chief as being Jats. (*Memoirs of Humayun*, p. 45). The editors of the *Journal of the Geographical Society* (xiv. 207 *n*.) derive *Jat* from the Sanskrit *Jyest'ha*, old, ancient, and so make the term equivalent to *aborigines;* but this etymology perhaps too hastily sets aside the sufficiently established facts of Getae and Yuechi emigrations, and the circumstance of Taimur's warfare with Jettehs in Central Asia.

Some of the most eminent of the Jat subdivisions in the Punjab are named Sindhu, Chineh, Varaitch, Chattheh, Sidhu, Kurrial, Gondul, &c. For some notices of the Jats of the Indus by early Muhammadan writers (about A.D. 977 and 1100) see Sir H. M. Elliot, *Historians of India*, pp. 69 and 270.

# APPENDIX II

## PROPORTIONS OF RACES AND FAITHS : POPULATION OF INDIA

OUT of 1,030 villages lying here and there between the Jumna and Sutlej, and which were under British management in 1844, there were found to be forty-one different tribes of *agriculturists*, in proportions as follows, after adding up fractions where any race composed a portion only of the whole community of any one village.

|  | | | | *Villages* |
|---|---|---|---|---:|
| Jats | .. | .. | .. | 443 |
| Rajputs | .. | .. | .. | 194 |
| Gujars | .. | .. | .. | 109 |
| Saiyids | .. | .. | .. | 17 |
| Shaikhs | .. | .. | .. | 25 |
| Pathans | .. | .. | .. | 8 |
| Mughals | .. | .. | .. | 5 |
| Brahmans | .. | .. | .. | 28 |
| Kshattriyas | .. | .. | .. | 6 |
| Rains (or Arains) | .. | .. | 47 |
| Kambos | .. | .. | .. | 19 |
| Malis | .. | .. | .. | 12 |
| Rors | .. | .. | .. | 33 |
| Dogras (Muhammadans claiming Kshattriya origin) | .. | .. | 28 |
| Kalals | .. | .. | .. | 5 |

|                                          | *Villages* |
|------------------------------------------|-----------|
| Gusain  religionists         ..   ..   .. | 3         |
| Bairagi religionists          ..   ..   .. | 2         |
| 24 miscellaneous tribes occupying equal to | 46        |
|                                          |           |
|                            Total         | 1,030     |

A classification of the tribes of India according to position, origin, and faith is much wanted, and is indeed necessary to a proper comprehension of the history of the country. The Revenue Survey, as conducted in the upper provinces of the Ganges, enumerates several castes or at least the predominant ones, in each village, and the lists might easily be rendered more complete, and afterwards made available by publication for purposes of inquiry and deduction.

The Sikh population of the Punjab and adjoining districts has usually been estimated at 500,000 souls in all (cf. Burnes, *Travels*, i. 289; and Elphinstone, *History of India*, ii. 275 *n.*), but the number seems too small by a half or a third. There are, indeed, no exact data on which to found an opinion; but the Sikh armies have never been held to contain fewer than 70,000 fighting men; they have been given as high as 250,000, and there is no reason to doubt that between the Jhelum and Jumna they could muster nearly half the latter number of soldiers of their own faith, while it is certain that of an agricultural people no member of some families may engage in arms, and that one adult at least of other families will always remain behind to till the ground. The gross Sikh population may probably be considered to amount to a million and a quarter or a million and a half of souls, men, women, and children.

The proportion of Hindus to Muhammadans throughout India generally has been variously estimated. The Emperor Jahingir (*Memoirs*, p. 29) held them to be as five to one, which is perhaps more unequal than the present proportion in the valley of the Ganges. Mr. Elphinstone (*History of India*, ii. 238 and notes) takes the relative numbers for the whole country to be eight to one. From p. 169 of the *Statistics of the NW. Provinces*, printed in 1848 and published in 1849 by the Indian Government, it appears that out of a population of 23,199,668 dwelling between Ghazipur and Hardwar, and in the direct or active occupation of about 72,000 square miles of country, there are 19,452,646 Hindus and 3,747,022 Muhammadans, 'and others not Hindus'—the others forming, doubtless, a fraction so small that they may be here disregarded.

This gives somewhat more than five Hindus to one Muhammadan, and so differs but little from the estimate of the Emperor Jahangir above quoted, and which probably had reference to the same tract of country. The revenue of the Upper Provinces amounts to about £4,700,000, which gives a taxation of about five shillings a head. Throughout India the state of industry and the system of revenue is nearly the same; and taking the gross income of the whole country at forty millions sterling (22 British and 18 native princes), it will result that the population amounts to two hundred millions in all, or double what it is commonly believed to be. The calculation, however, is borne out by the analogous condition of affairs in Germany. In Prussia the taxation is about eleven shillings a head, and the proportion seems to hold good in the other component states of the empire.

[The Census of 1911 shows the population and proportion as follows. A total population of 23,807,750, distributed in the following proportions :

Muhammadans roughly one-half.
Hindus          „      three-eighths.
Sikhs           „      one-eighth.—Ed.]

# APPENDIX III

## THE KSHATTRIYAS AND ARORAS OF THE PUNJAB

THE *Kshattriyas* of the Punjab maintain the purity of their descent, and the legend is that they represent those of the warrior race who yielded to Paras Ram and were spared by him. The tribe is numerous in the Upper Punjab and about Delhi and Hardwar. Kshattriyas are found in towns along the Ganges as far as Benares and Patna; but in Bengal, in Central India, and in the Deccan they seem to be strangers, or only to be represented by ruling families claiming a solar or lunar origin. In the Punjab the religious capital of the Kshattriyas seems to be the ancient Dipalpur. The Kshattriyas divide themselves into three principal classes : (1) the Charjatis, or the four clans; (2) the Barajatis, or the twelve clans; and (3) the Bawanjais, or fifty-two clans. The *Charjatis* are, 1st, the Seths;

2nd, the Merhotas; 3rd, the Khannas; and 4th, the
Kapurs, who are again divided, the first into two, and
the others into three classes. The principal of the
*Barajati* subdivisions are Chopra, Talwar, Tunnuhn,
Seighul, Kakar, Mahta, &c. Some of the *Bawanjais* are
as follows : Bhandari, Mahendro, Sethis, Suri, Sahni,
Anand, Bhasin, Sodhi, Bedi, Tihan, Bhallah, &c.

The *Aroras* claim to be the offspring of Kshattriya
fathers and of Vaisya or Sudra mothers, and their
legend is that they were settled in numbers about Uch,
when the Kshattriyas, being expelled from Delhi,
migrated to Tatta and other places in Sind, and subsequently to Multan. During their wars the Kshattriyas asked the aid of the Aroras, but they were
refused assistance. The Kshattriyas in consequence
induced the Brahmans to debar the Aroras from the
exercise of religious rites, and they thus remained
proscribed for three hundred years, until Sidh Bhoja
and Sidh Siama of Dipalpur readmitted them within
the pale of Hinduism. The Hindu bankers of Shikarpur are Aroras, and the Hindu shopkeepers of Khorasan and Bokhara are likewise held by the people of
the Punjab to be of the same race. The Aroras divide
themselves into two main classes : (1) *Utradi*, or of
the north, and (2) *Dakhni*, or of the south, and the
latter has likewise an important subdivision named
*Duhuni*.

In the Lower Punjab and in Sind the whole Hindu
trading population is included by the Muhammadans
under the term 'Kirar'. In the Upper Punjab the word
is used to denote a coward or one base and abject, and
about Multan it is likewise expressive of contempt as
well of a Hindu or a trafficker. In Central India the
Kirars form a tribe, but the term there literally means
dalesmen or foresters, although it has become the name
of a class or tribe in the lapse of centuries. Professor
Wilson somewhere, I think, identifies them with the
Chirrhadae of the ancients, and indeed *Kerat* is one
of the five *Prasthas* or regions of the Hindus, these
being Chin Prasth, Yavan Prasth, Indr Prasth, Dak-
shan Prasth, and Kerat Prasth, which last is understood
by the Indians to apply to the country between Ujjain
and Orissa. (Cf. Wilson, *Vishnu Puran*, p. 175 *n.*, for
the Keratas of that book). Further, the Brahmanical
Gonds of the Nerbudda are styled 'Raj Gonds', while
those who have not adopted Hinduism continue to be
called 'Kirria Gonds', a term which seems to have a
relation to their unaltered condition.

## APPENDIX IV

## CASTE IN INDIA

THE system of *caste*, as it has become developed in India, as it obtained in Egypt and in Persia, as it was exemplified in an ancient 'Gens' with its separate religious rites and hereditary usages, as it partially obtained in Europe during the Middle Ages, and as it exists even now, is worthy of an essay distinguished by the ripest scholarship, and by the widest experience of life and knowledge of the human mind. In India it has evidently been an institution of gradual progress up to the pernicious perfection of later days, and in early times the bounds were less markedly defined, or less carefully observed, than during the last few hundred years. The instance of Viswamitra's acquisition of Brahmanhood is well known, as is Vikramajit's almost successful desire of attaining to the same eminence. Vyasa likewise raised a Sudra to an equality with the priestly class, and his descendants are still looked upon as Brahmans, although inferior in degree. (Ward, *The Hindus*, i. 85; and see Manu, *Institutes*, chap. x, 42-72, &c., for admissions that merit could open the ranks of caste.) Even in the present generation some members of the Jat Sikh family of Sindhianwala, related to that of Ranjit Singh, made an attempt to be admitted to a participation in the social rites of Kshattriyas; and it may be assumed as certain that had the conquering Mughals and Pathans been without a vivid belief and an organized priesthood, they would have adopted Vedism and have become enrolled among the Kshattriyas or ruling races.

Perhaps the reformer Ramanand expressed the original principle of Indian sacerdotal caste when he said that Kabir the weaver had become a Brahman by knowing Brahm or God. (*The Dabistan*, ii. 188.)

The Muhammadans of India fancifully divide themselves into four classes, after the manner of the Hindus, viz. Saiyids, Shaikhs, Mughals, and Pathans. All are noble, indeed, but the former two, as representing the tribe of Muhammad and the direct progeny of Ali his son-in-law, are pre-eminent. It is likewise a fact, at least in the north-west, that a Kshattriya convert from Hinduism, or any convert from Sikhism, is styled a Shaikh, and that converts of inferior races are classed as Mughals and Pathans. Doubtless a Brahman who should become a Muhammadan would at once be classed among the Saiyids.

Mr. Hodgson (*Aborigines of India*, p. 144) shows that the Koch princes of Assam were admitted to be Rajputs on embracing Hinduism, although they are of the Tamil and not of the Arya race; but even the Jews were not altogether inflexible in former times, and Bossuet notices the conversion of the Idumaeans and Philistines, and sees their change of faith foretold by the prophets (*Universal History*, Translation of 1810, pp. 142 and 154).

[Possibly in his reference to Society in mediaeval Europe the author has not laid sufficient stress upon the rigid nature of what has been called the 'horizontal' division of Society during that period. The caste barrier that separated the knight from the merchant of his own country was a very real thing.—ED.]

## APPENDIX V

## THE PHILOSOPHICAL SYSTEMS OF THE INDIANS

THE six orthodox schools will be found, among them, to partially represent the three great philosophic systems of the Greeks—the ethical, the logical, and the physical; or to be severally founded, in more modern language, on revelation or morality, reason, and sense. Thus the first and second Mimamsa, being based on the Vedas, correspond in a measure with the school of Pythagoras, which identified itself so closely with the belief and institutions of the age. The Nyaya and Vaiseshika systems of Gautama and Kanadia which treat primarily of mind or reason, resemble th' dialectics of Xenophanes, while the Sankhya doctrines of Kapal and Patanjali, which labour with the inertness and modifications of matter, correspond with the physical school of Thales, as taught by Anaxagoras. Mr. Elphinstone (*History of India*, i. 234) has some good observations on the marked correspondence of the Indian and Greek metaphysics, and Mr. Ward (*Hindus*, ii. 113) attempts a specific comparison with a series of individual reasoners, but too little is yet known, especially of Brahmanical speculation, to render such parallels either exact or important.

The triple division of the schools which is adopted by the Indians themselves may here be given as some help to a better understanding of the doctrines of the modern reformers. They separate the systems into Arumbwad, Purnamwad, and Vivurtwad, or the simple atomic, the modified material, and the illusory. The 'Arumbwad' includes the first Mimamsa, the Nyaya, and the Vaiseshika, and it teaches the indestructibility of matter, while it leaves the atoms without any other inherent quality, and attributes their various shapes and developments to the exercise of God's will. The 'Purnamwad' includes the Sankhya and Yoga systems, and teaches that matter has not only a power of resistance, but a law of aggregation or development, or that it can only have forms given to it by God in accordance with its inherent nature. The modern Vaishnavas are mostly adherents of this doctrine, but they somewhat modify it, and say that the sensible world is God, so imbued with matter that he is himself manifest in all things, but under such varying forms and appearances as may suit his design. The 'Vivurtwad', or the second Mimamsa, which is orthodox Vedantism, or the system of Shankar Acharj, teaches that God changes not his shape, but is himself at once both spirit and matter, although to the sense of man he is variously manifested by means of 'Maya', his power or essence, his image or reflection—under the guise of the heavens and the earth, or as inorganic rocks and as sentient animals.

Another division of the schools is also made into 'Astik', and 'Nastik', or deist and atheist, so as to include doctrines not Brahmanical. Thus the 'Astik comprehends all the six 'Dursuns', and some modern reasoners further admit Muhammadanism and Christianity, considered as speculative systems, into this theistic or partially orthodox pale. The Nastik comprehends primarily the Buddhist and Jain systems, with the addition sometimes of the Charvak, which has never been popularized; but Hindu zealots make it secondarily to include not only Muhammadanism and Christianity, but also the sects of Gorakh, Kabir, and Nanak, as being irrespective of or repugnant to the Vedas, while similarly they place the Poorv and Utar Mimamsa above the mere deism of reason, as being the direct revelation of God.

The Buddhists are subdivided into four schools —the Sautrantik, the Waibhashik, the Yogachar, and the Madiamit. All agree in compounding animal existence of five essences or qualities : (1) independent consciousness, or soul, or self; (2) perception of form, or of external objects; (3) sensation, pleasure, or pain —the action of matter on mind; (4) understanding or comprehension, the reaction of mind on matter, or mind pervaded with the qualities of matter; (5)

passion, volition, action, or mind, vital and motive Scholars thus consider the present subjection of matter to mind as the greatest happiness of which man is capable, and they declare death to be the utter dissolution of the individual; while the Buddhas of vulgar adoration become simply revered memories or remembrances with the learned. The first section holds that intelligence, or the joint perception of the object and subject, is the soul or distinguishing characteristic of humanity; the second gives the preference to simple consciousness; the third prefers objective sensation, and the fourth teaches that the fact or the phenomenon of the assemblage of the component qualities is the only spirit; or, indeed, that there is naught permanent or characteristic save nonentity, or the void of non-being. This last evidently merges into the Charvak school, and it is also called the 'Shunyabad' system, or the doctrine of vacuity or non-existence, and an attempt was recently made to popularize it in Upper India, by one Bakhtawar, and his patron, the Chief of Hattrass (Wilson, *As. Res.*, xvii. 305); nor is it difficult to perceive that practically it would resolve itself into the principle of self-reliance, or perhaps the 'know-thyself' of the Greek sage.

The Jains base human existence on the aggregation of nine phenomena, or principles, one of which, Jiv, vitality, may by merit become a Jin, or an immortal spirit. The two great divisions, 'Swetambar', the white clothed, and 'Digambar', the naked, seem to have few important metaphysical differences, except that the latter refuses emancipation to the Jiv, or vital power, in woman, or denies that woman has a soul capable of immortality.

The six heretical systems of Indian speculation thus comprise the four Buddhist and two Jain schools; or, if the Jain be held to be one, the sixth is obtained by including the Charvak.

The tendency of Indian speculation lies doubtless towards materialism, and the learned say the *mind* cannot grasp that which is without qualities, or which has force without form, and is irrespective of space. In how much does the philosophy of Humboldt differ from this, when he says he confidently expects what Socrates once desired, 'that Reason shall be the sole interpreter of Nature'? (*Kosmos*, Sabine's trans., i. 154.)

## APPENDIX VI

## ON THE MAYA OF THE INDIANS

THE *Maya* of the Hindus may be considered under a threefold aspect, or morally, poetically, and philosophically.

*Morally*, it means no more than the vanity of Solomon (Ecclesiastes i and ii), or the nothingness of this world; and thus Kabir likens it to delusion or evil. or to moral error in the abstract. (*As. Res.*, xvi. 161.) The Indian reformers, indeed, made a use of *Maya* corresponding with the use made by the Apostle Saint John of the Logos of Plato, as Mr. Milman very judiciously observes. (Note in Gibbon, *History*, iii. 312.) The one adapted *Maya* to the Hindu notions of a sinful world, and the other explained to Greek and Roman understandings the nature of Christ's relation to God by representing the divine intellience to be manifested in the Messiah.

*Poetically*, Maya is used to denote a film before the eyes of gods and heroes, which limits their sight or sets bounds to their senses (Heereer, *Asiatic Nations*. iii. 203); and similarly Pallas dispel a mist from before the eyes of Diomed, and makes ne ethereal forms of divinities apparent to a mortal. (*Iliad*, v.) The popular speech of all countries contains proof of the persuasion that the imperfect powers of men render them unable to appreciate the world around them.

*Philosophically*, the Maya of the Vedant system (which corresponds to a certain extent with the Prakriti of the Sankhya school, and with the Cosmic substance of Xenophanes, or more exactly with the Play of the Infinite Being of Heraclitus), seems identical with the idealism of Berkeley. The doctrine seems also to have had the same origin as the 'Idola' system of Bacon; and thus, as an illusion or a false appearance, Maya is the opposite of Plato's 'Idea' or the True. Ordinarily, Maya is simply held to denote the apparent or sensible in opposition to the real, as when, according to the common illustration, a rope is taken for a snake, while in another point of view it is regarded as the Agent or Medium of God's manifestation in the universe, either as merely exhibiting images, or as really and actively mixed up with the production of worlds. It is curious that in England and in India the same material argument should have been used to confute Berkeley's theory of dreams and the Brahmanical theory of illusion. An elephant was impelled against Shankar Acharj, who maintained the unreal nature of his own body and of all around him; and Dr. Johnson considered that he demolished the doctrine when, striking a stone with his foot, he showed that he recoiled from it. But Shankar Acharj had a readier wit than the supporters of the bishop, and *he* retorted upon his adversaries when they ridiculed his nimble steps to avoid the beast, that *all* was a fancy; there was no Shankar, no elephant, no flight—all was a delusion (*Dabistan*, ii. 103.)

*Maya* may also be said to be used in a fourth or political sense by the Indians, as in the Sahit or Niti section of the 'Arth Shastra', or fourth 'Upved', which treats, among other things, of the duties of rulers, it is allowed as one of the modes of gaining an end. But Maya, in the science in question, is used to signify rather secrecy, or strategy, or dexterous diplomacy, than gross deceit; for fraud and falsehood are among the prohibited ways. Maya, it is said, may be employed to delude an enemy or to secure the obedience of subjects. Socrates admits that, under similar circumstances, such deceit would be fitting and proper, or that in his scheme it would come under the category of justice. (*Memorabilia*, book iv, chap. ii.)

# APPENDIX VII

## THE METAPHYSICS OF INDIAN REFORMERS

WHAT has been said in the text about the modern reformers relates chiefly to the popular theology. Some of them, however, likewise philosophized or speculated on the origin of things, and thus the 'Utar Mimamsa' school is sometimes subdivided into several branches, known (1) as the 'Adweit', or pure system of Shankar; and (2) as the 'Madhavadweit', the 'Vusisht-adweit', and the 'Shud-adweit', or modified systems of Unity of Madhav, Ramanuj, and Vallabh respectively. Shankar Acharj taught that God is the original of all things, and is in reality unchangeable in form; wherefore, when oblivious (*aghian*) of himself, he variously becomes manifest as vitality and matter, he does so as 'Maya', or as Images, or as the mirror reflecting all things, yet remaining itself the same. Life and the Soul are one in this system, and salvation becomes absorption, while, as a proof that the same vitality may put on different shapes, he quotes the instance of the caterpillar, the chrysalis, and the butterfly. Madhav holds Life to be distinct from Spirit, and with him the purified soul dwells with God without being absorbed, but he gives prominence to 'Maya' as coexistent with God, or as the moving and brooding spirit which gives form to matter; and thus the followers of Ramanuj extend Madhav's notion, and talk of God, Maya, and Life, as well as of Atoms. Vallabh and the Vishnu-swamins or the Shudadweits likewise maintain the distinct nature of Life or of the human Soul, and make salvation a dwelling with God without liability to reap-pearance; but the doctrine of 'Maya' is almost wholly rejected in favour of a Material Pantheism, as that the light which illumines a room is the same with the illu-minating principle of the transmitting flame, and hence that what man perceives is actual and not illusory. For some partial notices of these reasonings see Wilson, *As. Res.*, xvi. 34, 89, and 104; and they may be perused at length in the Commentaries of the several specula-tors on the 'Bhagavadgita', in the 'Urth Punchuk" of Ramanuj, and in the 'Dusha Slok' of Vishnuswami.

# APPENDIX VIII

## NANAK'S PHILOSOPHICAL ALLUSIONS POPULAR OR MORAL RATHER THAN SCIENTIFIC

PROFESSOR WILSON (*As. Res.*, xvii. 233, and conti-nuation of Mill's *History of India*, vii. 101, 102) would appear to think slightingly of the doctrines of Nanak, as being mere metaphysical notions founded on the abstractions of Sufism and the Vedant philosophy; but it is difficult for any one to write about the omnipot-ence of God and the hopes of man, without laying him-self open to a charge of belonging to one speculative school or another. Milton. the poet and statesman, indeed, may have had a particular leaning. when he thought of 'body working up to spirit' (*Paradise Lost*, v); but is St. Paul, the reformer and enthusiast. to be contemned, or is he to be misunderstood when he says. 'It is sown a natural body, and is raised a spiritual body' ? (1 Corinthians xv. 44). Similarly such expres-sions as 'Doth not the Lord fill heaven and earth?' (Jeremiah xxiii. 24), 'God, in whom we live and move

and have our being' (Acts, xvii. 28), and 'Of him, and
to him, and through him are all things' (Romans xi.
36), might be used to declare the prophet and the
apostle to be Pantheists or Materialists; but it nevertheless seems plain that Jeremiah and Paul, and likewise Nanak, had another object in view than scholastic
dogmatism, and that they simply desired to impress
mankind with exalted notions of the greatness and
goodness of God, by a vague employment of general
language which they knew would never mislead the
multitude.

Professor Wilson (*As. Res.*, xvii. 233, 237, 238) and
Muhsin Fani (*Dabistan*, ii. 269, 270, 285, 286) may be
compared together, and the *Siar ul Mutakharin* (i. 110)
may be compared with both, with reference to the contradictory views taken of the similarity or difference
respectively between Sikhism and Brahmanism. Each
is right, the one with regard to the imperfect faith or
the corrupt practices, especially of the Sikhs in the
Gangetic provinces, and the other with regard to the
admitted doctrines of Nanak, as they will always be
explained by any qualified person.

It is to be remembered that the Sikhs regard the
mission of Nanak and Gobind as the consummation of
other dispensations, including that of Muhammad; and
their talk, therefore, of Brahma and Vishnu and various heavenly powers is no more unreasonable than the
deference of Christians to Moses and Abraham and to
the archangels Michael and Gabriel.  Such allusions
are perhaps, indeed, more excusable in the Sikhs than
'that singular polytheism' of our mediaeval divines,
which they 'grafted on the language rather (indeed)
than on the principles of Christianity'. (Hallam, *Middle Ages*, iii. 346.)

For an instance of the moral application which
Nanak was wont to give to mythological stories see
Ward, *Hindus*, iii. 465. Nanak, indeed, refers continually to Hindu notions, but he was not therefore an
idolater; and it should further be borne in mind that
as St. John could draw illustrations from Greek philosophy, so could St. Paul make an advantageous use of
the Greek poets, as was long ago observed upon in a
right spirit by Milton (Speech for the Liberty of un-
licensed Printing).  In the early ages of Christianity,
moreover, the Sibylline leaves were referred to as fore-
telling the mission of Jesus; but although the spurious-
ness of the passages is now admitted, the fathers are
not accused of polytheism, or of holding Amalthaea,

the nurse of Jupiter, to be a real type of the Virgin Mary! In truth, all religious systems not possessed of a body of literature or philosophy proper to themselves seek elsewhere for support in such matters. Thus the Chevalier Bunsen (*Egypt*, i. 194, &c.) observes that the early Christians were even desirous of reconciling Scripture with Greek *history;* and Ranke (*Hist. of the Popes*, ed. 1843, p. 125) says that the Church, so late as the sixteenth century, was willing to rest its dogmas and doctrines on the metaphysics of the Ancients.

# APPENDIX IX

## THE TERMS RAJ AND JOG, DEG AND TEGH

THE warlike resistance of Har Gobind, or the arming of the Sikhs by that teacher, is mainly attributed by Malcolm (*Sketch*, pp. 34, 35) and Forster (*Travels*, i. 298, 299) to his personal feelings of revenge for the death of his father, although religious animosity against Muhammadans is allowed to have had some share in bringing about the change. The circumstance of the Guru's military array does not appear to have struck Muhsin Fani as strange or unusual, and his work, the *Dabistan*, does not therefore endeavour to account for it. The Sikhs themselves connect the modification of Nanak's system with the double nature of the mythological Janak of Mithila, whose released soul, indeed, is held to have animated the body of their first teacher (*Dabistan*, ii. 268), and they have encumbered their *ideal* of a ruler with the following *personal* anecdote: The wife of Arjun was without children, and she began to despair of ever becoming a mother. She went to Bhai Buddha, the ancient and only surviving companion of Nanak, to beseech his blessing; but he, disliking the degree of state she assumed and her costly offerings, would not notice her. She afterwards went barefooted and alone to his presence, carrying on her head the ordinary food of peasants. The Bhai smiled benignly upon her, and said she should have a son, who would be master both of the *Deg* and *Tegh;* that is, simply of a vessel for food and a sword, but typically of grace and power, the terms corresponding in significance with the 'Raj' and 'Jog' of Janak,[1] the 'Piri'

[1] 'Raj men jog kumaio,' to attain immortal purity or virtue, or to dwell in grace while exercising earthly sway. It is an expression of not infrequent use, and which occurs in the

and 'Miri' of Indian Muhammadans, and with the idea
of the priesthood and kingship residing in Melchisedec
and in the expected Messiah of the Jews. Thus Har
Gobind is commonly said to have worn two swords, one
to denote his spiritual, and the other his temporal
power; or, as he may sometimes have chosen to express
it, one to avenge his father, and the other to destroy
Muhammadanism. (See Malcolm, *Sketch*, p. 35.)

The fate of Arjun, and the personal character of
his son, had doubtless some share in leading the Sikhs
to take up arms; but the whole progress of the change
is not yet apparent, nor perhaps do the means exist of
tracing it. The same remark applies to the early
Christian history, and we are left in ignorance of how
that modification of feeling and principle was brought
about, which made those who were so averse to the
'business of war and government' in the time of the
[early] Caesars, fill the armies of the empire in the
reign of Diocletian, and at last give a military master
to the western world in the person of Constantine. (Cf.
Gibbon, *History*, ed. 1838, ii. 325, 375.)


# APPENDIX X

## CASTE AMONG THE SIKHS

IT may nevertheless be justly observed that Gobind
abolished *caste* rather by implication than by a direct
enactment, and it may be justly objected that the Sikhs
still uphold the principal distinctions at least of race.
Thus the Gurus nowhere say that Brahmans and Sudras
are to inter-marry, or that they are daily to partake
together of the same food; but that they laid a good
foundation for the practical obliteration of all differences will be evident from the following quotations,
bearing in mind the vast pre-eminence which they
assign to religious unity and truth over social same-
ness or political equality:

*Adi Granth*, in the 'Sawayas', by certain Bhats. Thus one Bika
says, Ram Das (the fourth Guru) got the 'Takht', or throne,
of 'Raj' and 'Jog', from Amar Das. 'Deg', as above stated,
means simply a vessel for food, and thence, metaphorically,
*abundance* on earth, and *grace* on the part of God. The two
terms are clearly synonymous, and thus Thomson writes of
the sun as the
　　　. . . 'great delegated source
　　Of light, and life, and *grace*, and joy below.'
　　　　　　　　THE SEASONS—*Summer.*

'Think not of caste : abase thyself, and attain to sa'vation.'—NANAK, *Sarang Rag*.

'God will not ask man of what race he is; he will ask him what has he done?'—NANAK, *Parbhati Ragni*.

' Of the impure among the noblest,
   Heed not the injunction;
   Of one pure among the most despised,
   Nanak will become the footstool.'

NANAK, *Malhar Rag*.

' All of the seed of Brahm (God) are Brahmans :
   They say there are four races,
   But all are of the seed of Brahm.'

AMAR DAS, *Bhairav*.

'Kshattriya, Brahman, Sudra, Veisya, whoever remembers the name of God. who worships him always, &c., &c., shall attain to salvation.'—RAM DAS, *Bilawal*.

' The four races shall be one,
   All shall call on the Guru.'

GOBIND, in the *Rahat Nama*
(not in the *Granth*).

Compare Malcolm (*Sketch*, p. 45 *n*.) for a saying attributed to Gobind, that the castes would become one when well mixed, as the four components of the 'Pan-Supari', or betel, of the Hindus, became of one colour when well chewed.

The Sikhs of course partake in common of the Prasad (vulg. Parshad) or consecrated food, which is ordinarily composed of flour, coarse sugar, and clarified butter. Several, perhaps all, Hindu sects, however, do the same. (See Wilson, *As. Res.*. xvi. 83 *n*., and xvii. 239 *n*.)

# APPENDIX XI

## RITES OF INITIATION INTO SIKHISM

SIKHS are not ordinarily initiated until they reach the age of discrimination and remembrance, or not before they are seven years of age, or sometimes until they have attained to manhood. But there is no authoritative rule on the subject, nor is there any declaratory ceremonial of detail which can be followed. The essentials are that five Sikhs at least should be assembled, and it is generally arranged that one of the num-

ber is of some religious repute. Some sugar and water
are stirred together in a vessel of any kind, commonly
with a two-edged dagger, but any iron weapon will
answer. The noviciate stands with his hands joined
in an attitude of humility or supplication, and he repeats after the elder or minister the main articles of
his faith. Some of the water is sprinkled on his face
and person; he drinks the remainder, and exclaims,
Hail Guru! and the ceremony concludes with an injunction that he be true to God and to his duty as a Sikh.
For details of particular modes followed, see Forster
(*Travels*, i. 307), Malcolm (*Sketch*, p. 182), and Prinsep's edition of Murray's *Life of Ranjit Singh* (p. 217),
where an Indian compiler is quoted.

The original practice of using the water in which
the feet of a Sikh had been washed was soon abandoned, and the subsequent custom of touching the
water with the toe seems now almost wholly forgotten.
The first rule was perhaps instituted to denote the
humbleness of spirit of the disciples, or both it and the
second practice may have originated in that feeling of
the Hindus which attaches virtue to water in which
the thumb of a Brahman has been dipped. It seems
in every way probable that Gobind substituted the
dagger for the foot or the toe, thus giving further pre-
eminence to his emblematic iron.

Women are not usually, but they are sometimes,
initiated in form as professors of the Sikh faith. In
mingling the sugar and water for women, a one-edged,
and not a two-edged, dagger is used.

# APPENDIX XII

## THE EXCLAMATION WAH GURU AND
## THE EXPRESSION DEG, TEGH, FATH

THE proper exclamation of community of faith of
the Sikhs as a sect is simply, 'Wah Guru!' that is, O
Guru! or Hail Guru! The lengthened exclamations
of 'Wah! Guru ki Fath!' and 'Wah! Guru ka Khalsa!'
(Hail! Virtue or power of the Guru! or Hail! Guru
and Victory! and Hail to the state or church of the
Guru!) are not authoritative, although the former has
become customary, and its use, as completing the idea
embraced in 'Deg' and 'Tegh' (see *ante*, Appendix IX)
naturally arose out of the notions diffused by Gobind,

if he did not ordain it as the proper salutation of believers.

Many of the chapters or books into which the *Adi Granth* is divided, begin with the expression 'Eko Unkar, Sat Guru Prasad', which may be interpreted to mean, 'The One God, and the grace of the blessed Guru'. Some of the chapters of the *Daswen Padshah ka Granth* begin with 'Eko Unkar, Wah Guru ki Fath', that is, 'The One God and the power of the Guru'.

The Sikh author of the *Gur Ratnawali* gives the following fanciful and trivial origin of the salutation Wah Guru !

Wasdev, the exclamation of the first age, or Satyug;
Har Har, the exclamation of the second age;
Gobind Gobind, the exclamation of the third age;

Ram Ram, the exclamation of the fourth age, or Kalyug; whence Wah Guru in the fifth age, or under the new dispensation.

# APPENDIX XIII

## THE SIKH DEVOTION TO STEEL, AND THE TERM 'SACHCHA PADSHAH'

For allusions to this devotion to steel see Malcolm, *Sketch*, pp. 48, 117 *n.*, 182 *n.*

The meaning given in the text to the principle inculcated seems to be the true one. Throughout India the implements of any calling are in a manner worshipped, or in Western moderation of phrase, they are blessed or consecrated. This is especially noticeable among merchants, who annually perform religious ceremonies before a heap of gold; among hereditary clerks or writers, who similarly idolize their inkhorn, and among soldiers and military leaders, who on the festival of the Das-hara consecrate their banners and piled-up weapons. Gobind withdrew his followers from that undivided attention which their fathers had given to the plough, the loom, and the pen, and he urged them to regard the sword as their principal stay in this world. The sentiment of veneration for that which gives us power, or safety, or our daily bread, may be traced in all countries. In our own a sailor impersonates, or almost deifies, his ship, and in India the custom of hereditary callings has heightened that feeling, which, expressed in the language of philosophy,

becomes the dogmå admitting the soul to be increate
indeed, but enveloped in the understanding, which
again is designed for our use in human affairs, or until
our bliss is perfect. It is this external or inferior spirit,
so to speak, which must devote its energies to the service and contemplation of steel, while the increate soul
contemplates God. [Compare also the mediaeval ceremony of 'watching his arms' regularly undergone by
the candidate for knighthood.—ED.]

The import of the term *Sachcha Padshah,* or True
King, seems to be explained in the same way. A spiritual king, or Guru, rules the eternal soul, or guides it
to salvation, while a temporal monarch controls our
finite faculties only, or puts restraints upon the play
of our passions and the enjoyment of our senses. The
Muhammadans have the same idea and a corresponding
**term, viz.** *Malik Hakiki.*


# APPENDIX XIV

## DISTINCTIVE USAGES OF THE SIKHS

THESE and many other distinctions of Sikhs may
be seen in the Rehet and Tankha Namas of Gobind,
forming part of Appendix XX of this volume.

Unshorn locks and a blue dress, as the characteristics of a believer, do not appear as direct injunctions
in any extant writing attributed to Gobind, and they
seem chiefly to have derived their distinction as marks
from custom or usage, while the propriety of wearing
a blue dress is now regarded as less obligatory than
formerly. Both usages appear to have originated in a
spirit of opposition to Hinduism, for many Brahmanical
devotees keep their heads carefully shaved, and all
Hindus are shaven when initiated into their religious
duties or responsibilities, or on the death of a near
relative. It is also curious, with regard to colour, that
many religious, or indeed simply respectable Hindus,
have still an aversion to blue, so much so indeed that
a Rajput farmer will demur about sowing his fields
with indigo. The Muhammadans, again, prefer blue
dresses, and perhaps the dislike of the Hindus arose
during the Musalman conquest, as Krishna himself,
among others, is described as blue clothed. Thus the
Sikh author, Bhai Gurdas Bhalla, says of Nanak, 'Again
he went to Mecca, blue clothing he had like Krishna'.

Similarly, no Sikh will wear clothes of a 'suhi' colour, i.e. dyed with safflower, such having long been the favourite colour with Hindu devotees, as it is gradually becoming with Muhammadan ascetics. As a distinction of race, if not of creed, the unshorn locks of Sikhs have a parallel in the long hair of the Frankish nobles and freemen. The contrasting terms 'crinosus' and 'tonsoratus' arose in mediaeval Europe, and the virtue or privilege due to flowing hair was so great that Childebert talked of having his brother's children either *cropped or put to death.* (Hallam, *Middle Ages,* notes to Chap. II.)

The Sikhs continue to refrain from tobacco, nor do they smoke drugs of any kind, although tobacco itself seems to have been originally included as *snuff* only among proscribed things. Tobacco was first introduced into India about 1617. (M'Culloc, *Commercial Dictionary,* art. 'Tobacco'.) It was, I think, idly denounced in form by one of Akbar's successors, but its use is now universal among Indian Muhammadans.

Another point of difference which may be noticed is that the Sikhs wear a kind of breeches, or now many wear a sort of pantaloons, instead of girding up their loins after the manner of the Hindus. The adoption of the 'kachh', or breeches, is of as much importance to a Sikh boy as was the investiture with the 'toga virilis' to a Roman youth.

The Sikh women are distinguished from Hindus of their sex by some variety of dress, but chiefly by a higher topknot of hair.


# APPENDIX XV

## ON THE USE OF ARABIC AND SANSKRIT FOR THE PURPOSES OF EDUCATION IN INDIA

Up to the present time England has made no great and lasting impress on the Indians, except as the introducer of an improved and effective military system; although she has also done much to exalt her character as a governing power, by her generally scrupulous adherence to formal engagements.

The Indian mind has not yet been suffused or saturated by the genuis of the English, nor can the light of European knowledge be spread over the country, until both the Sanskrit and Arabic (Persian) languages are made the vehicles of instructing the *learned*. These tongues should thus be assiduously cultivated, although not so much for what they contain as for what they may be made the means of conveying. The hierarchies of 'Gymnosophists' and 'Ulema' will the more readily assent to mathematical or logical deductions, if couched in words identified in their eyes with scientific research; and they in time must of necessity make known the truths learned to the mass of the people. The present system of endeavouring to diffuse knowledge by means of the rude and imperfect vernacular tongues can succeed but slowly, for it seems to be undertaken in a spirit of opposition to the influential classes; and it is not likely to succeed at all until expositions of the sciences, with ample proofs and illustrations, are rendered complete, instead of partial and elementary only, or indeed meagre and inaccurate in the extreme, as many of the authorized school-books are. If there was Sanskrit or Arabic counterparts to these much-required elaborate treatises, the predilections of the learned Indians would be overcome with comparative ease.

The fact that the astronomy of Ptolemy and the geometry of Euclid are recognized in their Sanskrit dress as text-books of science even among the Brahmans, should not be lost upon the promoters of education in the present age. The philosophy of facts and the truths of physical science had to be made known by Copernicus and Galileo, Bacon and Newton, through the medium of the Latin tongue; and the first teachers and upholders of Christianity preferred the admired and widely spoken Roman and Greek, both to the antique Hebrew and to the imperfect dialects of Gaul and Syria, Africa, and Asia Minor. In either case the language recommended the doctrine, and added to the conviction of Origen and Irenaeus, Tertullian and Clement of Rome, as well as to the belief of the scholar of more modern times. Similarly in India the use of Sanskrit and Arabic and Persian would give weight to the most obvious principles and completeness to the most logical demonstrations.

That in Calcutta the study of the sciences is pursued with some success through the joint medium of the English language and local dialects, and that in especial the tact and perseverance of the professors of the Medical College have induced Indians of family or caste to dissect the human body, do not militate against the views expressed above, but rather serve as exceptions to prove their truth. In Calcutta Englishmen are numerous, and their wealth, intelligence, and political position render their influence overwhelming; but this mental predominance decreases so rapidly that it is unfelt in fair-sized towns within fifty miles of the capital, and is but faintly revived in the populous cities of Benares, Delhi, Puna, and Hyderabad.

## APPENDIX XVI

### ON THE LAND-TAX IN INDIA

THE proportions of the land-tax to the general revenues of British India are nearly as follows :

Bengal, 2/5; Bombay, 2/3; Madras, 3/5; Agra, 4/5. Average = 3/5 of the whole.

In some European states the proportions are nearly as below :

England, 1/24; France, 1/4; Spain, 1/17 (perhaps some error); Belgium, 2/11; Prussia, 2/11; Naples, 1/4; Austria, 1/2.

In the United States of America the revenue is almost wholly derived from customs.

It is now idle to revert to the theory of the ancient laws of the Hindus, or of the more recent institutes of the Muhammadans, although much clearness of view has resulted from the learned researches or laborious inquiries of Briggs and Munro, of Sykes and Halhed and Galloway. It is also idle to dispute whether the Indian farmer pays a 'rent' or a 'tax' in a technical sense, since, practically, it is certain (1) that the government (or its assign, the jagirdar or grantee) gets in nearly all instances almost the whole surplus produce of the land; and (2) that the state, if the owner, does not perform its duty by not furnishing from its capital wells and other things, which correspond in difficulty of provision with barns and drains in England. In India no one thinks of investing capital or of spending money on the improvement of the land, excepting, directly, a few patriarchal chiefs through love of their homes; and indirectly, the wealthy speculators in opium, sugar, &c., through the love of gain. An ordinary village 'head-man', or the still poorer 'ryot', whether paying direct to government or through a revenue farmer, has just so much of the produce left as will enable him to provide the necessary seed, his own inferior food, and the most simple requisites of tillage; and as he has thus no means, he cannot incur the expense or run the risk of introducing improvements.

Hence it behoves England, if in doubt about Oriental 'socage' and 'freehold' tenures, to redistribute her taxation, to diminish her assessment on the soil, and to give her multitudes of subjects, who are practically 'copyholders', at least a permanent interest in the land, as she has done so largely by customary' leaseholders within her own proper dominion. There should likewise be a limit to which such estates might be divided, and this could be advantageously done, by allowing the owner of a petty holding to dispose as he pleased, not of the land itself, but of what it might bring when sold.

For some just observations on the land tenures of India see Lieut.-Col. Sleeman's *Rambles and Recollections of an Indian Official* (Oxford, 1915), pp. 58, 561. 571; while, for a *fiscal* description of the transition system now in force in the North-Western Provinces, the present Lieut.-Governor's *Directions for Settlement Officers* and his *Remarks on the Revenue System* may be profitably consulted (1849).

## APPENDIX XVII

## THE *ADI GRANTH*, OR FIRST BOOK; OR, THE BOOK OF NANAK, THE FIRST GURU, OR TEACHER OF THE SIKHS

NOTE.—The first *Granth* is nowhere narrative or historical. It throws no light, by direct exposition, upon the political state of India during the sixteenth and seventeenth centuries, although it contains many allusions illustrative of the condition of society and of the religious feelings of the times. Its teaching is to the general purport that God is to be worshipped in spirit and in truth, with little reference to particular forms, and that salvation is unattainable without grace, faith, and good works.

The *Adi Granth* comprises, first, the writings attributed to Nanak, and the succeeding teachers of the Sikh faith up to the ninth Guru, Tegh Bahadur, omitting the sixth, seventh, and eighth, but with perhaps some additions and emendations by Gobind;

secondly, the compositions of certain 'Bhagats', or saints, mostly sectarian Hindus, and who are usually given as sixteen in number; and, thirdly, the verses of certain 'Bhats', or rhapsodists, followers of Nanak and of some of his successors. The numbers, and even the names of the 'Bhagats', or saints, are not always the same in copies of the *Granth;* and thus modern compilers or copyists have assumed to themselves the power of rejecting or sanctioning particular writings. To the sixteen Bhagats are usually added two 'Doms', or chanters, who recited before Arjun, and who caught some of his spirit; and a 'Rababi', or player upon a stringed instrument, who became similarly inspired.

The *Granth* sometimes includes an appendix, containing works the authenticity of which is doubtful, or the propriety of admitting which is disputed on other grounds.

The *Granth* was originally compiled by Arjun, the fifth Guru; but it subsequently received a few additions at the hands of his successors.

The *Granth* is written wholly in verse; but the forms of versification are numerous. The language used is rather the Hindi of Upper India generally, than the particular dialect of the Punjab; but some portions, especially of the last ection, are composed in Sanskrit. The written character is nevertheless throughout the Punjabi, one of the several varieties of alphabets now current in India, and which, from its use by the Sikh Gurus, is sometimes called Gurmukhi' a term likewise applied to the dialect of the Punjab. The language of the writings of Nanak is thought by modern Sikhs to abound with provincialisms of the country southwest of Lahore, and the dialect of Arjun is held to be the most pure.

The *Granth* usually forms a quarto volume of about 1,232 pages, each page containing 24 lines, and each line containing about 35 letters. The extra books increase the pages to 1,240 only.

### Contents of the Adi Granth

1st. The *'Japji'*, or simply the *'Jap'*, called also *Guru Mantr*, or the special prayer of initiation of the Guru. It occupies about 7 pages, and consists of 40 sloks, called *Pauri*, of irregular lengths, some of two, and some of several lines. It means, literally, the remembrancer or admonisher, from *jap*, to remember. It was

written by Nanak, and is believed to have been appointed by him to be repeated each morning, as every
pious Sikh now does.  The mode of composition implies
the presence of a questioner and an answerer, and the
Sikhs believe the questioner to have been the disciple
Angad.

2nd. '*Sudar Rah Ras*'—the evening prayer of the
Sikhs.  It occupies about 3½ pages, and it was composed by Nanak, but has additions by Ram Das and
Arjun, and some, it is said, by Guru Gobind.  The additions attributed to Gobind are, however, more frequently given when the Rah Ras forms a separate pamphlet
or book. *Sardar*, a particular kind of verse; *Rah*, admonisher; *Ras*, the expression used for the play or
recitative of Krishna.  It is sometimes corruptly called
the 'Rowh Ras', from *Rowh,* the Punjabi for a road.

3rd. '*Kirit Sohila*'—a prayer repeated before going
to rest.  It occupies a page and a line or two more.  It
was composed by Nanak, but has additions by Ram Das
and Arjun, and one verse is attributed to Gobind.
*Kirit*, from Sanskrit *Kirti*, to praise, to celebrate; and
*Sohila*, a marriage song, a song of rejoicing.

4th.  The next portion of the *Granth* is divided
into thirty-one sections, known by their distinguishing
forms of verse, as follows :

| | |
|---|---|
| 1. Sri Rag. | 17. Gaund. |
| 2. Maj. | 18. Ram Kali. |
| 3. Gauri. | 19. Nat Narayan. |
| 4. Asa. | 20. Mali Gaura. |
| 5. Gujri. | 21. Maru. |
| 6. Dev Gandhari. | 22. Tukhari. |
| 7. Bihagra. | 23. Kedara. |
| 8. Wad Hans. | 24. Bhairon. |
| 9. Sorath (or Sort). | 25. Basant. |
| 10. Dhanasri. | 26. Sarang. |
| 11. Jait Sri. | 27. Malhar. |
| 12. Todi. | 28. Kanhra. |
| 13. Bairari. | 29. Kalian. |
| 14. Tailang. | 30. Parbhati. |
| 15. Sudhi. | 31. Jai Jaiwanti. |
| 16. Bilawal. | |

The whole occupies about 1,154 pages, or by far
the greater portion of the entire *Granth*.  Each subdivision is the composition of one or more Gurus, or of
one or more Bhagats or holy men, or of a Guru with
or without the aid of a Bhagat.

The contributors among the Gurus were as follows:

1. Nanak.                     5. Arjun.
2. Angad.                     6. Tegh Bahadur (with,
3. Amar Das.                     perhaps, emendations
4. Ram Das.                      by Gobind).

The Bhagats or saints, and others who contributed agreeably to the ordinary copies of the *Granth*, are enumerated below :

1. Kabir (the well-known reformer).
2. Trilochan, a Brahman.
3. Beni.
4. Rav Das, a Chamar, or leather dresser.
5. Namdev, a Chhipa, or cloth printer.
6. Dhanna, a Jat.
7. Shah Farid, a Muhammadan pir, or saint.
8. Jaidev, a Brahman.
9. Bhikan.
10. Sain, a barber.
11. Pipa (a Jogi?).
12. Sadhna, a butcher.
13. Ramanand Bairagi (a well-known reformer).
14. Parmanand.
15. Sur Das (a blind man).
16. Miran Bai, a Bhagatni, or holy woman.
17. Balwand, and
18. Satta, 'Doms' or chanters who recited before Arjun.
19. Sundar Das, Rababi, or player upon a stringed instrument. He is not properly one of the Bhagats.

5th. The *'Bhog'*. In Sanskrit t is word means to enjoy anything, but it is commonly used to denote the conclusion of any sacred writing, both by Hindus and Sikhs. The Bhog occupies about 66 pages, and besides the writings of Nanak and Arjun, of Kabir, Shah Farid, and other reformers, it contains the compositions of nine Bhats or rhapsodists who attached themselves to Amar Das, Ram Das, and Arjun.

The Bhog commences with 4 sloks in Sanskrit by Nanak, which are followed by 67 Sanskrit sloks in one metre by Arjun, and then by 24 in another metre by the same Guru. There are also 23 sloks in Punjabi or Hindi by Arjun, which contain praises of Amritsar. These are soon followed by 243 sloks by Kabir, and 130 by Shah Farid, and others, containing some sayings of Arjun. Afterwards the writings of Kall and the other Bhats follow, intermixed with portions by Arjun, and so on to the end.

The nine Bhats who contributed to the Bhog are named as follows :

1. Bhikha, a follower of Amar Das.
2. Kall, a follower of Ram Das.

3. Kall Sahar.                    6. Nall.
4. Jalap, a follower of           7. Mathra.
   Arjun.                         8. Ball.
5. Sall, a follower of            9. Kirit.
   Arjun.

The names are evidently fanciful, and perhaps
fictitious. In the book called the *Guru Bilas* eight Bhats
only are enumerated, and all the names except Ball
are different from those in the *Granth*.

### Supplement to the Granth

6th. '*Bhog ki Bani*', or Epilogue or the Conclusion.
It comprises about 7 pages, and contains, first, some
preliminary sloks, called 'Slok Mahal Pahla', or Hymn
of the first Woman or Slave; secondly, Nanak's Admonition to Malhar Raja; thirdly, the 'Ratan Mala' of
Nanak, i.e. the Rosary of Jewels, or string of (religious) worthies, which simply shows, however, what
should be the true characteristics or qualities of religious devotees; and, fourthly, the 'Hakikat', or Circumstances of Sivnab, Raja of Ceylon, with reference to a
'Pothi' or sacred writing known as 'Pran Sangli'. This
last is said to have been composed by one Bhai Bhannu
in the time of Gobind.

The Ratan Mala is said to have been originally
written in Turki, or to have been abstracted from a
Turki original.

## APPENDIX XVIII

### THE *DASWIN PADSHAH KA GRANTH*, OR, BOOK OF THE TENTH KING, OR SOVEREIGN PONTIFF, THAT IS, OF GURU GOBIND SINGH

NOTE.—Like the *Adi Granth*, the book of Gobind is
metrical throughout, but the versification frequently
varies.

It is written in the Hindi dialect, and in the Punjabi character, excepting the concluding portion, the
language of which is Persian, while the alphabet continues the Gurmukhi. The Hindi of Gobind is almost
such as is spoken in the Gangetic provinces, and has
few peculiarities of the Punjabi dialect.

One chapter of the Book of the Tenth King may
be considered to be narrative and historical, viz. the

*Vichitr Natak*, written by Gobind himself; but the Persian *Hikayats*, or stories, also partake of that character, from the circumstances attending their composition and the nature of some allusions made in them. The other portions of this *Granth* are more mythological than the first book, and it also partakes more of a worldly character throughout, although it contains many noble allusions to the unity of the Godhead, and to the greatness and goodness of the Ruler of the Universe.

Five chapters, or portions only, and the commencement of a sixth, are attributed to Gobind himself; the remainder, i.e. by far the larger portion, is said to have been composed by four scribes in the service of the Guru; partly, perhaps, agreeably to his dictation. The names of Sham and Ram occur as two of the writers, but, in truth, little is known of the authorship of the portions in question.

The *Daswin Padshah ka Granth* forms a quarto volume of 1,066 pages, each page consisting of 23 lines, and each line of from 38 to 41 letters.

## Contents of the Book of the Tenth King

1st. The '*Japji*', or simply the '*Jap*', the supplement or complement of the *Japji* of Nanak—a prayer to be read or repeated in the morning, as it continues to be by pious Sikhs. It comprises 198 distichs, and occupies about 7 pages, the termination of a verse and the end of a line not being the same. The *Japji* was composed by Guru Gobind.

2nd. '*Akal Stut*', or the Praises of the Almighty—a hymn commonly read in the morning. It occupies 23 pages, and the initiatory verse alone is the composition of Gobind.

3rd. The '*Vichitr Natak*', i.e. the Wondrous Tale. This was written by Gobind himself, and it gives, first, the mythological history of his family or race; secondly, an account of his mission of reformation; and, thirdly, a description of his warfare with the Himalayan chiefs and the Imperial forces. It is divided into fourteen sections; but the first is devoted to the praises of the Almighty, and the last is of a similar tenor, with an addition to the effect that he would hereafter relate his visions of the past and his experience of the present world. The *Vichitr Natak* occupies about 24 pages of the *Granth*.

4th. 'Chandi Charitr', or the Wonders of Chandi or the Goddess. There are two portions called Chandi Charitr, of which this is considered the greater. It relates the destruction of eight Titans or Deityas by Chandi the Goddess. It occupies about 20 pages, and it is understood to be the translation of a Sanskrit legend, executed, some are willing to believe, by Gobind himself.

The names of the Deityas destroyed are as follows:

1. Madhu Kaitab.          6. Raka' Bij.
2. Mah Khasur.            7. Nishumbh.
3. Dhumar Loehan.        8. Shumbh.
4 and 5. Chand and Mund.

5th. 'Chandi Charitr' the lesser. The same legends as the greater Chandi, narrated in a different metre. It occupies about 14 pages.

6th. 'Chandi ki Var.' A supplement to the legends of Chandi. It occupies about 6 pages.

7th. 'Gyan Prabodh', or the Excellence of Wisdom. Praises of the Almighty, with allusions to ancient kings, taken mostly from the Mahabharat. It occupies about 21 pages.

8th. Chaupayan Chaubis Avataran Kian'. or Quatrains relating to the Twenty-four Manifestations (Avatars). These Chaupays' occupy about 348 pages, and they are considered to be the work of one by name Sham.

The names of the incarnations are as follows :

1. The fish, or Machh.
2. The tortoise, or Kachh.
3. The lion, or Nar.
4. Narayan.
5. Mohani.
6. The boar, or Varah.
7. The man-lion, or Nur-singh.
8. The dwarf, or Bawan.
9. Paras Ram.
10. Brahma.
11. Rudr.
12. Jalandhar.
13. Vishnu.
14. No name specified, but understood to be a manifestation of Vishnu.
15. Arhant Dev (considered to be the founder of the sect of Saraugis of the Jain persuasion, or, indeed the great Jain prophet himself)
16. Man Raja.
17. Dhanantai (the doctor, or physician).
18. The sun, or Suraj.
19. The moon, or Chandarma.

20. Rama.
21. Krishna.
22. Nàr (meaning Arjun).
23. Bodh.

24. Kalki; to appear at the end of the Kalyug, or when the sins of men are at their height.

9th. No name entered, but known as 'Mihdi Mir' A supplement to the Twenty-four Incarnations. Mihdi, it is said, will appear when the mission of Kalki is fulfilled. The name and the idea are borrowed from the Shia Muhammadans. It occupies somewhat less than a page.

10th. No name entered, but known as the 'Avatars of Brahma'. An account of seven incarnations of Brahma, followed by some account of eight Rajas of bygone times. It occupies about 18 pages.

The names of the incarnations are as follows :

1. Valmik.
2. Kashap.
3. Shukar.
4. Batchess.
5. Vyasi.
6. Khasht Rikhi (or the Six Sages).
7. Kaul Das.

The kings are enumerated below :

1. Manu.
2. Prithu.
3. Sagar.
4. Ben.
5. Mandhat.
6. Dalip.
7. Ragh.
8. Aj.

11th. No name entered, but known as the 'Avatars of Rudr or Siva'. It comprises 56 pages; and two incarnations only are mentioned, namely, Dat and Parasnath.

12th. 'Shastr Nam Mala', or the Name-string of Weapons. The names of the various weapons are recapitulated, the weapons are praised, and Gobind terms them collectively his Guru or guide. The composition nevertheless is not attributed to Gobind. It occupies about 68 pages.

13th. 'Sri Mukh Vak, Sawaya Battis', or the Voice of the Guru (Gobind) himself, in thirty-two verses. These verses were composed by Gobind as declared, and they are condemnatory of the Vedas, the Purans, and the Kuran. They occupy about 3½ pages.

14th. 'Hazara Shabd', or the Thousand Verses of the Metre called Shabd. There are, however, but ten verses only in most Granths, occupying about 2 pages. Hazar is not understood in its literal sense of a thousand, but as implying invaluable or excellent. They are laudatory of the Creator and creation, and depre-

cate the adoration of saints and limitary divinities.
They were written by Guru Gobind.

15th. *'Istri Charitr'*, or Tales of Women. There
are 404 stories, illustrative of the character and disposition of women. A stepmother became enamoured of
her stepson, the heir of a monarchy, who, however
would not gratify her desires, whereupon she represented to her husband that his first-born had made
attempts upon her honour. The Raja ordered his son
to be put to death; but his ministers interfered, and
procured a respite. They then enlarged in a series of
stories upon the nature of women, and at length the
Raja became sensible of the guilt of his wife's mind,
and of his own rashness. These stories occupy 446
pages, or nearly half of the *Granth*. The name of Sham
also occurs as the writer of one or more of them.

16th. The *'Hikayats'*, or Tales. These comprise
twelve stories in 866 sloks of two lines each. They are
written in the Persian language and Gurmukhi character, and they were composed by Gobind himself as
admonitory of Aurangzeb, and were sent to the emperor by the hands of Daya Singh and four other Sikhs.
The tales were accompanied by a letter written in a
pointed manner, which, however, does not form a
portion of the *Granth*.

These tales occupy about 30 pages, and conclude
the *Granth* of Guru Gobind.

# APPENDIX XIX

## SOME PRINCIPLES OF BELIEF AND PRACTICE, AS EXEMPLIFIED IN THE OPINIONS OF THE SIKH GURUS OR TEACHERS

With an Addendum, showing the modes in which
the missions of Nanak and Gobind are
represented or regarded by the Sikhs

### 1.   *God—the Godhead*

THE True Name is God; without fear, without enmity;
   the Being without Death, the Giver of Salvation;
   the Guru and Grace.
Remember the primal Truth; Truth which was before
   the world began.
Truth which is, and Truth, O Nanak! which will
   remain.

By reflection it cannot be understood, if times innumerable it be considered.

By meditation it cannot be attained, how much soever the attention be fixed.

A hundred wisdoms, even a hundred thousand, not one accompanies the dead.

How can Truth be told. how can falsehood be unravelled ?

O Nanak! by following the will of God, as by Him ordained.

> NANAK. *Adi Granth*, Japji (commencement of

One, Self-existent. Himself the Creator.

O Nanak! one continueth, another never was and never will be.

> NANAK, *Adi Granth*, Gauri Rag.

Thou art in each thing, and in all places.

O God! thou art the one Existent Being.

> RAM DAS, *Adi Granth*, Asa Rag.

My mind dwells upon One,

He who gave the Soul and the body.

> ARJUN, *Adi Granth*, Sri Rag.

Time is the only God; the First and the Last, the Endless Being; the Creator, the Destroyer; He who can make and unmake.

God who created Angels and Demons, who created the East and the West, the North and the South, how can He be expressed by words?

> GOBIND, *Hazar ι Shabd*.

God is one image (or Being), how can He be conceived in another form?     GOBIND, *Vichitr Natak*.

### 2. *Incarnations, Saints, and Prophets; the Hindu Avatars, Muhammad, and Sidhs, and Pirs*

Numerous Muhammads have there been, and multitudes of Brahmas, Vishnus, and Sivas,

Thousands of Pirs and Prophets, and tens of thousands of Saints and Holy men :

But the Chief of Lords is the One Lord, the true Name of God.

O Nanak! of God, His qualities, without end, beyond reckoning, who can understand ?

> NANAK, *Ratan Mala* (extra to the *Granth*).

Many Brahmas wearied themselves with the study
    of the Vedas, but found not the value of an oil seed.
Holy men and Saints sought about anxiously, but they
    were deceived by Maya.
There have been, and there have passed away, ten
    regent Avatars and the wondrous Mahadev.
Even they, wearied with the application of ashes, could
    not find Thee.        ARJUN, *Adi Granth*, Suhi.

Surs and Sidhs and the Devtas of Siva; Shaikhs and
    Pirs and men of might,
Have come and have gone, and others are likewise
    passing by.        ARJUN, *Adi Granth*, Sri Rag.

Krishna indeed slew demons; he performed wonders, and he declared himself to be Brahm; yet he
should not be regarded as the Lord. He himself died;
how can he save those who put faith in him? How can
one sunk in the ocean sustain another above the waves?
God alone is all-powerful : he can create, and he can
destroy.        GOBIND, *Hazara Shabd.*

God, without friends, without enemies,
Who heeds not praise, nor is moved by curses,
How could He become manifest as Krishna ?
How could He, without parents, without offspring, be-
    come born to a 'Devki' ?
              GOBIND, *Hazara Shabd.*

Ram and Rahim[1] (names repeated) cannot give
    salvation.
Brahma, Vishnu and Siva, the Sun and the Moon, all
    are in the power of Death.
              GOBIND. *Hazara Shabd.*

### 3.  *The Sikh Gurus not to be worshipped*

He who speaks of me as the Lord,
Him will I sink into the pit of Hell !
Consider me as the slave of God :
Of that have no doubt in thy mind.
I am but the slave of the Lord,
Come to behold the wonders of Creation.
             GOBIND, *Vichitr Natak.*

### 4.  *Images, and the Worship of Saints*

Worship not another (than God) ; bow not to the Dead.
           NANAK, *Adi Granth*, Sorth Ragni.

[1] The Merciful, i.e. the God of the Muhammadans.

To worship an image, to make pilgrimages to a shrine, to remain in a desert and yet to have the mind impure, is all in vain, and thus thou canst not be accepted. To be saved thou must worship Truth (God).
—NANAK, *Adi Granth*, Bhog; in which, however, he professes to quote a learned Brahman.

Man, who is a beast of the field, cannot comprehend Him whose power is of the Past, the Present, and the Future.

God is worshipped, that by worship salvation may be attained.
Fall at the feet of God; in senseless stone Got is not.
                                        GOBIND, *Vichitr Natak.*

### 5. *Miracles*

To possess the power of a Sidhi (or changer of shapes),
To be as a Ridhi (or giver away of never-ending stores),
And yet to be ignorant of God, I do not desire.
All such things are vain.
                              NANAK, *Adi Granth*, Sri Rag.

Dwell thou in flames uninjured,
Remain unharmed amid ice eternal,
Make blocks of stone thy daily food,
Spurn the Earth before thee with thy foot,
Weigh the Heavens in a balance;
And then ask of me to perform miracles.
                    NANAK, *to a challenger about miracles;*
                              *Adi Granth*, Majh Var.

### 6. *Transmigration*

Life is like the wheel circling on its pivot,
O Nanak ! of going and coming there is no end.
          NANAK, *Adi Granth*, Asa. (Numerous other
              passages of a like kind might be quoted
              from Nanak and his successors.)

He who knows not the One God
Will be born again times innumerable.
                              GOBIND, *Mihdi Mir.*

### 7. *Faith*

Eat and clothe thyself, and thou may'st be happy;
But without fear and faith there is no salvation.
                    NANAK. *Adi Granth*. Sohila Maru Rag.

## 8. *Grace*

O Nanak ! he, on whom God looks, finds the Lord.

NANAK, *Adi Granth*, Asa Rag.

O Nanak ! he on whom God looks, will fix his mind
on the Lord.

AMAR DAS, *Adi Granth*, Bilawal.

## 9. *Predestination*

According to the fate of each, dependent on his
actions, are his coming and going determined.

NANAK, *Adi Granth*, Asa.

How can Truth be told ? how can falsehood be
unravelled ?
O Nanak ! by following the will of God, as by Him
ordained.

NANAK, *Adi Granth*, Japji.

## 10. *The Vedas, the Purans, and the Koran.*

Pothis, Simrats Vedas, Purans,
Are all as nothing, if unleavened by God.

NANAK, *Adi Granth*, Gauri Rag.

Give ear to Shastars and Vedas, and Korans,
And thou may'st reach 'Swarg and Nark'.
     (i.e. to the necessity of coming back again.)
Without God, salvation is unattainable.

NANAK, *Ratan Mala* (an Extra book<br>of the *Adi Granth*).

Since he fell at the feet of God, no one has appeared
great in his eyes.
Ram and Rahim, the Purans, and the Koran, have
many votaries, but neither does he regard.
Simrats, Shastars, and Vedas, differ in many things;
not one does he heed.
O God ! under Thy favour has all been done; naught
is of myself.

GOBIND, *Rah Ras*.

## 11. *Asceticism*

A householder [1] who does no evil,
Who is ever intent upon good,

---

[1] I.e. in English idiom, one of the laity; one who fulfils the
ordinary duties of life.

Who continually exerciseth charity,
Such a householder is pure as the Ganges.

NANAK, *Adi Granth*, Ram Kali Ragni.

Householders and Hermits are equal, whoever calls on
the name of the Lord.

NANAK, *Adi Granth*, Asa Ragni.

Be 'Udas' (i.e. disinterested) in thy mind in the midst
of householdership.

AMAR DAS, *Adi Granth*, Sri Rag.

## 12. *Caste*

Think not of race, abase thyself, and attain to salvation.

NANAK, *Adi Granth*, Sarang Rag.

God will not ask man of his birth,
He will ask him what has he done.

NANAK, *Adi Granth*, Parbhati Ragni

Of the impure among the noblest
Heed not the injunction;
Of one pure among the most despised
Nanak will become the footstool.

NANAK, *Adi Granth*, Malhar Rag.

All say that there are four races,
But all are of the seed of Brahm.
The world is but clay,
And of similar clay many pots are made.
Nanak says man will be judged by his actions,
And that without finding God there will be
no salvation.
The body of man is composed of the five elements;
Who can say that one is high and another low?

AMAR DAS, *Adi Granth*, Bhairav.

I will make the four races of one colour,
I will cause them to remember the words, 'Wah Guru.

GOBIND, in the *Rahat Nama*, which, however, is not included in the *Granth*.

## 13. *Food*

O Nanak! the right of strangers is the one the Ox,
and the other the Swine.
Gurus and Pirs will bear witness to their disciples
when they eat naught which had enjoyed life.

NANAK, *Adi Granth*, Maj.

An animal slain without cause cannot be proper food.
O Nanak ! from evil doth evil ever come.

NANAK, Adi Granth, Maj.

### 14. *Brahmans, Saints, &c.*

That Brahman is a son of Brahm,
Whose rules of action are devotion, prayer, and purity.
Whose principles of faith are humility, and contentment.
Such a Brahman may break prescribed rules, and yet
find salvation.     NANAK, *Adi Granth*, Bhog.

The cotton [1] should be mercy, the thread contentedness,
and the seven knots virtue.
If there is such a 'Janeu' of the heart, wear it;
It will neither break, nor burn, nor decay, nor become
impure.
O Nanak ! he who wears such a thread is to be numbered with the holy.

NANAK, Adi Granth, Asa.

Devotion is not in the Kinta (or ragged garment),
nor in the Danda (or staff), nor in Bhasm (or ashes),
nor in the shaven head (Mundi), nor in the sounding
of horns (Singheh weieh).

NANAK, Adi Granth, Suhi.

In this age few Brahmans are of Brahm (i.e. are pure
and holy).     AMAR DAS, *Adi Granth*, Bilawal.

The Sanyasi should consider his home the jungle.
His heart should not yearn after material forms :
Gyan (or Truth) should be his Guru.
His Bhabut (or ashes) should be the name of God,
And he should neither be held to be 'Sat-juni', nor
'Raj-juni', nor 'Tamh-juni' (that is, should neither
seem good for his own profit only, nor good or bad
as seemed expedient at the time, nor bad that he
might thereby gain his ends).

GOBIND, Hazara Shabd.

### 15. *Infanticide*

——With the slayers of daughters
Whoever has intercourse, him do I curse.
And again—

Whosoever takes food from the slayers of daughters,
Shall die unabsolved.

GOBIND, Rahat Nama. (Extra to the Granth).

---

[1] Viz. the cotton of the Brahmanical thread, or janeu.

## 16. *Sati*

They are not Satis who perish in the flames.
O Nanak ! Satis are those who die of a broken heart.
And again—

The loving wife perishes with the body of her husband.
But were her thoughts bent upon God, her sorrows
would be alleviated.

AMAR DAS. *Adi Granth,* Suhi.

ADDENDUM

*Bhai Gurdas Bhalla's mode of representing the
Mission of Nanak*

There were four races and four creeds [1] in the world
among Hindus and Muhammadans;
Selfishness, jealousy, and pride drew all of them
strongly
The Hindus dwelt on Benares and the Ganges, the
Muhammadans on the Kaba;
The Muhammadans held by circumcision, the Hindus
by strings and frontal marks.
They each called on Ram and Rahim, one name, and
yet both forgot the road.
Forgetting the Vedas and the Koran, they were inveig-
led in the snares of the world.
Truth remained on one side, while Mullas and Brah-
mans disputed,
And Salvation was not attained.

. . . .
. . . .

God heard the complaint (of virtue or truth), and
Nanak was sent into the world.
He established the custom that the disciple should wash
the feet of his Guru, and drink the water;
Par Brahm and Puran Brahm, in this Kalyug, he
showed were one,
The four Feet (of the animal sustaining the world)
were made of Faith; the four castes were made one;

[1] The four *races* of Saiyids, Shaikhs, Mughals, and Pathans
are here termed as of four creeds, and likened to the four
castes or races of the Hindus. It is, indeed, a common saying
that such a thing is 'haram-i-char Mazhab', or forbidden
among the four faiths or sects of Muhammadans. Originally
the expression had reference to the four orthodox schools of
Sunnis, formed by the expounders Abu Hanifa, Hanbal, Shafei,
and Malik, and it still has such an application among the
learned, but the commonalty of India understand it to apply
to the four castes or races into which they have divided themselves.

The high and the low became equal; the salutation of
the feet (among disciples) he established in the
world : [1]

Contrary to the nature of man, the feet were exalted
above the head.
In the Kalyug he gave salvation : using the only true
Name, he taught men to worship the Lord.
To give salvation in the Kalyug Guru Nanak came.

NOTE.—The above extracts, and several others from
the book of Bhai Gurdas, may be seen in Malcolm's
*Sketch of the Sikhs*, p. 152, &c.; rendered, however, in
a less literal manner than has here been attempted.

The book contains forty chapters, written in different kinds of verse, and it is the repository of many
stories about Nanak which the Sikhs delight to repeat.
One of these is as follows :

Nanak again went to Mecca; blue clothing he wore,
like Krishna;
A staff in his hand, a book by his side; the pot, the
cup, and the mat, he also took :
He sat where the Pilgrims completed the final act of
their pilgrimage,
And when he slept at night he lay with his feet towards
the front.
Jiwan struck him with his foot, saying, 'Ho ! what
infidel sleeps here,
With his feet towards the Lord, like an evil doer?'
—Seizing him by the leg, he drew him aside; then
Mecca also turned, and a miracle was declared.
All were astonished, &c., &c.

*Guru Gobind's mode of representing his Mission.*
(From the *Vichitr Natak*, with an extract from the
Twenty-four Incarnations, regarding the last Ava-
tar and the succeeding Mihdi Mir.)

NOTE.—The first four chapters are occupied with a
mythological account of the Sodhi and Bedi subdivisions of the Kshattriya race, the rulers of the Punjab
at Lahore and Kasur, and the descendants of Lau and
Kusu, the sons of Ram, who traced his descent through
Dasrath, Raghu, Suraj, and others, to Kalsain, a primaeval monarch. So far as regards the present object,
the contents may be summed up in the promise or pro-

The Akalis still follow this custom.

phecy, that in the Kalyug Nanak would bestow blessings on the Sodhis, and would, on his fourth mortal
appearance, become one of that tribe.[1]

*Chapter V* (abstract).—The Brahmans began to
follow the ways of Sudras, and Kshattriya of Vaisas,
and, similarly, the Sudras did as Brahmans, and the
Vaisas as Kshattriyas. In the fullness of time Nanak
came and established his own sect in the world. He
died, but he was born again as Angad, and a third time
as Amar Das, and at last he appeared as Ram Das, as
had been declared, and the Guruship became inherent
in the Sodhis. Nanak thus put on other habiliments,
as one lamp is lighted at another. Apparently there
were four Gurus, but, in truth, in each body there was
the soul of Guru Nanak. When Ram Das departed,
his son Arjun became Guru, who was followed successively by Har Gobind, Har Rai, Har Kishan, and Tegh
Bahadur, who gave his life for his faith in Delhi, having been put to death by the Muhammadans.

*Chapter VI* (abstract).—In the Bhim Khund, near
the Seven Sring (or Peaks), where the Pandus exercised sovereignty (the unembodied soul of) Guru
Gobind Singh implored the Almighty, and became
absorbed in the Divine essence (or obtained salvation
without the necessity of again appearing on earth).
Likewise the parents of the Guru prayed to the Lord
continually. God looked on them with favour, and
(the soul of) Gobind was called from the Seven Peaks
to become one of mankind.

Then my wish was not to reappear,
For my thoughts were bent upon the feet of the
    Almighty;
But God made known to me his desires.

The Lord said, 'When mankind was created, the
Daitayas were sent for the punishment of the wicked,
but the Daitayas being strong, forgot me their God
Then the Devtas were sent, but they caused themselves
to be worshipped by men as Siva and Brahma, and
Vishnu. The Sidhs were afterwards born, but they,
following different ways, established many sects.
Afterwards Gorakhnath appeared in the world, and he,
making many kings his disciples, established the sect
of Joghis. Ramanand then came into the world, and
he established the sect of Bairagis after his own

[1] Of. the translations given in Malcolm's *Sketch*, p. 174, &c.

fashion. Muhadin (Muhammad) too was born, and became lord of Arabia. He established a sect, and required his followers to repeat his name. Thus, they who were sent to guide mankind, perversely adopted modes of their own, and misled the world. None taught the right way to the ignorant; wherefore thou, O Gobind! hast been called, that thou mayst propagate the worship of the One True God, and guide those who have lost the road.' Hence I, Gobind, have come into the world, and have established a sect, and have laid down its customs; but whosoever regards me as the Lord shall be dashed into the pit of hell, for I am but as other men, a beholder of the wonders of creation.

[Gobind goes on to declare that he regarded the religions of the Hindus and Muhammadans as naught; that Jogis, and the readers of Korans and Purans, were but deceivers; that no faith was to be put in the worship of images and stones. All religions, he says, had become corrupt; the Sannyasi and Bairagi equally showed the wrong way, and the modes of worship of Brahmans and Kshattriyas and others were idle and vain. 'All shall pass into hell, for God is not in books and scriptures, but in humility and truthfulness.'

The subsequent chapters, to the 13th inclusive, relate the wars in which Gobind was engaged with the Rajas of the hills and the imperial forces.]

*Chapter XIV* (abstract).—O God! thou who hast always preserved thy worshippers from evil, and hast inflicted punishment on the wicked; who hast regarded me as thy devoted slave and hast served me with thine own hand, now all that I have beheld, and all thy glories which I have witnessed, will I faithfully relate. What I beheld in the former world, by the blessing of God will I make known. In all my undertakings the goodness of the Lord hath been showered upon me. Loh (iron) has been my preserver. Through the goodness of God have I been strong, and all that I have seen during the various ages will I put in a book; everything shall be fully made known.

### Extract from the Twenty-four Avatars

*Kalki* (conclusion of).—Kalki at last became strong and proud, and the Lord was displeased, and created another Being. Mihdi Mir was created, great and powerful, who destroyed Kalki, and became mas-

ter of the world. All is in the hands of God. In this
manner passed away the twenty-four manifestations.

*Mihdi Mir.*—In such manner was Kalki destroyed,
but God manifests himself at all times, and at the end
of the Kalyug, all will be his own.[1] When Mihdi Mir
had vanquished the world he became raised up in his
mind. He assumed to himself the crown of greatness
and power, and all bowed to him. He regarded himself as supreme. He taught not of God, but considered
himself to be in all things and to exist everywhere.
Then the Almighty seized the fool. God is One. He
is without a second. He is everywhere, in the water
and under the earth. He who knows not the One God,
will be born again times innumerable. In the end God
took away the power of Mihdi Mir, and destroyed him
utterly.

> A creeping worm did the Lord create;
> By the ear of Mihdi it went and stayed :
> The worm entered by his ear,
> And he was wholly subdued.


# APPENDIX XX

## THE ADMONITORY LETTERS OF NANAK TO THE FABULOUS MONARCH KARUN; AND THE PRESCRIPTIVE LETTERS O. GOBIND FOR THE GUIDANCE OF THE SIKHS.

NOTE.—Two letters to Karun are attributed to
Nanak. The first is styled the 'Nasihat Nama', or Letter
of Admonition and Advice. The second is styled simply the 'Reply of Nanak', and professes to be spoken.
Karun may possibly be a corruption of Harun, the
'Harun el Rashid' of European and Asiatic fame. Both
compositions are of course fabulous as regards Nanak,
and appear to be the compositions of the commencement or middle of the last century.

The two letters of Gobind are termed the 'Rahat
Nama' and the 'Tankha Nama', or the Letter of Rules
and the Letter of Fines respectively; and while they
are adapted for general guidance, they profess to have
been drawn up in reply to questions put by individuals,
or for the satisfaction of particular inquirers. There
is no evidence that they were composed by Gobind
himself; but they may be held to represent his views
and the principles of Sikhism.

[1] Nij jot, jot suman.

1. *The Nasihat Nama of Nanak, or the Letter to Karun, the Mighty Prince, possessing forty Capital Cities replenished with Treasure.* (Extracts from.)

Alone man comes, alone he goes.
When he departs naught will avail him (or bear him witness).
When the reckoning is taken, what answer will he give ?
If then only he repents, he shall be punished.

.          .          .

.          .          .

Karun paid no devotions; he kept not faith :
The world exclaimed he ruled not justly.
He was called a Ruler, but he governed not well,
For the pleasures of the world ensnared him.
He plundered the earth : hell-fire shall torment him.

.          .          .

.          .          .

Man should do good, so that he be not ashamed.
Repent—and oppress not,
Otherwise hell-fire shall seize thee, even in the grave.

.          .          .

Holy men, Prophets, Shahs, and Khans,
The mark of not one remaineth in the world;
For man is but as the passing shade of the flying bird.

.          .          .

Thou rejoicest in thy Forty Treasures,
See, oh people ! Karun utterly confounded.
O Nanak ! pray unto God, and seek God as thy refuge.

2. *The Reply of Nanak to Karun, the Lord of Medina.*

First, Nanak went to Mecca;
Medina he afterwards visited.
The lord of Mecca and Medina,
Karun, he made his disciple.
When Nanak was about to depart,
Karun, the fortunate, thus spoke :
Now thou art about to go,
But when wilt thou return?
Then the Guru thus answered :
When I put on my tenth dress
I shall be called Gobind Singh;
Then shall all Singhs wear their hair;
They shall accept the 'Pahal' of the two-edged dagger
Then shall the sect of the Khalsa be established;

Then shall men exclaim, 'Victory, O Guru !'
The four races shall become one and the same;
The five weapons shall be worn by all.
In the Kalyug they shall array themselves in vestments
of blue;
The name of the Khalsa shall be everywhere.
In the time of Aurangzeb
The wondrous Khalsa shall arise.
Then shall battles be waged,
Endless war shall ensue,
And fighting shall follow year after year.
They shall place the name of Gobind Singh in their
hearts,
Many heads shall be rendered up,
And the empire of the Khalsa shall prevail.
First, the Punjab shall become the land of the Sikhs;
Then other countries shall be theirs;
Hindustan and the North shall be possessed by them;
Then the West shall bow to them.
When they enter Khorasan,
Kabul and Kandahar shall lie low.
When Iran [1] has been laid prostrate,
Mecca shall be beheld,
And Medina shall be seized.
Mighty shall be the rejoicing,
And all shall exclaim, 'Hail, Guru !'
Unbelievers shall everywhere be destroyed;
The holy Khalsa shall be exalted;
Beasts, and birds, and creeping things, shall tremble
(in the presence of the Lord)
Men and women shall everywhere call on God.
The earth, the ocean, and the heavens, shall call on God.
By calling on the Guru shall men be blessed.
Every faith shall become of the Khalsa;
No other religion will remain.
'Wah Guru' shall everywhere be repeated.
And Pain and Trouble shall depart.
In the Kalyug shall the Kingdom be established
Which Nanak received from the Lord.
Worthless, I fall before God;
Nanak, the slave, cannot comprehend the ways of the
Lord.

[1] Persia.

3. *The Rahat Nama of Guru Gobind.* (Extracts from. and abstracts of portions.)

Written for Dariyai Udasi, and repeated to Prahlad Singh at Apchalnagar (Nader on the Godavery).

The Guru, being seated at Apchalnagar, spake to Prahlad Singh, saying, that through the favour of Nanak there was a sect or faith in the world for which rules (rahat) should be established.

A Sikh who puts a cap (topi)[1] on his head, shall die seven deaths of dropsy.
Whosoever wears a thread round his neck is on the way to damnation.

[It is forbidden to take off the turban (pag) while eating, to have intercourse with Minas, Massandis, and Kurimars (children slayers), and to play at chess with women.
No prayers are to be offered up without using the name of the Guru, and he who heeds not the Guru, and serves not the disciples faithfully, is a Mlechh indeed.
A Sikh who does not acknowledge the Hukamnama (requisition for benevolences or contributions) of the Guru shall fall under displeasure.]

First the Guru (*Granth* or Book) and Khalsa, which I have placed in the world,
Whosoever denies or betrays either shall be driven forth and dashed into hell.

[It is forbidden to wear clothing dyed with safflower (i.e. of a 'Suhi' colour), to wear charms on the head, to break the fast without reciting the Jap (the prayer of Nanak), to neglect reading prayers in the morning, to take the evening meal without reciting the Rah Ras, to leave Akal Purukh (the Timeless Being) and worship other Gods, to worship stones, to make obeisance to any not a Sikh, to forget the *Granth,* and to deceive the Khalsa.
All Hukamnamas (calls for tithes or contributions) given by the posterity of Nanak, of Angad, and of Amar Das, shall be heeded as his own : whosoever disregards them shall perish.

[1] Referring partciularly to Hindu ascetics; but perhaps, also to the Muhammadans, who formerly wore skull-caps alone, and now generally wind their turbans round a covering of the kind. The Sikh contempt for either kind of 'topi' has been thrown into the shade by their repugnance, in common with all other Indians, to the English cap or hat.

The things which he had placed in the world (viz.,
the *Granth* and the Khalsa) are to be worshipped.
Strange Gods are not to be heeded, and the Sikh who
forsakes his faith shall be punished in the world to
come.

He who worships graves and dead men ('gor' and
'murri', referring to Muhammadans and Hindus), or
he who worships temples (mosques) or stones (images), is not a Sikh. .

The Sikh who makes obeisance or bows down to
the wearer of a cap (topi) is a resident of hell.]

Consider the Khalsa as the Guru, as the very embodi-
ment of the Guru :
He who wishes to see the Guru will find him in the
Khalsa.

[Trust not Jogi or Turks.' Remember the writings
of the Guru only. Regard not the six Darsans (or systems of faith or speculation). Without the Guru, all
Deities are as naught. The Image of the Almighty is
the visible body (pragat deh) of the immortal Khalsa
(Akal). The Khalsa is everything, other divinities are
as sand, which slips through the fingers. By the order
of God the Panth (or sect) of Sikhs has been established. All Sikhs must believe the Guru and the *Granth*.
They should bow to the *Granth* alone. All prayers save
the prayers of the Guru are idle and vain.

He who gives the 'Pahal' to another shall reap
innumerable blessings. He who instructs in the prayers
and scriptures of the Gurus shall attain salvation.
Gobind will reverence the Sikh who chafes the hands
and the feet of the wearied Sikh traveller. The Sikh
who gives food to other Sikhs, on him will the Guru
look with favour.

Delivered on Thursday the 5th day of the dark
phase of the Moon of Magh in the Sambat year 1752
(beginning of A.D. 1696). He who heeds these injunctions is a Sikh of Guru Gobind Singh. The orders of
the Guru are as himself. Depend on God.]

#### 4. *The Tankha Nama, or Letter of Fines or Restrictions on Sikhs.* (Abstract of.)

Written in reply to the question of Bhai Nand Lal, who had
asked Guru Gobind what it was proper for a Sikh to do,
and what to refrain from.

Nand Lal asked, &c.: and the Guru replied that
such were to be the acts of the Sikhs. A Sikh should

set his heart on God, on charity, and on purity (Nam, Dan, Ishnan). He who in the morning does not repair to some temple, or visit some holy man, is greatly to blame. He who does not allow the poor a place (in his heart) is to blame. Without the favour of God nothing can be accomplished. He who bows his head (i.e. humbles himself) after having offered up prayers is a man of holiness. Charity (Karah Prasad, i.e. food) should be distributed in singleness of mind to all comers equally. Prasad should be prepared of equal parts of flour, sugar, and butter. The preparer should first bathe, and while cooking it he should repeat 'Wah Guru' continually. When ready, the food should be put on a round place.

The Sikh who wears the (written) charms of the Turks, or who touches iron with his feet, is to be condemned. He who wears clothing dyed with safflower (of the colour called Suhi), and he who takes snuff (naswar), is to be condemned.[1]

He who looks lustfully upon the mother or sister of one of the brethren—he who does not bestow his daughter becomingly in marriage—he who takes to himself the property of a sister or daughter—he who wears not iron in some shape—he who robs or oppresses the poor, and he who makes obeisance to a Turk, is to be punished.

A Sikh should comb his locks, and fold and unfold his turban twice a day. Twice also should he wash his mouth.

One tenth of all goods should be given (in charity) in the name of the Guru.

Sikhs should bathe in cold water : they should not break their fast until they have repeated the Jap. In the morning Jap, in the evening, Rah Ras, and before retiring to rest, Sohila should always be repeated.

No Sikh should speak false of his neighbour. Promises should be carefully fulfilled.

No Sikh should eat flesh from the hands of the Turks.

A Sikh should not delight in women, nor give himself up to them.

The Sikh who calls himself a Sadh (or Holy man) should act in strict accordance with his professions.

A journey should not be undertaken, nor should

[1] This is the only recorded prohibition against tobacco, to refrain from which in every shape is now a rule. The Afghans of Peshawar and Kabul continue to take snuff, a practice but little known to the Indians.

business be set about, nor should food be eaten, without first remembering or calling on God.

A Sikh should enjoy the society of his own wife only. He should not desire other women.

He who sees a poor man and gives him not something, shall not behold the presence of God.

He who neglects to pray, or who abuses the holy, or who gambles, or who listens to those who speak evil of the Gurus, is no Sikh.

Daily, some portion of what is gained is to be set aside in the name of the Lord, but all business must be carried on in sincerity and truth.

Flame should not be extinguished with the breath, nor should fire be put out with water, a portion of which has been drunk.

Before meals the name of the Guru should be repeated. The society of prostitutes is to be avoided, nor is adultery to be committed with the wife of another. The Guru is not to be forsaken, and others followed. No Sikh should expose his person; he should not bathe in a state of nudity, nor when distributing food should he be naked.[1] His head should always be covered.

> He is of the Khalsa,
> Who speaks evil to none,
> Who combats in the van,
> Who gives in charity,
> Who slays a Khan,
> Who subdues his passions,
> Who burns the 'Karms',[2]
> Who does not yield to superstitions,[3]
> Who is awake day and night,
> Who delights in the sayings of the Gurus,
> And who never fears, although often overcome.
> Considering all as created by the Lord,
> Give offence to none, otherwise the Lord will Himself be offended.

> He is of the Khalsa,
> Who protects the poor,
> Who combats evil,
> Who remembers God,

---

[1] The practices of many Hindu ascetics are mainly aimed at.

[2] i.e. who despises the ceremonial forms of the Brahmans.

[3] Hindi Aan, said to correspond with the meaning of the Arabic Aar—one who does not affect to be in any way protected by saints or others. The same term is applied to the brotherhood or mutual dependence of a chief and his followers.

Who achieves greatness,[1]
Who is intent upon the Lord,
Who is wholly unfettered,
Who mounts the war horse,
Who is ever waging battle,
Who is continually armed,
Who slays the Turks,
Who extends the faith,
And who gives his head with what is upon it.
The name of God shall be proclaimed;
No one shall speak against Him;
The rivers and the mountains shall remember Him;
All who call upon Him shall be saved.

O Nand Lal ! attend to what is said;
My own rule will I establish,
The four races shall be one,
I will cause all to repeat the prayer of 'Wah Guru'.
The Sikhs of Gobind shall bestride horses, and bear
    hawks upon their hands,
The Turks who behold them shall fly,
One shall combat a multitude,
And the Sikh who thus perishes shall be blessed for
    ever.
At the doorway of a Sikh shall wait elephants
    caparisoned,
And horsemen with spears, and there shall be music
    over his gateway.
When myriads of matches burn together,
Then shall the Khalsa conquer East and West.
The Khalsa shall rule; none can resist :
The rebellious shall be destroyed, and the obedient
    shall have favours heaped upon them.


# APPENDIX XXI

## A LIST OF SOME SIKH SECTS OR DENOMINATIONS

(In which, however, some Names or Titles not properly
distinctive of an Order are also inserted)

1st. *Udasi.*—Founded by Sri Chand, a son of
Nanak. The Udasis were rejected by Amar Das, as not
being genuine Sikhs.

2nd. *Bedi.*—Founded by Lakshmi Das, another
son of Nanak.

Literally, who resides in state.

3rd.  *Tehun.*—Founded by Guru Angad.
4th.  *Bhalla.*—Founded by Guru Amar Das.
5th.  *Sodhi.*—Founded by Guru Ram Das.

NOTE.—The Bedis, Tihans, Bhallas, and Sodhis are rather Sikhs of the subdivisions of Kshattriyas, so called (i.e. of the tribes of certain Gurus), than distinct sects.

6th.  *Ramraiya,* seceders who adhered to Ram Rai when Tegh Bahadur became Guru. They have a considerable establishment in the Lower Himalayas, near Hardwar.

7th.  *Banda-Panthi,* i.e. of the sect of Banda, who succeeded Gobind as a temporal leader.

8th.  *Masandi.*—Masand is simply the name of a sub-division of the Kshattriya race; but it is also specially applied to the followers of those who resisted Gobind; some say as adherents of Ram Rai, and others as instigators of the Guru's son to opposition.  The more common story, however, is that the Masands were the hereditary stewards of the household of the several Gurus, and that they became proud and dissipated, but nevertheless arrogated sanctity to themselves, and personally ill-used many Sikhs for not deferring to them; whereupon Gobind, regarding them as irreclaimable, expelled them all except two or three.

9th.  *Rangrheta.*—Converts of the Sweeper and some other inferior castes are so called. (See note 2, p. 64, *ante.*)

10th.  *Ramdasi,* i.e. Rao or Rai Dasi.—Sikhs of the class of Chamars, or leather-dressers, and who trace to the Rao Das, or Rai Das, whose writings are inserted in the *Granth.*

11th.  *Mazhabi.*—Converts from Muhammadanism are so called.

12th.  *Akali.*—Worshippers of Akal (God), the most eminent of the orders of Purists or Ascetics.

13th.  *Nihang.*—The naked, or pure.

14th.  *Nirmale.*—The sinless. One who has acquired this title usually administers the Pahal to others.

15th.  *Gyani.*—The wise, or perfect. A term sometimes applied to Sikhs who are at once learned and pious,

16th.  *Suthra Shahi.*—The true, or pure : said to have been founded by one Sucha, a Brahman.  (See *ante,* note 5, p. 55.)

17th.  *Suchidari.*—Likewise the true, or pure : the founder not ascertained.

18th. *Bhai.*—Literally, brother. The ordinary title of all Sikhs who have acquired a name for holiness; and it is scarcely the distinctive title of a sect, or even of an order.

To these may perhaps be added bodies of men who attach themselves to particular temples, or who claim to have been founded by particular disciples of eminence, or by followers who obtained any distinctive title from a Guru. Thus some claim to represent *Ram Das,* the companion of Nanak, who lived till the time of Arjun, and who obtained the title of 'Budha', or Ancient. Also many hereditary musicians call themselves *Rababi Sikhs,* from the Rabab, or particular instrument on which they play; and these affect to regard Mardana, the companion of Nanak, as their founder. Others are called *Diwane,* or the Simple or Mad, from one assiduous as a collector of the contributions of the faithful for the service of the Gurus, and who, while so employed, placed a peacock's feather in his turban. Another class is called *Musaddi* (or, perhaps, Mutasaddi, i.e. the clerk or writer order), and it is stated to be composed of devotees of the Muhammadan religion, who have adopted the 'Jap' of Nanak as their rule of faith. The Musaddis are further said to have fixed abodes in the countries westward of the Indus.

# APPENDIX XXIII

## THE TREATY WITH LAHORE OF 1806

*Treaty of Friendship and Unity between the Honourable East India Company and the Sardars Ranjit Singh and Fateh Singh.* (1st January 1806.)

SARDAR Ranjit Singh and Sardar Fateh Singh have consented to the following articles of agreement, concluded by Lieutenant-Colonel John Malcolm, under the special authority of the Right Honourable Lord Lake, himself duly authorized by the Honourable Sir George Hilaro Barlow, Bart., Governor-General, and Sardar Fateh Singh, as principal on the part of himself, and plenipotentiary on the part of Ranjit Singh :

Article 1.—Sardar Ranjit Singh and Sardar Fateh Singh Ahluwalia, hereby agree that they will cause Jaswant Rao Holkar to remove with his army to the distance of thirty coss from Amritsar immediately, and will never hereafter hold any further connexion with him, or aid or assist him with troops, or in any other manner whatever; and they further agree that they will not in any way molest such of Jaswant Rao Holkar's followers or troops as are desirous of returning to their homes in the Deccan, but, on the contrary, will render them every assistance in their power for carrying such intention into execution.

Article 2.—The British Government hereby agrees, that in case a pacification should not be effected between that Government and Jaswant Rao Holkar, the British army shall move from its present encampment, on the banks of the river Biah, as soon as Jaswant Rao Holkar aforesaid shall have marched his army to the distance of thirty coss from Amritsar; and that, in any treaty which may hereafter be concluded between the British Government and Jaswant Rao Holkar, it shall be stipulated that, immediately after the conclusion of the said treaty, Holkar shall evacuate the territories of the Sikhs, and march towards his own, and that he shall in no way whatever injure or destroy such parts of the Sikh country as may lie in his route. The British Government further agrees that, as long as the said Chieftains, Ranjit Singh and Fateh Singh, abstain from holding any friendly connexion with the enemies of that Government, or from committing any act of hostility on their own parts against the said Government, the British armies shall never enter the territories of the said Chieftains, nor will the British Government form any plans for the seizure or sequestration of their possessions or property.

Dated 1st January 1806.

# APPENDIX XXIV

## SIR DAVID OCHTERLONY'S PROCLAMATION
## OF 1809

*Precept or 'Ittila Nama', under the Seal of General St. Leger, and under the Seal and Signature of Colonel Ochterlony; written the 9th of February 1809, corresponding to the 23rd Zi Hijeh, 1223, Hijri.*

THE British army having encamped near the frontiers of the Maharaja Ranjit Singh, it has been thought proper to signify the pleasure of the British Government, by means of this precept, in order to make all the Chiefs of the Maharaja acquainted with the sentiments of the British Government, which have solely for their object and aim to confirm the friendship with the Maharaja, and to prevent any injury to his country, the preservation of friendship between the two States depending on particular conditions which are hereby detailed.

The Thanas in the fortress of Kharar, Khanpur, and other places on this side of the river Sutlej, which have been placed in the hands of the dependants of the Maharaja, shall be razed, and the same places restored to their ancient possessors.

The force of cavalry and infantry which may have crossed to this side of the Sutlej must be recalled to the other side, to the country of the Maharaja.

The troops stationed at the Ghat of Phillaur must march thence, and depart to the other side of the river as described, and in future the troops of the Maharaja shall never advance into the country of the Chiefs situated on this side of the river, who have called in for their security and protection Thanas of the British Government; but if in the manner that the British have placed Thanas of moderate number on this side of the Sutlej, if in like manner a small force by way of Thana be stationed at the Ghat of Phillaur, it will not be objected to.

If the Maharaja persevere in the fulfilment of the above stipulations, which he so repeatedly professed to do in presence of Mr. Metcalfe, such fulfilment will confirm the mutual friendship. In case of non-compliance with these stipulations, then shall it be plain that the Maharaja has no regard for the friendship of the British, but, on the contrary, resolves on enmity. In such case the victorious British army shall commence every mode of defence.

The communication of this precept is solely with the view of publishing the sentiments of the British, and to know those of the Maharaja. The British are confident that the Maharaja will consider the contents of this precept as abounding to his real advantage, and as affording a conspicuous proof of their friendship: that with their capacity for war, they are also intent on peace.

NOTE.—The recorded translation of this document has been preserved, although somewhat defective in style.

# APPENDIX XXV

## THE TREATY WITH LAHORE OF 1809

*Treaty between the British Government and the Raja
of Lahore.* (Dated 25th April 1809.)

WHEREAS certain differences which had arisen between the British Government and the Raja of Lahore
have been happily and amicably adjusted; and both
parties being anxious to maintain relations of perfect
amity and concord, the following articles of treaty,
which shall be binding on the heirs and successors of
the two parties, have been concluded by the Raja
Ranjit Singh in person, and by the agency of C. T.
Metcalfe, Esquire, on the part of the British
Government.

Article 1.—Perpetual friendship shall subsist between the British Government and the State of Lahore :
the latter shall be considered, with respect to the former, to be on the footing of the most favoured powers,
and the British Government will have no concern with
the territories and subjects of the Raja to the northward of the river Sutlej.

Article 2.—The Raja will never maintain in the
territory which he occupies on the left bank of the
river Sutlej more troops than are necessary for the
internal duties of that territory, nor commit or suffer
any encroachments on the possessions or rights of the
Chiefs in its vicinity.

Article 3.—In the event of a violation of any of the
preceding articles, or of a departure from the rules of
friendship, this treaty shall be considered null and void.

Article 4.—This treaty, consisting of four articles,
having been settled and concluded at Amritsar, on the
25th day of April 1809, Mr. C. T. Metcalfe has delivered
to the Raja of Lahore a copy of the same in English
and Persian, under his seal and signature; and the
Raja has delivered another copy of the same under his
seal and signature, and Mr. C. T. Metcalfe engages to
procure within the space of two months a copy of the
same, duly ratified by the Right Honourable the Governor-General in Council, on the receipt of which by
the Raja, the present treaty shall be deemed complete
and binding on both parties, and the copy of it now
delivered to the Raja shall be returned.

# APPENDIX XXVI

## PROCLAMATION OF PROTECTION TO CIS-SUTLEJ STATES AGAINST LAHORE. (Dated 1809)

*Translation of an 'Ittila Nama', addressed to the Chiefs of the Country of Malwa and Sirhind, on this Side of the River Sutlej.   (3rd May 1809.)*

IT is clearer than the sun, and better proved that the existence of yesterday, that the marching of a detachment of British troops to this side of the river Sutlej was entirely at the application and earnest entreaty of the several Chiefs, and originated solely from friendly considerations in the British Government, to preserve them in their possessions and independence.   A treaty having been concluded, on the 25th of April 1809, between Mr. Metcalfe on the part of the British Government, and Maharaja Ranjit Singh, agreeably to the orders of the Right Honourable the Governor-General in Council, I have the pleasure of publishing, for the satisfaction of the Chiefs of the country of Malwa and Sirhind, the pleasure and resolutions of the British Government, as contained in the seven following articles :

Article 1.—The country of the Chiefs of Malwa and Sirhind having entered under the British protection, they shall in future be secured from the authority and influence of Maharaja Ranjit Singh, conformably to the terms of the treaty.

Article 2.—All the country of the Chiefs thus taken under protection shall be exempted from all pecuniary tribute to the British Government.

Article 3.—The Chiefs shall remain in the full exercise of the same rights and authority in their own possessions which they enjoyed before they were received under the British protection.

Article 4.—Should a British force, on purposes of general welfare, be required to march through the country of the said Chiefs, it is necessary and incumbent that every Chief shall, within his own possessions, assist and furnish, to the full of his power, such force with supplies of grain and other necessaries which may be demanded.

Article 5.—Should an enemy approach from any quarter, for the purpose of conquering this country, friendship and mutual interest require that the Chiefs join the British army with all their force, and, exerting themselves in expelling the enemy, act under discipline and proper obedience.

Article 6.—All European articles brought by merchants from the eastern districts, for the use of the army, shall be allowed to pass, by the Thanedars and Sardars of the several Chiefs, without molestation or the demand of duty.

Article 7.—All horses purchased for the use of cavalry regiments, whether in the district of Sirhind or elsewhere, the bringers of which being provided with sealed 'Rahdaris' from the Resident at Delhi, or officer commanding at Sirhind, shall be allowed to pass through the country of the said Chiefs without molestation or the demand of duty.

# APPENDIX XXVII

## PROCLAMATION OF PROTECTION TO CIS-SUTLEJ STATES AGAINST ONE ANOTHER. (Dated 1811)

*For the Information and Assurance of the Protected Chiefs of the Plains between the Sutlej and Jumna.* (22nd August, 1811.)

ON the 3rd of May 1809 an 'Ittila Nama' comprised of seven articles, was issued by the orders of the British Government, purporting that the country of the Sardars of Sirhind and Malwa having come under their protection, Raja Ranjit Singh, agreeably to treaty, had no concern with the possessions of the above Sardars; That the British Government had no intention of claiming Peshkashs or Nazarana, and that they should continue in the full control and enjoyment of their respective possessions : The publication of the above 'Ittila Nama' was intended to afford every confidence to the Sardars, that the protection of the country was the sole object, that they had no intention of control, and that those having possessions should remain in full and complete enjoyment thereof.

Whereas several Zamindars and other subjects of the Chiefs of this country have preferred complaints to the officers of the British Government, who, having in view the tenor of the above 'Ittila Nama', have not attended, and will not in future pay attention to them; for instance, on the 15th of June 1811, Dilawar Ali Khan of Samana complained to the Resident of Delhi against the officers of Raja Sahib Singh for jewels and other property said to have been seized by them, who, in reply, observed that the 'Kasba of Samana being in the Amaldari of Raja Sahib Singh, his complaint should be made to him'; and also, on the 12th of July 1811, Dasaundha Singh and Gurmukh Singh complained to Colonel Ochterlony, agent to the Governor-General, against Sardar Charat Singh, for their shares of property, &c.; and, in reply, it was written on the back of their arzi, 'that since, during the period of three years, no claim was preferred against Charat Singh by any of his brothers, nor even the name of any co-partner mentioned; and since it was advertised in the 'Ittila Nama' delivered to the Sardars, that every Chief should remain in the quiet and full enjoyment of his domains, the petition could not be attended to,'—the insertion of these answers to complaints is intended as examples, and also that it may be impressed on the minds of every Zamindar and other subject, that the attainment of justice is to be expected from their respective Chiefs only, that they may not, in the smallest degree, swerve from the observation of subordination, —It is, therefore, highly incumbent upon the Rajas and other Sardars of this side of the river Sutlej, that they explain this to their respective subjects, and court their confidence, that it may be clear to them, that complaints to the officers of the British Government will be of no avail, and that they consider their respective Sardars as the source of justice, and that, of their free will and accord, they observe uniform obedience.

And whereas, according to the first proclamation, it is not the intention of the British Government to interfere in the possessions of the Sardars of this country, it is nevertheless, for the purpose of meliorating the condition of the community, particularly necessary to give general information, that several Sardars have, since the last incursion of Raja Ranjit Singh, wrested the estates of others, and deprived them of their lawful possessions, and that in the restoration, they have used delays until detachments of the British army have been sent to effect restitution, as in the case of the Rani of Tirah, the Sikhs of Chulian, the Talukas of Karauli and Chehloundy, and the village of Chiba; and the reason of such delays and evasions can only be attributed to the temporary enjoyment of the revenues, and subjecting the owners to irremediable losses,—It is, therefore, by order of the British Government, hereby proclaimed that if any one of the Sardars or others has forcibly taken possession of the estates of others, or otherwise injured the lawful owners, it is necessary that, before the occurrence of any complaint, the proprietor should be satisfied, and by no means to defer the restoration of the property,—in which, however, should delays be made, and the interference of the British authority become requisite, the revenues of the estate from the date of ejection of the lawful proprietor, together with whatever other losses the inhabitants of that place may sustain from the march of troops, shall without scruple be demanded from the offending party; and for disobedience of the present orders, a penalty, according to the circumstances of the case and of the offender, shall be levied, agreeably to the decision of the British Government.

## APPENDIX XXVIII

### INDUS NAVIGATION TREATY OF 1832

*Articles of a Convention established between the Honourable the East India Company, and his Highness the Maharaja Ranjit Singh, the Ruler of the Punjab, for the opening of the Iavigation of the Rivers Indus and Sutlej.* (Orig .ally drafted 26th December 1832.)

BY the grace of God, the relations of firm alliance and indissoluble ties of friendship existing between the Honourable the East India Company and his Highness the Maharaja Ranjit Singh, founded on the auspicious treaty formerly concluded by Sir T. C. Metcalfe, Bart.. and since confirmed in the written pledge of sincere amity presented by the Right Honourable Lord W. G. Bentinck, G.C.B. and G.C.H., Governor-General of British India, at the meeting at Rupar, are, like the sun, clear and manifest to the whole world, and will continue unimpaired, and increasing in strength from generation to generation :—By virtue of these firmly established bonds of friendship, since the opening of the navigation of the rivers Indus proper (i.e. Indus below the confluence of the Panjnad) and Sutlej (a measure deemed expedient by both States, with a view to promote the general interests of commerce),—has lately been effected through the agency of Captain C. M. Wade, Political Agent at Ludhiana, deputed by the Right Honourable the Governor-General for that purpose. The following Articles, explanatory of the conditions by which the said navigation is to be regulated, as concerns the nomination of officers, the mode of collecting the duties, and the protection of the trade by that route, have been framed,' in order that the officers of the two States employed in their execution may act accordingly :

Article 1.—The provisions of the existing treaty relative to the right bank of the river Sutlej and all its stipulations, together with the contents of the friendly pledge already mentioned, shall remain binding, and a strict regard to preserve the relations of friendship between the two States shall be the ruling principle of action. In accordance with that treaty, the Honourable Company has not, nor will have any concern with the right bank of the river Sutlej.

Article 2.—The tariff which is to be established for the line of navigation in question is intended to apply exclusively to the passage of merchandise by that route, and not to interfere with the transit duties levied on goods proceeding from one bank of the river to the other, nor with the places fixed for their collection : they are to remain as heretofore.

Article 3.—Merchants frequenting the same route, while within the limits of the Maharaja's government, are required to show a due regard to his authority, as is done by merchants generally, and not to commit any acts offensive to the civil and religious institutions of the Sikhs.

Article 4.—Any one purposing to go the said route will intimate his intention to the agent of either State, and apply for a passport, agreeably to a form to be laid down; having obtained which, he may proceed on his journey. The merchants coming from Amritsar, and other parts on the right bank of the river Sutlej, are to intimate their intentions to the agent of the Maharaja, at Harike, or other appointed places, and obtain a passport through him; and merchants coming from Hindustan, or other parts on the left bank of the river Sutlej, will intimate their intentions to the Honourable Company's agent, and obtain a passport through him. As foreigners, and Hindustanis, and Sardars of the protected Sikh States and elsewhere, are not in the habit of crossing the Sutlej without a passport from the Maharaja's officers, it is expected that such persons will hereafter also conform to the same rule, and not cross without the usual passports.

Article 5.—A tariff shall be established exhibiting the rate of duties leviable on each description of merchandise, which, after having been approved by both Governments, is to be the standard by which the superintendents and collectors of customs are to be guided.

Article 6.—Merchants are invited to adopt the new route with perfect confidence : no one shall be suffered to molest them or unnecessarily impede their progress, care being taken that they are only detained for the collection of the duties, in the manner stipulated, at the established stations.

Article 7.—The officers who are to be entrusted with the collection of the duties and examination of the goods on the right bank of the river shall be stationed at Mithankot and Harike; at no other places but these two shall boats in transit on the river be liable to examination or stoppage. When the persons in charge of boats stop of their own accord to take in or give out cargo, the goods will be liable to the local transit duty of the Maharaja's government, previously to their being landed, as provided in Article 2. The superintendent stationed at Mithankot, having examined the cargo, will levy the established duty, and grant a passport, with a written account of the cargo and freight. On the arrival of the boat at Harike, the superintendent of that station will compare the passport with the cargo; and whatever goods are found in excess will be liable to the payment of the established duty, while the rest, having already paid duty at Mithankot, will pass on free. The same rule shall be observed in respect to merchandise conveyed from Harike by the way of the rivers towards Sind, that whatever may be fixed as the share of duties on the right bank of the river Sutlej, in right of the Maharaja's own dominions and of those in allegiance to him, the Maharaja's officers will collect it at the places appointed. With regard to the security and safety of merchants who may adopt this route, the Maharaja's officers shall afford them every protection in their power; and merchants, on halting for the night on either bank of the Sutlej, are required, with reference to the treaty of friendship which exists between the two States, to give notice, and to show their passport to the Thanedar, or officers in authority at the place, and request protection for themselves : if, notwithstanding this precaution, loss should at any time occur, a strict inquiry will be made, and reclamation sought from those who are blameable. The articles of the present treaty for opening the navigation of the rivers above mentioned, having, agreeably to subsisting relations, been approved by the Right

Honourable the Governor-General, shall be carried into execution accordingly.

Dated at Lahore the 26th of December 1832.

[Seal and signature at the top.]

## APPENDIX XXIX

## SUPPLEMENTARY INDUS NAVIGATION TREATY OF 1834

*Draft of a Supplementary Treaty between the British Government and Maharaja Ranjit Singh for establishing a Toll on the Indus. (29th November 1834.)*

IN conformity with the subsisting relations of friendship, as established and confirmed by former treaties, between the Honourable the East India Company and his Highness Maharaja Ranjit Singh; and whereas in the 5th article of the treaty concluded at Lahore on the 26th day of December 1832, it was stipulated that a moderate scale of duties should be fixed by the two Governments in concert, to be levied on all merchandise on transit up and down the rivers Indus and Sutlej; the said Governments, being now of opinion that, owing to the inexperience of the people of these countries in such matters, the mode of levying duties then proposed (viz. on the value and quantity of goods) could not fail to give rise to mutual misunderstandings and reclamations, have, with a view to prevent these results, determined to substitute a toll, which shall be levied on all boats, with whatever merchandise laden. The following articles have therefore been adopted as supplementary to the former treaty; and, in conformity with them, each Government engages that the toll shall be levied, and its amount neither be increased nor diminished except by mutual consent.

Article 1.—A toll of 570 Rs. shall be levied on all boats laden with merchandise in transit on the rivers Indus and Sutlej between the sea and Rupar, without reference to their size, or to the weight or value of their cargo; the above toll to be divided among the different States in proportion to the extent of territory which they possess on the banks of these rivers.

Article 2.—The portion of the above toll appertaining to the Lahore Chief in right of his territory on both banks of these rivers, as determined in the subjoined scale, shall be levied opposite to Mithankot on boats coming from the sea towards Rupar, and in the vicinity of Harike-Pattan on boats going from Rupar towards the sea, and at no other place :--

| In right of territory on the right bank of the rivers Indus and Sutlej, 155 Rs. 4 ans. | In right of territory on the left bank of the rivers Indus and Sutlej, the Maharaja's share, of 67 Rs. 15 ans. 9 pie. |
|---|---|

Article 3.—In order to facilitate the realization of the toll due to the different States, as well as for the speedy and satisfactory adjustment of any disputes which may arise connected with the safety of the navigation and the welfare of the trade by the new route, a British officer will reside opposite to Mithankot, and a native agent on the part of the British Government opposite to Harike-Pattan. These officers will be subject to the orders of the British agent at Ludhiana; and the agents who may be appointed to reside at those places on the part of the other States concerned in the navigation, viz. Bahawalpur and Sind, together with those of Lahore, will co-operate with them in the execution of their duties.

Article 4.—In order to guard against imposition on the part of merchants in making false complaints of being plundered of property which formed no part of their cargoes, they are required, when taking out their passports, to produce an invoice of their cargo, which being duly authenticated, a copy of it will be annexed to their passports; and wherever their boats may be brought to for the night, they are required to give immediate notice to the Thanedars or officers of the place, and to request protection for themselves, at the same time showing the passports they may have received at Mithankot or Harike, as the case may be.

Article 5.—Such parts of the 5th, 7th, 9th, and 10th articles of the treaty of the 26th of December 1832 as have reference to the fixing a duty on the value and quantity of merchandise, and to the mode of its collection, are hereby rescinded, and the foregoing articles substituted in their place, agreeably to which and the conditions of the preamble the toll will be levied.

N.B.—A distribution of the shares due to the British protected States and the feudatories of the Maharaja on the left bank of the Sutlej will be determined hereafter.

## APPENDIX XXX

### THE TRIPARTITE TREATY WITH RANJIT SINGH AND SHAH SHUJA OF 1838

*Treaty of Alliance and Friendship between Maharaja Ranjit Singh and Shah Shuja-ul-Mulk, with the approbation of and in concert with the British Government.*

(Done at Lahore, 26th June 1838, signed at Simla, 25th June 1838.)

WHEREAS a treaty was formerly concluded between Maharaja Ranjit Singh and Shah Shuja-ul-Mulk, consisting of fourteen articles, exclusive of the preamble and the conclusion : And whereas the execution of the provisions of the said treaty was suspended for certain reasons : And whereas at this time, Mr. W. H. Macnaghten having been deputed by the Right Honourable George, Lord Auckland, G.C.B., Governor-General of India, to the presence of Maharaja Ranjit Singh, and vested with full powers to form a treaty, in a manner consistent with the friendly engagements subsisting between the two States, the treaty aforesaid is revived, and concluded with certain modifications, and four new articles have been added thereto, with the approbation of and in concert with the British Government, the provisions whereof, ascertained in the following eighteen articles, will be duly and faithfully observed :

Article 1.—Shah Shuja-ul-Mulk disclaims all title on the part of himself, his heirs and successors, and all the Saddozies, to all the territories lying on either bank of the river Indus, that may be possessed by the Maharaja, viz. Kashmir, including its limits, E., W., N., S., together with the fort of Attock, Chach-Hazara, Khabal, Amb, with its dependencies, on the left bank of the aforesaid river, and on the right bank Peshawar, with the Usufzais territory, the Khataks, Hashtnagar, Michni, Kohat, Hanggu, and all places dependent on Peshawar, as far as the Khaibar pass, Bannu, the Vaziri's territory, Daur-Tank, Garang, Kalabagh, and Khushalgarh, with their dependent districts, Dera Ismail Khan, and its dependency, Kot Mithan, Umar Kot, and their dependent territory; Sanghar, Harrand-Dajal, Hajipur, Rajanpur, and the three Kaches, as well as Mankehra, with its district, and the province of Multan, situated on the left bank. These countries and

places are considered to be the property, and to form
the estate, of the Maharaja : the Shah neither has nor
will have any concern with them; they belong to the
Maharaja and his posterity from generation to
generation.

Article 2.—The people of the country on the other
side of Khaibar will not be suffered to commit rob-
beries, or aggressions, or any disturbances on this side.
If any defaulter of either State, who has embezzled
the revenue, take refuge in the territory of the other,
each party engages to surrender him, and no person
shall obstruct the passage of the stream which issues
out of the Khaibar defile, and supplies the fort of
Fatehgarh with water according to ancient usage.

Article 3.—As, agreeably to the treaty established
between the British Government and the Maharaja,
no one can cross from the left to the right bank of the
Sutlej without a passport from the Maharaja, the same
rule shall be observed regarding the passage of the
Indus, whose waters join the Sutlej, and no one shall
be allowed to cross the Indus without the Maharaja's
permission.

Article 4.—Regarding Shikarpur and the territory
of Sind, on the right bank of the Indus, the Shah will
agree to abide by whatever may be settled as right
and proper, in conformity with the happy relations of
friendship subsisting between the British Government
and the Maharaja through Captain Wade.

Article 5.—When the Shah shall have established
his authority in Kabul and Kandahar, he will annually
send the Maharaja the following articles, viz. 55 high-
bred horses of approved colour, and pleasant paces; 11
Persian scimetars; 7 Persian poniards; 25 good mules;
fruits of various kinds, both dry and fresh; and Sardas
or Musk melons, of a sweet and delicate flavour (to be
sent throughout the year by the way of the Kabul river
to Peshawar); grapes, pomegranates, apples, quinces,
almonds, raisins, pistahs or chestnuts, an abundant
supply of each; as well as pieces of satin of every
colour; chogas of fur; kimkhabs wrought with gold and
silver; and Persian carpets, altogether to the number
of 101 pieces,—all these articles the Shah will continue
to send every year to the Maharaja.

Article 6.—Each party shall address the other on
terms of equality.

Article 7.—Merchants of Afghanistan who may be
desirous of trading to Lahore, Amritsar, or any other
parts of the Maharaja's possessions, shall not be stop-

ped or molested on their way; on the contrary, strict orders shall be issued to facilitate their intercourse, and the Maharaja engages to observe the same line of conduct on his part, in respect to traders who may wish to proceed to Afghanistan.

Article 8.—The Maharaja will yearly send to the Shah the following articles in the way of friendship : 55 pieces of shawls; 25 pieces of muslin; 11 dupattas; 5 pieces of kamkhab; 5 scrafs; 5 turbans; 55 loads of Bara rice (peculiar to Peshawar).

Article 9.—Any of the Maharaja's officers, who may be deputed to Afghanistan to purchase horses, or on any other business, as well as those who may be sent by the Shah into the Punjab, for the purpose of purchasing piece goods, or shawls, &c., to the amount of 11,000 rupees, will be treated by both sides with due attention, and every facility will be afforded to them in the execution of their commission.

Article 10.—Whenever the armies of the two States may happen to be assembled at the same place, on no account shall the slaughter of kine be permitted to take place.

Article 11.—In the event of the Shah taking an auxiliary force from the Maharaja, whatever booty may be acquired from the Barakzais in jewels, horses, arms, great and small, shall be equally divided between the two contracting parties. If the Shah should succeed in obtaining possession of their property, without the assistance of the Maharaja's troops, the Shah agrees to send a portion of it by his own agent to the Maharaja in the way of friendship.

Article 12.—An exchange of missions charged with letters and presents shall constantly take place between the two parties.

Article 13.—Should the Maharaja require the aid of any of the Shah's troops in furtherance of the objects contemplated by this treaty, the Shah engages to send a force commanded by one of his principal officers : in like manner the Maharaja will furnish the Shah, when required, with an auxiliary force, composed of Muhammadans, and commanded by one of the principal officers, as far as Kabul, in furtherance of the objects contemplated by this treaty. When the Maharaja may go to Peshawar, the Shah will depute a Shahzada to visit him, on which occasions the Maharaja will receive and dismiss him with the honour and consideration due to his rank and dignity.

Article 14.—The friends and enemies of each of the three high powers, that is to say, the British and Sikh Governments, and Shah Shuja-ul-Mulk, shall be the friends and enemies of all.

Article 15.—Shah Shuja-ul-Mulk engages, after the attainment of his object, to pay without fail to the Maharaja the sum of two lacs of rupees, of the Nanakshahi or Kaldar currency, calc lating from the date on which the Sikh troops may be dispatched for the purpose of reinstating his Majesty in Kabul, in consideration of the Maharaja stationing a force of not less than 5,000 men, cavalry and infantry, of the Muhammadan persuasion, within the limits of the Peshawar territory, for the support of the Shah, and to be sent to the aid of his Majesty, whenever the British Government, in concert and counsel with the Maharaja, shall deem their aid necessary; and when any matter of great importance may arise to the westward, such measures will be adopted with regard to it as may seem expedient and proper at the time to the British and Sikh Governments. In the event of the Maharaja's requiring the aid of any of the Shah's troops, a deduction shall be made from the subsidy proportioned to the period for which such aid may be afforded, and the British Government holds itself responsible for the punctual payment of the above sum annually to the Maharaja, so long as the provisions of this treaty are duly observed.

Article 16.—Shah Shuja-ul-Mulk agrees to relinquish for himself, his heirs, and successors, all claims of supremacy and arrears of tribute over the country now held by the Amirs of Sind (which will continue to belong to the Amirs and their successors in perpetuity), on condition of the payment to him by the Amirs of such a sum as may be determined under the mediation of the British Government; 1,500,000 of rupees of such payment being made over by him to Maharaja Ranjit Singh. On these payments being completed, article 4th of the treaty of the 12th March 1833 [1] will be considered cancelled, and the customary interchange of letters and suitable presents between the Maharaja and the Amirs of Sind shall be maintained as heretofore.

Article 17.—When Shah Shuja-ul-Mulk shall have succeeded in establishing his authority in Afghanistan, he shall not attack or molest his nephew, the ruler of

[1] Between Shah Shuja and Ranjit Singh.

Herat, in the possession of the territories now subject to his Government.

Article 18.—Shah Shuja-ul-Mulk binds himself, his heirs, and successors, to refrain from entering into negotiations with any foreign State without the knowledge and consent of the British and Sikh Governments, and to oppose any power having the design to invade the British and Sikh territories by force of arms, to the utmost of his ability.

The three powers, parties to this treaty, namely, the British Government, Maharaja Ranjit Singh, and Shah Shuja-ul-Mulk, cordially agree to the foregoing articles. There shall be no deviations from them, and in that case the present treaty shall be considered binding for ever, and this treaty shall come into operation from and after the date on which the seals and signatures of the three contracting parties shall have been affixed thereto.

Done at Lahore, this 26th day of June, in the year of our Lord 1838, corresponding with the 15th of the month of Asarh 1895, era of Bikarmajit.

Ratified by the Right Honourable the Governor-General at Simla, on the 23rd day of July, A.D. 1838.

(Signed)    AUCKLAND.
RANJIT SINGH.
SHUJA-UL-MULK.

# APPENDIX XXXI

## INDUS AND SUTLEJ TOLL AGREEMENT OF 1839

*Agreement entered into with the Government of Lahore, regarding the Duties to be levied on the Transit of Merchandise by the Rivers Sutlej and Indus, in modification of the Supplementary Articles of the Treaty of 1832. (Dated 19th May 1839.)*

OBJECTIONS having been urged against the levy of the same duty on a boat of a small as on one of a large size, and the merchants having solicited that the duties might be levied on the maundage, or measurement, of the boats, or on the value of the goods, it is therefore agreed, that hereafter the whole duty shall be paid at one place, and either at Ludhiana, or Ferozepore, or at

Mithankot; and that the duty be levied on the merchandise, and not on the boats, as follows :—

| | | | | |
|---|---|---|---|---|
| Pashmina | . . | *per maund* | 10 | rupees. |
| Opium | . . . | " | 7½ | rupees. |
| Indigo | . . . | " | 2½ | rupees. |
| Dried fruits | . . | " | 1 | rupee. |
| Superior silks, muslins, broad-cloth, &c. | . | " | 6 | annas. |
| Inferior silks, cottons, chintzes | . . . | " | 4 | annas. |

*On Exports from the Punjab*

| | | | | |
|---|---|---|---|---|
| Sugar, ghi, oil, drugs, ginger, saffron, and cotton | . . . | *per maund* | 4 | annas. |
| Madder | . . . | " | 8 | annas. |
| Grain | . . . | " | 2 | annas. |

*On Imports from Bombay*

| | | | | |
|---|---|---|---|---|
| All imports whatever | . *per maund* | 4 | annas. |

# APPENDIX XXXII

## INDUS AND SUTLEJ TOLL AGREEMENT OF 1840

*Treaty between the Lahore and British Governments, regarding the levy of Transit Duties on Boats navigating the Sutlej and Indus. (Dated 27th June 1840.)*

FORMERLY a treaty was executed by the Right Honourable Lord W. Cavendish Bentinck, the Governor-General of India, on the 14th of Pus Sambat 1889 (corresponding with A.D. 1832) through Colonel, then Captain, Wade, concerning the navigation of the Sutlej and the Sind rivers in the Khalsa territory, in concurrence with the wishes of both the friendly and allied Governments. Another treaty on the subject was subsequently executed, through the same officer, in Sambat 1891 (corresponding with A.D. 1834), fixing a duty on every mercantile boat, independent of the quantity of its freight and the nature of its merchandise. A third treaty was executed on this subject, in accordance with the wishes of both Governments, on the arrival of Mr. Clerk, Agent to the Governor-General at the Durbar, in May 1839, adjusting the rate of duties on merchandise according to quantity and kind; and it was also

specified that no further reduction of those rates should
be proposed between the two Governments.  On the
visit of that gentleman to the Khalsa Durbar at Amritsar, in Jith Sambat 1897 (corresponding with May
1840), the difficulties and inconveniences which seemed
to result to trade under the system proposed last year,
in consequence of the obstruction to boats for the purpose of search, and the ignorance of traders, and the
difficulty of adjusting duties according to the different
kinds of articles freighted in these boats, were all
stated; and that gentleman proposed to revise that
system, by fixing a scale of duties proportionate to the
measurement of boats, and not on the kind of com-
modities, if this arrangement should be approved of
by both Governments.  Having reported to his Government the circumstance of the case, he now drew up a
schedule of the rate of duties on the mercantile boats
navigating the rivers Sind and Sutlej, and forwarded it
for the consideration of this friendly Durbar; the
Khalsa Government, therefore, with a due regard to
the established alliance, having added a few sentences
in accordance with the late treaties, and agreeably to
what is already well understood, has signed and sealed
the schedule; and it shall never be liable to any contradiction, difference, change, or alteration without the
concurrence and consent of both Governments, in consideration of mutual advantages, upon condition it does
not interfere with the established custom duties at
Amritsar, Lahore, and other inland places, or the other
rivers in the Khalsa territory.

Article 1.—Grain, wood, limestone, will be free
from duty.

Article 2.—With exception of the above, every
commodity to pay duty according to the measurement
of the boat.

Article 3.—Duty on a boat not exceeding 50 maunds
of freight proceeding from the foot of the Hills, Rupar,
or Ludhiana to Mithankot or Rojhan, or from Rojhan
or Mithankot to the foot of the Hills, Rupar, or
Ludhiana, will be 50 rupees; viz.

| | |
|---|---|
| From the foot of the Hills to Ferozepore, or back | 20 rupees. |
| From Ferozepore to Bahawalpur, or back | 15  ,, |
| From Bahawalpur to Mithankot or Rojhan, or back | 15  ,, |
| The whole trip, up or down | 50 rupees. |

Duty on a boat above 250 maunds, but not exceding 500 maunds : from the foot of the Hills, Rupar, or Ludhiana to Mithankot or Rojhan, or from Rojhan or Mithankot to the foot of the Hills, Rupar, or Ludhiana, will be 100 rupees, viz.

From the foot of the Hills to Ferozepore or back . . . . . 40 rupees.
From Ferozepore to Bahawalpur or back    30    „
From Bahawalpur to Mithankot or Rojhan, or back . . . . . 30    „

               The whole trip, up or down 100    „

Duty on all boats above 500 maunds will be 150 rupees, viz.

From the foot of the Hills to Ferozepore, or back . . . . . 60 rupees.
From Ferozepore to Bahawalpur, or back    45    „
From Bahawalpur to Mithankot or Rojhan, or back . . . . . 45    „

               The whole trip, up or down   150 rupees.

Article 4.—Boats to be classed 1, 2, or 3, and the same to be written on the boat, and every boat to be registered.

Article 5.—These duties on merchandise frequenting the Sutlej and Sind are not to interfere with the duties on the banks of other rivers, or with the established inland custom-houses throughout the Khalsa territory, which will remain on their usual footing.

Dated 13th Asar Sambat 1897, corresponding with 27th June 1840.

# APPENDIX XXXIII

## DECLARATION OF WAR OF 1845

*Proclamation by the Governor-General of India*

Camp, Lashkari Khan ki Sarai,
December 13th, 1845.

THE British Government has ever been on terms of friendship with that of the Punjab.

In the year 1809, a treaty of amity and concord was concluded between the British Government and the late Maharaja Ranjit Singh, the conditions of which have always been faithfully observed by the British

Government, and were scrupulously fulfilled by the late Maharaja.

The same friendly relations have been maintained with the successors of Maharaja Ranjit Singh by the British Government up to the present time.

Since the death of the late Maharaja Sher Singh, the disorganized state of the Lahore Government has made it incumbent on the Governor-General in Council to adopt precautionary measures for the protection of the British frontier : the nature of these measures, and the cause of their adoption, were, at the time, fully explained to the Lahore Durbar.

Notwithstanding the disorganized state of the Lahore Government during the last two years, and many most unfriendly proceedings on the part of the Durbar, the Governor-General in Council has continued to evince his desire to maintain the relations of amity and concord which had so long existed between the two States, for the mutual interests and happiness of both. He has shown, on every occasion, the utmost forbearance, and consideration to the helpless state of the infant Maharaja Dalip Singh, whom the British Government had recognized as the successor to the late Maharaja Sher Singh.

The Governor-General in Council sincerely desired to see a strong Sikh Government re-established in the Punjab, able to control its army, and to protect its subjects; he had not, up to the present moment, abandoned the hope of seeing that important object effected by the patriotic efforts of the Chiefs and people of that country.

The Sikh army recently marched from Lahore towards the British frontier, as it was alleged, by the orders of the Durbar, for the purpose of invading the British territory.

The Governor-General's agent, by direction of the Governor-General, demanded an explanation of this movement, and no reply being returned within a reasonable time, the demand was repeated. The Governor-General, unwilling to believe in the hostile intentions of the Sikh Government, to which no provocation had been given, refrained from taking any measures which might have a tendency to embarrass the Government of the Maharaja, or to induce collision between the two States.

When no reply was given to the repeated demand for explanation, while active military preparations ere continued at Lahore, the Governor-General considered it necessary to order the advance of troops towards the frontier, to reinforce the frontier posts.

The Sikh army has now, without a shadow of provocation, invaded the British territories.

The Governor-General must therefore take measures for effectually protecting the British provinces, for vindicating the authority of the British Government, and for punishing the violators of treaties and the disturbers of the public peace.

The Governor-General hereby declares the possessions of Maharaja Dalip Singh, on the left or British bank of the Sutlej, confiscated and annexed to the British territories.

The Governor-General will respect the existing rights of all Jagirdars. Zamindars. and tenants in the said possessions, who, by the course they now pursue, evince their fidelity to the British Government.

The Governor-General hereby calls upon all the Chiefs and Sardars in the protected territories to cooperate cordially with the British Government for the punishment of the common enemy, and for the maintenance of order in these States. Those of the Chiefs who show alacrity and fidelity in the discharge of this duty, which they owe to the protecting power, will find their interests promoted thereby; and those who take a contrary course will be treated as enemies to the British Government, and will be punished accordingly.

The inhabitants of all the territories on the left bank of the Sutlej are hereby directed to abide peaceably in their respective villages, where they will receive efficient protection by the British Government. All parties of men found in armed bands, who can give no satisfactory account of their proceedings, will be treated as disturbers of the public peace.

All subjects of the British Government, and those who possess estates on both sides the river Sutlej, who, by their faithful adherence to the British Government, may be liable to sustain loss, shall be indemnified and secured in all their just rights and privileges.

On the other hand, all subjects of the British Government who shall continue in the service of the Lahore State, and who disobey the proclamation by not immediately returning to their allegiance, will be liable to have their property on this side the Sutlej confiscated, and themselves declared to be aliens and enemies of the British Government.

# APPENDIX XXXIV

## FIRST TREATY WITH LAHORE OF 1846

*Treaty between the British Government and the State of Lahore, concluded at Lahore, on March 9th, 1846.*

WHEREAS the treaty of amity and concord, which was concluded between the British Government and the late Maharaja Ranjit Singh, the ruler of Lahore, in 1809, was broken by the unprovoked aggression on the British provinces of the Sikh army, in December last : And whereas, on that occasion, by the proclamation dated the 13th of December, the territories then in the occupation of the Maharaja of Lahore, on the left or British bank of the river Sutlej, were confiscated and annexed to the British provinces; and, since that time, hostile operations have been prosecuted by the two Governments, the one against the other, which have resulted in the occupation of Lahore by the British troops : And whereas it has been determined that, upon certain conditions, peace shall be re-established between the two Governments, the following treaty of peace between the Honourable English East India Company, and Maharaja Dalip Singh Bahadur, and his children, heirs, and successors, has been concluded, on the part of the Honourable Company, by Frederick Currie, Esq., and Brevet-Major Henry Montgomery Lawrence, by virtue of full powers to that effect vested in them by the Right Honourable Sir Henry Hardinge, G.C.B., one of Her Britannic Majesty's most Honourable Privy Council, Governor-General, appointed by the Honourable Company to direct and control all their affairs in the East Indies; and, on the part of his Highness the Maharaja Dalip Singh, by Bhai Ram Singh, Raja Lal Singh, Sardar Tej Singh, Sardar Chattar Singh Atariwala, Sardar Ranjor Singh Majithia, Diwan Dina Nath, and Fakir Nur-ud-din, vested with full powers and authority on the part of his Highness.

Article 1.—There shall be perpetual peace and friendship between the British Government, on the one part, and Maharaja Dalip Singh, his heirs and successors, on the other.

Article 2.—The Maharaja of Lahore renounces for himself, his heirs and successors, all claim to, or connexion with, the territories lying to the south of the river Sutlej, and engages never to have any concern with those territories, or the inhabitants thereof.

Article 3.—The Maharaja cedes to the Honourable Company, in perpetual sovereignty, all his forts, territories, and rights, in the Doab, or country, hill and plain, situate between the rivers Beas and Sutlej.

Article 4.—The British Government having demanded from the Lahore State, as indemnification for the expenses of the war, in addition to the cession of territory described in Article 3, payment of one and a half crores of rupees; and the Lahore Government being unable to pay the whole of this sum at this time, or to give security satisfactory to the British Government for its eventual payment; the Maharaja cedes to the Honourable Company, in perpetual sovereignty, as equivalent for one crore of rupees, all his forts, territories, rights, and interests, in the hill countries which are situate between the rivers Beas and Indus, including the provinces of Kashmir and Hazara.

Article 5.—The Maharaja will pay to the British Government the sum of fifty lacs of rupees, on or before the ratification of this treaty.

Article 6.—The Maharaja engages to disband the mutinous troops of the Lahore army, taking from them their arms; and his Highness agrees to reorganize the regular, or Ain, regiments of infantry, upon the system, and according to the regulations as o pay and allowances, observed in the time of the la e Maharaja Ranjit Singh. The Maharaja further engages to pay up all arrears to the soldiers that are discharged under the provisions of this article.

Article 7.—The regular army of the Lahore State shall henceforth be limited to 25 battalions of infantry, consisting of 800 bayonets each, with 12,000 cavalry : this number at no time to be exceeded without the concurrence of the British Government. Should it be necessary at any time, for any special cause, that this force should be increased, the cause shall be fully explained to the British Government; and, when the special necessity shall have passed, the regular troops shall be again reduced to the standard specified in the former clause of this article.

Article 8.—The Maharaja will surrender to the British Government all the guns, thirty-six in number, which have been pointed against the British troops, and which, having been placed on the right bank of the river Sutlej, were not captured at the battle of Sobraon.

Article 9.—The control of the rivers Beas

Sutlej, with the continuations of the latter river, commonly called the Ghara and Panjnad, to the confluence of the Indus at Mithankot, and the control of the Indus from Mithankot to the borders of Baluchistan, shall, in respect to tolls and ferries, rest with the British Government. The provisions of this article shall not interfere with the passage of boats belonging to the Lahore Government on the said rivers, for the purposes of traffic, or the conveyance of passengers up and down their course. Regarding the ferries between the two countries respectively, at the several ghats of the said rivers, it is agreed that the British Government, after defraying all the expenses of management and establishments, shall account to the Lahore Government for one-half of the net profits of the ferry collections. The provisions of this article have no reference to the ferries on that part of the river Sutlej which forms the boundary of Bahawalpur and Lahore respectively.

Article 10.—If the British Government should, at any time, desire to pass troops through the territories of his Highness the Maharaja for the protection of the British territories, or those of their allies, the British troops shall, on such special occasions, due notice being given, be allowed to pass through the Lahore territories. In such case, the officers of the Lahore State will afford facilities in providing supplies and boats for the passage of rivers; and the British Government will pay the full price of all such provisions and boats, and will make fair compensation for all private property that may be endamaged. The British Government will moreover observe all due consideration to the religious feelings of the inhabitants of those tracts through which the army may pass.

Article 11.—The Maharaja engages never to take, or retain, in his service, any British subject, nor the subject of any European or American State, without the consent of the British Government.

Article 12.—In consideration of the services rendered by Raja Gulab Singh of Jammu to the Lahore State, towards procuring the restoration of the relations of amity between the Lahore and British Governments, the Maharaja hereby agrees to recognize the independent sovereignty of Raja Gulab Singh, in such territories and districts in the hills as may be made over to the said Raja Gulab Singh by separate agreement between himself and the British Government, with the dependencies thereof, which may have been in the Raja's possession since the time of the late

Maharaja Kharak Singh : and the British Government, in consideration of the good conduct of Raja Gulab Singh, also agrees to recognize his independence in such territories, and to admit him to the privileges of a separate treaty with the British Government.

Article 13.—In the event of any dispute or difference arising between the Lahore State and Raja Gulab Singh, the same shall be referred to the arbitration of the British Government; and by its decision the Maharaja engages to abide.

Article 14.—The limits of the Lahore territories shall not be at any time, changed, without the concurrence of the British Government.

Article 15.—The British Government will not exercise any interference in the internal administration of the Lahore State; but in all cases or questions which may be referred to the British Government, the Governor-General will give the aid of his advice and good offices for the furtherance of the interests of the Lahore Government.

Article 16.—The subjects of either State shall, on visiting the territories of the other, be on the footing of the subjects of the most favoured nation.

This treaty, consisting of sixteen articles, has been this day settled by Frederick Currie, Esq., and Brevet-Major Henry Montgomery Lawrence, acting under the directions of the Right Honourable Sir Henry Hardinge, G.C.B., Governor-General, on the part of the British Government; and by Bhai Ram Singh, Raja Lal Singh, Sardar Tej Singh, Sardar Chattar Singh Atariwala, Sardar Ranjor Singh Majithia, Diwan Dina Nath, and Fakir Nur-ud-din, on the part of the Maharaja Dalip Singh; and the said treaty has been this day ratified by the seal of the Right Honourable Sir Henry Hardinge, G.C.B., Governor-General, and by that of his Highness Maharaja Dalip Singh.

Done at Lahore, this 9th day of March, in the year of our Lord 1846, corresponding with the 10th day of Rabi-ul-awal 1262, Hijri, and ratified on the same day.

# APPENDIX XXXV

## SUPPLEMENTARY ARTICLES TO FIRST TREATY WITH LAHORE OF 1846

*Articles of Agreement concluded between the British Government and the Lahore Durbar, on the 11th of March 1846.*

WHEREAS the Lahore Government has solicited the Governor-General to leave a British force at Lahore, for the protection of the Maharaja's person and of the capital, till the reorganization of the Lahore army, according to the provisions of Article 6 of the treaty of Lahore, dated the 9th instant : And whereas the Governor-General has, on certain conditions, consented to the measure : And whereas it is expedient that certain matters concerning the territories ceded by Articles 3 and 4 of the aforesaid treaty should be specifically determined; the following eight articles of agreement have this day been concluded between the aforementioned contracting parties.

Article 1.—The British Government shall leave at Lahore, till the close of the current year, A.D. 1846, such force as shall seem to the Governor-General adequate for the purpose of protecting the person of the Maharaja, and the inhabitants of the city of Lahore, during the reorganization of the Sikh army, in accordance with the provisions of Article 6 of the treaty of Lahore; that force to be withdrawan at any convenient time before the expiration of the year, if the object to be fulfilled shall, in the opinion of the Durbar, have been obtained; but the force shall not be detained at Lahore beyond the expiration of the current year.

Article 2.—The Lahore Government agrees that the force left at Lahore, for the purpose specified in the foregoing article, shall be placed in full possession of the fort and the city of Lahore, and that the Lahore troops shall be removed from within the city. The Lahore Government engages to furnish convenient quarters for the officers and men of the said force, and to pay the British Government all the extra expenses, in regard to the said force, which may be incurred by the British Government, in consequence of their troops being employed away from their own cantonments, and in a foreign territory.

Article 3.—The Lahore Government engages to apply itself immediately and earnestly to the reorganization of its army, according to the prescribed conditions, and to communicate fully with the British authorities left at Lahore, as to the progress of such reorganization, and as to the location of the troops.

Article 4.—If the Lahore Government fails in the performance of the conditions of the foregoing article, the British Government shall be at liberty to withdraw the force from Lahore, at any time before the expiration of the period specified in Article 1.

Article 5.—The British Government agrees to respect the bona fide rights of those Jagirdars within the territories ceded by Articles 3 and 4 of the treaty of Lahore, dated 9th instant, who were attached to the families of the late Maharaja Ranjit Singh, Kharak Singh, and Sher Singh; and the British Government will maintain those Jagirdars in their bona fide possessions, during their lives.

Article 6.—The Lahore Government shall receive the assistance of the British local authorities in recovering the arrears of revenue justly due to the Lahore Government from their Kardars and managers in the territories ceded by the provisions of Articles 3 and 4 of the treaty of Lahore, to the close of the Kharif harvest of the current year, viz. 1902 of the Sambat Bikarmajit.

Article 7.—The Lahore Government shall be at liberty to remove from the forts in the territories specified in the foregoing article, all treasure and state property, with the exception of guns. Should, however, the British Government desire to retain any part of the said property, they shall be at liberty to do so, paying for the same at a fair valuation; and the British officers shall give their assistance to the Lahore Government, in disposing on the spot of such part of the aforesaid property as the Lahore Government may not wish to remove, and the British officers may not desire to retain.

Article 8.—Commissioners shall be immediately appointed by the two Governments, to settle and lay down the boundary between the two States, as defined by Article 4 of the treaty of Lahore, dated 9th March 1846.

# APPENDIX XXXVI

## TREATY WITH GULAB SINGH OF 1846

*Treaty between the British Government and Maharaja Gulab Singh, concluded at Amritsar, on 16th March 1846.*

TREATY between the British Government on the one part, and Maharaja Gulab Singh of Jammu on the other, concluded, on the part of the British Government, by Frederick Currie, Esq., and Brevet-Major Henry Montgomery Lawrence, acting under the orders of the Right Honourable Sir Henry Hardinge, G.C.B., one of Her Britannic Majesty's most Honourable Privy Council, Governor-General, appointed by the Honourable Company to direct and control all their affairs in the East Indies, and by Maharaja Gulab Singh in person.

Article 1.—The British Government transfers and makes over, for ever, in independent possession, to Maharaja Gulab Singh, and the heirs male of his body, all the hilly or mountainous country, with its dependencies, situated to the eastward of the river Indus, and westward of the river Ravi, including Chamba and excluding Lahul, being part of the territory ceded to the British Government by the Lahore State, according to the provisions of Article 4 of the treaty of Lahore, dated 9th March 1846.

Article 2.—The eastern boundary of the tract transferred by the foregoing article to Maharaja Gulab Singh shall be laid down by commissioners appointed by the British Government and Maharaja Gulab Singh respectively, for that purpose, and shall be defined in a separate engagement, after survey.

Article 3.—In consideration of the transfer made to him and his heirs by the provisions of the foregoing articles, Maharaja Gulab Singh will pay to the British Government the sum of seventy-five lacs of rupees (Nanakshahi), fifty lacs to be paid on ratification of this treaty, and twenty-five lacs on or before the 1st of October of the current year, A.D. 1846.

Article 4.—The limits of the territories of Maharaja Gulab Singh shall not be at any time changed without the concurrence of the British Government.

Article 5.—Maharaja Gulab Singh will refer to the arbitration of the British Government any disputes or questions that may arise between himself and the Government of Lahore, or any other neighbouring State, and will abide by the decision of the British Government.

Article 6.—Maharaja Gulab Singh engages for himself and heirs, to join, with the whole of his military force, the British troops, when employed within the hills, or in the territories adjoining his possessions.

Article 7.—Maharaja Gulab Singh .engages never to take, or retain, in his service any British subject, nor the subject of any European or American State, without the consent of the British Government.

Article 8.—Maharaja Gulab Singh engages to respect, in regard to the territory transferred to him, 'ie provisions of Articles 5, 6 and 7, of the separate engagement between the British Government and the Lahore Durbar, dated 11th March 1846.

Article 9.—The British Government will give its aid to Maharaja Gulab Singh, in protecting his territories from external enemies.

Article 10.—Maharaja Gulab Singh acknowledges the supremacy of the British Government, and will, in token of such supremacy, present annually to the British Government one horse, twelve perfect shawl goats of approved breed (six male and six female), and three pairs of Kashmir shawls.

This treaty, consisting of ten articles, has been this day settled by Frederick Currie, Esq., and Brevet-Major Henry Montgomery Lawrence, acting under the directions of the Right Honourable Sir Henry Hardinge, G.C.B., Governor-General, on the part of the British Government, and by Maharaja Gulab Singh in person; and the said treaty has been this day ratified by the seal of the Right Honourable Sir Henry Hardinge. G.C.B., Governor-General.

Done at Amritsar, this 16th day of March, in the year of our Lord 1846, corresponding with the 17th day of Rabi-ul-awal, 1262, Hijri.

# APPENDIX XXXVII

## SECOND TREATY WITH LAHORE OF 1846

*Foreign Department, Camp, Bhyrowal Ghat, on the left Bank of the Beas, the 22nd December 1846.*

THE late Governor of Kashmir, on the part of the Lahore State, Shaikh Imam-ud-din, having resisted by force of arms the occupation of the province of Kash-

mir by Maharaja Gulab Singh, the Lahore Government was called upon to coerce their subject, and to
make over the province to the representative of the
British Government, in fulfilment of the conditions of
the treaty of Lahore, dated 9th March 1846.

A British force was employed to support and aid,
if necessary, the combined forces of the Lahore State
and Maharaja Gulab Singh in the above operations.

Shaikh Imam-ud-din intimated to the British Government that he was acting under orders received from
the Lahore Durbar in the course he was pursuing; and
stated that the insurrection had been instigated by
written instructions received by him from the Wazir
Raja Lal Singh.

Shaikh Imam-ud-din surrendered to the British
agent on a guarantee from that officer, that if the
Shaikh could, as he asserted, prove that his acts were in
accordance with his instructions, and that the opposition was instigated by the Lahore minister, the Durbar
should not be permitted to inflict upon him, either in
his person or his property, any penalty on account of
his conduct on this occasion. The British agent pledged
his Government to a full and impartial investigation
of the matter.

A public inquiry was instituted into the facts
adduced by Shaikh Imam-ud-din, and it was fully
established that Raja Lal Singh did secretly instigate
the Shaikh to oppose the occupation by Maharaja
Gulab Singh of the province of Kashmir.

The Governor-General immediately demanded
that the Ministers and Chiefs of the Lahore State
should depose and exile to the British provinces the
Wazir Raja Lal Singh.

His Lordship consented to accept the deposition of
Raja Lal Singh as an atonement for the attempt to
infringe the treaty by the secret intrigues and machinations of the Wazir. It was not proved that the other
members of the Durbar had cognizance of the Wazir's
proceedings; and the conduct of the Sardars, and of the
Sikh army in the late operations for quelling the Kashmir insurrection, and removing the obstacles to the
fulfilment of the treaty, proved that the criminality of
the Wazir was not participated in by the Sikh nation.

The Ministers and Chiefs unanimously decreed,
and carried into immediate effect, the deposition of
the Wazir.

After a few days' deliberations, relative to the
means of forming a government at Lahore, the remain

ing members of the Durbar, in concert with all the
Sardars and Chiefs of the State, solicited the interference and aid of the British Government for the
maintenance of an administration, and the protection
of the Maharaja Dalip Singh during the minority of
his Highness.

This solicitation by the Durbar and Chiefs has led
to the temporary modification of the relations between
the British Government and that of Lahore, established
by the treaty of the 9th March of the present year.

The terms and conditions of this modification are
set forth in the following articles of agreement.

*Articles of Agreement concluded between the British*
*Government and the Lahore Durbar on*
*16th December 1846.*

Whereas the Lahore Durbar and the principal
Chiefs and Sardars of the State have, in express terms,
communicated to the British Government their anxious
desire that the Governor-General should give his aid
and his assistance to maintain the administration of
the Lahore State during the minority of Maharaja
Dalip Singh, and have declared this measure to be indispensable for the maintenance of the government :
And whereas the Governor-General has, under certain
conditions, consented to give the aid and assistance
solicited, the following articles of agreement, in modification of the articles of agreement executed at Lahore
on the 11th March last, have been concluded, on the
part of the British Government, by Frederick Currie,
Esq., Secretary to the Government of India, and
Lieutenant-Colonel Henry Montgomery Lawrence,
C.B., Agent to the Governor-General, North-West
Frontier, by virtue of full powers to that effect vested
in them by the Right Honourable Viscount Hardinge,
G.C.B., Governor-General, and on the part of his
Highness Maharaja Dalip Singh, by Sardar Tej Singh,
Sardar Sher Singh, Diwan Dina Nath, Fakir Nur-ud-
din, Rai Kishan Chand. Sardar Ranjor Singh Majithia,
Sardar Atar Singh Kaliwala, Bhai Nidhan Singh,
Sardar Khan Singh Majithia, Sardar Shamsher Singh,
Sardar Lal Singh Muraria. Sardar Kehar Singh Sin-
dhianwala, Sardar Arjun Singh Rangranglia, acting
with the unanimous consent and concurrence of the
Chiefs and Sardars of the State assembled at Lahore.

Article 1.—All and every part of the treaty of
peace between the British Government and the State

of Lahore, bearing date the 9th day of March 1846, except in so far as it may be temporarily modified in respect to clause 15 of the said treaty by this engagement, shall remain binding upon the two Governments.

Article 2.—A British officer, with an efficient establishment of assistants, shall be appointed by the Governor-General to remain at Lahore, which officer shall have full authority to direct and control all matters in every department of the State.

Article 3.—Every attention shall be paid, in conducting the administration, to the feelings of the people, to preserving the national institutions and customs, and to maintain the just rights of all classes.

Article 4.—Changes in the mode and details of administration shall not be made, except when found necessary for effecting the objects set forth in the foregoing clause, and for securing the just dues of the Lahore Government. These details shall be conducted by native officers as at present, who shall be appointed and superintended by a Council of Regency, composed of leading Chiefs and Sardars, acting under the control and guidance of the British Resident.

Article 5.—The following persons shall in the first instance constitute the Council of Regency, viz., Sardar Tej Singh, Sardar Sher Singh Atariwala, Diwan Dina Nath, Fakir Nur-ud-din, Sardar Ranjor Singh Majithia, Bhai Nihan Singh, Sardar Atar Singh Kaliwala, Sardar Shamsher Singh Sindhianwala; and no change shall be made in the persons thus nominated, without the consent of the British Resident, acting under the orders of the Governor-General.

Article 6.—The administration of the country shall be conducted by this Council of Regency in such manner as may be determined on by themselves in consultation with the British Resident, who shall have full authority to direct and control the duties of every department.

Article 7.—A British force, of such strength and numbers, and in such positions, as the Governor-General may think fit, shall remain at Lahore for the protection of the Maharaja, and the preservation of the peace of the country.

Article 8.—The Governor-General shall be at liberty to occupy with British soldiers any fort or military post in the Lahore territories, the occupation of which may be deemed necessary by the British Government for the security of the capital, or for maintaining the peace of the country.

Article 9.—The Lahore State shall pay to the British Government twenty-two lacs of new Nanak-shahi rupees of full tale and weight per annum for the maintenance of this force, and to meet the expenses incurred by the British Government; such sum to be paid by two instalments, or 13 lacs and 20,000 in May or June, and 8 lacs and 80,000 in November or December of each year.

Article 10.—Inasmuch as it is fitting that her Highness the Maharani, the mother of Maharaja Dalip Singh, should have a proper provision made for the maintenance of herself and dependents, the sum of 1 lac and 50,000 rupees shall be set apart annually for that purpose, and shall be at her Highness's disposal.

Article 11.—The provisions of this engagement shall have effect during the minority of his Highness Maharaja Dalip Singh, and shall cease and terminate on his Highness attaining the full age of 16 years, or on the 4th September of the year 1854; but it shall be competent to the Governor-General to cause the arrangement to cease, at any period prior to the coming of age of his Highness, at which the Governor-General and the Lahore Durbar may be satisfied that the interposition of the British Government is no longer necessary for maintaining the government of his Highness the Maharaja.

This agreement, consisting of eleven articles, was settled and executed at Lahore, by the officers and Chiefs and Sardars above named, on the 16th day of December 1846.

# APPENDIX XXXVIII

## REVENUES OF THE PUNJAB, AS ESTIMATED IN 1844

### TRIBUTARY STATES

|  | Rupees. | Rupees. |
|---|---|---|
| Bilaspur. Tribute, 10,000. Under Lahna Singh | 70,000 | |
| Suket. Tribute, 25,000. Under Lahna Singh | 70,000 | |
| Chamba. Not known. Under Gulab Singh | 2,00,000 | |
| Rajauri. Not known. Under Gulab Singh | 1,00,000 | |
| Ladakh. Tribute, 42,000. Under Gulab Singh | 1,00,000 | |
| Iskardu. Tribute, 7,000. Under Gulab Singh | 25,000 | 5,65,000 |

Note..—All of these States, excepting Bilaspur, may be regarded rather as farms held by the Chiefs than as tributary principalities; and, ordinarily, all the resources of the Chiefs being at the disposal of the government representative, the probable revenues have therefore been entered in full, instead of the mere pecuniary payment.

### LAND REVENUE

#### Farms.

| | |
|---|---|
| Mandi. Farm with the Raja of Mandi, who was allowed one lac out of the four for his expenses | 4,00,000 |
| Kullu. The members of the family had pensions | 1,20,000 |
| Jaswan. The family had a Jagir | 1,25,000 |
| Kangra. The family had a Jagir, not included in the farm | 6,00,000 |
| Kutlahar. The family had a Jagir | 25,000 |
| Siba. The family may almost be regarded as Jagirdars for the whole estate : they served with horse | 20,000 |
| Nurpur. The family had a Jagir | 3,00,000 |
| Haripur. The family had a Jagir | 1,00,000 |
| Datarpur. The family had a Jagir | 50,000 |
| Katlah. The family had a Jagir | 20,000 |

Note.—The above were all under Lahna Singh Majithia.

| | Rupees. | Rupees. |
|---|---|---|
| Bisohli. Family at large : was held by Raja Hira Singh . . . . | | 75,000 |
| Kashmir. Shaikh Ghulam Muhi-ud-din: | | |
| Contract . 21,00,000 | | |
| Troops . . 5,00,000 | | |
| Assignments . 4,00,000 | | 30,00,000 |
| Muzaffarabad, &c. (Under Kashmir.) The Muzaffarabad Chief a Jagirdar | | 1,00,000 |
| Chach-Hazara and Pakhli Dhamtaur. { RajaGulab Singh. The Gandghar and Tarnauli Chiefs have Jagirs; but they are almost independent freebooters } | | 1,50,000 |
| Rawalpindi. Diwan Hakim Rai . . | | 1,00,000 |
| Hasan Abdal, Khatir, and Ghipi. { Diwan Mul Raj: he lately held Chatch-Hazara also } | | 1,00,000 |
| Dhanni, Katas, and Chakwal. } Raja Gulab Singh | | 1,00,000 |
| Peshawar. Sardar Tej Singh. The Barakzais have Jagirs | | 10,00,000 |
| Tank-Bannu. Diwan Daulat Rai. The Chief fled; his brother a Jagir . | | 2,50,000 |
| Dera Ismail Khan. Diwan Daulat Rai. Chief a Jagir . . . | | 4,50,000 |
| Multan, Dera Ghazi Khan, Mankera. } Diwan Sawan Mal | | |
| Contract . 36,00,000 | | |
| Troops . 7,00,000 | | |
| Assignments, &c. 2,00,000 | | 45,00,000 |
| Ramnagar, &c. Diwan Sawan Mal . | 3,00,000 | |
| Mitta Tuwana. The late Dhian Singh | 1,00,000 | |
| Bhera Khushab. Raja Gulab Singh . | 1,00,000 | |
| Pind Dadan Khan. Raja Gulab Singh | 50,000 | |
| Gujrat. Raja Gulab Singh . . | 3,00,000 | |
| Wazirabad, &c. The late Suchet Singh | 9,00,000 | |
| Sialkot. Raja Gulab Singh . | 50,000 | |
| Jullundur Doab. Shaikh Imam-ud-din | 22,00,000 | |
| Shekhupura, &c. Shaikh Imam-ud-din | 2,50,000 | |
| Cis-Sutlej farms . . . . | 6,50,000 | |
| Miscellaneous farms in the Punjab . | 15,00,000 | 1,79,85,000 |

| LAND REVENUE (Continued) | Rupees. | Rupees. |
|---|---|---|

**Religious Grants.**

| | | |
|---|---|---|
| Held by 'Sodhis' . . . . | 5,00,000 | |
| Held by 'Bedis' . . . . | 4,00,000 | |
| Miscellaneous; viz. Akalis, Fakirs, Brahmans, and the lands attached to Amritsar, &c. &c. . . . | 11,00,000 | 20,00,000 |

**Hill Jagirs of the Jammu Rajas.**

| | | |
|---|---|---|
| Jesrota, &c. Hira Singh. The Chief a Jagir . . . . . | 1,25,000 | |
| Pader, and other districts of Chamba. } Gulab Singh | 1,00,000 | |
| Bhadarwa. Gulab Singh (in Jagir with uncle of Chamba Raja) . . | 50,000 | |
| Mankot. The late Suchet Singh. Family a Jagir . . . . . | 50,000 | |
| Bhaddu. The late Suchet Singh. Family a Jagir . . . . . | 50,000 | |
| Bandralta. The late Suchet Singh. Family a Jagir . . . . | 1,25,000 | |
| Chanini (Ramnagar). } Gulab Singh. Family a Jagir . | 30,000 | |
| Jammu and Riasi. } Gulab Singh. Family mostly refugees . | 4,00,000 | |
| Samba. The late Suchet Singh. Family extinct or fled . . . . | 40.000 | |
| Kishtwar. Gulab Singh. Family refugees | 1,50,000 | |
| Akhnur, including Chakkana, with Kesri Singh's family. } Gulab Singh. Family a Jagir . | 50,000 | |
| Bhimbar. The late Dhian Singh. Some members of family Jagirs; others refugees . . . . . | 1,50,000 | |
| The Chibh-Bhau tribes. The late Dhian Singh. Family Jag.rs . . | 1,00,000 | |
| Kotli. The late Dhian Singh. Family Jagirs . . . . . | 30,000 | |
| Sunach. The late Dhian Singh. Family perhaps refugees . . . | 70,000 | |
| Dang'i, Khanpur, &c. Gulab Singh. Some members of family Jagirs; others prisoners; others refugees . | 1,00,000 | 16,20,000 |

**Jagirs.**

| | | |
|---|---|---|
| Various Jagirs held by the Jammu Rajas (in the plains) . . . | 5,00,000 | |
| The Kangra Rajas (Ranbir Chand, &c.) | 1,00,000 | |

| LAND REVENUE—Jagirs (continued) | Rupees. | Rupees. |
|---|---|---|
| Sardar Lahna Singh Majithia . . | 3,50,000 | |
| Sardar Nihal Singh Ahluwalia . . | 9,00,000 | |
| Sardar Kishan Singh (son of Jamadar Khushal Singh) . . . . | 1,20,000 | |
| Sardar Tej Singh . . . | 60,000 | |
| Sardars Sham Singh and Chattar Singh Atariwala . . . . . | 1,20,000 | |
| Sardar Shamsher Singh Sindhianwala | 15,000 | |
| Sardar Arjun Singh, and other sons of Hari Singh . . . . | 15,000 | |
| Kanwar Peshaura Singh . . | 5,000 | |
| Kanwar Tara Singh . . . | 20,000 | |
| Sardar Jawahar Singh (uncle of Dalip Singh) . . . . . . | 50,000 | |
| Sardar Mangal Singh . . . | 50,000 | |
| Sardar Fateh Singh Man . . . | 50,000 | |
| Sardar Attar Singh Kalanwala . . | 50,000 | |
| Sardar Hukam Singh Mulwai . . | 50,000 | |
| Sardar Bela Singh Mokal . . . | 50,000 | |
| Sardars Sultan Muhammad, Saiyid Muhammad, and Pir Muhammad Khans . . . . . . | 1,50,000 | |
| Sardar Jamal-ud-din Khan . . . | 1,10,000 | |
| Shaikh Ghulam Muhi-ud-din . . | 30,000 | |
| Fakir Aziz-ud-din and his brothers . | 1,00,000 | |
| Diwan Sawan Mal . . . . | 20,000 | |
| Miscellaneous . . . . . | 50,00,000 | 79,15,000 |
| | | |
| CUSTOMS, &c. | | |
| | | |
| Salt Mines. Raja Gulab Singh . . | 8,00,000 | |
| Town Duties. Amritsar. The late Dhian Singh . . . . . . | 5,50,000 | |
| Town Duties. Lahore. The late Dhian Singh . . . . . . | 1,50,000 | |
| Miscellaneous Town Duties . . . | 1,00,000 | |
| 'Abkari' (Excise), &c. &c. Lahore . | 50,000 | |
| Transit Duties. Ludhiana to Peshawar | 5,00,000 | |
| 'Mohurana' (Stamps) . . . . | 2,50,000 | 24,00,000 |
| | | |
| Total . . . . . . | | 3,24,75,000 |

Note.—As noted in the Preface, the whole of the papers of the administration of Ranjit Singh now under examination and subsequent investigation may considerably modify some of these figures.—Ed.

### RECAPITULATION

| Land Revenue : | Rupees. |
|---|---|
| Tributary States | 5,65,000 |
| Farms | 1,79,85,000 |
| Eleemosynary | 20,00,000 |
| Jagirs | 95,25,000 |
| Customs, &c. | 24,00,000 |
| **Total** | **3,24,75,000** |

# APPENDIX XXXIX

# THE ARMY OF LAHORE, AS RECORDED IN 1844

| The Regular Army. | | Infantry Regiments. | Cavalry Regiments. | Light Artillery. | Heavy Guns. | |
|---|---|---|---|---|---|---|
| Commandants of Corps. | Description or Race of Men. | | | | Field. | Garrison. |
| Sardar Tej Singh | Sikhs | 4 | 1 | 10 | 0 | 0 |
| Gen. Pertab Singh Patti-wala | Sikhs | 3 | 0 | 0 | 0 | 0 |
| Gen. Jawala Singh | Inf. Sikhs; Art. Sikhs and Muhammadans | 2 | 2 | 4 | 0 | 0 |
| Shaikh Imam-ud-din | Muhammadans | 3 | 0 | 4 | 0 | 0 |
| Sardar Lahna Singh Majithia | Inf. Sikhs; Guns, chiefly Sikhs | 2 | 0 | 10 | 3 | 2 |
| Gen. Bishan Singh | Muhammadans; a few Sikhs | 2 | 0 | 3 | 0 | 0 |
| Gen. Gulab Singh Puhu-vindhia | 3 Muhammadans; Guns, Sikhs & Muhammadans | 3* | 0 | 14 | 0 | 0 |
| Gen. Mahtab Singh Majithia | Inf. Sikhs; Cav. mixed; Art. Sikhs and Muham. | 4 | 1 | 12 | 0 | 0 |
| Gen. Gurdut Singh Majithia | Inf. chiefly Sikhs; Guns, Sikhs & Muhammadans | 3 | 0 | 0 | 0 | 0 |
| Col. John Holmes | Formerly under General Court | 1 | 0 | 10 | 0 | 0 |
| Gen. Dhaukal Singh | Hindustanis; a few Sikhs; | 2 | 0 | 0 | 0 | 0 |
| Col. Cortlandt (discharged) | Inf. Sikhs & Hind.; Guns, Sikhs & Muhammadans | 2 | 0 | 10 | 0 | 0 |
| Shaikh Ghulam Muhi-ud-din | Inf. Sikhs? Guns, Sikhs and Muhammadans | 1 | 0 | 6 | 8 | 0 |
| | Carried forward | 32 | 2 | 83 | 11 | 2 |

* Shaikh Imam-ud-din subsequently raised a fourth regiment.

| The Regular Army. | | Infantry Regiments. | Cavalry Regiments. | Light Artillery. | Heavy Guns. | |
|---|---|---|---|---|---|---|
| Commandants of Corps. | Description or Race of Men. | | | | Field. | Garrison. |
| | Brought forward . | 32 | 2 | 83 | 11 | 2 |
| Diwan Adjudhia Parshad; Guns under Ilahi Bakhsh, General . . | Inf. Sikhs; Art. Sikhs and Muhammadans (Gen. Ventura) . . | 4 | 2 | 12 | 22 | 0 |
| Gen. Gulab Singh Calcuttawala (deceased) . | Sikhs . . . . | 4 | 1 | 16 | 0 | 0 |
| Diwan Jodha Ram . . | Sikhs, Muham., Hill men (Gen. Avitabile) . | 4 | 1 | 12 | 3 | 0 |
| Gen. Kanh Singh Man . | Sikhs & Muhammadans . | 4 | 0 | 10 | 0 | 0 |
| Sardar Nihal Singh Ahluwalia . . . . | Inf. Sikhs & Muham.; Art. chiefly Muhammadans | 1 | 0 | 4 | 11 | 0 |
| Diwan Sawan Mal . . | Muham. and some Sikhs . | 3 | 0 | 6 | 0 | 40 |
| Raja Hira Singh . . | Hill men, some Muh., &c. | 2 | 1 | 0 | 3 | 5 |
| Raja Gulab Singh . . | „ „ „ . | 3 | 0 | 15 | 0 | 40 |
| Raja Suchet Singh (dec.) | „ „ „ . | 2 | 1 | 4 | 0 | 10 |
| Capt. Kuldip Singh . . | Gurkhas . . | 1 | 0 | 0 | 0 | 0 |
| Commandant Bhag Singh | Sikhs and Muhammadans . | 0 | 0 | 6 | 0 | 0 |
| Commandant Shev Parshad . . . . | „ „ „ . | 0 | 0 | 8 | 0 | 0 |
| Missar Lal Singh . . | „ „ „ . | 0 | 0 | 10 | 0 | 0 |
| Sardar Kishan Singh . | Muham. and Hindustanis | 0 | 0 | 0 | 0 | 2 |
| Gen Kishan Singh . . | Sikhs and Muhammadans | 0 | 0 | 22 | 0 | 0 |
| Sardar Sham Singh Atariwala . . . . | „ „ „ . | 0 | 0 | 0 | 10 | 0 |
| Mian Pirthi Singh . . | Chiefly Muhammadans . | 0 | 0 | 0 | 56 | 0 |
| Gen. Mahwa Singh . . | Sikhs and Muhammadans | 0 | 0 | 10 | 10 | 0 |
| Col. Amir Chand . . | Chiefly Muhammadans . | 0 | 0 | 0 | 10 | 0 |
| Commandant Mazhar Ali | Muham. and Hindustanis | 0 | 0 | 10 | 0 | 0 |
| Jawahir Mal Mistri (Lahore) . . . . | Muhammadans; a few Sikhs . . . . | 0 | 0 | 0 | 20 | 12 |
| Commandant Sukhu Singh (Amritsar) . . . | Sikhs, and some Hindustanis . . . . | 0 | 0 | 0 | 0 | 10 |
| Miscellan. Garrison Guns | . . . . | 0 | 0 | 0 | 0 | 50 |
| | Total . | 60 | 8 | 223 | 156 | 171 |

## Abstract of the whole Army.

| | | |
|---|---|---|
| Sixty Regiments Infantry, at 700 . | 42,000 | |
| Ramghols, Akalis . . . . | 5,000 | |
| Irreg. Levies, Garrison Companies, &c. . | 45,000 | |
| | | 92,000 Infantry. |
| Eight Regiments Cavalry, at 600 . . | 4,800 | |
| Ghurcharhas' (Horse) . . . . | 12,000 | |
| Jagirdari Horse . . . . | 15,000 | |
| | | 31,800 Cavalry. |
| Field Artillery . . . . . | | 384 Guns |

[By the courtesy of the Government of the Punjab I am enabled to add to this appendix the statement recently compiled by L. Sita Ram Kohly, M.A., who has been conducting some researches into the MS. records lying in the Punjab Secretariat. There are many hundreds of these records still to be examined, and further investigation will no doubt yield important results. In the meantime it may be of interest to the reader to compare the actual figures for 1844, as obtained from these records, with those given by the author.—Ed.]

YEAR COMMENCING WITH KATIK 1900 AND ENDING WITH HSUJ 1901 B.S. (A.D. 1844)

| Commandant. | Inf. batts. | Cav. regts. | Artillery. | Total strength. | Expenditure |
|---|---|---|---|---|---|
| | | | | | Rs. A. P. |
| Special Brigade: Gen. Ventura . . . | 4 | 3 | Belonging to Ilahi Baksh | 4,415 | 83,609 8 8 |
| Diwan Jodha Ram . . | 4 | 1 | 10 guns, 294 men | 4,374 | 58,952 12 0 |
| Gen. Gulab Singh, acting for Gen. Court. . . | 4 | 1 | 392 | 3,882 | 54,751 4 0 |
| Gen. Dhaukal Singh . | 2 | 0 | 0 | 1,763 | 23,159 15 0 |
| Gen. Jawala Singh . . | 2 | 0 | 0 | 1,811 | 22,285 12 0 |
| Gen. S. Tej Singh . . | 4 | 0 | 2 field guns, 293 men, light artillery | 3,602 | 45,171 13 6 |
| Gen. Kanh Singh Man . | 4 | 1 | 264 | 4,154 | 61,248 0 0 |
| Gen. Mahtab Singh Majithia . . . . | 4 | 1 | 366 | 3,879 | 59,582 1 0 |
| Gen. Pertab Singh of Punach . . . | 3 | 0 | 250 | 2,690 | 32,743 1 0 |
| Gen. Gurdit Singh Majithia . . . . | 3 | 0 | 194 | 2,872 | 35,679 7 0 |
| Gen. Courtlandt . . | 2* | 0 | 0 | 1,698 | 14,163 14 6 |
| Gen. Gulab Singh Puhuvindhia . . . | 4 | 0 | 360 | 3,467 | 43,273 6 0 |
| Gen. Bishan Singh . . | 2 | 0 | 0 | 1,561 | 19,191 8 0 |
| Gen. Kishan Singh . . | 1 | 1 | 467 | 1,381 | 20,782 1 0 |
| Raja Hira Singh under Col. Jagat Singh | 0 | 2 | 0 | 1,030 | 29,572 8 0 |
| Rai Kesari Singh of Naulakha Cantt, formerly nr. Railway Station, Lahore . . . | 0 | 1 | 90 | 444 | 20,894 0 0 |
| Sardar Lahna Singh Majithia. . . . | 1 | 0 | 340 | 1,258 | 11,865 14 0 |
| Missa Lal Singh † . . | Different Companies | | | 303 | 3,477 6 0 |
| Miscellaneous Companies and soldiers . . | 17 Companies | | | 1,577 | 18,410 11 0 |

Total No. of Battalions : 45. Round No. 40,000 men.
" " " Regiments :    Approx. No. 6,000 men.
" " " Artillery :    plus 126 = 230.
A number of mortars and Camel Swivels are not included in these computations.

* Plus 8th Company of Ramghoal Battalion.
it seems that Lal Singh had to pay these soldiers quartered on his farms.
He farmed out certain districts

## YEAR COMMENCING WITH KATIK 1900 AND ENDING WITH HSUJ 1901 B.S. (A.D. 1844)

### ARTILLERY CORPS

| Commandant. | Guns. | Strength. | Expenditure. | | Jagir assignments. |
|---|---|---|---|---|---|
| | Rs. | | Rs. | A. | Rs. Per Year. |
| Lal Jawahir Mal in charge of Mistri Khana. | | | | | 620 |
| 1. M. Muz.hr Ali Beg. | 390 | 13 | | | |
| 2. B. Ishwar Singh, Col. | 210 | 10 | | | |
| 3. Meva Singh, Gen. | 100 | 12 | | | |
| | —35 | 1,014 | 10,284 | 10 | 5,400 |
| Sultan Muhd., Gen. Commanding heavy guns. | | | | | |
| 1. Bakhtawarkhan. | 165 | 13* | | | 9,000 |
| 2. Muhammad Baksh, Col. | 205 | 12 | | | 1,980 |
| 3. —— | | | | | 1,140 |
| | —25* | 622 | 6,673 | 0 | |
| Illahi Baksh Khan, Gen | | | | | |
| 1. M. Illahi Baksh | 510 | 18* | | | 4,120 |
| 2. Sikandar Khan, son of Illahi Baksh. | | | | | |
| 3. Fateh Khan and Lahora Singh. | 125 }<br>120 } | 12 | | | |
| | —30* | 1,026 | 10,842 | 4 | |
| Amir Chand, Col. | | | | | |
| Amir Chand, Col. | 0 | 15 | | | |
| | —15 | 400 | 3,436 | 0 | 3,040 |
| Fateh Singh and Mubarak Khan. | | | | | |
| Fateh Singh. | 310 } | | | | |
| Mubarak Khan. | 210 } | 21 | | | |
| | —21* | 620 | 6,237 | 0 | 2,580 |
| Total number of guns | 126 | | | | (made up o[f] smaller assignments.) |

 

|  | | Rs. | A. | P. |
|---|---|---|---|---|
| Infantry. Monthly expenditure | | 4,43,892 | 14 | 6 |
| Cavalry.   ,,   ,, | | 1,62,811 | 5 | 0 |
| Artillery.   ,,   ,, | | 67,030 | 10 | 0 |

**Grand Total :**

| | Rs. | A. | P. |
|---|---|---|---|
| (a) Annual land assignment to the military officers | 2,02,439 | 4 | 0 |
| (b) Cash disbursement | 83,69,109 | 10 | 0 |
| | 85,71,448 | 14 | 0 |

Total number of men, 51,050     15,22,627   9   9

Total number of guns, 230, not including mortars and swivels.

**Total for the Year**     1,00,94,076   7   9

---

\* Plus one mortar.

# APPENDIX XL

## THE LAHORE FAMILY

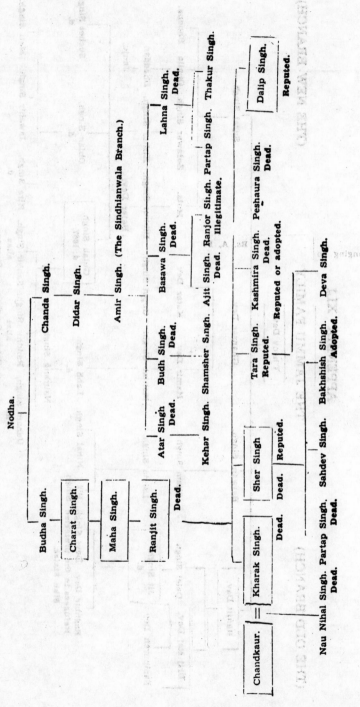

# APPENDIX XLI

## THE JAMMU FAMILY

(THE OLD BRANCH)                                    (THE NEW BRANCH)

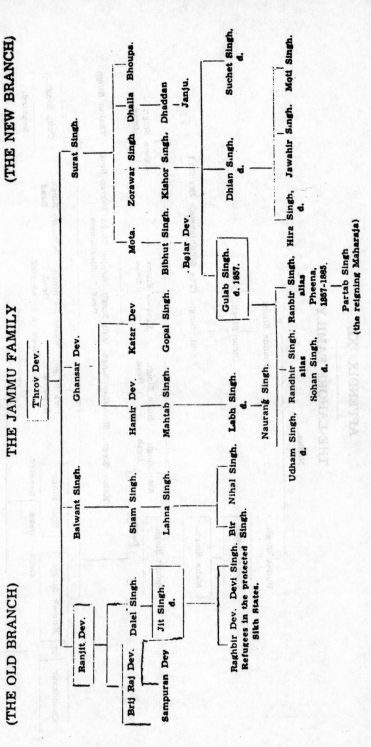

# INDEX

Jains, 16 n., 19 n., 22, 22 n., 41 n., 307.
Jaipur, 6 n., 57.
Jalalabad, surrender of, 222 n.; question of, 225.
Jalla, 239, 240.
Jammu, 6, 77, 106; tributary to the Sikhs, 103; Ranjit Singh confers it on his favourites, 161, 167; Rajas reduce Ladakh, 181; independent, 201; and Nau Nihal Singh, 207.
Jamrud, battle of, 190.
Janjuas, 5.
Jassa Singh, the Carpenter, 87; leads the Sikhs, 89, 96; defeated, 103, 105; his son, 121.
Jassa Singh Kalal (Ahluwalia), 85, 103.
Jats, 299.
Jats, 1, 4, 5, 7, 299; religion, 8, 16; yeomen, 12; origin, 18.n., Gobind intends to form a kingdom of, 68; rise of, 82; defeated, 93.
Jawahir Singh, 233, 240; Wazir, 242; execution, 246; intemperance, 257 n.
Jawala Singh, 230 n.
Jhanda Singh, 103.
Jhelum, 6, 7, 8.
Jind, 111.
Jindiala, 91.
Jodh Singh Kalsia, 125, 127.
Jodh Singh Ramgarhia, 121, 140.
Jodhpur, 149.
Jogis, 32.
Johiyas, 6, 6 n., 102 n.; migration, 15.
Jullundur Doab, 13 n., 55 n., 85.
Juns, 6, 14.

Kabir, 32, 33 n., 304, 306, 308.
Kabul, 2n., 3; taken by the English, 200; insurrection in, 222; recapture, 225.
Kabuli Mal, 92, 93.
Kafirs, 15.
Kahlur, Raja of, 143.
Kaithal, family, 55 n.
Kalabagh, 5, 104.
Kalhoras, 176, 182.
Kamran, 142, 190.
Kanauj, 28.
Kandahar, 170.
Kanets, 6.
Kangra, 103; obtained by Sansar Chand, 106; besieged by

the Gurkhas, 121.
Kanhayas, 97, 103, 118.
Kanjar, 8.
Karauli, 6 n.
Karnal retaken, 104.
Kartarpur, 37 n., 55 n.
Karon, 39 n., 340.
Kasauli, 55 n., 272 n.
Kash [Katch] tribes, 5.
Kashkar, 5.
Kashmir, 2 n., 3, 3 n., 5, 8, 51, 68, 78; annexed by Ahmad Shah, 87; Shah Shuja, a prisoner in, 135; Ranjit Singh and, 139, 142; the English in, 237; transferred to Gulab Singh, 288.
Kashmira Singh, 233.
Kashmiri, 7; mechanics, 13.
Kasur, 6 n., 7, 92, 103, 121.
Kathis, 6, 14.
Katotch, 102, 103, 147.
Kaura Mal, 85, 87; follower of Nanak, 85 n.; killed, 87.
Kelmaks, 17 n.
Khaibar Pass, 1, 223.
Khairabad, 142, 144.
Khairpur, 148, 170.
Khalils, 5.
Khalsa, 12, 63; derivation, 63 n.; Gobind founds, 65, 74, 81 n., army of the, 85; coinage, 89; meetings of, 94; Ranjit Singh and, 151, 152; army becomes the, 216.
Kharak Singh, 132, 173; attacks Multan, 141; invasion of Kashmir, 142; friendly to Katotch, 147; married, 159; apprehensive of Jammu Rajas, 182 n.; threat to Sindh, 185; proclaimed Maharaja, 202.
Khattaks, 5.
Khattars, 5.
Khiljis, 28.
Khorasan, 3 n., 249, 256 n.
Khushab, 7.
Khushal Singh, 160.
Khusru, 47.
Khwaja Obed, 91.
Kiratpur, 53, 55, 57.
Kishtwar, 8.
Kohat, 5.
Koh-i-nur, 137, 138.
Kohlis, 6.
Kot Kapura, incident at, 253.
Krishna, 6 n.; the infant Krishna, 34.